THE EPIC GAZE

The epic genre has at its heart a fascination with the horror of viewing death. Epic heroes have active visual power, yet become objects, turned into monuments, watched by two main audiences: the gods above and the women on the sidelines. This stimulating, ambitious study investigates the theme of vision in Greek and Latin epic from Homer to Nonnus, bringing the edges of epic into dialogue with the most celebrated moments (the visual confrontation of Hector and Achilles, the failure of Turnus' gaze), revealing epic as massive assertion of authority and fractured representation. Helen Lovatt demonstrates the complexity of epic constructions of gender: from Apollonius' Medea toppling Talos with her eyes to Parthenopaeus as object of desire. She discusses mortals appropriating the divine gaze, prophets as both penetrative viewers and rape victims, explores the divine authority of epic ecphrasis, and exposes the way that heroic bodies are fragmented and fetishised.

HELEN LOVATT is Associate Professor of Classics at the University of Nottingham and her teaching includes epic and its reception. She is the author of *Statius and Epic Games* (Cambridge, 2005), and co-editor, with Caroline Vout, of *Epic Visions* (Cambridge, forthcoming).

THE EPIC GAZE

Vision, Gender and Narrative in Ancient Epic

HELEN LOVATT

CAMBRIDGE UNIVERSITY PRESS
Cambridge, New York, Melbourne, Madrid, Cape Town,
Singapore, São Paulo, Delhi, Mexico City

Cambridge University Press
The Edinburgh Building, Cambridge CB2 8RU, UK

Published in the United States of America by Cambridge University Press, New York

www.cambridge.org
Information on this title: www.cambridge.org/9781107016118

© Helen Lovatt 2013

This publication is in copyright. Subject to statutory exception
and to the provisions of relevant collective licensing agreements,
no reproduction of any part may take place without the written
permission of Cambridge University Press.

First published 2013

Printed and bound by CPI Group (UK) Ltd, Croydon CR0 4YY

A catalogue record for this publication is available from the British Library

ISBN 978-1-107-01611-8 Hardback

Cambridge University Press has no responsibility for the persistence or
accuracy of URLs for external or third-party internet websites referred to
in this publication, and does not guarantee that any content on such
websites is, or will remain, accurate or appropriate.

Contents

Preface		*page* vii
List of texts and abbreviations		ix
1	Introduction	1
2	The divine gaze	29
3	The mortal gaze	78
4	The prophetic gaze	122
5	Ecphrasis and the Other	162
6	The female gaze	205
7	Heroic bodies on display	262
8	The assaultive gaze	310
9	Fixing it for good: Medusa and monumentality	347
Bibliography		375
Index locorum		402
General index		407

Preface

While I was writing this book, I was diagnosed with a visual impairment. Since I am already very short-sighted and now in addition suffer from retinitis pigmentosa, a progressive eye condition in which parts of your retina (the edges, to start with) simply cease to work, there is a certain irony in writing a book on vision. Do I have the requisite clarity of perception to make declarations on the workings of viewing and visual power? Or should I hurry it along while I can still watch films and see my computer screen? Or are the lurking measles on my retina as meaningless as the lichen on a gravestone? Am I going blind, or am I only just a bit more blind than I was before? Or will I fall off a cliff tomorrow, not seeing it beneath my feet, leaving only this unfinished manuscript as my own monument?

This project has been an epic of everyday life, attempting to juggle all the commitments of academic, personal and family life. I owe thanks to many people for helping to create the space and time for thinking and writing, as well as the impetus and stimulus for actually doing it. Murray Edwards College, Cambridge, gave me a Junior Research Fellowship, which allowed me to start thinking, and meant that I was able to stay in the game at all. The Dean's Fund at the University of Nottingham and the generosity of my colleagues at the department of Classics cleared me an extra semester of much-needed time, without which this book would be much poorer, if not still stuck indefinitely in never-land. It is my particular pleasure to thank friends and colleagues at the University of Sydney, who flew me out, put me up, showed me around, listened to me and fed me exceptionally well – Alastair Blanshard, Bob Cowan, Paul Roche, Frances Muecke and especially Anne Rogerson. My colleagues past and present have made me think: especially Carrie Vout, Lynn Fotheringham, Susanne Turner and Katharina Lorenz. Students have argued with me and inspired me: I can pick out my third-year special subject group of 2007–8, and Alice White and Andy Valner in 2009. Audiences in various locations (Groningen, Manchester, Exeter, Lampeter, Cork, Cardiff, Santiago de Compostela, and especially

Sydney) have listened and viewed with scepticism and enthusiasm: Hans Smolenaars, Federico Santangelo, Douglas Cairns and Daniel Ogden offered helpful thoughts and advice. Stephen Wheeler helped kick me off in the right direction. Tim Stover, Tobias Myers and Robin Osborne kindly allowed me to look at work in advance of publication. Mentors and friends have cast sharp eyes over drafts: John Henderson, Helen Van Noorden, Helen Asquith, Judith Mossman, Alan Sommerstein, Patrick Finglass. The anonymous reader for Cambridge University Press provided very constructive and helpful comments. Michael Sharp has been supportive, patient and encouraging. Thank you to Anna Hodson for keen-eyed copy-editing. In particular I would like to thank Philip Hardie for making me feel perennially inadequate in the best possible way, who has read it all, some of it several times, and improved it immeasurably. The (no doubt many) errors that still remain, are, of course, my own responsibility. Most importantly my love and thanks go to my family for support and encouragement: from parents to children and children to parents. My mother, who voluntarily reads my work; my father, who is always there; Andrew, who took the strain when I was out of the picture; Jonathan, who looks at the world with bright eyes; and Caroline, who enjoys being looked at but is equally capable of turning her gaze away: it is to them that I dedicate this book.

Texts and abbreviations

For the main epic poems in this study the following texts have been used:

Homer: Monro, D. B. and Allen, T. W. (1920) *Homeri Opera*. Oxford.
Apollonius: Fraenkel, H. (1961) *Apollonii Rhodii Argonautica*. Oxford.
Lucretius: Martin, J. (1969) *T. Lucreti Cari De Rerum Natura*. Leipzig.
Virgil *Georgics*: Mynors, R. A. B. (1969) *P. Vergili Maronis Opera*. Oxford.
  Aeneid: Conte, G. B. (2009) *P. Vergilius Maro Aeneis*. Berlin.
Ovid: Tarrant, R. J. (2004) *P. Ovidi Nasonis Metamorphoses*. Oxford.
Lucan: Housman, A. E. (1927) *M. Annaei Lucani Belli Civilis Libri Decem*. Oxford.
Valerius Flaccus: Liberman, G. (1997–2002) *Valerius Flaccus: Argonautiques*. Paris.
Statius *Thebaid*: Hill, D. E. (ed.) (1983) *P. Papinii Stati Thebaidos Libri XII*. Leiden.
  Achilleid: Shackleton Bailey, D. R. (2003) *Statius Achilleid*. Cambridge, MA.
Silius Italicus: Delz, J. (1987) *Silius Italicus Punica*. Stuttgart.
Quintus Smyrnaeus: Vian, F. (1963–9) *Quintus de Smyrne: La Suite d'Homère*. Paris.
Nonnus: Gerbeau, J. and Vian, F. (1992) *Nonnos de Panopolis: Les Dionysiaques, Tome VII, Chants XVIII–XIX*. Paris.
  Vian, F. (1990) *Nonnos de Panopolis: Les Dionysiaques, Tome IX, Chants XXV–XXIX*. Paris.
  Frangoulis, H. and Gerlaud, B. (2006) *Nonnos de Panopolis: Les Dionysiaques, Tome XII, Chants XXXV et XXXVI*. Paris.
  Fayant, M.-C. (2000) *Nonnos de Panopolis: Les Dionysiaques, Tome XVII, Chant XLVII*. Paris.

Abbreviations in general follow the *Oxford Classical Dictionary*, but be aware of the following:

AR	Apollonius of Rhodes
BC	Lucan, *Bellum civile*

LfrgrE	Snell, B., Fleischer, U. and Mette, H. J. (eds.) (1959) *Lexikon des frühgriechischen Epos*. Göttingen.
LIMC	*Lexicon Iconographicum Mythologiae Classicae* (1981–2009). Zurich.
LSJ	Liddell and Scott, *Greek–English Lexicon*, rev. H. Stuart Jones (1925–40); Supplement by E. A. Barber and others (1968). Oxford.
OLD	Glare, P. G. W. (ed.) (1982) *Oxford Latin Dictionary*. Oxford.
PH	*Posthomerica*
QS	Quintus Smyrnaeus
VF	Valerius Flaccus

CHAPTER I

Introduction

Epic is an omniscient and objective narrative, one that looks down on its characters, and turns them into objects of its gaze, although the characters themselves strive to stand out.[1] The protagonists of epic are action heroes, fighting, doing, going places, changing the world around them. Yet the aim of epic glory requires them to be transfixed, becoming monuments, poetic artefacts. The narrative of epic is structured by the gazes of those watching, not just the gods (and goddesses) on the mountains above, but also the women (and old men) on the walls at the edge. Readers of epic acknowledge its characteristic mix of wonder (or shock) with pity and fear.[2] Two brief cameos to get the action going: Achilles on the walls in *Iliad* 18 and Parthenopaeus stripping in *Thebaid* 9.

Patroclus is dead and Hector is on the point of winning his body; Achilles cannot join the fighting because Hector has taken his armour. So Hera sends Iris to encourage him to intervene by other means, using his passive visual power:

Ἡ μὲν ἄρ' ὣς εἰποῦσ' ἀπέβη πόδας ὠκέα Ἶρις,
αὐτὰρ Ἀχιλλεὺς ὦρτο Διῒ φίλος· ἀμφὶ δ' Ἀθήνη
ὤμοις ἰφθίμοισι βάλ' αἰγίδα θυσσανόεσσαν,
ἀμφὶ δέ οἱ κεφαλῇ νέφος ἔστεφε δῖα θεάων
χρύσεον, ἐκ δ'αὐτοῦ δαῖε φλόγα παμφανόωσαν.

---

[1] This is in contrast to the first-person fictions of love elegy, or the mimetic performance of tragedy, or even the detached but determinedly human perspective of historiography. On definitions of epic, see Martin 2005a. Other discussions of the nature of epic: Oberhelman, Kelly and Golsan 1994, Beissinger, Tylus and Wofford 1999, Foley 2005, King 2009
[2] Aristotle *Poetics* 1460a12 talks of τὸ θαυμαστόν ('the wondrous') in both epic and tragedy, but τὸ ἄλογον ('the improbable/contrary to nature') is particularly epic. See Feeney 1991: 28–9. On wonder, see Prier 1989. Another key word is ἔκπληξις ('astonishment'), literally striking you out of your normal state of mind. *On the sublime* 15.2 associates it with poetry, while prose aims for ἐνάργεια ('vividness'); most of the examples, however, are from tragedy, and the text does not separate out here the different visual effects of different poetic genres. In fact, Plutarch (*Mor.* 347a) uses the same concept of ἔκπληξις of Thucydides, therefore blurring even the distinction between poetry and prose. For rhetorical theory itself as persuasion, see Goldhill 2007.

ὡς δ' ὅτε καπνὸς ἰὼν ἐξ ἄστεος αἰθέρ' ἵκηται,
τηλόθεν ἐκ νήσου, τὴν δήϊοι ἀμφιμάχωνται,
οἵ τε πανημέριοι στυγερῷ κρίνονται Ἄρηϊ
ἄστεος ἐκ σφετέρου· ἅμα δ' ἠελίῳ καταδύντι
πυρσοί τε φλεγέθουσιν ἐπήτριμοι, ὑψόσε δ' αὐγὴ
γίγνεται ἀΐσσουσα περικτιόνεσσιν ἰδέσθαι,
αἴ κέν πως σὺν νηυσὶν ἄρεω ἀλκτῆρες ἵκωνται·
ὣς ἀπ' Ἀχιλλῆος κεφαλῆς σέλας αἰθέρ' ἵκανε.

(*Iliad* 18.202–14)

So speaking Iris of the swift feet went away from him;
but Achilles, the beloved of Zeus, rose up, and Athene
swept about his powerful shoulders the fluttering aegis;
and she, the divine among goddesses, about his head circled
a golden cloud, and kindled from it a flame far-shining.
As when a flare goes up into the high air from a city
from an island far away, with enemies fighting about it
who all day long are in the hateful division of Ares
fighting from their own city, but as soon as the sun goes down signal
fires blaze out one after another, so that the glare goes
pulsing high for men of the neighbouring islands to see it,
in case they might come over in ships to beat off the enemy;
so from the head of Achilles the blaze shot into the bright air.

(trans. Lattimore)[3]

The effects of this intervention are dramatic: the charioteers are put to rout; twelve Trojans are accidentally killed by their own side. From his vantage point on the walls, Achilles weeps at the sight of Patroclus. The change of scenes is complete when Hera drives the sun prematurely to its setting, and the Trojans assemble:

ὀρθῶν δ' ἑσταότων ἀγορὴ γένετ', οὐδέ τις ἔτλη
ἕζεσθαι· πάντας γὰρ ἔχε τρόμος, οὕνεκ' Ἀχιλλεὺς
ἐξεφάνη, δηρὸν δὲ μάχης ἐπέπαυτ' ἀλεγεινῆς.

(*Iliad* 18.246–8)

They stood on their feet in assembly, nor did any man have the patience
to sit down, but the terror was on them all, seeing that Achilleus
had appeared, after he had stayed so long from the difficult fighting.

Many things in this passage anticipate arguments to come: the change of scene, the connection between the divine and the heroic gaze, beauty and terror. But first I want to emphasise the sheer visual power of

---

[3] All translations of the *Iliad* and *Odyssey* are from Lattimore 1951 and Lattimore 1967 respectively. Translations of Quintus of Smyrna are from James 2004, of Nonnus from Rouse 1940. The rest are my own, drawing heavily on previous versions.

Achilles.⁴ Just seeing him from a distance terrifies the Trojans to such an extent that they not only retreat, but in the confusion some fall victim to their own weapons. This visual power is made concrete in the image of the flare (σέλας) and the aegis: Athene does not just protect and sponsor Achilles, she marks him out with a fiery halo. The simile of the beacon suggests that this is both a sign and an act that has concrete effects. It signals the need for help to the allies and their imminent destruction to the enemies, and causes this destruction actually to happen. Achilles' blaze signals his anger, his divine favour and his potential destructiveness. He is like a god in his terrifying visual power.⁵ The simile also moves the reader, in the wake of the narrator, out far beyond the immediacy of Achilles' vision, to dip briefly into another story, to be aware of the crafted nature of epic narrative. The roles of Hera, Iris and Athene have the simultaneous effects of raising Achilles beyond the normal mortal level, and making of him an object for their manipulation. Hera and Athene have opposed his plan, sponsored by Zeus, to make the Greeks feel his absence, throughout the earlier books of the *Iliad*. For them, Achilles is a means to an end, and that end is the destruction of Troy. This scene also shows the structural significance of divine viewing, with Hera's ox-eyed gaze (βοῶπις πότνια Ἥρη, 'lady Hera of the ox-eyes', 239) intervening briefly to drive the sunset between the situation on the Greek side, focalised by Achilles, and the assembly of the Trojans. Achilles' gaze also follows more than one epic pattern: the blazing of the angry hero, whose gaze can form an assaultive weapon;⁶ the mourning of the concerned watcher who laments the deaths of their loved ones. His physical position, on the walls, moving to the ditch, mirrors his position in the poem between mortal and immortal, active hero and lamenting lover.

The second cameo appearance belongs to Parthenopaeus, the beautiful boy hero of Statius' *Thebaid*.⁷ In book 9 he performs his insubstantial *aristeia* before an admiring audience of other warriors, nymphs and gods. Statius' poem is roughly structured around the deaths of each of the seven heroes; in the first half of book 9 it is the death of Hippomedon. The change to the new narrative unit is mediated by two visual incidents: the ill-omened vision of Parthenopaeus' mother Atalanta, and the protective viewing of

---

⁴ Sound is also very important in this episode (217–24); sound and vision can never be entirely separated as means of communication and perception. See further below, p.23.
⁵ Edwards 1991: 169 calls this moment 'a kind of epiphany'; Griffin 1980: 38–9 cites similarities with descriptions of warrior gods.
⁶ Clarke 2004: 83: 'he enters a state that stretches the limits of human nature . . . Achilles is transfigured, superhuman, blazing.'
⁷ See Lovatt 2005: 67–71, arguing that Parthenopaeus is the beloved of the audience. The love relationship becomes hollow, when it is reduced to a visual encounter. See also Jamset 2004.

Diana on Olympus. We then move back to the Theban battlefield, now following Parthenopaeus. Although he is the object of the gaze, subjectivity is injected into the details of his finery: his cloak, which is the only item of female work produced by the huntress Atalanta (690–2); his drooping shield and too-heavy sword (693–4); his pleasure in the golden clasp on his belt (694–5) and the sounds of his armour:

> interdum cristas hilaris iactare comantes
> et pictum gemmis galeae iubar. ast ubi pugna
> cassis anhela calet, resoluto uertice nudus
> exoritur: tunc dulce comae radiisque trementes
> dulce nitent uisus et, quas dolet ipse morari,
> nondum mutatae rosea lanugine malae.
> nec formae sibi laude placet multumque seueris
> asperat ora minis, sed frontis seruat honorem
> ira decens. dat sponte locum Thebana iuuentus,
> natorum memores, intentaque tela retorquent;
> sed premit et saeuas miserantibus ingerit hastas.
> illum et Sidoniae iuga per Teumesia Nymphae
> bellantem atque ipso sudore et puluere gratum
> laudant, et tacito ducunt suspiria uoto.
> talia cernenti mitis subit alta Dianae
> corda dolor, fletuque genas uiolata . . .   (*Thebaid* 9.698–713)

> Meanwhile it pleases him joyfully to toss his plumed crest
> and the radiance of his helmet decorated with gems. But when
> the helmet grows hot in breathless battle, he rises up naked with head
> released: then sweetly shines his hair with trembling rays
> and sweetly shines his gaze, and, which grieve him by their delaying,
> his cheeks not yet changed by rosy down.
> Nor is he pleasing to himself through praise of his beauty and he makes
> his face very harsh with stern threats, but righteous anger guards
> the honour of his brow. The Theban youth give ground voluntarily,
> mindful of their children, and turn back the weapons they had aimed;
> but he presses on and piles on the savage spears against those who pity him.
> Even the Sidonian Nymphs on the Teumesian ridges praise him
> as he fights, made more attractive even by sweat and dust
> itself, and they draw their sighs with silent prayer.
> For Diana, seeing these things, a gentle grief steals
> into the depths of her heart, and she violates her cheeks with weeping . . .

The double perspective of this passage represents him as an erotic object and a child to be wept over; he is both summed up by his clothes, accoutrements and parts of his body, and made more attractive by his subjectivity, strongly characterised by his resistance to his own typecasting. He refuses to admit that his role is that of the beautiful boy, even as he enjoys his own glamour. To admit it would be to have foreknowledge of his own inevitable death, to encounter heroic mortality. He is his own audience, looking at himself and listening to the sounds he generates. But he is also at the centre of a nest of audiences, like a gladiator or actor on display, watching himself and surrounded by ranks of different watchers. The other fighters are closest, then the nymphs on the ridges, then out to the goddess, and finally to us, the readers. The emotional responses of all these audiences tend to inspire emotion in us: pity from the warriors, and identification with their own children; desire and anxiety from the nymphs; grief from Diana. He is a substitute son for Diana, hence violating her untouchable virginity (and godhead) with a grief she should not have to feel. She responds by going down into the battle herself, like Athene looking after Telemachus, and protecting his body with ambrosia, as if he is a version of the dead Patroclus or Hector, before he has even died:

> ambrosio tunc spargit membra liquore,
> spargit equum, ne quo uioletur uulnere corpus
> ante necem, cantusque sacros et conscia miscet
> murmura, secretis quae Colchidas ipsa sub antris
> nocte docet monstratque feras quaerentibus herbas. (*Thebaid* 9.731–5)

Then she scatters his limbs with ambrosial liquor,
and she scatters his horse, so that his body will not be violated by any wound
before death, and she mixes sacred chants with knowledgeable
whispers, which she herself teaches the Colchian women at night
in their secret caves and shows wild herbs to those searching.

The Colchian reference evokes the *Argonautica* and Medea's love for Jason, also expressed by making his body inviolable, further racking up the apparently erotic involvement of the goddess. This erotic viewing of the hero has the potential to blur the distinction between women and warriors, gods and mortals. Epic is, in its own way, a story of desire.[8]

But that is a tendentious statement: epic, as we all know, is about gods, kings and heroes, battles and journeys. The question of genre, how it is performed, constructed and contested, is central.[9] In a sense, it is an artificial way to limit this study: rather than trying to look at all of ancient literature, or indeed all literature, I have chosen to focus on a group of texts from the ancient world which announce their affinity with each other. There is often as much difference between the different texts studied here as there is continuity:

---

[8] See for instance Pavlock 1990, Reed 2007.   [9] On genre: Fowler 1982, Depew and Obbink 2000.

but the *Iliad* is an important influence on them all; and for later Roman writers, the *Aeneid* always intervenes. We might debate whether Catullus 64, Ovid *Metamorphoses*, Lucretius *De rerum natura* and Hesiod count as epic: and definitions of epic changed over this enormous period. *Epos* is a much more capacious concept in Archaic Greece than epic after Virgil. But despite these differences, there is a great deal of continuity: the *Iliad* already contains many of the tropes and ideas that I will follow through the later poems, if they are adapted to new contexts in often surprising ways. Genre is an elusive concept, a weave of absences and denials, as much as a self-conscious stealing of other people's ideas. Perhaps it is the generic coherence of epic that makes it difficult for modern readers to take: not another set of games; not more gods intervening. On the other hand size is important: and the size of epic allows it to consume other genres. So tragedy, originally preying on epic itself, becomes the victim of Apollonius and Virgil, only to turn the tables (arguably) in Statius' *Thebaid*.[10] The grand narratives of history, too, have always had a close relationship with the grandeur of epic, even in its mythological form.[11] The generic frame has proved more productive than problematic for this book. Whether or not 'the epic gaze' is ultimately fragmented, tracing the uses of vision in this high-profile ancient genre holds enduring fascination.[12] On the optimistic side, reading around in other genres suggests that epic uses lines of sight and ideas of viewing in distinctive ways. If the *Iliad* and the *Odyssey* form two contrasting patterns of epic, battle narrative and quest epic, they both produce visual scenarios: the siege, with city looking out against attackers looking in, two armies drawn up in face-to-face confrontation, is a theatre of war; while the journey, whether towards home or away from it, is defined by a stream of new sights, monstrosities and marvels.[13] The practicalities of dramatic performance have their own effects, creating important similarities and differences; other contrasts, for instance with Latin elegy, or Hellenistic epigram, can bring out the flavour of epic. There are numerous sieges in historical narratives, for instance, yet the women on the walls are much less prominent as viewers. This book focuses on the internal dynamics of epic, but uses comparison with other genres where necessary.

---

[10] Excellent discussion of tragedy and epic, looking both forwards and backwards, in Schiesaro 2003.
[11] See for instance Ash 2002, Konstan and Raaflaub 2010, Miller and Woodman 2010. 'As in tragedy and history, so in Homer glory contains the promise of failure or death; and this is one important way in which the tragic habit of thought contributes to a historical concept of causation.' Macleod 1983: 157.
[12] I have decided in general to use 'vision' rather than 'visuality' because this is a book about how seeing is represented in literature, not about cultures of viewing in themselves. On the difference see Zanker 2004: 5: '"Visuality" denotes the way of seeing in a particular historical period; "vision" the way of seeing which essentializes and universalizes.'
[13] On the *Iliad* and the theatre of war, see Clay 2011; on different paths, see Purves 2010.

Approaches to vision and theories of 'the gaze'

'The gaze' once seemed a mysterious, exciting and confusing idea. This confusion results from the many different versions and theories of 'the gaze', all of which use similar terminology to mean quite different things. So what is 'the gaze'? We could start in any number of places or times: with Greek philosophers, early modern artists, twentieth-century psychoanalysts.[14] However, the phrase 'the gaze' is probably most often associated with the seminal article by feminist film theorist Laura Mulvey from 1975 ('Visual pleasure and narrative cinema'), which argues that the gaze of classic narrative cinema is masculine and active, while the feminine becomes a passive object to be looked at.[15] Mulvey used Freudian ideas about scopophilia (morbid pleasure in looking), through voyeurism (the desire to see the forbidden, especially the genitals and the primal scene – other people, especially your parents, having sex) and fetishism (in which sexual desire is transferred onto something other than the obviously sexual, i.e. feet, or shoes, or books) to analyse the pleasure of watching classic Hollywood cinema. The voyeuristic side of pleasure in watching the narrative and identifying with the male hero comes, in Mulvey's version, from a sadistic pleasure in gaining sexual power over the woman. The fetishistic side, on the other hand, takes us outside narrative, breaks the illusion of reality, with a two-dimensional fragmentation of the female body. The apparatus of the cinema is particularly appropriate for this sort of narrative pleasure: it puts the spectator in a position of power by keeping him hidden in the dark, by stitching together the gazes of audience, camera and male protagonist.

Mulvey's work is used in a classical context by Salzman-Mitchell 2005, which approaches Ovid's *Metamorphoses* as an interplay of intrusive and fixing gazes. Salzman-Mitchell develops Mulvey with her emphasis on sisterhood and women telling stories for each other, invoking criticisms of the monolithic nature of Mulvey's notion of the gaze: arguably a resisting reading of Ovid, for whose text rape is clearly a major source of narrative pleasure. It is certainly true that identification is a complex process, also true that viewers can identify with main characters, both male and female, with the setting and story as a whole, or change their identification from moment

---

[14] For a differently slanted introduction to the gaze, see Fredrick 2002: 1–30, which concentrates on the tensions between essentialism and constructionism in applying psychoanalytical theory to the specific cultural context of ancient Rome, and on differentiating Rome and Greece. See also Bartsch 2006, with a philosophical and scientific emphasis.
[15] Mulvey 1975.

to moment.[16] Just as there is no one reader and no one reading, so there is no one viewer and one process of viewing.[17]

This is not the place to tell the story of feminist film criticism: there are good introductory books to do that.[18] This introduction lays out different ideas that can lie behind the term 'the gaze' and offers some orientation amongst the vast and still growing literature on the subject. Mulvey is only one starting point. We might attempt to understand the psychoanalytical substructure of her argument, which invokes both Freud and Lacan, and instantly antagonises many.[19] But must we believe that the fetishised female represents the male fear of castration in order to agree that men find powerful female sexuality disturbing? The superstructure of the argument may retain its strength, even if we do not accept the Freudian underpinnings. Freud is not the only source of psychoanalytic inspiration: Lacan's work is also importantly concerned with vision.[20]

The work of Kaja Silverman, for instance, draws a great deal from Lacan.[21] Lacan's influential notion of the gaze develops not just Freud, but also phenomenology and Sartre.[22] In this version, looking and being looked at are reciprocal relationships. Lacan's 'gaze' describes a Sartrean field of vision, in which the self is paralysed by awareness of being looked at by everything that is other.[23] We might conceptualise this as a triangle with the field of vision converging on the subject who is being looked at. On the other side is the 'look' which is the word Silverman uses to convey the desiring gaze, from the subject to the single object. For Lacan the two types of looking are inextricable; we are always both looking and being looked at.

---

[16] As incidentally suggested in Penley 1994.

[17] Other developments of film theory are related to the post-colonial turn: emphasis on structures of power other than gender, different social and cultural contexts, especially the developing world. See for instance hooks 1996, Kaplan 1997, Furby and Randell 2005.

[18] For instance Penley 1988, Humm 1997, Thornham 1999. There has also been a backlash against 'theory': Bordwell and Carroll 1996. But McGowan 2003 argues that this results from incorrect application of Lacan's ideas about 'the gaze'. Those who deplore psychoanalysis continue to disagree: see for instance Currie 1995 and Currie 2010 for a philosophical approach to the cognitive turn in film theory and literature.

[19] See Oliensis 2009 for the appeal and limitations of Freudian approaches to ancient literature and the idea that literary critics may be looking for a 'textual subconscious', the meaning that lurks under the surface of a text, whether or not intended by its author.

[20] Lacan and Miller 1978: 67–122 on the gaze. Other models are also available, such as Nancy Chodorow's sociological feminist psychoanalysis: Chodorow 1994.

[21] Silverman 1988a, Silverman 1988b, Silverman 1992, Silverman 1994.

[22] Sartre 1966, Merleau-Ponty 1968.

[23] Lacan's concept of the 'mirror stage' is also important in forming concepts of identification in film theory.

McGowan 2007 takes a different Lacanian perspective: he focuses on Lacan's concept of the gaze as the *objet petit a* in the field of vision. Every aspect of our experience requires us to negotiate with otherness, both the 'big Other', which embodies authority and the symbolic order, associated with writing and masculinity, but also the inaccessible, incomprehensible desire of the other. The *objet petit a* is this gap, this lack, this thing which does not exist, despite the fact that we imagine it does. Lacan's gaze, therefore, in McGowan's account, is the distortion in the field of vision caused by the imagined desire of the other. McGowan 2003 uses Spielberg's first feature, *Duel* (1970), to exemplify the Lacanian gaze: in this film, the Other is the driver of the truck which pursues David Mann, for no apparent reason, threatening, terrifying in his hidden inexplicability. From high in his cab, he looks down on Mann, who cannot see him (and neither can we). Neither audience nor protagonist ever find out why the truck driver is trying to kill him.[24] McGowan 2007 argues that confrontation with the gaze allows the subject to move beyond the domestication of fantasy, and the eternal repetition of desire, to take pleasure in the process of desire itself: film can act as a sort of psychoanalysis.[25]

While various scholars have approached elegy from a Lacanian perspective, there has not been a great deal of work on epic.[26] Augoustakis 2010 uses Kristeva's concept of otherness to think about gender and nationality in Statius and Silius. Kristeva's idea of the abject is closely related to the Lacanian gaze, in that it too stages a confrontation with the Real. Augoustakis' approach to gender has been particularly helpful, although vision is not at the forefront of his study.

---

[24] Another example is Demme's *Silence of the Lambs* (1991), in which Hannibal Lecter is the desired and inexplicable 'other', of whom we are terrified, and whom we cannot understand. 'By enticing spectators to desire Lecter, the film impels them to acknowledge their affinity with a serial killer, thereby disrupting any sense of spectatorship from a safe distance.' McGowan 2003: 29.

[25] While McGowan's typology of film (cinema of fantasy, epitomised by Spike Lee and Fellini; cinema of desire, Orson Welles; cinema of integration, mainstream Hollywood, for instance *Schindler's List*; cinema of intersection, David Lynch) might be too schematic, it does offer a variety of psychoanalytical models for thinking about narrative. Fantasy is the spectacle too full to retain meaning; desire the ever-receding absence; integration solves desire by applying fantasy; intersection sets the two against each other to make us uncomfortably aware of the whole process. My feeling is that epic is continually mixing fantasy and desire: tentatively I associate the *Dionysiaca* with the epic of fantasy; Apollonius' *Argonautica* with desire; the *Odyssey* and the *Punica* with the epic of integration; the others all, in their different ways, create collisions between fantasy and desire.

[26] Especially Janan 1994, Janan 2001 and Miller 2004. On Ovidian epic Hardie 2002b, Janan 2009. Janan moves from interpersonal to political desire, also a feature of McGowan 2007; 224–51 explores the epic successors of Ovid to show how 'the intractable paradoxes on which epic dreams of a harmonious, organically-united polity are so uneasily founded'. (225)

A phenomenological theoretical background lies behind Smith's reading of Virgil's *Aeneid*.[27] He reads Aeneas as Merleau-Ponty's *voyant-visible* and conveys the way that the hero is both powerful because spectacular, and disempowered by being watched.[28] Smith joins the contest of words versus vision that has been ongoing since antiquity, coming down squarely on the side of vision, at least in Augustan Rome. Words are deceptive, while vision successfully persuades.[29] He successfully shows the importance and pervasiveness of vision in the *Aeneid*, but he does not set this in the context of the epic genre (is the *Aeneid* really that much more visual than the *Iliad*?).

Persuasion is only one part of the workings of vision, one that owes more to the discourse of ecphrasis than is acknowledged. 'Ecphrasis' means different things in different times and places: there is a clear disciplinary disjunction between classicists, for whom ecphrasis can be a description of any sort (of a place, a person, a work of art) and those studying English literature, for instance, for whom ecphrasis usually refers to the description of a work of art in a text, and is essentially about the interaction of media.[30] For epic, the shield of Achilles forms the set-piece ecphrasis, making 'art and text' an important reference point. The insights of art historians into modes and varieties of viewing inform the way we talk about descriptions of works of art in texts, as do changes in viewing cultures, which I discuss below. The importance of the 'art and text' discourse is not limited to ecphrasis. Cultures of viewing have a close relationship to cultures of reading; thinking about approaches to art can also illuminate approaches to performance (and reading).

Not only art is on display in the ancient world: spectacle is equally important, from sacrifice and ritual in the Homeric poems, to grand Alexandrian processions, to Roman games, in theatre, circus and amphitheatre.[31] Performance is another important aspect of viewing, and brings us to social history (or body history, as Fredrick calls it).[32] Foucault cannot be ignored, although feminist film theory resists historicist models.[33] Foucault desired to mark off the ancient world from the modern: yet the Roman

---

[27] Smith 2005.   [28] See Rogerson 2007.
[29] Drawing on Feeney 1990. But as Rogerson points out, vision is even more open than words to multiple interpretation.
[30] Webb 2009 reclaimed the term, with Goldhill's *BMCR* review, which defines the disjunction as one within classics; also Goldhill 2007. For a thoughtful survey of the issues, see Elsner 2002, Squire 2009.
[31] Nightingale 2004 on Classical Greek cultures of viewing and their philosophical resonances; Stewart 1993 on Hellenistic spectacle; Leigh 1997 on Lucan; Bartsch 1994 on imperial spectacle.
[32] Fredrick 2002: 7–10. On theatrical performance, especially Shakespeare, and the gaze, see Freedman 1991, Armstrong 2000.
[33] For a confrontation between the two, see Copjec 1994.

Cultures of viewing 11

arena can persuasively be read as a 'Panopticon' in Foucauldian terms.[34] Although not designed, like the prison, to offer a vantage point from which one person can see and control others while remaining unseen, the invisible viewer holding power over those watched, the arena puts all of Roman society on display in order to define and maintain power structures. The ideas in *Discipline and Punish* and *The Eye of Power* have been influential on discussion of the spectacle culture of ancient Rome.[35] The figure of the emperor is a spectacle for contemporaries as well as posterity.[36] This body of theory connects vision and power differently. Rather than relying on the idea that there is an essential similarity in the psychological development of all human beings which forms their visual response to the world, the relationship between power and vision is seen as socially constructed and specific to the society in question. Almost certainly a little of both is true: there clearly are continuities between societies as well as differences. What interests me is the way that these social and historical phenomena are represented, refracted and even created in literature. Epic is a particularly fascinating genre because of its privileged relationship with the powerful elite and its importance in education, both Greek and Roman.[37] The study of vision in epic offers insights into Greek and Roman society more broadly.

Cultures of viewing

The material of this book comes from a period of over a thousand years (Homer in the sixth to the eighth century BC, through to Nonnus in the fourth or early fifth century AD). Geographically it ranges from Asia (Quintus of Smyrna) and Africa (Apollonius, presumably based in Alexandria) to Greece and Italy. Although one can fairly describe all these texts as participating in one broadly defined Greco-Roman culture, there are still huge differences between their contexts.[38] The strong sense of literary affiliation that links them, descent from the *Iliad*, serves to minimise these differences,

---

[34] See Clavel-Lévêque 1984.
[35] Foucault 1979, Foucault 1980. On Foucault and classics, see Detel 1998, Larmour, Miller and Platter 1998, Porter 2006; inspired by Foucault: Halperin 1990, Goldhill 1995; discussing Foucault from a classical perspective: Halperin 1995; Bartsch 2006: 136–9 and 251–5 engages with Foucault.
[36] See Bartsch 1994, Elsner and Masters 1994, Bartsch 2006; Vout 2007, for instance, gives an erotic slant to this visibility.
[37] On the Roman side, see Keith 2000. On Greek and Roman, see Cribiore 2001, Too 2001.
[38] Elsner 1998: 8–24 argues for continuity in late antiquity, in a strong affiliation to Classical culture, and prominent engagement with pagan myth. Cribiore 2001: 8 argues that the conservative nature of education acted as a strong force for cultural continuity: 'Greek education in antiquity was virtually independent of societal changes and geography.' Literary production and reception, however, is not just a function of education, and changing contexts clearly do create changing poetic practices.

and it is tempting to see them as one enormous super-text. Yet even within the closely related subset of the epic genre which is now referred to as 'Flavian epic', three poets writing within the same political dynasty (Vespasian to Domitian) at the end of the first century AD, in Rome, there are very significant differences brought about by the different social statuses and literary self-positioning of their respective authors. Silius had a political career and his *Punica* draws extensively on historiography; it is difficult to sustain a pessimistic reading of his approach to Rome and politics.[39] We know very little about Valerius Flaccus; he has been read as a new Virgil for the Flavian age, and, as with Virgil, his poem can be read in more than one way: as carefully worked out propaganda, and as a subversive, alternative epic.[40] Statius, as a professional poet of Greek heritage based in Rome and receiving patronage from the emperor as well as many leading Romans, is different again, with the strongest tendency to merge Greek and Roman practices and culture; yet his epic is also the most difficult to read as positive political endorsement for anything.[41] For all three the figures of Homer, Virgil and Ovid loom large, while Apollonius is important for Valerius Flaccus and Statius, but less so for Silius. Literary contexts and socio-political contexts are both significant in appreciating any one epic's response to 'the epic gaze'.

Imperial Greek epic has received less attention than Flavian epic, now arguably the flavour of the moment. Amongst the hexameter poetry of late antiquity, the *Posthomerica* of Quintus of Smyrna and the *Dionysiaca* of Nonnus stand out for their size and their self-conscious continuation of the classical epic genre.[42] One particular problem associated with these poems raises its head in this study: were later Greek writers aware of Latin literature? There is a range of opinions: there is little evidence of knowledge of Latin in the Greek East, but we might make an exception in the case of Virgil.[43] Quintus Smyrnaeus' fourteen-book epic on the events between the end of the *Iliad* and the beginning of the *Odyssey* seems to date from the second or third century AD.[44] Quintus' choice to write a much more direct sequel to Homer than Virgil's puts him in direct competition with the *Aeneid*; his description of

---

[39] Though Tipping 2010 more or less manages; Marks 2005 is much more optimistic, while Augoustakis 2010 attempts to strike a balance.
[40] New Virgil: Stover forthcoming; subversive and alternative: Buckley forthcoming.
[41] For the strongest negative readings see Dominik 1994, and with more complexity, Ganiban 2007.
[42] I would also like to have considered Tryphiodorus and Claudian, possibly also Colluthus and Oppian, but time and space kept me in check.
[43] Gärtner 2005 concludes that Greek speakers might have known Virgil, at least. But she argues that each apparent allusion must be judged on its own merits.
[44] On Quintus, Baumbach and Dümmler 2007, Carvounis 2008, Bär 2010, Maciver 2012. On context, see Hadjittofi 2007.

Cultures of viewing

the sack of Troy in particular seems impossible to read without thinking about Virgil.[45] Nonnus' style and attitude is remarkably Ovidian: but does this simply reflect a shared love of Hellenistic poetry?[46] His forty-eight-book epic of Dionysus is as polymorphous as the god, as capacious as any other epic.[47] Shorrock remains convinced that Nonnus was not a connoisseur of Latin epic, but others have disagreed.[48] As James points out, much of the reluctance among Hellenists to see engagement with Latin poetry stems from an assumption of the low literary quality of later epic, no doubt in some cases combined with a distaste for Latin literature. However, if we embrace a more generous definition of intertextuality, these questions become less pressing, and for the purposes of this project comparison and similarity are the point, rather than intentional allusion. I am sympathetic to the idea that Quintus and Nonnus echo Latin epic, but I am not making a case here, only pointing out areas of common ground.

My decision to organise this book on thematic lines might tend to emphasise continuities rather than differences. If, like Feeney's *The Gods in Epic* (1991), the book had a chapter on each poet (or half a chapter), then there might have been a clearer sense of what is distinctive about each poet's approach to vision. On the other hand, looking at the same phenomena across the whole genre allows differences to be put into relief. Since it is very difficult to do justice to such a range of contexts, I here offer a few reminders about change and difference. It is important to remember, of course, that individual viewers and readers, even living at the same time and in the same place, might have responded differently to these texts; that there are as many 'scopic regimes' as there are people to live in them.

An attempt to define the different visual cultures of the periods under consideration might talk about stylistic development: from the *kouroi* of Archaic Greece, to the naturalism of the Classical period, and the mannered realism of the Hellenistic time, each of which makes different demands of viewers, and creates different viewing attitudes.[49] In Rome, the Augustan emphasis on the political use of images creates a political viewer; while

---

[45] On Quintus and Virgil see Gärtner 2005, James 2007.
[46] Knox 1988 is also sceptical, arguing against Braune 1935; but Hardie 2005: 129 leaves room for further investigation.
[47] Shorrock 2011 sets the *Dionysiaca* in its fifth-century context, through its engagement with both pagan and Christian *topoi*, stimulated by Nonnus' probable authorship of a *Paraphrase of St John's Gospel*.
[48] Shorrock 2011: 10–11, though he allows that the process of exploring similarities may in itself be fruitful. '[T]here is a growing feeling among literary critics that later Greek poetry does perhaps owe a larger debt to Latin literature than we have been prepared to acknowledge.' (10)
[49] On Greek visual culture, see Goldhill and Osborne 1994, Goldhill 2001, Steiner 2001, Zanker 2004.

Hadrian's scattering of the empire with relics of his beloved Antinous links power and desire; the move from illusionistic to symbolic art in late antiquity tells a different story.[50] Equally important are the huge variations in any given time and place: from grand public monuments, enormous temples, for instance, to miniature, private, ephemeral objects. Throughout, the interactions between context, commissioner and viewer make people look at the world in particular ways.

Gender is an important concern for this project, both femininity and masculinity;[51] there is so little evidence for what female readers (or viewers) in the ancient world might have thought, women's viewing cannot emerge as a distinct category.[52] Literary evidence is almost entirely male-authored, and even that which might have been written by a woman inevitably partakes in male discourse. If epic was used to teach masculinity, then its importance for women must clearly have been different to its significance for men. We have some evidence (however problematic) for female readers or audiences of epic: for instance, the story that Octavia, the sister of Augustus and mother of Marcellus, fainted at the words *tu Marcellus eris* (*Aen.* 6.883).[53] Propertius represents the *puella* as a reader of poetry, and sometimes epic poetry.[54] At 2.1.49–50 he portrays her reading the *Iliad*, critically, but as a love poem: *si memini solet illa leuis culpare puellas, | et totam ex Helena non probit Iliada*. ('If I remember correctly, she is accustomed to blame fickle girls, and did not approve of the whole *Iliad* because of Helen.') Within epic, representations of poetry recitals at banquets include women in the audience: most notably, Dido in *Aeneid* 1.[55] The question of women's participation in and viewing of spectacle is also important: did women attend the performances of tragedy?[56] Greek women were broadly less able to go out in public than Roman women, but they still had an important role in ritual, and certainly Theocritus

---

[50] See further Zanker 1988, Elsner 1996, Elsner 1998, Vout 2007.
[51] On femininity: Butler 1990; on masculinity: Connell 1995.
[52] See for instance Dixon 2001 for a negative take on the possibilities of retrieving any sort of unmediated female experience.
[53] In Suetonius *Life of Virgil* 32; cf. Servius *ad Aen.* 6.861, in which her excessive weeping makes Augustus order her to be silent until Virgil has finished speaking; this version models her on the mother of Euryalus (*Aen.* 9.498–502). Is this the role imagined for women readers? To listen for their personal connections and respond emotionally. On Virgilian lives, see Horsfall 1995: 1–26, Stok 2010.
[54] See James 2003. James focuses on the thread of elegiac discourse that makes the poems' persuasion and love poetry the only type of poetry a girl is interested in (e.g. Prop. 2.34b.41–6; 1.9.13–14; 1.7.9–11; Ovid *Am.* 2.1.19–22, 29–32).
[55] *Aen.* 1.748–50. Although Nausicaa and Arete may well listen to the songs of Demodocus (and the story of Odysseus), there is no focus on them as audience members; at *Od.* 1.325–44 Penelope comes down from her room where she has been upset by hearing the song Phemius sings to the banqueters. On female narrators in Ovid, see Salzman-Mitchell 2005: 150–206.
[56] Two representative positions, sceptical: Goldhill 1994 and less so: Henderson 1991b.

represents women attending processions in Alexandria (*Idylls* 15).⁵⁷ In Rome women were certainly present at Circus games (Ovid *Am.* 3.2 imagines seduction at the circus; see Henderson 2002); they were probably not allowed to watch athletic games, and were secluded in the highest seating of the gladiatorial games.⁵⁸

The degree to which women were required to be unseen was also important. Veiling is one useful cultural signifier of the relationship between gender, respectability and vision. Llewellyn-Jones shows that veiling was an important part of 'a male ideology that required women to be silent and invisible creatures, like mute tortoises contained and hidden within their shells'.⁵⁹ Veiling is already common in the *Iliad* and the *Odyssey*; for instance, Circe and Penelope at *Od.* 5.230–2 and 10.543–5 wear a veil as part of their costume; Hecuba and Andromache's veils come under scrutiny during the process of lamenting Hector (*Il.* 22.406, 22.468–70); when Helen walks to the ramparts in *Il.* 3.139–44, she is veiled as well as chaperoned. Cairns acutely observes the multivalence of this particular episode: 'The gesture is an ordinary manifestation of women's modesty ... but Helen is also weeping, and veiling is often a means of concealing one's tears.'⁶⁰ Not only women covered their faces in order to hide emotion: Odysseus too veils his tears in the banquets of the Phaeacians, specifically a response to epic poetry (*Od.* 8.83–92). Practices of veiling in the Greek world change over time, coming to a climax in the fourth century BC when face-covering veils became more prevalent.⁶¹ In Roman culture, veiling seems to be associated almost entirely with religious practices, even among women.⁶² Veiling, then, seems to have meant different things at different times, and in different cultures and contexts.

Greco-Roman religion was varied and ever-changing: cults grew, from Cybele to Christianity, and faded. There was already huge variation from place to place, with local deities and religious practices, gradually mixed in with Panhellenic and empire-wide ritual, like imperial cult. The Jupiter of the *Aeneid* is not straightforwardly the same as the Zeus of the *Iliad*,

---

⁵⁷ Although Lambert 2001 argues that this is more parody than reality.
⁵⁸ On women as gladiatorial audience, Petr. *Sat.* 126, Martial 5.24.10, *CIL* 4.4342, 4345, 4356, with Watson and Watson 1996.
⁵⁹ Llewellyn-Jones 2003: 1.   ⁶⁰ Cairns 2002: 74.   ⁶¹ Llewellyn-Jones 2003: 67.
⁶² Glinister 2009 identifies at least nine contexts in which Romans used veiling: consecration of property (Cic. *Dom.* 124); declaring war (Livy 1.32.5–6); expiating a crime (Livy 1.26.13); *deuotio* (Cic. *Nat. D.* 2.10); sacrificing and murdering, as in the deaths of Pompey, Caesar and Gracchus (Livy 1.21.4; Serv. *Aen.* 1.292); vestals punished for losing their virginity were buried alive fully veiled (Plut. *Num.* 10.7); bride or indeed bride and groom (Serv. *Aen.* 4.374); prayer (Ovid *Fasti* 3.363); augury (Livy 1.18.6–10).

let alone that of the *Dionysiaca*. The gods of the epic world were less subject to change than the gods of the real world, insulated by tradition and the separation between literature and reality. But Apollonius already includes a great deal of specific reference to Ptolemaic cult and Hellenistic practices.[63] The Virgilian Venus is almost unrecognisable as a Roman version of Homer's and Apollonius' Aphrodite:[64] a driving narrative force, an interfering political patroness, even in Valerius Flaccus a terrifying fury-like avenger, rather than the pathetic wounded female of *Iliad* 5.[65]

Class has an important impact on viewing: respectable women would have been more secluded than their less well-off equivalents. Social class might also have had an impact on processes of identification, at least where epic is made accessible to often illiterate lower classes.[66] A Homeric hero might be the property of a whole community,[67] yet Trimalchio's misreadings of Homer in Petronius' *Satyricon* show that epic is cultural capital, easily mishandled (e.g. 48.7; 59.4–5).[68] Only for the (former) political elite in Rome is epic likely to have a value as an oppositional form, a complex critique of imperial power structures. For those less invested in their own power, it might tend instead to reassure and give prestige, to those praised, and to those who read, understand and display their knowledge of it.[69] Whether or not Alexandrian poetry is an insider's literary game, only available to a tiny cultured elite, Roman Callimacheanism clearly appealed to a reasonably wide audience, at least in terms of the readers of poetry.[70]

---

[63] See for instance Mori 2008: 140–86.

[64] On the Hellenistic representation of Aphrodite, and 'fascination with her playful superficiality on the one hand and her irresistible potency on the other' see Zanker 2004: 144–52.

[65] General on Aphrodite: Cyrino 2010, Smith and Pickup 2010; on Venus in Valerius Flaccus see Elm von der Osten 2007.

[66] Class had a massive impact on education, of women as well as men. On women and education see Cribiore 2001: 74–101. Ford 1999 discusses the extent to which Homer is a democratic text in classical Athens: 'if Homer was common coin in the democratic exchange of ideas, each transaction was also a social exchange of status and ideology'. (234–5)

[67] Homer is the most popular author among surviving papyri; this pattern also matches quotation in extant literary authors. There are a thousand Homeric papyri, ten times as many as the next most popular author, Euripides. The *Iliad* outshines the *Odyssey* at a rate of three to one, and the earlier books of the *Iliad*, especially books 1 and 2, are most popular by far. See further Cribiore 2001: 194–7.

[68] See Smith 1975, who adds the historical example of Calvisius Sabinus in Sen. *Epist*. 27.5–8, who bought slaves to know Homer and Hesiod for him. On the concept of cultural capital, see Guillory 1993.

[69] In democratic Athens, knowledge of epic shows your social status and leisured access to education: 'simply by virtue of its omnipresence, epic could serve not only as a medium of cultural exchange, but also as an arena for winning social distinction', Ford 1999: 233.

[70] On Roman Alexandrianism, see Hunter 2006. Literacy levels remained low; though many would be aware of epic without reading. Harris 1989: 323–37 summarises the growth, high points and decline of literacy in Greece and Rome; in classical Athens it was likely to have been 10–15%; Hellenistic Greece may have reached 30–40%; in the Roman period there was a lower level, with female literacy likely to have been as low as 5%.

Roman art must have reached a wider audience; Roman spectacle certainly did, as graffiti in Pompeii reveal.[71]

Political structures, too, varied wildly over this period. There is a huge difference between the culture of Archaic Greece, in which relatively small communities focused on kings, whom we might today view more as tribal leaders, and the enormous world cities of Alexandria and Rome.[72] Yet the differences between centre and periphery must also have been very significant. The relatively subtle difference between Republican and early Imperial Rome has been called revolution.[73] How much more important, then, is the difference between Athenian democracy, Ptolemaic kingship and Roman empire?[74] Some things, however, display continuity: the prestige of Homer; the importance of rhetorical and literary education; the use of epic as political and cultural capital.[75] In this situation, and given the strong claims of continuity and affiliation displayed in the texts themselves, it does make sense to study ancient epic as a whole.

Ancient thinking about vision

Scholarship, rhetoric, philosophy and scientific thinking influence epic, as well as a less well-articulated but nonetheless influential folk culture. Feeney has effectively shown how the scholia can illuminate (and influence) the workings of the poet;[76] Virgil's clear relationship to philosophical contexts has been explored with many different conclusions;[77] Lucan, as the nephew of Seneca, always offers the tantalising possibility that Stoic philosophy might be the key to his poem;[78] Statius' *Thebaid*, too, has been influentially

---

[71] There was a great deal of mythological and particularly epic material in surviving art, not just in Rome and Italy (especially Pompeii), but also in the provinces. Cribiore 2001: 195 gives this example: 'When in a papyrus letter a man, Capiton, asked a friend what type of murals he would like on the walls of his house – scenes from the *Iliad* perhaps? – for "the place demands it," one catches a tangible glimpse of the place this epic occupied in the lives of provincials in the Eastern part of the empire.' Epic material in Pompeian art: Lorenz forthcoming; on the *tabulae Iliacae*, see Squire 2011. On the popularity of gladiators in Pompeii, see Beard 2008: 259–75; on Virgil in Pompeian graffiti, see Gigante 1979: 163–83, Franklin 1997.
[72] On politics and the *Iliad*, see Hammer 2002 and in a more general Greek context Barker 2009. On Rome as cosmopolis see Edwards and Woolf 2003; Stephens 2003 on Alexandria.
[73] Syme 1939, interrogated by Habinek and Schiesaro 1997. On the 'Athenian revolution', see Osborne 2007, though with no essay on epic: is it inherently an anti-democratic form?
[74] Politics and literature in Rome: Habinek 1998, Dominik, Garthwaite and Roche 2009; on epic, Boyle 1993, Quint 1993; on Virgil, Stahl 1998; on Ovid, Feldherr 2010; on Lucan, Bartsch 1997.
[75] On the ancient reception of Homer, see Lamberton and Keaney 1992, Graziosi 2008.
[76] Feeney 1991. On Virgil and the Homeric scholia, see Schmit-Neuerburg 1999; for an introduction, Hexter 2010.
[77] For instance, Galinsky 1994, D. Armstrong 2004.
[78] See for instance, Marti 1945, D'Alessandro Behr 2007.

read as a Stoic text.[79] While the identification of one poet (or poem) with one philosophical affiliation is not my concern here, awareness of the changing, complex and thought-provoking intellectual contexts of these poems is clearly important. Different approaches to vision are expressed in various ancient contexts: the philosophical, scientific, mathematical and medical; the folk models of vision give a different slant, as do the metaphors of vision that are formed and expressed in literature, and the rhetorical treatises in which the relation between vision and text is theorised.

It is difficult to write about Greek and Roman theories of vision without too much oversimplification.[80] Most importantly nearly all the different theories assume some sort of physical contact between the thing viewed and the eye, even if mediated by the air; and second, that most theories fall into (or between) one of two groups: intromission (which envisages the eye as passive receiver of impressions from outside) and extramission (in which the eye sends out an active ray).

For example, Empedocles, as quoted by Aristotle at *Sens.* 2.437b–438a, seems to view the eye as a sort of lantern that sees by shining on external objects; the early Pythagoreans, as discussed by Theophrastus at *De sensu* 26, also seemed to think that the eye produced fire which flashed out. Most theorists seem to move between extramission and intromission, or to combine the two.[81] Plato in the *Timaeus*, for instance (45b–c), posits a fire from the eye coalescing with daylight to produce a continuous link between eye and object; at *Theaetetus* 156d–e colour is produced by an interaction between the eye and the object, both of which together are responsible for seeing.[82] Aristotle is difficult to pigeonhole, because he sometimes denies the role of touch in explaining sight altogether (*Sens.* 2.438a–b), but at other times suggests that the eye sends out visual rays (for instance, at *Mete.* 2.9.370a–374b).[83]

The Epicureans, following the atomists Democritus and Leucippus, are clearly intromissionists: we have not only fragments of Epicurus, but large parts of Lucretius book 4 concerned with vision. In their account, objects of vision emit *simulacra* or *eidola* (a sort of onion skin, atom-thick film, which retains the shape of the object) which strike the eye and cause vision (see e.g. Epicurus *Letter to Herodotus* in Diogenes Laertins *Lives* 10.48–9; Lucretius

---

[79] Vessey 1973; see also Billerbeck 1985.
[80] For a lucid introduction, see Bartsch 2006: 58–67, to which my summary here is indebted; other recent summaries: Morales 2004: 15–18, Cairns 2005: 138–9; for more detail, see van Hoorn 1972, Simon 1988, Rakoczy 1996; for a broader context: Lindberg 1976, Park 1997, Simon 2003; for a useful collection of optical sources: Smith 1999. Park 1997: 2 gives a useful diagram of the relative chronology of different ancient visual theorists.
[81] Smith 1999: 28.   [82] See Lindberg 1976: 3–6.
[83] Bartsch 2006: 64; see also Rakoczy 1996: 28–31. See also *De insomnis* 2.459b–460a.

4.54–61).⁸⁴ The Stoic position is less clear, partly because sources are late and obscure: they talk of a visual *pneuma* which emanates from the eye, causing a tension (*synentasis*, or in Latin, *intentio*) which acts upon the air. The idea that vision is a ray from the eye is persistent and difficult to dislodge.⁸⁵

One important folk concept of vision sees it as a locus of contagion. Cairns lists various literary texts which envisage pollution, shame and even diseases such as *ophthalmia* and epilepsy, as transmissible by sight.⁸⁶ Epic is notably absent from this list, but I will investigate below (Chapter 2, pp.71–7) ideas of visual pollution in epic, which are especially important with regard to the gods. The turning away of the gaze might not be an expression of relative status, or social rejection, but rather the desire to avoid contagion (or all three at once).

Bartsch 2006: 138–52 examines the penetrating gaze as part of Roman social regulation, suggesting that the huge number of images of eyes being pierced or attacked might be apotropaic devices, designed to turn away the piercing or attacking qualities of the eyes of envious onlookers. Chapter 8 will focus on the hostile gaze and the idea of the evil eye in epic. The evil eye is the folk conception that an envious gaze from afar, often not perceived by its object, can cause literal harm, either passing on the pollution associated with the negative emotion, or causing specific evil events to befall the object. Just as extramission shades into intromission, so the passive visual power of the hero as object on display shades into the active, penetrating gaze of berserk warriors, gods and monsters.

Considering metaphors and images used of vision, we have already thought about the active gaze as a ray.⁸⁷ The gaze is also associated with weapons, wounding and sharpness. The wound of love is a classic *topos*, and it can be imagined as being inflicted by the eyes of the beloved.⁸⁸ Bartsch discusses instances of the gaze as *acies*, or conceptualised as blunt (*hebes*) in Roman culture.⁸⁹ The gaze can also torture ([Quint.] *Decl.* 19) or burn (Pers. 2.34).⁹⁰

---

⁸⁴ Bartsch 2006: 59–62.
⁸⁵ Smith 1999 suggests Euclid and Hero of Alexandria as pure emissionists (28).
⁸⁶ Cairns 2005: 149 n.61: Soph. *OT* 1384–5; Eur. *Hipp.* 1437–8; *HF* 1153–62; *IT* 1217–8; Theophrastus *Char.* 16.14; Heliod. *Aeth.* 3.7.4.
⁸⁷ See Morales 1996, Morales 2004. Bartsch 2006: 145–52 also has many good observations on different metaphors associated with the gaze in Greek and Roman literature.
⁸⁸ Lucr. 4.1045–56, with Brown 1987: 132–3.
⁸⁹ Bartsch 2006: 149. *Aetna* 349; Hor. *Ep.* 1.14.37–8 (of the gaze as something that can be scraped); Pliny *HN* 23.59, 24.99, 29.132.
⁹⁰ Cf. also the sharp, blinding gaze of Augustus at Suet. *Aug.* 79.3 and Trajan's effective assaultive gaze in Pliny *Pan.* 17.3. Bartsch 2006: 149. See also Rakoczy 1996: 33–5, Barton 2001: 248–50. A striking metaphor found by Bartsch (150) in a fourth-century CE commentator on Plato's *Timaeus*, Chalcidius (*SVF* 2.863) characterises the gaze as 'a reptilian force invading the body'.

Steiner argues that sight and stoning are conceptual equivalents in Greek myth.[91] Another important metaphor of vision is that of the consumptive gaze, which feeds on desired objects or spectacles of pain.[92]

Finally, ancient rhetorical theorists discuss *ecphrasis* (description), *phantasia* (the internal image) and *enargeia* (bringing events before the eyes). As Goldhill rightly cautions, handbooks dating from the later centuries CE are no straightforward guide to the interpretation of sophisticated literary texts from a range of contexts and a particular genre.[93] Hoewever, Webb's treatment of *phantasia*, for instance, links epistemological theories of sense-perception to rhetorical theories of persuasion.[94] Webb argues strongly that visualisation played a huge part in the ancient discourse on and experience of reading and/or listening to poetry.[95] She builds on modern studies of visuality and reader response, as well as her own anecdotal evidence, gathered from students, to suggest that the ancient response privileged visualisation much more than modern discourse about reading.[96]

Homer is frequently present in the rhetorical handbooks as an example of effective *enargeia* (description that brings things before the eyes), along with Thucydides and the orators.[97] The boxing in *Aeneid* 5 is the first example in Quintilian's discussion of *enargeia* (*Inst. or.* 8.3.63 quoting *Aen.* 5.426).[98] Webb's desire to move away from the 'modern' definition of ecphrasis, which privileges epic and sets up the shield of Achilles as the Ur-text of ecphrasis, leads her to concentrate on history and oratory in opposition. Yet epic was hugely influential on other genres, and loomed large in the education system and ancient experiences of reading/listening. I am interested in all the visual tactics of epic, not just descriptions of works of art, and I will be examining Ovid's use of ecphrasis more broadly in articulating his narrative structure, as well as reflecting on the relationship between craftsmanship and poetry.

---

[91] Steiner 1995.
[92] Morales 1996. Examples: Cic. *Verr.* 2.5.65.12; Petr. *Sat.* 96.4; Suet. *Vit.* 14.2.6; Livy 24.14.2; Nepos *Eum.* 11.2.2; [Quint.] *Decl.* 7.10.20, 7.18.10; Calp. Flacc. *Decl.* 4.9; Tac. *Hist.* 1.44.2; Cic. *Mil.* 58.9; Cic. *Phil.* 11.7–8; Val. Max. 9.2.1. Bartsch 2006: 151 n.85; see also Leigh 1997: 171–97.
[93] Goldhill 2009. [94] Webb 2009: 107–30. [95] Webb 2009: 13–28.
[96] Esrock 1994; Small 1997: 130–1 on Michel Denis.
[97] Webb 2009: 19 cites the death of Patroclus and the making of the shield of Achilles; her appendix on subjects for ecphrasis (213–14) includes: Eurybates (*Od.* 19.246); Thersites (*Il.* 2.219); and the shield of Achilles.
[98] Virgil is frequently quoted by Quintilian, perhaps showing his pervasiveness in Roman education: in this section we also see *Aen.* 3.29–30 and 7.518; the next section on simile includes 2.355–6; 4.254–5; 4.143–4; *Georgics* 1.512–4. Quintilian even chastises himself for using too much Virgil, when he should be talking about oratory: *Cuius praeclara apud Vergilium multa reperio exempla, sed oratoriis potius utendum est.* ('I find many outstanding examples of this in Virgil, but examples from the orators ought rather to be used.' *Inst. or.* 8.3.79).

If ancient readers were particularly visual in their responses to texts, this may be attributable to available technologies. What would it be like to experience an epic or a tragedy (whether read silently, or aloud; in a recitation, a performance, or at home) in a world without film and television? Even the theatre must be a vastly different experience without darkness, the fourth wall and realist conventions. That rhetorical handbooks offer a formula for stirring the emotions in order to persuade, which might suggest that the analogy between listeners/readers of poems or speeches in the ancient world and viewers of cinema in the last hundred years or so is closer and more persuasive than is immediately obvious.[99] The cinema's heightened emotionality and processes of identification are perhaps even intensified by the active involvement of the reader/listener in producing images from his or her own store of *phantasiai*. Speaking from my personal experience as a reader of books and a viewer of films, both can have a similar effect of stimulating intense engagement.[100] The phenomenon of the disappearance of the cinematic apparatus from the consciousness of the viewer, the immersion of the viewer in the film world (or 'suture'), is something that can also happen, at least to me, when reading. The awareness of turning pages, seeing words and lines, disappears, and emotional involvement intensifies to the point of laughing, crying and gasping along with the characters. The anecdote above (p.14) of Octavia fainting during the recitation of *Aeneid* 6 might suggest that it was at least possible for ancient listeners to achieve the same sort of immersion.

Methodology

Is it anachronistic to read ancient texts in the light of modern theory? Bartsch justifies her exclusion of feminist film theory and psychoanalysis from her discussion of the gaze on the grounds that she wants to read texts from the ancient world as much as possible on their own terms. I agree that this is one laudable aim, although I am not convinced that excluding any particular part of modern theory makes it more achievable. In practice, Bartsch does use a wide range of modern ideas and approaches. Our readings of the ancient world are always a dialogue between their ways of thinking and ours; we can never come to the material as if innocent, unaffected by our own culture. The fascination of working on the ancient world is partly generated by the

---

[99] Webb 2009: 24–5 discusses the disjunction in ancient and modern critical responses to visualisation, arguing that critics in our culture tend to marginalise visual responses to texts, to emphasise their individual resonance, in contrast to ancient critics, who assume a degree of predictability in visual responses. Are modern readers disavowing the ways that film and television influence their reading?
[100] On the embodied nature of spectatorship and reading, see Esrock 1994.

interplay of difference and similarity, the attempt to think ourselves into their *schemata* and thought patterns, while remaining aware of our own. For this project, all sorts of theoretical writings are invaluable. Anyone who claims not to be using a 'theory' in their work is being disingenuous, or rhetorical. I have tried not to impose an idea on the material, but to balance what I look for in the texts against what I happen to find.

My approach to theory is consciously eclectic: I use modern ideas as ways to think about things, to start a dialogue with ancient material, as heuristic tools. This may be open to the charge of lack of commitment, to the suggestion that my approach is under-theorised rather than over-theorised. My decision not to stick with one set of ideas, but to read more broadly in the field of visual theory, leaves me open to the accusation that I am not really engaging with any one of those ideas. It is certainly possible to take one theory and pursue in depth the way it affects readings of texts, but this imposes its own limits. In any case, many of these theories are closely related to each other, and it seems artificial to pick one and exclude everything else. Film theory is closely related to literary theory, which also draws heavily on social history, art history and philosophy. Further, different material, different themes and ideas work better with different approaches. My aim is exploratory and provocative; the book is intended to make people think, and if others take these ideas further, and perhaps more systematically, then it will have succeeded.[101]

Narratology has provided useful insights, but I am not a narratologist. Focalisation, in particular, relates closely to my subject: representations of seeing in the text. By reflecting on the character in the text through whom the reader views the narrative, I explore multiple models for audience engagement. Narratologists often ask 'who speaks?'; one of my basic questions has been 'who sees?' at any given point, and, in particular, I look for multiple or competing viewers and viewpoints. How do lines of sight create structures in the narrative? In what different ways do lines of sight link characters and audiences together? How do lines of sight define power relationships? In this sense, my work is concerned with narrative and its workings, but is aware of its own subjectivity. Determining 'who sees' is always an act of interpretation, and in general I avoid attempts at quantitative answers. Rather this is a qualitative investigation, an attempt to ask how these lines of sight work. I want to follow through the numerous effects of vision, viewing and spectatorship as a theme of the poems. Matthew Leigh's work on amphitheatrical

---

[101] I have also tried to explain myself clearly and not rely on jargon to obfuscate meaning: I may not always have succeeded in doing this, but it is not my aim to mystify.

spectatorship in Lucan is an exemplary exploration of the political ramifications of one form of viewing in one poem.[102] I set multiple models in dialogue with each other across the genre of epic.

Neither am I taking a linguistic approach, as Prier, for instance, does (in a way) to the *Iliad* and *Odyssey*.[103] Words of vision do interest me, but I have not carried out a systematic study of the different words of vision and their implications.[104] I am rather concerned with larger-scale thematic and narrative structures. A word of vision often strengthens my argument, but is not necessary to enable a visual reading. The *phantasiai* are there even without specific visual words to activate them. Zeus may well be looking, even if it does not say so, and Apollo must surely be looking if he fires an arrow, even without a word to describe it. The relationships of power and knowledge which are crucial to the gaze are not always visual: the aural is also important, and the two overlap and interact. However, here I emphasise the visual aspect and explore its characteristic effects. Not all of these phenomena are exclusively epic manifestations, and this approach might be expanded fruitfully to other genres. But this book explores a selection of the characteristic ways of viewing (in) epic, in a way that offers a new perspective on epic, and on individual epic poems.

I have not tried to be comprehensive, either: in a book of this size, on material of this range, it would be impossible. However, ancient epic is represented in all its variety, from central and very well-studied texts, like Homer and Virgil, to the tangentially epic, such as Hesiod, Lucretius, Ovid and Catullus 64, to the sadly fragmentary, like Ennius and the epic cycle, and the extant poems which many may wish had disappeared, such as Silius Italicus, Quintus Smyrnaeus and Nonnus, and the newly recanonised, such as Apollonius, Lucan, Valerius Flaccus and Statius.

'The gaze' has been a fashionable phrase, that may already have had its day: books such as Reed 2007, *Virgil's Gaze*, seem to evoke the body of theory without actually engaging with it, showing how resonant the idea is. Reed's work was essential for my chapter on heroic bodies, but is really a book about the relationship between Virgil and Hellenistic poetry, focusing on the death of the beautiful boy, rather than a study of vision. Salzman-Mitchell 2005 is much more centrally relevant, and valuable for my understanding of Ovid, along with Hardie 2002b, although I aim to set Ovid within the epic tradition, rather than engaging with the body of his work as a whole. Clay

---

[102] Leigh 1997.   [103] Prier 1989.
[104] Thank you to the audience at Manchester in November 2009, especially David Langslow, for a stimulating discussion of this issue.

2011 was particularly useful for thinking about Homeric visions. Fredrick 2002 has generated a sense of what is distinctively Roman about the Latin epics I am studying; there is as yet no Greek equivalent, although the work of Goldhill and Osborne is important in different ways, and a collection of essays on Greek vision, resulting from the Celtic conference in Classics at Cork in 2008, is forthcoming.[105] Despite all the work on vision in individual epic poets, this book offers something different by putting them all together. My original aim, to gain a stronger sense of what is epic about epic, even to redefine our sense of the genre, might seem hubristic, but pursuing this theme across so many epic poems has certainly brought into relief the central structures of the genre and their many variations and subversions.

Film and text

To sum up: there are various advantages and disadvantages of using theories developed in relation to film to read ancient epic poems. First, theories of film are often closely related to theories of narrative. Currie's cognitive approach to film, which was a polemical response to psychoanalytical film theory, led to his rethinking of narrative.[106] There is a similar cognitive turn in the study of oral poetry, which, among other things, shows that seeing in the mind's eye or mental visual representation is 'a system analogous to perception' and 'uses the same parts of the brain as visual perception'.[107] Further, Bakker argues from discourse analysis that 'epic narrative is typically presented as, in narratological terms, a *description of things seen*, with the narrator (performer) posing as eyewitness'.[108] Arguably, the oral origins of epic make it more, rather than less, visual as a genre.

Later epic continues to play with ideas of performance and witnessing.[109] Traditions of rhapsodic performance and, later, *recitatio* continue to make

---

[105] Goldhill and Osborne 1994, Blundell, Cairns and Rabinowitz forthcoming.
[106] Currie 1995 developed into Currie 2010. These philosophical approaches, based on cognitive psychology, do give some consideration to effects specific to the medium, for instance the question of whether or not film (along with photography) presents rather than representing (i.e. are films and photographs in some sense 'real', putting their subject itself before us, rather than producing an image of it?). The same possibility exists, of course, for direct speech, which might well be 'real', i.e. a record of speeches which were actually made, or conversations which actually took place, but within narrative still constitute representation. So medium is still not crucial here.
[107] Clay 2011: 27, citing Rubin 1995: 57. Cognitive work on Homer includes: Minchin 2001: esp.132–60, Heiden 2008.
[108] Bakker 1993: 15. See further Bakker 2005 on Homeric performance and visualisation, esp. ch. 8, 'Remembering the god's arrival'.
[109] On Ovid, see Wheeler 1999. It would be profitable to pursue this in other Hellenistic and Roman epics.

epic performance more than simply imaginary.[110] Modern readers have often seen affinities between cinematic and epic techniques.[111] More tendentiously, one might argue that narrative poetry in the ancient world has the same cultural hegemony, penetration and prestige as cinema has in ours. Filmmakers and promoters have adopted the word 'epic' to connote grandeur of ambition, an association with the past, heroism that goes beyond the bounds of normal humanity.[112] Studies of the ancient world on film explore the relationship between films and texts.[113] For all the similarities, the differences between film and epic are equally important: by drawing out the visual side of epic, ideas from film studies and other visual theories take us away from words and the poet, and instead privilege the reader or listener as spectator. The problems of anachronism, particular generic expectations and the lack of a mass audience in antiquity are mitigated by attention to context, literary and historical. The essentialism of psychoanalysis, the idea that we are all, at base, the same, is offset by a clear sense of the cultural specificity of ancient epic.

Chapter summaries

The book begins from Zeus, and the idea of the divine gaze. The gods in epic, as in Greco-Roman culture and society in general, are imagined as watching over mortals with the potential to intervene. What is special about epic is that this is mimetically represented, and an important structuring device in the narrative. A change of scene is often modulated by going up to the divine level and back down elsewhere on the human level. This is typified by the *Iliad*, and later epics respond in different ways, which I trace in Chapter 2. After the gaze of Zeus, structure and transition, comes a brief survey of the figure of divine audience, exploring the already complex and fractious spectatorship of groups of gods in the *Iliad* and later epic. Gender has less effect on the vision of different gods than relative position within hierarchies of divine power: there follows a case study of Hera/Juno. Goddesses are often characterised as looking askance or aslant, in comparison to the downward vertical gaze of gods. However, the associations between rape and the imperial gaze are generally the preserve of gods. For goddesses, rape and other violations are

---

[110] See Collins 2004 on Greece; Markus 2000 on Rome.
[111] Mench 1969, Fitzgerald 1995: 147; on Homer, Latacz 1977: 78, Van Wees 1997: 673–4, Winkler 2007: 46–63, Clay 2011: 36–7.
[112] As in Elley 1984.
[113] Winkler 1991, Wyke 1997, Solomon 2001 with sections on mythology and 'muscleman epic', Winkler 2004, Winkler 2007. Winkler 2009 attempts a philological reading of film, which approaches the question in the opposite direction. For film and epic, see Paul 2013, which was not yet published at time of writing.

sites rather of dangerous pollution, and the chapter finishes with an investigation of passages in which gods and goddesses avert their gazes, coming to a climax with Statius' removal of the whole epic pantheon in *Thebaid* 11. The divine gaze is a site of vulnerability as well as power.

Chapter 3 looks at what happens when mortals look at gods and even, on occasion, challenge the divine control of viewing. It begins by exploring the problems of visualising the gods in representations of epiphany, where the incomprehensibility of divine desires fits well with McGowan's presentation of the Lacanian gaze as a distortion of the field of vision. Taking this further, the chapter investigates three explicit examples of mortal heroes granted partial versions of the divine gaze: Diomedes in *Iliad* 5, Aeneas in *Aeneid* 2 and Hannibal in *Punica* 12. This makes clearer the differences between mortal and divine vision, and investigates the plays on power and knowledge in these (limited) allowances of divine viewing privileges. It moves on to mortals who attempt, often with little success, to appropriate the divine perspective, in particular examining the tradition of heroes who scorn the gods, from philosophers, and especially Lucretius' Epicurus, to figures such as Ovid's Pythagoras and Statius' Capaneus, and finishes with the absence of the divine in Lucan's narrative.

If heroes often come between gods and men, prophets offer a channel of communication between them. Chapter 4 examines vision in a prophetic context, showing both the powerful, penetrative gaze of prophet figures, and its circumscription, especially by blindness, sexual violence and the abject. While gods decree, mortal prophets have visions; madness is mostly associated with women and only enters epic later in the tradition. Prophets can see into parts that are hidden from others: not just the future, but the underworld, the inside of the body, and other parts of the world. However, the problems and difficulties of persuasion and interpretation are continually highlighted, and both male and female prophets are excluded from society and associated with the abject. So the power of the prophet also forms a distortion in the field of epic vision, emphasising the vulnerability of poetic power.

Chapter 5 focuses on ecphrasis, and its close connection to the authorising power of the divine gaze. This is the inset image at the heart of the book, a pause which looks back and forward to other chapters. Beginning with Catullus' Ariadne, it starts from the idea of ecphrasis as containment and objectification of the other, but moves on to explore the fragmentation and complexity of the different ways ecphrasis is used in epic narrative. Different objects described, and different types of ecphrasis, have different effects. The shield is often apotropaic, designed to induce terror and to emphasise associations with the divine. The cloak has feminine connections, while ecphrases of spaces emphasise the poet as creator of his own universe. The chapter explores the transitional use of ecphrases, particularly in Ovid, and associates this with his subversive representation of the divine. It investigates the representation of gender and ethnicity in ecphrases, and what happens when the ecphrastic subject breaks out of the frame or draws the viewer in by returning their gaze.

In Chapter 6, the female gaze comes to the fore, and the figure of the teichoscopy (looking out from the walls over the besieging troops, often used as an expository device). Those who watch from the walls are usually women or old men and children; their marginal position equates to their exclusion from the main action of epic. In contrast to the gods, they are not able to break the frame and enter the world of battle, although the power of grief and the performance of lament does allow limited incursions (those of Priam and Argia are particularly important). However, women on the walls become surrogates of the narrator, taking on poetic power as they explain what they see, analogous to prophets and seers. Yet there are different models of viewing, and the perspective of the women on the walls is distinct from that of the heroes themselves, the gods and even the old men. Their concern is with personal relationships, and this often shades over into erotic viewing. Teichoscopy is a central epic trope, and yet it is always at the margins of epic, threatening to become tragedy or even elegy. We watch how Helen's teichoscopy in *Iliad* 3 is transformed by tragedians, elegists, and Ovid, all of which have their influence on the Flavian epicists, Statius and Valerius Flaccus, ending with the passage in Quintus Smyrnaeus' *Posthomerica* in which the Trojan women threaten to break into the fighting, which shows that Quintus is no pale imitation of Homer.

The female gaze is equally important in Chapter 7, which looks at the other side of the coin: the hero as 'to-be-looked-at'. Heroes in ancient epic are erotic objects, not just in explicit narratives of eros, but also in mainstream battle narrative. They are the objects of the gaze not just of women (and gods) in the text, but also of the audience. The chapter begins by taking a cluster of images in which gods beautifying heroes are compared to craftsmen creating works of art. The association between women in epic and statues is matched by an association between heroes and art objects. Is there a homoerotic agenda in at least some of ancient epic? (For those who hear *The epic gaze* as *The epic gays*, this is your section.) It takes the imagery of art objects and extends it to other metaphors of nurture and cultivation, especially the comparison of dying heroes to flowers and trees. This chapter takes theory about fetishisation and female bodies in film and applies it to the (mainly) male bodies of epic heroes. It suggests that epic narrative is inherently masochistic, in the alternation between victor and victim, killer and dying. It finishes by looking once more at the importance of gender, by interrogating examples of action heroines, from Camilla in Virgil to Penthesilea in Quintus and Nicaea in Nonnus. Are women on the battlefield treated any differently to men and what significance does this have?

This representation of epic masculinity as compromised and problematic is, of course, only one part of the story. Chapter 8 offers the normative version of the heroic gaze, and the perspective of the killer and victor, coming back to the powerful gaze as exemplified earlier in the book by that of Zeus. The assaultive gaze links vision and violence, in a pattern of causation and analogy. Viewing leads to killing, and viewing can be in itself a sort of violence, a sort of violation. This chapter investigates the visual power of the epic hero and its significance in the light of ancient theories of vision. It focuses on the idea of the blazing eyes of the hero and their effects in battle, not just as signifier, but also as agent, like the shield, of violence. Battles are not always physical; sometimes the most important confrontations are decided on the field of vision. This chapter investigates the role of ancient ideas about the evil eye in epic, culminating in Medea's conquest of Talos, the ultimate battle of the gaze. It ends with examples of battles of the gaze, from Hector and Achilles, to Aeneas and Turnus, Tisiphone and *Pietas* in *Thebaid* 11.

The final chapter brings the female gaze and the male gaze together, in the duo of Perseus and Medusa, to interrogate epic monumentality. The chapter thinks about the different ways Medusa's gaze is represented, her agency or lack of it, her identity as a rape victim, and the way she is used by Perseus. Ovid and Lucan, epic's most incisive and insistent critics and practitioners, also give us the two main surviving accounts of the Medusa myth. Ovid's Perseus episode, in particular, parodies, questions and complicates epic. How does this fit into wider epic attitudes towards monuments? What happens when the epic hero ceases to do things and becomes fixed, looked at and admired as a monument? We then turn once more to Lucan, and his reluctant burial of Pompey. Finally, back to Achilles and his ongoing burial and monumentalisation in the *Odyssey*, the *Metamorphoses* and the *Posthomerica*: is ancient epic, in the end, always struggling to finish off the *Iliad*? Statius' Parthenopaeus has the last word: object and subject of desire, emblem of mortality. Just as Medusa's gaze is appropriated and yet its continued effectiveness suggests she is not entirely disempowered, so heroes turned into the material of epic are both its objects and subjects.

CHAPTER 2

The divine gaze

The gods of epic gaze endlessly at the action: Zeus sits on Mount Ida, watches Hector and manipulates his mind (*Iliad* 11.336–7). Athene perches in the form of a swallow in the rafters of Odysseus' palace, drinking in the slaughter below (*Odyssey* 22.240). Juno on a cloud is the impotent spectator of Aeneas' duel with Turnus (*Aeneid* 12.791). Mercury flies over the earth with the predatory gaze of a bird of prey, only to fall in love (*Metamorphoses* 2.708). Jupiter orders the gods to remove their eyes from the *nefas* at Thebes (*Thebaid* 11.126). While Zeus gazes in desire at Semele, Eros watches him (Nonnus *Dionysiaca* 7.190). These moments of divine viewing are emblematic of their respective epics.

The gods are one of the defining features of the epic genre:[1] divine action creates the quintessentially epic effect of ἔκπληξις, the thrill of shock and wonder.[2] When Athene flashes down like a shooting star to disrupt the aftermath of the duel between Paris and Menelaus in *Iliad* 3, the sight paralyses the watching Trojans and Achaeans with θάμβος (*Il.* 3.79). Prier reads this feeling of wonder as a sense of the otherness of the universe pressing down on the viewer.[3] The word ὄπις, 'the vengeance of the gods' (LSJ), has a visual element.[4] It refers both to the vengeance of gods on men, and to the awe men feel towards gods, and the existence of this concept suggests that the Greeks felt themselves to be objects of the divine gaze.[5]

---

[1] Feeney 1991: 301 discusses Lucan's *Civil war* as 'history' rather than epic because of its disavowal of divine action; Servius 1.4.4–6 defines the heroic thus: *est autem heroicum quod constat ex diuinis humanisque personis continens uera cum fictis* ('it is heroic because it consists of divine and human characters, containing truth alongside created things'). Feeney 1991: 36.

[2] Feeney 1991: 52 citing Arist. *Poet.* 1460a11–17; Polybius 34.41; Dio 12.67; Plut. *Quomodo adul.* 17f, 20f, 25d; Heinze 1915: 466 n.1.

[3] Prier 1989.

[4] *LfgrE* links the word etymologically to the root of ὄψομαι; the first meaning given is 'kontrollierender *Blick* der Götter', although *op* may also refer to voice rather than gaze, as εὐρύοπα.

[5] See Burkert 1981; Rakoczy 1996: 67–71 discusses the visual aspect of the word.

The gods in epic can work on a number of levels: as characters taking full part in the story; as allegorical representations of human emotions (anger, wisdom, love); as embodiments of the natural world; as cultic presences, worshipped by readers outside the poems. It is often difficult to distinguish between these modes, and a god in epic can be more than one thing at a time. Gods also have a special way of looking. The divine gaze is characterised as clearer, more penetrative and more effective than that of mortals. Gods disguise themselves, or conceal themselves or their protégés with clouds; Athena removes the cloud that blunts Diomedes' vision at *Iliad* 5.121–32, so that he can see and attack the other gods. Only by wearing the helmet of Hades can a god hide from another god (5.844–5).

When Feeney put his stamp on *The Gods in Epic*, one of his central concerns was the problem of propriety and fiction in representing the gods: what sort of varying responses did Homer's gods inspire? Why did ancient readers find them problematic? How did later writers of epic respond?[6] Critics of Homer complain that the gods are stripped of their majesty when they are displayed feasting, laughing and committing adultery. For instance, Xenophanes' observation that:[7]

> πάντα θεοῖσ' ἀνέθηκαν Ὅμηρός θ' Ἡσίοδός τε,
> ὅσσα παρ' ἀνθρώποισιν ὀνείδεα καὶ ψόγος ἐστίν,
> κλέπτειν μοιχεύειν τε καὶ ἀλλήλους ἀπατεύειν.   (Fr. 11 DK)
>
> Homer and Hesiod attributed to the gods everything,
> as many things as are a disgrace and a reproach to men,
> stealing, adultery and deceiving one another.

leads into a rejection of anthropomorphism, and is thought to have inspired allegorical readings of the gods.[8] The scholia, too, complain of impropriety and unseemliness.[9] Yet the gods remain incomprehensibly powerful to the human characters, who for the most part cannot even look upon them.[10]

What I will suggest in this chapter and the next is that the gods in epic function like the 'big Other' in Lacanian film theory. McGowan's account of 'The Real Gaze' champions Lacanian psychoanalysis against those who argue that 'Film Theory' is no longer possible or desirable.[11] By going

---

[6] Feeney 1991: 5–56. More recent interventions include: Allan 2006, Turkeltaub 2007.
[7] On Xenophanes, see Kirk, Raven and Schofield 1983: 163–80, Feeney 1991: 6–8.
[8] Feeney 1991: 8–12, 19–20.
[9] Feeney 1991: 36 citing Porph. 226.9–10, A 3.423; bT 4.4; bT 19.407; bT 24.23.
[10] On epiphany and its problems, see below, Chapter 2, pp.79–85.
[11] McGowan 2003 responding to Bordwell and Carroll 1996; developed further in McGowan 2007. Another influential account of cinematic subjectivity is Silverman 1988a.

further into Lacan's ideas about 'the gaze' he offers an alternative model to Mulvey's mastering gaze. 'The gaze is not the look of the subject at the object, but the point at which the object looks back.'[12] It is the moment of distortion in the field of vision, when we attempt to imagine the desire of the other that remains always inaccessible. The incomprehensibility of divine power to characters in epic is very similar to the effect of the unknown and unknowable truck driver in Spielberg's first feature, *Duel* (1970), in which the protagonist, David Mann, is pursued inexplicably by an enormous truck, whose driver neither he nor the audience ever see.[13]

The gods are a source of authority, for kings, men and the epic genre, yet they are also distant, difficult (if not impossible) to represent and fully understand. Confronting divinity contains the discomfiture and deferral encountered in confrontations with the gaze of the Other, the perpetually inaccessible Real. The ancient awareness of existing in a field of vision is closely tied to the divine gaze. What is so disturbing about the gods is that characters can never really understand why they act or predict reliably what they will do. For readers, the clash between the trivial, anthropomorphised gods and the awe-inspiring, incomprehensibly powerful representations of the arbitrariness of life, fate and natural forces creates a vertiginous sense of inadequacy in the face of the universe.

McGowan suggests that the comforting cinema of mass-market Hollywood aims at domestication and integration of the gaze; so in *Schindler's List*, for instance, the father figure of Schindler makes bearable the horrors of the Holocaust. We might see the Homeric 'taming' of the gods, in scenes of feasting, laughter and rivalry, as a form of fantasy, not dissimilar to that offered in many Hollywood films, not least Harryhausen's *Clash of the Titans* (1981). Yet, like all fantasies, by making the gods comprehensible in human terms, by countering the terror and awe that they induce, this fantasy contains the seeds of its own dissolution.[14] Readers cannot accept this representation as the full story, and the incongruity of the narrator's visions of the gods (almost comic in tone), set in contrast with the human characters' experiences of the gods or their casual almost cosmic destruction (the *theomachy* in *Iliad* 20 is perhaps the best example of this), undoes the fantasy, creating an awareness of textuality, and of the impossiblity of adequate representation.[15]

---

[12] McGowan 2003: 28–9.   [13] See further above, p.9.
[14] Aristotle regards Homer's poetic sweetness as covering up the implausible in the narrative (*Poet.* 1460a 35–b 2).
[15] Criticism of the *theomachy*: Porph. 2.226.9–14.

The presence of the gods in epic both authorises and problematises the genre.[16] The importance of the gods as intermediate audience has a number of contradictory narrative effects: on the one hand we are drawn to empathise with Zeus' anger on waking up in *Iliad* 15, or Juno's grievances at the beginning of the *Aeneid*, or Diana's sorrow at the death of Camilla, or Parthenopaeus. Yet on the other hand we are always continually aware of the incommensurability of the divine perspective. The gods serve to heighten epic emotion and simultaneously to alienate. The objectivity of the epic narrator is an item of faith: but in practice focalisation works in many different ways to offer blurred and layered subjectivities. To watch with the gods is always to be aware of being watched by the gods. Temporarily to aspire to an immortal perspective is to be permanently aware of mortality. The presence of the divine gaze in epic is important for establishing both the pain and the pleasure of the text.

The aim of this chapter is to explore the workings of the divine gaze in epic, its role in epic narrative, the relationship between the narrator and the gods. The chapter begins from Zeus, as the normative centre of visual power and control, and goes on to bring out the complexities, problems and fragmentations of that normative power. Epic is a massive assertion of authority and an ongoing subversion of that authority, and already within the dynamics of the divine audience, before mortals fully enter the equation, we can see that opposition at work. The second section sets up the structural importance of the divine gaze in the *Iliad* and elsewhere in epic. Although De Jong 1987 argues that only 12% of the *Iliad* is focalised by the gods, the divine audience is continually evoked as a mediating presence, like that of the narrator, if indirectly.[17] What sort of mediation do these divine audiences provide? Often divine viewing is characterised by dissent and conflict, and the following section discusses a selection of divine audiences. Hera and Juno, in particular, often oppose and rival the control of Zeus and Jupiter. The next section asks to what extent this rivalry is gendered, and whether Hera and Juno have feminine gazes. The divine gaze has its limits; Juno's lack of agency at the end of the *Aeneid* is one notorious instance of this. The next section engages with divine blind spots, moments of fallibility and confrontations with the limits of divine power, especially the relationship between narrative and fate. The last section looks at the divine gaze as

---

[16] This approach brings Ovid's *Metamorphoses* into line with other epic, more self-consciously aware, but still playing the same game. Lucan, then, looks like the most radical reinterpreter of Homeric epic.

[17] De Jong 1987: 228–9 decides that 'the *Iliad* mainly presents a human vision of the events around Troy'. Pucci 2002 makes a strong argument for the gods as spectators in the *Iliad* as a mediating audience.

vulnerable, especially to pollution, and examples of gods averting their gaze, either as an expression of power, or from fear of contamination. Viewing in the ancient world is not entirely a one-way process, and it is difficult to separate the passive visual power of the gods, as they create awe, wonder and terror, from their active, penetrating gazes, which see through to the fabric of reality and lead to action and accomplishment, but my focus here is on the gods as active viewers, and in the third chapter, 'The mortal gaze', on the gods as objects of the gaze, in which we, and epic, as well as its heroes, look back at the gods.

The gaze of Zeus

The controlling gaze of Zeus/Jupiter watches over much ancient epic. The plot of the *Iliad* is, at least on some level, the unfolding of the plan of Zeus (1.5). Even if Zeus' control and visual power are less prominent in the *Iliad* than they are in the Hesiodic corpus, especially the *Theogony*, the gaze of Zeus is still at the heart of the *Iliad*.[18] Zeus' epithet εὐρύοπα can be translated as 'far-seeing'.[19] Although the narrative begins with Apollo and Hera, it moves up to Zeus with the supplication of Thetis; the first book ends with Zeus falling asleep and the second book begins with him lying awake worrying, deciding to send down the deceptive dream to Agamemnon. We can think of the gaze of Zeus, along with the gaze of the narrator, as overseeing the whole narrative, even if (or perhaps because) he does not intervene as much as other gods.

Book 11 shows a sequence of close (if atypical) involvement: at 11.3–4 Zeus sends Eris down to the battlefield, and at 73–83 vision links Zeus and Eris, as they rejoice in watching the battle, while the other gods sit apart, forbidden to intervene. Zeus' separation from the other gods is an emphatic index of his power and control over them and the narrative. He continues as audience through the book: at 163–5 he rescues Hector; panoramic similes, for instance that of a forest fire describing Agamemnon's *aristeia* at 155–9, associate the narrator's perspective with that of Zeus; at 181–94 his assumption of a more effective viewing position on Mount Ida, although without a specific verb of vision, leads to his intervention by sending down Iris with instructions to Hector; at 335–6 Zeus is explicitly viewing again as he holds

---

[18] See Lovatt forthcoming-c on the divine gaze in Hesiod.
[19] Alternatively it might mean far-sounding: see LSJ *ad loc. LfgrE* suggests 'breitgesichtig, mit weitem Blick' or 'mit weitreichender Stimmer'. Used always of Zeus in the Homeric corpus: see *Il.* 1.498, 5.265, 8.206, 8.442, 9.419, 9.686, 13.732, 14.203, 14.265, 15.152, 15.724, 16.241, 17.545, 24.98, 24.296, 24.331; *Od.* 2.146, 3.288, 4.173; *Hom. Hymns* 2.3, 2.335, 2.442, 2.461, 3.340, 4.540, 23.2, 23.4.

the balance between the two sides; and at 544 he is called ὑψίζυγος (seated on a high ridge) as he drives fear onto Ajax. At 598 Achilles takes over as focaliser of the action, with a narratorial comment which points out his lack of control (602–3). The movement from viewing to controlling is typical of the divine gaze, and while Zeus' awareness of the action is not always cast in visual terms (the gods also hear events on the battlefield), the emphasis on position and vertical perspective often implies vision. So at the beginning of book 20, Zeus summons a council 'from the many folded peak of Olympus' (κρατὸς ἀπ' Οὐλύμποιο πολυπτύχου· 20.5), and later points out to the gods that he will use this as his vantage point to watch them as they intervene: ἀλλ' ἤτοι μὲν ἐγὼ μενέω πτυχὶ Οὐλύμποιο / ἥμενος, ἔνθ' ὁρόων φρένα τέρψομαι· ('Even so, I shall stay here upon the fold of Olympus, sitting still, watching, to pleasure my heart.' 20.22–3). Later, as the gods fight, Zeus is still watching, and listening, on Olympus:

ἄϊε δὲ Ζεὺς
ἥμενος Οὐλύμπῳ· ἐγέλασσε δέ οἱ φίλον ἦτορ
γηθοσύνῃ, ὅθ' ὁρᾶτο θεοὺς ἔριδι ξυνιόντας.   (*Iliad* 21.388–90)

Zeus heard it
from where he sat on Olympus, and was amused in his deep heart
for pleasure, as he watched the gods' collision in conflict.

Zeus is represented as separate from the other gods and in control of them, watching them along with the mortals, showing his control over both realms, mortal and immortal, by the fact that he does not need to act. His predominant emotion in these passages is joy, a response to his own power and control, although elsewhere he watches with frustration, sorrow and pity.[20] What sort of effect might the mediating internal audience of Zeus have on the experience of the external audience (readers or listeners)? Does it create a sense of alienation, or can we identify with his joy? The external audience are not in any way in control of the narrative, but rather, like the other gods in book 11, they must watch but not intervene.

The gaze of Zeus continues to be important after the *Iliad*, and its prominence is one index of the epic nature of a text.[21] So epics of the

---

[20] See below, pp.42, 73.
[21] The gaze of Zeus is closely related to the will (or mind, or plan) of Zeus. 'As the νόος or βουλή of Zeus reaches its fulfilment (τέλος, *telos*), so does the plot of an epic.' (Feeney 1991: 58) However, the gaze also marks his direct involvement, manifestation and representation in the narrative. The plan of Zeus may lie behind a text like Apollonius' *Argonautica*, or even Lucan's *Bellum civile*, but the display of Zeus gazing is an index of the epic poet's commitment to the epic genre, his removal from tragedy and historiography and other ways of writing about the gods.

alternative stream that begins with the *Odyssey* offer less access to the viewpoint of Zeus, and a much less secure sense of the authority which derives from the poet's association with Zeus.[22] The *Odyssey* itself begins with Poseidon leaving (1.22–6), just as Zeus averts his gaze in *Iliad* 13, but focuses on presence rather than viewing; Athene tends to take on a persona and join the action, rather than watching it (for example, as Mentes at 1.105). After the divine council at 1.22–95, the poem operates for the most part at one remove from Zeus; the vertical gaze of Athene instead takes centre stage.[23] Similarly in Apollonius' *Argonautica*, various gods look down, but Zeus, although apparently concerned, is not on display.[24] In the *Aeneid*, however, the gaze of Jupiter regains its prominence.[25] Although, as we will discuss below, Juno is the first divine audience in the poem, at 1.223–6 the transition to Olympus is achieved not through the concerned viewing of Venus, who will shortly supplicate him, but through the powerful gaze of Jupiter:

> Et iam finis erat, cum Iuppiter aethere summo
> despiciens mare ueliuolum terrasque iacentis
> litoraque et latos populos, sic uertice caeli
> constitit et Libyae defixit lumina regnis. (*Aeneid* 1.223–6)

> And now there was an end, when Jupiter from the high ether
> looking down on the sea with its winged sails and the low-lying lands
> and the shores and the broadly spread peoples, thus at the peak of the sky
> he stood and fixed his eyes on the kingdom of Libya.

Jupiter's power is emphasised by his vertical perspective: not just in *aethere summo* and *uertice caeli*, but also in the description of the world spread out beneath him, and the repetition of the *de-* prefix in *despiciens* and *defixit*. Venus' eyes, in contrast, are full of shining tears (228), which Jupiter calms as he calms the elements (254–6). Another structurally important moment

---

[22] The gaze of Zeus features in the cyclic *Cypria*: in fr. 1 West, Zeus sees the overcrowded earth and takes pity, deciding to reduce the human race by means of war: Ζεὺς δὲ ἰδὼν ἐλέησε ('Zeus saw and pitied', 3).

[23] Zeus does appear at *Od.* 13.125–58, though in response to Poseidon, and not apparently viewing events in the mortal realm himself. Poseidon and Athene are the most active divine viewers; Poseidon watches Odysseus at 5.282–4 and 375–8. Athene's gaze seems almost like an extension of, or replacement for, the gaze of Zeus: she has a powerful vertical gaze, for instance, at 22.205–9, 236–40, 297 and 24.472–88.

[24] Feeney 1991: 56–69 on the absence of Zeus in the *Argonautica*. Zeus is called by the epithet Ἐπόψιος (the one who watches over) at 2.1123, but there are no actual scenes of Zeus watching. At 2.237–48, Athene's viewing of the Argo after they leave Phineus is combined with her presence; her movement down from Olympus is compared to a man thinking about and straining to see his way home. At 3.6–10 Hera and Athene watch the Argonauts as they hide in the reeds. At 4.54–6 the moon watches Medea as she flees; at 475–6 the *Erinys* watches Jason and Medea kill Apsyrtus.

[25] On Jupiter in the *Aeneid*, see Hejduk 2009, tendentious but with further bibliography.

is at 219–21, when Jupiter hears the prayer of Iarbas, and directs his gaze to Carthage (*oculosque ad moenia torsit | regia et oblitos famae melioris amantis*, 'he turned his eyes to the royal walls and the lovers forgetful of good reputation', 220–1), before sending Mercury down to dispatch Aeneas. The transition to Olympus at the beginning of book 10 is also achieved through the powerful gaze of Jupiter, who calls a council of the gods:

> sideream in sedem, terras unde arduus omnis
> castraque Dardanidum aspectat populosque Latinos.   (*Aeneid* 10.3–4)
>
> in his starry seat, from where on high he turns his gaze on
> all lands and the camp of the Dardanians and the Latin peoples.

Book 12 makes Juno's viewing explicit (see below), but leaves Jupiter's implicit: at 725–7 Jupiter weighs the fates of Turnus and Aeneas in the scales, as if responding to the noise of battle (*fragor*, 724), but without explicit verbs of either hearing or seeing. After the reconciliation of Juno, she turns her gaze away (*mentem . . . retorsit*, 841; *nubemque relinquit*, 842, picking up on *de nube tuentem*, 792), and Jupiter replaces her by sending down a *Dira*. This act of sending is equated in a simile to a Parthian shooting a poisoned arrow (853–60).[26] This evocation of visual intention, of the assaultive gaze (see below, pp.310–46), is reinforced by verbal connections to previous mentions of the divine gaze of Jupiter: *ab aethere summo*, at the end of line 853 recalls the end of line 1.223, and the use of the verb *torsit* for the Parthian shooting the arrow, at the end of line 858, recalls *torsit* at the end of 4.420. The sending of the *Dira* then becomes an act of divine closure, imposing Jupiter's authority on the narrative, as he promised in books 1, 4 and 10. Aeneas' spear throw can be read as an extension of the assaultive gaze of Jupiter, fulfilling his purpose and penetrating Turnus' body as the *Dira* penetrates and debilitates his mind.

In the *Metamorphoses*, the scenes of Jupiter gazing take place in the early books, suggesting that Ovid moves from one type of epic to another, perhaps from a Hesiodic mode towards something more Apollonian.[27] Lucan's evocation of the divine gaze of Jupiter comes at the height of the narrator's bitter criticism of the gods for allowing Pharsalia to take place, at

---

[26] More strictly, the flight of the *Dira* is equated to the flight of the arrow, but there is emphasis on the Parthian shooting the arrow, as on Jupiter sending the *Dira*.

[27] Book 1 contains three scenes, all with explicit verbs of vision: 1.163 (Lycaon, *uidit*); 1.324–6 (Deucalion and Pyrrha, *uidet*); 1.588–9 (Io, *uiderat*). In book 2, when he shoots down Phaethon at 304–13, all the elements of the assaultive divine gaze are present, including his vertical position, but there is no verb of vision, only the moment when he calls on the other gods to bear witness to the necessity of his action; at 2.401–10 he inspects the damage and catches sight of Callisto (see below, pp.68–9).

the moment he appears to espouse an Epicurean position that the gods are not interested in mortal affairs: *spectabit ab alto | aethere Thessalicas, teneat cum fulmina, caedes?* ('Will he watch the Thessalian slaughter from the high ether, and yet hold onto his thunderbolts?', 7.447–8). Valerius Flaccus returns to a much more Virgilian model, with his Jupiter gazing from the starry citadel (*siderea arce*, 498) at 1.498–500 before he sets out his world plan (even if the verb of gazing, *tuens*, recalls rather Virgil's Juno); at the beginning of book 4, the Apollonian revelation from Glaucus that the loss of Hylas and Hercules was part of the plan of Zeus is turned into a rather Homeric divine scene, with Jupiter watching, pitying (4.1–3) and rebuking Juno (4.4–14). Both of these episodes articulate the structure of the epic, and enact a change of scene, as well as emphasising Jupiter's control and authority. Silius too presents a largely Virgilian Jupiter, gazing at Scipio in danger (4.417–19), watching from the Alban mount as he turns Hannibal from Rome (6.595–9).[28] Quintus is rather more sparing with his use of the gaze of Zeus.[29] And Nonnus presents a Zeus as much gazed at as gazing.[30]

This section ends with a brief case study of the gaze of Zeus at the beginning of the second half of the *Thebaid*, a gaze which will be averted later in the poem and the chapter.[31] The games have finished, and the scene shifts from the Argive camp, delayed on their march to Thebes, to Olympus:

> Atque ea cunctantes Tyrii primordia belli
> Iuppiter haud aequo respexit corde Pelasgos,
> concussitque caput motu quo celsa laborant
> sidera proclamatque adici cervicibus Atlans.   (*Thebaid* 7.1–4)

---

[28] Further examples: 12.605–8; 17.341–3 (where Juno watches the battle of Zama, and Jupiter watches her, as in *Aeneid* 12); though the last word is left for Juno (see below).

[29] The only concrete example of Zeus watching the battle comes at 10.47–9, just before an expanded focus on the figure of Eris (53–65). Divine audiences are more frequent: 2.492–3; 3.90; 8.194–6; 8.430; 12.438; 13.416–19; 14.95–6.

[30] At 1.64 Zeus is a *thauma* watched by the nymphs; at 1.324 Hera watches Zeus watching Europa; at 7.190–279 Zeus watches Semele, but Eros watches Zeus. But at 2.436 Zeus watches the battle, at 5.609 he watches Persephone; at 6.207 he watches the death of Zagreus; 9.180–3 watching Dionysus; at 24.73–108 Zeus's pitying gaze inspires a mass divine intervention, a baroque reworking of the passage in *Iliad* 22 in which Hera warns him that if he rescues Hector, all the gods will feel entitled to rescue their favourites; here it actually happens. At 27.241–341 Zeus breaks up a divine banquet to insist that all the gods should watch the battle and intervene. At 32.38–41 his eyes are enslaved by Hera in a repetition of the *Dios apate*.

[31] On the poetics of delay in this section, see McNelis 2007: 97–101. McNelis argues that the shift at the beginning of book 7 is partly generic, from a Callimachean to an epic mode, from aetiology to battle narrative, evoking the seventh books of Virgil and Ennius with their martial subject matter. The emphasis on the gaze of Zeus fits into that movement, as do the Iliadic moments also pointed out by McNelis.

> And as they were delaying those first beginnings of the Theban war,
> Jupiter with unbalanced heart looked back to the Pelasgians,
> and shook his head with that movement at which the high stars
> struggle and Atlas proclaims that weight has been added to his neck.

Jupiter here is a cosmic, Lucretian god, not composing the universe but throwing it into confusion, looking back rather than looking forward or looking down.[32] He creates narrative momentum from uneasy energy, through a complex, layered divine machine, sending Mercury to stir Mars into action; paradoxically, this narrative thrust takes us into the pause of ecphrasis, as we view the palace of Mars, into the territory of Ovid.[33] The end of the episode is articulated by a return to the gaze of Jupiter (*uidit pater altus*, 'the high father sees', 84), combined with a sea simile (86–9), leading into a return to the Argives (90–105). Quick-response Mars on the mountain of Acrocorinth sends Panic (*Pauor*) with a visual and aural illusion of Theban troops on the plain of Nemea. This stimulates a mad rush towards, rather than away from, battle, brought to an end with another sea simile (139–44), which gives a panoramic view of the Argive expedition in disarray, as if on the point of setting out again, compared to sailors setting sail into a storm. The scene changes back to Olympus via the gaze of Bacchus: *uiderat Inachias rapidum glomerare cohortes | Bacchus iter* ('Bacchus had seen the Inachian cohorts gathering for a swift journey', 145–6), whose misery and supplication make him an object of our gaze and that of Jupiter (151–4). Jupiter builds up the impression of his control by denying that Juno has influenced him (195–7), and holding up implacable fate as his own justification (197–8; 215–18), even as his less than subtle rhetoric accuses Bacchus (208–14). His special pleading of his own clemency (199–208) leaves us with the strong impression of his autocratic and arbitrary power (and possibly a sense of insecurity?). Finally we make it to Thebes at the end of the supplication scene (227), the ultimate scene change, as if the readers are undertaking their own epic journey, from *Odyssey* to *Iliad*, from journey to arrival. The proliferation of scene-changing moves is typically Statian, making us go up to Olympus and back twice, mixing divine instructions, supplication and prophecy, with ecphrasis and the action of personified

---

[32] The Lucretian vocabulary (*primordia* and *motu* occur frequently) does not match any particular passage or idea in a straightforward way: two well-known passages (1.907–14 – atoms as elements, like letters; 2.308–32 – looking at atoms with the human eye is like looking at sheep from the top of a mountain) combine these words with vocabulary of vision (also *concussa* at 1.919). We are at the limits of allusion; *primordia* is used not in its Lucretian sense, but rather in its narrative, historical sense. Jupiter is emblematic of the malevolent divine gaze which Lucretius reviles (see below, pp.99–101).

[33] On this ecphrasis, see below, p.171.

Pauor. The complex tone of the representation of Jupiter suggests the uneasy relationship between the *Thebaid* and the tradition of epic authority, which we will come back to when we address Jupiter's refusal to watch, or to allow the other gods to watch, the end of the poem.[34]

The normative controlling gaze of the king of gods and men is a key ingredient of epic. When Zeus or Jupiter is watching the unfolding of his plan, all is epic in the text. By shying away from the gaze of the supreme god, poets shy away from the full, heavy-handed power of epic. The relationship between divine gaze and structure is emerging: epic narrative often follows lines of sight, turns away from one object to another, following the gaze of the gods.

Structure, transition and the divine gaze

The divine gaze structures and frames the *Iliad*. In particular, the scene often changes by moving along the line of sight to the gods in Olympus, or positioned elsewhere vertically above the plain of the narrative, and back down to focus on a different person, or place. Elsewhere, generalising similes perform a similar function, moving the listener out to a panoramic perspective, before taking them back in to a different part of the action.[35] This pattern is particularly prominent at the beginnings of books, which suggests that Hellenistic editors (and later readers and writers of epic) took it as a structural marker.[36] For instance, at 4.1–4 the gaze of the gods links the duel of Menelaus and Paris to the divine council. At the end of the scene (75–80) the transition back to the battlefield is achieved by following Athene as she does Zeus' bidding, and by watching her from the mortal perspective, in puzzlement. Here the mortal gaze is set against the divine gaze (see further below, Chapter 3). The beginning of book 20, too, cuts from Xanthus' prophecy of Achilles' death to the divine council, via Zeus,

---

[34] See below, pp.71–7.
[35] See Clay 2011: 21, 64–5. Martin 1997: 144 proposes a 'rhythmic' function of Homeric similes: 'they punctuate the narrative, giving it an almost musical rhythm and providing episodic definition'. He even uses a cinematic analogy: 'Similes are not like freeze-frames or slow-motion sequences in film, but like transition shots, often accompanied by theme music.' (146)
[36] For this study, the *Iliad* as foundation of the epic tradition is key. Since evidence from Apollonius shows that Homeric book divisions (or 'segment markers' as Heiden prefers) were already fair game for intertextual play by that stage according to De Jong 1996, it matters little who actually devised the divisions, or even precisely when. The idea of Homer is more important here than the 'real' Homer, if he ever existed. For an introduction to the debate, see Heiden 2000. See further Taplin 1992: 285–93, Stanley 1993: 249–93, Olson 1995: 228–39, Heiden 1998, Jensen 1999, De Jong 2001, Edwards 2002: 38–61, Heiden 2008. We should take book divisions seriously as part of the architectural design of the poems, especially the *Iliad*, at whatever stage in the tradition they were introduced, and as a fascinating aspect of narrative transition.

whose viewing is highlighted at 22–3. A stronger example, which stays on the battlefield, but moves from the Greeks to the Trojans, occurs between books 12 and 13. At the end of book 12, Hector is in the process of breaking through the Greek wall (462–71), and we are watching from the Trojan perspective. At the beginning of book 13, Zeus turns away his eyes:

> Ζεὺς δ' ἐπεὶ οὖν Τρῶάς τε καὶ Ἕκτορα νηυσὶ πέλασσε,
> τοὺς μὲν ἔα παρὰ τῇσι πόνον τ' ἐχέμεν καὶ ὀϊζὺν
> νωλεμέως, αὐτὸς δὲ πάλιν τρέπεν ὄσσε φαεινώ,
> νόσφιν ἐφ' ἱπποπόλων Θρῃκῶν καθορώμενος αἶαν
> Μυσῶν τ' ἀγχεμάχων καὶ ἀγαυῶν Ἱππημολγῶν
> γλακτοφάγων, Ἀβίων τε δικαιοτάτων ἀνθρώπων.
> ἐς Τροίην δ' οὐ πάμπαν ἔτι τρέπεν ὄσσε φαεινώ·
> οὐ γὰρ ὅ γ' ἀθανάτων τινα ἔλπετο ὃν κατὰ θυμὸν
> ἐλθόντ' ἢ Τρώεσσιν ἀρηξέμεν ἢ Δαναοῖσιν. (*Iliad* 13.1–9)

> When Zeus had driven against the ships the Trojans and Hector
> he left them beside these to endure the hard work and sorrow
> of fighting without respite, and himself turned his eyes shining
> far away, looking out over the land of the Thracian riders
> and the Musians who fight at close quarters, and the proud Hippomolgoi,
> drinkers of milk, and the Abioi, most righteous of all men.
> He did not at all now turn his shining eyes upon Troy land
> for he had no idea in mind that any one of the immortals
> would come down to stand by either the Danaans or the Trojans.

This transition begins the second half of the poem, and a major segment of the narrative; appropriately the first word is Zeus. He is the agent, as discussed above, but showing his power by turning his gaze away. With anthropological detachment, he looks rather at faraway tribes, reinforcing his global perspective. He is bigger than this story. The repetition of τρέπεν ὄσσε φαεινώ emphasises his visual power. Then Poseidon comes into the picture, taking his place as chief viewer:

> Οὐδ' ἀλαοσκοπιὴν εἶχε κρείων ἐνοσίχθων·
> καὶ γὰρ ὁ θαυμάζων ἧστο πτόλεμόν τε μάχην τε
> ὑψοῦ ἐπ' ἀκροτάτης κορυφῆς Σάμου ὑληέσσης
> Θρηϊκίης· ἔνθεν γὰρ ἐφαίνετο πᾶσα μὲν Ἴδη,
> φαίνετο δὲ Πριάμοιο πόλις καὶ νῆες Ἀχαιῶν.
> ἔνθ' ἄρ' ὅ γ' ἐξ ἁλὸς ἕζετ' ἰών, ἐλέαιρε δ' Ἀχαιοὺς
> Τρωσὶν δαμναμένους, Διὶ δὲ κρατερῶς ἐνεμέσσα. (*Iliad* 13.10–16)

> Neither did the powerful shaker of the earth keep blind watch;
> for he sat and wondered at the fighting and the run of the battle,
> aloft on top of the highest summit of timbered Samos,

the Thracian place; and from there all Ida appeared before him,
and the city of Priam was plain to see and the ships of the Achaeans.
There he came up out of the water, and sat, and pitied the Achaeans
who were beaten by the Trojans, and blamed Zeus for it in bitterness.

οὐδ' ἀλαοσκοπιήν implies the watchfulness of a guard, here noticing an opportunity. His viewing contains both the distance and wonder of the detached divine audience, and the pity and engagement which leads to intervention; finally, back down to the Greek camp, when Poseidon inspires Ajax (43–75). The narrative has moved from Trojans attacking the Greek wall to Zeus on Ida, to Poseidon on Samos, back to the mortal level, but this time from the Greek perspective, and from Zeus in control to Poseidon in control; all this has been mediated and initiated by divine viewing.

At the beginning of book 15 Zeus awakes and there is a strong transition from Hera and Poseidon ascendant to the resumption of Zeus' plan, from the Achaeans triumphant and the Trojans in disarray, to Hector's incursion on the Greek ships, which will finally stimulate Patroclus' intervention and Achilles' return to battle.

> ἔγρετο δὲ Ζεὺς
> Ἴδης ἐν κορυφῇσι παρὰ χρυσοθρόνου Ἥρης,
> στῆ δ' ἄρ' ἀναΐξας, ἴδε δὲ Τρῶας καὶ Ἀχαιούς,
> τοὺς μὲν ὀρινομένους, τοὺς δὲ κλονέοντας ὄπισθεν
> Ἀργείους, μετὰ δέ σφι Ποσειδάωνα ἄνακτα·
> Ἕκτορα δ' ἐν πεδίῳ ἴδε κείμενον, ἀμφὶ δ' ἑταῖροι
> ἥαθ', ὁ δ' ἀργαλέῳ ἔχετ' ἄσθματι κῆρ ἀπινύσσων,
> αἷμ' ἐμέων, ἐπεὶ οὔ μιν ἀφαυρότατος βάλ' Ἀχαιῶν.
> τὸν δὲ ἰδὼν ἐλέησε πατὴρ ἀνδρῶν τε θεῶν τε,
> δεινὰ δ' ὑπόδρα ἰδὼν Ἥρην πρὸς μῦθον ἔειπεν·   (*Iliad* 15.4–13)

> But now Zeus wakened
> on the high places of Ida, by Hera of the golden throne,
> and stood suddenly upright, and he saw the Trojans and the Achaeans,
> those driven to flight, the others harrying them in confusion,
> these last Argives, and among them Lord Poseidon.
> And he saw Hector lying on the plain, his companions sitting
> around him, he dazed at heart and breathing painfully,
> vomiting blood, since not the weakest of the Achaeans had hit him.
> And the father of men and gods saw him and pitied him,
> and looking terribly under his eyebrows at Hera, he spoke a word to her:

Zeus' resumption of the gaze equates to his resumption of control over the narrative. He looks at the Trojans and Achaeans, Poseidon, Hector and finally Hera; the passage runs through the panoply of different types of viewing: an unmarked gaze, to a pitying gaze, to a threatening gaze. We are made to participate in his viewing, with the Trojans and Achaeans separated and yet confused; the delay of Ἀργείους until line 8 creates a sense of visual arrangement; keeping Poseidon back until even after that emphasises the shock and anger of Zeus; even more so, the sight of Hector wounded is what engages him emotionally and brings his anger at Hera to a climax.[37] This moment of gazing has two effects: it brings to an end the *Dios apate*, the episode of the deception of Zeus, and it shifts the scene from mortal battles to Olympus, to which Hera now flees; after a number of divine messages, Poseidon leaves and is replaced by Apollo; the focus on the Argives is replaced by a focus on Hector. This is a pivotal moment of divine gazing.

The Iliadic narrator shares this divine perspective, using the god's-eye view (or the bird's-eye view) to give a broad overview of the action, before swooping in to pick out a particular narrative focus. The bird's-eye view brings the narrator and the gods particularly close together. The narrative focus changes from the particular to the general; the scope of the narrative pans out, as if we cut from a zoom to a wide-angled lens.[38] So in book 11, at 67–73 the focus moves from the Trojans, and Hector in particular, to a general sense of the whole battle spread out below us, via a simile of two lines of reapers facing each other. At 72–3 it becomes clear that this simile is focalised through Eris, and probably Zeus, as she watches and delights in the spectacle of battle. So at 155–62 the general effect of Agamemnon's *aristeia* is conveyed from above as a forest fire, which turns out at 163–4 also to be focalised through Zeus. This particular transition is eased and complicated emotionally by the reference to vultures at 161–2:

> οἱ δ' ἐπὶ γαίῃ
> κείατο, γύπεσσιν πολὺ φίλτεροι ἢ ἀλόχοισιν.   (*Iliad* 11.161–2)
>
> who were lying on the ground
> much dearer now to the vultures than to their wives.

---

[37] Hera's epithet (βοῶπις) appears at these two key moments, among others: when she lies to Zeus about involvement with Poseidon (34); and when Zeus responds to her heavily spun words (49) and may imply a deceptive gaze.

[38] Richardson 1990: 119–23 points out that the bird's-eye view in Homer occurs when people gather for battle, when they scatter or when they fight (120). He also points out the prevalence of similes (120) and marks out the bird's-eye view as a framing or transitional device. 'The bird's-eye view frames a scene of mass movement, usually only at the beginning or at the end, and serves as a transition between episodes.' (121) He also makes the link with the gods: 'Because we are accustomed in Homer to supernatural flight and to the gods' distant perspective, the sudden ascent to a bird's-eye view does not so much highlight the narrator's manipulation of our perception of the story as it establishes a strong relationship between the narrator and the gods'. (122)

Structure, transition and the divine gaze 43

The predatory birds, too, are looking down from above, so that this simile which pans out is quite literally a bird's-eye view. The gods are often represented as, or represented by, birds.[39] Not just any bird, either, but almost invariably a predatory bird, whose extraordinarily sharp gaze picks out the movements of the small and weak and gives them the ultimate punishment.[40] The bird's-eye view, then, suggests the power of the gods over what they watch: at any moment, suspended in the air above the scene, we might swoop and destroy. Not every bird's-eye view in the *Iliad* is juxtaposed with a transition to a viewing god, but the two are closely associated with each other, in a way that continually reminds the reader of the mediating divine audience. So at 4.422–45 the Danaans prepare for battle; at 422–6 they are compared to waves beating against the shore; at 433–6 the Trojans are like a myriad of sheep bleating for their lambs; at 439–45 the gods associated with each side are introduced, reaching a climax once more with Eris swelling up into the heavens and hurling down bitterness on both sides. The great general battle-scene, the enormity of which is conveyed in contrast to the similes from nature and farming, is focalised through divine viewers.[41]

The divine audience is so structurally important to the *Iliad* that it functions as a level of viewing in the poem, always potentially there, a constant mediation between story and audience, an alternative to the narrator (or implied author).[42] The Muses who inspire the epic poet are represented as witnesses of the story, for instance at *Il.* 2.484–92.[43] Later epic poems, especially the *Aeneid*, always responding to the *Iliad*, pick up on this phenomenon, so that it becomes a marker of the epic nature of a text.

---

[39] Gods as birds: 7.58–66 (Athene and Apollo watch the duel as vultures in a tree, and also watch the massed ranks of the Achaeans, who are compared to a wind darkening the waters of the sea, 63–6); 14.286–91 (Sleep hiding from Zeus becomes a songbird up a tree); 15.236–8 (Apollo as hawk); 18.615–16 (Thetis delivers the armour like a hawk); 19.349–51 (Athene goes down like a hawk to give Achilles divine nourishment).

[40] Lonsdale 1989 associates the penetrating gaze of the gods with birds of prey, in particular the eagle of Zeus.

[41] Another example: at 13.330–60, from Idomeneus we move to a general battle, described by a simile at 334–7 as like whirlwinds raising dust in a great cloud; then back to the perspective of individual warriors, blinded by the sunlight on the weapons (341–4), and finally to the gods behind it all, Zeus, Poseidon and their rivalry (345–60), whose perspective is contrasted with a potential mortal viewer: μάλα κεν θρασυκάρδιος εἴη / ὅς μιν ἄδην ἐλόωσι καὶ ἐν σταδίῃ ὑσμίνῃ. ('That man would have to be very bold-hearted who could be cheerful and not stricken looking on that struggle.' 13.343–4). Clay 2011: 64–5 discusses transitional similes, for example 12.278–89. Here Zeus is included in the simile, creating the snow storm and the rain, and a few lines later at 292 he drives on Sarpedon to attack the Greeks. The transitional vision includes the perspective of Zeus, even though an explicit verb of vision is not applied to him.

[42] Myers forthcoming deals with the gods as mediating audience in more detail.

[43] See Clay 2011: 15–17. For the relationship between muse and poet see Spentzou and Fowler 2002.

44   The divine gaze

The *Odyssey* works rather differently: for instance at 4.625, the move from Telemachus and Nestor in Pylos to the suitors back on Ithaca is achieved by a simple δέ (Lattimore adds 'meanwhile'). Beginnings of books focus on time and space.[44] Athene thinks and moves, intervening like a character rather than a member of the audience who has broken into the story, and the divine gaze, when it does occur, is more often in its assaultive mode.[45] Apollonius has one crucial but atypical structural moment of divine gazing, when Hera and Athene watch the Argonauts as they hide in the reeds at Colchis, and go apart to devise their plan:

> Ὣς οἱ μὲν πυκινοῖσιν ἀνωίστως δονάκεσσιν
> μίμνον ἀριστῆες λελοχημένοι αἱ δ' ἐνόησαν,
> Ἥρη Ἀθηναίη τε, Διὸς δ' αὐτοῖο καὶ ἄλλων
> ἀθανάτων ἀπονόσφι θεῶν θάλαμόνδε κιοῦσαι
> βούλευον.   (AR *Argonautica* 3.6–10)
>
> In this way, the heroes were waiting unexpected
> in the dense reeds, in ambush, but they noticed them,
> Hera and Athene, and went to a room apart from Zeus himself
> and the other immortal gods and began to plan.

Vision is emphasised by the heroes hiding in the reeds, in ambush; the use of ἐνόησαν recalls many Homeric instances of the divine gaze. This introduces the first and only narrative excursus up to Olympus, and motivates the action of the second half of the poem, changing at a stroke the tone of the narrative.[46] Ironically enough, it is with this distinctively Iliadic scene that the most Hellenistic focus on love (and tragedy) begins. The structural similarities bring out the differences in approach and attitude. In Virgil, by contrast, the moments of divine gazing cluster around the beginning, the climax and turning points in the poem, in a manner very similar to the *Iliad*.

The later Latin tradition, excluding Lucan and Ovid for the moment as special cases, largely follows Virgil.[47] Some examples: at Valerius Flaccus 1.574–7 Boreas spies out the Argo (*Pangaea Boreas speculatus ab arce*, 'Boreas,

---

[44] See Heiden 2000, who argues that the *Odyssey* is different from the *Iliad*, in which 'segment markers' come after 'low consequence' scenes (i.e. the shield of Achilles) and before 'high consequence scenes' (i.e. the death of Hector). Dawn begins books 2, 5, 8 and 17. Arrivals mark books 4, 10, 12, 14, 16 and 18. Departures: 6, 7, 11, 14 and 15. The only books that begin with gods are books 15 (Athene departs for Sparta), 21 (Athene puts the contest into the mind of Penelope) and 24 (Hermes leads the souls of the suitors down to the underworld). Only the latter has a focus on vision, with the staff of Hermes that confuses the eyes.

[45] See Lonsdale 1989 for Odyssean material.

[46] Hunter 1989: 24, who takes ἀνωίστως as 'out of sight' (97).

[47] Ovid uses many different transitional devices, and treats his gods in a typically slippery manner. He is the master of changing scenes, changing stories and changing everything else: which make his epic

having seen from his Pangaean citadel...', 575) and starts a new episode with his demand for a Virgilian epic storm. Bacchus kicks off the Nemean episode at *Thebaid* 4.664–7 when he catches sight (*conspicit*, 665) of the Argive expedition, causing a drought and the events of books 5 and 6. Statius' *Achilleid* plays with the divine gaze at 25–6 by placing Thetis, as she panics at the sight of Paris' ship, underneath rather than above the action, looking up from the bottom of the sea, leading into the main action of the poem. Silius has Venus watching during the storm which threatens Hannibal at the end of the poem, as he leaves Italy (17.283), and pleading for him to be saved, paradoxically, so that the Romans can prove their military prowess by defeating him (part of Silius' closural reworking of *Aeneid* 1).

Quintus Smyrnaeus is appropriately Iliadic, with numerous instances of the divine gaze.[48] A good example is the moment when Apollo cuts off the *aristeia* of Achilles at 3.29–30, horrified by piles of Trojan corpses as he fights Memnon, which leads into the death of Achilles. From this survey, the sense that there are two streams of epic, the normative, Iliadic stream, and the subversive, Odyssean one, is strengthened. One would tentatively include Apollonius and Ovid, but surprisingly none of the Flavian epics, not even the *Achilleid*, in the Odyssean stream.[49] This is inevitably an oversimplification, but it does underline the way that opposition and complication are built into the epic genre from as early as the *Odyssey*, and that responding to the *Iliad* is always in a sense subverting it.

Fractious viewing: divine audiences and dissent

The classic moment of divine viewing in the *Iliad* is at 22.158–66, when a simile describing Hector and Achilles racing around Troy as competitors at an athletic festival modulates into the gods watching them, with the implication that what is deadly serious for mortals is a game for the gods.[50] This contrast, however, is far from being the whole story. For the divine audience, the sight stimulates a debate about whether or not to intervene, showing Zeus in disagreement with Athene, who speaks for the other gods. Far from rejoicing, Zeus mourns for Hector in this passage (ἐμὸν

---

credentials difficult to assess, although he elevates ecphrasis above the divine gaze in his transitions and hence gives precedence to the authority of poet over the authority of muse and god. See Chapter 5, pp.177–80. On Lucan and the divine gaze, see below, pp.111–20.

[48] 1.184–5; 2.492–3; 3.30–1, 91–2; 7.556–63; 8.24–5, 191–2, 430; 9.182–3; 10.47–9; 11.168–9; 12.437–9; 13.416–29.

[49] On the *Achilleid* and 'alternative' epic, Hinds 2000.

[50] Griffin 1978, Griffin 1980: 144–204. On the divine audience as spectators at games, see Lovatt 2005: 80–100. Myers forthcoming will change the game.

δ' ὀλοφύρεται ἦτορ / Ἕκτορος, 'My heart grieves for Hector', 169–70). In fact, this is a passage which focuses on the inevitability of epic narrative, even for Zeus, and he gives Athene dispensation to go down to the battlefield and assist the story in following its course. The controlling gaze of Zeus is tempered by the corporate gaze of the gods, by which his actions, too, are held accountable.[51] The powerful emotions stimulated by viewing threaten to make Zeus act irrationally and outside the remits of what has been decided. The *Iliad* is characterised by gods viewing as a group, and disagreeing about it. The sight of the duel in book 3 leads to the disagreement between Zeus and Hera at 4.1–84; at 7.442–63 Zeus and Poseidon watch the Greeks build their wall and argue about it; at 8.1–52 Zeus forbids the other gods to intervene; at 12.176–8, the narrator wishes for divine powers to tell the story, but the Achaean gods are dejected; at 20.4–32 Zeus watches, but sends the other gods to join in; at 24.23–76 the gods watch Achilles mistreating the corpse of Hector, and discuss what to do.[52] Above all the events are represented as stirring up strong emotions and viewers as being drawn into the action: whether it is joy, anger or sorrow, even (in later epics) love, viewing epic is not a neutral experience. Mixtures of these emotions may create even more powerful paradoxical responses.

There is a self-conscious and complex play on divine viewing in the song of Ares and Aphrodite at *Od.* 8.266–369.[53] Here the audience of gods is called together to laugh at the adulterers caught in the golden net, rather than to lament the deaths of great heroes. Rinon reads this second of the three songs of Demodocus as a *mise-en-abyme* of the *Odyssey*, while the other two songs reflect on the relationship with the *Iliad*.[54] However, intertextuality with the *Iliad* is still clearly important here. In *Iliad* 1 Hephaestus was a figure who inspired uncontrollable laughter (ἄσβεστος γέλως, 1.599), a peacemaker who reconciles differences, but takes on the role of a servant, bustling (ποιπνύοντα) about the palace (1.597–600). Now he is putting on the show, but it is not clear whether the uncontrollable laughter of the gods at the sight is entirely directed against Ares and Aphrodite:[55]

> ἔσταν δ' ἐν προθύροισι θεοί, δωτῆρες ἑάων·
> ἄσβεστος δ' ἄρ' ἐνῶρτο γέλως μακάρεσσι θεοῖσι
> τέχνας εἰσορόωσι πολύφρονος Ἡφαίστοιο.   (*Odyssey* 8.325–7)

---

[51] See Morrison 1997, Van Erp Taalman Kip 2000.
[52] Clay 2011: 6 suggests that the internal audience of mortals in the chariot race is the equivalent, in which an argument breaks out over predictions of who will win, and that the device of the internal audience creates *enargeia* (vividness).
[53] On Ares and Aphrodite Burkert 1960, Braswell 1982, Olson 1989, Alden 1997.   [54] Rinon 2006.
[55] On the laughter of the gods, see Brown 1989.

Fractious viewing: divine audiences and dissent 47

> The gods, the givers of good things, stood there in the forecourt,
> and among the blessed immortals uncontrollable laughter
> went up as they saw the handiwork of subtle Hephaistos.

Further, when Ares catches sight of Hephaestus leaving, so that he can have his way with Aphrodite, the same phrase describes him as Poseidon stealing a march on Zeus at *Il.* 13.10:

> οὐδ' ἀλαοσκοπιὴν εἶχε χρυσήνιος Ἄρης,
> ὡς ἴδεν Ἥφαιστον κλυτοτέχνην νόσφι κιόντα·   (*Odyssey* 8.285–6)
>
> Nor did Ares of the golden reins keep a blind watch on him,
> as he saw Hephaistos the glorious smith go away.

So Hephaestus, controlling the plot with his artful technology, becomes not just a figure of the poet, but also a figure of Zeus. He is temporarily deceived by Ares and deceives him in his turn. In both episodes the erotics of epic come to the surface. Yet Hera only has agency to hide the activities of Poseidon, rather than acting herself, and Aphrodite is the object of laughter and the lascivious gazes of the male gods, for female gods are specifically excluded from this audience: θηλύτεραι δὲ θεαὶ μένον αἰδοῖ οἴκοι ἑκάστη. ('but the female gods remained each at her home, for modesty.', *Od.* 8.324). This clearly underlines the ways that gender roles are a strong part of the anthropomorphic characterisation of the gods in epic. Goddesses may have power over mortals, but they stand in relation to gods much as women stand in relation to men. This song is a pleasurable episode for its male audience, in which the laughter of the gods is echoed by the enjoyment of Odysseus and the Phaeacians (367–9). But for Hephaestus (and Aphrodite), both in a way at the centre of this nest of gazes, this is no laughing matter: his anger, like that of Achilles, is savage (χόλος δέ μιν ἄγριος ᾕρει· 'with the savage anger upon him', 304), as if attempting to return to properly epic territory. Poseidon, too, takes the episode as a serious affront to divine dignity, and demands that Hephaestus release them immediately (343–58).

Different members of the audience respond very differently to what they see. Aphrodite's response to being looked at, when she reaches the safety of Paphos, is to wash (362–6), demonstrating a connection between pollution and being the object of the gaze. This is not just a way of drawing a strong contrast between gods and mortals; the similarities between Hephaestus and Odysseus, both wronged husbands taking their revenge, argue for the story's relevance to the wider text of the *Odyssey*. This episode was considered out of place by ancient critics, as was the *Dios apate*.⁵⁶ Yet it is highly attractive to and influential on later epic poets. Epic is always more multiform and more provocative than the notions of the critics devising the categories might suggest.

How is the idea of the divine audience used as the epic tradition develops? In Apollonius' *Argonautica*, for instance, it is largely significant for its absence;⁵⁷ apart from Hera and Athene (see above, p.44), the only real incident of divine viewing in the poem marks the departure of the Argo as a sublime epic moment:⁵⁸

> πάντες δ' οὐρανόθεν λεῦσσον θεοὶ ἤματι κείνῳ
> νῆα καὶ ἡμιθέων ἀνδρῶν γένος, οἳ τότ' ἄριστοι
> πόντον ἐπιπλώεσκον·   (AR *Argonautica* 1.547–9)

And all the gods looked down from heaven on that day
on the ship and the race of the semi-divine heroes, the best men then
who sailed on the sea.

As well as the gods, the nymphs watch from Pelion, marvelling at the ship as divine work and the heroes themselves, presumably, though not explicitly, as erotic objects (549–52). The audience of gods, in this text that eschews omniscient narrative, and prefers the limited perspective of its puzzled characters, authenticates the epic credentials of expedition, heroes and poem, though it also misleads us, by implying that it will be more Iliadic than it actually is.

It is notable that in Valerius Flaccus' version of this scene, the divine viewing is the moment of a scene change to Olympus and a full divine council, complete with competing divine factions, prophecy and world-plan, dragging the *Argonautica* into the mainstream of epic in the Homeric–Virgilian tradition:⁵⁹

> Siderea tunc arce pater pulcherrima Graium
> coepta tuens tantamque operis consurgere molem

---

⁵⁶ Ares and Aphrodite: Zoilus of Amphipolis, fr. 38 in Friedländer 1895; Plato *Rep*. 389a, 390c. Feeney 1991: 30, Jolivet 2005.
⁵⁷ Another notable absence is in Ovid's 'Iliad': in *Metamorphoses* 12, the figure of Fama replaces the watching divine audience; at 150–4 there is a sacrifice, but no divine response; during the whole Cycnus episode, and obviously throughout Nestor's narrative, the divine audience are absent. It is not until the capricious Apollo and Neptune appear at 12.580–611 in order to kill off Achilles that we have a sense we are still in epic territory.
⁵⁸ Hunter 1993: 78. Occasional moments of single gods viewing: Athena watches the Argonauts leave Phineus and accompanies them (2.537–48); Artemis as the moon watches Medea fleeing (4.57–65); Hephaestus, Hera and Athene watch the Nereids bouncing the Argo through the wandering rocks in amazement and terror (4.956–60). None of these, though, are scenes of group watching and discussion, as in the *Iliad*.
⁵⁹ On the prophecy of Jupiter, see Hershkowitz 1998b: 239–41. Zissos 2008: 302: 'The switch to Olympian focalization . . . achieves an elegant change of scene.'

laetatur (patrii neque enim probat otia regni).
una omnes gaudent superi uenturaque mundo
tempora quaeque uias cernunt sibi crescere Parcae.

(VF *Argonautica* 1.498–502)

Then the father looking down from his starry citadel is happy at
the beautiful undertakings of the Greeks and that such a great mass of work
rises up; for he did not approve the leisure of his father's reign.
Together all the gods rejoice and the Fates see times to come
for the world and the roads growing for their own benefit.

Here the figure of Jupiter, initially on his own, seems in imperial control, and the other gods provide nothing more than assent; yet the *Parcae* seem to have their own agenda, once more foregrounding the problematic issue of Jupiter's narrative control. Both see this as marking the end of the golden age, the first ship opening up the sea to work, commerce and war;[60] *molem operis* ('the mass of work') might also imply the beginnings of epic; the phrase *tantae molis erat Romanam condere gentem* ('Such a great labour it was to found the Roman race', 1.33) sums up the opening of the *Aeneid*; *coepta* is also a key word in the proem of Ovid's *Metamorphoses* (*coeptis*, *Met.* 1.2).[61] Jupiter's prophecy goes on to explicitly position the *Argonautica* as the first beginnings of epic, leading to the Trojan war (545–54), and the Roman empire (555–60): or in poetic terms, the *Iliad* and the *Aeneid*.[62] The reinstatement of the epic narrator's special relationship with the gods is one of Valerius' ways of re-epicising Apollonius, and scenes of divine viewing are much more frequent throughout the poem than in the Hellenistic *Argonautica*.[63]

However, there is a difference between the Iliadic model and the much more Virgilian approach of Valerius. Valerius makes his Jupiter the principal owner of the gaze, but the whole pantheon watch together, and respond in unanimity (*una omnes gaudent superi*, 'All the gods rejoice together', 1.501). We have seen above the importance of Jupiter's gaze in Virgil, but there is far less emphasis on the group watching so prominent in the *Iliad*. Jupiter's gaze leads into the council of book 10, but the other gods are not

---

[60] For this Roman trope in Augustan poetry, see Fabre-Serris 2008.
[61] For metapoetic treatment of the Argonautic myth in earlier Roman poetry see Harrison 2007.
[62] It is also notable that Valerius replaces the admiring nymphs of Apollonius' version, and the baby Achilles, with the women on the shore (494–7). The grieving gaze of the worried mothers and wives left behind is set in contrast to the joy of the gods. The blazing limbs of Apollonius' rowers are replaced by the more threatening sails (reminiscent of Catullus 64) and shields of Valerius' Argonauts.
[63] 1.120 (Juno watching Hercules); 1.598 (Boreas sees and asks for storm); 3.487 (Juno watching Hercules); 4.1 (Jupiter watching); 4.131 (Neptune turns gaze away from Amycus); 4.667 (the gods watching); 5.617 (Mars watching); 6.621 (Jupiter watching); 7.153 and 7.190–2 (Juno watching); 7.193 (Venus looking at Colchis); 8.318 (Juno watching and intervening).

represented as watching. As their speeches make clear, both Venus and Juno are well aware of the action currently under-way, and the other gods do respond to the emotional viewing of the two goddesses, but there is no description of them watching. Virgil emphasises the potential for discord and disruption in their responses:

> Talibus orabat Iuno, cunctique fremebant
> caelicolae adsensu uario, ceu flamina prima
> cum deprensa fremunt siluis et caeca uolutant
> murmura uenturos nautis prodentia uentos   (*Aeneid* 10.96–9)

> Juno was making her plea in such words, and all the gods
> were raging with varied assent, as if the first breaths of wind
> when caught by the woods rage and roll around blind
> murmurs betraying winds to come to sailors.

The blindness of the storm suggests an arbitrary threatening violence, and it is hard to know what the function of the internal observer is here (a counterpart of the unwary mortals? Of Jupiter himself?). But Jupiter's response is calculated to seem even-handed and quell the threatened storm (his function of bringer of calm weather is emphasised in the matching lines at 101–3). Jupiter is still scrutinised by wider divine society in this passage; if he is too arbitrary, chaos and civil war in heaven will be the result. However, there are still far fewer scenes of group watching, discussion and dissent in the *Aeneid* than in the *Iliad*.

Valerius' divine audience gives a flavour of later first century epic. In *Metamorphoses* 1, for instance, Jupiter's gaze (1.163) precedes the divine council, which he calls. His ability to calm the cosmos is transformed into the ability to shake it, and becomes an opening gambit before he has even spoken (179–80). There is no sense that the other gods have been watching; he simply informs them what will happen, and they ratify his decisions. The uproar at 199 (*confremuere omnes*) consists of unanimous outrage at the actions he has already punished, and he calms it with the briefest gesture (205–6). The two alternative responses to his final speech (*pars . . . partes*, 244–5) express their approval in different ways, although they do at least question his decision to destroy the human race, and are answered. The only other example of group watching from the divine audience in the *Metamorphoses* is their fear at the sufferings of Hercules, as he is consumed by flames on Mount Oeta (*timuere dei pro uindice terrae*, 'the gods feared for the defender of the earth', 9.241). But what may initially seem like an independent reaction is immediately read by Jupiter as an imperial compliment (243–58): *nostra est timor iste uoluptas* ('that fear is our pleasure', 243).⁶⁴ So perhaps Valerius should be characterised as Ovidian, rather than Virgilian. The political situation of imperial Rome clearly influences the divine gaze, as is made manifest by Ovid's comparison of Olympus to the Palatine (1.176), and the comparison of the outrage of the gods at Lycaon's crime to the outrage of the Roman senate at the assassination of Julius Caesar (200–6).⁶⁵ Statius' divine council at 1.197–302 takes this tendency even further, by removing even Jupiter's gaze from the equation: the god is so far removed from the world of men that he is not even looking, let alone allowing others to watch.⁶⁶ The divine audiences seem to be looking at Jupiter looking at them, rather than looking at the action. Knowledge without vision expresses even greater power than divine vision.

One exception to this is the other instance of group viewing in Valerius Flaccus, at 4.667–85, when the gods watch the Argo approach the clashing rocks. There is no mention of Jupiter, simply *dei*; they are benevolent and in suspense, a strong model internal audience. Minerva and Juno intervene, first by sending a sign, and then by holding back the rocks themselves. This recalls the other instance of group watching in Apollonius (4.956–60): Hephaestus, Hera and Athene all watch as the Argo negotiates the Planctae, and Hera clutches Athene in her terror: ἀμφὶ δ'Ἀθήνῃ / βάλλε χέρας, τοῖόν μιν ἔχεν δέος εἰσορόωσαν. ('She threw her arms around Athene, such fear held her as she watched', 4.959–60). This is a remarkably anthropomorphic and feminine moment. When the workings of power and hierarchies are removed from the equation, the response of the gods is assimilated to that of the women on the walls. But Valerius makes his goddesses more masculine and more active: they take control of the situation, and give the seal of their intervention to the sublime moment when the Argo passes through the clashing rocks, in contrast to Apollonius, who displaces the viewing scene onto the much less well-known incident of the Planctae.

More complex is the Capaneus episode in *Thebaid* 10. Here the fractious audience is combined with an autocratic Jupiter. As Capaneus rails at the gods from the walls of Thebes, they are far from unified in their response:

> iamque Iouem circa studiis diuersa fremebant
> Argolici Tyriique dei; pater, aequus utrisque,
> aspicit ingentes ardentum comminus iras
> seque obstare uidet.   (*Thebaid* 10.883–6)

---

⁶⁴ There is, therefore, a great deal of irony in Ajax's comment at 13.70 that 'the gods watch mortal things with their just eyes' (*aspiciunt oculis superi mortalia iustis*).
⁶⁵ Feeney 1991: 198–200, Habinek 2002, Feldherr 2010: 143–4.
⁶⁶ Dominik 1994: 4–7; Ganiban 2007: 52; Keith 2007.

And now the Argive and Theban gods were raging around
Jupiter, partisans drawn in different directions; the father, fair to each side,
watched the enormous angers at close hand of those burning with rage
and sees that he stands in the way.

The Virgilian sense of civil war about to break out is tempered by the cool gaze of Jupiter. The different rivalries are represented in visual terms: Bacchus, for instance, looks obliquely back at his father (*obliquo respectans lumine patrem*, 887), reduced to a powerless and feminine model of vision; similarly Venus stands far away and looks back at Mars with silent anger (*stat procul et tacita Gradiuum respicit ira.* 894).[67] Both are marginalised and disempowered. Jupiter, by contrast, is the only god not to react in a highly emotional fashion: *non tamen haec turbant pacem Iouis* ('These things, however, do not disturb the peace of Jove', 897). When Capaneus taunts them again, *dolor* overwhelms the other gods (907), but Jupiter maintains his calm (*ipse furentem | risit*, 'he laughed at him as he rages', 907–8). After the battle, they congratulate Jupiter as if he has refought the gigantomachy (11.7–8). The extreme separation between Jupiter and the other gods has the effect of partially undermining the contrast between gods and mortals. Statius, as often, manages to be more Iliadic than Virgil, and produce something quite different from either.

In Silius there is very little group viewing among the gods. The best example is inspired not by Hannibal's crossing of the Alps, but by that of Hercules before him. The divine audience creates sublimity. Already in Livy, Feldherr argues, Hannibal is a version of Lucretius' Epicurus, breaking through the bounds of the world and challenging the gods.[68] Silius plays with his position in the epic tradition and Hannibal's relationship with the past, by having the gods explicitly watch Hercules' earlier crossing of the Alps:

> caligat in altis
> obtutus saxis, abeuntque in nubila montes.
> mixtus Athos Tauro Rhodopeque adiuncta Mimanti
> Ossaque cum Pelio cumque Haemo cesserit Othrys.
> primus inexpertas adiit Tirynthius arces.
> scindentem nubes frangentemque ardua montis
> spectarunt superi longisque ab origine saeclis
> intemerata gradu magna vi saxa domantem.   (*Punica* 3.492–99)

The gaze grows dark on the high rocks, and the mountains
disappear in the clouds. Athos mixed with Taurus, Rhodope joined to Mimas,
Ossa with Pelion, and Othrys on Haemus – yield to the Alps.

---

[67] On Capaneus' gaze, see below (pp.108–11).   [68] Feldherr 2009.

> First and the Tirynthian approached the inexperienced summits.
> Cutting through the clouds and breaking the steeps of the mountain,
> the gods watched him with great force taming the rocks,
> unchallenged by any step from their origins long ages ago.

In these lines, we reach the climax of Silius' description of the Alps, and their sublimity is both visual and generic. The human gaze is conquered by them, and their enormity amounts to a multiplication of the gigantomachic challenge. Hercules, like Epicurus and Lucretius, is an avatar of the poet, breaking new ground, and the gods watch him literally dismantling the landscape, as he does in *Aeneid* 8.[69] Hannibal, however, still finds a way to be the first (3.513–17), taking a new route. In his speech to his men, he equates their assault on the Alps to an attack on Capitoline Jupiter (509–10). The ongoing ascent becomes a battle of vision (530: *aperit*, 'opened'; 532: *respexisse*, 'looked back'; 532–3: *tanta formidine plana | exterrent repetita oculis*, 'the repeated surfaces terrify the eyes with such great fear'; 534–5: *atque una pruinae | canentis, quacumque datur promittere uisus, | ingeritur facies*. 'and wherever the gaze is allowed to proceed, one sight of white frost is heaped.') in which fear is caused by sight and the relentless repetitiveness of the landscape wears them down. This is followed by a sea image, of a sailor looking over the boundless sea and turning to the equally featureless sky to refresh his vision (3.535–9). Both mountain and ocean are images of alienation in extremes of nature, of the oppression caused by the grandeur of the natural world. Silius' vision so far has excluded the gods from Hannibal's crossing, but it turns out they have been watching all along: at *Punica* 3.557–69, Venus appears *ancipiti mentem labefacta timore* ('her mind slipping with double-headed fear', 557), as if she was in fear for Hannibal, rather than afraid of him. This leads into Jupiter's great prophecy (570–630), placed at the summit of the Alps, as if the readers have strayed the few extra feet upwards from Hannibal and his army into Olympus. The conditions of mortal vision are made physical in the cloud, snow and storm of the Alps: in epic, mortals live in a state of reduced visibility, unable to see far beyond their noses, while gods can pick them out from above only too clearly.

Quintus Smyrnaeus is again much more Iliadic. At 2.490–513, for instance, the gods watch with pleasure, some supporting Achilles, others supporting Memnon; parallel fear assaults Thetis (497–9) and Dawn (500–1). The rivalries, threatening to become violent, are put to rest when Zeus sends a Fate to each warrior, in a variation of Zeus' weighing of the fates at *Il.* 22.208–13. The other gods respond emotionally, with grief set against

---

[69] On Hannibal and Hercules, Tipping 2010: 20, 70–80.

triumph. This careful parallel arrangement is characteristic of Quintus' divine audiences, in contrast to the *Iliad* in which mixed emotions seem more prominent: Zeus pities Hector, but endorses his death. At 3.91–5, for instance, they respond to Apollo's killing of Achilles in a strictly partisan and split way. Differently, the sight of the Trojans dragging the horse into the city inspires delight from the divine audience, giving only the Greek perspective:

> Ἐγέλασσε δ' Ἐνυὼ
> δερκομένη πολέμοιο κακὸν τέλος· ὑψόθι δ' Ἥρη
> τέρπετ', Ἀθηναίη δ' ἐπεγήθεεν. Οἳ δὲ μολόντες
> ἄστυ ποτὶ σφέτερον μεγάλης κρήδεμνα πόληος
> λυσάμενοι λυγρὸν ἵππον ἐσήγαγον· αἳ δ' ὀλόλυξαν
> Τρωιάδες, πᾶσαι δὲ περισταδὸν εἰσορόωσαι
> θάμβεον ὄβριμον ἔργον ὃ δή σφισιν ἔκρυφε πῆμα.
> (*Posthomerica* 12.437–43)

> The goddess of warfare laughed
> to see that war's bad outcome, while on high
> Athena and Hera were both delighted. When the Trojans
> Arrived at their own great city, they breached its crown of walls
> And brought the baneful horse inside. The women of Troy
> All raised a cry and, as they gathered round to look,
> Admired that mighty work in which their ruin was hidden.

The Trojan women represent the other side of the conflict, the opposite end of the spectrum of epic viewers. Gods and women look on in admiration at the immense work of craftsmanship and what it represents, but dramatic irony divides the two audiences. The gods rejoice in their knowledge of destruction to come, while the women can only see the horse as a representation of the end of the Trojan war. In fact it is a new beginning. The Trojan horse is also an incarnation of the sublime epic moment, a work of craftsmanship which contains within it a war, larger than life, divinely endorsed.

This survey of divine group viewing has shown how the audience of gods does much more than reflect on the tragic contrast between mortals and immortals. We have seen the power relationships between gods, especially that between Zeus/Jupiter and the other gods. The power differential on display is only one aspect; equally the viewing gods heighten epic sublimity, make good the claim of epic to its position at the summit of the generic hierarchy. These moments, therefore, tend to be marked as among the most significant in any particular epic: which is why it is so loaded that Apollonius' major scene of divine viewing is not a grand duel, but the machinations of two goddesses making a mortal woman fall in love.

Hera and Juno: alternative centres of visual power

Goddesses may not feel it appropriate to view Ares and Aphrodite trapped in the midst of their love-making by Hephaestus, but epic battle is certainly fit matter for a female audience. Hera and Athene are very frequently to be found viewing events of epic poems, and often working together, whether in support of the Greeks at Troy or the Argonauts. If Feeney's *Gods in Epic* has a hero, it is surely Juno. Or should one call her a 'heroine'?[70] Or does this already elide the difference between goddesses and mortal women? Or is she an anti-hero? In any case, she takes up a great deal of time and space, and is instrumental in moving along the plot.[71] Feeney's reading of Hera/Juno as essentially malevolent may betray the masculine perspective of epic, in which women who assume agency must be getting in the way of the march of male progress.[72] It must be possible to read Hera/Juno against the grain as an underdog struggling to assert herself in a masculine universe.[73] Why is it Juno who is despised for punishing Io, when it was Jupiter who raped her in the first place? In a system of competitive acquisition and display of power and status, gender is only one marker; mortality another. If heroes compete for *kleos* (fame), gods compete for power and influence over mortals and each other. This section explores the gaze of Hera/Juno in the epic tradition and sets it against that of Jupiter/Zeus to investigate the nuances of gender relationships among immortals.

Tensions between Hera and Zeus are important in the *Iliad*. Zeus is the first god to be mentioned in the poem (Διὸς δ'ἐτελείετο βουλή, 1.5), but Hera enters the poem in person before Zeus; after Apollo's anger, she inspires Achilles to call an assembly, after watching and pitying the deaths of the Greeks (κήδετο γὰρ Δαναῶν, ὅτι ῥα θνήσκοντας ὁρᾶτο. *Il.* 53–6).[74]

---

[70] On the vexed and complex question of the relationship between gender and immortality, see Lyons 1997; see also Blundell and Williamson 1998, Deacy and Villing 2001.

[71] Feeney 1991: 62–4 on Hera in Apollonius; 116–17 on Juno in Naevius; 125–8 on Ennius; 130–41 on the *Aeneid*; 149–51 Hera and Juno in general; 201–3 on Ovid; 303–4 on Silius; 325–8 on Valerius Flaccus; 354–5 on the *Thebaid*.

[72] Of Hera in Apollonius: 'Once her instrument of vengeance is safely married to the transport, she disappears from the story, now fully assimilated to her standard pattern of malevolence, with the anomaly of her initial beneficence removed.' (Feeney 1991: 63 citing Burkert 1985: 134)

[73] Salzman-Mitchell 2005, for instance at 27, 29, 174.

[74] Zeus is the most frequent and important divine viewer in the *Iliad*: 2.1–15; 8.41–52, 397; 11.80–3, 181, 336–7, 543–5; 13.1–9; 15.4–13, 599–600; 16.431, 644–58; 17.198–208, 441; 19.340; 21.388–90; 24.331–2. However, Hera is one of the three gods who, separately and jointly, are most often represented viewing after Zeus: Hera: 1.56; 5.711; 8.350; 14.153; 16.439; Athene and Hera: 5.418; Apollo: 1.47–51; 4.507; 5.460; 10.515–16; 15.320; Apollo and Athene: 7.58–62; Athene: 1.193–200; 7.17; 19.349–51; 23.388; Poseidon: 13.10–16; 14.135; 20.291. Aphrodite: 3.374; 5.312; Ares: 5.846; Iris: 2.800–1.

Zeus' first response to Thetis is that she will put him in conflict with Hera (1.518–19) and at 536–8 his prediction is fulfilled; Hera has seen him with Thetis (ἰδοῦσ', 537). Hera's most celebrated intervention in the *Iliad* is the *Dios apate*, which is also (see above, p.41) an important episode for the gaze of Zeus. Hera sees the narrative situation, watching Zeus looking elsewhere and Poseidon busy on the battlefield, and decides to seduce Zeus away from watching the battlefield:

> Ἥρη δ' εἰσεῖδε χρυσόθρονος ὀφθαλμοῖσι
> στᾶσ' ἐξ Οὐλύμποιο ἀπὸ ῥίου· αὐτίκα δ' ἔγνω
> τὸν μὲν ποιπνύοντα μάχην ἀνὰ κυδιάνειραν
> αὐτοκασίγνητον καὶ δαέρα, χαῖρε δὲ θυμῷ·
> Ζῆνα δ' ἐπ' ἀκροτάτης κορυφῆς πολυπίδακος Ἴδης
> ἥμενον εἰσεῖδε, στυγερὸς δέ οἱ ἔπλετο θυμῷ.
> μερμήριξε δ' ἔπειτα βοῶπις πότνια Ἥρη
> ὅππως ἐξαπάφοιτο Διὸς νόον αἰγιόχοιο·   (*Iliad* 14.153–60)

> Now Hera, she of the golden throne, standing on Olympos'
> horn, looked out with her eyes, and saw at once how Poseidon,
> who was her very brother and her lord's brother, was bustling
> about the battle where men win glory, and her heart was happy.
> Then she saw Zeus, sitting along the loftiest summit
> on Ida of the springs, and in her eyes he was hateful.
> And now the lady ox-eyed Hera was divided in purpose
> as to how she could beguile the brain in Zeus of the aegis.

Her position on Olympus rivals Zeus' vertical perspective; she gazes at him as well as Poseidon, a viewer with agency and the intention to act. She uses her beauty to distract him and deceive him into hiding himself from the other gods, which equally blinds him to what Poseidon is doing. This was clearly a serious affront, as his anger on waking shows; he gazes terribly at her (δεινὰ δ' ὑπόδρα ἰδὼν Ἥρην, *Il.* 15.13), threatens to whip her (17) and reminds her of the time when he suspended her from Olympus (18–30) for persecuting Hercules against his will, the ultimate objectification and assertion of power. In the heroic past, it seems, conflict between Zeus and Hera was more grave, a threat to the cosmos;[75] now their antagonism is fought out on the level of vision, concealment and threat.

Hera's gaze is structurally and thematically significant in Apollonius' *Argonautica*, as we have seen (p.44). Her underlying motive of vengeance

---

[75] Also recalled by Hephaestus at *Il.* 1.590–4. See Feeney 1991: 150 on the allegorisation of the antagonism of Zeus and Hera, Jupiter and Juno as the stormy relationship between *aether* and *aer*; and 329 on allegorical readings of this passage in antiquity, and their development by Valerius Flaccus at *Arg.* 2.82–6.

against Pelias drives the narrative. The invocation of Erato and the mention of Cypris at 3.1–5 insist on the importance of Aphrodite at this crux of the poem; however it is the joint gazes of Hera and Athene that motivate the scene change to Olympus at 3.6–10, as quoted above. In this duo of goddesses, Hera takes the lead, both now, and in devising a plan (3.23). Juno's gaze is crucial, too, at the beginning of the *Aeneid*: as Syed argues, 'Juno's gaze is the first gaze of a fictional character in the story and the reader shares this gaze.'[76] Although here, as often, there are no verbs of gazing, Virgil offers us two sights from the perspective of Juno. He sets up the focus on Juno's emotions with the invocation at 1.8–11 (*numine laeso*, 'with divine power wounded', 8; *dolens*, 'grieving', 9; *irae*, 'angers', 11). Then he presents an ecphrastic description of Carthage (*Vrbs antiqua fuit*, 'There was an ancient city', 12), with a return to the focalisation of Juno at 15 (*quam Iuno...* 'which Juno...'). Again she is an emotional viewer: *tenditque fouetque* ('she strives for it and cherishes it', 18); fear (*metuens*, 23) for Carthage, allusively recalling her bargain with Zeus in *Iliad* 4 in which she allows him to destroy Argos in return for her destruction of Troy (24), is mixed with anger and grief, and jealousy of the honour paid to Ganymede. *his accensa* ('set on fire by these things', 29) emphasises her extreme emotion, and leads into the image of the Trojans tossed on the waves as she keeps them away from Latium, implying a Lucretian vertical gaze, which has been following them for many years.[77] Our gaze (and the narrator's) is aligned with hers at 34–5 as we look down on Aeneas and his men, and they look back to the receding shore of Sicily, with the *cum Iuno* at 36, which leads into her raising of the storm. The storm can be read as an explosion of feminine emotion, in contrast to the peaceful gaze of Neptune: *et alto prospiciens summa placidum caput extulit unda* ('and looking out from the deep he raised his peaceful head out to the waters above', 126–7), who can also see through to Juno's motivations (130). As he leaves, he is again *prospiciens*, this time assimilated to Jupiter by the epithet *genitor* (155). When Jupiter is revealed to have been watching all along, his gaze is equally unemotional (223–6), especially in contrast to Venus (227–9), and his smile as he addresses her is associated with the serenity of the cosmos:

---

[76] Syed 2005: 111. Syed also argues for the importance of gender: 'Juno's passion is peculiarly female, her resentments reflect the specific concerns of women in the roles assigned to them in ancient culture.' (110) But Juno is a goddess and is fundamentally concerned with power: the slight to her beauty represents a loss of face in her relationships with Venus and Minerva; the influence of Ganymede corresponds to a threat to her position as consort of Jupiter, and her influence over him.
[77] On Lucretian viewing in this passage, see Hardie 2009b: 160–2.

> Olli subridens hominum sator atque deorum
> uultu, quo caelum tempestatesque serenat,
> oscula libauit natae, dehinc talia fatur: (*Aeneid* 1.254–6)
>
> Smiling at her, the father of men and gods,
> with his face, which calms the sky and storms,
> he offered kisses to his daughter, then said these things:

There is a clear distinction between the masculine, controlled and controlling gazes of Jupiter and Neptune, who close things down, and the powerful emotions associated with the gaze of Juno, who opens the story. Similarly in book 12, Jupiter watches Juno with the emphasis on his power (*rex omnipotentis Olympi*, 'king of all-powerful Olympus', 791) and his smiling composure is contrasted with her emotion (*olli subridens hominum rerum repertor*, 'smiling at her the author of men and things', 829). Feeney had already made a strong case for a sort of ring composition in the divine action of the poem, from Juno's anger to Jupiter's accommodation of Juno's anger, in which Jupiter's sending of the *Dira* at the end of book 12 from the high heaven (*ab aethere summo*, 12.853) recalls his first vertical perspective on the Trojans (*ab aethere summo*, 1.223), in which Jupiter is assimilated to Juno in the final action of the poem.[78] Similarly the narrator's opening question (*tantaene animis caelestibus irae?* 'Is there such great anger in heavenly minds?', 1.11) is echoed in his despairing question halfway through book 12 (*tanton placuit concurrere motu, | Iuppiter, aeterna gentis in pace futuras?* 'Did it please you, Jupiter, to set in conflict with such a great clash races about to be in eternal peace?', 12.503–4).[79] While Syed sees Juno's gaze as a spectacle of emotions which inevitably distances the Roman reader, Feeney holds that 'even [Jupiter's] perspective is unavailable as a neutral, dispassionate vantage-point. There is no Archimedean hypothetical point in space from which to regard the action of the poem and evaluate it. Every vantage-point the poem offers is

---

[78] Silius reads this link as significant when he echoes the idea of the poisoned arrow in his own first simile (Hannibal compared to a Dacian using poisoned arrows: 1.324–6).

[79] Feeney 1991: 151–5. Jupiter's sending down of the *Dira* is also assimilated to the opening of the *Iliad* by the simile which compares the descent of the *Dira* to an arrow (12.856–60); this is another reference which unsettles any sense of closure: war starting over just at the end, in the same way that the *Dira* is extraordinarily similar to Allecto. Feeney 1991: 151 struggles with this similarity, following Hübner 1970 in saying that 'one brings disruption while the other imposes final order'; his solution is to say that 'the Dira stands to Allecto as Jupiter stands to Juno: they are siblings and share many qualities and effects, but have different functions'. The arrow image conveys the idea of the divine gaze as penetrative, powerful and, in this case, malevolent, underlined by the provenance of the arrow as Parthian and its power as coming from poison.

inextricable, part of a competition of views.' (155) This seems to me much the more satisfying reading, and offers a sense of the tension between the *Aeneid*'s claim to epic high ground and the text's (and its readers') discomfort with the god's-eye-view, objective narrator of one concept of epic. Jupiter's vision ought to authenticate that of the epic narrator, but instead the narrator seems to question it.[80]

If, we feel, even the *Aeneid* does not conform to the ideal of the epic gaze, with the narrator's top–down perspective mapping on to that of the gods, this still allows later poets in the epic tradition to 'flatten out some of the complexities' of the *Aeneid* in order to react against it.[81] We will look at Juno's gaze in Ovid later, but for now I want briefly to mention the role of Juno's gaze in Flavian epic. In both Valerius Flaccus' *Argonautica* and Statius' *Thebaid* Juno combines her self-consciously Virgilian (and Ovidian) inheritance with a surprisingly positive representation. As the traditional sponsor of the Argonauts, her role in Valerius Flaccus is not in conflict with Jupiter; yet her enmity to Hercules allows her to play a Virgilian role. In the *Thebaid* her patronage of the Argives brings her into conflict with Jupiter's plan to destroy them along with Thebes. In Silius, too, she is Hannibal's protector. In Valerius Flaccus' *Argonautica*, Juno's gaze is both the protective gaze of the patron goddess, as for Turnus in the *Aeneid*, and the hostile gaze of the jealous wife. It is striking that her hostility to Hercules, which is one element of the Apollonian Argonautic story that Valerius Flaccus magnifies beyond recognition, is given as much prominence as her protection of Jason, which would seem more central. Juno's most striking moment of protective spectatorship comes at 7.189–92 when she decides to call in Venus herself as reinforcement, to make sure Medea really has fallen in love, after more than a book of personal intervention;[82] now she can only sit and watch:

> Protinus hinc Iris Minyas, Cytherea petiuit
> Colchida, Caucaseis speculatrix Iuno resedit
> rupibus, attonitos Aeaea in moenia uultus
> speque metuque tenens et adhuc ignara futuri.
>
> (VF *Argonautica* 7.189–92)

---

[80] See also Feeney 1991: 180–7 on prophecy and omens, gaps in knowledge. He emphasises the Apollonian side of the *Aeneid*, even suggesting that 'Vergil follows his master Apollonius in setting puzzles for the reader.' (183–4) On prophecy, see below, Chapter 4, pp.122–61.

[81] 'Flatten': Gale 2006: 107; Gale also comments that 'it could be argued that the poet – by giving us our first glimpse of the Trojans through the eyes of a hostile, passionate, female subject – in fact invites or challenges the Roman reader to *question* his natural biases'. (107)

[82] This repetition and multiplication is typical of Valerius and of Flavian epic; Statius too has his fury call for reinforcements at *Theb.* 11.57–61.

> Immediately then Iris sought the Minyans and Cytherea
> Colchis; Juno the female spy sat back on the Caucasian
> cliffs, holding her gaze, struck dumb by hope and fear,
> on the Aeaean walls, and still not knowing the future.

Here Juno is not suffering fear for the imminent danger of someone she loves, like the women on the walls, or like the tension felt by Apollonius' Hera and Athena, watching the Argo in danger at 4.956–60.[83] Instead her angst is generated by tension about whether or not her own plans will succeed; her ignorance of the future is loaded with irony in this overdetermined myth with its multiple literary predecessors, both epic and tragic.[84] Her Virgilian heritage comes across much more strongly in the two episodes of hostile gazing that define her enmity towards Hercules: at 1.111–20, having taken on the role of *Fama* to stir up participation in the voyage, she sees Hercules on his way, breaks out into her *solitos questus* ('standard laments', 112) that her loyalty to the rest of the crew forbids her from enacting her Virgilian role and embroiling them in a storm.[85] The Hylas episode is her opportunity to engineer Hercules' removal:

> Illum ubi Iuno poli summo de uertice puppem
> deseruisse uidet, tempus rata diua nocendi
> Pallada consortem curis cursusque regentem,
> nequa inde inceptis fieret mora, fallere prima
> molitur caroque dolis auertere fratri. (VF *Argonautica* 3.487–91)

> When Juno sees him desert the ship, from the high
> summit of the heavenly axis, the goddess, thinking it time for harming,
> first works to deceive Pallas, her accomplice in worries,
> and guiding his course, so that no delay should arise from that for the expedition,
> and to turn her away from her dear brother by tricks.

The Apollonian pairing is split, turning Pallas into a Juturna, and Juno's method of deception is to send Pallas off to prepare for the next great Valerian digression, the civil war between Perses and Aeetes. At 522 she takes inspiration from the sight of the nymphs (*respicit*) to offer Hylas as a husband to Dryope, or in fact to claim he had always been destined to be her husband, thus performing an Ovidian gender reversal, reminiscent of Salmacis and Hermaphroditus, as well as Echo and Narcissus, of Juno's

---

[83] See above, p.51.
[84] Two other examples of protective watching, both with Virgilian overtones: at 5.399–401, Juno protects Jason with mist at Colchis, like Venus in *Aeneid* 1; at 8.318–24 she sees the Argonauts under threat from the pursuing Colchians, breaks open the gates of the storms, fusing together the gates of war (*Aen.* 7.601–22) with the storm.
[85] Zissos 2008: xl.

offer of a bride to Aeolus in *Aeneid* 1.[86] Hylas is the object of the gazes of both Juno and Dryope, and equally another Ascanius or Actaeon, chasing after his stag with fatal consequences.[87] Jupiter's rage at Hylas' loss (4.1–14) is inspired by the sight of Hercules' grief (1–3); he accuses Juno of improperly imitating the *Aeneid* (*sic arma uiro sociosque ministrat*, 'Thus you supply arms and allies to a hero', 4.8). Juno's hostile gaze in this episode performs a sort of indirect rape, stealing his beloved from Hercules, and causing a boy to be stolen away by a desiring female. This leads directly to the frustrated anxiety of her protective viewing in the second half of the poem: Jupiter is now the agent of delay, making Juno's plans less certain and effective.

In the *Thebaid*, Juno is one goddess among many divine patrons: Apollo cannot save Amphiaraus, Pallas is disgusted by Tydeus, Diana avenges Parthenopaeus through the penetrative gaze of her nymph Opis, Capaneus is bizarrely paired with his arch-enemy Jupiter, just as Polynices and Eteocles receive the furies they deserve. Juno too watches Hippomedon in his river battle (9.519–20) and begs Jupiter to allow him to die on land. But when it comes to book 10, she takes on something of the special status familiar from other epics. Here the Argive women make an offering of a robe to her, just as the Trojan women propitiate Minerva in *Iliad* 6. At 10.70–83 Juno takes inspiration from her vision of the guards unsleeping on the walls of the Theban camp (*uidet alto ex aethere*, 'she sees from the high heaven', 73),[88] and sends Iris to cajole Sleep on her behalf, to set up a massacre, which entirely fails to make a difference to the plot. Instead the episode channels her anger that Jupiter's plans go against her, and her anger is explicitly compared to that which she felt at Jupiter's double night with Alcmene (10.76–8), thus creating a link to the Valerian Juno. This Juno savage on behalf of the Argive army, with whom the reader has mainly been led to sympathise, is a typically discomforting Statian character. The discomfort is increased by the contrast with the ecphrasis on the *peplum* (56–64) which shows an idealised innocent Juno: *lumine demisso pueri Iouis oscula libat | simplex et nondum furtis offensa mariti* ('with eyes looking down, uncomplicated, she tastes the kisses of the boy Jove, not yet made hostile by the thefts of her husband', 63–4). The downcast gaze of feminine modesty has given way to a vertical gaze downwards from a position of power, even if compromised by her inevitable submission to Jupiter. Just as Juno's anger and its eventual reconciliation takes up the same space as the plot of the *Aeneid*, so the narrator of the

---

[86] Heerink 2007 for Ovidian intertexts and metapoetic play.
[87] See Heerink 2007: 617 on Ascanius.
[88] As Philip Hardie points out *per litteras*, she here occupies the Virgilian position of Jupiter.

Thebaid seems to take a Junonian perspective. The *Thebaid*, with its focus on the Argives, aligns itself with Juno, in contrast to the *Aeneid*, which for the most part aligns itself with Aeneas and his men.

In Silius Italicus' *Punica*, too, the gaze of Juno frames the narrative, following the *Aeneid* closely as ever.[89] The vast majority of the divine gazing in the rest of the poem belongs to Jupiter, but Juno starts and closes proceedings.[90] There is noticeably less emphasis on the divine gaze, which must represent Silius' generic affiliation with history. Silius' proem explicitly foregrounds the epic poet's right to knowledge of divine motivations, in terms reminiscent of both the *Aeneid* and Phineus:

> tantarum causas irarum odiumque perenni
> seruatum studio et mandata nepotibus arma
> fas aperire mihi superasque recludere mentes.   (*Punica* 1.17–19)
>
> The causes of such great angers and of hatred kept
> with enduring enthusiasm and weapons entrusted to descendants
> it is right for me to open out and to reveal divine minds.

When Silius does invoke the figure of Juno with her opening force, she is indirectly represented; he reports her anger rather than putting it on show. Nevertheless, Juno watches Rome at 1.29–33. At the end of the poem, she is watching still; at 17.341, she is on her cloud watching Hannibal's speech before the battle of Zama, observed by Jupiter (17.341–3). After re-reconciliation, Juno leads Hannibal from the battle with a phantom Scipio, and he watches from a hill, as Juno does at *Aen.* 12.134–7.

> At fessum tumulo tandem regina propinquo
> sistit Iuno ducem, facies unde omnis et atrae
> apparent admota oculis vestigia pugnae.   (*Punica* 17.597–9)
>
> But at last queen Juno stops the tired leader
> on a nearby mound, from where the whole appearance
> and the moving traces of that black battle appear before his eyes.

Hannibal thus becomes an avatar of Juno, and appropriates the perspective of the narrator and makes his own immortality in the memories of men a challenge to the dominance of Jupiter.[91]

The gaze of Hera is also a key structuring force in the *Dionysiaca* of Nonnus. Here, again, Hera is the jealous stepmother: Dionysus is arguably

---

[89] Jupiter is again mentioned first (1.9) but Juno is the first god as character (1.26–33).
[90] Jupiter gazing: 3.574; 4.417; 6.595–9; 12.605; with Juno: 17.341. Juno: 1.31; 12.201 and 704–5 (see below); 17.597ff. Vulcan: 4.667; Venus: 17.283.
[91] See below on the feminised gaze of Hannibal (p.257).

Hera and Juno: alternative centres of visual power 63

the most successful of Zeus' ambitious offspring, and the whole narrative, as with Hercules, is the story of his battle against her hostility to prove himself worthy of immortality. A brief selective dip into the *Dionysiaca*, focusing on Nonnus' reworking of the *Dios apate*, Hera's deception of Zeus at *Iliad* 14–15 (see above, pp.41, 56).[92] This complex episode, with the characteristic expansion and multiplication of Nonnus' Dionysiac poetics, begins with a vivid evocation of Hera's painful spectatorship:

Ἥρη δὲ φθονεροῖσιν ἀνοιδαίνουσα μερίμναις
<ἄκρον> ἀπειλητῆρι κατέγραφεν ἠέρα ταρσῷ,
αὐτόθι παπταίνουσα πολυσπερέων στρατὸν Ἰνδῶν
θύρσοις ἀνδροφόνοισιν ἀλοιηθέντα Λυαίου.
Καὶ χόλον ἄλλον ἔγειρεν Ἐρυθραίῳ παρὰ πόντῳ
Ἀνδρομέδης ὀρόωσα πολύπλοκα λείψανα δεσμῶν
καὶ λίθον ἐν ψαμάθῳ, βλοσυρὸν τέρας Ἐννοσιγαίου.
Ἀχνυμένη δ' ἑὸν ὄμμα παρέτραπε, μὴ παρὰ πόντῳ
Γοργοφόνου Περσῆος ἴδῃ χαλκήλατον ἅρπην.   (*Dionysiaca* 31.3–11)

But Hera, swelling with jealous passions,
scored the air with menacing sole,
when she beheld the host of scattered Indians beaten like corn
in the threshing where they stood, by the manslaying thyrsus of Dionysus.
And she awakened a new resentment when she saw
the heap of Andromeda's broken chains beside the Erythraean sea,
and that rock on the sand, the monstrous lump of the earth-shaker.
Bitterly she turned her eye aside, so she might not see beside the sea
the bronze-forged sickle of Gorgon-slaying Perseus.

Hera is relentlessly battered by the sight of Zeus' triumphant by-blows, so much so that she cannot bear to look further at Perseus.[93] Another emotional Hera turns her gaze away in acknowledgement of the limits of her power. The resemblances between Nonnus' version and that in the *Iliad* are remarkably close, even down to Hera's offer of the nymph Pasithea to Sleep for his assistance in both poems.[94] Nonnus adds an extra layer of complexity: instead of aiding Poseidon in a battle he has already started, Nonnus' Hera is cooking up a new plan, introducing Megaera as an agent to make

---

[92] On this episode's Homeric underpinnings, see the lucid and concise account in Shorrock 2001: 75–81; on Dionysus as Achilles in this episode (μανία as μῆνις) see Hopkinson 1994.
[93] The threshing image aligns her with the narrator in the *Iliad*, who finishes book 20 with a distant view of Achilles slaughtering the Trojans, first as a forest fire (20.490–2), and then as a farmer using oxen to thresh grain (20.495–503).
[94] Presumably, then, Nonnus views his version as replacing the *Iliad*; after all you cannot marry the same person twice.

Dionysus mad, in the tradition of Ovid and Statius.⁹⁵ The visual element is also greatly increased: Zeus is enchanted via the eyes (31.26; 32.38–41);⁹⁶ Dionysus' madness is configured in visual terms, like that of Pentheus in the *Bacchae*.⁹⁷ The description of Iris looking for Sleep emphasises her powerful investigatory gaze:

> Ὣς φαμένης πεπότητο θεὰ χρυσόπτερος Ἶρις
> ἠέρα παπταίνουσα, καὶ εἰς Πάφον, εἰς χθόνα Κύπρου
> ἀπλανὲς ὄμμα τίταινε, τὸ δὲ πλέον ὑψόθι Βύβλου
> Ἀσσυρίου σκοπίαζεν Ἀδώνιδος εὔγαμον ὕδωρ,
> διζομένη περίφοιτον ἀλήμονος ἴχνιον Ὕπνου.   (*Dionysiaca* 31.124–8)

> At these words, Iris the golden-winged goddess flew away
> glancing around through the air, and she directed her unwavering eye
> to Paphos, to the land of Cyprus, and most of all she spied out
> Byblos on the well-married water of Assyrian Adonis,
> seeking the wandering track of vagrant Sleep.

Iris' unerring gaze pursues wandering sleep, as if pinning down the meandering poetics of the *Dionysiaca*. The god flying over the landscape, taking a broad aerial view, searching, conveys the pervasiveness of divine power. The equivalent passage in the *Iliad* (14.224–30) shows Hera speeding over Pieria, Emathia and Thrace to Lemnos, but the predatory gaze is absent. However, the passage at 32.9–37 in which Nonnus gives us a heavily eroticised description of Hera dressing (or arming for the erotic battle), is very similar to *Iliad* 14.166–86; in both the readers are encouraged to gaze at the goddess as an erotic object, though the continual references to ambrosia (170, 172, 177, 178) in the *Iliad* underline her difference from us. A striking addition to the story is that when Megaera is driving Dionysus mad, another watching god almost intervenes to put a stop to it:

> Τὸν μὲν ἀμερσινόοιο κατάσχετον ἄλματι λύσσης
> Ἄρτεμις ἐσκοπίαζε, καὶ ἤθελε λύσσαν ἐλάσσαι,
> ἀλλά μιν ἐπτοίησε βαρύκτυπος ὑψόθεν Ἥρη,
> πυρσὸν ἀκοντίζουσα·   (*Dionysiaca* 32.110–13)

> But Artemis spied out Dionysus caught in a fit of
> mind-marauding madness, and wanted to drive the madness away,

---

⁹⁵ See Introduction pp.12–13 for discussion of relationship between later Greek epic and Latin poetry.
⁹⁶ At *Il.* 14.160 it is Zeus' mind Hera intends to attack (νόον), though Hera does ask Sleep to work on the shining eyes of Zeus at 14.236.
⁹⁷ 31.72–4: Megaera's evil eye (βάσκανον ὄμμα, 74) will fulfil Hera's plan of making Dionysus mad; 32.102: Megaera attacks Dionysus' eyes; 32.119–24: Dionysus' madness represented as primarily visual, though the other senses are also brought in.

> but Hera, heavy-thundering from above cast a burning brand at her
> and scared her off.

This moment underlines Hera's similarity and subordination to Zeus: her power to intimidate Artemis is compromised by the use of the 'burning brand' (πυρσὸν) rather than a thunderbolt, as Athene does against Ajax Oileus, to assert her control. Nonnus has recontextualised this episode from the *Iliad* into a poem where it feels completely in place, and complicated the visual structures in the process, fragmenting the divine audience, and using representatives to increase the sense of Hera's imperial power.

We have seen many different types of divine gazing in these representations of Hera and Juno: the jealous gaze of the hostile stepmother; the awe-inspiring visual power of the god above; the protective gaze of the sponsor; the pitying and loving gaze of the wife and mother. Her primary relationship of antagonism to Jupiter/Zeus makes her an important force in the development of the epic plot. Her gaze can be surprisingly similar to that of Jupiter/Zeus, a senior goddess with a great deal of power. But her passions are contrasted with the serenity of Jupiter in the Latin tradition, if Zeus can be equally emotional in Greek epic.

Jupiter and Juno in Ovid: rape and the imperial gaze

Throughout this study Ovid's *Metamorphoses* recurs as a complex, atypical and influential engagement with ideas of epic. The rival gazes of Jupiter and Juno are still important, especially in the early stages of the poem. However, they function differently from the Homeric/Virgilian 'norm': Jupiter is explicitly the predatory rapist while Juno is characterised as the jealous spouse, looking obliquely on Jupiter's conquests. In the *Aeneid*, Juno's hatred of the Trojans might well be motivated by the same feminine concerns of jealousy and desire, but her desire is more explicitly a masculine desire for power and *imperium*. In Ovid we lose sight of the grander dynastic and historical aims and instead lose ourselves in the farcical moment, in which Juno might at any second walk in on her husband as he has his wicked way.[98]

Salzman-Mitchell analyses the Io episode as an example of Juno's gaze: taking her ability to see through Jupiter's transformation of Io into a cow as

---

[98] On Juno in Ovid, see Janan 2009: 87–113, in which she reads Juno and Jupiter as incarnations of incomplete desire, but does not acknowledge the obsession with power and control highlighted so well by Hejduk 2009 with respect to Virgil's Jupiter. On Ovid's Thebes and Juno see also Hardie 1990, Wheeler 2000: 70–106.

oblique viewing 'seeing what is underneath the appearances' (24); this askance position offers a feminine alternative way of seeing.[99] 'Juno's "suspicion" can then be taken as meta-literary and programmatic.'[100] However her gaze is not characterised that differently from that of the male gods: she looks down (*despexit*, 1.601) and looks around (*circumspicit*, 1.605). Salzman-Mitchell suggests that her vertical gaze has a different significance from Jupiter's: 'The vertical gaze pertains to deities and males but is felt as devious in women.' (24) But this fails to look the issue in the face. In fact, there is a great deal of similarity between Juno's gaze and Jupiter's, and if she was able to see what was going on, sisterhood would be the least likely response.[101] For instance, her vengeance on Ino, for having been the nurse of Dionysus, is motivated by a glimpse of her good fortune:

> aspicit hanc natis thalamoque Athamantis habentem
> sublimes animos et alumno numine Iuno
> nec tulit   (*Metamorphoses* 4.420–2)

> Juno caught sight of this woman with her children, having
> Athamas in her bedroom and her spirit raised by her divine nursling
> and could not bear it.

It is her lack of power that she laments:

> nil poterit Iuno nisi inultos flere dolores?
> idque mihi satis est? haec una potentia nostra?   (*Metamorphoses* 4.426–7)

> Can Juno do nothing except weep for her griefs unavenged?
> Is that enough for me? Is this our one power?

This sight inspires Juno to enact a katabasis in search of Tisiphone to madden Ino and Athamas and destroy their family. The verb *aspicio* ('catch sight of'), which might be read, as Salzman-Mitchell reads *suspicio*, as an index of obliqueness, or at least a less straightforward and empowered sort of seeing, is in fact used across the whole range of Ovidian visual situations, even the gaze of the rapist. In particular, it is used of Mercury at 2.714, when he sees Herse at the start of the Aglauros episode. Casualness can be an index of power. The comparison of Mercury to a bird of prey (716–19) makes this a particularly striking use of the predatory gaze of the

---

[99] Although Juno could not see through Jupiter's cloud which he puts in place at *Met.* 1.599–600, the absence of Jupiter which it creates is itself a giveaway, so in a way she sees through that too.
[100] Salzman-Mitchell 2005: 25.
[101] Salzman-Mitchell 2005: 27 says that Ovid implies at 2.435 that if Juno had seen Callisto being raped, she would have been kinder, but 'Jupiter is here preventing sisterhood and asserting the power of the phallus over feminine alliances'. (27)

rapist, combined in the image with the consumptive gaze of the bird, desiring to eat the entrails, and the god desiring the offerings of mortals. Juno's gaze, then, is described in terms which are not distinct from the male gaze.[102] The ecphrasis of Hades which follows her glimpse of Ino (432–63) aligns the gaze of narrator and readers firmly with that of Juno, who replaces Aeneas with typically Ovidian irony as the tourist in the underworld. The sights she sees there serve to confirm her resolve:

> Quos omnes acie postquam Saturnia torua
> uidit et ante omnes Ixiona, rursus ab illo
> Sisyphon aspiciens 'cur hic e fratribus' inquit
> 'perpetuas patitur poenas' (*Metamorphoses* 4.464–7)

> Then Saturnia saw all those with her fierce
> gaze, and above all Ixion, again after him
> catching sight of Sisyphus 'Why should only this one of the brothers,' she said
> 'suffer perpetual punishment'

The figure of Ixion, a mortal who attempted to rape Juno, emphasises her vulnerability; in the end, even as a goddess inspecting the underworld she partakes in femininity, and her relationship to Tisiphone is not securely that of superior to inferior: her exit from the underworld has a hint of flight about it (*laeta redit Iuno*, 4.479). This episode has strong structural similarities to *Aeneid* 7, in which she also catches sight of Aeneas' good fortune when he has landed in Italy, soliloquises about her own impotence and immediately seeks out Allecto:

> Ecce autem Inachiis sese referebat ab Argis
> saeva Iovis coniunx aurasque invecta tenebat,
> et laetum Aenean classemque ex aethere longe
> Dardaniam Siculo prospexit ab usque Pachyno.
> moliri iam tecta videt, iam fidere terrae,
> deseruisse rates: stetit acri fixa dolore. (*Aeneid* 7.286–91)

---

[102] Other predatory uses of *aspicit*: 2.443: Diana sees Callisto; 2.748: Aglauros sees Mercury; 3.356: Echo sees Narcissus; 3.479: Narcissus sees himself; 3.577: Pentheus sees the bound Bacchus; 11.395: Neptune and Apollo plan to kill Achilles. Less predatory: 2.228: Phaethon looks at the destruction around him; 2.283: Earth asks Jupiter to look at her burnt hair; 3.725: Pentheus calling on Agave to recognise him; 6.14: Nymphs eager to watch Arachne weave; 6.34: Arachne looks scornfully at Pallas; 6.248: Alphenor (son of Niobe) watches his brothers die; 7.70: Medea urges herself to look at her own crimes; 11.395: Peleus and friends watch a wolf ravaging cattle; 13.520 and 536: Hecuba sees death of Polyxena and Polydorus' corpse; 13.591: Aurora addresses Jupiter; 13.842: Polyphemus asks Galatea to look at him; 14.61: Scylla looking at transformed body; 14.168: Achaemenides catching sight of Polyphemus; 14.323: Picus as statue; 15.200: speech of Pythagoras; 15.765: Venus to gods on assassination of Julius Caesar. There is a dichotomy of predators and victims; this reflects on the nature of the *Metamorphoses* as much as the nature of relationships of sight.

> Look, however, the savage spouse of Jove was bringing
> herself back from Inachian Argos and was transported, carried on the winds,
> and she looked out over happy Aeneas, and his Dardanian fleet
> from far in the aether as far as Pachynian Sicily.
> Now she sees buildings constructed, now trust in the land,
> the ships deserted: she stood fixed by a fierce grief.

Here too Juno is like Aeneas (*Aen.* 1.495, *defixus*; and other paralysed viewers: see below, pp.201–3), a viewer for whom the sight is penetrative, causing pain and paralysis. The text makes much of her divine mobility, but her grief fixes her, moving her from the framework of divine ease onto the plain of mortal pain. But here there is no erotic element to the narrative: she is purely concerned with power.

'The rape of Proserpina', as told by Calliope in the Muses' account to Minerva of their song-battle with the Pierides, in book 5 of Ovid's *Metamorphoses*, shows the connections between divine rape and the imperial gaze, and the complications that ensue.[103] The song begins with cosmic order: at 341–5, Ceres is worthy of song because she is the origin of laws as well as agriculture. The mission of Dis, when he goes to Sicily, is to inspect the boundaries of his kingdom which have been shaken by Typhon struggling in his prison:

> inde tremit tellus, et rex pauet ipse silentum
> ne pateat latoque solum retegatur hiatu
> immissusque dies trepidantes terreat umbras.
> hanc metuens cladem tenebrosa sede tyrannus
> exierat curruque atrorum uectus equorum
> ambibat Siculae cautus fundamina terrae. (*Metamorphoses* 5.356–61)

> From this the earth trembles, and the king of the silent ones himself is afraid
> that the soil might open and be uncovered in a huge chasm
> and the daylight sent in might terrify the panicking shades.
> Fearing this disaster the tyrant had left his shadowy
> seat and born on his chariot with its black horses
> was going around the foundation rocks of the Sicilian land.

Here the gaze of Dis, implicit in his touring, is that of a king, safeguarding his kingdom and his power over it.[104]

The episode of Jupiter and Callisto, three books earlier, starts similarly. It is while he reorders the cosmos after Phaethon's disastrous flight, that Jupiter catches sight of Callisto:

---

[103] See Johnson 1996 for a strong reading of Venus' imperial gaze as a political critique of Augustus' moral reforms and republican imperialism, as emblematised by Verres.

[104] On the importance of surveying in the Roman Empire, see Nicolet 1991: 95.

Jupiter and Juno: rape and the imperial gaze

> At pater omnipotens ingentia moenia caeli
> circuit et ne quid labefactum uiribus ignis
> corruat explorat; quae postquam firma suique
> roboris esse uidet, terras hominumque labores
> perspicit. Arcadiae tamen est impensior illi
> cura suae; fontesque et nondum audentia labi
> flumina restituit, dat terrae gramina, frondes
> arboribus, laesasque iubet reuirescere siluas.
> dum redit itque frequens, in uirgine Nonacrina
> haesit et accepti caluere sub ossibus ignes.   (*Metamorphoses* 2.401–10)

> But the omnipotent father went around the huge walls
> of the sky and investigated whether anything had been made to slip
> and would fall down from the strength of the fires; and after he sees that it is
> firm and strong in itself, he probes the lands and the labours
> of men. However, his particular care is for his own
> Arcadia; and he restored the fountains and the rivers that did not yet
> dare to flow, gives grass to the land, leaves
> to the trees, and orders the wounded woods to grow green again.
> While he comes and goes often, he gets caught on a Nonacrian
> virgin, and the welcomed fires grow hot in his bones.

Here too the verbs of viewing (*explorat, uidet, perspicit*) construct an imperial gaze, concerned with aggressively policing and containing his kingdom (he has just struck Phaethon with a thunderbolt, after all), but equally with beneficently protecting it. Jupiter goes a step further than Hades, becoming a creative source of order, life and nourishment.[105] Yet this positive sense of ownership easily elides into a destructive control: it is while he looks after the land of his birth that he looks in a predatory fashion on Callisto. Even though he is described as if affected by a work of art, a passive viewer receiving the fires of love, he will actively take her; consciously deciding to ignore Juno's displeasure (423–4), he halts her and silences her (*qua uenata foret silua narrare parantem | impedit amplexu*, 'He stops her with her embrace as she prepares to tell where she went in the woods while hunting', 432–3). As he goes back to the heavens, he is called victor (*superum petit aethera uictor | Iuppiter*, 437–8).

Coming back to Dis and Proserpina, we might expect this scene of imperial viewing to end in Dis catching sight of Proserpina by chance and replicating Jupiter's victory. However, Ovid is playing a little game of his

---

[105] On Jupiter as demiurge rebuilding Arcadia, see Hinds 2002: 129: 'Jupiter's manipulation of "real" space tends to read as mimicry of the ecphrastic manipulation of rhetorical space, rather than *vice versa*.' Cf. 2.455–8 where Diana also rhetoricises the landscape.

own (or is it Calliope?),[106] and instead Dis becomes the object of the imperial gaze of another divine viewer, Venus:

> postquam exploratum satis est loca nulla labare
> depositoque metu, uidet hunc Erycina uagantem
> monte suo residens natumque amplexa uolucrem
> 'arma manusque meae, mea, nate, potentia' dixit,
> 'illa, quibus superas omnes, cape tela, Cupido,
> inque dei pectus celeres molire sagittas,
> cui triplicis cessit fortuna nouissima regni.
> tu superos ipsumque Iouem, tu numina ponti
> uicta domus ipsumque regit qui numina ponti.
> Tartara quid cessant? cur non matrisque tuumque
> imperium profers? agitur pars tertia mundi.' (*Metamorphoses* 5.362–72)

> After he had explored enough to see that no place was slipping
> and set aside his fear, Erycina sees him wandering
> sitting on her own mountain and embracing her swift son
> 'My arms and hands, son, my power' she said,
> 'take these weapons, Cupid, by which you conquer all,
> and send the swift arrows into the heart of the god
> to whom fortune yielded the most recent of the triple kingdoms.
> You conquer the gods above and Jupiter himself; you conquer the powers
> of the sea, their home, and he himself who rules the sea.
> Why should Tartarus escape? Why not extend your rule
> and your mother's? A third part of the world is at stake.'

Venus on the mountain from which her epithet comes (Eryx) calls on the epic powers of Cupid (*arma manusque* is metrically equivalent to *arma uirumque*) to extend their empire by taking power over the king of the underworld. Dis is the object of their gaze in more than one sense, as Cupid aims the arrows of love at him. The rapacious gaze of Dis, then, is deferred upwards onto the rapacious gaze of Venus, taking pleasure in having power over other gods. Yet Dis is still a destructive force: when the nymph Cyane stands in his way, he figuratively violates her by opening a tunnel to the underworld through her pool with his royal sceptre:[107]

> haud ultra tenuit Saturnius iram
> terribilesque hortatus equos in gurgitis ima
> contortum ualido sceptrum regale lacerto
> condidit; icta uiam tellus in Tartara fecit
> et pronos currus medio cratere recepit. (*Metamorphoses* 5.420–4)

---

[106] Johnson 1996 suggests various possible motives for Calliope, including a shared sense of virginal vulnerability with her various audiences, nymphs and Minerva.
[107] Segal 1969: 55.

> Saturnius could no longer bear his anger
> and urging his terrifying horses into the depths of the pool
> hurled the royal sceptre with strong arm
> and buried it; the earth was struck and he made a way to Tartarus
> and it received the headlong chariot in the middle of its crater.

Here Hades is son of Saturn, but it is Juno who is more normally known as *Saturnia* (e.g. *Aen.* 1.23); he is explicitly tyrannical, with his *sceptrum regale*, causing the very rift from the upper world to the lower which he had initially set out to prevent. So in the Ovidian world, Venus and Cupid have the most powerful gazes; it is not clear after all that any world-plan of Jupiter's (or Juno's) could stand up to them. The Muses in their song do not seem to offer any straightforward hierarchy of the gaze among different divinities, male or female. A god or goddess might extend a powerful gaze at one moment, and become the object of another god's gaze at another. In this way, Ovid in particular undermines epic (political and imperial) authority.

Limits of power and averting the gaze

Epic narrative is often characterised as omniscient, the prototype of the omniscient aspect of the Western novel.[108] But the divine gaze is neither omniscient or omnipotent. Often the gods turn their gaze away, for various reasons. I have begun to explore the complexity of the Iliadic narrator's relationship with the gods above:[109] the narrative device of the bird's-eye view is often associated with a focalising god, or gods; the narrator's reliance on the Muses for knowledge is matched by his assumption of the divine perspective to create narrative authority.[110] However, he occasionally feels overwhelmed by the responsibility of this close association (*Il.* 12.176–80). The limits of knowledge and power are also significant. Models of non-verbal behaviour include the gaze as a marker of social interactions.[111] For the most part, in Greek culture at least, a direct gaze indicates either a close connection, or shamelessness, while averted gaze signifies modesty and respect. But this is not entirely the case: Cairns 2005: 133–7 argues that averting the gaze can also

---

[108] On the Iliadic invocation as establishing omniscient narrative: see Ford 1992: 23.
[109] Clay 1997: 9–25 sets up a comparison between the gaze of the (blind) epic poet, inspired by the muse, encompassing the deeds of both men and gods, and the gaze of the far-seeing gods, especially Zeus and Helios, which nevertheless has blind spots.
[110] Similarly, Wheeler 1999: 190 suggests that Ovid's multiplication of narrators in *Metamorphoses* 12–14 operates to 'break down epic omniscience, or the memory of the Muses, into a set of different personal memories that are not unified by the single authoritative point of view of the epic poet'.
[111] On non-verbal behaviour see Lateiner 1995, Ricottilli 2000. Cairns 2005 on the gaze and social behaviour in Greek culture.

be a sign of power. When at *Iliad* 13.1–9 (quoted above, p.40) Zeus looks away from Troy to the Ethiopians and other faraway peoples, he does so not from lack of interest, horror, sorrow, but simply because he cannot imagine any of the gods obstructing his expressed will (8–9). Zeus' averted gaze here is an expression of power and confidence in himself. But when Jupiter decides to avert his gaze from the fratricidal duel of Polynices and Eteocles at *Theb.* 11.119–35, at the same time ordering the other gods to turn away their eyes, it is much less clear how it should be interpreted.[112] Bernstein 2004 has read the progressive removal of the authorising gazes of Jocasta, Adrastus, Jupiter and others as an undermining of epic authority; Ganiban 2007: 176–206 reads it as 'the rout of Jupiter', in which the Furies and Dis take control of the poem, and Jupiter is disempowered. I now look at ways of thinking about the averted gaze of both gods and humans, in order to come back to this episode with the full complexity of the gesture in mind, beginning with sorrow and disempowerment, moving through assertions of power and refusal, to ideas of pollution, infection and contamination.

The gods of the *Iliad* are not omniscient. Zeus himself is blinded by his lust for Hera in books 13 to 15, as we have seen.[113] The relationship between Zeus, knowledge and the unrolling of the narrative is never clearly articulated, just as the relationship between Jupiter and fate in the *Aeneid* is continually problematic.[114] At times Jupiter and Zeus can be identified with knowledge, power and narrative control; at others they seem to be

---

[112] There may be a precedent in the cyclic *Iliou Persis* in which Electra, the catasterised ancestress of the Trojan royal family, refuses to watch the sack of Troy and leaves the heavens (fr. 5 West = Schol. (D) *Il.* 18.486a).

[113] Other examples of divine blind spots: Ares does not know about the death of his son Ascalaphus at *Il.* 13.521–5; Poseidon must deduce from his sighting of Odysseus' raft at *Od.* 5.282–90 that the council of the gods has authorised his return home; Apollo at *Met.* 4.234–46 does not know that his lover Leucothoe is being buried alive until too late (Salzman-Mitchell 2005: 97–101 equates this to 'a failure of the masculine gaze') and the parallel case in Statius' *Thebaid* 1, although this is represented as a failure of knowledge rather than vision. Apollo, like Zeus, has particularly powerful vision, because he is equated with the sun who sees all things, as, for instance, Helios at *Od.* 12.323, even though he still needs a messenger to tell him about Odysseus' men eating his cattle (12.374–5).

[114] On Zeus and fate in the *Iliad*, see as a starting point Morrison 1997, Van Erp Taalman Kip 2000. On the *Aeneid*, Neri 1986, Feeney 1991: 139–40, 154–5. 'Jupiter's perspective is, naturally, a commanding one. It is the perspective Fate, of Time, of history.... He regards events from a height that shrinks human values. Yet it is not a perspective from which problems disappear.' (155) Ganiban 2007 throughout equates Jupiter and fate, and associates them with the forces of order typical of an Augustan reading of the *Aeneid*, as in Hardie 1986. The poetics of *nefas* in Statius' *Thebaid*, in his argument, are truly controlled by Dis and the underworld. But we might also see Dis as a syncretistic alternative version of Jupiter. And does Jupiter really control fate? Ganiban argues that Jupiter is both malevolent and incompetent, associating malevolence with the early stages of the poem: see especially ch. 3, 44–70, and powerlessness with book 11 and the aversion of the gaze, where he argues that the Furies take control (176–206).

characters within the narrative, struggling along with the rest of the characters against the tide of events. Zeus cannot rescue Sarpedon at *Il.* 16.462–507; Jupiter in the *Aeneid* remembers this moment when he consoles Hercules, who cannot answer the prayer of Pallas at 10.466–73: *sic ait, atque oculos Rutulorum reicit aruis.* ('So he spoke, and turned his eyes back to the fields of the Rutulians.', 10.473).[115] The agency of the gods as they watch the narrative unfold is not uncomplicated: it is not straightforwardly the case that they can intervene, while we cannot (and neither can the women on the walls). Some things can be changed and others cannot: more like the relationship of the poet to his material.[116] The narrator watches, and can change some things, but if he changed too much the story would become unrecognisable or implausible. The gods, like the readers and the poet, feel a sense of external inevitability pressing down upon them. Or is it merely that they must live with their own decisions?

In this context, the aversion of the divine gaze is often associated with sorrow and disempowerment. So Harrison reads Jupiter's refusal to watch the battle in *Aeneid* 10 above.[117] Similarly, Juno at 12.151 cannot bear to watch: *non pugnam aspicere hanc oculis, non foedera possum.* ('I cannot look at this fight with my eyes, nor at this treaty.').[118] At *Met.* 13.583 Aurora cannot bear to watch Memnon's funeral, and Neptune at VF *Arg.* 4.131 decides not to watch Amycus in the boxing match, because he is powerless against Jupiter, whose son, Pollux, will defeat him. And in the *Thebaid* at 7.789, Apollo cannot bear to watch the death of Amphiaraus and the Dioscuri cannot watch the death of Alcidamas (10.502).[119] In Quintus, too, Ganymede cannot bear to watch the Trojan defeat, and begs Zeus to help (8.428–43). These scenes make the divine viewers less straightforwardly a source of epic authority and more effective as a mediating audience. They invite the readers to reflect on the workings of causation and narrative.

However, lack of power is only one aspect of the averted gaze. Cairns 2005 has persuasively shown that 'both turning the head aside and inclining

---

[115] A further reflection on this scene at *Theb.* 9.659–62 when Statius' Apollo advises Diana that she cannot protect Parthenopaeus from death.
[116] This is the position of Morrison 1997 and Myers forthcoming.
[117] Harrison 1991: 193. 'Jupiter turns his eyes away from the battle in sorrow, not with the detachment of the Homeric Zeus. . . . the contrast with Homer's divine audience is characteristically Vergilian.' But Zeus in *Iliad* 16 and 22 is equally sorrowful. However, there does seem to be an increased emphasis in Latin epic on the distinction between Jupiter (and the other gods) and fate.
[118] Mortals in the *Aeneid* also avert their gaze for sorrow: at 2.403–5 Coroebus cannot bear to watch as Cassandra is dragged from the temple (evoking, but not explicitly, the tradition which we will examine below of her rape by Ajax Oileus); at 4.451 Dido cannot bear to look at heaven, in a reversal of the divine gaze.
[119] Henderson 1991a: 59, 77, n.173 suggests that aversion of the divine gaze is the Theban pattern.

it forward are ways of directing the look of the eyes in such a way that it expresses a degree of rejection for and disrespect for its target' (137).[120] The divine gaze is a mark of favour, and gods can express the removal of favour by looking away.[121] In particular, cult statues (on some level, a version of the gods themselves) turn their gaze away when they reject offerings: at *Aen.* 1.482, the image on the frescos in the temple of Juno represents the scene of the Trojan women presenting a robe to Pallas, and the statue refusing it: *diua solo fixos oculos auersa tenebat*, 'the goddess, turned away, was holding her eyes fixed on the ground'.[122] This image evokes the moment in the *Iliad* at 6.311 in which Pallas Athene 'nods backwards' ἀνένευε in response to the prayer of Theano.[123] With this in mind, Jupiter's averted gaze in *Thebaid* 11 can be read as both punishment and sign of hostility towards Thebes and Argos, and therefore quite consistent with his earlier malevolence.

However, his rhetoric is not about hostility, but about pollution:

> nunc etiam turbanda dies: mala nubila, tellus,
> accipe, secedantque poli: stat parcere mundo
> caelitibusque meis; saltem ne uirginis almae
> sidera, Ledaei uideant neu talia fratres.   (*Thebaid* 11.130–3)

> Now even the day must be thrown into disorder: the evil clouds, earth,
> receive them, let the heavens withdraw; it remains to spare the world
> and my heavenly ones; at least the stars of the gentle virgin,
> at least the Ledaean brothers should not see such things.

The comparison with Tantalus, Lycaon and Thyestes, all occasions on which the sun was eclipsed, combine a rhetoric of intertextual competition with one of pollution.[124] Jupiter both disavows authority, and takes a perverse pride in the narrative. The implication is that the sight will actually be dangerous for the divine viewers. Other examples of this usually refer to

---

[120] Mortal characters express anger and contempt by withdrawing or averting the gaze: *Il.* 3.216–20 (Odysseus looks angry because he is looking at the ground); 3.426–7 (Helen avoids Paris' gaze); Dido expresses her rejection of Aeneas in their final encounter in the underworld at 6.469 (*illa solo fixos oculos auersa tenebat*, 'she, turned away, was holding her eyes fixed on the ground'); similarly as the two talk past each other in book 4, both avert their gazes (4.331–2, Aeneas holds his eyes unmoved; *immota tenebat | lumina*; Dido at 4.362: *talia dicentem iamdudum auersa tuetur*, 'she gazed away for a while as he said such things'). All these moments evoke the Ajax of *Odyssey* 11, who refuses to speak to Odysseus in his anger (11.563). Similar to these examples is Athene's expression of disdain for Ares at *Il.* 21.415.

[121] Cairns 2005: 137: 'Gods avert their eyes from those whom they do not wish to support, whose prayers they reject, or whose conduct they find reprehensible.'

[122] The near repetition of this line in Dido's rejection of Aeneas at 6.469 emphasises Dido's power.

[123] Barchiesi 1998.

[124] Jupiter is a poet figure whose rhetoric echoes that of Dis at 8.34–79 and of the narrator himself, for instance, at 10.827–36, taking greater inspiration for the madness of Capaneus, or at 11.574–9, reflecting on the negative exemplarity of Polynices and Eteocles. Dis (and Jupiter?) as poet figure: Ganiban 2007: 182.

rape, particularly on sacred ground. The story of Cassandra's rape by Ajax Oileus, mentioned by Juno at the very beginning of the *Aeneid*, as the inspiration for Athene's destruction of the returning Greeks, and therefore her own attempted destruction of the Trojans, must already have been well known. We have Quintus' version, at 13.415–30, in which the gods are in mourning at the sight of the destruction of Troy, except for Hera and Athene, who rejoice, but Athene's viewing is compromised by the rape:

> Οὐδὲ οἱ ἔργον ἀεικὲς· ἐσέδρακεν, ἀλλά οἱ αἰδὼς
> καὶ χόλος ἀμφεχύθη, βλοσυρὰς δ' ἔστρεψεν ὀπωπὰς
> νηὸν ἐς ὑψόροφον, περὶ δ' ἔβραχε θεῖον ἄγαλμα,
> καὶ δάπεδον νηοῖο μέγ' ἔτρεμεν: (*Posthomerica* 13.425–8)

> Nor would she willingly look on the deed, but she wrapped herself
> in shame and anger: she turned her stern eyes
> to the high roof of the temple: she made the holy statue groan
> and floor of the temple tremble:

Similarly in Ovid *Metamorphoses* 4, Medusa is punished by Athena's anger, when Neptune rapes her in the temple of the goddess:

> hanc pelagi rector templo uitiasse Mineruae
> dicitur: auersa est et castos aegide uultus
> nata Iouis texit, neue hoc inpune fuisset,
> Gorgoneum crinem turpes mutauit in hydros. (*Metamorphoses* 4.798–801)

> This girl the ruler of the sea is said to have violated in the temple
> of Minerva: the daughter of Jupiter turned away and covered her chaste
> face with the aegis, and so that this would not happen without punishment,
> she changed the Gorgon's hair into foul snakes.

Is Ovid tendentious here in punishing Medusa for being raped, or is it the pollution which is punished? Similarly, Hippomenes and Atalanta have consensual sex in the temple of Cybele, having angered Venus for their ingratitude; Cybele turns away her gaze (*sacra retorserunt oculos*, 10.696) and transforms them into lions. In all these cases of pollution, the divine gaze must be averted: the implication is the pollution can enter via the eyes, and that gods are in danger of being contaminated by it. Earlier in the *Thebaid*, Athena has removed her gaze (and her favour) from Tydeus after his cannibalistic frenzy threatened to pollute her:[125]

> atque illum effracti perfusum tabe cerebri
> aspicit et uiuo scelerantem sanguine fauces

---

[125] This episode is already present in the cyclic *Thebaid* (fr. 9 West).

> (nec comites auferre ualent): stetit aspera Gorgon
> crinibus emissis rectique ante ora cerastae
> uelauere deam; fugit auersata iacentem,
> nec prius astra subit quam mystica lampas et insons
> Ilissos multa purgauit lumina lympha. (*Thebaid* 8.760–6)
>
> But when she catches sight of him drenched in the gore
> of the broken brain and his throat defiled by living blood
> (nor are his companions strong enough to take it away): the harsh Gorgon's
> hair stands on end and erect snakes veil the face
> of the goddess; she flees, having turned away from him as he lies there,
> and she did not go back up to the stars before the mystic lamp
> and innocent Ilissos had purified her with much liquid light.

Pallas is actually polluted by the sight of Tydeus and must undergo ritual purification. The divine gaze can be a site of vulnerability as well as an index of power and authority.

With all this in mind, let us return to Jupiter in *Thebaid* 11, and examine the interplay of power and vulnerability in his speech. The section begins at 119 with a clear expression of Jupiter's powerful gaze: *illas ut summo uidit pater altus Olympo*, ('when the high father saw them from the top of Olympus',); his fierce face (*toruo ore*, 121) as he speaks, continues the emphasis on his powerful (even assaultive) gaze. Yet the narrator's description of what he sees: *incestare diem trepidumque Hyperionis orbem | suffundi maculis* ('that the day is polluted and the panicked orb of Hyperion is suffused with stains', 120–1) intervenes, already implying that the universe (of which the sun is the emblem) is physically embroiled in the narrative. This is clearly focalised through Jupiter, but it does seem to suggest, as does the similarity of Jupiter's rhetoric of intertextual one-upmanship to that of the narrator elsewhere, that the narrator shares Jupiter's sense of pollution and vulnerability. However, the first three lines of the speech, in which Jupiter constructs an opposition between the lawful battles so far, which have been fine to watch, and this war, which is a step too far, are made problematic by his mention of Capaneus' *impia bella*. This has always been an epic which goes too far, straying into the tragic; Dis has taken credit for every *nefas* since the death of Amphiaraus. Jupiter's decision to stop watching now seems arbitrary. The final lines of the speech evoke the Hesiodic universe of the absolute power of Zeus;[126] he is called *pater omnipotens* (134), and his gaze removes sweet serenity (*dulci sereno*, 135) from the guilty fields (*nocentibus aruis*). He is both powerful (indifferent, hostile) as he removes his gaze, and disempowered (polluted, out of control). He expresses disgust, sorrow, fear and disapproval. The narrator

---

[126] *Works and Days* 197–200: Aidos and Nemesis veil their heads at the state of the world; cf. Astraea. Virg. *Ecl.* 4.6–7.

loves his story and hates it; so the removal of Jupiter's gaze is an expression of the split voice of Statius: part of the narrator is now absent. This is an intensification of night covering the acts of Atreus: not just the sun but all of the gods have turned away. All comes together to highlight the intense paradox of the pleasure and horror of watching.

Further, the ambivalence of the representation of Jupiter and his actions induces a keen sense of subjection: the subject of power cannot know whether the agent is malevolent or incompetent, because, however motivations are articulated, they are always uncertain. The reader and the narrator are subject to the arbitrary tyranny of the text. Jupiter's gaze is an act of poetic disavowal: gods, but no gods, in the tradition of Lucan and Ovid, and the complex Virgil of no clear vantage point. Where Virgil's Jupiter removes Juno, Statius' Jupiter goes one step further by removing himself.

Conclusions

From the controlling gaze of Zeus in the *Iliad* to the averted gaze of Statius' Jupiter, the chapter has explored the structural importance of the divine gaze, demonstrating how epic uses the divine audience as mediating frame between narrator and listener/reader. The association between transitions, divine viewing and similes and other narrative devices which give a view from above, shows how the epic narrator plays with a divine perspective. Group responses emphasise the power of Zeus, but also the complexity of different emotional reactions available in response to the narrative. Gender is still important, even among deities, as the case of Hera shows. And the controlling gaze, the male gaze, the divine gaze, is also often the gaze of the rapist, using disempowered objects, women and the universe, for their own fulfilment. The power of the divine gaze can be circumscribed, and throughout the epic tradition fate (and narrative compulsion) have their own force. But epic is a genre closely associated with the divine gaze, the genre which most clearly aspires to apotheosis: epic requires and desires authority. The effects of epic wonder and terror are closely bound up with the divine gaze which holds the world in its grasp, but the interplay of divine gazes is an exploration of the complex workings of power. Loss of power for the gods is their closest equivalent to mortality. As part of the cosmos, control is always incomplete; separation from mortals is equally incomplete. Epic gods are cosmic and incomprehensible; involved and compromised. In the next chapter, I will investigate what happens when mortals are granted, or attempt to appropriate, this divine gaze, and the power of epic along with it.

CHAPTER 3

The mortal gaze

The previous chapter focused on the gods as active viewers, the divine audience. This chapter looks at their passive visual power and mortal attempts to appropriate the divine gaze. The divine gaze is characterised by verticality (the gods tend to be above the action, often on a mountain or hill), and often a distant, 'birds-eye' view, clarity and penetration (seeing through to the true nature of what is on display), agency and effectiveness. When gods see something, they act on it. It is often to be found at turning points in the plot and scene changes, and closely associated with narrative authority. The narrator of epic calls upon the Muses to share what they have witnessed;[1] and he too sees through to reality, and from above, to display his mastery of the material. The divine gaze signals generic sublimity, and calls attention to the poet's bid for his poem to surpass the rest. It can be protective, aggressive, jealous or pitying, emotional or distant. We have examined the interplay between divine gaze and power, but what happens when mortals look at gods? Occasionally mortals are granted divine vision by the gods; what effect does this have on them, and on the narrative? What of those who appropriate the divine gaze imperfectly, illegitimately or against the will of the gods? The section begins with a brief discussion of epiphany, moves on to Diomedes, Aeneas and Hannibal, and their divinely sponsored visions. It discusses philosophy and gazes set in opposition to the gods, starting with Lucretius' Epicurus and his battle against *Religio*, and Statius' Capaneus. Finally, there is a case study of Lucan, which brings together this chapter and the last to think about the absence of the gods, and Caesar's appropriation of the divine gaze.

Looking at gods: visual epiphanies and poetic visions

In the previous chapter I briefly discussed the inset story of Ares and Aphrodite in *Odyssey* 8, to show the complexity of divine viewing in epic. Ares and Aphrodite

[1] See Halliwell 2011: 36–92 on Homeric poetics.

are not just on display to the other gods, however; they are also on display to the internal narrator and his audience, to the *Odyssey* poet and his audience. If Actaeon, Tiresias and others can be viciously punished for looking at naked gods, why can we look at Love and War through the window of epic? Or are we seeing a deeper reality, an epiphanic vision of the Empedoclean universe? We gain a frisson from sharing the visual pleasure of the male gods, but the poet risks loss of gravity and narrative authority (hence distancing himself from the story by inserting a secondary narrator). Arachne's tapestry in Ovid's *Metamorphoses* is doubly transgressive, not just for competing with Minerva, but also for containing, displaying and denigrating divine power. By illustrating scenes of divine rape and questioning theodicy, Arachne inevitably lays herself open to destruction. As a figure of Ovid himself, she shows that he is keenly aware of the issue of epic (political and theological) propriety, but is unlikely to toe the line.

We have seen something of the powerful, and often assaultive, gaze of the gods, and we will see more below. However, they also create powerful effects simply by being seen, revealing themselves. As Hera points out to the other gods, Achilles should be frightened of them: χαλεποὶ δὲ θεοὶ φαίνεσθαι ἐναργεῖς. 'The gods are dangerous when they appear clearly.' (*Il.* 20.131). The overwhelming effects of epiphany are most clearly portrayed in the *Homeric Hymns* to Demeter and Aphrodite: Demeter fills the house with light and Metaneira gives way at the knees (*Hom. Hymns Demeter* 275–83); Anchises averts his gaze and fears retribution when he sees Aphrodite's stature filling the house, and the brilliance of her beauty (*Hom. Hymns* 5.168–90). Steiner points out the way that cult statues, with their colossal size, and brilliant materials, replicate the imagined visual experience of epiphany; this is why the gods disguise themselves: 'The blindness, paralysis, or unconsciousness that seizes those to whom the gods do display themselves (even fleetingly) in full majesty provides one rationale for disguise: such is the brilliance and power of divinities that mortals are incapable of sustaining their gaze and must immediately turn away in reverence and fear if they are to escape the consequences of the encounter.'[2]

It is important that this sort of full-face epiphany does not really occur in the *Iliad*, where representation of physical presence is 'always weak and arbitrary'.[3] In Apollonius' *Argonautica*, a fuller epiphany occurs, in which

---

[2] Steiner 2001: 80–1. Like ecphrasis, however, the attempt to portray divine power in visual art is always only partially successful. For a discussion of ecphrasis and epiphany, see Platt 2002; Platt 2011 had not quite arrived at time of writing this. For historical context on representations of epiphany, see Lane Fox 1988: 102–67.

[3] Pucci 1997: 69. Also Pucci 1994: 17 'Only in the *Homeric Hymns*, though rarely, do they manifest the full presence of the divine persona as being visible – and also confusing – to mortals.' (17) The best discussion of Homeric epiphany remains that of Pucci: on the *Iliad*, Pucci 1997: 69–96; and on the *Odyssey*, Pucci 1987: 110–23.

the Argonauts see Apollo of the dawn on the island of Thynias; they are struck with θάμβος, but bow their heads:[4]

> τοὺς δ' ἕλε θάμβος ἰδόντας ἀμήχανον· οὐδέ τις ἔτλη
> ἀντίον αὐγάσσασθαι ἐς ὄμματα καλὰ θεοῖο.
> στὰν δὲ κάτω νεύσαντες ἐπὶ χθονός· αὐτὰρ ὁ τηλοῦ
> βῆ ῥ' ἴμεναι πόντονδε δι' ἠέρος·   (AR *Argonautica* 2.681–4)

> And helpless wonder held them as they looked; nor did anyone dare
> to gaze face to face into the fair eyes of the god.
> And they stood with heads bowed to the ground. But he far off
> went on to the sea through the air.

Apollo is both a representation of sunlight and a physical presence of the uncanny, inspiring a sense of overpowering otherness, while he remains far off and apparently unaware of the viewers.[5] Apollonius here, as often, allies the gaze of his narrator and audience with the internal viewers, limiting their knowledge, vision and understanding to the same level as that of the characters. We, too, experience helpless wonder at the glory of Apollo/dawn; the narrator tells us where he is going, but we do not know what motivates his movements.[6]

The most extreme example of full epiphany ought to be Ovid's Semele (*Met.* 3.253–315), who is literally consumed by Jupiter's fire, when she asks him to come to her in the same manner that he goes to Juno. Semele suffers two divine encounters: first that of the deceptive, disguised Juno, who offers a rationalisation of her lover, Jupiter, as a lying mortal. This is represented in traditional visual terms: Juno first disguises herself (275–8), then removes her cloud (*nubes remouit*, 274), but still witholds her true appearances, playing Semele's nurse Beroe. Jupiter's manifestation eludes visualisation, must be conveyed metaphorically. When he takes up his insignia (*insignia sumat*, 286) he becomes the storm (298–309): *corpus mortale tumultus | non tulit aetherios donisque iugalibus arsit*. ('Her mortal body did not bear the heavenly storm and she burnt with the bridal gifts', 308–9). The fullness of his presence goes beyond visuality: in order to completely understand, you

---

[4] Hunter 2009: 143–9 argues that this passage is less sublime than Homeric epiphanies because Apollo is too precisely visualised, but acknowledges that it has its own force.
[5] On this passage, see Feeney 1991: 75, Hunter 1993: 76, 84–5.
[6] But intertextuality gives us an edge: the contrast with Apollo's appearance in *Iliad* I, in which he comes down 'like night' (1.47), gives us a sense that Jason will make it to adulthood. It might also reflect the poetics of distance in Apollonius: Apollo is the figure who both begins and ends the epic (1.1, 4.1747; Hunter 1993: 65), and the elusive aesthetic of Apollonius which both distances and creates awe at his scholarship and craftsmanship is well represented by a figure who passes by without noticing his audience.

Visual epiphanies and poetic visions 81

must feel it, be consumed by it. Ovid enjoys the impossibility of representation, combining epiphany and sex with typically Ovidian virtuosity.[7]

Pucci points out the rhetorical evasiveness which characterises descriptions of epiphany: the tendency to slip sideways into synecdoche, 'conspicuous silence' and comparison (metaphor and metonym).[8] This evasiveness must partly be focalised through the watching mortals; the *Iliad* describes gods in a great deal of visual detail: at 14.170–86 Hera decks herself out to seduce Zeus; at 5.733–47 Athene arms for battle.[9] The gods are visualised very similarly to heroes elsewhere. Turkeltaub 2007: 76 argues that the poet of the *Iliad* presents the audience of epic as being like the common soldiers of the poem, while he experiences aural epiphanies, like a favoured hero. But it seems difficult to separate out the aural epiphany of the Muses from the visualisation of the poet: the poet's ability to describe the gods suggests that he is more godlike than heroic. Turkeltaub emphasises the suturing effects of epiphany in epic, which functions to smooth over difference, and use religious awe and emotion to create identification with characters and authority for the poet. Pucci 1997: 78 analyses this tendency, but suggests that the creation of such a 'comforting and rational Iliadic theology' is skin-deep at best.[10] Rather, epiphany with all its problems and difficulties implies that 'the divine has forces in reserve, powers and intentions that escape the control of even the most favoured mortal. . . . This could correspond in turn to the poets' consciousness that their own texts create effects not entirely within their control, and that the Muses, whatever power or function they represent, have a power that surpasses the control of even the most favoured θεράπων.' (80) Hence representing the gods both creates narrative authority and undermines it.

Epiphany in poetry seems to have strong poetic associations with epic. In a later article, Pucci uses his work on epic epiphany to reflect on the relationship between epic and tragedy. He concludes that tragic epiphany tends to be marginal, and marked by allusion as epic.[11]

---

[7] In *Am.* 1.5 Ovid also plays with the limits of representation: who does not know the rest? On epiphany in *Am.* 1.5 see Papanghelis 1989.
[8] Pucci 1997: 70.
[9] On the elusiveness of the *Iliad*'s visual representation of the gods, see Smith 1988.
[10] Further, Pucci argues that the *Iliad* strives to create the belief that 'The world of the heroes and that of the gods duplicate one another. Naturally they differ in occupying the divergent levels of mortality and immortality, but in other respects they are fully parallel, without gaps or discontinuities, guaranteeing to one another the sublime virtues of beauty and nobility, attesting to each other's reality (and, I am tempted to add, historicity) and to the wondrous and perfect manner in which both exist and function. Theology, history, and story become a seamless whole.'
[11] Epiphany is also used by poets to justify their poetic choices: the Muses appear to Hesiod; Apollo appears to Callimachus in *Aetia* fr. 1, and Cupid appears to Ovid in order to steal a foot of his second

Epiphanies are not always visual, of course: I am interested in moments when mortals look at gods, not in dreams, which will be covered below (pp.206–16), but in the waking narrative. Turkeltaub's typology of epiphany for the *Iliad* ranks visual epiphany more highly than aural in terms of closeness to the divine: those to whom the gods appear in disguise, and who only recognise them later, or by deduction, are furthest away, and likely to be in for a difficult time (if not to die); only particularly favoured heroes (Odysseus, Diomedes and Hector) hear the voice of the gods and recognise it; demigods (Achilles, Helen and Aeneas) see visual epiphanies and recognise the gods by sight; only Achilles interacts with gods like another god, having a conversation with Iris, as well as Thetis. While this typology may smooth over the complexities too much, it does offer food for thought about the later epic tradition. To explore these implications, I briefly discuss three examples of divine epiphany: first that of Athene to Achilles in *Iliad* 1, then Venus and Aeneas in *Aeneid* 1, and finally Virtus in *Thebaid* 10.

When Achilles is deciding whether or not to draw his sword and attack Agamemnon in the assembly of *Iliad* 1, Athene comes down to stop him:[12]

στῆ δ' ὄπιθεν, ξανθῆς δὲ κόμης ἕλε Πηλεΐωνα
οἴῳ φαινομένη· τῶν δ' ἄλλων οὔ τις ὁρᾶτο.
θάμβησεν δ' Ἀχιλεύς, μετὰ δ' ἐτράπετ', αὐτίκα δ' ἔγνω
Παλλάδ' Ἀθηναίην· δεινὼ δέ οἱ ὄσσε φάανθεν·   (*Iliad* 1.197–200)

She stood behind him, and seized the blonde hair of the son of Peleus
appearing to him alone. None of others saw her.
Achilles was struck by wonder, and turned behind, and immediately recognised
Pallas Athene; and (his or her?) eyes blazed terribly.

Her appearance to Achilles alone marks him out as special, but her positioning behind him is arguably threatening: her anger at him, marked by the seizing of his hair, matches his anger at Agamemnon. The blazing eyes, which may belong to Achilles, would then imply the immensity of Achilles' anger; most read them as belonging to Athene, and a sign of divine power and intensity. However, Achilles is not afraid, but amazed. The psychologising reading of this scene as the intervention of Achilles' rationality fails to account for the tone of the encounter.[13] As Pucci convincingly argues 'The ironic, mocking appearance of the goddess at Achilles' shoulder and her message (fraudulent on any objective view, a piece of coercion on a

---

line in *Am.* 1.1, turning his poem from epic into elegy. These poetic epiphanies are bound up with adopting or refusing the epic voice. On Ovid's marginalisation of Apollo as poetic and political move, see R. Armstrong 2004, with further bibliography on poetic epiphanies.

[12] On this passage, see Turkeltaub 2007: 63; and the more detailed discussion of Pucci 1997: 71–5.
[13] For bibliography on this reading, see Turkeltaub 2007: 61 n.30.

subjective one) together form a structure that, as a whole, is ambivalent and ironic.' (77) If Achilles had simply killed Agamemnon, the whole *Iliad* would have been finessed, and perhaps Troy would still stand. Achilles' epiphany, far from creating authority for the poem, gives a sense of narrative contingency. Achilles is close to the gods, terrifying enough to be an avatar of them for ordinary mortals, but also immeasurably inferior to them.

In this context, the extraordinarily problematic nature of Venus' encounter with Aeneas in *Aeneid* 1 becomes clearer: she is not just the prologue of a tragedy, inserting herself into the love story as if with potentially incestuous intentions, but her appearance to Aeneas in disguise, only revealing herself as she leaves (1.402–5), suggests that her plans for him are not entirely benevolent.[14] Aeneas' accusation of cruelty (407–9) seems justified: he is not an Achilles, or even an Odysseus in this passage, and he only sees the true goddess (*uera dea*, 405) at the end of the episode. Virgil stresses throughout that she is his mother: *cui mater* (314) begins the meeting; after she removes her disguise *ille ubi matrem | agnouit* ('he when he recognises his mother', 405–6) places *matrem* emphatically at the end of the line. Smith justifies her distancing epiphany in the vaguest terms.[15] The description of Venus' unveiling is vivid but elusive:

> Dixit et auertens rosea ceruice refulsit,
> ambrosiaeque comae diuinum uertice odorem
> spirauere; pedes uestis defluxit ad imos,
> et uera incessu patuit dea.   (*Aeneid* 1.402–5)

> She spoke and turning away she sent out light from her rosy neck,
> and her ambrosial hair breathed out a divine scent
> from her head; her clothes flowed down to the soles of her feet;
> and the true goddess lay open as she went.

Both Demeter and Aphrodite in the *Homeric Hymns* only reveal themselves as they leave. Here too the revelation is embedded in the departure. The text specifies very little: colour, light and an indescribable scent; are her clothes changing into divine clothes, or disappearing entirely, like those of Ariadne in Catullus 64? Perhaps we should see Venus' agenda as actively destructive: has she planned all along the downfall of Dido and Carthage? Later in book

---

[14] On this passage see Reckford 1995–6, Smith 2005: 24–8 with further bibliography, Hardie 2006: 26 on the sexual overtones of the meeting.

[15] '[D]eception is necessary for Venus to convey information about Dido to Aeneas without the distraction that the epiphany of a goddess would have engendered. Recognition of Venus might have prompted Aeneas to seek the direct help and guidance that she chooses to provide less directly, for Venus understands that, to achieve his destiny, Aeneas must first undergo trials.' Smith 2005: 28.

8 Aeneas is becoming an *alius Achilles* when the gift of the divine weapons at 608–16 is accompanied by an embrace; but at 12.411–19 she wraps herself in a cloud and adds the divine ingredient to Iapyx' medicine *occulte* (418) – unlike Hermes in *Odyssey* 10, who appears to Odysseus to reveal how he can counter Circe's magic.

The epiphany of Virtus to Menoeceus in *Thebaid* 10 gives a different slant on the problems of looking at gods in epic.[16] Virtus disguises herself as Manto deceitfully (*fraude*, 640) and in her female and mortal trappings, she is compared to Hercules in women's clothes (10.646–9). This almost overdetermined description, which refers to her insignia (sword, 643; laurel, 645), is still difficult to pin down: how can she take off her face (*priores exuitur uultus*, 640–1)? What does it mean that her clothes descend (to cover or uncover? *descendunt uestes*, 644)? How can her eyes display horror and vigour (*abiit horrorque uigorque | ex oculis*. 'The horror and vigour is gone from her eyes', 641–2). In what way does she look like Hercules in women's clothes? The description gives a strong impression of threat and incongruity, but serves mainly to underline the indescribability (and incomprehensibility?) of the divine. Like Athene with Achilles, she touches Menoeceus, stops his hand from fighting (661); then strokes herself into his heart, now an Allecto (672–3).[17] Menoeceus only recognises her as a god as she turns away, and grows into the clouds, like Homer's Eris and Virgil's Fama:

> ut uero auersae gressumque habitumque notauit
> et subitam a terris in nubila crescere Manto
> obstipuit.   (*Thebaid* 10.678–80)

> As he noted her step and appearance while she turned away
> and that Manto suddenly grew from the earth into the clouds,
> he was dumbfounded.

The links to problematic and malevolent epiphany support the negative reading of Menoeceus as defrauded and destroyed, driven to a suicide which will cause as many problems as it solves. The paralysis caused by the vision is compared to the effect of being struck by lightning (674–7), bringing out an equivalence between the destructive penetrative gaze of Jupiter with his

---

[16] On this passage see Fantham 1997, Ganiban 2007: 143–4.
[17] Ganiban 2007: 143 emphasises the resemblance to the *Dirae* and Allecto of the *Aeneid* in his account of Statius' poetics of the underworld. But her resemblance also to Athene and Venus might seem even more worrying: you cannot exonerate Statius' gods by putting the blame on the underworld; the gods and the furies are all part of the same outfit.

thunderbolt and the passive visual power of divine manipulation of appearances.

Epic epiphany shows how difficult it is for mortals (the readers of epic included) to look at gods. The gods are absent presences, too real to be conveyed by description, like pain, or love, always metonymic and at one remove. We gain a clear sense from these passages of the powerful impact that seeing a god (or thinking you have seen a god) can have. Often, however, such encounters do not bring meaningful understanding, but rather activate processes of divine control. Epiphany stages the passive visual power of the gods; to-be-looked-at does not necessarily mean to-be-disempowered. When mortals try to borrow or appropriate the divine gaze, to see penetratively into reality, and to see the gods at work in the heart of the narrative, is this another process of control?

The divine gaze and theomachy: Diomedes in *Iliad* 5

The *aristeia* of Diomedes in *Iliad* 5 is the original example of a mortal given temporary access to the divine gaze.[18] After being wounded by Pandarus, he prays to Athene (115–20) who hears his prayer and responds:

> ἀχλὺν δ' αὖ τοι ἀπ' ὀφθαλμῶν ἕλον, ἣ πρὶν ἐπῆεν,
> ὄφρ' εὖ γιγνώσκῃς ἠμὲν θεὸν ἠδὲ καὶ ἄνδρα.
> τῷ νῦν, αἴ κε θεὸς πειρώμενος ἐνθάδ' ἵκηται,
> μή τι σύ γ' ἀθανάτοισι θεοῖς ἀντικρὺ μάχεσθαι
> τοῖς ἄλλοις· ἀτὰρ εἴ κε Διὸς θυγάτηρ Ἀφροδίτη
> ἔλθῃσ' ἐς πόλεμον, τήν γ' οὐτάμεν ὀξέϊ χαλκῷ. (*Iliad* 5.127–32)

> I have taken away the mist from your eyes, that before now
> was there, so that you may well recognise the god and the mortal.
> Therefore now, if a god making trial of you comes hither
> do you not do battle head on with the gods immortal,
> not with the rest; but only if Aphrodite, Zeus' daughter
> comes to the fighting, her at least you may stab with the sharp bronze.

Diomedes' rather conventional prayer receives more response than he bargained for: on one level Athene allows him to protect himself better in battle by recognising when he is fighting against a god. On another, she has

---

[18] On Diomedes' *aristeia* in *Iliad* 5 see Bernadete 1968, Andersen 1978: 47–94, Linares and Saconi 1996. Taplin 1992: 106–9 sees the episode as unspoken revenge on Pandarus for breaking the truce. Alden 2000: 112–52 reads Diomedes as someone stuck in the double bind of divine instructions, who will be punished for fighting the gods. At *Aen.* 11.271–7 Diomedes makes much of his punishment for wounding Venus, but his *nostos* is much less disastrous than many; in several versions he lives to a ripe old age.

her own agenda: for Aphrodite to be attacked by a mortal. Diomedes has the divine gaze only to the extent that he can distinguish between gods and mortals in battle. He has no broader perspective, no view from above, just a particular tool to help him in fighting. Some scholars read this passage as a metaphor illustrating the limitations of mortality.[19]

When Aphrodite does (inevitably) join the battle, Diomedes recognises her and immediately attacks. He does not just see her, but recognises her as a god less powerful in battle, wounds her hand and taunts her. His gaze has become penetrative, assaultive and effective. When Apollo steps in to look after Aeneas, he covers him with a dark mist (345), but Diomedes tries to kill Aeneas anyway (434–5), even though he can see Apollo.[20] He can see through the cloud, but his ability to see gods does not lead to an understanding of where his own limits lie. Three times he attacks, 'equal to a *daimon*' (δαίμονι ἶσος, 438), but on the fourth Apollo frightens him off (438–42).[21] Though he can see Apollo, the divine gaze does not make much difference; it is the supernatural voice of Apollo which succeeds in deterring him. Ironically when Ares does take over as the god against Diomedes, he covers the battle in dark night (506–7) – which of course is little good as a tactic against Diomedes who is still endowed with the divine gaze.[22] In fact, it is his sight which now enables him to recognise Ares and encourage a retreat:

> Τὸν δὲ ἰδὼν ῥίγησε βοὴν ἀγαθὸς Διομήδης·
> ὡς δ' ὅτ' ἀνὴρ ἀπάλαμνος, ἰὼν πολέος πεδίοιο,
> στήῃ ἐπ' ὠκυρόῳ ποταμῷ ἅλαδε προρέοντι,
> ἀφρῷ μορμύροντα ἰδών, ἀνά τ' ἔδραμ' ὀπίσσω,
> ὣς τότε Τυδεΐδης ἀναχάζετο, εἶπέ τε λαῷ·   (*Iliad* 5.596–600)

Diomedes of the great war-cry shivered as he saw him
and like a man in his helplessness, who, crossing a great plain,
stands at the edge of a fast-running river that dashes seaward,
and watches it thundering into white water, and leaps a pace backward,
so now Tydeus' son gave back and spoke to his people:

---

[19] Clay 1997: 16–18, Turkeltaub 2007: 51.
[20] Kirk 1990: 106 points out connections with 16.702–6, 16.784–6 and 20.445–9 via the 'thrice . . . thrice' motif.
[21] Turkeltaub 2007: 67 suggests that the hero in an *aristeia* is semi-divine 'imbued with divine strength by the gods and often radiating light as do the gods in the *Homeric Hymns*'. Oversimplified, but certainly the penetrative gaze of the hero relates to the destructive gaze of the gods.
[22] Scholarship has long seen Homeric description of gods as moving between metaphor and literal transformation: Bowra 1952: 267, 'When Homer's gods descend like the night or rise like the mist, they are for the moment almost equated with night or mist and have such a look and movement.' For context on comparison in Homer see Ready 2008.

His vision of Ares creates a sense of smallness in the face of incommensurable power. Possession of the divine gaze, here, merely allows him to be more aware of mortal limitations and the impossibility of measuring up to the gods. Athene then returns to rebuke him for not attacking Ares. But this was not part of the deal: Hera has gained special permission from Zeus for Athene to attack Ares, of which Diomedes cannot be expected to be aware (5.755–66). This change in the direction of the narrative, which seemed to be focused on Athene and Aphrodite, but now brings Hera and Ares into play, alienates Diomedes. He is clearly separate from the narrator and this lack of narrative understanding is exacerbated by the limited divine vision that he borrows. Athene puts on the 'helmet of Hades' (844–5), allowing her to limit the vision of other gods, and especially preventing Ares from seeing her helping Diomedes. Together they wound Ares:

δεύτερος αὖθ' ὡρμᾶτο βοὴν ἀγαθὸς Διομήδης
ἔγχεϊ χαλκείῳ· ἐπέρεισε δὲ Παλλὰς Ἀθήνη
νείατον ἐς κενεῶνα, ὅθι ζωννύσκετο μίτρῃ·
τῇ ῥά μιν οὖτα τυχών, διὰ δὲ χρόα καλὸν ἔδαψεν,
ἐκ δὲ δόρυ σπάσεν αὖτις. (*Iliad* 5.855–9)

After him Diomedes of the great war-cry drove forward
with the bronze spear; and Pallas Athene, leaning in on it,
drove it into the depth of the belly, where the war-belt girt him.
Picking this place, he stabbed, and driving it deep in the fair flesh
wrenched the spear out again.

Here we can see the overdetermination of epic causation in action: the spear is driven by both Diomedes and Athene, but although Diomedes seems to take the initiative, it is the gaze of Athene that determines how hard it stabs and where. Her choice of where to place the wound, and the focus on Ares' clothing, objectifies and fragments the god, like a mortal hero.[23] The emphasis on his beautiful flesh is not just an index of his divinity, but also a trope of Homeric killing. Beauty and fragility go hand in hand, and even Ares is not exempt when a more powerful god, sanctioned by Zeus, is against him. But Athene's decision to wear the helmet of Hades is more than just a practical tactic: it also suggests that this sequence is outside the normal rules of epic engagement; by allowing Diomedes to see and wound her fellow gods, Athene is compromising divine etiquette, and asserting her own power within the hierarchy of the gods.

---

[23] On bodies and fragmentation, see below, pp.293–302.

88   The mortal gaze

What difference, then, does Athene's gift of divine vision to Diomedes make? Diomedes on his own manages merely to graze Aphrodite's hand, while he needs the impetus of Athene to bury his spear in Ares' belly. The emphasis on Aphrodite's *ichor* spilt from the wound makes even this small penetration extremely physical. Equally Diomedes takes on power when he takes on the divine gaze: he becomes equal to a *daimon*, something rather more than a hero and less than a god.[24] However this power is circumscribed and limited: Apollo's shout can still deter him, and he needs further encouragement and help to attack Ares. His penetrative gaze, which goes beyond the surface of appearances to see the gods and their actions beneath, is literalised with Athene's help.

What does he gain from this episode? Glory (*kleos*) is the stated aim of Athene's first intervention (5.3). But Diomedes is also used and put at risk in the service of Athene's machinations. He does achieve revenge against Pandarus and wins the important prize of Aeneas' horses. But Dione in her consolation of Aphrodite suggests that he will be punished for it (406–15), and almost all versions of his story leave him in exile in Italy. In some versions the exile is caused by the unfaithfulness of his wife Aigialea and can be read as Aphrodite's revenge. By borrowing the divine gaze, Diomedes allows himself to be exposed to divine wrath. Ultimately his subjectivity is unimportant to Athene, so that she even seems to rebuke him for not knowing in advance that she would change her mind about her injunction only to attack Aphrodite and no other god. He does not have any wider awareness of the significance of his actions through his borrowing of the divine gaze, nor any real knowledge except the specific ability to detect gods and mortals.

Seeing the gods in *Aeneid* 2

In *Aeneid* 2, this motif becomes part of Aeneas' narrative to Dido of the fall of Troy. When Venus catches Aeneas, viewing events from the top of Priam's palace, about to kill Helen, she shows him the gods destroying Troy, to persuade him to follow her commands:

> aspice (namque omnem, quae nunc obducta tuenti
> mortalis hebetat uisus tibi et umida circum
> caligat, nubem eripiam; tu ne qua parentis
> iussa time neu praeceptis parere recusa):   (*Aeneid* 2.604–7)

---

[24] Linares and Saconi 1996 suggest that he approaches divine power and is assimilated to Ares as the book goes on.

Look (for the whole cloud, which now obstructing you as you gaze
blunts your mortal vision and wraps moist darkness
around, I will snatch away; and you should not fear
any orders of your mother nor refuse to obey my commands);

Venus describes what he will see: not rocks and destruction, but Neptune destroying the walls with his trident, Juno calling her allies from the Scaean gates, Pallas occupying the highest citadel and Jupiter himself inspiring the Greeks. Finally we see through his changed vision:

apparent dirae facies inimicaque Troiae
numina magna deum.
   Tum uero omne mihi uisum considere in ignis
Ilium et ex imo uerti Neptunia Troia: (*Aeneid* 2.622–5)

The dread visions appear and, hostile to Troy,
the great powers of the gods.
   Then indeed all Ilium seemed to me to settle down
into the flames and Neptunian Troy to be overturned from its foundation:

The passage finishes with one of the most memorable similes of *Aeneid* 2, that of Troy cut down by the gods as an ash tree cut down by farmers with axes.

This whole episode is overshadowed by its textual problems.[25] Current orthodoxy (in the shape of Mynors' Oxford Classical Text) treats the Helen episode as spurious, while Venus' epiphany has always been accepted as Virgilian.[26] The two passages are closely related; arguments about continuity are important. If a later poet chose this point to make an interpolation, that may reflect on the importance of Venus' intervention: the power of the vision of destruction, the special authority which Venus' revelation gives to Aeneas' narrative, the insight to realities behind appearances, make this an important passage.[27] One intertextual link is with Athene's epiphany to

---

[25] For recent contributions to this debate with further bibliography see Horsfall 2008: 553–67, Fish 2004, Murgia 2003, Egan 1996, Berres 1992, Conte 1986: 196–207, Goold 1970.

[26] The Helen passage is not in the manuscripts, but only preserved in Servius *auctus* on 2.566, who claims it was originally written by Virgil but was cut out by Varius and Tucca. Goold 1970 suggests that it might have been written soon after the *Aeneid*, possibly even by Lucan, in whose poetry we have the first evidence of imitation of it; Murgia 2003 argues it was composed later. Horsfall 2008: 563 suggests that the language is too saturated with Virgilian stylistic tics to be Virgilian; too paradoxical? But his analysis of the problems of continuity and understanding between the Helen epiosde and the wider text are convincing. He holds to the idea that it was composed to fill a lacuna and several times points out the unfinished nature of the passage; but see O'Hara 2007 on the weakness of inconsistency as justification. Fish 2004 argues that it was a 'prop' and therefore the unfinished work of Virgil, and that it is an important part of Virgil's use of Philodemus' discussion of anger.

[27] Conte's final comment is the most important one for this study: 'In any case, this Virgilian draft is the textual "facies" (surface) beyond which the philologist's probe cannot go: the final surface for readers

Achilles in *Iliad* 1.²⁸ The allegorisation of this epiphany as clarity of mind, the return of reason, is relevant here too. Before Venus appears, Aeneas has a maddened mind (*furiata mente*, 588) and her manifestation is the epitome of clarity:

> cum mihi se, non ante oculis tam clara, uidendam
> obtulit et pura per noctem in luce refulsit
> alma parens, confessa deam qualisque uideri
> caelicolis et quanta solet,   (*Aeneid* 2.589–92)

> when she presented herself to me to be seen, not before so clear
> in my eyes, and she shone in pure light through the night,
> my gentle parent, manifesting herself as a goddess, in the same manner
> and size as she was accustomed to be seen by the heaven dwellers.

The image of light shining through darkness, *pura* and *clara*, suggests knowledge and revelation. However the emphasis is on Aeneas' remarkably unmediated access to his mother: he has never before seen her so clearly. By revealing herself as a goddess she makes a particular claim of truth and authority for this speech – while also emphasising her own power both over Aeneas and to protect him. By making Venus reveal herself as a goddess, Aeneas makes a particular claim of truth and authority both for this speech and his own narrative, while emphasising his own privileged connection with the divine. For the primary narrator, this passage is a claim to the sublimity of epic, at a moment when his narrative of defeat might seem to yield to the *Iliad*.

Virgil's engagement with the divine gaze here emphasises the synaesthetic qualities of epic viewing. The normal state of mortal vision is blunt and wrapped in moist darkness. The idea that mortal vision is 'blunt' evokes the use of *acies* (primary meaning: sharpness, cutting edge) to mean keenness of vision, the eye and even keenness of the mind.²⁹ The image of ignorance as a dark mist is a motif common in Homer.³⁰ When Venus removes the mist on Aeneas' vision, she makes a strong claim to be showing him the inner

---

who wish to interpret these lines, although it was not final in the intention of their author.' (Conte 1986: 207) Does Virgil's intention or the reader's interpretation make the text? By an accident of preservation (or a specific interpolation) we have these lines: whatever we think of their provenance they are now irrevocably part of the tradition of the *Aeneid* (though the decision about whether or not to print them in the main text clearly makes an important difference).

[28] Conte 1986: 200–2 makes this the keystone of his argument that the two halves of this episode are inseparable; *contra* Murgia 2003: 405 n.2.

[29] On the assaultive gaze, see below, pp.310–46.

[30] Other Homeric examples: 5.506–7: Ares covers the battle with night; 15.668–70: Athene removes a divine cloud of mist from the Achaeans' eyes; 16.567–8: Zeus spreads destructive night over the fighting round Sarpedon's body, and similarly around Patroclus' at 17.268–70. See further Kirk 1990: 69.

reality of the Trojan war. Yet gods often play with mortal vision and perhaps we should be wary of divine visions: the episode's status as part of a first-person narrative gives the authority of autopsy, but undermines the reassurance of epic omniscience. Aeneas is telling us what he thinks happened, or he wants to think happened, but he may have got it wrong. In this case, Venus has a specific agenda: she wants Aeneas to follow her commands. We know from book 1 that her protection of Aeneas is not straightforwardly a manifestation of motherly love; she desires the foundation of Rome, and is willing to use Aeneas for that purpose. She may also (if we accept the Helen passage) want to protect Helen. However, Venus' representation of the responsibilities for the destruction of Troy remains partial: if Juno and Minerva are hostile to Troy, this must surely be partly because of Venus' own victory in the judgement of Paris – of which Paris' abduction of Helen is a symptom. Paris and Helen themselves may not be to blame, but if so, this is because they were the pawns of Venus in divine rivalries. By showing Aeneas the image of the gods destroying Troy, Venus clearly reveals its inevitability, but also occludes her own part in causing the war and Troy's ultimate destruction. The rhetoric of Venus' speech suggests that she is giving Aeneas an insight into reality: but how can he (and the reader) be sure that she is not really showing him a vision?

This impression is emphasised by the only partial visualisation received by the reader. The only description of what Aeneas sees comes in the voice of Venus: Venus describes what he should see. What Aeneas himself sees is described as *dirae facies* ('terrible faces'? or 'terrible appearances'?) and *numina magna deum* ('the great powers of the gods'). The first indicates that he sees something specific, that he recognises the gods, but does not pass the details on to us; the second makes abstract the anthropomorphic divinities, turning them back from personalities into unformed power. He does describe the physical destruction of Troy (settling down into the flames) but not the divine 'reality' behind it. Aeneas is only capable of portraying his understanding of Venus' vision through a simile, at one remove further from direct visualisation. And the majority of the simile (628–31) focuses on the ash tree itself, trembling, groaning and dragging down ruin. Through the simile, Aeneas' vision achieves an emotional, but not visual, directness, conveying the impact of Venus' revelation. The simile displays a vivid image, but it is not the gods, rather the violence of divine destruction. This deferred visuality is partly an index of sublimity:[31] how can

---

[31] Harrison 1990 calls this 'the high-point of Virgil's use of the *Iliad* as a guide in book 2' and makes the link with Diomede in *Iliad* 5: 'the great apocalypse that forms the unforgettable climax of the book'.

it be possible to convey adequately the enormous workings of the universe without making them banal or ridiculous? Virgil, through Aeneas, gestures towards the ineffable awesomeness of divine action: even Venus' speech might give us too much for comfort.[32]

As a first-person narrative it allows Aeneas the narrator a specially privileged viewing to pass on to his audience, and ultimately readers. Aeneas is given authority by his access to the divine gaze; he becomes a special reader of the events that he witnesses, a step closer to an inspired epic poet himself. Yet this passage also puts strains on his narrative. Venus' intervention offers authorisation for Aeneas' version of events from a divine source: it explains why he did not fight to the death in defence of his city. Yet Venus' intervention, too, is within Aeneas' narrative; her epiphany was seen only by him, as was the vision she granted him. The sense of authorisation is essentially circular: this sublime vision, in the words of Heinze 'almost too vast for the imagination to grasp' is both impossible to believe, and not to believe.[33] Yet the very daring of his image and the sublimity itself acts as its own authorisation: by 'concentrating the mighty struggle into one magnificent symbol' (Heinze 1993: 53) Aeneas and Virgil go beyond issues of credibility and falsehood to reach for the truth of fiction.

Aeneas surely gains power and prestige in the eyes of his audience(s) – both the immediate audience at Carthage, including and especially Dido, and the Roman audience contemporary to Virgil. By adopting, no matter how briefly and imperfectly, the divine gaze, Aeneas becomes a more powerful hero, closer to the gods and further removed from men. Venus' gift of allowing him to see her unmediated marks him out already as especially favoured; his assumption of the divine gaze takes him further than Diomedes, who can see only those gods fighting in the battle that he needs to see and for Athene's clearly defined purposes. Aeneas can see (some of) the structuring realities behind the narrative. Yet he does not have Diomedes' agency: he can do nothing, and is persuaded against fighting further, or punishing Helen. He too is at the mercy of a goddess; Aeneas is emphatically the object of Venus' gaze. And when she has finished speaking she immediately returns to the mists of darkness that her epiphany dispersed – continuing to hide herself from Aeneas. Aeneas as narrator is an imperfect epic poet and vision will continue to cause problems in the rest of *Aeneid* 2, particularly in the escape from Troy itself when what he sees or thinks he sees (or believes that Anchises sees) will lead to the loss of Creusa

---

[32] Feeney 1991: 143 finds that 'this shift in perspective is dismaying'; cf. Austin 1964: xx–xxi.
[33] Heinze 1993: 51–3 (original page numbers).

(2.730–40). Aeneas never really looks like a god: his vertical perspective is limited to the top of a building, and his reaction to what he sees marks him out as inevitably mortal with the perspective of a mortal.[34]

The other important intertext in this passage is Lucretius: allusions to two important passages of the *De rerum natura* set this vision in dialogue with those of Epicurus and Lucretius.

> apparent dirae facies inimicaque Troiae
> numina magna deum.
>   Tum uero omne mihi uisum considere in ignis
> Ilium et ex imo uerti Neptunia Troia: (*Aeneid* 2.622–5)

> Dread visions appear and, hostile to Troy,
> the great powers of the gods.
>   Then indeed all Ilium seemed to me to settle down
> into the flames and Neptunian Troy to be overturned from its foundation:

contains two Lucretian verbal reminiscences. The first, from the climax of the praise of Epicurus at the beginning of book 3, evokes Lucretius' ecstatic vision of divine peace and pleasure:

> nam simul ac ratio tua coepit vociferari
> naturam rerum, divina mente coorta,
> diffugiunt animi terrores, moenia mundi
> discedunt. totum video per inane geri res.
> apparet divum numen sedesque quietae
> quas neque concutiunt venti nec nubila nimbis
> aspergunt   (*De rerum natura* 3.14–19)

> For as soon as your reason begins to shout out
> the nature of things, originating from your divine mind,
> the fears of the mind flee away, the walls of the world
> depart, I see things done throughout the whole void.
> The power of the gods appears and their peaceful palaces
> which the winds do not shake, nor clouds scatter
> with snow

Epicurus is the equivalent of Venus, Lucretius a version of Aeneas; fear and materiality are a rationalisation of the Homeric mist, which disperses under the intellectual light of Epicurean philosophy; the dwellings of the gods, unlike Troy as ash tree, are not shaken or confounded.[35] The use of the tag

---

[34] On Lucretius in this passage, see Delvigo 2005, Horsfall 2008: 446–8, Hardie 2009b: 168–9.
[35] Horsfall 2008: 418 calls this 'A clear (and exquisitely paradoxical) verbal debt to Lucretius' radically unVirgilian view of the *sedes quietae* of the gods (3.18) suggests . . . a further analogy between the cloud here dispersed and the removal of obstacles to a clearer view of the *natura rerum*.'

natura rerum adds a level of self-reflexivity: by Lucretius' poetry, we can share in light and revelation. The second echo comes from another passage about the gods (5.146–99) in which he argues that the gods did not make the world for mortals, and must be removed from the world, another description of divine *ataraxia*. His statement of the belief, with which he disagrees, that the gods made the world to be eternal and never to be overthrown contains the phrase: *sollicitare suis ulla vi ex sedibus umquam | nec verbis vexare et ab imo evertere summa* ('not by any violence ever to be shaken from its foundations nor to trouble it by words and to overturn it from top to bottom', *DRN* 5.162–3). Hardie 2009b 168–9 discusses these passages, and suggests that Aeneas' 'pointedly anti-Lucretian vision of the gods' can be recuperated by reading the fall of Troy as a Lucretian apocalypse. He goes on to read Aeneas as an active Lucretian enquirer elsewhere in the poem.[36] If Aeneas seems to be using Epicurean vision to see epic sights, this has a paradoxical effect on the issues of authority and credibility that have been our theme. Venus, after all, authorises and provides inspiration for the whole *De rerum natura*. The reference to the false vision of a world that cannot be overthrown is set against the negative reference to philosophical enlightenment, to create an exquisitely paradoxical sense that true vision is only possible through illusion. There is a sort of philosophical irony here, as if Virgil (or Aeneas) is trying to have his gods and disbelieve them (or have his epic and discredit it). As we will see below, Lucretius has a powerful impact on the mortal gaze: the relatively modest iconoclasm of Aeneas will grow into other, madder ecstatic visions.

Troy and Rome: Hannibal and Juno in Silius' *Punica* 12

Hannibal in *Punica* 12 is a good example of this; in this episode Hannibal is given the divine gaze despite his challenge, visual and otherwise, to the gods.[37] We have already seen him reaching for the sublime as he crosses the Alps (pp.52–3), and later we will see him watching his own defeat at the battle of Zama (pp.62, 257–61). Silius replays the passage from *Aeneid* 2 at a crucial turning point of Hannibal's campaign in Italy: the nearest he came to besieging and taking Rome. Here too the divine gaze is used to mark out significant moments.

Hannibal's allies at Capua are under siege by the rejuvenated Roman forces and he marches on Rome. On two succeeding days huge thunderstorms make

---

[36] See also Delvigo 2005: 71–5.
[37] Cowan 2007: 1 on this visual confrontation between Hannibal and Jupiter as the turning point of the epic.

battle impossible, only to disperse leaving clear skies when the two armies withdraw. Hannibal decides to pull back and never comes so close to taking Rome again. In Livy's version (Livy 26.11), the weather is simply bad weather, and Hannibal's superstition plays its part in his decision to withdraw. Silius takes this episode and adds full divine machinery. First Jupiter defends Rome single-handedly; the storms become the weapon of his wrath. Then Hannibal's patron goddess, Juno, talks her protégé out of inevitable destruction, which she does by revealing herself in her full divine form and showing him the Roman gods protecting their city: Apollo on the Palatine, Diana on the Aventine, Mars on the Campus Martius, Janus on the Janiculum, Quirinus on the Quirinal; finally, set above all, angry Jupiter blazing with his thunderbolts. Hannibal leaves; the Romans suspect a trick; finally they come out of the city and go to look at his camp.

In many obvious ways this passage reverses *Aeneid* 2.[38] Juno, not Venus, is at work. Rather than destroying Troy, Juno reveals the gods protecting Rome. The Roman reaction to Hannibal's departure is analogous to the Trojan reaction to the Greek departure at *Aeneid* 2.27–30. Both are reluctant to believe their enemy has really left, both suspect a trick. The fall of Troy is undone: the Trojans were right to suspect a trick, but the Romans really are being protected by the gods. Silius draws on the *Aeneid* to represent escape from Hannibal as a 're-founding' of Rome.

Silius is much less interested in the visuality of the episode. Juno's epiphany to Hannibal occurs in brackets, as it were, between the two parts of her speech:

                              Iuno inquit et atram
        dimouit nubem ueroque apparuit ore.   (*Punica* 12.704–5)

                    Juno spoke and removed the black cloud
        and appeared with her true face.

The black cloud is unexplained: is it a reference to the general insufficiency of mortal sight, or just to the clouds gods often use to cover themselves or their protégés? Juno's explanation of the revelation is also much abbreviated:

            (namque oculis amota nube parumper
    cernere cuncta dabo)   (*Punica* 12.707–8)

            For with the cloud removed from your eyes for a little,
    I will grant that you see all things.

---

[38] On the relationship with Virgil, see Marks 2005: 197 n.87, Tipping 2010: 87. Elsewhere in book 12, Silius plays with *Aeneid* 8; see Pomeroy 2000.

The revelation again occurs in Juno's speech, although when we return to focalise it through Hannibal we do receive some telling visual detail. Hannibal 'wonders at the faces of the gods and their fiery limbs' (*mirantem superum uultus et flammea membra*, *Punica*, 12.727).[39] This allows the reader of the epic to see the gods, too, through Hannibal's eyes, moving away from the Virgilian sublimity of vision too great to express.

Juno's revelation itself, like that of Venus, culminates with Jupiter. Virgil's Jupiter inspires the Greeks, but Silius' Jupiter dominates the whole, ordered scene:[40]

> sed enim aspice, quantus
> aegida commoueat nimbos flammasque uomentem
> Iupiter et quantis pascat ferus ignibus iras.
> huc uultus flecte atque aude spectare Tonantem:
> quas hiemes, quantos concusso uertice cernis
> sub nutu tonitrus! oculis qui fulgurat ignis!
> cede deis tandem et Titania desine bella.   (*Punica* 12.719–25)

> But look at him too, how great Jupiter is,
> how he stirs up the aegis, vomiting clouds and flames,
> and savagely feeds his angers with such great fires.
> Turn your face here and dare to watch the Thunderer:
> What storms you see, how great the thunders ruled by his nod
> when he has shaken his head! What fire flashes from his eyes!
> Yield to the gods at last and cease from Titanic war.

Jupiter's fiery violence recalls the Jupiter of the *Theogony*.[41] Silius has represented the violent storms which prevented battle as manifestations of Jupiter's concrete anger (605–26). At 622–6 Jupiter even strikes Hannibal himself with a thunderbolt and destroys his sword and spear. Hannibal's reaction to this is close to the epic *contemptor deum* (see below, p.320);[42] he insists that the storm is only weather:[43]

> sistebat socios et caecum e nubibus ignem
> murmuraque a uentis misceri uana docebat.   (*Punica* 12.628–9)

> He made his allies stand and taught them that the fire from heaven
> was blind and the murmurs from the winds mixed up empty things.

---

[39] This suggests that Silius at least read Virgil's *dirae facies* as the faces of the gods.
[40] Heinze 1993: 52.
[41] On Zeus' fiery battles in Hesiod, see Lovatt forthcoming-c. Jupiter is vomiting flame, like Augustus at *Aen.* 8.680–1; cf. Aeneas at *Aen.* 10.270–1.
[42] Mezentius has also been read as an Epicurean: Kronenberg 2005.
[43] On Hannibal and gigantomachy, see Fucecchi 1990.

Hannibal claims that the gods have no power and threatens Rome that he will capture her 'even if Jupiter himself descends to the earth' (*descendat Iupiter ipse | in terras licet*, 635–6). These lines echo Iarbas' accusation of Jupiter in *Aeneid* 4:

> an te, genitor, cum fulmina torques,
> nequiquam horremus, caecique in nubibus ignes
> terrificant animos et inania murmura miscent? (*Aeneid* 4.208–10)

> Do we shudder in vain at you, father, when you hurl
> the thunderbolts, and the blind fires in the clouds
> terrify our minds and mix in empty murmurs?

Hardie has pointed out the Epicurean overtones of Iarbas' speech, in which he draws on allegorisations of the Phaeacian episode in Homer as a diatribe against luxury, in order to condemn Aeneas' luxurious stay with Dido.[44] Iarbas threatens the epic gods with a dissolution of their power into allegorisations or philosophical separation: to which Jupiter responds by refocusing his gaze on Carthage and taking action. This is an apt moment of tangential Silian intertextuality: as an African unafraid to threaten the gods, Iarbas is an appropriate avatar of Hannibal. But his position of hostility to Dido sets him in the other camp, and his condemnation of luxury sits uneasily with Hannibal's recent stay in Capua, precisely presented as his Phaeacia, his Carthage, the dissolution of his military power in luxury. Jupiter's gaze in the *Aeneid* proves his power, and Hannibal will fail in his battle of the gazes against Jupiter, no matter how hard he tries to rationalise.

After the second storm Hannibal must convince his men to carry on fighting – asking where Jupiter was at Cannae and Lake Trasimene.[45] As he waits out the night he seems to have internalised the storm, becoming mad (as Statius characterises Capaneus when he assaults the walls of Thebes):

> nec nox composuit curas somnusue frementem
> ausus adire uirum, et redeunt cum luce furores.
> rursus in arma uocat trepidos clipeoque tremendum
> increpat atque †armis† imitatur murmura caeli. (*Punica* 12.682–5)

> Nor did night settle his cares, or sleep dare
> to approach the raging man, and his madness returns with the light.
> Again he calls his fearful men to arms and crashes his terrifying
> shield and imitates the rumbles of the sky with his weapons.

---

[44] Hardie 1999: 99. See also Dyson 1996 on Lucretius and Epicureanism in *Aeneid* 4, and Esteves 1982 on Jupiter's gaze.

[45] Hannibal anticipates critics such as Feeney 1991 whose scathing paragraph on Silius' Jupiter complains that his 'motives oscillate meaninglessly between purgative zeal and protective concern'. Is Silius' Hannibal making a metapoetic comment on the implausibility of epic divine machinery?

Light does not bring sanity but more madness; he uses his weapons as rival thunder, trying to become a version of Jupiter himself.[46] When Juno first accosts Hannibal, she calls him mad and demands whether he will attempt greater wars than are allowed to mortals (*quo ruis, o uecors? maioraque bella capessis | mortali quam ferre datum?*, 12.703–4).[47] The removal of the cloud from his mortal vision seems less a favour than a threat. The confrontation is transferred onto a different level: that of the hostile gaze.[48] The visible power of Jupiter is made manifest through vomiting flames. Looking at Jupiter is like looking into lightning. Juno suggests that even with her consent, the act of looking at Jupiter is itself daring (perhaps blasphemous): *aude spectare Tonantem* ('Dare to watch the Thunderer', 722). The storms and lightning of Jupiter's power become fires flashing in his eyes – the iconic image of the hostile gaze of the warrior gone beserk. By looking at Jupiter, Hannibal fights his promised battle with him, and is bested by the sheer power of his gaze.

Hannibal, then, does not seem to own the divine gaze in any way – but rather to be exposed to it. Yet he does not lose his status as viewing subject: even as he agrees reluctantly to retreat, he looks back and swears he will return (*respectans abit*, 729). Hannibal's position as anti-hero complicates the processes of identification: the whole episode is focalised simultaneously through Hannibal, Juno and the besieged Romans.[49] The Roman reader sees a construction of his city with its protecting gods, yet might simultaneously hate and despise Hannibal for his blasphemous tendencies, and respect and admire him for his daring. Hannibal, unlike Aeneas, does not share the epic poet's vision, and is reluctant to buy into the epic gaze; he would rather follow the historical–scientific gaze of Livy or Lucretius. But Juno forces him back into the world of epic (as do his superstitious men in Livy's account). Hannibal is a resisting viewer.

---

[46] Here Hannibal goes further than Capaneus, whose identification with Jupiter is largely implicit, to become a version of Salmoneus, who was struck by lightning for attempting to be Jupiter. Salmoneus features in a storm scene in Valerius at 1.662–4; see Shelton 1974: 18.

[47] This line evokes the discourse of civil war: Horace *Ep.* 7.1 (*quo, quo scelesti ruitis?*); Lucan's proem (*bella plus quam ciuilia*, BC 1.1; *Quis furor, o ciues*, 1.8), and Statius' demand for greater poetic powers to tell of Capaneus (*maior ab Aoniis poscenda amentia lucis: | mecum omnes audete deae! Theb.* 10.830–1).

[48] On battles of the gaze, see below, pp.337–46.

[49] The concepts of 'alignment' and 'allegiance', offered by Smith 1996, for instance, do not particularly help here. We are not necessarily aligned with Hannibal, though his is the primary focalisation, but allegiance is complicated. We are offered multiple audience positions, in which we both love and hate, admire and despise Hannibal. The intertextual play in which he is both Aeneas and Turnus exemplifies the complexity of allegiance here.

Philosophy and the divine gaze

Hannibal's disavowal of epic traditions of divine intervention is one manifestation of the influence of Lucretius in Latin epic.[50] Lucretius has a tendency to turn to the Trojan war and epic battle as an illustration of what is wrong with attitudes towards the gods.[51] Furthermore he portrays Epicurus' philosophical achievements as a visual battle against the vertical divine gaze of personified superstition (Religio):

> humana ante oculos foede cum vita iaceret
> in terris oppressa gravi sub religione,
> quae caput a caeli regionibus ostendebat
> horribili super aspectu mortalibus instans,
> primum Graius homo mortalis tollere contra
> est oculos ausus primusque obsistere contra,
> quem neque fama deum nec fulmina nec minitanti
> murmure compressit caelum, sed eo magis acrem
> inritat animi virtutem, effringere ut arta
> naturae primus portarum claustra cupiret.   (*De rerum natura* 1.62–71)

> When human life lay before the eyes of all foully
> weighed down to the ground by burdensome superstition,
> who was showing her head from the regions of heaven
> pressing down with shudder-inspiring gaze upon mortals,
> the Greek man, first among mortals dared to raise mortal
> eyes against her and first stood against her,
> whom neither the rumours/epic fame of the gods nor the thunderbolt
> nor heaven with its threatening murmur suppressed, but by so much the more
> it stimulated the keen courage of his mind, so that he first desired
> to break out from the narrow bars of the gates of nature.

Epicurus' visual confrontation with Religio is an epic duel, in which the losing fighter is trampled underfoot, but in this case is able to look up and stand against the threat from above. He not only defeats the divine gaze, but appropriates it. His miraculous mental journey at 1.74 (*omne immensum peragravit mente animoque,*

---

[50] See Hardie 2009a, especially 'Lucretian visions in Virgil' and 'Virgil's *fama* and the Lucretian and Ennian sublime', Gillespie and Hardie 2007, and, for an earlier layer, Hardie 1986.

[51] The myth of Iphigenia reflects the dangers of superstition: *DRN* 1.80–101. Although Iphigenia is more tragic than epic, Lucretius focuses on her role as sacrifice to kick-start the Trojan war (100), which also makes her potent in tragedy's reflections on epic. At 102–6 he specifies the *uates* as the source of superstitions: not just epic poets, but the sacred poet–prophet was important in epic self-fashioning. At 1.464–82 Helen, Paris and the causes of the Trojan war are an example of the inconsequentiality of history in comparison to the great everlasting truths of natural science. The distant views of 2.1–19 also pick two quintessentially epic moments: the man in a storm at sea and warfare on the plains (perhaps corresponding to the *Odyssey* and the *Iliad*).

'he travels through the immense universe with his mind and spirit') is the equivalent of the miraculous divine journeys of epic gods. He also activates the penetrative gaze which is associated with the gods, seeing clearly through illusion and appearance to the reality of things.

Not just Epicurus, but his followers, especially Lucretius, and, through him, his readers, can all partake in this clarity of vision. For instance at the end of book 1:

> namque alid ex alio clarescet, nec tibi caeca
> nox iter eripiet, quin ultima naturai
> pervideas: ita res accendent lumina rebus.
>
> (*De rerum natura* 1.1115–17)

> For one thing will grow clear from another, and blind night
> will not snatch the way from you to stop you seeing through into the uttermost
> recesses of nature: thus things will set light on fire for other things.

The arguments of religious men are equated to dreams and visions (1.104–5), the deceptive side of epic divine machinery. The progressive clarity of vision achieved by Lucretius leads to the gradual assimilation of Epicurus to a god. In the ecstatic proem of book 3 (1–30), Lucretius begins by praising Epicurus in hymnic fashion for lifting a light to break through the darkness (1–3); through his words Lucretius can see reality (*DRN* 3.14–17). The divine mind of Epicurus gives a comprehensive vision of reality to Lucretius, including the gods, peaceful and separate from the world (18–24), in perfect undisturbed bliss.

Lucretius himself approaches divine pleasure from his revelation:

> his ibi me rebus quaedam divina voluptas
> percipit atque horror, quod sic natura tua vi
> tam manifesta patens ex omni parte retecta est.
>
> (*De rerum natura* 3.28–30)

> Then from these things a sort of divine joy
> thoroughly seizes me and a shuddering, because nature thus
> by your force is lying so open, uncovered in all its parts.

By book 5.1–55, Lucretius makes a forceful argument that Epicurus should be considered literally as a god: his discoveries equate to those of Ceres or Bacchus (13–21), he was far superior in his heroism to Hercules (22–42). The philosophical struggles to purge the mind and live the good life are of equal stature to epic battles and monster-slaying (*proelia atque pericula*, 43–4).

If Epicurus, and through him Lucretius, take on the divine gaze, they also tend to view the world from a distance, as if they were the equivalent of the audience of epic gods.[52] Here the obvious example is the proem of book 2

---

[52] De Lacy 1964, Hardie 2009a: 154–5.

(1–19) when the distant view of the sea storm and the battle allow detachment; equally at 2.308–32 the *primordia* seen from a distance are compared to sheep or battle on a plain. The *De rerum natura* is not just superficially related to epic: it participates in the visual structures of epic, only to turn them on their heads, to take them and use them for other purposes.[53] Lucretius does not straightforwardly deconstruct the epic gaze; rather he uses it for new endeavours, taking epic authority and turning it into philosophical and didactic authority; challenging the gods, yet using them as an illustrative example.

This Lucretian 'drama of vision' is hugely influential in Virgil's *Aeneid*, as Hardie has shown.[54] Ovid, too, follows in the footsteps of Epicurus/ Lucretius.[55] Pythagoras, whose philosophical tour de force sums up and complicates the *Metamorphoses* in book 15, emulates Lucretius' Epicurus in his sublime incursion into divine territory:[56]

isque licet caeli regione remotos
mente deos adiit et quae natura negabat
uisibus humanis, oculis ea pectoris hausit.
cumque animo et uigili perspexerat omnia cura,
in medium discenda dabat coetusque silentum
dictaque mirantum magni primordia mundi
et rerum causas et quid natura docebat, ...   (*Metamorphoses* 15.62–8)

And he, though removed from the heavenly region,
approached the gods with his mind and what nature was denying
to human vision, he drained those things with the eyes of his heart.
And when he had looked through all cares with a watchful spirit,
he put them in the middle so that they might be learnt and he used to teach
the gatherings of silent men and those wondering at his words the first beginnings
of the great world, the causes of things, what nature is ...

He can see what nature denies to human sight; the emphasis on nature's concealment and his revelation of these things to others suggests that he is a Prometheus or a Phineus figure, spilling the beans about the workings of the

---

[53] Another example: at 3.642–56 a remarkably 'Silver' epic passage describes the mutilation of bodies in battle, to prove that the spirit can also be cut into pieces, and therefore is mortal.
[54] The phrase is that of Gildenhard 2004; Hardie 2009b prefers 'epic of vision'; he puts on display various Lucretian visual moments in the *Aeneid*: distant views in the storm of (1.118–19); Aeneas as detached Epicurean viewer (1.127, 155) and looking at the Carthaginians as bees (1.418–19); Dido looking at the departing Trojans as ants (4.402–11). The Lucretian penetrative gaze comes when the palace of Priam is opened up (2.483–4); Laocoon's failed penetration of the Trojan horse (2.40–9); the bleeding bush at 3.26–48; Hercules tearing open Cacus' cave (8.241–6).
[55] Hardie 1995 puts the emphasis on Empedocles, but Lucretius is also much in evidence.
[56] On Ovid's Pythagoras episode, see: Miller 1994, Hardie 1995, Hardie 1997b, Galinsky 1998, Segal 2001, Oberrauch 2005, Feldherr 2010: 33, 65–6.

universe. The inclusion of *rerum natura* in line 68, along with *primordia mundi* in 67, suggests the Lucretian parallel. This is even clearer in Pythagoras' account:

'Et quoniam deus ora mouet, sequar ora mouentem
rite deum Delphosque meos ipsumque recludam
aethera et augustae reserabo oracula mentis.
magna nec ingeniis inuestigata priorum
quaeque diu latuere, canam; iuuat ire per alta
astra, iuuat terris et inerti sede relicta
nube uehi ualidique umeris insistere Atlantis,
palantesque homines passim et rationis egentes
despectare procul trepidosque obitumque timentes
sic exhortari seriemque euoluere fati:' (*Metamorphoses* 15.143–52)

'And since a god moves my mouth, I follow the god moving my mouth
duly and I shall open up my own Delphi and the god himself,
and I will unbar the heavens and oracles of a reverend mind.
Great things not found out by the talents of former men,
things which lay hidden for a long time, I will sing; it pleases me to go through
the high stars, it pleases me to leave behind earth and its inactive seat,
to be borne on a cloud and to stand on the shoulders of strong Atlas,
to look down from afar on men wandering everywhere
and lacking reason, panicking and fearing death,
to encourage them thus and roll out the episodes of fate:'

Pythagoras has been read as a surrogate of Ovid, and here he echoes Ovid's proem, as well as taking on the mantle of prophet, in a specifically visual way (opening up, uncovering), which also evokes Ennius and Lucretius.[57] He makes the traditional claim for priority, and trumps that with an image of his mental flight through the heavens, taking on the divine epic perspective, the distant view on men and their fears of death. He looks back on the *Metamorphoses* as well as the previous traditions of epic and didactic poetry, even as his speech is a sort of *mise-en-abyme* of Ovid's epic. Is Pythagoras becoming a god, challenging the gods, or using the gods as authority for his own peculiar brand of didactic message? Segal argues that Ovid's play on Pythagoras as an alternative poet figure, a version of Lucretius whose didactic message is directly in contradiction to that of Lucretius, and a version of Ovid who nevertheless is only partial and compromised, allows Ovid to reflect on mortality and immortality, and in particular to stake a

---

[57] *nos ausi reserare*, Ennius *Ann*. fr. 208–10 Sk., with Lucretius' poetic praise of Ennius at 1.117–19, and Hinds 1998: 53.

claim to his own poetic immortality.⁵⁸ However, Ovid does not directly endorse Lucretius' challenge to the divine machinery of epic (or religion); his Pythagoras is brought down to earth by the bathos of his overall message.⁵⁹

Flying beyond the world and gazing like a god is dangerous in Ovid: Phaethon exemplifies the failure to match up to the divine gaze of his father, the sun. At 2.21–3, when he first arrives at the palace, he cannot come close to Phoebus because he cannot bear the light. His failure to drive the chariot is repeatedly portrayed as a failure of the gaze:

> ut uero summo despexit ab aethere terras
> infelix Phaethon penitus penitusque patentes,
> palluit et subito genua intremuere timore
> suntque oculis tenebrae per tantum lumen obortae.
>
> (*Metamorphoses* 2.178–81)
>
> But when unfortunate Phaethon looked down from the top of heaven
> on the lands lying open far, far below,
> he grew pale and suddenly his knees trembled with fear
> and over his eyes darkness rose up from too much light.

The divine perspective is not just dizzying but terrifying: the sublime gap between Phaethon and the earth induces a sort of Lucretian vertigo: for the lands lie open, and he has the chance to observe them: but in fact he is not brought from darkness into light, but rather brought into darkness by light. His Epicurean daring is his undoing. He gives up any attempt to control the chariot at 198–200, driven further into terror by the sight of Scorpio.⁶⁰ In contrast, Jupiter, when he finally admits he must intervene, takes his traditional epic perspective: *summum petit arduus arcem, | unde solet nubes latis inducere terris, | unde mouet tonitrus uibrataque fulmina iactat* ('he goes high and seeks the highest citadel, from where he is accustomed to gather together the clouds over the wide lands, from where he stirs up the thunder, brandishes the thunderbolt and hurls it', 2.306–8).

---

⁵⁸ Segal 2001; e.g. 'Ovid can both complement and surpass Lucretius in this one deeply rooted theme of the epic tradition, the immortality of the poet in the lasting glory of his work.' (99)

⁵⁹ This can be extended to his politics: Feldherr 2010 shows that Pythagoras can be read as both Augustan and anti-Augustan. Is there a pun in *augustae mentis* (145)? 'Pythagoras's contrasting insistence that nothing perishes can also be read as establishing an opposition between the soul and the material world that provides scope for an individual resistance to the imposition of external authority.' (33)

⁶⁰ Other visual references: *Met.* 2.188, 190, 191, 194, 227–8, 233–4.

We might, then, sense a degree of anxiety about the apotheosis of Julius Caesar, also portrayed in visual terms. There is an uneasiness in the application of epic divine machinery to such recent historical events. Venus' anxiety over Caesar's assassination expresses itself in a desire to extract him in a cloud, like Paris or Aeneas in the *Iliad* (15.803–6).[61] Jupiter's address to Venus, in which he emphasises the inevitability of fate by calling on Venus to witness the decrees engraved on adamant, stages a version of Aeneas' vision of the inevitability of the fall of Troy, in which Venus becomes the viewer instead of the author of the vision.[62] Julius Caesar, like Augustus on the shield of Aeneas (*Aen.* 8.720–2), Jupiter says, will become a divine viewer:

> hanc animam interea caeso de corpore raptam
> fac iubar, ut semper Capitolia nostra forumque
> Diuus ab excelsa prospectet Iulius aede.   (*Metamorphoses* 15.840–2)

> When you have snatched this soul up, cut from its body,
> make it a star, so that always Divus Julius might look out
> from his high seat onto our Capitol and the forum.

A few lines later he is looking out over Augustus (850–1). Ovid is too tactful a poet to suggest, as Lucan does (*BC* 1.45–66), that the deified emperor might reenact Phaethon or unbalance the cosmos.[63] Yet it is notable that Ovid's own apotheosis is limited and specific; he will be borne up above the stars: *parte tamen meliore mei super alta perennis | astra ferar* (15.875–6) but it is his name that will survive; he will be read, he will live on in *fama*, but he will not look down on the earth and assume the divine gaze of epic as (dead) poet as well as narrator. There is, then, distance between Ovid and Pythagoras, just as he does not claim he is a reincarnation of any particular poet, and a distance between the daring of Phaethon and the daring of Ovid; there is a gap, too, between the epic gaze of the narrator and the mortal gaze of the poet.[64] Just as the poem dances along the line of what can remain epic, so the persona of Ovid as poet does not fully endorse his own epic voice.

---

[61] Feldherr 2010: 65–83 examines this uneasy relationship between poet and emperor, poetry and power in the apotheoses of book 15.
[62] On Venus here as Virgil's Juno from *Aeneid* 1, see Feldherr 2010: 68: 'we are watching an *Aeneid* where the roles are inverted, and we are watching it in reverse'.
[63] See further below, p.115.
[64] Feldherr 2010: 65:'Ovid's exposure of imperial fictions to poetic deconstruction will be balanced by an anxiety that he has made himself emperor of nothing, that the type of immortality he creates for himself depends entirely on his own words, that is, on keeping the reader's perspective located within his literary horizons.'

Philosophical heroes in Flavian epic: Prometheus and Archimedes

The philosophical or scientific hero who relies on his own intellect rather than the power of the gods is not common. Two examples from Flavian epic are Prometheus (books 4 and 5 of Valerius Flaccus' *Argonautica*) and Archimedes (book 14 of Silius Italicus' *Punica*). Prometheus is a Valerian addition to the Argonautic myth. Valerius' Aeschylean combination of Hercules, Prometheus and Io offers a tragic reflection on the fallibility of Zeus/Jupiter.[65] This Jupiter is a tyrant practising clemency rather than reaching reconciliation with a previous generation of defeated enemies. The weeping of Latona and Diana, combined with the words and *honor* of Apollo, cause Jupiter to decree the release of Prometheus, rather than the Titan's deployment of his own knowledge. Prometheus does not confront Jupiter with his gaze, but supplicates him:

> e scopulis media inter pabula diri
> uulturis ipse etiam gemitu maestaque fatigat
> uoce Iouem saeuis releuans ambusta pruinis
> lumina   (VF *Argonautica* 4.68–71)

> from the crags and in the middle of the hideous vulture's
> banquet he himself, even, tires Jupiter with his groan
> and sad voice lifting up once more his eyes seared
> by savage frosts

Prometheus is a god (called *dei* at 4.72) but his liminal status as benefactor of humanity compromises his divinity. His position on the heights of the Caucasus is elevated, but his eyes are ineffective, even damaged, and the pain of his torture makes him unable to focus on anything else. When Hercules frees Prometheus, at 5.154–76, the feat is presented elliptically through the ignorant hearing and viewing of the Argonauts. Although the passage focuses primarily on the sounds of cosmic disintegration and pain (*consonat*, 5.160; *fit fragor*, 163; *horruit . . . horruit . . . recusso*, 165–6; *gemitu . . . audiri . . . uociferans*, 168–70), it finishes with vision:

> tantum mirantur ab alto
> litora discussa sterni niue ruptaque saxa
> et simul ingentem moribundae desuper umbram
> alitis atque atris rorantes imbribus auras.   (VF *Argonautica* 5.173–6)

> only they wonder from the deep
> at the shaken out snow lying on the shore and the broken rocks

---

[65] On the Prometheus episode in Valerius Flaccus, see Hershkowitz 1998b: 158–9, 195–7, Zissos 2004. On Io in Valerius Flaccus, see Davis 2009.

106   The mortal gaze

> and at the same time from above the huge shadow of the dying
> bird and breezes bedewed with black showers.

Zissos argues well that Valerius turns around the Apollonian version by making the Argonauts the audience of the liberation of Prometheus rather than his ongoing, inevitable, cyclical torture. But Valerius' Argonauts, looking from below at the shadow of the bird they cannot know is dying, and the debris raining down from the cosmic disturbance of Hercules' heroism, are not even granted the degree of revelation given to the Italian natives in *Aeneid* 8, who see the monstrous head/corpse of Cacus. Despite the poet's revitalisation of the divine machinery, the Argonauts are no more aware than their Apollonian counterparts, and the deliberate obscurity of Valerius' style and his elliptical digressions might well leave readers with a similar feeling of confusion. The extreme pain and destructiveness of Prometheus' liberation does not offer much hope for the validation of the imperial Jupiter's clemency.

Another cameo from a Lucretian scientific hero is the brief appearance of Archimedes in Silius book 14. Marcellus is besieging Syracuse unwillingly.[66] We are first introduced to Archimedes through the tower that he has built to enable the Syracusans to rain down destruction on their attackers (14.300–2); he is described as *Graius*, and the tower is *multiplici surgens ad sidera tecto* ('rising to the stars in multiple storeys'); the tower, however, is destroyed by fire (307–15) and collapses as if struck by a thunderbolt. The vertical gaze of the Syracusans appears to have been trumped by the Roman avatars of Jupiter. Archimedes' other devices also suggest an intrusive vertical gaze: the claw that descends from above to grab men and ships before smashing back into the sea (320–32), and the holes in the wall that allow archers to shoot unseen (333–7).[67] This is again called simply Greek cleverness (*calliditate Graia*, 337). Archimedes' anonymity and Greekness make him a version of Epicurus; this becomes more obvious in the passage of praise (341–52) in which he becomes a natural scientist (*caelum terraeque paterent*, 'the sky and the lands lie open to him', 343).[68] After the Carthaginian fleet are defeated in the sea battle, and the city is taken, Marcellus assumes almost divine power:

---

[66] On Marcellus' capture of Syracuse, see Marks 2005: 259–62, though not Archimedes, whose death might detract from the idealism of Marcellus' representation. For a nuanced reading of Silius' Archimedes, see Jaeger 2008: 93–100.

[67] This gaze is also present in Livy's account, in which Archimedes is presented as himself the one shooting the missiles (*emittebat ... petebat telis*, 24.34.8).

[68] Livy, too, calls him *unicus spectator caeli siderumque* ('the unique spectator of the sky and the stars', 24.34.2); he also refers to his unique skill (*Archimedis unica arte*, 24.34.14).

> His tectis opibusque potitus
> Ausonius ductor, postquam sublimis ab alto
> aggere despexit trepidam clangoribus urbem,
> inque suo positum nutu, stent moenia regum
> an nullos oriens uideat lux crastina muros,
> ingemuit nimio iuris tantumque licere
> horruit   (*Punica* 14.665–71)

> The Ausonian leader had taken power over these buildings
> and this wealth, and afterwards he looked down on high
> from a lofty rampart on the town panicked with its clamour,
> and set on his own nod, whether the fortifications of the kings should stand,
> or whether tomorrow's rising light should see no walls,
> he groaned at too much responsibility and shuddered at how much
> he might have allowed

This passage is loaded with words of divine gazing: not only does he look down (*despexit*) he is also *sublimis* and on a high rampart (*alto aggere*).[69] The comparison with the gods is explicit in *nutu* (nod) and his reflection on his own power;[70] he is even in a position to offer charity to gods themselves (672–3). The passage ends with the death of Archimedes, becoming a pitiable spectacle for Marcellus:[71]

> tu quoque ductoris lacrimas, memorande, tulisti,
> defensor patriae, meditantem in puluere formas
> nec turbatum animi tanta feriente ruina.   (*Punica* 14.676–8)

> You also bore the tears of the leader, o worthy of remembrance,
> defender of your fatherland, contemplating shapes in the dust
> and not disturbed in the mind, with such great ruin striking.

The downward gaze of Archimedes and his lack of concern about his surroundings suggest that he is killed from above, unaware, whether literally by falling debris, or by the metaphorical ruin of death. His unawareness of the battle could be read as a failure of the gaze, just as the soldier who kills him in Livy is unable to distinguish true value: the genius who needed to be

---

[69] This is, of course, also the gaze of the general on the hill: cf. Pompey (*stetit aggere campi*, *BC* 7.649) and Flaminius (*Pun.* 5.378).

[70] Jaeger 2008: 96 draws a parallel between Marcellus and Jupiter, and between Marcellus and Archimedes, who also looks down. Marcellus' control over his soldiers in Silius (not in Livy) equates to his control over cosmic order.

[71] Livy separates Marcellus' quasi-divine view over the city (25.24.11) from the death of Archimedes, which happens during the sack (25.31.8–11). In Livy, his death is instead associated with the negative *exempla* of greed and anger produced, like a spectacle, by the sack (*Cum multa irae, multa auaritiae foeda exempla ederentur* . . ., 25.31.9).

preserved. Silius emphasises his detachment and the impersonal nature of destruction: his mind is not bound to the world, and the images represent his intellectual freedom, while *nec turbatum animi* suggests emotional distance from the overthrow of his city.[72] Science may not stand up to force (knowledge is not power), but Archimedes is worth remembering just like an epic hero, crushed by the divinely endorsed juggernaut of Roman imperialism.[73] Jaeger's discussion of the workings of epic memorialisation in this passage points out that the *tu quoque . . . memorande* of Silius' lament evokes Virgil's Icarus (6.30–1) and Lausus (*nec te, iuuenis memorande, silebo*, 'nor will I be silent about you, young man worthy of memory', *Aen.* 10.793); Archimedes, then, in a typically Silian tangential connection, is both craftsman and Epicurean hero, as he melds together the characteristics of both pairs of fathers and sons.

The gaze of Capaneus

Statius' Capaneus is also a Lucretian hero, and perhaps Marcellus is a reversal of him.[74] Leigh has demonstrated his sublimity, and connected him to the Lucretian Epicurus.[75] The workings of spectacle and the gaze in this passage are complex and thought-provoking. Before Menoeceus' sacrifice, Capaneus is in control of the battle (*Theb.* 10.739–41), orchestrating the movements of different types of troops, a successful general, a Lucanian Julius Caesar (see below). Like a force of nature, his destructiveness threatens the landscape (742–3). Leigh pointed out the moment where he throws a javelin at the walls, as he masters all the missiles, with the adjective *sublime*: *nunc iaculum excusso rotat in sublime lacerto* ('now he whirls a javelin on high with outshaken arm', 745). This might also evoke the Lucretian thought-experiment of the javelin thrown beyond the boundaries of the universe (*DRN* 1.968–83).[76] A more concrete echo comes at 753 when no one can stand against him (*obsistere contra*, 753, end of line; cf. Lucretius *DRN* 1.67, also end of line, of Epicurus standing against *Religio*). At the end of the passage, we move to look at him

---

[72] Evoking Hor. *Odes* 3.3.1–8 on the unshaken leader; the imminent apotheosis of Augustus and the destruction of Troy in the rest of the poem might well form a reflection on Marcellus and Carthage.

[73] Jaeger 2008: 96 on Marcellus' gaze: 'now the peculiar and almost divine genius of benevolent Roman imperialism dwarfs Greek intellectual power'.

[74] Capaneus, too, looks down on the trembling town of Thebes: *trepidamque adsurgens desuper urbem | uidit*, 'rising up, he saw the panicked town from above' (871–2). Both authors put *urbem* as the final word in the line. This is an example of a moment where it would be nice to see Statius coming after Silius, Capaneus as it were failing to live up to Marcellus; for the relationship between Statius and Silius, see Lovatt 2010.

[75] Leigh 2006. [76] For resonances of this passage in *Aeneid* 12 see Hardie 2009b.

with the Thebans, from afar (*procul arma furentis* | *terribilesque iubas et frontem cassidis horrent*. 'From afar they shudder at the weapons of the raging man and his terrifying crests and the front of the helmet.' 754–5).

This, like many other things, as Heinrich and others have shown, serves to assimilate Capaneus to Menoeceus, also the object of the gaze of others from afar.[77] Menoeceus is *sacer aspectu solitoque augustior ore* ('sacred to see and with a more venerable face than normal', 757), like a god to look upon, revealing himself by removing his helmet (*exempta manifestus casside nosci*, 'with his helmet removed he is clearly shown to be recognised', 759).[78] He does look down at 760 (*despexit*) but this is his only active verb of vision, and it is swiftly followed by the silence of the army, so that we are always looking at him through their eyes.

In comparison, Capaneus owns and acts upon his gaze, a philosopher–poet–hero, the madness of poetic inspiration and battle fury also finding its equivalent in stories of the mad poet Lucretius.[79] At 839 Capaneus is growing tired of standard battle and looks back at the heavens (*respexit*). His engagement begins on a visual level:

> ardua mox toruo metitur culmina uisu,
> innumerosque gradus gemina latus arbore clausos
> aerium sibi portat iter, longeque timendus (*Thebaid* 10.840–2)

> soon he is measuring the high roofs with a fierce gaze,
> innumerable steps shut in at the side by a twin tree
> he carries as an airy route for himself, deserving to be feared from afar

The prosaic ladder of many a historiographical siege narrative becomes a Lucretian measure of the universe, his airy way suggesting the flights of the mind we saw above. But his attempt to measure with his mind is already doomed to fail in this the most hyperbolic of epic feats: the innumerable steps of the ladder imply the impossibility of actually climbing it. This sense of sublime escape is intensified at 860–3, when he is pounded by missiles from above, but seems to float through them:

> ille nec ingestis nec terga sequentibus umquam
> detrahitur telis, uacuoque sub aere pendens
> plana uelut terra certus uestigia figat,
> tendit et ingenti subit occurrente ruina: (*Thebaid* 10.860–3)

---

[77] Heinrich 1999, Ganiban 2007: 136–9.
[78] On Parthenopaeus' similar gesture at 9.699–703, see pp.3–5.
[79] The story is not certainly attested before Jerome, but Horace may have been alluding to it in his tale of Empedocles' mad suicide; see Hardie 2009a: 212–13. Statius refers to the *docti furor arduus Lucreti* ('high madness of learned Lucretius', *Silvae* 2.7.76). *Arduus* is also a word associated with Capaneus (10.840, 845); as is *furor* and its cognates (10.486, 753, 754, 832, 907). Worth noting also that Juno is *furibunda* at 896.

> No weapons heaped from above nor following him from behind
> ever drag him down, and hanging on/under the empty air,
> confident, he fixed his steps as if on smooth land,
> stretched and went up under the huge debris coming to meet him.

While Archimedes is struck down, Capaneus miraculously comes through, walking on the empty air, like Pythagoras on the clouds.[80] Once he reaches the top he literally tears the city apart (877–82).[81]

This is the high point of his anti-religious campaign: and now we take the perspective of the epic narrator, watching through the eyes of the audience of gods.[82] The dissenting audience of gods compete for the attention of a Jupiter, who is the authoritative Jupiter of the *Aeneid* (*rex Iuppiter omnibus idem*, *Aen.* 10.112). In contrast stands the silent figure of Juno, whose oblique gaze has been usurped by Bacchus. When Jupiter reaches for his weapon, Juno no longer stands in the way: *nec iam audet fatis turbata obsistere coniunx* ('no longer does his disturbed wife dare to stand in the way of the fates', 912). Juno has Capaneus' daring, and resists Jupiter and fate, just as Capaneus' opponents cannot stand up to him, but Epicurus stands up to Religio.[83] Capaneus appears to have found his way onto the Caucasus: *in media uertigine mundi* (918); and the wondering gods (*mirantur taciti et dubio pro fulmine pallent*, 920) are reduced to the state of the citizens of Thebes: *tunc uero attoniti fatorum in cardine summo* ('then indeed struck dumb on the final cusp of their fate', 853). Capaneus turns into Bellona (854–5), becoming an incarnation of war, while the gods have lost their position of distanced spectators, and, apart from Jupiter, are little different from the women on the walls.

Capaneus' gaze fails: as the storm gathers, he holds the walls but cannot see them (*tenet ille tamen, quas non uidet, arces*, 923) and his last claim that he will use the thunderbolt to renew (*renouare*) his own Bellona-esque torch betrays the fact that the renewal is Jupiter's, striking Thebes once again. Even so, not all of Capaneus falls to earth. His crest flees to the clouds

---

[80] Or hanging like Juno suspended by Jupiter. See above, p.51 for Juno's sympathy for Capaneus.

[81] Like Lucretius seeing into the building-blocks of the world? *Moenia mundi* is the metaphor for Epicurus' escape beyond the boundaries of the normal mental universe (*DRN* 1.73). The river simile at 864–9 is another way of casting Capaneus as a sublime natural force. There may also be an echo of the Virgilian invocation of Lucretian destruction in the simile of the ash tree at *Aen.* 2.609 (*auulsaque saxis | saxa*) with Lucretius 4.140–1 (*montes auolsaque saxa | montibus*), which is set in gigantomachic context (see Hardie 1986: 212–13). This would have the pleasing effect of linking Capaneus to a Virgilian moment in which the gods perform the destruction carried out by giants in Lucretius.

[82] See above, pp.51–2.

[83] A mention of Iapetus (915–16) connects to Prometheus, who pleads on his son's behalf at VF *Arg.* 4.73–5.

(*primae fugere in nubila cristae*, 928) and his final breath goes against (but not up to) the stars (*extremumque in sidera uersus anhelat*, 935). Though he cannot escape the walls of the world, his death does mark the walls of the city (*signauit muros ultricis semita flammae*, 'the path of the avenging flame marked the walls', 11.4), creating his own perverse monument. As he holds onto the fragments of the city, his gaze is still fierce (*ille iacet lacerae complexus fragmina turris | toruus adhuc uisu memorandaque facta relinquens*, 'he lies embracing the broken parts of the torn up tower, still fierce in his gaze and leaving behind deeds worthy of remembering', 11.9–10) and the spectacle of his dead body is like the body of Tityos for the vultures coming out of the enormous liver of the giant. Capaneus has finally lost his claim to Promethean heroism and become only an icon of violence.

This characteristically rich and densely textured Statian passage, which has not been neglected in the secondary literature, yields yet more rewarding food for thought when probed in this particular framework. The mortal gaze is given quite a different flavour by the directness of the challenge to poetic (and particularly epic) representations of the gods in Lucretius. Is Statius undoing Lucretius by associating him with Capaneus, turning him into a *contemptor divum*? A hard Stoic reading of Statius might find this attractive. But how does that fit with the evocations of Prometheus, and the extent to which we have allegiance to Capaneus? Matthew Leigh concludes that Statius is 'of the devil's party' – but what does this say about his relationship to epic authority?

We have seen in the previous chapter the power and complexity of the divine gaze; this chapter has examined the difficulty and danger of looking at gods, and battles of vision between gods and mortals. The importance of Lucretius' Epicurus in providing a model of independent mortal vision is striking. Roman epic is torn between the desire for authority and authenticity provided by the gods, and a yearning to break free from the divine framework.

Lucan, Caesar and the absence of a divine audience

This last section examines three mortal gazes, bringing together divine vision and mortal vision: the mortal gaze of the poet Lucan who refuses the epic poet's vision of the gods, and the divine gazes of Caesar, who embraces it, and Pompey, who struggles with it.[84] Lucan notoriously excluded mimetic representations of divine action from his epic. Feeney masterfully expounds the effects of this decision on Lucan's epic voice: 'the

[84] On Caesar as Jupiter see Nix 2008. On spectacle in Lucan, see below, pp.283–93.

discordant spurning of divine inspiration and epic insight, together with the selection of Nero as substitute, combine to create an epic voice without precedent' (276); instead of 'the omniscient, divinely-guaranteed perspective of the archetypal epic poet' Lucan produces an 'ignorant narrator' with a 'belligerently fallible voice' (280). Feeney argues that Lucan uses the absence of the gods to avoid making a decision about how responsible they are for the civil war: are they actively malevolent, or merely distanced Epicurean spectators?[85] This absence is importantly qualified: the narrator does not tell us what they are doing, but both characters and narrator talk about them as if they are there. What remains of the divine gaze? If we cannot look down on the gods, what difference does it make to the workings of epic?

The gods are certainly envisaged by both narrator and characters as an audience. Most strikingly the narrator rants thus in the middle of the battle of Pharsalia itself:

> sunt nobis nulla profecto
> numina: cum caeco rapiantur saecula casu,
> mentimur regnare Iouem. spectabit ab alto
> aethere Thessalicas, teneat cum fulmina, caedes?
> scilicet ipse petet Pholoen, petet ignibus Oeten
> immeritaeque nemus Rhodopes pinusque Mimantis,
> Cassius hoc potius feriet caput? astra Thyestae
> intulit et subitis damnauit noctibus Argos:
> tot similes fratrum gladios patrumque gerenti
> Thessaliae dabit ille diem? mortalia nulli
> sunt curata deo.
>
> (*Bellum civile* 7.445–55)

> Of course there are no divine powers
> for us: when the ages are snatched by blind disaster,
> we lie that Jupiter rules. Will he watch from the high
> heaven the Thessalian slaughter, while he holds on to his thunderbolt?
> Surely he himself will aim at Pholoe, at Oete with its fires
> and the undeserving groves of Rhodope and the pines of Mimas,
> and will Cassius rather strike this head? He brought on the stars
> for Thyestes and condemned Argos to sudden night:
> will he give daylight to so many matching swords of brothers
> and fathers brandished at Thessaly? Mortal things are worth
> nothing to the god.

This is the climax of the Lucanian narrator's interventions, the most extreme denial of divine providence, in which a Lucretian resistance against

---

[85] Feeney 1991: 281–3. See also Fantham 2003.

the gods of poetry (epic and tragedy) is staged.[86] The figure of Jupiter as divine audience, at this sublime epic moment, is evoked to inspire contempt rather than awe. The potentially malevolent divine gaze would here be welcome: the gigantomachic figure of Caesar should be struck down by Jupiter's thunderbolt.[87] Like Virgil's Iarbas, he calls on Jupiter to prove his existence, only to be answered by a thunderous silence. Chance is specifically blind (*caeco casu*), like the thunderbolts of Iarbas' and Hannibal's speeches; lack of vision is equivalent to lack of *telos*, lack of aim, lack of order. Leigh has well demonstrated Lucan's undoing of Augustan poetic teleology, not just that found in Virgil, but also Horace and Ovid.[88] But I find this a more destructive move than Leigh implies: Jupiter does not just represent Lucan's condemnation of passive spectatorship in the face of political tyranny. Rather his lack of care (and potential malevolence) undermine epic authority and causality. Lucan reverses the normal equation between political longevity and epic's power to memorialise: instead the gods will have to face Caesars as their *pares* (matches/equals, 7.455–9).

The gods are also envisaged as the audience of a gladiatorial spectacle. At the beginning of book 6, the two armies draw up opposite each other and the stage is set for one of Lucan's many narrative delays:

> Postquam castra duces pugnae iam mente propinquis
> inposuere iugis admotaque comminus arma,
> parque suum uidere dei,   (*Bellum civile* 6.1–3)

> Afterwards the leaders, now with a mind for battle, set down
> their camps on neighbouring ridges, and moved their weapons face to face,
> and the gods saw their own pair

This classic opening to an epic book raises audience expectations: we should either be given a battle, or a council of the gods now, but in fact we receive neither. Instead the leaders disengage again and start a long siege. The hint of divine spectatorship never goes beyond the potentially metaphorical: the watching gods are (just) a figure of speech. Two more examples of Lucan playing around with a more traditional epic mode: at 7.192–206, Lucan reflects on the Patavian augur who knew of the battle when it was occurring and flirts with the idea of a heavenly audience:

> si cuncta perito
> augure mens hominum caeli noua signa notasset,

---

[86] On this whole passage, see Leigh 1997: 82–99.
[87] Which is surely the import of the stray mountain *Mimas*, also the name of one of the giants who fought against the gods. See Leigh 1997: 97.
[88] Leigh 1997: 89–91.

> spectari toto potuit Pharsalia mundo.
> o summos hominum, quorum fortuna per orbem
> signa dedit, quorum fatis caelum omne uacauit!
>
> (*Bellum civile* 7.202–6)
>
> if the mind of men,
> skilled in augury, had noted all the new signs in the sky,
> Pharsalia could be watched by the whole world.
> O highest of men, whose fortune produced signs
> throughout the world, for whose fates the whole sky was at leisure!

Here Lucan twists the epic universe; instead of gaining sublimity and power for his epic through the divine audience, the sky is empty to stage their battles: not just that it has space, but also hinting that the gods are not there to watch it.[89] This democratises the divine audience: the whole world can watch like gods, just as the participants are *summos*, not the gods. Similarly, at 7.475–84 the noise of battle strikes the heaven; this too should herald a transition to Olympus, but the only reaction in the text is the self-reflexive terror of the armies themselves: *uocesque furoris | expauere sui tota tellure relatas*. ('they panic at their own voices of rage carried throughout the land', 7.483–4).

When the narrator mentions the gods, there is often a threatening gaze from above. At 1.524–5 the gods fill the universe with portentous signs: *superique minaces | prodigiis terras impleurunt, aethera, pontum.* ('The threatening gods have filled the lands, heavens and sea with prodigies.')[90] Nigidius Figulus blames the gods for what he foresees: *quod cladis genus, o superi, qua peste paratis | saeuitiam?* ('What kind of disaster, o gods, are you preparing? What savagery from what plague?', 1.649–50). Now it seems precisely as if Phaethon was once more running wild in the heavens (1.655–60) as the constellations burn and flee.[91] When we do receive a clear reference to effective divine power in the narrator's text, it is the destructive and rapacious prophetic possession of Apollo (5.165–74).[92]

Not much remains, then, of the divine gaze. Although reference to, and accusations of, the gods are frequent, they rarely receive narratorial

---

[89] Feeney 1991: 'it [epic] achieves its characteristic effects principally through stunning and extraordinary displays of power, to which the gods above all contribute' (262); 'he [Lucan] is straining to an epic status and power which he can never attain, and is therefore for ever falling short of something he ought to be hitting' (285). I would see Lucan as redirecting, twisting and appropriating epic sublimity rather than falling short.

[90] See also Pompey at 3.36, feeling threatened by the gods.

[91] Cato, too, accuses the gods: at 2.288 he accuses them of making him guilty. To watch the civil war would be like watching the sky fall (2.289–92), or sitting on one's hands while the universe disintegrates. Indifference is the *furor* from which Cato begs the gods to keep him (2.295–7).

[92] The narrator mentions gods as audience by imagining Jupiter marvelling at Erichtho (6.464–5).

endorsement and can often be read as metaphorical. What is there constantly presents the dark side of the divine gaze, coming from above, powerful, threatening, destructive and largely incomprehensible. For the narrator often protests ignorance (e.g. 1.234–5; 9.621–2); at 1.419, the gods are represented as wanting explanations of the natural world to stay hidden.[93] In this context, the heavens are the right place for Lucan's deified Nero, exchanging his earthly vigilance (*statione peracta*, 1.45–6) for the divine gaze. Lucan asks him not to look obliquely on Rome, a Juno as well as an Apollo:

> sed neque in Arctoo sedem tibi legeris orbe
> nec polus aversi calidus qua uergitur Austri,
> unde tuam uideas obliquo sidere Romam.
> (*Bellum civile* 1.53–5)

> But do not choose your seat in the northern hemisphere,
> or where the hot pole of the opposing south inclines,
> from where you would look on your Rome with star aslant.

As well as destabilising the universe and offering another potentially hostile gaze on mortals below, Nero will also be the object of our gaze:

> pars aetheris illa sereni
> tota uacet nullaeque obstent a Caesare nubes.
> (*Bellum civile* 1.58–9)

> May that whole part of the peaceful aether
> remain empty, and may no clouds stand in the way of Caesar.

The hyperbolic and potentially humorous (if vitriolic) tone of this passage works to objectify Nero.[94] His divine pretensions might make him ridiculous, but his imperial gaze is very real, as the dead Lucan might testify.

Something of this paradox is seen in the gazes of Caesar and Pompey, both of whom display the divine (and imperial) gaze in different ways.[95] Both are visual phenomena in book 1: Pompey as the tree inspires awe, but is an empty appearance (*magni nominis umbra*, 'the shadow of a great name', famously, 1.135); while Caesar as lightning bolt is pure visual power, assaulting the eyes of those who look at him (1.153–4). Pompey's tree is *sublimis* (136); he is also high on a horse at 7.342 (*sublimi praeuectus equo*) after

---

[93] Other examples of the narrator asking unanswered questions are numerous, including 5.244–7.
[94] Dewar 1994.
[95] Cato is also an important spectator, especially of his men's sublime heroism at 9.881–9; his appropriation and problematisation of the gaze of the philosophical epic hero needs to be explored further, but for now I focus on Caesar and Pompey, who need to be read in apposition to each other.

standing paralysed by the sight of Caesar's army and the imminent battle (*uidit . . . superis placuisse diem, stat corde gelato | attonitus*, 'he saw that the day pleased the gods, and stands thunderstruck with frozen heart', 7.339–40). Within the logic of the epic gaze, it makes perfect sense that Pompey should be viewing from the hill as the defeat of Pharsalia unfolds (7.647–711).[96] He is both the general on the hill (Leigh compares him with Camillus at Livy 6.23.10–12) and a version of Virgil's Juno, almost unable to watch, impotent and horrified. The perspective seems too far away to be realistic:

> stetit aggere campi,
> eminus unde omnes sparsas per Thessala rura
> aspiceret clades, quae bello obstante latebant.
>
> (*Bellum civile* 7.649–51)
>
> He stood on a rampart of the field,
> from where he might watch from a distance the whole disaster
> scattered through the Thessalian countryside, which was lying hidden with the war in the way.

This is a Lucretian perspective, seeing through the close-packed battle to the scattered disaster underneath.[97] The war which stands in the way is like the epic terror occluding a clear view of the workings of the universe, the mortal mist. Yet he is not a detached godlike viewer: instead he over-identifies, feels that the army is literally his body, that he himself is being killed (652–3).[98] For Leigh this represents Pompey's monarchical perspective, his epic pretensions. He wants to be the synecdochic hero, to die one for all, or even be a Patroclus figure, for whose body all are fighting. In reality all he can do is watch, wish and think. Instead, Leigh argues, he is that suspect figure, the general who survives defeat (like Aeneas in *Aeneid* 2 and Hannibal). If we see Pompey as godlike in this passage it offers a possible way out of the dilemma between detachment and engagement. Like Virgil's Juno, he is prevented from acting by Fate, and by the stronger figure of the Jupiter-like Caesar. The artificial view from the hill allows a different way of matching *Bellum civile* against the *Aeneid*, presenting civil war as an un-founding of Rome.[99] Pompey paradoxically gazes in godlike

---

[96] Leigh's chapter on Pompey focuses on this: Leigh 1997: 110–57, emphasising Lucan's originality.
[97] See above, pp.99–101.
[98] Leigh 1997: 154–7 argues that this is 'a terrible delusion, and, worse, one that is thoroughly Augustan, thoroughly Vergilian in character' (154).
[99] The artificiality is underlined by the way that Pompey does not stay far away, and does not go straight into retreat; instead at 666–9 he is going around the troops trying to persuade them not to die for him. Leigh 1997: 128–39 reads Pompey's retreat as a sort of reverse *deuotio*.

serenity: despite the emotional turmoil of his thoughts, he is undisturbed by what he sees:

> non gemitus, non fletus erat, saluaque uerendus
> maiestate dolor, qualem te, Magne, decebat
> Romanis praestare malis. non inpare uoltu
> aspicis Emathiam: nec te uidere superbum
> prospera bellorum nec fractum aduersa uidebunt;
>
> *(Bellum civile 7.680–4)*

> There was no groaning, no weeping, a grief deserving of respect
> with dignity preserved, such as is appropriate for you, Magnus,
> to offer for Roman evils. Not with unequal face
> do you look on Emathia: success in battle did not see you
> proud, and defeat will not see you broken.

Pompey here becomes an *exemplum* for the reader, giving an appropriate response, and one which demands not engagement but lack of emotion in the face of defeat. He is a model Roman reader, but also on display. Unlike Juno, he is not hidden in a cloud; his eminence makes him only too visible. In the end his objectification is emblematised by his severed head, kept to display to Caesar, to which event Lucan looks forward at 7.673–5. This is not to downplay the unease of the narrator's complex manoeuvrings around his defeated hero: but in the last move (698–711) we come back to the idea that heroism and epic victory are utterly undermined by the civil war context:

> nonne iuuat pulsum bellis cessisse nec istud
> perspectasse nefas? spumantes caede cateruas
> respice, turbatos incursu sanguinis amnes,
> et soceri miserere tui. quo pectore Romam
> intrabit factus campis felicior istis?
>
> *(Bellum civile 7.698–702)*

> Surely it pleases you that you have yielded, put to flight in war, and that you
> did not have to gaze on that unspeakable horror? Look back at the squadrons
> foaming with gore, the rivers overthrown by the inrush of blood,
> and pity your father-in-law. With what heart will he enter
> Rome, since he had been made luckier on those fields?

Pompey's inability to watch to the end is actually lucky: in civil war, victory is defeat and defeat is a sort of victory. By winning, Caesar becomes the guilty party. The divine perspective mixes wonder and pity; here Pompey is given that perspective back as he is asked to pity the victor. Death is all that is needed to set a seal on his Lucanian apotheosis.[100]

---

[100] See concluding chapter, pp.364–8.

Caesar, in contrast, shares in the divine gaze; not a god watching from the mountain, but more like a god intervening in the battle.[101] The key passage for this is 7.557–81, in which Caesar personally inspects, motivates, staunches wounds and supplies weapons, even compared to Bellona or Mars at 567–73.[102] His gaze is also imperial and oppressive:

inspicit et gladios, qui toti sanguine manent,
qui niteant primo tantum mucrone cruenti,
quae presso tremat ense manus, quis languida tela,
quis contenta ferat, quis praestet bella iubenti,
quem pugnare iuuet, quis uoltum ciue perempto
mutet;
(*Bellum civile* 7.560–5)

He inspects the swords too: which are wholly wet with blood,
which shine with only the first point bloody,
which hands tremble as they press the sword, who bears their weapon slackly,
who bears it intently, who offers war to one ordering,
whom it pleases to fight, who changes his face when a citizen
has been slaughtered;

Caesar is not just motivating his troops, but looking for evidence of their emotional commitment to civil war, like an informer in their midst.[103] His intervention has visual effects, as if he were the Homeric Ares: *nox ingens scelerum est* ('a huge night of crime arises', 7.571), though, like divine manifestations, it also works aurally (7.571–3).

Caesar also implicitly claims that he has been given the divine gaze in his pre-battle speech: *haud umquam uidi tam magna daturos | tam prope me superos* ('I have never seen the gods about to give such great things and so close to me', 7.297–8). A way of speaking, perhaps, but Caesar often usurps the epic voice, claims the knowledge and certainty that the narrator denies himself. So in book 1, when Caesar persuades his men to join him in starting the civil war, he narrates the actions of the gods: *nunc, cum fortuna secundis | mecum rebus agat, superique ad summa uocantes, | temptamur* ('Now, when fortune drives me with favouring circumstances, and the gods above are calling me to the summit, I am challenged', 1.309–11). He goes on to

---

[101] Gods motivating: Athene and Diomedes earlier in this chapter (*Il.* 5.120–32); Apollo and Hector (*Il.* 15.220–70); Enyo and Ares leading the Trojans (*Il.* 5.590–5). Inspecting: Athene and Apollo sitting in the tree (*Il.* 7.58–66), watching the duel between Hector and Ajax. Staunching wounds: Venus with Aeneas (*Il.* 12.411–24); supplying weapons: Athene and Achilles (*Il.* 22.273–7).

[102] 'Here Caesar acts exactly as an epic god acts, supplying the necessary inspiration and equipment.' Feeney 1991: 296. On the whole passage see Leigh 1997: 99–109. On Caesar as godlike, see also Ahl 1976: 284–5, Henderson 1987: 146. General on Caesar: Rossi 2001, Walde 2006, Nix 2008.

[103] See Bartsch 1994: 28–31, and more generally; Suet. *Nero* 23, *Domit.* 10; Pliny *Pan.* 33.3–4.

compare Pompey to a tiger at 327–31, an extended epic simile within his speech.

Caesar is like a god, appropriates the divine perspective, and something of the omniscience of the epic narrator. In the storm of book 5 he runs the risk of becoming a Salmoneus or a Capaneus,[104] but book 3, where he exercises a divine and imperial gaze over Rome itself, sees him at his most secure and Augustan. He begins with a distant view of Rome:

> excelsa de rupe procul iam conspicit urbem
> Arctoi toto non uisam tempore belli
> miratusque suae sic fatur moenia Romae:
>
> *(Bellum civile* 3.88–90)

> From a high cliff far away now he gets a full sight of the city,
> which he had not seen throughout the whole time of the Northern war,
> and, having wondered at the walls of his own Rome, he addresses it thus:

The *suae* expresses his sense of ownership. This stands in contrast to Aeneas looking down at a city which belongs to others, Carthage (*Aen.* 1.419–22). Caesar calls Rome *deum sedes* ('the home of gods', 91) yet he will shortly be despoiling the Roman treasure in the temple of Saturn (114–19). The vertical perspective of his gaze is that of the attacking army or the hostile god. At 103–9 Lucan's description of Caesar calling an assembly in the temple of Apollo on the Palatine assimilates him to Ovid's Jupiter as Augustus (*Met.* 1.163–76), and Feeney has shown how Caesar is elsewhere similar to Ovid's Jupiter.[105] This is followed by two contrasting passages which emphasise the Roman empire's relationship to the known world: the plunder which Caesar takes from the temple was taken from all corners of the world by imperial Romans (154–68); the world turns out in answer to Pompey's call for help (177–297). Although Lucan's narrator has denied himself the divine level, he still encompasses the world within his sight.

After Pharsalia, Caesar's viewing of the battlefield and the world subsiding into gore becomes a final act of aggression against the gods:

> fortunam superosque suos in sanguine cernit.
> ac, ne laeta furens scelerum spectacula perdat,
> inuidet igne rogi miseris caeloque nocenti
> ingerit Emathiam.   *(Bellum civile* 7.796–9)

---

[104] On the storm, see Pitcher 2008.
[105] Feeney 1991: 295–7. For instance, *Met.* 1.166 = *BC* 1.183–5. He argues that Caesar has undertaken a sort of successful gigantomachy, perverting Ovid's euhemeristic apotheoses: 'Here is the full development of Ovid's perspectives, expressed with a despairing bitterness which Ovid never felt, or never cared to express.' (298)

> He diagnoses his Fortuna and his own gods in the blood.
> And so that, raging, he does not lose the joyful spectacle of crime,
> he begrudges the fire of a pyre to the wretched men and heaps Emathia
> on the guilty heavens.

He is a perversion of the philosopher hero, whose joy arises not from looking through to reality, but from staying on the surface, a pointed contrast to Pompey (7.750–1), who looks through to the implications for Rome, and is reluctant to see the slaughter (7.698–9). Caesar sees the blood and dead bodies as an index of his own success, and perhaps a sort of epiphany, revealing his divine sponsorship, or an act of revenge.

Even without the formal structures of epic divine apparatus, the divine audience are often on the minds of characters and narrators, and Lucan engages with the epic tradition of divine viewers productively (or perhaps rather with gruesome destructiveness). Pompey's view from the hill sets him somewhere between the divine gaze and that of the women on the walls, disempowered, but maintaining his emotional distance. Caesar, in contrast, is immersed and yet has agency. Lucan has separated out different aspects of the philosophical epic hero: Pompey has all the philosophy, Caesar all the success. Caesar challenges the gods, Pompey pays the price, and the narrator is overshadowed by his heroes.

Conclusions

This chapter has explored the difficulties of looking back at the gods: the elusiveness of epiphany, the way that gods are visualised indirectly through metaphor and allegorisation; the limits of the mortal gaze, even when augmented by temporary divine vision; the associations between divine vision and authority, illusion and deception. From Diomedes onwards, there is a close link between looking at the gods and attacking the gods. Both Aeneas and Hannibal have affinities with Lucretius' Epicurus, who stands first in a strong line of philosophical heroes, culminating with Statius' Capaneus, who breaks free (or attempts to break free) from the conventions of religion and epic. Lucan the narrator fits into this tradition, while Pompey and Caesar both act (and look) like gods in their own ways.

Just as women in film who attempt to appropriate the male gaze are often destroyed, so mortals who reach for the divine gaze, or even look directly at the gods, run the risk of destruction. The gaze of Zeus/Jupiter is the essence of visual power: in its field even the other gods are objectified (and particularly when Jupiter in Roman epic becomes an avatar of the imperial gaze). Yet despite the awareness in readers of epic of being immeasurably small in the gaze of the universe, readers are also tempted, even encouraged, to look at the world through the eyes of the gods.

The concept of identification is still much under discussion among those who study film: is it just a matter of empathising or sympathising with fictional characters portrayed on screen?[106] Or is it something more than that, defined by the workings of the psyche? For Feldherr identification in tragedy is 'the capacity for those in the audience to recognize themselves in the figures they see on stage'.[107] Recognition is a useful concept here: understanding, familiarity, a conscious decision to want to be like someone, an awareness of differences, as well as empathy and sympathy. We might empathise with Zeus' sorrow for Sarpedon and Hector, but the move from there to identification is a large leap. Yet as the epic tradition goes on, characters in epic become readers of previous epics. The *poeta creator* takes part in his text by means of his avatars, characters who are versions of him. After Lucretius, and even more so after Lucan, the option of challenging the gods, becoming the god of your own epic world is always available: but it is frequently, repeatedly countered by the reassertion of Jupiter's gaze, the thunderbolt, the awareness of failure in the face of power.

---

[106] Neill 1996 sets out the problem; see also Currie 1995, with response from Vaage 2009.
[107] Feldherr 2010: 31.

CHAPTER 4

The prophetic gaze

Between gods and mortals come the prophets: close to the gods, they share in the divine ability to see through to further realities; nonetheless they are vulnerable, sometimes violated and abased. Prophetic visions allow epic narrative its totalising reach and contribute to epic authority. Epic is based in the heroic past; prophecy allows the poet to articulate a relationship with the present, the future, and all that comes in between. But prophecy, like fantasy, is often characterised by problems and gaps. The authority of the prophet is hedged about with qualifications: for instance, O'Hara points to the way that prophecy in the *Aeneid* often comes with a *si non vana* ('if it's not empty/meaningless') qualification.[1] This is not just a Virgilian feature: when Odysseus remembers Calchas' interpretation of the omen at Aulis, he wonders whether it might be wrong: 'Endure, my friends and stay for a time, that we may know whether the prophecies of Calchas are true or not.' (τλῆτε, φίλοι, καὶ μείνατ' ἐπὶ χρόνον, ὄφρα δαῶμεν / ἢ ἐτεὸν Κάλχας μαντεύεται, ἦε καὶ οὐκί. *Il.* 2.299–300). This is just one way that the power and knowledge of the prophet are undermined and complicated: this chapter shows how his (or her) gaze is both powerful and compromised.

The prophetic gaze is an important aspect of the epic gaze: the prophet is a doublet for the epic poet, the poet can be a sort of prophet.[2] The process of inspiration produces similar confusions and power dynamics in the case of both poetry and prophecy. The prophet's simultaneous power and powerlessness is often related to the poet's anxiety about the truth and effectiveness of poetry.[3] So the Sibyl makes a declaration of poetic inadequacy at the moment of her deepest penetration into the underworld (*Aen.* 6.625–7).[4] In the last line of Ovid's *Metamorphoses* there is a *si non vana* motif, qualifying and emphasising his own poetic immortality:

---

[1] O'Hara 1990: 55–6 gives examples of this motif in the *Aeneid* and Augustan poetry.
[2] Particularly in Latin poetry: see Newman 1967, Lovatt 2007.
[3] By, for example, O'Higgins 1988, O'Hara 1990 and Fantham 2006.   [4] Gowers 2005.

> quaque patet domitis Romana potentia terris
> ore legar populi, perque omnia saecula fama
> (si quid habent ueri uatum praesagia) uiuam.   (*Metamorphoses* 15.877–9)

> Wherever Roman power lies open in tamed lands
> I am read by the mouths of the people, through all the ages, in my fame,
> (if the foretellings of prophets have any truth) I shall live.

Just after the death of the prophet Bogus in the battle of Lake Trasimene, Silius is struck by traditional poetic anxiety:

> Quis deus, o Musae, paribus tot funera uerbis
> euoluat, tantisque umbris in carmine digna
> quis lamenta ferat?   (*Punica* 5.420–2)

> What god, o Muses, might roll out so many deaths
> with equal words? Which poet might bring laments in song
> worthy of such great shades?

Valerius Flaccus, in the middle of the Lemnian episode, envisages his own narrative as a dream:

> unde ego tot scelerum facies, tot fata iacentum
> exsequar? heu, uatem monstris quibus intulit ordo,
> quae se aperit series! o qui me uera canentem
> sistat et hac nostras exsoluat imagine noctes.   (VF *Argonautica* 2.216–19)

> From where should I follow the appearance of so many crimes, so many deaths
> of those just lying there? Alas to what horrors the poem's course brings the poet!
> What a series opens itself! O who might stop me as I sing
> true things and release my nights from this vision!

He seems overwhelmed by his subject matter, calling himself by implication a *uates*; the process of revelation is like the opening of hell, and his inspiration a nightmare: but it is emphatically a true nightmare (*uera canentem*), and this reluctance to sing is also a claim of authority and authenticity, despite the emphasis on appearance (*facies*) and the idea of the dream, which might equally be an illusion.

Lucretius talks about the visions of prophets and poets as dreams in his anti-mythological proem:

> Tutemet a nobis iam quouis tempore uatum
> terriloquis uictus dictis desciscere quaeres.
> quippe etenim quam multa tibi iam fingere possunt
> somnia, quae uitae rationes uertere possint
> fortunasque tuas omnis turbare timore!   (*De rerum natura* 1.102–6)

> You yourself at some point not far from now will seek
> to fall away from us, conquered by the terrifying words of prophets/poets.

> For how many dreams can they now create
> for you, which can upturn the reasoning of life
> and overthrow all your fortunes with fear.

Ennius in particular, and his version of the underworld, in which the figure of Homer unfolds the workings of the universe (*DRN* 1.117–26), stands against Lucretius' poetic agenda (127–35) and his anxiety about its difficulty (136–45). Clarity of mind is of utmost importance to Lucretius, light out of darkness. For Latin epic in particular the issue of the truth and reliability of poetry and man's communications with the divine is at the centre of establishing, maintaining and questioning poetic authority.

The prophetic gaze is an important way of constituting and negotiating these relationships of power, authority and credibility: both powerful and disturbing, it offers knowledge to the reader and encapsulates the incomprehensibility of the other. Many ways of foretelling the future are inherently visual: the internal, verbalised visions of prophets, dreams of worried mothers, omens, portents or auguries. Prophets and interpreters of omens function as an internal audience, in apposition to the poet/narrator. A special relationship with the divine gives prophet figures authority and privileged knowledge of things far away, deep inside and to come, but they lack the agency of divine viewers. Prophets are also often objects of the gaze, separated from society, by madness, blindness, seclusion, gender and sexual violence. This element of abjection, this association with the uncanny, functions like the Lacanian gaze, the distortion in the field of vision which evokes the unpalatable real, the impossibility of ever achieving complete knowledge and control, and the inevitability of death.

This chapter explores the importance of vision and viewing for understanding the representation of foretelling the future in epic. It begins by briefly examining the nature of prophecy, its relationship with divine plans, and moves on to a case study of Virgil's Sibyl. It then tackles the issue of the gendered representation of the prophetic gaze, starting with the way that prophetesses are characterised by madness and lack of control, in contrast to the much more varied representation of prophets, who often have a powerful gaze in space as well as time. It pursues the relationship between navigation, prophecy and narrative, and looks into the prophetic gaze as penetrative. In contrast, inspiration can be represented as a sort of penetration, a sort of sexual violation. For male prophets, however, blindness and social exclusion seem to be the price to pay for prophetic power. The chapter finishes with two case studies of the uncanny in episodes of necromancy.

Prophecy between gods and mortals: seeing and decreeing

When the Cumaean Sibyl makes her prophecy about the Trojans in Italy to Aeneas at the beginning of *Aeneid* 6, she famously says: *bella, horrida bella, | et Thybrim multo spumantem sanguine cerno* ('War, bristling war, and the Tiber foaming with much blood I see', *Aen.* 6.86–7). The language of making things out through vision, judging, sifting, is accompanied by vivid visualisation.[5] Although, as we shall see below, she is represented in part as a vessel for the words of Apollo, she also has an active gaze, which allows her to understand the future.

The προφήτης (from πρό, φημί) is 'one who speaks for a god and interprets his will to man' (LSJ 2 II), though the word might also imply speaking beforehand. Gods foretell the future, but for them it is a matter of fact and knowledge (or planning and decision-making) rather than scrying and interpreting. In Jupiter's prophecies in books 1 and 10 of the *Aeneid*, he does not see, but rather decrees. In his prophecy to Venus at *Aen.* 1.257–96, the only literal verb of seeing refers to Venus (258: *cernes urbem et promissa Lauini | moenia*). Jupiter, speaking *fatum*, is described as *talia fatur* ('speaking these things', 256), a verb which he recapitulates with *fabor enim* ('for I will speak', 261), combined with a metaphor from reading and writing: *longius et uoluens fatorum arcana mouebo* ('unrolling the far secrets of the fates, I will stir them up', 262).[6] Later the active first-person verbs emphasise that he is the one who actually makes things happen (*pono, dedi*, 278–9). Similarly at 10.11–15 he moves from stating what will happen, to issuing orders so that it does. Although he ends his rather autocratic mediation between Venus and Juno by implying that he will not intervene (*nullo discrimine habebo . . . soluo . . . rex Iuppiter omnibus idem. | fata uiam inuenient*. 'I will make no distinction . . . I let go . . . king Jupiter is the same for all. The fates will find a way', 10.108–13), in fact he closely equates his own decisions with fate.[7]

In the *Aeneid* and later Latin epic, the divine gaze often leads to or frames a divine prophecy. Jupiter's prophecy in *Aeneid* 1 begins with the passage of divine gazing examined above (*Aen.* 1.223–6). Similarly at 10.2–3 he is looking from on high at the camp of the Trojans and the Latin people (*sideream in sedem, terras unde arduus omnis | castraque Dardanidum aspectat*

---

[5] *OLD s.v. cerno*: 1. to sift; 2. to distinguish; 5. to distinguish with the eyes.
[6] On Jupiter and fate: Wilson 1979, Feeney 1991: 139–40, 152–5. On fate and writing: Lowrie 2009: 3–5.
[7] Celaeno, chief of the Harpies, emphasises Jupiter's ultimate authority in matters of prophecy. At *Aen.* 3.250–2, from her location high on a cliff (245–6), she talks of prophecy coming from Jupiter, to Apollo, from Apollo to her, and from her to Aeneas and his men.

populosque Latinos). But this connection is not the case in the *Iliad* and *Odyssey*, where divine vision is rather equated with lack of knowledge and the attempt to regain control of the narrative. So in *Iliad* 15, when Zeus awakes from his sexually induced oblivion, his return to awareness is presented by his vision of the Trojans in disarray (4–12); after rebuking Hera, he takes back control of the poem, and his prophecy at 49–77 looks forward to the deaths of Patroclus and Hector and the fall of Troy. In *Odyssey* 5, Poseidon catches sight of Odysseus when he returns from the Ethiopians (5.282–90), and realises that he has been excluded from the divine decision-making process. Why is the panoptic gaze of Jupiter so much more prominent in Latin epic than that of Zeus in Greek epic? Why is there so little prophecy in the *Iliad*, most of it focusing on the action of the poem itself, or certainly not much further than the sack of Troy?

In order to understand the significance of the gaze here, we need to consider the relationship of epic to its political context. The Homeric epics are set in the heroic past; they are separate from any particular political situation.[8] Although they may reflect in an indirect way political developments, they do not have an immediate relationship with a single overriding source of power.[9] They question and critique power structures; Agamemnon is no avatar of Zeus.[10] Their cultural force comes from the appropriation of a long oral tradition and from their Panhellenic status.[11] In contrast, even Apollonius is much more firmly embedded in the context of Ptolemaic Alexandria;[12] while Ennius and Virgil (and later Latin poets) are entangled in the Roman culture of patronage. Prophecy in epic is particularly political: scenes of prophecy represent negotiations between men of words and men of power, while prophecies themselves enable epic to reflect on times and places outside the immediate narrative context.[13]

Divine plans and intentions are turned into action via words, drawing on the authority of the written or spoken words of the fates or Jupiter, and how the divine gaze inspires and mediates divine action. In contrast, mortal

---

[8] This is not quite the same as the argument that the *Iliad* is pre-political: for a summary of that position see Hammer 2002: 20–5.
[9] On the politics of the *Iliad*, see Van Wees 1992, Thalmann 1998, Raaflaub 1998, Hammer 2002 with Buchan 2003, Wilson 2002, Christensen 2007: esp. 29–40, Barker 2009.
[10] Christensen 2007: 196: 'Agamemnon is unlike Hesiod's muse-inspired king and the central king of the *Theogony*, Zeus.'
[11] Christensen 2007: 35: 'The audience of the epic in its final form was Panhellenic, the poem's world is a Panhellenic pastiche.'
[12] See Mori 2008, but also Hunter 1993.
[13] Prophecy is also used by other genres of praise poetry, as an important tactic of praise (such as Pindar in *Pythian* 4, or Horace in *Odes* 3.3); this too may have had an influence on Apollonius, Virgil and later poets.

prophets struggle to attain knowledge of the divine mind; rather than just speaking for the gods, they often seem to see into the mind of the gods. There is an emphasis on vision, to create authority, immediacy and vividness. From this stems a focus on the problems and difficulties for mortals of turning vision into knowledge, and of understanding and interpreting both visions and words (including the poems themselves).

Mortal prophets and the powerful gaze

Prophets operate in various ways, to foretell the future, interpret the will (or anger) of the gods, warn and advise. Many types of divination are inherently visual: the interpretation of omens and portents sometimes involves strange noises, but mostly marvellous sights; scrutinising the entrails of sacrificed animals, observing the flight of birds and watching the movements of flames are necessarily visual practices. Dreams, too, are almost always visual, although words can be an important part of dream communication, too.[14] Necromancy, kledonomancy, prophecies of people about to die, and oracles are the least visual forms of divination: here interpretation is applied instead to verbal pyrotechnics and riddling conundrums. However, different types of prophecy are often combined (an omen to confirm a verbal statement) or blurred together (Odysseus calls up the spirits of the dead to obtain a verbal prophecy from Tiresias; the Sibyl offers a verbal prophecy, followed by an ecphrasis of Tartarus and the panorama from Anchises in *Aeneid* 6; Calchas observes and interprets omens, but also offers straight verbal advice and prophecy). This section explores the gaze of the prophet and the way it is both powerful and powerless.

The Sibyl of *Aeneid* 6 is probably the most famous and enduring prophetic figure from antiquity. Gowers points out her doubleness and marginality, and this quality is also reflected in her gaze.[15] We have already seen the climactic *cerno* of her prophecy to Aeneas at 6.86–7, and vision is equally important when she acts as Aeneas' guide to and through the underworld, culminating in her ecphrastic description of Tartarus at 6.548–627. She comes on the scene as an authoritative figure, who begins by ordering Aeneas away from the images created by Daedalus (6.37–9), disrupting his pleasurable viewing and indulgence in emotion, forcing instead a focus on the incomprehensible desires of the gods. She is addressed

---

[14] See below, Chapter 6, pp.206–16.
[15] Gowers 2005: 170–1, 177. On Virgil's Sibyl, see also Merkelbach 1961, Garstang 1963, Quiter 1984, Parke 1988: 71–99.

by Aeneas as *sanctissima uates* (65). Her initial inspiration brings out her separation from the mortal world:

> cui talia fanti
> ante fores subito non uultus, non color unus,
> non comptae mansere comae; sed pectus anhelum,
> et rabie fera corda tument, maiorque uideri
> nec mortale sonans, adflata est numine quando
> iam propiore dei.   (*Aeneid* 6.46–51)

Speaking such things, suddenly, in front of the doors, her face
and her colour were not the same, her hair did not remain kempt; but her breast
was gasping, her wild heart swells with madness, and she seemed greater
and no longer sounded mortal, when she was breathed through by the divine power
of the god, now close at hand.

The signs of madness are uncanny, but also give increased stature; even so she is represented as the passive recipient of the god's power. Later, at 77–80, her madness increases (*bacchatur uates*, 78), and Apollo tames, presses and forms her (*fera corda domans, fingitque premendo*, 80).[16] Her doubleness comes out well here: as prophetess of Apollo, she is a vessel of his words; yet she also participates in the tradition of powerful priestesses of Hecate (following Circe and Medea), and her emphatic *cerno* seems to represent her own vision, not that of Apollo.

In the journey to the underworld, too, she opens up closed things, lights up the darkness and reveals things concealed.[17] In particular, metaphors of bodily penetration, opening of mouths and throats, characterise the journey and they come to a climax with the opening of the gates of Hell (574).[18] Yet the narrative focus is on the speech of the Sibyl and the gaze of Aeneas: she has seen it all before, and he is the reader's surrogate.[19] Only for Tartarus,

---

[16] For readings of sexual undertones in these lines, see Gowers 2005: 178–9, citing Norden 1916: *ad* 6.77–80, and the dismissal of Austin 1977: *ad loc.*

[17] On opening and concealment Gowers 2005: 176–7. Tropes and metaphors of vision, darkness, revelation and hiding at *Aen.* 6.12 (*aperit*), 27–9 (*resoluit*), 81 (*patuere*), 100 (*obscuris*), 127 (*patet*), 138–9 (*tegit . . . obscuris*), 141 (*telluris operta*), 157–8 (*caecos*), 262 (*aperto*), 406 (*aperit . . . latebat*), 574 (*panduntur*), 578 (*patet*).

[18] Gowers 2005: 180 emphasises 'the foul gaping jaws, yawning chasms, and belching gullets of its geographical and bestial fixtures'.

[19] At 37–9 she speaks to stop Aeneas viewing (*perlegerent oculis*, 34); at 125–55 she repeatedly constructs Aeneas as viewer (134, *uidere*; 145, *oculis*; 155, *aspicies*); similarly at 322–30 (323, *uides*; 325, *cernis*). Other Sibylline speeches at 539–43, 562–627. Aeneas as viewer at 108 (in his own speech, 103–23); 317 (*miratus*); 333 (*cernit*); 452–5 (Apollonius' image of Lynceus catching a far glimpse of Hercules at 4.1477–80, used here for Aeneas' recognition of Dido); 495 (*uidit*); 548–9 (*respicit . . . uidet*). For the agency of the Sibyl, see for instance briskly hurrying Aeneas on (37, 539, 629–30); breaking off dialogue with Palinurus (372–81); negotiating with Charon (399–407), overcoming Cerberus (419–21).

where he may not penetrate, does she offer her own vision, provided for her by the tutelary figure of Hecate:

> nulli fas casto sceleratum insistere limen
> sed me cum lucis Hecate praefecit Auernis,
> ipsa deum poenas docuit perque omnia duxit. (*Aeneid* 6.563–5)

> It is not right for any chaste man to stand on that criminal threshold;
> but when Hecate made me in charge of the Avernian grove,
> she herself taught me the punishments of the gods and led me through all.

Gowers points out the sublimity of this ecphrasis: the yawning chasm between earth and Tartarus, twice as deep as the distance between Olympus and earth.

> hic genus antiquum Terrae, Titania pubes,
> fulmine deiecti fundo uoluuntur in imo,
> hic et Aloidas geminos immania uidi
> corpora ...
> uidi et crudelis dantem Salmonea poenas, ... (*Aeneid* 6.580–5)

> Here I saw the ancient race of the Earth, the Titanic youth,
> thrown down by the thunderbolt, they roll in the profound depth,
> here too I saw the twin Aloides and their immeasurable
> bodies ...
> I saw too Salmoneus giving cruel punishments, ...

Here at the deepest point, the furthest in, the Sibyl acts as a witness to the fixation and humiliation of those who challenge the gods, finishing, most penetratively of all, with the ever-regenerating liver of Tityos, marked by an ecphrastic *cernere erat* (596). The Sibyl's triply repeated *uidi* is the authenticating personal view of the didactic poet. This vividly visualised description is an 'extended *praeteritio*', a Hellenistic condensation of all the underworld journeys before it, and a metapoetic reflection on the process of writing epic.[20] Yet even the Sibyl cannot tell all: a narrative of mystic initiation lurks.[21] Against the eternal, sublime divine perspective of the prophet stands the confused, labyrinthine and ephemeral understanding of mortal interpreters, as symbolised by Helenus' representation of the Sibyl writing on leaves, which are scattered by even a breath of wind (3.441–62).[22] Ovid's Sibyl, in contrast, expands on her own story, after the underworld, on the return journey (*Met.* 14.101–57), when Virgil's Sibyl has become much less prominent.[23] Virgil's

---

[20] Most 1992b, Gowers 2005: 176–8.
[21] Gowers 2005: 176, particularly on *Aen.* 6.266–7. See also Quiter 1984: 85–91, Zetzel 1989: 377.
[22] Gowers 2005: 174; see also Fowler 1997: 268–9, Hershkowitz 1998a: 105 n.121.
[23] In Ovid, Aeneas regards the Sibyl as an image of divine power (*numinis instar eris semper mihi, Met.* 14.124), and she looks back at him (*respicit hunc uates*, 129) as she tells him her own story, of Phoebus'

Sibyl, then, does have a powerful gaze: her vision, authenticated by prophetic possession and signs of madness, allows her to penetrate the depths of the underworld, as well as understand the workings of the future, even if she is also an object of the gaze in her madness, and objectified by the power of the god. She disrupts the visual pleasure of Aeneas, but not that of the reader.

Madness and the gaze

In later epic prophetic madness is an essential part of the package, but the image of the inspired prophet, characterised by signs of madness, is not found in Homeric epic or Apollonius' *Argonautica*, and first surfaces in tragedy.[24] This generic marking of madness is important for thinking about the relationship between madness and the epic gaze.[25] Cassandra is mentioned twice in the *Iliad*, at 13.366 (betrothed to Othryoneus) and 24.699 (first to catch sight of Priam returning with Hector's body, from the walls), in both cases conforming to female roles.[26] There are some signs that it might have been different in the cyclic epics: the summary of the *Cypria* in Proclus' *Chrestomathy* mentions prophecies from both Helenus and Cassandra.[27] In Aeschylus' *Agamemnon*, however, Cassandra is clearly characterised by her mad visions (1114, 1125, 1217–18).[28] By the time of Quintus Smyrnaeus, however, Cassandra's epic and tragic modes have merged:

---

offer of eternal life, her refusal of his love, and decline into a thousand years of old age, shrinking into only a voice (147–53). Ovid's Sibyl dramatises the uneasy (eroticised) relationship between prophetess and god, even as she forms a feminine counterpart to Ovid's own imagined literary immortality. On Ovid's Sibyl see Galinsky 1975: 226–9, Ellsworth 1988, Salzman-Mitchell 2005: 203–6 (as story-teller), Myers 2009: 77–88.

[24] With the partial exception of Theoclymenus, on whose vision of the death of the suitors (*Od.* 20.345–70), see below. However, there is no description of his prophetic inspiration; rather Athene inspires the suitors with a sort of madness. Plato at *Phaedrus* 244A speaks of the madness of priestesses at Delphi and Dodona, as well as the Sibyl 'prophesying in divine possession'. Padel 1995: 83. See also Heraclitus fr. 92 DK.

[25] Hershkowitz 1998a suggests that the epic voice itself is mad (hyperbolic, extreme, maniacal), but relies on Latin epic to make her point: she acknowledges that '[t]he most notable thing about madness in the *Iliad* and the *Odyssey* is that there is not very much of it' (126) and suggests that madness is 'considered unheroic or undignified for that poetic world' (153).

[26] On the poet's knowledge of the tradition of Cassandra as prophet, see Richardson 1993: 348. At *Od.* 11.421–3, Agamemnon mentions the death of Cassandra along with his own death at the hands of Clytemnestra, but here too does not hint at her prophetic role.

[27] West 2003: 67–8. There seem to have been more prophecies in the cyclic epics than in the *Iliad*: Calchas in the *Cypria* has two outings; in the *Little Iliad* Helenus is captured and forced to make a prophecy, according to Proclus (120–1).

[28] Padel 1995 speaks of Cassandra's 'spasms of frenzied vision' as an aspect of her relationship with Apollo in Euripides' *Troades* as well as Aeschylus. Lycophron's *Alexandra*, too, combines complex riddles with descriptions of what she sees (e.g. 86, 216).

> Οἵη δ' ἔμπεδον ἦτορ ἔχεν πινυτόν τε νόημα
> Κασσάνδρη, ...
> ἥ ῥ' ὅτε σήματα λυγρὰ κατὰ πτόλιν εἰσενόησεν
> εἰς ἓν ἅμ' ἀΐσσοντα, μέγ' ἴαχεν, εὖτε λέαινα,
> ἥν ῥά τ' ἐνὶ ξυλόχοισιν ἀνὴρ λελιημένος ἄγρης
> οὐτάσῃ ἠὲ βάλῃ, τῆς δ' ἐν φρεσὶ μαίνεται ἦτορ
> * * * * *
> πάντῃ ἀν' οὔρεα μακρά, πέλει δέ οἱ ἄσχετος ἀλκή·
> ὣς ἄρα μαιμώωσα θεόπροπον ἔνδοθεν ἦτορ
> ἤλυθεν ἐκ μεγάροιο· κόμαι δέ οἱ ἀμφεκέχυντο
> ὤμοις ἀργυφέοισι μετάφρενον ἄχρις ἰοῦσαι·
> ὄσσε δέ οἱ μάρμαιρεν ἀναιδέα· τῆς δ' ὑπὸ δειρῇ,
> ἐξ ἀνέμων ἅτε πρέμνον, ἄδην ἐλελίζετο πάντῃ. (*Posthomerica* 12.525–39)
>
> One heart alone was constant, one mind was lucid,
> Kassandra's. ...
> So when she saw these sinister portents in Troy converging
> To one conclusion, she cried aloud like a lioness,
> When in a woodland thicket it has been stabbed or shot
> By an eager hunter, so that her heart within her is maddened. ...
> All through the lofty hills with irresistible might.
> Kassandra like that, her prophetic heart within her raging,
> Came out of the palace. Her hair was streaming out
> Over her silvery shoulders all the way down her back.
> Her eyes were flashing fearlessly. Under her head her neck,
> Like the stem of a tree in a gale, kept writhing this way and that.
>
> (trans. James)

Her clarity of vision draws on omens for authority, and the signs of madness mark her genuine prophetic inspiration. As well as the cry, the wandering and the unkempt hair, the flashing eyes make her comparable to a berserk warrior, and suggest the power of her vision.[29] The image of the lioness also equates her to a heroic figure, although one who has been penetrated by prophetic madness from afar.[30] The erotic undertones of prophetic inspiration combine with the foreshadowing of tragic destruction, for both city and woman.[31] Cassandra's prophecy itself offers a vision of death and furies in the city:

---

[29] See below, Chapter 8, pp.311–24.
[30] This image can be productively read with the description of Dido at *Aen.* 4.68–73, wandering maddened through the city, like a deer hit unknowingly by a hunter, object of the gazes of Venus, Juno and Cupid, if not of Aeneas.
[31] Gärtner 2005 argues that Quintus' engagement with Virgil must be argued on a case-by-case basis; on this Cassandra episode, see 221–6 evoking a common source, but also acknowledging the possibility of Virgilian influence.

«Ἄ δειλοί, νῦν βῆμεν ὑπὸ ζόφον· ἀμφὶ γὰρ ἡμῖν
ἔμπλειον πυρὸς ἄστυ καὶ αἵματος ἠδὲ καὶ οἴτου
λευγαλέου· . . .
οὕνεκ' Ἐρινύες ἄμμι γάμου κεχολωμέναι αἰνοῦ
ἀμφ' Ἑλένης, καὶ Κῆρες ἀμείλιχοι ἀΐσσουσι
πάντη ἀνὰ πτολίεθρον· ἐπ' εἰλαπίνη δ' ἀλεγεινῇ
δαίνυσθ' ὕστατα δόρπα κακῷ πεφορυγμένα λύθρῳ
ἤδη ἐπιψαύοντες ὁμὴν ὁδὸν εἰδώλοισι.» (*Posthomerica* 12.540–2, 547–51)

'Poor fools, we've entered the realm of darkness. Round us
The city is filled with fire and blood and a doom
That is horrible. . . .
Because the spirits of vengeance, angry with us for Helen's
Fatal marriage, and the pitiless Fates are darting
Everywhere in the city. This miserable banquet of yours,
Fouled as it is with gore, is the last that you will enjoy.
The path you are on makes ghosts your companions now.'

Like the suitors in *Odyssey* 20 (see below), the Trojans dine as if already dead. Troy has become an underworld full of blood, flames and grief. Cassandra attempts to follow up her words with action, attacking the wooden horse with both fire and steel with the aim of opening it, revealing the truth (12.568–73), but her agency is removed by the community of Trojans, after a striking speech full of social disapprobation, calling her mad, and lacking in maidenly modesty (553–5). She is, in the end, objectified and impotent, sexually compromised and outside society.

Cassandra is not here compared to a maenad, but the imagery hints at it, and Dionysiac inspiration (and madness) is often important in the representation of prophets in Latin epic.[32] Virgil's Sibyl (*Aen.* 6.78) and Lucan's Phemonoe (*BC* 5.169–74) also rave like Bacchants, and I will return to Phemonoe below, in my discussion of sexual violation (pp.146–9). Lucan presents a figure who combines Apolline and Dionysiac inspiration, and seems to embody the powerful gaze of prophecy, the *matrona* at the end of book 1. She comes after a duo of male and relatively respectable prophets, Arruns the Etruscan diviner, and Nigidius Figulus the astrologer, and is compared to a Bacchant as she terrifies the Romans:

terruerant satis haec pauidam praesagia plebem,
sed maiora premunt. nam, qualis uertice Pindi

---

[32] Hershkowitz 1998a: 35–48 discusses the links between madness (of both Apolline and Dionysiac varieties) and prophecy. Other maenad images: Medea: VF *Arg.* 6.755–60; 8.446–9; Sen. *Med.* 382–6; Imilce: *Pun.* 4.774–7 with Augoustakis 2010: 200–13; Jocasta: *Theb.* 11.315–20; Argive women: 12.786–94. Argonauts: VF *Arg.* 3.257–8, 263–6.

> Edonis Ogygio decurrit plena Lyaeo,
> talis et attonitam rapitur matrona per urbem
> uocibus his prodens urguentem pectora Phoebum
>
> (*Bellum civile* 1.673–7)
>
> These omens had terrified the panicked people enough,
> but greater ones press them. For, just as an Edonian woman
> runs down from the peak of Pindus, full of Ogygian Lyaeo,
> so too a thunderstruck matron is snatched through the city
> betraying by these words that Phoebus is spurring on her breast

She has come down from a divine perspective, and the sexuality of her inspiration is implied in the adjective *plena* as well as *rapitur*.[33] She is an object of the people's gaze, an omen in her own right. But despite this apparent disempowerment, her vision is remarkably powerful: she flies, like Epicurus, throughout the whole world of the epic, carried by Apollo (*feror*, 678), but standing above the earth (678–9). She looks down on the mountains, like the gods (*Pangaea*, 679; *Haemi sub rupe*, 680; *Alpis*, 688; *Pyrenen*, 689). The verbs of movement are mostly in the passive (*feror, raptam*, 678; *feror, me ducis*, 683; *mutatur*, 684; *feror*, 686; *abripimur*, 690), but as the prophecy goes on she seems to take a more active role: the first-person plural of *abripimur* (690) suggests that both she and Apollo are being taken; *remeamus* (690) continues, while *eo* (693) seems to abandon Apollo altogether, even though she is in the process of demanding to go somewhere else. The verbs of perception, however, are active: *uideo* (679), *agnosco* (686), *uidi* (694); and she commands Apollo to explain what she sees (*doce*, 681) and take her somewhere else (*noua da mihi cernere litora ponti*, 693), even if neither command has any likelihood of success. Rather than simply being a vessel for the words of Apollo, she uses his power to appropriate a divine vision of the world, and, at the end of the book, she may lie passively (*lasso iacuit deserta furore*, 695), but we are not given any sense that she will suffer for her vision.[34]

So far the prophets with inspired vision we have looked at have all been female. Do men receive inspired prophetic visions, and if so, how are they

---

[33] On this passage see Hardie 1993: 107–8, Hershkowitz 1998a: 45–6; Fowler 2002 on *plena* and *rapitur*. *attonitam* also suggests penetration by thunderbolt, in the manner of Semele, as well as the more straightforward reading 'knocked out of her senses'.

[34] At *Theb.* 4.369–405, Statius adapts and recapitulates this scene. His Bacchant literalises Lucan's image and has a very different relationship with the god: she begins by calling him *omnipotens* but then accusing him of neglecting his home city. She demands that he carries her beyond the Caucasus, not to witness violence, but to be taken away from destruction at home (4.393–6). When she does have her vision, she complains that she is suffering from the wrong madness (396–7), and her vision (*uideo*, 397) is of an epic simile, the two competing would-be rulers of Thebes seen as bulls fighting for a meadow. See Hershkowitz 1998a: 46–7.

represented? In *Odyssey* 20, the seer Theoclymenus, guest-friend of Telemachus, has a vision in which he foretells the death of the suitors:

> « ἆ δειλοί, τί κακὸν τόδε πάσχετε; νυκτὶ μὲν ὑμέων
> εἰλύαται κεφαλαί τε πρόσωπά τε νέρθε τε γοῦνα.
> οἰμωγὴ δὲ δέδηε, δεδάκρυνται δὲ παρειαί,
> αἵματι δ' ἐρράδαται τοῖχοι καλαί τε μεσόδμαι·
> εἰδώλων δὲ πλέον πρόθυρον, πλείη δὲ καὶ αὐλή,
> ἱεμένων Ἔρεβόσδε ὑπὸ ζόφον· ἠέλιος δὲ
> οὐρανοῦ ἐξαπόλωλε, κακὴ δ' ἐπιδέδρομεν ἀχλύς.» (*Odyssey* 20.351–7)

> 'Poor wretches, what evil has come on you? Your heads and faces
> and the knees underneath you are shrouded in night and darkness;
> a sound of wailing has broken out, your cheeks are covered
> with tears, and the walls bleed, and the fine supporting pillars.
> All the forecourt is huddled with ghosts, the yard is full of them
> as they flock down to the underworld and the darkness. The sun
> has perished out of the sky, and a foul mist has come over.'

But he is emphatically not mad: when the suitors call him mad at 360, he calmly replies that he has eyes and ears and two feet, and will help himself out of the house, before they all die. Rather it is the suitors who suffer from divinely inspired madness:[35]

> μνηστῆρσι δὲ Παλλὰς Ἀθήνη
> ἄσβεστον γέλω ὦρσε, παρέπλαγξεν δὲ νόημα.
> οἱ δ' ἤδη γναθμοῖσι γελώων ἀλλοτρίοισιν,
> αἱμοφόρυκτα δὲ δὴ κρέα ἤσθιον· ὄσσε δ' ἄρα σφέων
> δακρυόφιν πίμπλαντο, γόον δ' ὠΐετο θυμός. (*Odyssey* 20.345–9)

> In the suitors Pallas Athene
> stirred up uncontrollable laughter, and addled their thinking.
> Now they laughed with jaws that were no longer their own.
> The meat they ate was a mess of blood, their eyes were bursting
> full of tears, and their laughter sounded like lamentation.

Theoclymenus himself is not given any of the markers of madness, and the narrator clearly shares Theoclymenus' vision, another aspect of this passage which differentiates it from later prophetic visions. The suitors are the objects of all gazes here, those of Athene, Telemachus and the readers, as well as Theoclymenus, while remaining unaware of their own strange behaviour.

The majority of male prophet figures do not suffer from the madness which often accompanies the prophetic visions of women. Calchas in the *Iliad* negotiates with Agamemnon and Achilles shrewdly, with no hint of

---

[35] Hershkowitz 1998a: 149–50; often called 'the most disturbing in the Homeric epics'. See also Fenik 1974: 233–44, Colakis 1985.

madness (*Il*.1.68–100); Phineus in Apollonius' *Argonautica* is abject and squalid in his blindness and poverty (see below, pp.150–1), but lists and describes the Argonauts' future journey without the need for inspired vision (AR *Arg*. 2.308–425); similarly, Virgil's Helenus makes no claim to divine inspiration or special vision. Flavian epic, however, offers several examples of male prophets suffering divine inspiration.[36] The prophetic contest between Mopsus and Idmon in Valerius Flaccus' *Argonautica* 1 sets the inspired Mopsus against the calm Idmon.[37] The power of Mopsus' vision is emphasised; equally he is presented as the object of the gaze himself:

> ecce sacer totusque dei per litora Mopsus,
> immanis uisu, uittamque comamque per auras
> surgentem laurusque rotat. uox reddita tandem,
> uox horrenda uiris; tum facta silentia uati.
> "heu quaenam aspicio! . . .
>   . . . quem circa uellera Martem
> aspicio? quaenam aligeris secat anguibus auras
> caede madens? quos ense ferit? miser eripe paruos
> Aesonide. cerno en thalamos ardere iugales." (VF *Argonautica* 1.207–11, 223–6)

Behold, sacred and wholly possessed by the god, Mopsus on the shore,
monstrous to see, with his fillets and hair rising through
the breezes as he whirls the laurel. At last his voice returns,
a voice terrifying to the heroes; then silence is made for the seer.
'Alas what things I see! . . .
                    . . . What battle do I see
around the fleece? What woman wet with slaughter cuts the breezes
with winged snakes? Which people does she strike with the sword? Wretched
son of Aeson, snatch away your little ones. Behold, I see the bridal bedroom
   burning.'

Idmon, in contrast, offers an optimistic, Virgilian prophecy, and is described with the emphasis on his lack of madness, learning and rationality:

> sed enim contra Phoebeius Idmon,
> non pallore uiris, non ullo horrore comarum
> terribilis, plenus fatis Phoeboque quieto,
> cui genitor tribuit monitu praenoscere diuum
> omina, seu flammas seu lubrica comminus exta
> seu plenum certis interroget aera pennis (VF *Argonautica* 1.228–33)

---

[36] Zissos 2008: 190 notes the popularity of ecstatic prophetic vision in 'Silver' Latin, citing Sen. *Ag*. 710–74; Luc. 1.674–95, 5.190–7; Stat. *Silv*. 4.3.121–63, *Ach*. 1.524–35, which he attributes to the influence of Virgil's Sibyl.
[37] On this passage see Zissos 2008: 186–202 and Stover 2009, with further bibliography.

But in opposition Phoebeian Idmon
not with paleness for the men watching, nor horrifying with any
bristling of the hair, full of the fates and a restful Phoebus,
to whom his father had allotted through instruction to know omens of the gods
beforehand, whether he questions flames or gets in close to slippery
entrails or reads the air full of certain wings

The internal mad, vision of Mopsus is strongly contrasted with Idmon's knowledge and scrutiny of external signs, which has been taught, but not necessarily inspired, by Apollo.

Valerius Flaccus' Phineus has a gaze which is powerful without signs of madness. Unlike Apollonius' Phineus he is not squalid, and is given a sense of renewal by the Argonauts' rescue:

ille ducem nec ferre preces nec dicere passus
amplius, hic demum vittas laurumque capessit
numina nota ciens. stupet Aesonis inclita proles
Phinea ceu numquam poenis nullaque gravatum
peste Iovis: tam largus honos, tam mira senectae
maiestas infusa; vigor novus auxerat artus. (VF *Argonautica* 4.547–52)

Then he could bear the leader no more nor allow him to make
prayers any further, and at last he took up the fillets and the laurel
stirring up the well-known divine power. The famous son of Aeson is amazed
at Phineus, looking as if he had never been weighed down by punishment
and the plague of Jupiter; a new vigour strengthened his limbs.

Like Virgil's Sibyl, he seems to grow bigger; inspiration here is a positive force rather than a maddening one. This renewal is read by Stover as a renewal of the role of the *uates* under the new Flavian regime; under the positive influence of the rescuing Argonauts prophecy becomes possible again, just as Augustus (and Vespasian) allow poetry through peace, making Valerius a Virgil for his times.[38] Stover suggests that the Prometheus-like liberation of Phineus from Zeus' punishment and restrictions on prophecy allows him to propel forward the action of the epic.[39] However if we look at the lines in context, a slightly different picture emerges:

---

[38] Stover forthcoming, ch. 4. Much of Stover's argument here is convincing, although his choice of Lucan's Phemonoe as comparandum for Phineus is rather tendentious. Phemonoe and Phineus are completely different types of prophet; as well as the gender difference, there is the type of prophecy. Phineus' navigational mode indeed owes more to Helenus, Tiresias and Circe (or possibly the Sibyl) than to Phemonoe – so comparison needs to be made with them.

[39] He also connects Phineus' feeling at 632–3 that he can see the sun again with Cassius Dio's story of Vespasian healing a blind man (65.8.1). 'In Valerius the renewed vigor, emancipated voice, and restored vision of the *vates* emerge as the key components in the consolidation of a new – and better – political order.' Stover forthcoming, ch. 4.

> me Pangaea super rursus iuga meque paterna
> stare Tyro dulcesque iterum mihi surgere soles
> nunc reor. exactae uerumne abiere uolucres?
> nec metuam tutaeque dapes? date tangere uultus,
> dem sinite amplexus, propiusque accedite dextrae.   (VF *Argonautica* 4.631–5)
>
> I think that now I stand again above the Pangaean ridge
> and paternal Tyre and sweet suns rise
> for me. Have the birds really been driven away?
> Should I fear no longer, are my meals safe? Give me your faces to touch,
> allow me to give embraces, and approach nearer to my right hand.

These lines equally echo Lucan's *matrona*, and although uplifting, might also suggest that Phineus is a Lucan figure, rather than a Virgil figure: Phineus has lost his homeland and his sight for good, just as Lucan feels civil war has destroyed Rome for good, by allowing the imperial system to take hold. There is a sense of Phineus' joy as illusory (the Harpies might yet return), yet the *matrona* really does see terrible things to come. The restoration of Phineus is limited: he has not regained his sight; he asks them to communicate with him by touch, to come to his hand, rather than bringing his hand to them, so his restored vision is strictly limited. In the same way, perhaps, the poet cannot be any more sure than Virgil that the optimism at the beginning of the new reign will bear fruit.[40]

Statius' *Thebaid* brings this tragic, ecstatic vision to a climax. Stover has already pointed out the way that the prophetic duo of Melampus and Amphiaraus in *Thebaid* 3 builds on the contest between Idmon and Mopsus in Valerius Flaccus: instead of presenting agonistic (and generic) ambivalence, Statius offers two reinforcing prophecies and an unremittingly tragic (and Tragic) vision of the future.[41] Similarly, Amphiaraus is the only rational guiding voice in the *Thebaid* (see below for his auspice taking), and he is graphically erased from the epic narrative by the resurgence of his traditional tragic fate (his wife Eriphyle betrays him for Harmonia's necklace, opening the way for his son to avenge himself on her), when he is swallowed up alive by the underworld.[42] Like the *Iliad*, the *Thebaid* does not look far beyond the boundaries of its own story. Its inward-facing plot is not a synecdoche for wider world narratives, but rather an incestuous focus on the mixed-up house

---

[40] Stover 2008 argues that the *Argonautica* is wholly a product of Vespasian's reign. I agree that the latest datable reference is to the explosion of Vesuvius, but it does not necessarily follow that the poem must have been complete within months of it. Those who argue that Valerius might still have been writing into the reign of Domitian cannot be absolutely proved wrong.
[41] Stover 2009.   [42] On Amphiaraus see Fantham 2006.

of Oedipus (*Oedipodae confusa domus*, *Theb.* 1.17), a refusal to follow Valerius in validating (even partially) Roman empire and Flavian regime.

One example from book 10: as the Argives recover from the deaths of Hippomedon and Parthenopaeus in book 9, Thiodamas, the new prophet figure, appears suddenly (*ecce repens*, 10.160) inspired (either by Juno or Apollo, comments the narrator) with *horror*. He is terrifying to see (164); his fragile mind cannot stand up to the god (165–6); his eyes, face and hair show the signs of madness (166–9). Most extraordinary in this passage, however, is the simile which compares him to a devotee of Cybele:

> sic Phryga terrificis genetrix Idaea cruentum
> elicit ex adytis consumptaque bracchia ferro
> scire uetat; quatit ille sacras in pectora pinus
> sanguineosque rotat crines et uulnera cursu
> exanimat: pauet omnis ager, respersaque cultrix
> arbor, et attoniti currum erexere leones.   (*Thebaid* 10.170–5)

> Just so the Phrygian mother on Ida summons the bloody man
> from the terrifying shrines and forbids him to know that his arms
> are consumed by iron; he shakes the sacred pine-brands against his breast
> and whirls his bloody hair and disempowers his wounds
> by running: the whole field panics, and the blood-spattered worshipping
> tree, and the lions rear from the chariot, thunderstruck.

This stunning simile brings out the uneasy relationship between inspiration and power, gender and violence, subject and object of the gaze. He has an enormous effect on those watching him, like Orpheus apparently animating the landscape. The violated devotee is forbidden to know what is happening to his body, like an Agave beheading herself. The sheer energy of his violence has the paradoxical effect of draining life not just from his body but from the wounds, as if they have become part of his body. The worshipping tree is female, as is the goddess, as mother offering renewal; but lurking behind the violence, blood and wounds is Attis of Catullus 63, who becomes grammatically female by castrating himself in his madness. The frenzied madness of prophecy prevents the prophet from realising that he is destroying himself. It is no surprise, then, that prophetic madness is often associated with women, and the increasing importance of masculine prophetic madness shows the complexity of gender in Flavian epic.

The inspired visions of prophets can be an index of their powerful gazes: madness advertises the prophet's closeness to the divine, and the outward signs have a powerful effect on their audiences. The prophet with his or her powerful gaze can see places, times and worlds that others cannot see; if he is blind, he seems to gain a sort of sight. However, inspiration (or madness) equally demonstrates powerlessness, in a lack of control. Madness can both authenticate the prophecy and undermine the authority of the prophet.

The mad prophet disturbs the narrative and the processes of identification in interesting ways. She brings the incomprehensibility of the divine onto the epic stage along with the incomprehensibility of madness. The ecphrastic description of a mad vision is never sufficient to experience what it is like to go out of your mind, to have one yourself. We see fragments but cannot wholly identify. Madness creates distance, objectification: which is why it is appropriate that in the *Odyssey* it is the suitors who are mad, not Theoclymenus, whose prophecy represents an allegorical understanding of the narrative to come – only he, and we through him, can see the suitors' madness.

Following McGowan's interpretation of the Lacanian gaze, madness is a moment when the uncanny realisation of the incomprehensibility of the other comes to the fore.[43] He gives the example of David Lynch's film *Blue Velvet* (1986), in which the naked, beaten and humiliated figure of Dorothy Vallens (Isabella Rosselini) sidles onto the scene and disrupts the narrative, stopping a fight between the central character Jeffrey and his rival, confusing and disturbing viewers, both internal and external.[44] Dorothy's status as victim of sexual violence and her madness, along with her distance from understanding and identification, offers a partial parallel with some of the prophetesses of epic. In the same way that Dorothy's presence shows the clash between fantasy and desire, the juxtaposition of the political power of prophecy and the disempowerment and madness of the prophet brings out the fissures in epic's assumptions of authority. Madness is the necessary result of the human mind attempting to truly encompass and understand the divine; following Hershkowitz, we might argue that the epic gaze, as well as the epic voice, is partly mad.[45] On the other hand, prophetic madness is constrained by gender and genre (often marked as tragic, mostly restricted to women), tamed and bounded by ritual.

Navigation

Finding the way is rarely a matter of internal vision, but rather of recognising landscape and reading signs, interpreting omens seen by the prophet, hence a

---

[43] McGowan 2003.
[44] McGowan 2003: 40–3. 'Jeffrey confronts the gaze in the figure of Dorothy: the film centers around her desire and her status as an emodiment of that gaze.' (41) 'As an embodiment of the *object petit a*, Dorothy intrudes into this fantasmatic realm [the ordered suburbia of Lumberton] and completely disrupts it, ripping apart the fantasy structure.' (42–3)
[45] See below on the visual aspect of battle madness (assaultive gaze, pp.311–24).

form of 'external prophecy'. It is a much more masculine and epic phenomenon than the internal visions of inspired prophets.[46] Here the prophet is an internal audience and a model for the reader. The calm and rational exposition of the meaning of things viewed allows prophets (and poets) to take on a controlling and almost scientific gaze. The taking of auspices and the reading of the stars require detailed specialist knowledge, while the study of entrails is like a medical investigation, scrutinising the inside of the body. However, all these practices are ultimately acts of interpretation, and are represented in epic poems as contingent and problematic: often contested, sometimes mistaken and confused, this mediation between story and audience puts a pessimistic slant on epic as monumental act of authoritative communication.

Processes of navigation are particularly interesting here: the storyline must move along, but where to?[47] Knowing the way without a map requires the ability either to look down from above or to go ahead in the mind; the guide needs a powerful gaze capable of seeing beyond the normal limits of vision. Calchas in the *Iliad* is renowned for his guidance of the Greek ships to Troy, as well as his knowledge of past and future (1.68–72); but he does not actually help to navigate.[48] The first clear navigational prophecies in the epic tradition are those of Circe and Tiresias in *Odyssey* 10 and 11, but both are concerned more with the direction of the story than with practical instructions for getting anywhere. At 10.487–574 Circe explains to Odysseus that he will need to go to the underworld and focuses on the rituals required. Tiresias' prophecy, too, (11.100–49) is full of instructions rather than visions: they must not eat the cattle of the sun; Odysseus may kill the suitors and must take a second journey far into the interior before he can settle down for a ripe old age.

Phineus at Apollonius' *Argonautica* 2.317–407, in contrast, gives a detailed, ecphrastic description of the Argonauts' journey to come, not just instructions on how (and whether) to attempt to go between the clashing rocks. The first few lines of Phineus' first speech allude to the proem of the whole *Argonautica*.[49] But in contrast to this powerful navigational vision, he

---

[46] See Zissos 2008: 187–8 on the contrast between internal and external prophecy.
[47] Prophets (and gods) often act as guides, but guides are not always prophetic: the helmsman, too, needs the powerful gaze of the navigator. There is often slippage, too, between the question of where to go and the question of what to do in order to get there. But navigational prophecy does seem to form a distinct category in epic: prophetic guides are rarely inspired, instead practical and focused. Navigational questions are much less emotional than other types of prophetic conundrums.
[48] Calchas may have been more of a guide in the *Cypria*; West 2003: 74–5 gives the summary of the argument from Proclus' *Chrestomathy*, in which Calchas guarantees the navigational guidance of Telephus to the Greek leaders. Similarly, the cyclic *Thebaid* (fr. 6 West) calls Amphiaraus 'the eye of the army' (στρατιᾶς ὀφθαλμὸν).
[49] For instance Hunter 1993: 91, Clare 2002: 74.

frequently reminds himself (and us) of his earlier punishment for telling too much (212–13, 311–16, 390–1); finally he finishes, despite Jason's request for more information about the return journey, by requesting them to ask him nothing further (425).⁵⁰ Is this part of Apollonius' poetic of elusiveness, the parsimonious communication between gods and mortals in the poem?⁵¹

Aeneid 3 displays a concentration of navigation and prophecy. Anchises' interpretation of the prophecy of Apollo (3.84–120) leads only to plague at Crete, and a vision from the Penates for Aeneas is needed to correct their aim.⁵² Smith argues that vision trumps words in this episode, but the dream contains both vision and words, and both are open to interpretation. Navigators, like prophets, combine a powerful gaze with a limited understanding of the implications of what they see, and appear particularly vulnerable: Palinurus, whose effective observation of the skies saves Aeneas' fleet from a storm at 5.8–34, and sets them on course for Italy, is the best example of this. He is cut down in the moment of arrival, the one sacrifice who guarantees the safety of the expedition. Further, the two Argonauts who die are Idmon (the prophet) and Tiphys (the helmsman), and the first of Statius' seven to die is Amphiaraus (the prophet).⁵³

Omens and augury

Navigational vision is only one aspect of the interpretation of omens and signs, important from the beginning of the epic tradition: we have seen already Odysseus' narrative of Calchas' interpretation of the omen of the snake and birds in *Iliad* 2 (see above, p.122). Later at 12.200–50, Polydamas and Hector clash over the interpretation of another bird omen (showing the prophet's vulnerability to those with power).⁵⁴ In the *Odyssey* and Apollonius' *Argonautica* omens are interpreted and disputed similarly.⁵⁵

---

⁵⁰ Hunter 1993: 92–4. Clare 2002: 79 suggests that Phineus 'retains some of the reticence of Homeric Circe and Teiresias'.
⁵¹ Knight 1995: 286–7: 'It is characteristic of Apollonius casually to mention a divine intervention after describing its effect.'
⁵² See Smith 2005, who argues that vision trumps words here, but vision does not seem to offer much more hope or understanding than words.
⁵³ In a rather more complex narrative movement, Hypsipyle's direction of the seven to a river to quench their thirst in *Thebaid* 4 diverts them from their journey, and leads to her narration (quenching their desire for knowledge), and indirectly to the death of the baby Opheltes, who was in her care.
⁵⁴ Other omens in the *Iliad*: 8.130–66, in which Nestor correctly interprets a lightning bolt from Jupiter, backed up by thunder, and Diomedes reluctantly believes him; 8.245–52, Zeus sends an omen to the Achaeans; 24.290–321, Priam asks for and receives a positive omen to confirm his plan of going to Achilles.
⁵⁵ *Od.* 2.146–207, 15.154–81, 15.525–34, 19.535–53; AR *Arg.* 1.435–47, 2.911–29, 3.521–63.

These omens are unasked for, but Roman divinatory culture makes the diviner more active: he scrutinises the skies, the behaviour of birds or the bodies of sacrificial victims, in order to answer a specific question. This emphasises the powerful gaze of the diviner who actively delves into the natural world and the minds of the gods. Yet this controlled and scientific divinatory method is combined with passivity. Perhaps the most famous augury scene from epic is in Ennius (72–91 Sk.) in which Romulus and Remus are competing to decide who names and becomes king of Rome. The fragment emphasises their care in looking: *curantes magna cum cura* ('careful with a great care', 80) and the suspense of the watching crowd (87–92), compared to the audience at a chariot race waiting for the consul to give the sign which starts the race. The consul implicitly represents Jupiter who will decide where and when to send birds, and although Romulus does catch sight of the birds (*conspicit*, 99), he is passively given rule (*sibi data esse*, 99).

Omens and auguries are often misread, deceptive and/or ineffective. The omen sent by Juturna and interpreted by Tolumnius at *Aen.* 12.244–56 is interpreted correctly but proceeds from a deceptive god; Tolumnius' penetrative gaze (he goes on to restart the war by piercing the body of a beautiful boy at 12.266–76) is ultimately ineffective because not sanctioned by the correct god. So Turnus' dream of Allecto disguised as Calybe (7.415–59) conveys instructions from Juno which are not at all in his best interest, but are not explicitly wrong either, and lead up to his misinterpretation of the transformation of Aeneas' ships into nymphs (9.126–58). Aeneas' misunderstandings (of the implications of the images in the temple of Juno, for instance; ignorance of the meaning of the shield) only lead to his own distress, rather than a significant narrative outcome, because his aims are made to coincide with divine plans. They do, however, contribute to the Apollonian atmosphere of mortal separation from and misunderstanding of the divine in the *Aeneid*.[56]

Lucan's male divinatory experts in book 1 are validated in the public arena, even though they foretell only destruction. Arruns, an Etruscan diviner, orders the purification of Rome, leading up to an ill-omened sacrifice. Lucan describes the entrails in a great deal of gory detail:

cor iacet, et saniem per hiantes uiscera rimas
emittunt, produntque suas omenta latebras.
quodque nefas nullis inpune apparuit extis,
ecce, uidet capiti fibrarum increscere molem
alterius capitis.
(*Bellum civile* 1.624–8)

---

[56] On prophecy in Silius see Lovatt forthcoming-a.

Omens and augury 143

The heart subsides, and the innards send out pus
through gaping cracks, and the caul betrays its own hiding places.
And an unspeakable thing, which has never before appeared unpunished in entrails,
behold, he sees a mass of segments growing on the lobe,
part of another lobe.

Flab and corruption equate to the state of the Roman senate; gaping and revelation, lack of strong separation, show the cosmos falling in on itself, and the climactic focus is on the malformed liver, which represents the vividly alive figure of Caesar parasitic upon the decaying figure of Pompey. These things Arruns sees but he can speak only in vague doom-laden words (637–8). Instead the body of the sacrificial animal appears to validate the poet's vision of the civil war; with *ecce*, Lucan's readers are drawn in to share the vision of Arruns, watching him as he looks.

Figulus, too, the astrologer who follows Arruns, is described as an authoritative expert who probes the secrets of the universe:

> at Figulus, cui cura deos secretaque caeli
> nosse fuit, quem non stellarum Aegyptia Memphis
> aequaret uisu numerisque <seque>ntibus astra   (*Bellum civile* 1.639–41)

> But Figulus, to whom it was given to know the cares of the gods
> and the secrets of heaven, whom Egyptian Memphis did not equal
> in sight of the stars and numbering the following constellations

His astrological knowledge is represented in visual terms as control over the universe, but his prophecy is presented as a series of ever madder questions, implying that the universe is about to be destroyed in any number of apocalyptic ways (641–58) and revealing only the imminence of war.

Statius' prophetic episode in *Thebaid* 3 uses both augury and extispicy, and draws extensively on Lucan.[57] The doubled prophets (Amphiaraus and Melampus) begin with an extispicy (456–8), and then go up to a mountain to carry out an augury.[58] Statius gives a brief ecphrasis of the mountain (*mons erat*, 460–69) and associates it with Perseus learning to fly:

> inde ferebant
> nubila suspenso celerem temerasse uolatu
> Persea, cum raptos pueri perterrita mater
> prospexit de rupe gradus ac paene secuta est.   (*Thebaid* 3.462–5)

---

[57] See Fantham 2006 and Stover 2009.
[58] The choice of augury might come from Sophocles, *Antigone* 998–1022 in which Tiresias, too, carries out extispicy and augury, and finds the same corrupted innards and carrion birds tearing each other to pieces.

> From there, they used to say, swift Perseus challenged the clouds
> with his hanging flight, while his mother, utterly terrified, looked out
> from the cliff at the snatched steps of the boy and almost followed.

The vertical perspectives of both Perseus and his mother suggest an appropriation of the divine gaze, and the element of challenge in Perseus' flight (*nubila temerasse*) links him to our mortal heroes. Yet the predominant gaze is the female gaze of his mother, watching in terror, excluded from his flight, yet vertiginously longing to join in, as if about to throw herself off the mountain. Later the prophets represent themselves in similar terms as intruding on the realm of the divine:

> piget irrupisse uolantum
> concilia et caelo mentem insertasse uetanti,
> auditique odere deos.   (*Thebaid* 3.549–51)

> They regret having broken in on the councils of the birds
> and intruding their gaze on the mind of heaven which had forbidden it,
> and they hate the gods who heard their prayers.

The prophets appear to be assaulting heaven by looking; they too take on the divine perspective by climbing the mountain. Adrastus has just recently been called the Perseian hero (*Perseius heros*, 441) and the implication must be that both prophets and Argives are reaching above themselves in their desire for epic glory. Later, Amphiaraus, in his speech to Capaneus, combines these two ideas (*Persei montis*, 633, and *superumque inrumpere coetus*, 634).

The augury itself is rich with description and visual language, both Melampus' ecphrasis of ill-omened birds attacking each other (502–15) and Amphiaraus' long narrative of the swans and eagles pre-enacting the events of the *Thebaid* (516–47).[59] Their initial professional confidence is brought out in Amphiaraus' long prayer to Jupiter at 471–98, in which he marshals the power of Hellenistic learning and claims the superiority of augury over every other form of divination. He even calls on unknown and mysterious dark powers (497–8) in the manner of Erichtho. As they set themselves up, the emphasis is on controlled ritual viewing:

> postquam rite diu partiti sidera, cunctas
> perlegere animis oculisque sequacibus auras   (*Thebaid* 3.499–500)

> After they had duly shared out the stars and for a long time
> read thoroughly all the breezes with minds and following eyes

---

[59] Visual language: *uides* (503); *huc aduerte animum* (524); *cernis* (536); *hic … illum … hic … hic … hic … illum … agnosco* (539–47); *certa sub imagine* (548).

Yet this professional, objective detachment falls to pieces in the moment of recognition at 546–7 when the prophet realises that the death he is foretelling is his own. From playing the role of Perseus' mother, he becomes instead Perseus himself, plummeting like Icarus from the sky.

After the augury scene, Melampus retires to the countryside, and Amphiaraus strips off his prophetic insignia (3.566–8), like Aeschylus' Cassandra (see below, p.148). His reticence is depicted in visual terms: he hides from the sight of the people (*aspectum uulgi*, 570), in darkness (*atra | sede tegi*, 571–2); when he finally speaks, he describes himself as called from the shadows (*elicior tenebris*, 623). There is considerable continuity with Lucan's Phemonoe: just as she is made to speak by Appius and by the force of Apollo, Amphiaraus is made to speak by the madness of the crowd.[60] Despite his acknowledgement that the prophecy is in vain, still Amphiaraus wheels out every prophetic tactic for establishing authority, especially eyewitness authority: like Virgil's Sibyl, he has penetrated the secrets of the world (*consulti testor penetralia mundi*, 637), but unlike her he has also broken in on the council of the gods (*superumque irrumpere coetus*, 634). He emphasises what he saw: *quae signa futuri | pertulerim* (639–40); *uidi . . . uidi* (640–1), as well as using the language of prophetic vision: *deus ecce furentibus obstat, | ecce deus!* ('the god, look, stands in your way as you rage, behold the god!', 643–4). Capaneus' response combines a sarcastic suggestion that Amphiaraus is a Lucretian Epicurus figure, who could use his words to influence the world (657–9), while simultaneously using Lucretian language himself to claim that fear created gods (*primus in orbe deos fecit timor!*, 661). The conflict between prophet and warrior over power and persuasion brings out the workings of the prophetic gaze, its power and vulnerability.[61]

Gender and the prophetic gaze

Prophets become objects of the gaze in different ways. Blindness, abjection and social exclusion characterise male prophets, while for female prophets, the prophetic experience itself is eroticised and dangerous: inspiration, like a

---

[60] Though sometimes it works in paradoxical ways: just as Virgil's Apollo forces the Sibyl to speak (*fingitque premendo*, *Aen*. 6.80) so Amphiaraus presses his own mouth shut (*premit ora*, 574).

[61] If Capaneus stimulates Amphiaraus to speak by impugning his virility (*Theb*. 3.611–16), Dido attempts to appropriate the masculine and public gaze of the augur in her private angst, but is instead penetrated by love. At *Aen*. 4.54–73, after Anna advised her to propitiate the gods, Dido sacrifices to various gods including Juno and attempts herself to read the insides of the animals (*Aeneid* 4.60, 63–7). Her power is private and undermined by her own penetration by love. She is *pulcherrima* (most beautiful), the object of our gaze, and madness (*furentem*) objectifies her. Despite the fact that she is the subject in the search for knowledge, she is incapable of learning, and is instead penetrated by madness.

disease (epilepsy?), penetrates the body, taking away the agency of the woman, and in extreme cases threatening her life. Fowler suggests that male poets are also disempowered by the emasculating force of inspiration, being penetrated by an external force, at the whim of female goddesses, unable to maintain the self-control crucial for masculinity.[62] But there is a clear difference between the ways men and women respond to inspiration: for men, madness, and the erotic overtones associated with it in this context, are much less pronounced. Eroticisation brings out the disturbing aspect of divine power behind the prophetic gaze: we never see the gods looking at the women they use, but rather the results. We are aware of their power, disturbed by the effects. In the logic of epic, the incomprehensibility of divine power lies behind the objectification of prophets.

Lucan's Phemonoe, in *Bellum civile* 5, is the clearest example of the inspired prophetess described with the language of rape.[63] Lucan sets up the narrative by describing the violence of inspiration, and comparing it to a volcanic eruption or earthquake (97–101); he explains that the oracle has been silent because death is the result of receiving the god (116–20), with emphasis on the violence to the human body and mind (*pulsusque deorum | concutiunt fragiles animas*, 'the beatings of the gods shake their fragile spirits', 119–20). Not only the god, but also Appius (127) and the priests (145–6) force Phemonoe to enter the inner sanctum and make a truly inspired prophecy. They watch her for the signs of madness, which authorise the prophecy: without these she is not believed to be a true prophet (146–57 lists the attributes missing which mark her prophecy as deceptive). At 165–9 Apollo finally overpowers Phemonoe:

> tandemque potitus
> pectore Cirrhaeo non umquam plenior artus
> Phoebados inrupit Paean mentemque priorem
> expulit atque hominem toto sibi cedere iussit
> pectore.   (*Bellum civile* 5.165–9)

> At last taking control
> never more fully in the Cirrhaean breast of the priestess
> Paean broke into her limbs and pushed out her former
> mind and ordered what was human in her to yield to himself
> in her breast.

This extraordinary display of power and domination is more horrifying than rape: her mind is displaced and she loses her humanity. The god violently

---

[62] Fowler 2002.
[63] See various: most importantly Masters 1993: 91–149; but see also O'Higgins 1988, Sharrock 2002.

penetrates her (*nec verbere solo | uteris et stimulis flammasque in uiscera mergis*, 'nor do you use whip alone, but you also use spurs and plunge flames into her entrails', 5.173–4), and the process comes to a climax with flowing madness, groaning, panting and wailing (5.190–3), an aural display that leaves the reader guessing about the visuals. At the end of the sequence, the lingering madness is focused on the eyes:

> illa feroces
> torquet adhuc oculos totoque uagantia caelo
> lumina, nunc uoltu pauido, nunc torua minaci;   (*Bellum civile* 5.211–13)
>
> She still twists her eyes and her gaze wanders over the whole
> sky, now with a panicked face, now fierce and threatening.

Here the ferocity of her gaze combined with terror brings out the prophet's simultaneous power and vulnerability. Her gaze is threatening, like a berserk hero, and *torquet* evokes the torturing gaze of Jupiter, but wandering and therefore out of control. The overall effect of this paradox equates to a disturbance in the visual field: we know that something powerful is happening, but not what it is or how it works. The desire for knowledge on behalf of the questioner will not be sated; the overall effect is not to reveal what will happen, but to reveal mortal powerlessness in the face of the ultimate otherness of the divine. Finally imagery of light and darkness at 219–20 emphasises her return to normality, only to be undercut as Apollo makes sure she cannot reveal too many secrets, by pouring the waters of Lethe into her insides (221–2). Lucan leaves it unclear whether she will die or not: Appius responds to the nearness of death (*uicinia leti*, 224) but she may well be recovering (*uixque refecta*, 224).

The strong sexualisation of the process of inspiration can be read back onto Virgil's Sibyl.[64] We have already seen at *Aen*. 6.77–80 the moment of her prophetic inspiration; the language of erotic madness (*bacchatur*, 78) and the image of taming are present (*domans*, 80); after the prophecy, at 101, Apollo turns his spurs in her breast (*stimulos sub pectore uertit*). But is this really an eroticisation of prophetic inspiration? Or is it rather that the same language is used to describe possession by the divine power of the prophetic god and the divine power of the erotic god? That both are afflictions which cause the subject to lose control of their reason? Either way, this possession disempowers the prophet and emphasises instead their domination by the violent power of the gods.

The language of taming (*Aen*. 6.80, *domans*; 100–1, *frena ... stimulos*) is literalised in Ovid's Ocyrhoe episode (*Met*. 2.633–75), when the daughter of Chiron is punished for going beyond the limits of prophecy by being turned

---

[64] See for instance Fowler 2002 and Sharrock 2002.

into a mare.⁶⁵ Ovid here comments on the objectification of the female prophet by taking it a stage further. Ocyrhoe decides to learn too much (638–9), going beyond what she should learn from her father into the *fatorum arcana*. The sight of the baby Aesculapius (*aspicit*, 642) causes the prophecy, which leads to her metamorphosis. She too is eroticised both by her madness (*uaticinos concepit mente furores | incaluitque deo*, 'she conceived prophetic madness in her mind and grew hot with the god', 2.640–1) and her transformation: the mare is associated with erotic magic, and horse similes which emphasise the prowess of heroes evoke the waiting mares in the meadows.⁶⁶ The concern with truth and authority associated with prophecy is transferred in a typically Ovidian and disturbing fashion onto the dissonant moment of metamorphosis, which continues to turn Ocyrhoe more completely into an object of the gaze as her body is itemised part by part in its extrusion into equine form.

The sexualisation of the relationship between Apollo and prophetess is authenticated by the myth of Cassandra, who famously suffers at the hands of Apollo, after she accepts his gift of prophecy but refuses his erotic advances. The strongest surviving representation of this is in Aeschylus' *Agamemnon* at 1202–13. The pain of the prophecy itself is emphasised (for instance at 1136, and 1256), and at 1266–76 she strips herself of her prophetic insignia, declaring that Apollo is undressing her. Prophetic possession in this scene seems to be a substitute for sexual possession. Ovid's Sibyl also tells a story of an erotic bargain with Apollo:⁶⁷

> lux aeterna mihi carituraque fine dabatur,
> si mea uirginitas Phoebo patuisset amanti.   (*Metamorphoses* 14.132–3)
>
> Eternal light would be given to me, so that I would lack an end,
> if my virginity would open up to Phoebus as lover.

The emphasis on light and opening act as a counterpart of the language of prophetic knowledge used, for instance, of Virgil's Sibyl. But since she, like Cassandra, refused Apollo, she gained immortality without youth, and will dwindle to nothingness: here Ovid looks aslant at the tradition of violent possession of prophetesses, and deprives the Sibyl of her erotic attractiveness, even as he inserts her words into erotic discourse, leaving her as mere voice. But Ovid's Sibyl and Aeschylus' Cassandra are not straightforwardly epic characters: the *Iliad* is careful to sanitise Cassandra, and Ovid

---

⁶⁵ See Heath 1994.
⁶⁶ On hippomanes as aphrodisiac, see Faraone 1999: 10, 21. On horse similes, see below, Chapter 7, pp.268–73.
⁶⁷ On Ovid's Sibyl, see Due 1974: 38–41, Ellsworth 1988, Baldo 1995: 80–8, Tissol 1997: 177–91, Papaioannou 2005: 43–74, Myers 2009: 76–88.

Blindness, prophecy and the abject 149

notoriously miniaturises, subverts and undercuts Virgil in his little *Aeneid*.[68] Cassandra will be a rape victim more overtly in Quintus Smyrnaeus, but even there the text passes quickly over the scene in the temple of Minerva in which Ajax Oileus rapes her (*PH* 13.420–9, but with the focus on the polluted gaze of Athena, and the maddened state of Ajax).

Epic has an uncomfortable relationship with prophecy; these scenes of violent, sexualised prophetic possession operate at the edge of the genre, and gesture towards a denial of the recuperative political power of prophecy.[69] The authorising function of prophecy and the closeness of prophet to poet make the difficulty of separating the authorising function of prophetic and poetic madness from the emasculating, maddening side of inspiration particularly uneasy.

Blindness, prophecy and the abject

If the female prophet is the eroticised, passive object of the predatory male god, along with the voyeuristic, objectifying gaze of the enquirer and the epic audience, the male prophet can equally become the object of the gaze, often without being able to return it. For there is a signficant connection between prophet figures and the motif of blindness. Blindness seems to be the masculine equivalent of rape; where women pay a sexual price for second sight, men seem to pay with their literal sight. Blindness is also associated with the abject: the emphasis in representations of blinding and blind prophets is often on closeness to death, physical squalor, pain and horror. Apollonius' Phineus, Statius' Oedipus and Quintus' Laocoon embody this complex of ideas. Kristeva's concept of the abject, an irruption of the Real, the pre-linguistic, into ordered lives and texts, is closely related to Lacan's *objet petit a*: not the other, but the desire of the other which is imagined but not comprehensible.[70] Representation of blindness is disturbing, exercises the fascination of a car crash, compelling that we look, but making us wish we could look away. The blindness of the prophet places him outside society and renders him a figure of otherness, as does madness, and for women, rape.[71] Not all prophets are blind, and not all blind

---

[68] On the 'Little Aeneid', see Papaioannou 2005, Myers 2009.
[69] Cassandra about to be raped is evoked at Ovid *Am.* 1.7.17–18, as a comparandum for the mistress when she has been attacked by Ovid.
[70] For Kristeva's ideas of the abject, see Kristeva 1982; for an introduction to Kristeva, Moi 1986; Augoustakis 2010 uses Kristeva's ideas of motherhood to approach Statius and Silius; see 19–20 on abjection.
[71] For a connection between the two, see Bernidaki-Aldous 1990: 57–93, which argues blindness was a punishment for sexual sins. Oedipus is the primary example; Tiresias loses his sight because of his

prophets are abject, but the horror of blindness brings out the uncanny aspect of prophecy, the disturbing pay-off to our desire for knowledge, and to epic's desire for authority.[72]

Phineus in the *Argonautica* of Apollonius Rhodius is vividly depicted as living in poverty, squalor and misery. Where Valerius sanitises and dignifies the figure of the prophet, turning him into a majestic old man, Apollonius focuses on the physicality of old age, near starvation and disability.[73] In Apollonius' version of the myth Apollo granted him the gift of prophecy, but Zeus punished him for prophesying the future too completely, by blinding him and making him the victim of the Harpies: bird–women who descend on any food and eat almost all of it, leaving the remains foully polluted, so he is forced to survive in horrific squalor and semi-starvation.[74] As he goes to meet the Argonauts he is vividly described:

> ὀρθωθεὶς δ' εὐνῆθεν, ἀκήριον ἠύτ' ὄνειρον,
> βάκτρῳ σκηπτόμενος ῥικνοῖς ποσὶν ἦε θύραζε,
> τοίχους ἀμφαφόων· τρέμε δ' ἅψεα νισσομένοιο
> ἀδρανίῃ γήραϊ τε· πίνῳ δέ οἱ αὐσταλέος χρὼς
> ἐσκλήκει, ῥινοὶ δὲ σὺν ὀστέα μοῦνον ἔεργον.
> ἐκ δ' ἐλθὼν μεγάροιο καθέζετο γοῦνα βαρυνθεὶς
> οὐδοῦ ἐπ' αὐλείοιο· κάρος δέ μιν ἀμφεκάλυψεν
> πορφύρεος, γαῖαν δὲ πέριξ ἐδόκησε φέρεσθαι
> νειόθεν, ἀβληχρῷ δ' ἐπὶ κώματι κέκλιτ' ἄναυδος.
> οἱ δέ μιν ὡς εἴδοντο, περισταδὸν ἠγερέθοντο
> καὶ τάφον.
> (AR *Argonautica* 2.197–207)

> He got up from his bed like an insubstantial dream,
> and leaning on a staff, went to the door on his shrivelled feet,
> feeling along the walls. His body was trembling with the
> weakness of old age. His dusty flesh was dried up with dirt,
> and his skin kept together nothing but bones.
> Coming out of the room, he sank down to his weary knees

---

transgressive vision of Pallas; Thamyris competes with the Muses in song and threatens to rape them if victorious; when he loses, the Muses both blind him and make him forget his song. For a broader typology of blindness as punishment see Tatti-Gartziou 2010.

[72] On blindness as an idea, see Barasch 2001; in Greek literature, see Buxton 1980, Bernidaki-Aldous 1990, Létoublon 2010.

[73] On the episode see especially excellent commentary by Cuypers 1997: 193–305; also Hunter 1993: 90–6, Knight 1995: 169–76, Clare 2002: 73–84.

[74] On other versions of the myth, see Cuypers 1997: 202–9. Apollonius' is the first surviving version, but Hesiod told about the Harpies, and both Sophocles and Aeschylus wrote plays about Phineus. The reasons for his punishment vary from telling Phrixus the way (Hesiod *Catalogue of Women*), choosing prophecy over eyesight (Hesiod *Cat.*), or blinding his own sons because their stepmother persuaded him (Sophocles). Since Apollonius' version, which links Phineus to Prometheus and Tiresias, does not seem to have much resonance in the later tradition (apart from Valerius Flaccus), Cuypers suggests that he may have made up the idea of being punished for abusing his prophetic powers.

> at the threshold of the court; a black dizziness immersed him,
> the earth beneath him seemed to swirl around,
> and unable to speak, he lay weak in the arms of unconsciousness.
> When they saw him thus, they gathered around him and gazed
> in amazement.

His state is so horrific that he becomes a freak to be stared at. He is also like a dream: Cuypers 1997 *ad loc.* points to the ambiguity of ἀκήριον which can mean both 'lifeless' and 'deathless', suggesting either that he looks dead like a ghost in a dream or that he looks paradoxically like a ghost who is not dead. He is in a state of living death.[75] The encounter with Phineus reminds both us and the Argonauts of our own mortality. Blindness has many associations with death: the epic formulae for dying frequently contain the idea of 'loss of light/sight'.[76] This description of Phineus invites us to view him as an object, to watch voyeuristically as he struggles out of his bed, and take in every detail of squalor and bodily disintegration,[77] but also asks us to experience what it is like to be Phineus from the inside, hearing the arrival of the Argonauts, feeling the walls, the trembling of the limbs, the earth spinning as he falls to the ground. The passage is focalised simultaneously through the Argonauts and through Phineus himself. We treat him as an object and experience what it is like to become an object. Phineus is a source of knowledge and guidance, and a poet figure, as well as a disturbing spectacle of abjection and bodily disintegration.

In *Thebaid* 8, Phineus is used as an image for Statius' Oedipus, rejoicing in the horrific destruction he has caused, just as Phineus rejoiced when the Argonauts rescued him (8.254–8).[78] While Statius' Oedipus is not a prophet, he is a poet figure: his curse initiates the events of the poem (1.46–87), and at 11.592 the whole fratricidal war is his *opus*.[79] His state of living death is continually emphasised, coming to a climax with his comparison to Charon at 11.587–93. Oedipus' exclusion from society and abjection are brought into relief when he makes his unaccustomed foray to join the celebratory banquet in book 8: he is 'always unseen and hiding in his grim lair' (*semper inaspectum diraque in sede latentem*, 241); his white hair is black with dirt, and it hangs loose around his filthy face (*canitiem nigram squalore sordida fusis | ora comis*

---

[75] Hunter 1993: 91.
[76] Bernidaki-Aldous 1990: 11–20 gives many examples from tragedy; Graziosi 2002: 143 does the same for epic. Phineus is a version of Tiresias (as well as a version of Circe) and the journey through the Symplegades is like a journey to the underworld; see Knight 1995: 175, Clare 2002: 75 n.74 on the journey's chthonic colouring.
[77] Later the Argonauts even wash the old man (2.301–3).
[78] On this simile, see Lovatt forthcoming-b.   [79] On Statius' Oedipus, see Ganiban 2007: 24–43.

laxasse manu, 243–4); his blinded eyes are marked by still undried blood (*quin hausisse dapes insiccatumque cruorem | deiecisse genis*, 246–7). Statius' Oedipus is a figure of horror, a walking monument of mortality and the impotence of even the politically powerful in the face of the gods and fate.

Blindness is also used as a punishment in the Laocoon episode of Quintus Smyrnaeus (*PH* 12.389–499).[80] Quintus' variation on the story seems to build on Virgil's version (*Aen.* 2.40–56, 199–231), in which Laocoon is a priest (*sacerdos*, 201), who immediately sees through the ruse of the horse (45–48) as if he can penetrate it with his gaze, and then literally penetrates it with his spear throw (50–3). In the *Aeneid* he is killed along with his sons in the poisonous embrace of two enormous serpents, who are never explicitly sent by Athene, but retire to her shrine (225–7). In the *Posthomerica*, Laocoon urges the Trojans to burn the horse, rather than attempting to penetrate it, but his first and immediate punishment is blindness, described in lavish detail:

> μέλαινα δέ οἱ περὶ κρατὶ
> νὺξ ἐχύθη· στυγερὸν δὲ κατὰ βλεφάρων πέσεν ἄλγος,
> σὺν δ' ἔχεεν λασίῃσιν ὑπ' ὀφρύσιν ὄμματα φωτός·
> γλῆναι δ' ἀργαλέῃσι πεπαρμέναι ἀμφ' ὀδύνῃσι
> ῥιζόθεν ἐκλονέοντο· περιστρωφῶντο δ' ὀπωπαὶ
> τειρόμεναι ὑπένερθεν· ἄχος δ' ἀλεγεινὸν ἵκανεν
> ἄχρι καὶ ἐς μήνιγγας ἰδ' ἐγκεφάλοιο θέμεθλα.
> Τοῦ δ' ὁτὲ μὲν φαίνοντο μεμιγμένοι αἵματι πολλῷ
> ὀφθαλμοί, ὁτὲ δ' αὖτε δυσαλθέα γλαυκιόωντες·
> πολλάκι δ' ἔρρεον, οἷον ὅτε στυφελῆς ἀπὸ πέτρης
> εἴβεται ἐξ ὀρέων νιφετῷ πεπαλαγμένον ὕδωρ.
> Μαινομένῳ δ' ἤικτο καὶ ἔδρακε διπλόα πάντα
> αἰνὰ μάλα στενάχων. Καὶ ἔτι Τρώεσσι κέλευεν
> οὐδ' ἀλέγιζε μόγοιο· φάος δέ οἱ ἐσθλὸν ἄμερσε
> δῖα θεή· λευκαὶ δ' ⟨ἄρ'⟩ ὑπὸ βλέφαρ' ἔσταν ὀπωπαὶ
> αἵματος ἐξ ὀλοοῖο.   (*Posthomerica* 12.400–15)

> Around his head was spread
> the blackness of night. A horrible pain shot through his eyelids
> and disordered the eyes beneath his shaggy brows.
> Stabbed with piercing pangs up from their roots,
> his pupils grew confused. His eyeballs started rolling
> with the deep affliction, and agonizing pain
> penetrated the membranes at the base of his brain.

---

[80] While he is not strictly a prophet, he shares many prophetic characteristics: a special connection with the gods, the ability apparently to see beyond normal barriers and to understand realities behind appearances. On this episode, see Gärtner 2009. He is called *mantis* by Apollodorus, in a section in which he seems to be summarising the cyclic *Iliou Persis*: West 2003: 144–5.

> His eyes appeared alternatively extremely bloodshot
> and, in contrast, covered with a sickly glaze.
> From them came a frequent discharge, just like water
> sprinkled with snow which flows from a rugged rock in the hills.
> He seemed to be demented, seeing everything double
> and uttering dreadful groans. But still he exhorted the Trojans,
> disregarding his misery. Robbed of their blessed light
> by the goddess, his eyes grew fixed and white beneath their lids
> after the fatal bleeding.

The process of blinding moves from the outside of the eyes deep within the brain; an almost medical gaze makes his eyes objects of scientific interest, almost as if no longer part of a person. He suffers some of the symptoms of inspiration (rolling eyeballs, pain) along with symptoms of madness (seeing double). The rush of water and the madness of prophecy suggest an emasculation: he is liquefied and out of control. His eyes themselves become omens: blindness here trumps death in the Virgilian narrative. Even after this, Laocoon does not give up his resistance to Athena (444–5), and now the serpents come from a dark, inaccessible cave (449–53). Their arrival in Troy induces panic (463–72) and paralysis (477–8) among the watching Trojans, an internal audience responding to the disturbance of the gaze. Laocoon and his sons are the objects of the assaultive gaze of the serpents (and implicitly the gods), and he cannot even watch his sons die, although they stretch their arms out to him (476–7). Finally the Trojans build an empty monument for the sons on the remaining trace of the serpents in front of the shrine of Apollo, as Laocoon sheds blind tears (480–99). The emptiness of the monument encapsulates the impotence of both blind man and mortal viewers. This entire scene, in both Quintus and Virgil, creates a deceptive omen which forces the Trojans towards their destruction. By adding the motif of blindness, Quintus makes Laocoon a much clearer parallel for Cassandra, and ties him in with the tradition of blindness as punishment for seeing too much, which we have already seen in the cases of Phineus and Tiresias.

Not all blind figures are abject: Demodocus the Odyssean poet, famously a model for Homer, is an honoured and almost divinised object of the gaze.[81] His blindness still separates him from society, but in a positive way. The epithets of Demodocus emphasise his fame (περικλυτός, *Od.* 8.83, 367, 521) and his closeness to divinity (θεῖος, 8.47, 87, 534). The audience at the banquet and the readers of Homer (or his audience at their banquet) watch at length as arrangements are made for him. Demodocus is famous, praised

---

[81] Graziosi 2002: 140–1 on his closeness to the divine and distance from humanity.

by Odysseus as representative of the race of poets and inspired by the Muses (479–98), but equally he too is a spectacle.

Like a statue or an image on a screen, the blind cannot return the gaze of those who look at them. Demodocus' status as a poet rescues him from the poverty and squalor of the blind in the ancient world.[82] If Homer is envisaged as blind, does this image relate to the ancient idea of epic? Is 'objectivity' partly a function of otherworldliness? Or is the otherness, the abjection of blind figures in post-Homeric epic rather an effect of their close connections with tragedy? Oedipus is a quintessentially tragic figure; Phineus had an alternative life in tragedy;[83] Tiresias, too, is more famous for his roles in Sophocles than in Ovid and Statius. Yet these figures have close connections with the persona of the epic poet. I want to finish this chapter by looking at Tiresias in Statius, his blindness and his use of necromancy (the art of foretelling the future by raising the dead), and, in apposition, another powerful poet figure, this time sighted and female: Lucan's transgressive and monstrous Erictho.

Necromancy

Lucan's Erichtho has been read as a figure of the poet and the hero of the poem.[84] As a witch, she has extensive control over the cosmos, heavenly, infernal and earthly, and she is brought tangentially into the action in the build-up to the battle of Pharsalia by Sextus Pompey's desire to know more about the outcome of the battle. The general description of Thessalian witchcraft (*BC* 6.434–506) focuses more on voice than gaze.[85] Erichtho's personal specialities (507–68) cluster mainly around touch: she penetrates bodies, but with her hands rather than her eyes.[86] She is the incarnation of abjection, a walking accumulation of bodily horrors, and the object of our gaze in her monstrousness (515–20), but when Sextus Pompey finds her she

---

[82] Both Bernidaki-Aldous 1990: 33–47 and Graziosi 2002: 150–9 emphasise the links between blindness, poverty and helplessness.

[83] See Gantz 1993: 349–56 for tragic fragments and other early references to Phineus. Aeschylus *Phineus* and Sophocles *Phineus A*, *Tympanistai* and *Phineus B* (probably) fragments. Hesiod *Cat.* fr. 157MW; *Megalai Ehoiai* fr. 254MW; Asklepiades 12F31; Diodorus 4.43.3–44.4; Cyzicene Epigrams *Palatine Anthology* 3.4; Odyssey Scholia Σ*Od.* 12.69 = 12F31; Apollodorus *Library* 1.9.21, 3.15.3.

[84] Johnson 1987, O'Higgins 1988, Masters 1993. See also Ogden 2001: 144–6 on Erichtho, 149–59 on Roman attitudes to necromancy.

[85] *carmina*, 444; *uox*, 445; *tetigit murmur*, 448; *carmine*, 452; *excantata*, 458; *audito carmine*, 463; *carmen*, 480; *carmina*, 497.

[86] Listening and speaking: *audire*, 513; *uoce . . . carmen . . . audire*, 527–8; *infudit murmura*, 567; touch: *rapit*, 534; *colligit*, 537; *inmergitque manus oculis gaudetque gelatos | effodisse orbes*, 541–2; *uolsit*, 546; *morsus*, 549; *erumpat*, 555; *extrahitur*, 558; *uolsit*, 561; *abscidit*, 562.

is sitting on a cliff above the battlefield, casting a spell to make sure the battle does not take place elsewhere, more like a god than a woman on the walls (573–87). She brings together divine power and feminine subversion: the emphasis on touch rather than vision may well represent a feminisation of the prophetic process.[87] This episode brings out the extremity of prophetic inspiration; Erichtho is the inspiring force, who controls not just the prophet but also the universe, while the corpse is as passive as can be.[88] Erichtho too performs a sort of katabasis: Sextus Pompey's request echoes Virgil (*Elysias resera sedes*, 600); the setting is a cavern, represented as close to the underworld (642–51); the moment when she is called *uates* is as Lucan speculates about whether or not she has actually gone down to see the dead or brought the underworld up (651–3, including a rare moment of Erichtho as subject of the gaze, *aspiciat*, 653). Mostly she is like part of the underworld that has strayed into earth: she watches Sextus' terror (658) and, like the Sibyl, tells him not to be afraid, but unlike the Sibyl it is because even if she showed him all the horrors of the underworld, none would be as horrific as she herself is (662–6). She penetrates the underworld with her voice and tongue (685–94), and when the ghost of the dead soldier hesitates to go back into the body, as Phemonoe attempts to evade inspiration, Erichtho's threats to the gods of the underworld are threats of exposure to the gaze (732–8) along with the revelation of secrets (739–42). For instance:

> tibi, pessime mundi
> arbiter, inmittam ruptis Titana cavernis,
> et subito feriere die.   (*Bellum civile* 6.742–4)

> For you, worst ruler of the world,
> I will send the Titan in to your broken caverns,
> and you will be struck with sudden day.

Finally the power of the unnamed god beneath all gods is visual: *qui Gorgona cernit apertam* ('He who looks at the Gorgon uncovered', 746). The corpse is the object of Erichtho's power but as *uates* witnesses the action and authenticates her claims. Stupefaction on returning to life (760) is transformed into vision and revelation of the underworld (*aspexi*, 778; *uidi*, 785; *uidimus*, 792; *uidi*, 795). This passage strikingly inverts the patterns of prophetic inspiration, bringing power up from below, and using darkness to obtain knowledge; it also inverts the gender dynamics of prophetic inspiration. Epic will never be the same after Lucan.

---

[87] On Erichtho and women, see Finiello 2005.
[88] O'Higgins 1988 points out that both are called *uates* (corpse at 628 and 812; Erichtho at 651) and treats them as a prophetic team, but in terms of the gaze there is a clear division between them.

Statius, for instance, follows Lucan with an important necromancy episode, featuring Tiresias, who is a good figure with which to bring together the threads of this chapter. Tiresias is probably the best-known blind prophet of antiquity; he appears in many texts, epic, tragic and other, most importantly Callimachus *Hymn* 5. The best-known version of the myth is that in Ovid's *Metamorphoses* 3.316–38 in which his vision of snakes mating causes him to cross and recross gender boundaries. As both man and woman he is called to resolve a dispute between Jupiter and Juno about who has the most pleasure in sex. When he replies that women do, she punishes him by blinding him. Jupiter, however, compensates him by giving him prophetic vision and fame as a prophet. Ovid once more puts the seams of epic on display, making the compensatory links between inner sight and literal vision only too concrete.

Ovid does not dwell for long on the story of Tiresias, but instead uses him as a structural feature in the narrative of book 3: Narcissus, Pentheus, Actaeon, Semele; the stories in *Metamorphoses* 3 are thematically related by vision and transgression, and the blind Tiresias functions as an emblem and structural linchpin in the book, in his knowledge and authority a version of the all-knowing narrator, but not actually telling the stories, merely witnessing them. He crosses both gender and genre. In epic, he is a non-epic figure, and his importance in Ovid and Statius reflects not just their Theban emphases, but the pervasive influence of tragedy in both.

Statius gives us a virtuoso exploration of the paradoxes of blind vision in the necromancy of *Theb.* 4.405–645. In the *Thebaid*, Tiresias is not the one called up from the underworld to make a prophecy, but rather the person who carries out the necromancy, complete with his own attendant (his daughter Manto) and the darker equivalent of Odysseus, Eteocles. Eteocles calls upon Tiresias for reassurance in the face of Theban panic at the approaching Argives. He is immediately given the tag *uates* (407) and his blindness itself is characterised as wisdom (*tenebrasque sagaces*, 407). The preparations for necromancy are described in detail and Tiresias, despite his blindness, is a hands-on seer: he prepares the Lethean rites (414–16), chooses the location and gives orders for sacrifice (443–6), garlands the sacrificial animals with his own hand (451). At 463 Manto takes over, but Tiresias continues to be in charge of proceedings despite relying on senses other than vision. Statius self-consciously plays with this paradox at 468–72:

> atque ipse sonantia flammis
> uirgulta et tristes crepuisse ut sensit aceruos
> Tiresias (illi nam plurimus ardor anhelat
> ante genas impletque cauos uapor igneus orbes)
> exclamat (tremuere rogi et uox terruit ignem): (*Thebaid* 4.468–72)

> And he himself senses the sticks crackling in the flames
> and the grim heaps roaring, Tiresias (for great heat
> gasps before his cheeks and fiery steam fills his hollow eyes)
> shouts out (and the pyres trembled and his voice terrified the fire):

The image of his empty eye-sockets filled with heat from the fires turns the eyes into vehicles of another sense, and makes the reader voyeuristically aware of his blindness. *Sonantia* ('sounding') and *crepuisse* ('roaring') already prepare us for his perception through senses other than sight, but the image of heat on his face is particularly intimate, while alluding to madness to come. His voice is enough to terrify the fires themselves. Statius' Tiresias is a powerful and sinister figure.

After Tiresias makes his first speech, Eteocles, like Sextus Pompey, is terrified (488–99). Both Tiresias and Manto are not afraid *quippe in corde deus* ('because the god is in their hearts', 490). The epic simile of the hunter waiting for a lion in terror (494–9) emphasises Eteocles' lack of epic stature. Manto's ecphrastic description makes her both Tiresias' guide and deputy (*o nostrae regimen uiresque senectae*, 'O guide and strength of my old age', 536). She enacts a revelation:

> panditur Elysium chaos, et telluris opertae
> dissilit umbra capax, siluaeque et nigra patescunt
> flumina: (*Thebaid* 4.520–2)

> The Elysian chaos lies open and the capacious shadows
> of the dark land jump apart, both the woods and the black rivers
> lie revealed.

This is a vision of things which should not be seen, emphasising the power of the prophetic gaze (and doing precisely what Erichtho had threatened to do: opening the underworld to our view). She brings before our eyes the rivers which structure the underworld: Acheron spewing up blue–black sand, Phlegethon rolling black fires and smoking, Styx separating shades from the underworld. Hades himself, the ruler of the underworld, surrounded by servants, furies and Persephone, is capped with a triumphant claim of visual power: *cerno*. The scene she describes is an interplay of powerful gazes, with Manto herself, and through her Tiresias, Eteocles and the reader, ultimately, looking down. Hades sits on his throne and presumably looks down at Persephone on her couch and the surrounding minions. 'Black Death' (*atra Mors*) is described as sitting on the look-out post (*in speculis*, 528), counting silent people for his master. Minos, the Gortynian judge, scrutinises the lives of those before him.

But Manto ceases her account of the underworld with a self-conscious *praeteritio*, like the Sibyl's declaration of poetic inadequacy. She is no Virgil and will not describe the punishments of Tartarus. But Tiresias makes this evasion an assertion of poetic originality: he orders her to avoid the paths trodden by the common crowd (*ne uulgata mihi*, 537), in an equally Callimachean and Horatian quip. Further, he carries on the list with Sisyphus, Tantalus (neither mentioned by name, to ram home the point), Tityos and Ixion. For he has literally seen them all before:

> ipse etiam, melior cum sanguis, opertas
> inspexi sedes, Hecate ducente, priusquam
> obruit ora deus totamque in pectora lucem
> detulit. (*Thebaid* 4.540–3)

> I myself, when my blood was better, have inspected
> the dark palaces, with Hecate leading me, before
> the god destroyed my eyes and brought all light
> into my chest.

This seems to rewrite the myth of Tiresias completely, or to suggest that he is an intertextual reincarnation of Virgil's Sibyl: he was already a *uates* if Hecate could lead him down to the underworld; prophecy then comes before blindness, in this version, more like Phineus, and not like the version in either Ovid or Callimachus. The pair together form a version of Virgil's Sibyl. Manto takes on the narratorial role, and even takes charge of the words (*carmenque serit*, 'she sows a song', 549), specifically compared to Medea and Circe. Her catalogue of Theban ghosts is a recapitulation of Ovid's Theban stories in *Metamorphoses* 3, told like the ecphrasis of a frieze. At this moment, Tiresias' inner vision transcends sight and he takes over:

> talia dum patri canit intemerata sacerdos,
> illius elatis tremefacta adsurgere uittis
> canities tenuisque impelli sanguine uultus.
> nec iam firmanti baculo nec uirgine fida
> nititur, erectusque solo, 'desiste canendo,
> nata,' ait, 'externae satis est mihi lucis, inertes
> discedunt nebulae, et uultum niger exuit aer.
> umbrisne an supero demissus Apolline complet
> spiritus? en uideo quaecumque audita.' (*Thebaid* 4.579–87)

> While the unviolated priestess is singing such things to her father,
> his white hair, trembling, stands up with fillets raised
> and his thin face is urged by blood.
> No longer does he lean on the strengthening staff or on the faithful
> virgin, but stands erect on the ground, 'Cease from singing,

daughter,' he said, 'there is enough external light for me, the inactive mists are leaving, and the black air strips off my face.
Does breath fill me from the shades or sent down from Apollo above? Look, I see whatever I was hearing.'

As with Phineus in Valerius Flaccus, Tiresias' old age is transformed by inspiration: he no longer needs to be supported by staff or guide. Yet when he describes it, the revelation is not inner vision trumping outer blindness, but outer blindness actually dissolving. It is external light which he sees; the clouds leave and the black air goes from his face. This is the *enargeia* of epic narrative taken to extremes: Manto has so successfully involved her audience that he can now actually see what she was talking about. But her compressed visual and literary allusions were the very opposite of *enargeia*: and the consequence of drawing her audience into her text is that she now loses control of the text and is not allowed to carry on singing. Tiresias authoritatively takes over, his supernatural vision trumping hers. What is more, he does not restrict himself to describing what he sees: he interprets and makes prophetic judgements. The Argive ghosts are sorrowful and have downturned eyes (*sed ecce | maerent Argolici deiecto lumine manes!*, 587–8); their grief signifies Theban victory: *auguror hinc Thebis belli meliora*. ('I prophesy from this the better of the war for Thebes.', 592). In the final lines of the speech he takes on the mantle of Virgil's Sibyl: they are better off dead, because what remains is *bella horrida nobis, | atque iterum Tydeus* ('Horrific wars for us, and Tydeus again/another Tydeus', 601–2).

Later at 10.589–605, as Thebes seems to be on the point of falling to the Argives, Tiresias provides another internal repetition, a second prophecy, leading to a second war. He represents himself as an Amphiaraus figure, whose warnings have been ignored (592–3), and gestures towards refusing to make a prophecy, but his imagination of enduring the sack of the city as a blind man convinces him to speak:

'te tamen, infelix,' inquit, 'perituraque Thebe,
si taceam, nequeo miser exaudire cadentem
Argolicumque oculis haurire uacantibus ignem.'   (*Thebaid* 10.594–6)

'But you, unlucky,' he said, 'and about to perish, Thebes,
if I am silent, I will not be able to bear hearing your wretched fall
and drinking in the Argive fire with my empty eyes.'

This image of drinking in the fire with his blind eyes strikingly anticipates the effects of the pyromancy. After Manto describes the appearance of the flames to him, his interpretation takes the form of an inspired prophecy (recapitulating both Idmon and Mopsus from Valerius Flaccus 1, as well as Phineus' revivification):

> ille coronatos iamdudum amplectitur ignes,
> fatidicum sorbens uultu flagrante uaporem.
> stant tristes horrore comae, uittasque trementes
> caesaries insana leuat: diducta putares
> lumina consumptumque genis rediisse nitorem. (*Thebaid* 10.604–8)

> He was already embracing the wreathed fires, and had been for a while,
> absorbing prophetic vapour with a flaming face.
> His grim hair stands in horror, the mad locks raise
> the trembling fillets: you would think that his eyes were opened
> and the consumed radiance had returned to his cheeks.

He shows the signs of madness, which give him life once more, and we look at him as if he is the object of ecphrasis. Figuratively he seems already to be witnessing the destruction of the city. His masculine self-sufficiency is compromised by his reliance on Manto, and this prophetic team crosses the gender boundaries (as Tiresias himself famously did in myth). Manto, Tiresias' daughter and surrogate eyes, shares her father's inspiration and is called *Phoebea uirgo* at 488: belonging to Apollo, but not raped by him. At the moment Tiresias interrupts her narrative with his own supernatural sight, she is called *intemerata sacerdos* ('unviolated priestess', 579). Tiresias suffers inspiration; Manto merely relays what she sees, like Erichtho's corpse.[89] She is a channel for information not even affected by the process of passing it on. She has neither the special authority nor the ambivalent suffering of the inspired prophet. It is as if her vision does not belong to her, even though her narrative is that of the artful and allusive poet. Relegated to playing supporting act, her prophetic and poetic gaze is not validated by suffering and loss.[90]

Tiresias is not abject, and Manto is not threatened by violence, but they exist within the dysfunctional tragic society of Thebes, and the dysfunctional epics of Ovid and Statius, and they are a channel for further violence in the narrative. Like other prophets, Tiresias is both powerful and powerless, begged by Eteocles but reliant on Manto; even better than Erictho, but no more effective in his prophecies than Phemonoe. He is the subject and the object of the Mulveyan gaze, and his sight itself encapsulates the

---

[89] In the cyclic *Epigoni*, Manto becomes an Andromache figure, sent to Apollo at Delphi as a votive offering by the successful Argives, being made to marry and founding a city (fr. 4 West).
[90] Perhaps she might still be a figure for Statius: the Statius who scorns himself for not being brave enough to sing a toga'd song in his praise of Lucan in *Silv.* 2.7.

uncanny nature of prophecy: the lack at the heart of epic authority, the ecphrastic failure of epic vision. Called upon for reassurance, Tiresias rather provides the opportunity for further destabilisation of his own poetic world.

Conclusions

In this chapter we have seen the rich complexity of epic prophecy, and the importance of vision for it: both prophet and poet can offset blindness with insight; their vision reaches parts of the universe not seen by other mortals (or genres). In both time and space, they have an otherworldly connection with the divine gaze. Yet prophets pay a price for their vision, and epic pays a price for its authoritative prophetic role. The relationship between prophet (male and female) and divine inspiration is ambivalent and complex just like the relationship between poet and muse. To possess a powerful gaze which sees further into the reality of things is a double-edged sword in the ancient world. There is a price to pay for power of vision: possessing the gaze exposes the viewer to danger. This price is gendered: for male prophets inner vision is usually set against blindness and social exclusion; for female prophets the price paid is usually sexual. The safety of anonymity in the darkened cinema is not available for the ancient viewer, who is more like the spectator in the amphitheatre, always potentially part of the spectacle. The constant unease in the face of the divine gaze is brought out strongly by the distortion in the field of vision created by the prophet's uncanny visions and his or her madness, abjection or violation.

CHAPTER 5

Ecphrasis and the Other

    Haec uestis priscis hominum uariata figuris
heroum mira uirtutes indicat arte.
namque fluentisono prospectans litore Diae
Thesea cedentem celeri cum classe tuetur
indomitos in corde gerens Ariadna furores,
necdum etiam sese quae uisit uisere credit,
ut pote fallaci quae tum primum excita somno
desertam in sola miseram se cernat harena.
immemor at iuuenis fugiens pellit uada remis,
irrita uentosae linquens promissa procellae.
Quem procul ex alga maestis Minois ocellis,
saxea ut effigies bacchantis, prospicit, eheu,
prospicit et magnis curarum fluctuat undis,
non flauo retinens subtilem uertice mitram,
non contecta leui uelatum pectus amictu,
non tereti strophio lactentis uincta papillas,
omnia quae toto delapsa e corpore passim
ipsius ante pedes fluctus salis adludebant.   (Catullus 64.50–67)

This cloak, decorated with ancient figures of men,
displays the manly virtues of heroes with wondrous skill.
For looking out from the wave-sounding shore of Samos,
at Theseus departing with his swift fleet she gazes,
bearing untamed furies in her heart, Ariadne,
and not yet even does she believe that she herself sees what she sees,
since only just woken from deceiving sleep
she sees herself, abandoned and wretched, on the lonely sand.
But unmindful, that young man, fleeing, forces the shallows with his oars,
leaving empty promises for the windy storms.
At him far away through the sea-weed, Minos' daughter with her sad eyes,
like the stony statue of a bacchant, gazes, alas,
gazes and tosses on great waves of sorrow,
with her blonde hair not held in its finely woven head-dress,
with her chest not covered, veiled by its light garment,

Ecphrasis and the Other 163

with her milky breasts not bound by a smooth wrapping,
everything had slipped everywhere from her whole body
and the salty waves were playing with them at her feet.

Is this the most famous passage of gazing in Latin literature?[1] Not epic, exactly, but closely related to epic, and important for the exploration of viewing and epic ecphrasis.[2] Catullus' longest poem notoriously inverts the relationship between ecphrasis and narrative characteristic of epic: the set-piece description of the coverlet on the marriage bed of Peleus and Thetis takes over the poem, becomes more important than the marriage itself.[3] We have here the beginning of the description of this work of art, one that lays claim to the territory of epic with the phrase *heroum uirtutes* ('the virtues/courage/manliness of heroes').[4] It displays, however, not the feats of a man, but the body of a woman: Ariadne, abandoned by Theseus on the island of Naxos, after she betrayed her father and helped Theseus kill the Minotaur.[5] This passage plays complicated games with art and text, focalisation and objectification. Fitzgerald sees these games as fundamentally cinematic.[6] On the one hand, Ariadne is very much a living person, from whose perspective we too look out over the waves. She is the subject of the sentences,

---

[1] The most satisfying reading of Catullus 64 as a poem of gazing is Fitzgerald 1995: 140–68. Further reflections, and comparison with Campanian wall-painting, in Elsner 2007.
[2] Fitzgerald 1995 approaches the poem in terms of myth and reality, alienation and separation, Greek and Roman: 'The mythical world, associated here with a great technological feat (sailing), is the object of a visual longing that is richly satisfied by the representational virtuosity of the poem, at the same time as the poem thematizes the desiring gaze in its narrative, producing a complex interplay between viewer and viewed, between the act of representation and the action represented. The matter of Catullus' epyllion is Greek myth, so the Roman reader is doubly removed from the world of heroes, both temporally and culturally; and yet counterpointing this removal is the position of the conquering Roman as the confident consumer and appropriator of Greek culture.' (167) The term 'epyllion' is not as fashionable as it once was, and much of the literature emphasises the continuity with epic, as well as the rivalry. For instance, Lyne 1978 describes epyllion as 'brief, highly wrought *epos* which more or less ostentatiously dissociates itself from traditional *epos*, concentrating on unheroic incidentals in the sagas of heroes, or on heroines as opposed to heroes, or on otherwise offbeat subject matter; employing a narrative technique that was often wilfully individual and selective, and yet largely maintaining epic language, metre and style' (172–3).
[3] The key narrative and ecphrastic reading is Laird 1993.
[4] The Argonautic voyage at the beginning, and the ending, with its vivid prophecy of the destructive feats of Achilles, insist that engagement with epic is central to Catullus' agenda.
[5] Fitzgerald 1995 focuses on the sensuous surface of the poem and engages with its bodily imagery: 'So from the half-naked bodies of the nymphs that mark the wonder of the first sea voyage to the sacrifice of Polyxena in honor of the dead Achilles, it is the woman's body on which the exploits of the heroes are registered and whose vulnerability compensates the viewer's debilitating longing for what has passed.' (165)
[6] For instance, on lines 63–7: 'the incantatory rhythm of the first three lines, with their subtle variations of grammatical structure, seems to hold Ariadne in a soft focus as the camera turns around her in slow motion ... The language of film immediately suggests itself in connection with this passage, which includes a closeup (Ariadne's nipples, 62) and even the thoroughly filmic shot of the water playing with the fallen clothes.' (147) This is not a natural move, but is determined by Fitzgerald's use of gaze theory, mainly Silverman 1988a, though he does also consider the relationship with ancient art. Elsner 2007 examines ecphrasis and art together as two semiotic systems that work in parallel; his analysis of the visual representations of Ariadne and their use of various viewing positions, internal and external,

while Theseus, in the accusative, is the object of her gaze. We experience her disorientation and emotion; the adjectives which describe Theseus are also focalised through Ariadne; he is *immemor* ('unmindful') and *fugiens* ('fleeing') and not much of a hero to her. Yet she is equally the object of our gaze, also in the accusative (*desertam*) as she looks at herself. At *saxea ut effigies bacchantis* ('like a rocky statue of a bacchant') we are crucially alienated from her.[7] This simile is not in her mind, and it is certainly not she who strips off items of clothing, moving down her body from head to feet, emphasising the sensuous play of colour and texture, with milky breasts and fine garments, culminating in total nakedness. The poem puts its reader into the position of the viewer of the artwork, looking at her as a work of art within a work of art. This passage is the *locus classicus* of ecphrasis objectifying woman. And yet we must not forget that the first line of the ecphrasis presents her looking out from the shore: at Theseus, yes, but also at us. She is not just sad, she is dangerously angry, and her fury will cause the death of Theseus' father Aegeus.

Fitzgerald uses the gaze as a way of unifying his reading of Catullus 64 as a whole: the visual plenty offered by Ariadne's body to the viewers offsets the barrenness caused by the farmers attending the wedding (Catullus 64.39–41; Fitzgerald 1995: 149). He replaces a moral reading of separation from the golden age with a literary one: the belated poet (and his readers) are always alienated from 'the beautiful but lost world of myth on which they long to feast their eyes' (140) but the 'representational virtuosity' (167) of Catullus' poetry gives its own satisfaction. However it seems to me that the transitions in his argument, like those in Catullus' poem, are problematic.[8] It seems disingenuous to dismiss the 'Hellenistic' qualities of the poem as hermeneutically unproductive; one of those qualities is the complex generic play of the poem. The lost alienated (bracketed) past of Catullus 64 is generically epic; the close involvement of gods with the lives of mortals is not just an index of the golden age, but also an index of the changes in the fictional worlds of *epos* from Hesiod to Homer to Apollonius. The grand ecphrasis of textile rather than shield, the focus on love, and the negative approach to epic battle all fit closely with the rejection of an enormous teleological heroic narrative. So the gap between ecphrasis and narrative is analogous to the gap between desire and fantasy. Catullus appropriates, trumps and subverts the epic gaze, and his adoption of Roman moral discourse seems as

---

suggests that the fragmentation and complexity of the gaze in Catullus' poem is not peculiar to Roman literary reflections on myth, but rather part of Roman culture (though most of the visual representations are rather later than Catullus).

[7] Griffin 1985: 98 already saw Catullus as an alienated viewer here: 'savouring the spectacle of her distress'.

[8] Fitzgerald 1995: 'Perhaps the most virtuosic element of Catullus' poem is its dazzling and unpredictable handling of transitions, between the various levels of the poem, between one story and another, and between the senses addressed.' (158)

much like a posture of self-loathing as anything else. This rejection of epic ecphrasis is underlined by what he does not say: there is no sense of how the *uestis* was made, and by whom, rendering it a purely poetic artefact. Similarly, we are not allowed to see Bacchus actually looking at Ariadne; the focus is displaced instead onto his companions and the noise they make. Fitzgerald points out the way that the simile at 269–75 works unexpectedly, by comparing the peaceful dispersal of the mortal guests to waves of the sea, used in Homer of gathering and clashing armies.[9] Catullus' narrative transitions also avoid using the divine gaze: instead the Thessalian youths, gazing and giving way to the gods, form the linchpin between ecphrasis and narrative (267–8). Similarly, his presentation of the *Parcae* creates an uncanny prophetic gaze, in which the divine prophets partake in the abjection and marginalisation typical of mortal prophets.[10] Desire for the unapproachable Ariadne and desire for the lost age of the mingling of gods and heroes are both equivalent to ecphrastic failure: Catullus 64 is epic (or epyllion) of desire.[11]

Here at the centre of the book lies a panel in which I examine the relationship between ecphrasis and the epic gaze. In an influential article, W. J. T. Mitchell has suggested that the object of ecphrasis is inevitably 'other', both in its visual nature and in a political sense: 'the "otherness" of visual representation may be anything from a professional competition [between poet and painter] ... to a relation of political, disciplinary or cultural domination in which the "self" is understood to be an active, speaking, seeing subject, while the "other" is projected as a passive, seen and (usually) silent object'.[12] The ecphrastic frame separates the image from the narrative and demands the self-conscious involvement of the reader in reflection on the relationship between the visual and the verbal. Ecphrasis is a technology of viewing (and reading), separating the reader from the text as the cinema screen separates the viewer from the action.[13] Yet ecphrasis has a number of narrative functions: it can be proleptic, displaying the course of things to come, either within or outside the narrative;[14] it can constitute a *mise-en-abyme*, a miniature version of the whole;[15] it can be a pause, a misdirection.[16]

---

[9] Fitzgerald 1995: 158 n.24, citing the similes at *Il.* 4.422–60 and 7.63–4.
[10] Fitzgerald 1995: 163: 'The Fates, who can see everything, are themselves the object of a way of seeing that mixes what would otherwise be separated in time or place: they are young and old; dancing and working (singing might appropriately accompany both activities); sexy and repulsive; goddesses and entertainers; dancing girls and spinning Roman matrons.'
[11] On McGowan's typology of cinema as cinema of fantasy, desire and the clash between the two, see above, Introduction, p.9.
[12] Mitchell 1992.
[13] For sophisticated reflection on the workings of ecphrasis, see Elsner 2002, Squire 2009.
[14] On the proleptic ecphrasis, see Harrison 2001 and now Harrison 2010.
[15] Some discussion in Lovatt 2002. On *mise-en-abyme* Fowler 2000a.
[16] On pause and progress, see Fowler 1991, and intelligent development in Putnam 1998b.

Ecphrasis in the ancient sense is not restricted to the description of works of art, although these ecphrases are most interesting for their representation of maker and viewer as versions of the poet and reader: the term also encompasses descriptions of the natural world, people, events and places.[17] In this chapter I want to explore the interrelation between the different types of ecphrasis in epic, how they function in the narrative, how they relate to the divine, prophetic and female gaze, and how they contribute to representations of epic viewing. Ovid, in particular, seems to use ecphrastic description as a transitional device, as important in the *Metamorphoses* as the divine gaze elsewhere. The viewer (internal or external) of the ecphrasis (or its object) seems to have all the power: yet often the sense of wonder generated can be transformed into paralysis or unsatisfied desire. Different objects have different effects, yet they can relate closely to each other: a shield is an apotropaic device, which generates visual power; yet a cloak can be a kind of shield, and a shield can be described as woven (*textum*, *Aen.* 8.625); a door marks the boundary and the crossing of it, just as a valley or a pool are self-contained spaces to be broken into. How does the representation of viewing in passages of ecphrasis contribute to the overall representation of viewing in epic? What effects do the objects described have on their viewers? And how do these descriptions of viewing act as models for the reading of epic?

The chapter begins with a survey of different types of things described to provide the framework. There follows a panel focused on makers and in particular the gods; between this and the next panel a border, on narrative transition, especially in Ovid, and the ideas of frames themselves (and breaking out from them). The next panel features cloaks, women and the objects of representation, moving from gender to ethnicity and the imperial gaze in the next part. Finally at the centre is the idea of the agency of art, how these representations look back at us, and affect the viewers internal and external.

Shields, cloaks and other things

The most famous and well-discussed, and arguably the most important, epic ecphrases are those of shields, especially those of Achilles (*Il.* 18.467–616) and Aeneas (*Aen.* 8.617–731). The size, reach and impact of these two shields make them key for understanding their poems and the nature of epic. Ecphrases of shields and armour continue to be important throughout

---

[17] Webb 2009 on ancient definitions of ecphrasis. Salzman-Mitchell 2005: 43–5 also integrates natural ecphrases with artistic ones; as she points out, Ovid almost demands it, with his continual play on the art of nature, and the nature of art.

ancient epic, at least in the military strand (following the 'code models' of the *Iliad* and *Aeneid*).[18] But the alternative stream of epic, initiated by the *Odyssey* and varied by Apollonius, replaces the military with the domestic, the warlike with the erotic. The two most important ecphrases in the *Odyssey* are of places: the cave of Calypso (5.55–75) and the palace of Alcinous (7.43–132), and Apollonius follows these with his description of the palace of Aeetes (AR *Arg.* 3.215–48). Hephaestus has a hand (at least) in the making of these buildings and their decorations, and the same language of wondering is used of the internal viewers.[19] Virgil's description of the frescos in the temple of Dido (*Aen.* 1.441–93) builds on these ecphrases, giving them a sacred and political resonance, and they are pervasively important, if not as iconic as shields, in the later tradition.[20] The dividing line between these buildings and their natural settings is not always clear, but Ovid takes the description of the natural world to new heights, and makes it his distinctive contribution to epic ecphrasis.[21] Apollonius' equivalent of the shield of Achilles, by which he subverts and eroticises the Homeric world, is the cloak of Jason, and the tradition of cloaks, tapestries and other items of personal adornment offers a

---

[18] Shields in the *Iliad*: Agamemnon's (11.36–7); the aegis of Athene (5.741–2); in the *Aeneid* that of Turnus (7.789–92). Statius has that of Capaneus (4.165–72); Hippomedon (4.128–35); Crenaeus (9.332–8); Theseus (12.665–71). The tragic tradition, exemplified in Aeschylus' *Septem contra Thebas* and Euripides. *Phoenissae*, is also important for Statius. Silius has the shield of Hannibal (2.395–457); Quintus Smyrnaeus is relentlessly Iliadic: armour of Achilles (5.1–120); Eurypylos (6.196–293); Achilles again (7.195–205) and Philoctetes (10.176–206). Nonnus is the typical exception, bridging the two streams of epic; despite his erotic and Hellenistic tendencies, he includes two shield ecphrases (Aiacus: 13.2104; Dionysus 25.384–572). These lists are intended to be representative rather than comprehensive.

[19] Hephaestus: *Od.* 7.92; AR *Arg.* 3.223, 228–9. Viewing and wonder: *Od.* 7.43–5, 84–5, 133–4; AR *Arg.* 3.215.

[20] The palace of Latinus is also important (*Aen.* 7.170–91). For liminality, the doors of the temple of Apollo at Cumae stand out (*Aen.* 6.14–41), as do the doors of the palace of Apollo at *Met.* 2.1–18; the cave of Sleep (11.592–615) and the house of *Fama* (12.39–63), like the cave of Calypso, lie somewhere between buildings and natural places. But the temple of Apollo at VF *Arg.* 5.407–56 is clearly in the tradition of Virgil. More Ovidian are Statius' palace of Mars (*Theb.* 7.34–63) and cave of Sleep (10.84–117). The *ara Clementiae* also partakes in this tradition (12.481–511). Silius' *Punica* has three temples, that of Dido (1.80–100), Hercules (3.32–44) and at Liternum (6.653–716). Nonnus returns to Odyssean mode, with two palaces (*Dion.* 3.131–79 and 18.67–92).

[21] In this category (arguably) Calypso's cave, definitely Virgil's harbour (*Aen.* 1.159–69) and ambush (11.522–31). In Ovid: Diana's pool (*Met.* 3.155–62); Narcissus' pool (3.407–12); Salmacis' pool (4.296–301); the path to Hades (4.432–45); the Calydonian boar's lair (8.329–39); the beach profaned by Peleus' rape of Thetis (11.229–36). Statius (most Ovidian of the Flavians) has the path up from the underworld (*Theb.* 2.32–70); the valley of the Sphinx (2.496–525); the mountain of Perseus (3.460–9). Silius' geographical ecphrasis of the tides of Gades (3.45–60) is rather Lucanian. Sacred groves and trees: Virgil's temple of Juno is situated in a sacred grove (*Aen.* 1.141) and the sacred laurel is important at *Aen.* 7.59–63; Erysichthon cuts down the grove at *Met.* 8.743–50; Caesar commits similar sacrilege at Lucan *BC* 3.399–425; trees are also felled for the building of the Argo at VF *Arg.* 1.120–6, and the building of Opheltes' bier at *Theb.* 6.54–125. A sacred grove contains the necromancy at *Theb.* 4.419–42; cf. Diana's sacred tree at 9.585–92. On Lucan and geography, see Masters 1993:150–78, Murgatroyd 2007; landscape: O'Gorman 1995, Bexley 2009.

feminine, slant-wise approach to epic ecphrasis.[22] The makers (and/or givers) of these cloaks are usually female: Helen and Andromache in the *Iliad*, Athene and the Graces (given by Hypsipyle) in Apollonius; Arachne and Minerva in the *Metamorphoses*; the Argive women at *Theb.* 10.56–64; Harmonia weaves a robe in *Dionysiaca* at 41.288–306.[23] Dido also makes cloaks for Aeneas, which he uses to bury Pallas (*Aen.* 11.72–5), although they are not described in any detail.[24] Cloaks are often associated with deception, abandonment and loss, while shields (often) offer divine power and plenitude; shields seem to partake in the divine gaze, while cloaks are more closely related to the female gaze.

Ecphrasis and divine authority

The fact that the most important objects of ecphrases are often made by gods is more than just an association: divine authorship gives the objects and their messages divine authority. The divine authority of Vulcan is particularly important in the *Aeneid*; when Venus gives the weapons to Aeneas, Vulcan is described as learned and prophetic:

> illic res Italas Romanorumque triumphos
> haud uatum ignarus uenturique inscius aeui
> fecerat ignipotens   (*Aeneid* 8.626–8)

> There the god powerful in fire had made
> Italian affairs and the triumphs of the Romans,
> not unaware of the prophets nor ignorant of the coming age

The shield symbolically represents the world and Rome's role in it. This builds on allegorical readings of the Homeric Hephaestus as creator of the

---

[22] Cloaks in Homer: those of Helen (*Il.* 3.125), Andromache (*Il.* 22.440–1), Odysseus (*Od.* 19.241–2); Apollonius' cloak of Jason (AR *Arg.* 1.721–68), of Dionysus (4.421–34). *Aeneid*: Cloanthus' prize (5.250–7); similarly a prize at *Theb.* 6.540–7; Jason's cloak at VF *Arg.* 2.408–17 is the gift of Hypsipyle; in Silius the cloak of Hasdrubal (*Pun.* 15.421–34).

[23] The close links between tapestry in general and cloaks in particular, the woven products of women, encourage me to include Arachne and Minerva. Others include the tapestries in Euripides' *Ion*, and the image of Adonis in Theocritus (*Idyll* 15.80–6). On historical references to tapestries, including the peplos woven by Athenian maidens and the tapestries of Ptolemy Philadelphus, see Shapiro 1980: 268–9.

[24] Other items of personal adornment include: the belt of Aphrodite (*Il.* 14.214–17); Odysseus' brooch (*Od.* 19.226–361); Heracles' belt (*Od.* 11.605–8), the sword-belt of Pallas (*Aen.* 10.495–505); the necklace of Harmonia (*Theb.* 2.269–305); another necklace of Harmonia (*Dion.* 5.136–89). Other luxury goods: Eros' golden ball (AR *Arg.* 3.135–41); the *crater* given by Anius to Aeneas at *Met.* 13.681–704; the *crateres* at *Theb.* 1.544–52 and 6.531–9; the ancestor statues at *Theb.* 2.213–25 and similar images at 6.268–95; Silvia's stag is included by Putnam 1998b, and Statius has matching tigresses (*Theb.* 7.564–81). Nonnus' dances (*Dion.* 19.198–236) and Valerius Flaccus' painted ship (AF *Arg.* 1.127–48) seem to be unique in the surviving tradition. On the ship, see Zissos 2008:152–69, with discussion of the evidence for historical painted ships, and literary ones (Hor. *Carm.* 1.14.14–15; Prop. 4.6.49–50).

universe, and the Homeric shield as a representation of the cosmos born in creative fire.[25] The cloak of Jason in Apollonius is the work of Pallas Athene herself (AR *Arg.* 1.721–4), and was also read by scholiasts as a cosmic allegory.[26] Nonnus' shield of Dionysus, also made by Hephaestus, is represented by its bearer, Attis, as a prophetic guarantee of imperial victory (*Dionysiaca* 25.351–67). These ecphrases represent a divine perspective both within and looking at epic. The shield of Achilles is bounded by Oceanus; it covers peace and war, city and country, and contains within it a miniature *Iliad* in the shape of the city under siege. It is both a microcosm of the poem and a frame for it: it represents a wider reality, the same reality of the similes, which goes beyond war and glory to bring in details of everyday life familiar to Homer's audience. Both the shield of Achilles and that of Aeneas play games with time: the shield of Achilles bridges the gap between daily life in the now of the narrator and the larger than life heroic legends of Troy past; the shield of Aeneas creates epic authority by situating what the Roman audience knew as historical facts in the prophetic future of the poem. This vertical divine perspective is offset by the minute detail on display and the close focus on the material of the shields and their making: divine vision is at once a satellite image of the planet and an x-ray microscopic vision of the miniature and the inside. By describing divine art, the epic narrator takes on the role of a godlike prophet. The text is the medium that presents divine craftsmanship to its viewers; the poet is a doublet of the god.

Hephaestus' involvement with the palaces of Alcinous and Aeetes is partial, and has a rather different function, in creating a sense of otherworldliness and emphasising the importance and divine connections of the kings. At *Od.* 7.91–4 he makes silver and gold dogs to guard the palace. They take the miracle of ecphrasis a step further by actually being alive, despite being crafted objects. His involvement with Aeetes' palace at AR *Arg.* 3.222–34 is deeper, but still circumscribed: he made the four miraculous fountains, and the bronze bulls. The palace of the sun at Ovid *Met.* 2.1–30 carries on the tradition of the naive guest arriving in another world, and offers a model of an ordered (even authoritarian) cosmos.[27] Brown argues that it can be read, too, as a version of the *Metamorphoses*, moving from order to chaos, and that it has affinities with the 'idyllic landscapes which often preface tales of rape and transformation ... throw into relief the theme of sexual violence'.[28] Phaethon's gaze, however, is importantly mortal, compared to Hermes wondering at Calypso's cave, for instance

---

[25] See Hardie 1986: 340–1.   [26] Shapiro 1980: 265. See also Bulloch 2006 with further reading.
[27] See Brown 1987.   [28] Brown 1987: 215.

(*Od.* 5.73–6); he is an intruder in a divine world. Unlike Odysseus, he is not even canny enough to be amazed by what he sees.[29]

In contrast, Valerius Flaccus' Jason, when confronted by the wonders of the Argo itself and the paintings upon it, avoids the stupefaction felt by others, and remains apprehensive about the dangers of journeying over the sea (VF *Arg.* 1.149–50). Phaethon's lack of awareness of the doors as boundary contrasts with Jason's understanding of the boundary they are violating by initiating sea travel. This is the first of two major divine-authored ecphrases in Valerius' *Argonautica*, and has double divine authorisation: Juno watches (120–1) as Athena, with Argus, builds the boat.[30] What these pictures give, though, is no straightforward authorisation, no representation of the cosmos. Rather the images are most importantly a recapitulation of Catullus 64, with various nods to Ovidian passages of rape and destruction: Thetis going through the sea on a dolphin evokes Ovid's version of Peleus' rape of Thetis; the Cyclops calling to Galatea reminds us of his violent destruction of Acis in *Metamorphoses* 13; the peaceful wedding banquet is interrupted not by Eris or the fates, but by a slip sideways to Ovid's banquet battle scene, the Lapiths and the Centaurs. The repetition of *hic . . . hic . . .* (at 144) to point out Peleus and Aeson carving out their heroic roles in the midst of the dining tables may be an ironic evocation of the epiphany of Augustus in *Aeneid* 6 (*hic uir, hic est*, 791), imperial destiny transformed into after-dinner entertainment. Similarly the temple of Apollo at VF *Arg.* 5.407–56 puts the divine maker in control (as in Ovid, but not, crucially, Virgil):[31] just as the scene shifts to our poem, to the ship setting off (and the previous ecphrasis), Hephaestus is called *praesaga Mulciber arte* ('Vulcan with his prescient skill', 437–8); but his knowledge is set against the viewers' ignorance:

> haec tum miracula Colchis
> struxerat Ignipotens nondum noscentibus, ille
> quis labor, aligeris aut quae secet anguibus auras
> caede madens; odere tamen uisusque reflectunt.   (5.451–4)

---

[29] Odysseus as wondering viewer: *Od.* 7.43–5, 133–4.
[30] At 126, she looks for a mast; the authorship of the paintings is not clear: *superaddit* (129) might refer to Argus, Pallas or even Juno. Argus was the most recent subject of a sentence, but Pallas looking for the mast intervenes in a subordinate clause. But if Argus does the painting, he clearly has the help and sponsorship of Pallas.
[31] Links to Ovid: VF *Arg.* 5.408–10 (brightness of the temple); 429–32 (Phaethon). Phaethon is out of place here: everything else is directly relevant to the story: the origins of the Colchians, the rape of the nymph Aea (aetiology of the city's name); then directly afterwards the *mise-en-abyme* of the present text, plus the *Medea* to come. This must hint at a move from order to chaos still to come, which we never quite reach in the surviving poem.

> The fire god had built these wonders then for the Colchians
> who did not yet know, what work that was, or which woman
> cuts through the breezes with winged serpents
> dripping with gore: but they hate it nevertheless and turn back their gazes.

This reverses the moment in *Aeneid* 8 where Aeneas does not understand the prophetic shield but rejoices in it (*miratur rerumque ignarus imagine gaudet*, 'he wonders and not knowing about the matter, rejoices in the image', *Aen.* 8.730). The wonder of the ecphrastic moment is destroyed by a sense of foreboding. If the Colchians had read their Apollonius, they would know that 5.441 closely echoes Medea's dream at AR *Arg.* 3.630–2, in which she decides to leave with Jason and her parents' cry wakes her. The contrast here between immortal knowledge and mortal ignorance is much more concretely tragic: it is not just a matter of leaving out the difficult parts, but rather the sense that real understanding might have unravelled the whole plot. If the ultimate *telos* is *Medea*, ecphrasis loses its epic authority.[32]

Statius' *Thebaid* takes this tendency even further: both of its divinely authored ecphrases are actively malevolent. The necklace of Harmonia (2.269–305) is extraordinary for turning Vulcan into a witch: like a doublet of Erichtho, he concocts the ingredients necessary to take revenge on the offspring of Mars and Venus; the close weaving of the necklace into the narrative, as a new version of the beginning of the epic, makes it become the motivation for the whole expedition (as well as Amphiaraus' destruction, through Eriphyle's tragic longing for the necklace).[33] As she watches, she cooks up her envy (*coquebat trucem inuidiam*, *Theb.* 2.300), looking askance on the tradition of dangerous satiety in ecphrastic viewing, which we will explore below. As in Valerius, this opening ecphrasis has its structural equivalent at the beginning of the second half of the poem, in the palace of Mars at 7.34–63.[34] Here Vulcan's involvement with building the palace is tendentiously highlighted by 7.60–3, in which Statius plays with ecphrastic time. Vulcan is happy to help Mars because the adultery with Venus has not yet happened; this adultery was the cause of Vulcan making the necklace, which helped to initiate the whole epic. Together the two objects emphasise the impotence of Vulcan's craftsmanship. The allusion to Virgil's (circular) shield with *cernere erat* (7.61, *Aen.* 8.676) marks this move as deliberately

---

[32] This section is indebted to the insights of Buckley forthcoming.   [33] McNelis 2007: 50–75.
[34] Structure is often subjective: although the necklace of Harmonia comes in book 2, it has a clear initiatory force. Structure is even more problematic with Valerius, in which we cannot securely pin down an end-point. The orthodox position is that Valerius intended to end the poem after eight books (though ten seems equally plausible to me). The fifth book can be seen to begin the second half. Although they do not reach Colchis until 5.184, and the second invocation is not until 217–21, there is Virgilian precedent for this structural slippage.

tendentious.³⁵ Further, Valerius' *praesaga Mulciber arte* (433) uses the same name and in the same metrical position as Virgil's *discinctos Mulciber Afros* (*Aen.* 8.274), as does Statius' *diuina Mulciber arte* (*Theb.* 7.61).³⁶ Statius' personifications take Discordia and Bellona from the shield of Aeneas (Bellona is bloody in both), and the Dirae, missing from Statius' long list, but present in Virgil, are there at VF *Arg.* 5.445. Mars' horrendous spoils (*Theb.* 7.55–60) then equate to Augustus' triumphal parade. Moreover, Augustus watches this parade from the temple of Apollo. The two Flavian poets seem to be working together to undo Virgilian teleology.

If Flavian epic tends to set Virgil up as the optimist to stand against their pessimistic texts, there is a great deal of complication already present in Virgil. The special relationship to narrative authority presented in the shield of Aeneas is not unproblematic: as we have seen in the chapter on prophecy, this power is often accompanied by danger and/or abjection. Homer's Hephaestus is a god, but not top rank. He combines glory with abjection: is strong-armed and famous, but crippled.³⁷ He agrees to help Thetis in return for the help she gave him when Hera threw him out of Olympus to try and hide her shame at her imperfect offspring (*Il.* 18.394–9). Virgil's Vulcan is strikingly feminised by the simile at *Aen.* 8.407–15, which compares him to a woman getting up early to do the housework.³⁸ Attis in the *Dionysiaca* embodies this ambivalence further: as Rheia/Cybele's priest, he castrated himself; Shorrock reads him as a flawed doublet of Dionysus, not just looking like a woman but unmanned and sterile.³⁹ Yet he can also represent the process of death and resurrection, which is so thematically important in Dionysus' shield. Divine authority is complicated by association with two categories of the 'other': the feminine and the bodily incomplete.

Mortal makers: the shield of Hannibal

The figure of the maker (or bearer, or giver) may be ambivalent, but the power of the ecphrasis remains. When Virgil (and Venus) give the shield to Aeneas, they are equally giving the world to Rome. The cosmos as depicted

---

[35] Smolenaars 1994: 22–3 on intertexts.
[36] Smolenaars 1994: 36 on the obscurity of *Mulciber*. He also adds *diuina arte* (*Aen.* 2.15 *diuina Palladis arte*), which further implies divine malevolence.
[37] Epithets used in this episode include: κυλλοποδίων ('crook-footed', 371); κλυτοτέχνην ('famous for his skill', 391); περικλυτὸς ἀμφιγυήεις ('famous and strong-armed', 393, 462, 587, 590); πέλωρ αἴητον χωλεύων ('hard-breathing monster, limping', 410–11); κλυτὸς ἀμφιγυήεις (614).
[38] See Lada-Richards 2004 on the complicated gender and generic negotiations in this passage, esp. 33–4 on the traditionally compromised masculinity of Hephaestus/Vulcan.
[39] Shorrock 2001: 177–8.

on the shield is a symbol of *imperium*, which is the divine destiny of Aeneas, Augustus and Rome.[40] The ecphrasis of the divine shield represents the ultimate god's-eye view of epic poetry. It is particularly important, then, that in all except Silius these are divine artefacts. Silius' shield offers a complex reflection on the *Iliad*, the *Aeneid* and the *Punica* itself.[41] The shield comes early on in the seventeen-book epic, during the siege of Saguntum in book 2, a gift to Hannibal sent as a tribute from Spanish neighbours. Hannibal, as an anti-hero, and an anti-Aeneas (and an anti-Achilles?) receives a shield made by humans, portraying neither the cosmos nor the future, but the past and the present of the poem itself.[42] The shield is divided into two sides: the right shows Virgil's Dido and Aeneas story, supplemented by Hannibal's oath and Hamilcar in Sicily; the left shows Xanthippus and Regulus from the First Punic War, an African pastoral scene, complete with lionesses and nomads, and Saguntum itself. The shield is eminently self-reflexive, and works on a number of levels, allowing us to look with and at the Carthaginians, and indeed the Saguntines. Regulus, for instance, can act as an example of Roman defeat, praising Carthage, or an example of Roman virtue and steadfastness, encouraging the Saguntine resistance. It is significant that the armour Silius creates for his anti-hero Hannibal, the enemy of Rome, is made not by divine but human creators.[43] Coming as it does immediately after Hannibal has made a quick raid to reinforce the loyalties of his allies (*Pun.* 2.392–3), this shield asks questions about the motives of its makers.[44] Perhaps they are not just buttering up a difficult and potentially tyrannous ruler, but deliberately attempting to induce in him a false sense of invincibility. Silius emphasises the earthly origins of the shield with *Callaicae telluris opus* ('the work of the Galician land', 397) and reminds us again at 417 that the hand of man not god is behind this revision of Virgil's Dido and Aeneas (*Callaicae fecere manus*). Vessey has shown how Hannibal's shield is full of bad omens which can be read both ways: the shouting and baying of hounds at the cave scene (417–18), the pyre of Dido (424–5), the grim face and burning eyes of Hamilcar (430–1),

---

[40] See Hardie 1986.
[41] Readings of the shield of Hannibal: most useful were Vessey 1975 and Venini 1991; see also Küppers 1986: 154–64, Laudizi 1989: 108–9, Devallet 1992, Pomeroy 2000: 156–8, Marks 2005: 89. Pomeroy 2000: 156 discusses the shield as part of Silius' 'reversal of Virgilian themes'.
[42] Vessey 1975: 401 on Hannibal and Aeneas; see also Venini 1991: 1191 n.2, Marks 2005: 89.
[43] Vessey 1975: 397: 'Gone is the cosmic and supernatural element in Virgil.' See also Küppers 1986: 157, Devallet 1992: 191–2.
[44] Not only Vessey sees the shield as actively false in its promises: 'Hannibal's shield is a *fraus*, its surface implications delusive.' Vessey 1975: 404. Also Devallet 1992: 198: 'Ce bouclier est donc bien celui de la fausse promesse de victoire.'

the victor Xanthippus (betrayer who is destined to be betrayed in his turn). In fact the whole shield shines *saevo fulgore* ('with a savage gleam', 395). Just as Dido looks at Aeneas *fronte serena* ('with a carefree face', 414), so Hannibal rejoices at the shield (*lustrat ovans oculis*, 'he pores over it, rejoicing', 405). The same verb (*ouat*, *Aen.* 10.500) is used of Turnus as he rejoices in the spoils taken from Pallas, in his ignorance of the implications of the image. Watchers in the image, viewers of the image, readers of the text: are all designed to be taken in by ecphrastic hope?[45] For ultimately, Dido dies, Hannibal is defeated and Carthage is destroyed. And on one reading of Silius, Rome, too, starts down the steep slope to corruption and moral desecration.[46] Ultimately, though, this is a more conservative approach than that of Valerius or Statius: by attributing the shield to mortal makers, Silius preserves the authority and benevolence of the gods.

The association between the divine gaze and the ecphrastic gaze is clearly important. It is no coincidence that Lucan's epic world, which is stripped of its divine apparatus, does not display any ecphrases of works of art.[47] Lucan abdicates the responsibility and authority of the epic narrator, while simultaneously undermining the whole structure. It is worth pointing out, however, that Virgil's shield is the exception rather than the rule in the *Aeneid*. The temple in *Aeneid* 1 was founded by Dido (1.446–7) and created by artists in rivalry (1.454–6), presumably Carthaginians; the auteurship of Daedalus is particularly important in the ecphrasis of the temple doors at 6.14–33;[48] finally, the sword-belt of Pallas at 10.495–505, like the belt of Heracles in *Odyssey* 11, has a negative impact (it – or the images on it – is *nefas* at 10.497), but is also explicitly made by a mortal, here named as Clonus Eurytides. The tragic material on the belt suggests that the poem is moving away from its epic high point at the end of book 8, back towards the greater complexity of the earlier mortal creations. Turnus' failure as a reader to see himself in the dead young men is repeated by Aeneas' failure to see Turnus as one of the tragic dead. The deaths on the sword-belt initiate further cycles of revenge. All three of these mortal images focus on deaths of the young (Troilus, and arguably Penthesilea; Icarus; the sons of Aegyptus)

---

[45] Here the phrase 'ecphrastic hope' is extended to imply not just the belief that it is possible to convey visual images in words, but also the belief that the apparently optimistic message of the visual image (and its description) will prove true.
[46] Negative readers of Silius include: Cowan 2007 and Tipping 2010.
[47] Dinter 2006: 169 discusses the lack of ecphrases; he argues that the battle scenes in book 7 contain a fragmented version of the shield of Aeneas, that Lucan turns the mutilated bodies of his fighters into warped works of art.
[48] The passage begins *Daedalus, ut fama est*, ... (14) and finishes with the emphatic image of artistic failure as he tries and fails to represent the fall of Icarus.

Representing the divine

set against epic glory and success. Is Lucan, then, extending a Virgilian insight, then, rather than reacting against it?

Representing the divine

We have already explored the complexities of the divine gaze, and the complications created by the epic poet and his reader/audience's observation of the gods. How does this play out in the tradition of the shield ecphrasis? In the shield of Achilles the focus is on mortals. The only divine actors are Athene and Ares:[49]

> ἦρχε δ' ἄρα σφιν Ἄρης καὶ Παλλὰς Ἀθήνη,
> ἄμφω χρυσείω, χρύσεια δὲ εἵματα ἔσθην,
> καλὼ καὶ μεγάλω σὺν τεύχεσιν, ὥς τε θεώ περ
> ἀμφὶς ἀριζήλω· λαοὶ δ' ὑπολίζονες ἦσαν.   (*Iliad* 18.516–19)
>
> Ares and Pallas Athena led them,
> both golden, clothed with golden cloaks,
> beautiful and huge with their weapons, and as Gods do,
> stand out above those around them. The people next to them seemed small.

The two gods who support opposing sides represent the general theme of divine intervention in battle. Their size, goldenness and beauty mark them out as separate from the mortals. The materiality of this representation suggests the conventions of art rather than the way that gods are usually represented in the rest of the poem, where often mortals cannot see them. These gods may be the object of representation but they clearly retain immense power over the people around them.

The shield of Aeneas expands to represent all three levels of the cosmos, with Tartarus at *Aen.* 8.666–70. In the climactic representation of the battle of Actium, the battle takes place on a divine and cosmic level as well as the human one. The monstrous Egyptian gods battle the Olympian deities, emphasising the otherness of Augustus' Actian foes:

> omnigenumque deum monstra et latrator Anubis
> contra Neptunum et Venerem contraque Mineruam
> tela tenent; saeuit medio in certamine Mauors
> caelatus ferro tristesque ex aethere Dirae,
> et scissa gaudens uadit Discordia palla,
> quam cum sanguineo sequitur Bellona flagello.
> Actius haec cernens arcum intendebat Apollo

---

[49] There are personifications at 535–8, but these lines are probably interpolated from the Ps-Hesiodic *Scutum* (see Edwards 1991: 220–1).

desuper; omnis eo terrore Aegyptus et Indi,
omnis Arabs, omnes uertebant terga Sabaei. (*Aeneid* 8.698–706)

All kinds of monstrous gods and even the barking Anubis
hold weapons against Neptune and Venus
and against Minerva. Mars rages in the middle of the struggle
engraved in iron, and, grim from the sky the Dirae,
and Discord is on the march, rejoicing in her tattered robe,
Bellona follows with her bloody whip.
Actian Apollo watching this aims his bow
from above; all Egypt at that terror and the Indians,
all Arabia, and all the Sabaeans turn their backs.

Within the ecphrasis, then, a game of gazing is played out. Apollo embodies the powerful divine gaze, looking from above and at the moment of taking action (stretching his bow). The conquest is already achieved by the power of vision: the enemy are so terrified that they are fleeing without the actual shooting. Virgil turns the golden Ares from Homer into an iron Mars, and adds in the personifications with their evocation of *amor martis*. According to Gransden 1976: 181, *Discordia* represents civil war, but the list of exotic peoples, with its emphatic anaphora of *omnis*, turns Actium into a synecdoche of Roman imperial conquest. It is as if Augustus, too, is a viewer of the shield as the text segues into the triple triumph, with the figure of Caesar appropriating the divine gaze of Apollo and watching the imperial roll call of nations:[50]

ipse sedens niueo candentis limine Phoebi
dona recognoscit populorum aptatque superbis
postibus; incedunt uictae longo ordine gentes,
quam uariae linguis, habitu tam uestis et armis.
hic Nomadum genus et discinctos Mulciber Afros,
hic Lelegas Carasque sagittiferosque Gelonos
finxerat; Euphrates ibat, iam mollior undis,
extremique hominum Morini, Rhenusque bicornis,
indomitique Dahae, et pontem indignatus Araxes. (*Aeneid* 8.720–8)

He himself, sitting on the snowy threshold of glowing Phoebus
recognises the gifts of the peoples and fits them to the proud
door-posts; the conquered tribes press on in a long line,
as varied in their tongues as in the appearance of their clothes and arms.
Here the race of the Nomads and the un-belted Africans,

---

[50] On Augustus as central subject and ideal viewer of the shield, Barchiesi 1997: 276. When Silius adapts this passage in his temple ecphrasis at *Pun.* 6.689–97 to describe the image of the defeated Carthaginian, he replaces Augustus' quasi-divine gaze with the actual divine gaze of Dione from Mount Eryx (6.696–7).

> here the Lelegae and the Carians and the arrow-bearing Geloni
> Mulciber had made; the Euphrates flows, now softer in his waves,
> and the Morini, at the edge of humanity, and the two-horned Rhine,
> and the un-tamed Dahae, and Araxes, angry at his bridge.

In place of Oceanus, the universal framing river, we have a multitude of conquered rivers, making the edge of empire into the edge of the shield (or the centre), encompassing the entire Roman world. The powerful centre looks down on the powerless periphery; imperial power is equated with divine power; the gaze embodies military power. The shield of Aeneas is the ultimate example of ecphrasis objectifying the other.

Natural spaces and narrative transition

The shield ecphrases have key structural significance: the shield of Aeneas comes at the end of the second tetrad, the positive (chronological) endpoint of the poem. The two ecphrases in Silius (Hannibal's shield at the end of the beginning, Hasdrubal's cloak at the beginning of the end) are also structural features. The shield of Achilles marks his imminent return to battle, and the turning point in the fortunes of Greeks and Trojans in the *Iliad*. Both Virgil and Ovid place decorated doors at the thresholds of new books (*Aeneid* 6 and *Metamorphoses* 2). Ecphrases of places often mark the beginning of a new sequence (the palaces of Alcinous and Aeetes, the temple of Juno in Carthage, the palace of Latinus, the house of Mars in *Thebaid* 7, the *ara Clementiae* in *Thebaid* 12). As a pause, a moment of self-conscious reflection on artistry, ecphrases invite structural readings.

Ovid in particular makes extensive use of ecphrasis to form a transition from one episode to the next; conversely he tends to avoid straightforward scenes of divine gazing as a transitional motif.[51] Most of these ecphrases

---

[51] Two examples in Virgil: the harbour at 1.159–69 (marked by *est in secessu longo locus*, 159; juxtaposed with the gaze of Neptune: *prospiciens genitor*, 155; marking the border between land and sea, and the return to safety after the storm); the ambush at 11.522–9 (marked by *est curuo anfractu ualles*, 522; comes at the end of Turnus' preparations for battle, just before the action moves to Opis and Diana). In both the landscape has a function in the plot, not just setting the scene. As well as *Met.* 2.1–18 (palace of the Sun), which takes Phaethon across the end of the book and crosses from mortal to divine realm, there are: 3.155–64 (valley and pool where Diana bathes; marked by *uallis erat*, 155; beginning of Actaeon story); 3.407–12 (pool of Narcissus; marked by *fons erat*, 407; turning point of Narcissus story); 4.432–45 (path to Hades; marked by *est uia*, 432; beginning Juno's katabasis); 6.1–145 (Arachne episode, although ecphrases of the tapestries themselves are less pivotal at 70–128); 8.329–37 (marsh of the Calydonian boar; marked by *silua*, 329; after the catalogue of heroes, marks the beginning of the hunt proper); 8.743–50 (the oak of Ceres; marked by *stabat . . . quercus*, 743; just after the beginning of the episode); 11.229–37 (bay and cave of Thetis; marked by *est sinus*, 229; beginning of Peleus' rape of

mark the beginning of an episode, though occasionally a transition within it, or an end.⁵² What are the implications of these observations?

The narrator in the *Metamorphoses* is not as closely connected to the gods, and the gods form the subject matter of the poem, which allows them to be objectified in works of art (both the tapestries of Minerva and Arachne, for instance), rather than functioning as a mediating and authorising internal audience as they do elsewhere in ancient epic. Instead the narrator takes his own authority over the natural world, and works to draw the reader into it, by making the settings a marker of each new story. The formulaic character of this figure makes it equally a marker of textuality and alienation.⁵³ The reader (and the narrator) never wholly identifies with Ovid's characters, but maintains an ironic distance.⁵⁴

Salzman-Mitchell puts her discussion of ecphrasis in Ovid into the context of 'the intrusive gaze', and figures the reader, like several of the characters, as an intruder into the frame of ecphrasis, the private space in the text, which is feminised by the fact that it is hidden and dark.⁵⁵ Her paradigm is Peleus and Thetis, where the reader's ecphrastic vision of the goddess bathing anticipates the assaultive gaze of Peleus, which leads directly to his rape of the goddess (44). Actaeon is another convincing example, although the intrusive gaze here leads not to rape, but to the dehumanisation of the viewing male: divine power trumps the masculine gaze.⁵⁶

There are various weaknesses in this argument; the most important problem here, though, is the equation of reading to an act of violent penetration. One might equally, or even more plausibly, see the reader as drawn in and trapped by the ecphrastic description. Salzman-Mitchell in her analysis of

---

Thetis); 11.592–615 (cave of Sleep; marked by *est prope Cimmerios*, 592; in the middle of the Ceyx and Alcyone episode, marks the beginning of the dream section); 12.39–63 (house of *Fama*; marked by *orbe locus medio est*, 39; beginning of the Trojan war).

⁵² Groves are enclosed in the middle of the story: Virgil's Carthaginian grove at 1.441–9 (marked by *Lucus in urbe fuit media*, 441) in the middle of Aeneas' arrival in Carthage; the sacred laurel at 7.59–63 (marked by *laurus erat*, 59) in the middle of the description of Latium begins the episode of the prophecy; the sacred grove at Massilia desecrated by Caesar in Lucan (*BC* 3.399–425) in the middle of the Massilian episode; the grove used by Tiresias in Statius *Thebaid* 4 comes as the second part of the episode, after Eteocles initiates the process (4.419–42, marked by *silua . . . stat*, 419–20); the sacred tree of Diana at *Theb.* 9.585–92 (*quercus erat*, 586) is part of the dream sequence of Atalanta. At *Pun.* 1.81–98 the temple (and grove) of Dido is within the sequence describing Hannibal's obsession with war (marked by *Urbe fuit media*, 81).

⁵³ On the *est locus* formula, see Hinds 1987: 36–8.

⁵⁴ Of Ovid's successors, Statius is the most Ovidian. The cave of Sleep retake (*Theb.* 10.84–117) comes, like many of Statius' ecphrases, second in the episode; see above on the palace of Mars (7.34–63, p.171); the altar of Clementia comes after the change of scene from Thebes to Athens at 464, at 12.482–511, beginning with *urbe fuit media* (482).

⁵⁵ Salzman-Mitchell 2005: 43–61.

⁵⁶ Other examples: Pentheus and Narcissus, and, less centrally, Arachne.

ecphrasis as a bounded space focuses on the initial marker of ecphrasis (*uallis erat, fons erat, est sinus*; see n.51). The closing boundary is often less easy to make out: it is usually a move from the general to the particular, drawing the reader on deeper into the story.[57] The temple or sacred grove and the ambush location both express a sense of threat: landscape is not here an inert object, but rather a site of awe and imminent violence.[58] For the most part it is not the place viewed but rather the viewer who is under threat: Peleus is the exception to the rule; only with the explicit dispensation of Jupiter and the divine help of Proteus can he overcome his awe of Thetis' divinity in order to carry out his violent intrusion.

Characters arriving in cities for the first time are in need of protection and aware of their own vulnerability. Even for divinities like Hermes, Juno and Iris, the ecphrasis usually marks their sense of dislocation and unease at entering the realm of another power. For the reader, the ecphrasis induces both wonder and suspense: this place must be significant because something will happen here. It is an index of the poet/narrator's control over the narrative and the emotional experience of his audience. The pleasure of the text is created by digression and delay, as well as *enargeia*, vivid visualisation, variety and the active involvement of the reader in forging connections between inset description and frame, just as with similes.

This applies most fruitfully to ecphrases of places, but also works for descriptions of works of art. The shield of Achilles delays the return of the terrifying hero to battle and builds up the anticipation of the audience, as they wait with delight and terror for the violence of his impact. Similarly, Statius' necklace of Harmonia sets the tone for the epic, creating a sense of foreboding and horror, as well as playing a role literally and symbolically in driving the plot onwards. Obviously these effects vary from case to case. The harbour in *Aeneid* 1 is a place of relative safety, although the tone of the description is not very optimistic.[59] The palace of Alcinous offers optimism and otherworldliness and promises an upturn in Odysseus' fortunes. Ecphrasis interacts with

---

[57] Some examples: *Aen.* 1.170, from harbour to the tired sailors now in it (*huc*); 11.530, from setting to plans for ambush (*huc*); *Met.* 2.19, from doors of sun to Phaethon approaching (*quo*); 3.173–4, from pool to Diana now bathing (*dumque . . . ecce*); 3.413, from the pool to Narcissus (*hic*); 4.447 (*illuc*); 8.338 (*hinc*); 11.238 (*illic*); 11.616 (*quo*). *Theb.* 2.55 (*hac*); 2.523 (*huc*); 10.118 (*huc*).
[58] Hinds 2002: 131: 'Inasmuch as the ideal landscape pattern functions in the *Met.* as a recurrent setting for erotic desire and violence, such landscapes come to provide a narratological "cue" for such action.'
[59] The cliffs threaten (*minantur*, 162); and there is an equally threatening grove (*horrentique atrum nemus imminet umbra*, 165). This ecphrasis foreshadows Carthage as a place of short-term safety, but long-term threat.

epic narrative in a number of ways: the places and objects described are not inert, but have effects on viewers in the text as well as readers.[60]

Breaking the frame

An ecphrasis is not just a site for intrusion: we can break in, but its objects can also break out. This is what happens in the Calydonian boar hunt, another Ovidian literalisation of a poetic mode, when the setting is precisely detailed in order to increase the impact of the boar's sudden charge out of hiding:

> hinc aper excitus medios uiolentus in hostes
> fertur ut excussis elisi nubibus ignes.
> sternitur incursu nemus et propulsa fragorem
> silua dat; exclamant iuuenes praetentaque forti
> tela tenent dextra lato uibrantia ferro.   (*Metamorphoses* 8.338–42)

> From here the boar, shaken up, is carried violently against
> his enemies just as fire is struck out from clashing clouds.
> The grove is laid low by his attack and the wood pushed forward
> gives a crash; the young men shout out and strong they hold
> weapons stretched out, brandishing broad iron in their right hands.

The boar explodes from the landscape into the middle of the group, suddenness and violence emphasised by the comparison with lightning; the landscape itself is under threat from its attack. The description of the landscape is a displacement of a description of the boar, who cannot yet be seen; the boar is the real object of the hunters' gaze, indescribable in his horror and fury as Narcissus is indescribable in his beauty. Yet the boar does not escape from his entrapment by the hunters, even if his violence seems to be transferred to Meleager (and Althaea).

Statius' Hermes, accompanied by Laius, breaks out from the underworld at *Theb.* 2.55–7, after the description of the path. More strikingly, Statius' ecphrasis of the retired tigers of Bacchus, described at 7.564–78, ends with the Fury whipping them into action (*has*, 279), so that they burst out into the uncomprehending landscape (*erumpunt non agnoscentibus agris*, 581). They, too, are like lightning bolts (582–5), seizing Amphiaraus' charioteer, and then pursued and pierced, themselves, they become objects of the gaze of the Argives, and the final proximate cause of the outbreak of actual hostilities.

---

[60] Descriptions of works of art, buildings or other spaces can have social functions just like actual examples. For art drawing its significance from involvement in social interactions, see Osborne and Tanner 2007, reflecting on the anthropological work of Gell 1998.

More subtle and metaphorical ways of breaking the frame of ecphrasis can also be figured as breaking out rather than breaking in: Hunter points out that Apollonius breaks the frame of the cloak, by removing Homer's internal audience of marvelling women at *Il.* 18.495–6 from within the shield to outside the cloak: at 1.782–5 the Lemnian women marvel at Jason as he walks through the city, while he is unable to sustain his gaze in the face of their intensity, but looks at the ground like a demure bride.[61] Similarly in *Odyssey* 11, the violent gaze of Hercules continues into the violent gazes of the beasts displayed on his belt: at *Od.* 11.608 Hercules is glaring around terribly (δεινὸν παπταίνων); the lions on the belt have flashing eyes (χαροποί τε λέοντες, 611). Just as Hercules terrifies the ghosts as he approaches (605–6), so the belt terrifies Odysseus (613–14).

In Silius' shield, the frame is marked by the Homeric reference in the river flowing around the edge:[62] not Oceanus, but the Spanish Ebro, which Hannibal crossed to break the treaty with Rome and kick-start the Punic war.[63] Hannibal's shield emphatically does not represent the cosmos: it is limited in its geographical and historical representations and focused on thematic links to the immediate story.[64] Yet despite (or perhaps because of) the limitations, this cosmos cannot contain Hannibal who breaks the boundaries of the ecphrasis as he breaks the treaty and crosses the threshold of the river banks:

> extrema clipei stagnabat Hiberus in ora
> curuatis claudens ingentem flexibus orbem.
> Hannibal abrupto transgressus foedere ripas
> Poenorum populos Romana in bella uocabat. (*Punica* 2.449–52)

> On the extreme edge of the shield, the Hiberus stood still
> Enclosing the huge sphere with its curved bends.
> Hannibal, treaty broken, transgressed the river banks,
> And was calling the Punic peoples to a Roman war.

The clear link with the Homeric passage:

> Ἐν δὲ τίθει ποταμοῖο μέγα σθένος Ὠκεανοῖο
> ἄντυγα πὰρ πυμάτην σάκεος πύκα ποιητοῖο. (*Iliad* 18.607–8)

> And he places the great strength of the river Oceanus
> On the extreme rim of the solidly made shield.

---

[61] Hunter 1993: 55.   [62] Küppers 1986: 162, Spaltenstein 1990: 150.
[63] Likened to Caesar's crossing of the Rubicon by e.g. Laudizi 1989: 109.
[64] Vessey 1975: 404: 'By comparison with Oceanus, Ebro implies limitation and restriction, not universality.' Note also the irony that it is the nomadic Phoenician herds which wander *fine sine ullo* ('without any boundary', 441), while the Carthaginian *imperium* will have a clear limit (cf. *Aen.* 1.279 *imperium sine fine dedi* ('I have given rule without end')).

in *extrema ora* (emphasised by its visual position at either edge of the line) brings out the differences between the shields of Hannibal and Achilles. Becker uses σθένος as an index of movement;[65] but the Hiberus *stagnabat* (which either suggests a stagnant pool, or overflowing, flooding water). In Virgil, the river Oceanus becomes a sea, which is the setting for the battle of Actium and the triumph of Augustus; readers often place it in the centre of the shield. So Silius is correcting Virgil by returning to the Homeric model, and setting up Hannibal (and by implication Caesar) as (negative) versions of Augustus. But he takes it a step further: Hannibal breaks out of the ecphrasis, as if no picture (or poem) could really contain him. Hannibal represents the other escaping from safely distanced representation and threatening action, threatening in this case to overturn history and destroy the Roman cosmos and *imperium* – though as we will see in the following chapter, his gaze is increasingly feminised and marginalised as the epic proceeeds.

Cloaks and the female gaze

Cloaks, in contrast, offer an oblique perspective on epic. The cloak of Jason in Apollonius is the code model for later cloak ecphrases, and is itself closely related to the Iliadic (and Hesiodic) shield ecphrases.[66] Jason's erotic arming is the equivalent of Homeric arming scenes.[67] The blinding brightness of the cloak (AR *Arg*. 1.725–6) evokes the terrifying brightness of Achilles (and later Aeneas) with his divine armour.[68] Its double purple (δίπλακα πορφυρέην, 722) is aurally similar to the τρίπλακα μαρμαρέην ('triple flashing', *Il*. 18.480) of the border in the Iliadic shield.[69] The cosmic reading of the shield can also be applied to the cloak, which begins from the Cyclopes forging a thunderbolt, and continues with the founding of a city, love and strife (Aphrodite in Ares' shield), and a cattle raid involving the Teleboans.[70] Hunter shows how Apollonius uses intertextual reminiscences to re-slant the all-encompassing epic nature of the shield. Here, for

---

[65] Becker 1995: 83: 'The noun *sthenos* (strength, force, vitality) gives a name to the ability to move implied in the verb *rhôonto* (417); *sthenos* is a requisite or potential for *kinesis* (movement).'
[66] I discuss the shield of Heracles in Lovatt forthcoming-c. The cloak of Jason has been much discussed: see Bulloch 2006 for further bibliography; most useful is still Hunter 1993: 52–9.
[67] Hunter 1993: 48.
[68] At *Il*. 19.14–17 the terror of the Myrmidons at the sight of the shield is juxtaposed with Achilles' glaring, shining anger; later at 20.46 the Trojans are terrified by Achilles 'shining in all his armour' (τεύχεσι λαμπόμενον). Aeneas' shield even vomits flames at 10.270–5. See below 'Returning the gaze', pp.198–201.
[69] Hunter 1993: 53.
[70] The weaving of Harmonia at Athene's loom (*Dion*. 41.294–306) takes the cosmic reading literally.

instance, Ares is a lover not a warrior. Similarly the cloak's relationship with the poem around it is oblique and complex: it forms a continuation of Orpheus' cosmic song (AR *Arg.* 1.496–511); each panel suggests connections with the plot to come, but none are straightforward or satisfying. Hunter's summary of the overall effect is apposite: 'The cloak thus presents scenes which are partial analogues of elements of the epic, with correspondences which are both oblique and polyvalent' (58); 'The scenes suggest doubt, conflict, deceit and the problematic of choice' (59). This cosmos, in contrast to that of the shield of Achilles is 'partial and unclarified' (59).[71]

Cloaks, and other products of weaving, are inevitably associated with the feminine: in the *Iliad* we have cloaks woven by Helen (3.125) and Andromache (22.440–1). Apollonius' cloak of Jason was made and given by the goddess Pallas Athene, and problematises gender categories. Athene is both warrior and weaver, just as Jason is both lover and hero. The cloak mentioned later at AR *Arg.* 4.421–34 was made by the Graces for Dionysus, and is characterised by an overpowering aroma from the time of Dionysus and Ariadne's love-making. It is first given by Hypsipyle to Jason (who abandons her) and then by Jason and Medea to Apsyrtus, to entice him into their ambush, an episode both immoral and unepic. In Valerius Flaccus' *Argonautica* Hypsipyle gives to Jason a cloak she has made herself (2.408–17), which combines her own greatest deed (the rescue of her father Thoas from the other Lemnian women) with an optimistic reprise of the abduction of Ganymede, which had already featured at *Aen.* 5.249–57. Rape scenes are already present in Apollonius, with Pelops abducting Hippodameia (AR. *Arg.* 1.752–8) and Apollo fighting off Tityos who is trying to rape Leto (759–62). While Virgil's Ganymede scene places the emphasis on the loss experienced by the Trojan viewers, Valerius gives us Ganymede as cupbearer, an icon of immortality (the immortality Jason will receive by pursuing his heroic ambitions? But at the cost of abandoning his human connections?).[72] The Apollonian scene presents Apollo in gigantomachic mode, a force of Olympian order, while Ganymede represents a divine rape, no matter how positive the outcome. In this context, the tapestries of Minerva and Arachne in Ovid *Metamorphoses* 6 seem gendered,

---

[71] Later shields refer back to Jason's cloak, thus emphasising the links between these two strands: for instance Vian 2008: 388 notes the influence of Jason's cloak on Quintus' ecphrasis of Eurypylos' shield in book 6, and more pervasively on the shield of Dionysus in Nonnus 25. Both have scenes of Amphion and Zethus (AR *Arg.* 1.735–41; *Dion.* 25.417–42); both reflect on sounds that might be heard by viewers (AR *Arg.* 1.765–7; *Dion.* 25.424–8) and the concluding lines contain verbal echoes (AR *Arg.* 1.768; *Dion.* 25.563).

[72] Further on Ganymede below at pp.189–91. On Virgil's Ganymede ecphrasis see Putnam 1998b: 55–74, with Hardie 2002a; Statius also reworked it, but on a cup at *Theb.* 1.544–52; see Lovatt 2002.

although the conflict is primarily between mortal and immortal.[73] Arachne's fluid rendering of scenes of divine rape, so often compared to Ovid's poem, takes that typically Ovidian oblique slant on epic, while Minerva's portrayal of divine order and punishment puts us back in a more conventional epic world.[74] This episode shows once more the radical nature of Ovid's engagement with the epic gaze: he displaces the divine gaze onto a tapestry, puts it in competition with a mortal woman, and creates a serious disjunction between the authorised divine view and that of his own poem. As ever, the seams of epic are prominently on display in the *Metamorphoses*.

Statius also produces an ecphrastic description of female weaving, in the *peplum* which the Argive women dedicate to Juno at *Theb*. 10.56–64. In this, we find the image of a gentle Juno:

> lumine demisso pueri Iouis oscula libat
> simplex et nondum furtis offensa mariti. (*Thebaid* 10.63–4)
>
> with downcast eyes she pours out kisses for the boy Jove,
> naive and not yet made hostile by the thefts of her husband.

This eroticisation of the relationship between Jupiter and Juno looks back to the *Iliad* and before it, imagining a world without the whole driving force of Roman epic, as well as alluding, slant-wise to the divine rapes of other cloaks. This image portrays an objectified Juno, following the norms of feminine submissiveness, yet still actively pursuing her desire, and it becomes a stimulus for action, persuading Juno to instigate the night-raid of *Thebaid* 10, which threatens to turn the war around (although it does not, of course, succeed).[75]

The gendered opposition between cloaks and shields only goes so far, of course: both the shields of Achilles and Aeneas are provided by their mothers, even if made by Vulcan, and shields too present rape scenes: the shield of Turnus at *Aen*. 7.789–92 features Io, while that of Crenaeus at *Theb*. 9.332–8 contains Europa. Just as Vulcan is feminised by his subservience to Venus, so Athene is masculinised by her close association with Zeus and her status as warrior. Cloaks (and other woven products), though, do seem to have a peculiar, oblique relationship to the power of epic ecphrasis. A cloak gives glamour to its wearer, without substance; a man in striking clothing is quite

---

[73] Pavlock 2009: 3–6 on gender and power; see also Leach 1974, Harries 1990 and Rosati 1999.
[74] For instance in Richlin 1992: 162. Although these are tapestries rather than cloaks, their woven nature links them with earlier scenes of weaving, like those featuring Helen and Andromache.
[75] An inset story of Aphrodite attempting to usurp Athene's position as goddess of weaving at *Dion*. 24.230–329 objectifies Aphrodite in a complex manner: it is a repeat of Demodocus' song of Ares and Aphrodite, only now she is the object of the ridicule of the other gods for her crude and unskilled weaving, while the cosmos is threatened by her absence.

different to a hero in divinely made armour. Jason in Apollonius' Lemnian episode is an erotic object, not simply using and abandoning Hypsipyle, but also being used and deceived. It is particularly appropriate, then, that Hypsipyle's cloak becomes a deceptive gift for Apsyrtus, whose killing will fatally compromise Jason's relationship with the gods and his heroic reputation.

A notable exception to the feminine associations of epic cloaks is the cloak of Hasdrubal at Silius *Punica* 15.421–34: it was a gift from Hannibal, made by Sicilian men, worn by Sicilian kings and given by the king of Sicily to Hannibal before he passed it on to his brother. The scenes on the cloak are Virgilian and Homeric: Ganymede briefly snatched, and a more developed Cyclops scene of gore and violence, at the moment just before his blinding. Where Valerius had looked at Apollonius' cosmogonic Cyclopes through an Ovidian lens in his ecphrasis of the paintings on the Argo (Polyphemus calls incidentally to Galatea as she passes in the distance: VF *Arg.* 1.135–6), Silius returns him to the world of heroic epic, about to be brought down by Odysseus as (the one-eyed) Hannibal will be brought down by Scipio.[76] This is the closural parallel for Hannibal's mortal shield in book 2, and Hasdrubal's pride in Hannibal (*fratris spirans ingentia facta*, 'breathing his brother's huge achievements', 411), along with his status as powerful object of the gaze, at the centre of the ceremony, admired for his striking cloak (433–4), stands just before his own defeat, and ultimate objectification as a head on a stake at 15.813–16.[77] The lack of immortal authorisation is matched by a lack of feminine attention: are they in fact two sides of the same coin?

Objects of ecphrasis: gender

The cloak is a feminine object: what is the significance of gender in approaching the depictions in ecphrases of art? This section explores the ways in which women (and disempowered men) are represented in ecphrases. How are they put on display and fetishised, and how does the inset play of gazes work? How does opposition between masculine and feminine interact with the other totalising polarities on display in the Homeric cosmos, peace and war, city and country, in the shield of Achilles?

Women feature as part of the recurring theme of courtship and marriage, which represents functioning society: at *Il.* 18.567–72 young women and men carry grapes and dance; at 590–605 dancing young women and men are described with equal elaboration. There is a visual balance between men and

---

[76] For connections to the wider *Punica* see Harrison 2010.
[77] On decapitation in Silius, see Marks 2008.

women in these passages, which suggests that women are not other but each gender is an equal half of the whole.[78] Both are doubly on display with an internal audience watching the dancing at 603–4. In the war passages of the shield, however, the protagonists are male, except for the goddesses, and, as in the *Iliad* itself, the women are there as the internal audience of epic, along with children and older men, the 'other' of warriors (τεῖχος μέν ῥ' ἄλοχοί τε φίλαι καὶ νήπια τέκνα ῥύατ' ἐφεσταότες, μετὰ δ' ἀνέρες οὓς ἔχε γῆρας· 'The dear wives and little children stood on the walls protecting them, and with them those men whom old age held', 514–15).

At 491–6 there is a more complicated scene of gendered gazing:

> ἐν τῇ μέν ῥα γάμοι τ' ἔσαν εἰλαπίναι τε,
> νύμφας δ' ἐκ θαλάμων δαΐδων ὕπο λαμπομενάων
> ἠγίνεον ἀνὰ ἄστυ, πολὺς δ' ὑμέναιος λαμπομενάων
> κοῦροι δ' ὀρχηστῆρες ἐδίνεον, ἐν δ' ἄρα τοῖσιν
> αὐλοὶ φόρμιγγές τε βοὴν ἔχον· αἱ δὲ γυναῖκες
> ἱστάμεναι θαύμαζον ἐπὶ προθύροισιν ἑκάστη. (*Iliad* 18.491–6)

And on it were weddings and festivals,
and they were leading the brides from their chambers
under the lit torches through the city, loud wedding song was rising;
and the dancing young men whirled, and among them
the flutes and lyres kept sounding; and women
standing each in their door gazed in wonder.

Who are the women looking at here? This does seem to be a wondering gaze of women at young men. Does it represent female desire? Or are the older women contrasted with both the young men and the young women? Are they wondering at the beauty of the scene, remembering the time when they too were the focus of attention, or enjoying a moment of voyeurism? This female audience, like many, is defined by its passivity: the brides are being led while the men dance energetically and the women stand and watch.

In the cloak of Jason these complex gender dynamics are combined with reflections on looking at gods by the representation of Aphrodite admiring herself in the shield of Ares.[79]

---

[78] ἠΐθεοι καὶ παρθένοι ('youths and maidens', 593); αἱ μὲν … οἱ δὲ ('the women on the one hand, the men on the other', 595, repeated at 597). At 558–60 there are clearly delineated gender roles, with women scattering barley while men slaughter oxen (though since a group which included both men and women is gendered masculine in Greek, we have no way of knowing if the sheaf-binders and reapers are entirely male, or also include women).

[79] Shapiro 1980 on the connections between the cloak and Hellenistic art; at 281–2 he connects this panel to representations of an armed Aphrodite, and a Pompeian wall-painting in Naples, showing Thetis looking at her own reflection in the shield of Achilles, a particularly Hellenistic element.

Ἑξείης δ' ἤσκητο βαθυπλόκαμος Κυθέρεια
Ἄρεος ὀχμάζουσα θοὸν σάκος· ἐκ δέ οἱ ὤμου
πῆχυν ἔπι σκαιὸν ξυνοχῇ κεχάλαστο χιτῶνος
νέρθε παρὲκ μαζοῖο· τὸ δ' ἀντίον ἀτρεκὲς αὔτως
χαλκείῃ δείκηλον ἐν ἀσπίδι φαίνετ' ἰδέσθαι.   (AR *Argonautica* 1.742–6)

Next was made deep-haired Cytherea
bearing the sharp shield of Ares; the binding of her tunic
had been loosened and it had come down from her shoulder over
her left arm to her breast; and opposite her a perfect
reflection appeared to be seen in the bronze shield.

Aphrodite is represented as an erotic object: the details of her unclothed breast, arm and shoulder expose her as feminine and to-be-looked-at. But the implication is that she nevertheless holds the power in the exchange of gazes. This is not just an allegorisation of love and war, but an image thematically relevant to its narrative context, and the personified power of love will enable Jason first to conquer Lemnos and then to achieve his quest by conquering Medea and through her the bulls, the dragon and Aeetes. Where, however, is Aphrodite looking? Is she using the shield of Ares as a mirror in which to admire herself? Or is she returning the gaze to the viewer, in disconcertingly double form? The inclusion of the shield is also a self-referential trumping of the shield of Achilles:[80] this shield, the shield of the god of war itself, is either functioning as a mirror to display the eroticised body of the goddess of love, or is appropriated by the goddess of love to turn herself into a power of war.[81] Aphrodite embodies the other in her divine inscrutability and her feminine allure, but she is far from objectified; she represents the power of erotic desire to affect the world around it. By looking at Venus you are in danger of succumbing to her spell.

On the shield of Aeneas, the first women on display are the Sabine women at *Aen.* 8.635–8 (*raptas sine more Sabinas*), forcibly removed from the audience and the safety of the games, passive cause of a war;[82] no mention is made of their role in ending it, which is a masculine affair of honorific names, treaties and sacrifices. In contrast Cloelia is an active woman, breaking her chains and swimming the river (651). Most significant, though, is Cleopatra (*Aegyptia coniunx*, 688), both foreign and female (doubly other), and further objectified by the periphrasis which avoids her

---

[80] The reflection works as a marker of intertextuality (Hunter 1993: 55), and of the doubleness of ecphrasis itself (both art and text).
[81] The eroticised body of Venus is also on display in the shield of Quintus Smyrnaeus at 5.69–72 where he seems to make a conscious reference to the famous painting of Venus Anadyomene, with Venus rising from the sea spattered with foam.
[82] Putnam 1998b: 123–4.

name.⁸³ This passage moves between alienation and identification with Cleopatra: she begins as a *nefas* (688), calls out to her troops with her inherited *sistrum* (696), a clear marker of otherness.⁸⁴ At 709–13, however, she becomes a figure of pathos in defeat: she is pale in anticipation of her death, and the reader is encouraged to sympathise with her and the other people defeated by looking at them through the eyes of the river-god Nile who grieves and opens his cloak to receive the defeated, like a mother looks after children.⁸⁵

The shield of Turnus represents his ancestress, Io (*Aen.* 7.789–92).⁸⁶ Io is an emblem of the objectified female: raped, transformed into an animal, placed under guard (the object of the gaze of all Argus' hundred eyes), driven mad by gadflies, and finally displaced to Egypt, although she there becomes a goddess, and the ancestress of the Danaids. This ecphrasis represents her at the moment of transformation (*iam saetis obsita, iam bos*, 'now covered in bristles, now a cow', 790), and equally transformed into epic material (*argumentum ingens*, 'a huge narrative', 791). The relationship with Moschus *Europa*, which tells the rape of Europa, with the story of Io as the illustration on her basket, suggests a re-epicisation of erotic and Hellenistic models, or perhaps rather a contamination of shields and other objects, epic and other genres.⁸⁷

Similarly, Statius reflects on these ideas by putting Europa the ancestral rape victim (*Theb.* 9.333) on display on the shield of Crenaeus, a beautiful boy about to be destroyed in epic battle.⁸⁸ Although Statius' shield gives us more than a glimpse of Europa's subjectivity (*blandi iuuenci*, 334; *secura maris*, 335), echoes of Catullus 64 underline the fact that she is to-be-looked-at. Statius takes this further by connecting the trust of the viewer in the reality of the image (and of the ecphrastic hope of the reader, which encourages her to believe that she can see the object, and through it the reality which it depicts) with the false confidence of Europa in her own safety: while she (unlike Crenaeus) will not die a watery death, she will find that the bull is not as

---

⁸³ Putnam 1998b: 142. On the broader use of Cleopatra in Augustan discourse, see Syed 2005: 177–93.
⁸⁴ The sistrum is associated with the worship of Isis, and the word is first used in Latin literature here and at Prop. 3.2.43, so that it is likely to have retained a sense of the alien. Putnam 1998b: 236 n.39.
⁸⁵ This is where I part company from Syed who sees Cleopatra and Dido as 'defining Others'; for instance, 'like Cleopatra, Dido enters the Roman discourse of imperialism as the representative of the vanquished, the Other, the East' (191). If Cleopatra and Dido are really so closely related, then the argument of mixed identification and alienation becomes even more compelling. Reed 2007, as often, offers a more satisfying approach in his demonstration of the way the doorposts of Augustus at 8.871–2 echo both those of Latinus and Priam (123–4), both Italian and oriental.
⁸⁶ Gale 1997, Putnam 1998b: 18–22; Reed 2007: 70–1 integrates this in his reading of Turnus as beautiful young man.
⁸⁷ Putnam 1998b: 22 reads this ecphrasis as part of a typically Virgilian 'pattern of emotional debasement', typified by the career of Turnus 'the final, passive, virginal target' of Aeneas and the gods.
⁸⁸ Faber 2006: 113 notes verbal connections between this shield and the shield of Turnus. See also Chinn 2010: 150.

blandus ('sweet') as she thought. The process of deception and enchantment central to ecphrasis risks objectifying the viewer.[89]

Rape is inevitably present in ecphrasis, as an important theme in Greek and Roman literature, a feature of numerous foundation narratives, and a particular leitmotif of Ovid's *Metamorphoses*.[90] But is there a stronger connection? Another favourite theme which crosses between shields and cloaks is the rape not of a woman, but of a boy: the story of Ganymede (featuring in the cloak of Cloanthus in *Aeneid* 5, the cup in Statius *Thebaid* 1 and the shield of Dionysus in Nonnus *Dionysiaca* 25, as well as an inset story at *Met.* 10.155–61, the first story in the song of Orpheus).[91] Ganymede is the archetypal beautiful boy, at the threshold in many different senses: boy and man, mortal and immortal, masculine and feminine, master and slave, hunter and hunted. Quintus Smyrnaeus includes the marriage of Peleus and Thetis in his shield, one point of origin of Hera's hatred and the Trojan war; Nonnus includes the rape of Ganymede as the other point of origin of Hera's hatred of Troy.

In Virgil's cloak, Ganymede begins as the focus of the image and the focaliser of the events, both subject and object at once:

> intextusque puer frondosa regius Ida
> uelocis iaculo ceruos cursuque fatigat
> acer, anhelanti similis, quem praepes ab Ida
> sublimem pedibus rapuit Iouis armiger uncis;
> longaeui palmas nequiquam ad sidera tendunt
> custodes, saeuitque canum latratus in auras. (*Aeneid* 5.252–7)

> And the royal boy woven on leafy Ida
> tires out the swift stags with his javelin and his pursuit,
> eager, as if panting for breath, whom headlong from Ida
> Jove's armour-bearer snatched with its curved talons on high;
> the old guards stretch their palms to the stars
> in vain, and the barking of the dogs rages against the breezes.

We zoom in on Ganymede: first a small figure on the mountain, then the same size as the stags, then in close-up on the word *acer*, intimately listening

---

[89] Faber 2006 connects this ecphrasis to the wider theme of the deceptiveness of the gods in Statius.
[90] Richlin 1992 is still provocative. 'In the *Met.*, rape keeps company with twisted loves, macabre and bloody deaths, cruel gods, cataclysms of nature ..., wars, and, of course, grotesque transformations.' (162) It is interesting to see the contrast with Hardie 2002b: 66–72, in which rape (and its repetition) in Ovid is read as a process of desire (the Lacanian lack: desire, inevitably for something not there, is always displaced and deferred, and therefore repeated), rather than an expression of power. Is rape part of the erotics of the *Metamorphoses*, or part of the violence of the poem? Can the two aspects be separated? Does the erotic charge stem from the violence on display? See Chapter 7, pp.293–302. 'The place of rape in Ovid's texts is thus one where pleasure and violence intersect. Fear is beautiful; violence against the body stands in for rape.' Richlin 1992: 165.
[91] See Hardie 2002a, responding to the chapter in Putnam 1998b. On the Statius passage, see Lovatt 2002.

to his breathing. Distance is created almost immediately by *similis*: he looks *like* he is breathing, but is not actually breathing. So ecphrastic hope and ecphrastic failure set in one two-word phrase. On *quem* he becomes the object and disappears from the text as well as from Mount Ida: now the focus is on the eagle, and we look through the eyes of the *custodes* and the dogs, barking at empty air. The gasping breath (*anhelanti*) also suggests an erotically sensual depiction: running, hot, heavy breathing.[92]

In Nonnus (*Dion.* 25.429–50) the story has two distinct stages, both images set among the stars (429): first the rape itself (οἷα καὶ ἐν γραφίδεσσι, 'as it is in pictures', 433), focusing on Zeus transformed into the eagle and his thoughts and anxieties as he carries the boy: worried that he might fall and become a version of Icarus, or Helle (434–41). The other half of the scene focuses on Ganymede installed in heaven, pouring the wine:[93]

> Οὐρανίης δ' ἤσκητο θεῶν παρὰ δαῖτα τραπέζης
> κοῦρος ἀφυσσομένῳ πανομοίιος· αὐτοχύτου δὲ
> νεκταρέης κρητῆρα βεβυσμένον εἶχεν ἐέρσης,
> καὶ Διὶ δαινυμένῳ δέπας ὤρεγεν· ἕζετο δ' Ἥρη
> οἷα χολωομένη καὶ ἐν ἀσπίδι, μάρτυρι μορφῇ
> ψυχῆς ζῆλον ἔχουσα, παρεζομένῃ δὲ θεαίνῃ
> Παλλάδι δείκνυε κοῦρον, ὅτι γλυκὺ νέκταρ Ὀλύμπου
> βουκόλος ἀστερόφοιτος ἐῳνοχόει Γανυμήδης
> πάλλων χειρὶ κύπελλα, τά περ λάχε παρθένος Ἥβη.   (*Dionysiaca* 25.442–50)

Next the boy was fashioned beside the feast of the heavenly
table, just like someone drawing liquid; and he had
a mixing bowl full of self-pouring dewy nectar,
and he offered a cup to Zeus as he was dining; and Hera sat,
looking angry even on the shield, with her shape bearing witness
that she had a jealous soul, and to the goddess sitting next to her,
Pallas, she pointed out the boy, saying that a cowherd walking
among the stars, Ganymede, was pouring out the sweet nectar of Olympus,
brandishing with his hand the cups which were the lot of the maiden Hebe.

---

[92] In Statius' version we come in at a later moment, as Ganymede flies through the air, and we carry on looking through his eyes: *Gargara desidunt surgenti et Troia recedit* ('Gargara fails him as he rises and Troy recedes', *Theb.* 1.549). Valerius' ecphrasis of the cloak given by Hypsipyle to Jason at 2.408–17 loads the actual rape with intertextual markers (*frondosae Idae* picks up on Virgil's *frondosa Ida*, while *inlustrem* highlights the self-consciousness of the allusion), but focuses on the happy (*laetus*) scene of Ganymede serving wine on Olympus.

[93] This is very similar to the passage in Ovid's song of Orpheus, which is focalised through Zeus, explaining his desire to change into the eagle, with emphasis on the deceptiveness of his shape (*mendacibus . . . pennis*, 'lying wings', 159), until the pay-off, at 160–1 (*qui nunc. . .*, 'who now'), in which Ganymede's role as mixer of wine is reflected in the poet's mixing of wine, Juno and Jupiter (*inuitaque Ioui nectar Iunone ministrat*, 'with Juno unwilling to Jupiter nectar he serves' – though Juno's unwillingness surrounds both Jupiter and the nectar).

Ganymede himself is not named until the second last line of the passage, and his presence in the text is elusive: he is little more than the sum of his function; more attention is paid to the nectar than to him. It is Hera's jealous gaze, the emotion conveyed by the art, which is the focus of the passage. The boy Ganymede is the object of a power struggle between Zeus and Hera, a possession to be displayed, with no real agency of his own. Hera uses his otherness in the context of Olympus to persuade Pallas. Nonnus transforms Virgil's earthly perspective into a heavenly one; where the Virgilian passage focuses on those left behind, even the rape itself in Nonnus' ecphrasis (as in Ovid's miniature) is focalised through Zeus.

The boy, Ganymede, then, is objectified in all three poets – put into a position of powerlessness, arguably feminised, and stripped of his subjectivity. His transition from boy to man is arrested; by becoming a god, he loses his masculinity and his power, moving from prince to slave. Even so his role is enviable: Hera suggests he has usurped Hebe. To be a god of any sort, even a feminised slave boy, is better than being a royal man. Ganymede is an ideal object of ecphrasis, a passive, aestheticised commodity. Ecphrasis, with its emphasis on the powers of art and text to persuade and deceive, is particularly hospitable to discourses of power and powerlessness.

Objects of ecphrasis: the imperial gaze

Gender is one index of otherness, as is divinity, represented and contained in ecphrasis. We can see how internal audiences structure (and complicate) our responses.[94] We began to look at the imperial gaze in the shield of Aeneas: I now take this further by exploring ecphrasis and 'other' worlds in Homer, Valerius, Silius and Nonnus.

The resolutely mortal shield of Hannibal contains two simultaneous imperial gazes: Hannibal looking at Rome, and Rome looking back at Hannibal. The Second Punic War is the turning point between two potential empires. This shield plays with time in a very different way from Virgil's and the contest between two rival gazes, the attempt to separate, contain and disempower, is both going on as we watch, and always already over. Let us consider what we should make in this context of Silius' African pastoral scene:

> laetior at circa facies, agitata ferarum
> agmina uenatu et caelata mapalia fulgent.

[94] For a complex and effective exploration of different levels of focalisation and different audiences in Silius' ecphrasis of a temple at Liternum, see Fowler 2000b. On otherness in Silius, see Augoustakis 2010, Keith 2010.

> nec procul usta cutem nigri soror horrida Mauri
> adsuetas mulcet patrio sermone leaenas.
> it liber campi pastor, cui fine sine ullo
> inuetitum saltus penetrat pecus; omnia Poenum
> armenti uigilem patrio de more sequuntur:
> gaesaque latratorque Cydon tectumque focique
> in silicis uenis et fistula nota iuuencis.
>
> *(Punica* 2.437–45)

> But around a more joyful appearance, columns of wild beasts
> stirred up by hunters and engraved huts shine out.
> Not far away, the bristly sister of the black Moor, with burnt skin,
> soothes the customary lionesses with her native speech.
> The shepherd goes free over the fields, and without any boundary
> his unforbidden herd penetrates the pastures; everything follows
> the Punic guard of the herd, in his inherited custom;
> spear, barking Cretan dog, roof and hearth
> in the veins of a flint and the pipe, well-known to his cattle.

Vessey reads it as simultaneously alien and yet idyllic, a scene of peace and joy contrasted with the violence of war, but one very far from Rome and Italy.[95] *Mapalia* is a Punic word emphasising difference, and set between two words which bring out the texture of the metal shield (*caelata* and *fulgent*): so far we can follow Mitchell's model of the other objectified in representation.[96]

But Silius' description clearly alludes to Virgil *Georgics* 3.339–48:

> Quid tibi pastores Libyae, quid pascua uersu
> prosequar et raris habitata mapalia tectis?
> saepe diem noctemque et totum ex ordine mensem
> pascitur itque pecus longa in deserta sine ullis
> hospitiis: tantum campi iacet. omnia secum
> armentarius Afer agit, tectumque laremque
> armaque Amyclaeumque canem Cressamque pharetram;
> non secus ac patriis acer Romanus in armis
> iniusto sub fasce uiam cum carpit, et hosti
> ante exspectatum positis stat in agmine castris.
>
> (*Georgics* 3.339–48)

> Why should I pursue for you in my verse the Libyan shepherds,
> their pastures and the huts they live in, with thin roofs?
> Often the grazing goes on, day and night and throughout the whole

---

[95] Vessey 1975: 403: 'The whole passage is redolent of an alien and exotic world, utterly strange to the Aeneadae, the men of Rome and Italy. But the epithet *laetior* is not inapt. Superficially the impression is idyllic, even though it is a foreign idyll with little in common with the Arcady of Virgil or Calpurnius.'

[96] Mitchell 1992.

> month, and the herd goes far into the desert without any
> refuge: it only lies in the fields. The African cattle-hand
> drives all with him, house, hearth,
> weapons, Spartan dog and Cretan quiver;
> no less fierce is the Roman in his inherited weapons
> when he seizes a way under an unjust rod and stands
> in a column, with the camp left aside, before the enemy expected.

Silius' passage, then, cannot be straight exoticism, the other on display: for Virgil assimilates the African shepherd with the Roman soldier. When Silius' shepherd 'penetrates' the countryside, he seems to be pursuing an imperial mission. *Patriis* in Virgil referred to the Roman patriarchal inheritance: in Silius it is transferred (twice) to the African. The double perspective of the shield, looking through both Carthaginian and Roman eyes, continues here: the African shepherd represents a 'golden age' idealisation of both Carthaginians and Romans; it is foreign and other, but also represents an idealised Roman military virtue. The scene of the *soror Mauri* soothing the lioness adds to this: she makes the representation doubly other, black-skinned (*usta cutem*; *nigri*) and female. On the other hand, she is Silius' reprise of the key first scene of Aeneas' shield, the she-wolf soothing Romulus and Remus (*Aen.* 8.630–4). Reversal is the key to this allusion. Whereas Virgil's wolf is an animal taking on human qualities and turning boys into wolf-like soldiers, Silius' African woman becomes beast-like by communicating with animals. North Africa was the main source of animals for the wild-beast hunts that took place in gladiatorial games: the shield can be an arena and the hunt a spectacle for the reader. *Agmina* as applied to the animals also plays on the breaking down of the distinction between man and beast. Significantly it recurs a few lines later in the description of Saguntum besieged (448). It sets up the *Punica* itself as a gladiatorial spectacle. Watching gladiators is a key index of Romanness and of empire (gladiators were not just classified by weapons but also by ethnic origins – e.g. Samnite, Gaul, Thracian).[97] The ambivalence which they inspired, as victims enslaved and forced to fight, yet noble moral exemplars and potential superstars, reflects the equivocal Roman attitude towards the barbarian other.

The shield of Aeneas equally reflects this attitude in the description of the Gauls attacking the citadel:[98]

---

[97] Types of weapons are also a stock in trade of ethnographic description. For the complex Roman attitudes to gladiators, see Barton 1993; for wild-beast hunts and the ideology of control over nature, see Wiedemann 1992: 65–7; on cultural identity, 41–7. For gladiatorial spectacle and epic see Zissos 2003.

[98] See Reed 2007: 56–7, who also argues that they are eroticised.

> Galli per dumos aderant arcemque tenebant
> defensi tenebris et dono noctis opacae:
> aurea caesaries ollis atque aurea uestis,
> uirgatis lucent sagulis, tum lactea colla
> auro innectuntur, duo quisque Alpina coruscant
> gaesa manu, scutis protecti corpora longis.   (*Aeneid* 8.657–62)
>
> The Gauls were at hand through the thickets, and were holding the citadel,
> defended by the shadows and the gift of dark night.
> Their hair was golden and golden their clothes,
> they glimmer with striped cloaks and their milky necks
> are entwined with gold, each one brandishes two Alpine
> javelins in his hand, his body protected by a long shield.

Silius alludes to this passage by providing his African *pastor* with a rather unlikely Gallic spear – *gaesa* (*Pun.* 2.444). The deadly beauty and glamour of the militarily successful and threatening barbarian in this passage offsets the depiction of defeated barbarian people filing past Augustus at *Aen.* 8.720–8, which we discussed above. Silius then, picks up on, and uses, the imperial gaze on display in the shield of Aeneas.

This imperial ethnographic gaze seems particularly Roman. The Homeric shield displays two cities, shifting focalisation to make the viewer empathise with both, and giving no sense of ethnic identity. Apollonius does introduce an ethnic dimension to his recapitulation of the Homeric cattle raid: the sons of Electryon are the defenders, and the Teleboans, also called Taphians, the foreign invaders, a horde overpowering the herdsmen (AR *Arg.* 1.747–51), although they are not ethnically other.[99]

Valerius Flaccus reworks Apollonius' interest in Greeks, barbarians and ethnography, by including the geographical (and ethnographic) digression of Argus at AR *Arg.* 4.257–93, in an ecphrasis. We have already mentioned above the temple of the sun in VF *Argonautica* 5; here the Argonauts learn about multiple stories of the origins of Colchis, with their own story set in counterpoint (possibly on the opposite door of the temple?).[100] A cosmic array of representations of earth, sky and sea leads into the images on the doors, which begin with two panels describing the Egyptian Sesostris' colonisation of Colchis (5.418–24). The Colchians, already on the edge of the known world, are made even more exotic by their connection with Africa and Egypt.[101] While for Aeneas, the images of the Trojan war on the temple of Dido are an

---

[99] See Bulloch 2006: 61–2 on the complex family relationship of the two sides.
[100] On this passage, see Wijsman 1996: 196–217.
[101] The mention of the Egyptians returning to Arsinoe, which is a Hellenistic city, may well be Valerius' comment on the Ptolemaic agenda behind this passage of Apollonius. On the politics of Apollonius see Mori 2008.

index of civilisation, here the images refer to the otherness of the Colchians, and the barbarity of Medea (and the Argonauts?) to come. This story of ethnic origins is then doubled (trumped? confirmed?) with a rape narrative, that of the nymph Aea by the river Phasis (425–8).[102] The first word of this panel describes the river as *barbarus* (425), and he is also *furens* (426); the nymph's futile attempt to hold onto the power of her gaze is represented by her haphazard, panicked firing of arrows.

But this temple, like Dido's, and like Silius' temple at Liternum, has multiple focalisers.[103] Jason is *laetus* ('joyful', 416) to see the images, but the ecphrasis has two sets of internal viewers: the Argonauts at the beginning, and the Colchians at the end (451–4), who hate the images despite their ignorance, and turn away their gaze. This *horror* is transferred to the Argonauts at 455. Similarly the two halves of the ecphrasis present two subjects: in the first half the Colchians, and the sun god (Phaethon as Ovidian intertextual referent, and also unsuccessful double of Medea, has come down to earth at 429–32); in the second half the Argonauts themselves unknowingly become subject matter, along with the tragedy of Medea. At 445 avenging Furies form an internal audience within the ecphrasis, watching from the roof of the house in Corinth. Aeneas' identification with the Trojan figures in Carthage, which leads him to identify too closely with Dido, is destabilised by connection with his ignorance of the images on the shield: neither the Colchians nor the Argonauts recognise or understand Vulcan's prophetic images. The two halves also reflect each other: Jason is a reversal of Sesostris, who will take away the future of Colchis (Medea, Apsyrtus and the fleece), while Medea reverses Aea, not raped but destructive. It is Medea whose quasi-divine gaze erupts from the ecphrasis, cutting through text and air, unidentified by the Colchians at 453–4, eluding both Colchians and Jason, subject matter apparently escaping from objectification, becoming a Phaethon who controls the chariot.[104]

Nonnus' Dionysus has unashamed imperial ambitions and the increased reach of Nonnus' cosmic description matches Dionysus' mission to conquer the world (represented by India) and gain apotheosis (like Julius Caesar and Augustus – not to mention Ovid – in the *Metamorphoses*). In Nonnus the Indian 'other' is not the object of ecphrasis: when Attis delivers the

---

[102] Wijsman 1996: 207 points out that the story is not elsewhere attested, but holds back from assuming that Valerius invented it.
[103] Fowler 2000b: 99: 'the characters in the pictures, the artists who made them, the receiving audience of Romans in Liternum, Hannibal and the Carthaginian viewers at the moment described by Silius, Silius himself as narrator and/or author, the contemporary Roman audience of the *Punica* implied and/or real – and ourselves'.
[104] See Buckley forthcoming.

shield, he first presents a complaint from Rheia that Dionysus has not yet conquered the Indians, in terms that clearly represent them as 'other':

> Ἀμπελόεις Διόνυσε, Διὸς τέκος, ἔγγονε Ῥείης,
> εἰπέ μοι εἰρομένῳ, πότε νόστιμος εἰς χθόνα Λυδῶν
> ἵξεαι οὐλοκάρηνον ἀιστώσας γένος Ἰνδῶν·
> οὔ πω ληιδίας κυανόχροας ἔδρακε Ῥείη ...   (*Dionysiaca* 25.326–9)

> Dionysus of the vine, son of Zeus, offspring of Rheia,
> tell me when I ask, when will you return to the land of the Lydians
> having destroyed the woolly-headed race of Indians?
> Not yet has Rheia seen your dark-skinned captives ...

He then follows with a prophecy (352–67) that the Indian city will be destroyed in the seventh year, in which the shield becomes the cosmos itself – not just representing Rheia/Cybele's female omnipotence, but shading into being it:

> Αἰθέρος ἀστερόεσσαν ἀνούτατον ἀσπίδα πάλλων,
> ὦ φίλος, οὐ τρομέεις χόλον Ἄρεος, οὐ φθόνον Ἥρης,
> οὐ μακάρων στίχα πᾶσαν, ἔχων παμμήτορα Ῥείην,
> οὐ στρατὸν ἀγχυλότοξον, ὅπως μὴ δούρατα πέμπων
> Ἠέλιον πλήξειεν ἢ οὐτήσειε Σελήνην.
> τίς ξίφος Ὠρίωνος ἀμαλδύνειε μαχαίρῃ,
> ἢ χθονίοις βελέεσσιν ὀιστεύσειε Βοώτην·
> ἀλλ' ἐρέεις γενέτην κεραελκέα Δηριαδῆος·
> Ὠκεανὸν φορέοντι τί σοι ῥέξειεν Ὑδάσπης·   (*Dionysiaca* 25.352–60)

> Brandishing this starry inviolate shield of the sky,
> my friend, you should not tremble at the anger of Ares, nor the envy of Hera,
> nor all the company of the blessed, holding the all-mother Rheia,
> nor the army with crescent bows, that they might, sending their spears,
> strike Helios or wound Selene.
> Who could soften the sword of Orion with a knife
> or shoot Bootes with earthly arrows?
> But you will say the strong-horned begetter of Deriades:
> what could Hydaspes do to you when you bring Oceanus?

The enemy army are imagined as fighting against Helios and Selene: the cosmic figures are reanimated and Oceanus himself fights off the Indian king's river-god father, Hydaspes. Dionysus does not just obtain the universe, but uses it to fight his battles. Nonnus turns the tables on ecphrasis and makes the image a literal actor in the narrative, more powerful than its contextual reality.[105]

---

[105] This is hyper-Ovidian: see Wheeler 2000: 12–23 on Ovid's cosmogony and the demiurge as artisan. 'Ovid does not present an evolutionary narrative, but an ecphrastic description of a state of nature that is the opposite of chaos.' (17)

Returning the gaze: the apotropaic shield

This is also a feminine cosmos, not just representing but also identified with the 'all-mother Rheia'. The shield contains images of the two key male–female divine rivalries that structure the *Dionysiaca*: the Ganymede panel, as we have seen, represents the conflict between Zeus and Hera that creates the labours of Dionysus. On the other side of the Moria and Tylus episode lies the battle between Cybele and Kronos, in which she deceives Kronos by substituting a stone for the newly born Zeus. Nonnus feminises Kronos by comparing his disgorging of the swallowed babies (and one stone) to labour:

> καὶ λίθον ἐν λαγόνεσσι μογοστόκον ἔνδον ἀείρων
> θλιβομένην πολύτεκνον ἀνηκόντιζε γενέθλην
> φόρτον ἀποπτύων, ἐγκύμονος ἀνθερεῶνος.   (*Dionysiaca* 25.560–2)
>
> There he was again in heavy labour with the stone inside him
> bringing up all those children squeezed together
> and disgorging the burden from his pregnant throat.

Verbal echoes link this contest to the rivalry between Amphion and Zethus earlier in the shield (413–28).[106] If Kronos is a version of Zethus, then Rheia becomes another in the line of Nonnus' figures: a very important one, as Dionysus' main divine sponsor, and significantly, feminine.[107] Poetic power is the equivalent of Cybele's female generative power; deception and illusion are ultimately creative.

Nonnus seems to reverse the relationship between ecphrasis and the other: the shield is envisaged as an active protagonist; the representations on it are closely linked to Dionysus himself, almost intertwined. In the same way that the ecphrasis picks on themes and stories that recur frequently in the poem, so the relationship between narrative and ecphrasis is reversed, dominating the visual description with an epyllion. The Indian 'other', then, is denied the power of inclusion in the ecphrasis: in Nonnus the inside is the powerful place to be; Olympus is part of this ecphrasis. The Indian audience stay on the outside, not contained but excluded.

Returning the gaze: the apotropaic shield

The object of ecphrasis (both physical objects and objects displayed in decoration) can gain power and agency: one way is through the malevolent

---

[106] Three echoes of line 418: θλιβομένη πετραῖον ἐπωμίδι φόρτον ἀείρων.
[107] Shorrock argues that one of the major poet figures in the poem is Dionysus himself: Nonnus represents himself as the generator of a Dionysiac poetics. Like Dionysus, then, perhaps he spans masculine and feminine.

gaze of image back at viewer. In Hannibal's shield the figure of Hamilcar has this effect:

> at senior Siculis exultat Hamilcar in aruis –
> spirantem credas certamina anhela mouere,
> ardor inest oculis, toruumque minatur imago. (*Punica* 2.429–31)
>
> But old Hamilcar rejoices in the Sicilian fields –
> you would believe that he was breathing and stirring up breathless conflicts,
> there is burning in his eyes, and the fierce image threatens.

The *topos* of ecphrastic realism slides into something different: he is not just breathing, but breathing war. Virgil's gasping Ganymede is replaced by the gasping of warriors and dying men. His burning eyes are not just the standard attribute of a ferocious warrior: he is the embodiment of the powerful, penetrating, hostile gaze. As a representation of Carthaginian victory, he threatens the Romans, and the watching Saguntines, who are envisaged, as we have seen, as one audience for the shield. Hannibal is another: the scene just before (1.70–139) shows Hannibal as a small boy, resolutely not terrified by the hellish temple and swearing *haud mollia dictu* ('things not soft in the saying', 113). Hamilcar is a model, but also a reminder and a threat for Hannibal.

Later in book 4 we see Hannibal's shield in action. At the battle of Ticinus, Hannibal goes into battle to re-invigorate his troops:

> Aduolat aurato praefulgens murice ductor
> Sidonius circaque Metus Terrorque Furorque.
> isque ubi Callaici radiantem tegminis orbem
> extulit et magno percussit lumine campos,
> spes uirtusque cadunt, trepidaque a mente recedit
> uertere terga pudor; nec leti cura decori
> sed fugere infixum est, terraeque optantur hiatus. (*Punica* 4.324–30)
>
> Gleaming out in gold and purple, the Sidonian leader
> flies close, and around him are Fear, Terror and Rage.
> And when he raised up the shining circle of his Gallician
> shield and struck the fields with great light,
> hope and courage fall, and shame about turning their backs
> retreats from the panicked minds; nor is there any care for a decent death
> but flight is fixed in, and they long for a chasm in the earth.

In 324–5 Hannibal is like an artefact from the Homeric shield, golden like Ares and Athena, the purple reflecting the dyed red cloak of Death at *Il.* 18.538, while *Metus, Terror* and *Furor* correspond to Ἔρις, Κυδοιμός, and

Κήρ (Strife, Din and Fate/Death) at 535.[108] The shield here acts as a weapon, and the verb of striking (*percussit*) turns it from a defensive to an aggressive object. The idea of light striking the fields suggests haptic theories of vision, in which light and vision are particles with physical impact on the world around them. Psychological defeat is equated with actual defeat. Fixation on the visual object turns into fixation on flight. The image has such an impact on its viewers here that it can be said to be active rather than passive, to be powerful and have agency.

The ecphrastic shield has long been read as an apotropaic device, designed to put the fear of god into those who face it.[109] The shield of Agamemnon has on it a Gorgon with a powerful gaze:[110]

> τῇ δ' ἐπὶ μὲν Γοργώ βλοσυρῶπις ἐστεφάνωτο
> δεινὸν δερκομένη, περὶ δὲ Δεῖμός τε Φόβος τε. (*Iliad* 11.36–7)
>
> And on it, at the centre, was the horrifying face of the Gorgon,
> gazing terribly, and around her were Terror and Fear.

This paralysing image of power and powerful image is a reflection of the aegis of Zeus, worn by Athene:

> ἐν δέ τε Γοργείη κεφαλὴ δεινοῖο πελώρου,
> δεινή τε σμερδνή τε, Διὸς τέρας αἰγιόχοιο. (*Iliad.* 5.741–2)
>
> and on it the Gorgon head of the terrible monster,
> terrifying and fear-inspiring, the omen of aegis-bearing Zeus.

Achilles' shield, too, terrifies even his own Myrmidons:

> Μυρμιδόνας δ' ἄρα πάντας ἕλε τρόμος, οὐδέ τις ἔτλη
> ἄντην εἰσιδέειν, ἀλλ' ἔτρεσαν. (*Iliad* 19.14–15)
>
> But trembling caught hold of all the Myrmidons, and not one dared
> to look at the shield, but they were afraid.

The wonder inspired by the divine glory and workmanship shades over into terror at divine power. The shield initiates a battle of gazes between the hero, standing in for his divine sponsor, and whoever is confronting him. The power of the divine gaze is encapsulated in the divine shield. You

---

[108] The corresponding passage in Virgil's shield (8.700–3) has Mars surrounded by Dirae, Discordia and Bellona (who has a bloody whip rather than a bloody cloak).

[109] See Harrison 2001 for T-scholia reading the shield of Agamemnon in this way.

[110] For more of Medusa, see below, Chapter 9, pp.353–7. Dead monsters are another way of objectifying otherness while terrifying your audience: see for instance the shield of Capaneus at *Theb.* 4.168–72 which enshrines the marvel of ecphrastic viewing in the dead (or dying) body of the horrifying monster. On this shield see Harrison 1992.

literally cannot look at it but must turn your eyes away and flee. Similarly, we have seen above the terrifying impact of the ghost of Heracles in *Odyssey* 11, and of his belt on Odysseus.

Likewise, when Aeneas arrives back at the Trojan camp in *Aeneid* 10, his shield, too, blazes with light and puts the enemy to flight:

> ardet apex capiti tristisque a uertice flamma
> funditur et uastos umbo uomit aureus ignis:
> non secus ac liquida si quando nocte cometae
> sanguinei lugubre rubent, aut Sirius ardor
> ille sitim morbosque ferens mortalibus aegris
> nascitur et laeuo contristat lumine caelum. (*Aeneid* 10.270–5)

> The peak of his helmet blazes and sad flame pours
> from the top and the golden boss spews out vast fire:
> no differently than when bloody comets glow grievously red
> in the clear night, or burning Sirius rises,
> bringing thirst and diseases to sick mortals
> and the sky sorrows with ominous light.

The flame is an omen that has the power to create the effects it predicts. The bloody comets echo Bellona with her bloody whip in the Actium scene of the shield (*sanguineo flagello*, *Aen.* 8.703); the red glow of the comet looks back to the red of the bloody Actian sea (*rubescunt*, 695); Aeneas' shield vomiting flame replicates Augustus at 680–1 (*geminas cui tempora flammas | laeta uomunt*). The shield is coming to life: this is not just typology, but a sort of eerie pre-incarnation. It is also a reprise of the heart of the *Iliad*, the moment where Hector finally confronts Achilles in book 22. Priam is the first to see him coming across the plain blazing like Sirius at 22.26–31: ὡς τοῦ χαλκὸς ἔλαμπε περὶ στήθεσσι θέοντος ('So the fire of the bronze shone around his chest as he was running', 22.32). As Hector waits and watches, we participate in his thought processes and he decides to stand his ground. But the sight is too much for him:

> Ὣς ὅρμαινε μένων, ὁ δέ οἱ σχεδὸν ἦλθεν Ἀχιλλεὺς
> ἶσος Ἐνυαλίῳ, κορυθάϊκι πτολεμιστῇ,
> σείων Πηλιάδα μελίην κατὰ δεξιὸν ὦμον
> δεινήν· ἀμφὶ δὲ χαλκὸς ἐλάμπετο εἴκελος αὐγῇ
> ἢ πυρὸς αἰθομένου ἢ ἠελίου ἀνιόντος.
> Ἕκτορα δ᾽, ὡς ἐνόησεν, ἕλε τρόμος· οὐδ᾽ ἄρ᾽ ἔτ᾽ ἔτλη
> αὖθι μένειν, ὀπίσω δὲ πύλας λίπε, βῆ δὲ φοβηθείς· (*Iliad* 22.131–7)

> So he pondered, waiting, but Achilleus was closing upon him
> in the likeness of the lord of battles, the helm-shining warrior,
> and shaking from above his shoulder the dangerous Pelian

ash spear, while the bronze that closed about him was shining
like the flare of blazing fire or the sun in its rising.
And the shivers took hold of Hector when he saw him, and he could no longer
stand his ground there, but left the gates behind, and fled, frightened

This clash of light versus gaze encapsulates the visual power of the hero. It is no coincidence that the erotic power of Jason as he approaches Hypsipyle on Lemnos, wearing his cloak, is described with a similar star image (AR *Arg.* 1.774–81).[111] The cloak is so bright that looking at it is like looking at the rising sun (725–6); it overpowers by beauty and intensity, not sheer power of light, as in the description of Achilles above.

The apotropaic power of the shield (and other ecphrases) is one effect on internal viewers of artefacts described in epic ecphrases. This paralysis or horror works in apposition to sensual dis/satisfaction, both of which show deep emotional engagement, often almost erotic.[112] When Achilles looks on his shield at *Il.* 19.19 he rejoices: αὐτὰρ ἐπεὶ φρεσὶν ᾗσι τετάρπετο δαίδαλα λεύσσων ('But when he had satisfied his heart with looking at the intricate armour'). τέρπω is used both to signify pleasure and satisfaction; it is often used in Homer of both food and sex.[113] While others are terrified, Achilles rejoices, no doubt in killing and vengeance to come, as well as divine recognition and heroic glory. Similarly, Odysseus wonders at and enjoys an unbroken view of Alcinous' palace (*Od.* 7.133–4), just as Hermes takes pleasure in the sight of Calypso's cave: ἔνθα κ' ἔπειτα καὶ ἀθάνατός περ ἐπελθών/θηήσαιτο ἰδὼν καὶ τερφθείη φρεσὶν ᾗσιν. ('Even an immortal arriving there would have wondered as he looked and satisfied the heart within him', *Od.* 5.73–4). Later in the tradition, satisfaction becomes endless dissatisfaction, the desire born out of lack: so in the description of the cloak of Dionysus which Hypsipyle gave to Jason: οὔ μιν ἀφάσσων οὔτε κεν εἰσορόων γλυκὺν ἵμερον ἐμπλήσειας· ('Neither by touching nor by looking might you fill out sweet desire', AR *Arg.* 4.428–9).[114] The cloak is so supernaturally attractive that it partakes in the insatiability of erotic desire, as if permeated by the lovemaking of Dionysus and Ariadne.[115]

---

[111] See below, Chapter 7, pp.265–8, on heroes and stars.
[112] Disgust and desire are two emotions important for designing and selling consumer products: Desmet 2002. On disgust see further Menninghaus 2003.
[113] Food and drink: *Il.* 9.705; *Od.* 1.26, 369, 3.70; sex: *Il.* 9.337; *Od.* 8.292; poetry: *Od.* 8.368; looking: *Il.* 20.23; *Od.* 16.26.
[114] This particular cloak is characterised by sensual overload: the divine fragrance (430), looking and touching (429). For Freud, vision replaced olfactory stimulation as the civilised driver of sexual desire.
[115] On the workings of desire and insatiable gazing, see Morales 2004: 105–6.

There has been much debate over the significance of *animum pictura pascit inani* at *Aen*. 1.464–5 ('He feeds his mind on the empty image').[116] The conjunction between language of feeding and the idea of lack of substance is important here: Virgil implicitly questions the Homeric equation of pleasure in viewing with bodily pleasure. The consumptive gaze is always destined to be disappointed. More importantly, visual pleasure is no guarantee of truth, reliability or satisfaction. Apollonius' insatiable gaze is connected with the deception of Apsyrtus, and the implication of Virgil's phrase is that Aeneas deceives himself in his onesided interpretation of these representations of his own past, which no longer belong to him alone in the public context of Carthage. The false ecphrastic hope on display asks readers of epic to beware, to resist the potential enchantment of epic's alignment with authority.[117]

The other effect of Dido's murals is to paralyse: *Haec dum Dardanio Aeneae miranda uidentur, | dum stupet obtutuque haeret defixus in uno* ('while these things seemed full of wonder for Dardanian Aeneas, while he is stupefied and unable to move, fixed in one gaze', 1.494–5). In his complete subjection to the viewing experience, he loses agency. Dido's arrival turns Aeneas' gaze from the images to her, but the viewing (and the paralysis) continues. Each in turn is stupefied by the sight of the other: *obstipuit* 513 (of Aeneas); 613 (of Dido), although this reciprocity is undone by the complicating factor of the other Trojans who appear between Aeneas' view of Dido and his reaction. It has been argued that the similarity between Penthesilea, object of the final panel of the ecphrasis, and Dido as Diana, who immediately follows, breaks the frame of the ecphrasis, and makes Dido part of its objectification.[118] Troilus and Hector already converted into body rather than actor, Penthesilea about to become erotic object in death, the Trojan women in a futile attempt to avoid enslavement, while Pallas averts her gaze, all encapsulate the objectification of the other in ecphrasis (especially given that they are all ethnically other for the Carthaginian artists, and part of that

---

[116] See Beck 2007: 539–40 on this phrase, with further bibliography on the passage and misinterpretation at 534. Her argument that the *Aeneid* gives a fundamentally more complex and problematic account of art and interpretation than Homeric epic flattens out the different aspects of Homeric epic too much, as well as ignoring the intervening influence of Apollonius, but is otherwise satisfying.

[117] There is an internal recapitulation of the motif of emptiness in the Troilus panel, where he is still attached to his empty chariot, and his spear makes meaningless marks in the dust: *curruque haeret resupinus inani* (476) ... *uersa puluis inscribitur hasta* (478). Read as an analogy for Aeneas' viewing of the images, Aeneas is passively dragged along by a driving visual force, that nevertheless has no real agenda, and is unable to create secure meaning himself, already embroiled in his own destruction. This takes the analogy too far, but there is certainly a thematic affinity between the two scenes.

[118] Putnam 1998a: 254–6, reprinted in Putnam 1998b. See also Bartsch 1998.

lost world of epic, which we saw in Catullus 64, for Dido already). Yet this objectification is transferred onto the viewer: Aeneas identifies with the subject matter, and his passivity in viewing is matched by his passivity in the narrative, manipulated and protected by Venus, object of Juno's hatred, used by Jupiter.

That the Sibyl moves him away from the paralysis of grief at 6.33–7, where Daedalus' inability to portray the death of Icarus is juxtaposed with the moment of Aeneas being prevented from 'reading' the images, with the word *spectacula* (37) implying an empty or even counter-productive viewing experience, suggests that he has not, by this point in the narrative, progressed. Perhaps his recognition of the sound of the omen at 8.530–1, when others are paralysed by the arrival of the shield, shows greater agency and determination. But the language of dissatisfaction remains: although Aeneas is *laetus* at 8.617, he cannot be satisfied (*expleri nequit*, 618) and the contrast between substance and image remains in his final reaction (*miratur rerumque ignarus imagine gaudet*, 'he wonders and ignorant of the matters, he rejoices in the image', 730). Is Aeneas' viewing any different from Turnus' viewing of the spoils he has taken from Pallas? At 10.500–5 Turnus rejoices in his power (*ouat spolio gaudetque potitus*, 500) but this is immediately followed by his ignorance of the future. In the context of this discussion, the verb *hausit* in the final confrontation with Turnus and the sword-belt of Pallas seems important:

> ille, oculis postquam saeui monimenta doloris
> exuuiasque hausit, furiis accensus et ira
> terribilis   (*Aeneid* 12.945–7)

> He, after he had drained down the reminder of savage grief
> and the spoils with his eyes, lit up by rage and terrifying
> in his anger

Here Aeneas fully consumes the image, letting go of any distance or restraint, not interrupted or moved on;[119] the result is the ultimate objectification of Turnus in violent death (or is it the consummation of Aeneas' epic heroism?).[120]

---

[119] Or does he fail to see the surface image at all, instead remembering his vividly visual grief at the death of Pallas (*Pallas, Euander, in ipsis | omnia sunt oculis*, 'Pallas, Evander, everything is in his eyes themselves', 10.515–16)? Not just competing interpretations, but competing visions are at work here.

[120] Ovid re-eroticises epic viewing, particularly in the Narcissus episode, where viewing and desire conjoined literally replace food and drink (*Met.* 3.437), and even then *spectat inexpleto lumine* ('he looks with unfulfilled/dissatisfied eye', 439).

Conclusions

This survey of epic ecphrases has led us into fascinating territory, if briefly and incompletely (Is satisfaction possible? Or even desirable?). We have seen the power of the image and the way that the ecphrastic gaze is intimately linked to the divine gaze. The problematic representations of maker and gods both in and around ecphrases complicate this relationship. Women and the conquered Other are not simply passive objects of ecphrasis; sometimes men, or boys, are; sometimes the other cannot be contained. The shield in particular is an icon of heroic force: it creates visual power, fixates and paralyses.

I finish with two brief moments of reflection on epic and ecphrasis in the final book of Statius' *Thebaid*. Book 12 of the *Thebaid* has been read as the redemption of this almost unmitigatingly dark poem, or as a recapitulation of battle and destruction, or both.[121] The importance of the Argive women (we will examine Argia's *aristeia* in the next chapter) offers a feminine alternative to epic violence.[122] In this context it seems noteworthy that Statius' description of the altar of Clemency, which lies at the heart of his alternative ending, his feminine re-slanting, explicitly eschews representative imagery. This long ecphrasis (*Theb.* 12.481–511) often focuses on what is not there. The refusal of incense and blood sacrifce (487–8) is matched by the undoing of visual art:

> nulla autem effigies, nulli commisa metallo
> forma dei: mentes habitare et pectora gaudet.   (*Thebaid* 12.493–4)
>
> But there are no statues, no forms of the god entrusted
> to metal: she rejoices to inhabit minds and hearts.

This is the anti-type of Virgil's temple of Juno, of Ovid's (and Valerius') temple of the sun, of Statius' own house of Mars and necklace of Harmonia, and an extension of Virgil's Daedalus: not enforced but chosen visual silence; a refusal to represent which matches (and trumps) the refusal to gaze. However this feminine redemption must be carried out by the masculine, military figure of Theseus, whose shield is a recapitulation of the epic shield (12.665–71), containing an image of Crete, the labyrinth and his own conquest of the Minotaur, in progress. This shield goes back to origins of epic ecphrasis; like Agamemnon's shield it exists to create terror: *terror habet populos* ('terror holds the peoples', 672). Epic violence, monstrosity and self-glorification efface Daedalus from the labyrinth, erase Ariadne from the story, and leave the epic hero centre-stage to complete the circle.

---

[121] On redemption, Braund 1997; on endlessness, Lovatt 1999.   [122] Dietrich 1999.

CHAPTER 6

The female gaze

The previous chapter began with a woman as the object of the gaze, and explored the workings of gender as one marker of otherness, contained and objectified in works of art. However, women are not the central subject matter of epic: the epic gaze is fundamentally concerned with looking at men, and this chapter discusses three different areas of female viewing in epic: dreams, teichoscopy and lament.

Since Mulvey's article, there has been much debate about whether the gaze must inevitably be male, whether there can be such a thing as a female gaze.[1] If a woman watches a film, is she inevitably taking on a masculine role, becoming the temporary wielder of the male gaze? Or can she 'look askance', take her own feminine perspective and use it to challenge the values of what she views? Following on from McGowan's Lacanian perspective (see Introduction, p.9), when you consider the gaze as a disturbance of the visual field, the gaze relates only indirectly to gender (as one index of otherness). However, the female perspective is centrifugal: it works against power, authority, structures of expectation. The female gaze is that point at which woman in particular forms a disturbance in the visual field, and this chapter shows quite how important that female gaze is in complicating epic.

The discussion of prophecy in Chapter 4 focused on the differences between male and female inspiration, and the different challenges facing male and female prophets. A particularly female space for engaging with the future is the dream: often interior, both psychologically and physically, dreams take place in the mind and in the bedroom. Dreams are private and only become public if the dreamer presents them to the world. While most

---

[1] For a good summary of the issues around spectatorship see Mayne 1998; specifically on the female gaze see: Doane 1982 and Doane 1988 both reprinted in Doane 1991, De Lauretis 1984, Modleski 1988: 5–9, essays by Crowie and Bergstrom in Penley 1988, essays by Gamman (Gamman 1988) and Moore (Moore 1988) in Gamman and Marshment 1988, Pribram 1988, Stacey 1994: 19–48, Polk 1997.

interpreters of omens are male, dreamers and their interpreters are often female. Dreams offer one way of approaching the female gaze in epic. Dreams in the ancient world are a channel of communication from gods to men, a visualisation of the incomprehensible desires of the other (both gods and women), and a disturbance of narrative causality.

Dreams are secluded and internal: the next section moves out of domestic space, and onto the marginal space of the walls and the shore. Scenes of women in epic watching men from the walls, either as they fight or as they leave, are frequent: the female perspective takes on a surprising importance, and women often take the reins of the narrative. Alternatively they become objects of the gaze: looking can expose them. Finally, this chapter investigates the visual aspects of lament and aftermath. Lament is women's work, and the state of mourning allows women the freedom to move beyond domestic spaces and even enter the battlefield. Does the power of grief empower the female gaze? How is viewing connected to mourning? By looking at these areas, I explore the operation of a female gaze in epic, whether women as viewers are always generically troubling, and how epic spaces are created and problematised by gender.

Dreams and female viewing

Dreams are often connected with film, as a metaphor for the subconscious.[2] In the ancient world, however, they are viewed rather differently, as another channel of communication between gods and men. Many dreams in ancient literature have prophetic elements.[3] Some contain omens; some, like omens, must be interpreted by prophets; others are more like private, inspired visions. Dreams are also associated with genres: the epic dream is exemplified by the dream of Agamemnon (*Il.* 2.5–34), in which Zeus sends a dream to Agamemnon to give him instructions which also imply a prophecy; Aeneas, too, has many of these 'message dreams', guiding him through the narrative towards the prophetic *telos*.[4] The tragic dream is exemplified by the dream of

---

[2] The *locus classicus* is Metz 1982: 101–28. Jung 2002 characterised dreams as theatrical: 'A dream is a theatre in which the dreamer is himself the scene, the player, the prompter, the author, the producer, the public, and the critic.' (54) On early cinema and dreams: Chanan 1996. Particular film-makers who considered the relationship between film and dreams important include Bergman, Fellini and Kurosawa. On actual use of dreams in film-making, see Pagel, Kwiatkowski and Broyles 1999.
[3] On dreams in the ancient world see Grillone 1967, Kessels 1978, Perutelli 1994, Bouquet 2001, Walde 2001, Harris 2009, Harrisson 2010.
[4] See Krevans 1993: 257 with bibliography. Classifying dreams often seems arbitrary: however, intertextual resonances with Homer or Virgil might justify calling a type of dream 'epic', while predominance or frequency in tragedy might suggest that 'tragic' is also a fair label.

Clytemnestra in Aeschylus *Choephori* (523–50) in which the sleeper awakes terrified, attempts to turn away the effects of the dream by ritual practices, it is told to a listener, and interpreted.[5] There is an association between gender and genre: the 'epic dreams' come more often to men, 'tragic dreams' more often to women.[6] We could deconstruct this opposition: in epic the dreamer does not need to tell his dream to a confidante; the narrator can narrate it. Tragic dreams also contain elements of the message dream, such as the dream of Clytemnestra at Sophocles' *Electra* 417–30 in which Agamemnon delivers a visual message. How do genre and gender interact in epic dreams? To what extent do dreams offer a centrifugal perspective, pulling away from the centre of power, towards the feminine margins? Do dreams in epic function as a disturbance in the field of vision?

In *Iliad* 2, Agamemnon's dream plays with the incomprehensibility of divine desires to mortals. Zeus deliberately and deceptively sends a dream to prophesy to Agamemnon that now is the right time to take Troy. In practice, Zeus has decided to honour Achilles at the expense of the other Greeks. Penelope has several dreams in the *Odyssey*, and is not a passive dreamer; in book 4 she questions her dream figure, and in book 19 she reflects self-consciously on the nature of dreams, as part of her power game with the disguised Odysseus. The dream at 4.795–841 is a message dream, sent by Athene, prophesying the safe return of Telemachus. Penelope questions the dream (810–11) and pushes it for further prophecies, challenging the dream to prove it is divine (831–4). This dreams is an epic dream (though it does not contain instructions or guidance, only comfort); the dream which Penelope sets out to Odysseus at 19.535–51 seems more 'tragic': she is telling her dream to a confidant, who interprets it. The dream contains a disturbing omen: in it, her favourite geese are slaughtered by an eagle, and she responds by weeping.[7] The eagle returns and offers her a comforting prophecy in the voice of Odysseus. Odysseus himself, still in disguise, interprets it as an omen that the suitors are about to be killed

---

[5] Another good example: Atossa at Aesch. *Persae* 176–211, in which she foresees the death of her son; visual language emphasises clarity, at 179, 188, 200. It is combined with an omen of a hawk and an eagle at 205–11. Other ways of classifying dreams: external (caused by a deity or similar) and internal (coming from the dreamer's own psyche); type-1 dreams (visitation) and type-2 (symbolic), as in Walde 2001, who genders type-1 male, and type-2 female.

[6] Kessels 1978: 163–5 argues that a change over time from male dreamers in the *Iliad* to female dreamers in the *Odyssey* and tragedy is implausible, and even by the time of Apollonius, in which the dream of Euphemus plays a prominent role, this seems far too schematic. Historiography complicates the picture still further: see Pelling 1996.

[7] On this dream see Rozokoki 2001. She interprets the gates of ivory and horn as, respectively, something grand and impressive which conceals deceit, and truth which often goes unseen. See also Rutherford 1992: 33–8.

(19.555–8). But Penelope does not accept this interpretation, just as she refuses to accept Odysseus as her husband until she has tested him in the dialogue about the bed. Instead she calls the dream ἀμήχανοι ἀκριτόμυθοι 'hard to interpret, hopeless to puzzle out' (560) and ἀμενηνῶν 'insubstantial' (562), and speaks of the gates of horn and ivory. Some dreams are true, others are deceptive, and she insists on putting this dream into the category of the deceptive dream. Does this represent her refusing to hope when her hope has so often been disappointed? Or taking back control of the situation from the interpreting figure of the disguised Odysseus? Does she really not recognise him, or is she playing his own game of deception against him?[8] And what of her emotional response to the death of the suitors in the dream? Is it fear, as the eagle diagnoses? Penelope herself relates it to her fondness for the geese. Does the return of Odysseus represent in fact a loss of control for Penelope? Penelope presents the female side of epic, the women left behind, and responding to male exploits and adventures, the domestic set against the warlike, which is not just a foreshadowing of many of the concerns of tragedy, but also an integral part of epic.

Dreams are important for the characterisation of Medea in Apollonius, and for Apollonius' engagement with the epic genre: her dream at 3.616–32 almost foreshadows what will happen (it is not strictly prophetic, but rather reflects her own emotional processes), and is not exactly tragic either. It is almost confessed to her sister (instead she misrepresents the dream at 688–92 as being about the death of Chalciope's sons).[9] We are not privy to the dream's causes (as in tragedy), but it might well have been sent by a god. Medea's powerful gaze will be on show later (pp.334–6, Talos episode), but here we can see her both powerful and powerless, taking action, but apparently at the mercy of the powers which inspired her dream.

The dream of Euphemus at 4.1731–45, which forms the last significant episode in the poem, is clearly symbolic: he dreams that he is breastfeeding the clod of earth given him by Triton, that it turns into a woman, and he rapes it. It even includes his emotional distress at having raped his own 'daughter'. The content of the dream combines male sexual violence with female fertility. It also represents an interesting interaction with Pindar *Pythian* 4, in which Medea's prophecy about Euphemus' founding of Cyrene is the main event, sidelining the more obvious parts of the

---

[8] This question has long been discussed: Harsh 1950; see also Winkler 1990: 129–61.
[9] Scioli 2010 argues that the inability to communicate effectively the content of dreams is related to the inability of the epic poet to convey fully his subject matter: but here, as elsewhere, it surely comes down to the transgressive desires of the dreamer and their inability to face up to it in social space.

Argonautic narrative. As a woman taking on a prophetic role in public and as part of a foundation myth, she very much stands against the general association of men with prophecies that lead to action, foundation and political agency. Yet in Apollonius' version, which in many respects is less epic than Pindar's lyric *Argonautica*, Jason takes back the role of prophetic interpreter, and his interpretation leads immediately to Euphemus' action of throwing the clod into the sea (contrasting obviously with Medea's complaint in Pindar that the Argonauts did not listen to her, and the clod accidentally fell into the sea).[10] Both of these dreams, like Penelope's, give us a clear sense of dreams as visual stimuli that summon up a strong emotional response (as does Penelope's dream at *Od.* 20.87–90, in which she wakes from a dream that Odysseus is beside her to find an empty bed, turning joy into misery).

Euphemus' dream, and Penelope's, also share the feature of narrative incongruity: the leap from one strange situation to another, the difficulty of rationalising and understanding it, which calls for interpretation. Dreams, like omens, share a causal relationship between interpretation and narrative. Within the story world, the reader knows that the dream must be significant, or the text would not highlight it. The interpretation of dreams is another aspect of over-coherent thinking, the faculty of the human brain which allows and encourages us to make narratives (and sense).[11] Medea's significant dream seems prophetic to us because it foretells what she will in fact do; it seems significant to her because it represents what she wants to do; and it becomes significant because she acts on it. Yet Penelope's emotional response seems to represent some unease about the narrative in which she is involved: as if she is a Nausicaa figure, about to be remarried to Odysseus.[12] Similarly, Apollonius plays with the Euphemus dream sequence by making it so disturbing and yet positive. The desire of the gods remains an uneasy matter; dreams are another disturbance in the field of epic vision.

The dream of Ilia, which is one of the most significant fragments of Ennius' *Annales* (34–50 Sk.), shows a similar anxiety and ambivalence, about the figure of her abductor, who is both beautiful (*pulcer*, 38) and threatening; about her family, who will desert her, and also redeem her, represented by the prophetic figure of her father Aeneas, whose prophecy comforts her with the prospect of founding Rome, but cannot be seen: *Nec sese dedit in conspectum corde cupitus* (47). Throughout her narrative of the dream to her sister, which marks the dream as both tragic and epic, the language of seeming and appearance emphasises the potential deceptiveness

---

[10] Pindar *Pyth.* 4.13–56.   [11] On this see Currie and Jureidini 2004.   [12] Krevans 1993: 262–3.

of vision (*uisus*, 38; *uidebar*, 40; *uidetur*, 43). Her straining and seeking, not just for her father, but for home and family (39–42) show a feminine perspective combined with lack of power and agency. Since we cannot easily fit this fragment into a wider context it is difficult to draw further conclusions, but for now I note the connection again between woman, prophecy and rape (see above, Chapter 4, pp.145–9).

Krevans argues that Ilia's dream has important implications for the understanding of dreams in the *Aeneid*. She suggests that Dido goes from being a foundation heroine, like Ilia, whose trials and tribulations will be rewarded by the political success of her descendants (dream of Sychaeus, narrated by Venus at *Aen*. 1.353–609), to become in *Aeneid* 4 a purely tragic heroine, whose omens, dreams and predictions lead only to her own death (dream sequence along with other omens at 4.465–8).[13] In contrast, Aeneas' dreams are mainly of the 'visitation' type, and Latinus, too, has a positive and prophetic dream of guidance.[14] However the most famous of these visitation dreams (the dream of Hector, 2.268–97) is linked in a number of ways to the 'tragic' dream tradition, especially that in Ennius. The tone of the initial vision is emotional and disorientating:

> in somnis ecce ante oculos maestissimus Hector
> uisus adesse mihi largosque effundere fletus,
> raptatus bigis ut quondam, aterque cruento
> puluere perque pedes traiectus lora tumentis.
> ei mihi, qualis erat, quantum mutatus ab illo
> Hectore qui redit exuuias indutus Achilli
> uel Danaum Phrygios iaculatus puppibus ignis,
> squalentem barbam et concretos sanguine crinis
> uulneraque illa gerens, quae circum plurima muros
> accepit patrios! ultro flens ipse uidebar
> compellare uirum et maestas expromere uoces:
> 'o lux Dardaniae . . .' (*Aeneid* 2.270–81)

> In my sleep, behold, before my eyes, most sorrowful Hector
> seemed to be present to me and to pour out generous tears,
> as he once was when he had been snatched by the chariot, black with blood
> and dust and his swollen feet pierced with thongs.
> Alas, what a state he was in, how changed from that
> Hector who returned wearing the spoils of Achilles
> or threw Phrygian fires against the ships of the Danaans,

---

[13] Krevans 1993: 266–71.
[14] Aeneas: Hector *Aen*. 2.268–97; Penates 3.147–78; Anchises and Mercury 4.351–3, 554–70; Anchises 5.721–45; Tiber 8.26–67. Latinus' incubation dream: 7.92–101.

his beard crusted and his hair solid with blood
bearing those wounds, those many wounds which he received
around his ancestral walls! Weeping I myself of my own accord seemed
to address the hero and speak sorrowful words:
'O light of Dardania . . .'

Echoes of Ennius complicate the effects of this vision.[15] Lines 279–80 echo 44 Sk. of the dream of Ilia, in which her father addresses her, both recalling the foundation heroine status of Ilia, and implicitly suggesting that Aeneas, like her about to suffer greatly in the cause of founding Rome, shares some of the passivity of a rape victim, although it is reversed to the extent that Aeneas addresses Hector, whereas Ilia's father Aeneas addresses her. The fact that Aeneas addresses the ghost, who refuses to answer his questions, also evokes Penelope; his disorientation (he appears not to remember Hector's death) evokes the emotional confusion of Penelope (and Ilia). One might argue that this initial tragic colouring only serves to emphasise the positive epic ending of the encounter, but in practice the whole of *Aeneid* 2 is characterised by failures of vision: the deception of wearing Greek armour and the resulting confusion, darkness, watching powerlessly the deaths of Polites and Priam, culminating in Aeneas' loss of Creusa (see above, pp.88–94 on Aeneas' short-lived divine vision). Does Aeneas have a female gaze? The gates of ivory at the end of book 6 refuse any security of interpretation.

A dream which contrives to be both true and deceptive offers us a way into Ovid's slant-wise take on the epic gaze, in the well-studied episode of Ceyx and Alcyone (*Met.* 11.410–748).[16] What is interesting about this episode is the way that prophecy, and epic, are gestured towards, but occluded. Ceyx voyages in search of a prophecy (410–14); Alcyone's forebodings are semi-prophetic, but could easily be dismissed as the rhetoric of a lover left behind, and never become a full prophecy (416–18, 457–8). The central dream, in which Juno sends Iris to Sleep, who chooses Morpheus to impersonate Ceyx, in order to tell Alcyone that her husband is dead, should be prophetic, but in fact tells only of things that have already happened. It is characterised by the layers of distance between the initial impetus and the dream itself, and Hardie has demonstrated

---

[15] Smith 2005: 66–70 assimilates this dream to the dream of the Penates in *Aeneid* 3, and treats it as a straightforward 'epic' dream, 'inspiring' Aeneas (70). For him the echoes of Ennius are part of the negotiation between past and future; as Hector represents the past glory of Troy and passes its future to Aeneas, so Virgil appropriates Ennius, the past of Roman epic (though Smith never quite goes as far as saying this).

[16] Hardie 2002b: 272–82 already traces many of the visual dynamics, especially those of absence and illusion.

the peculiar way in which the dream forms the central part of the deferral of contact between Ceyx and Alcyone:

> 'non haec tibi nuntiat auctor
> ambiguus, non ista uagis rumoribus audis;
> ipse ego fata tibi praesens mea naufragus edo.
> surge, age, da lacrimas lugubriaque indue nec me
> indeploratum sub inania Tartara mitte.'
> adicit his uocem Morpheus, quam coniugis illa
> conderet esse sui; fletus quoque fundere ueros
> uisus erat, gestumque manus Ceycis habebat. (*Metamorphoses* 11.666–73)

> 'No ambiguous author announces these things to you,
> you do not hear those things through vague rumours;
> I myself produce for you my own fate as a present shipwreck.
> Rise, come, give tears and put on mourning and do not send me
> unwept to the emptiness of Tartarus.'
> Morpheus added the voice to these words, which she would swear
> was the voice of her own husband; also he seemed to pour forth
> true tears, and he had the hand gestures of Ceyx.

Morpheus is both orator and actor, a walking ecphrasis; the text emphasises his distance from reality with every comment on how real he seemed. The dream uses the language of prophetic trickery to insist on its own truth, when it is both true and deceitful. Here too any sort of reunion is denied, just as reunion in metamorphosis denies any happy ending.[17] Generically, too, this episode flirts with epic only to deny it: Ceyx is no Agamemnon or Odysseus (or even a Jason). He does not even get as far as receiving an oracle to encourage him to make an epic voyage or undertake an expedition. The storm happens when they have only recently left the harbour, and is structured in the manner of an epic battle, building up to the climactic death of the hero, Ceyx. Drowning is the opposite of the beautiful epic death (Achilles at *Il.* 21.273–83, Odysseus at *Od.* 5.299–312 and Aeneas at *Aen.* 1.94–101 all contrast the two modes of death). The sounds of storm are equated to the sounds of siege weapons (507–9); the winds are described as lions (510–13). The tenth wave which breaches the ship is compared to the first soldier to scale a wall (525–32); the confusion of the crew is like the confusion of defenders when a city has been infiltrated (533–6). The final wave which sinks the ship is compared to a victorious soldier standing over

---

[17] A sort of epic monumentality is achieved; the *alycones* will continue to remind us of the story. But for other stories transformed into birds (Tereus, Procne and Philomela; Nisus and Scylla) continuity seems not to have an emotional payload.

his spoils (551–7), adopting the gaze from above which characterises both victorious epic heroes and gods. The storm is also characterised throughout by darkness and causes inability to communicate (480, 484–5, 520–3, 540–2, 549–50, 570–2). It is framed by Alcyone's perceptions: at 463–73 she strains her eyes to keep watching the departing Ceyx, as he gradually moves away;[18] at 573–6 she is unaware, counting the days and blithely weaving (like Helen and Andromache in the *Iliad*). The episode as a whole focuses on love: separation, absence, longing and finally a sort of reunion. The gods enter late and offer cold comfort. The main point of the story is not the heroic journey, but the woman left behind, who can also be equated to the elegiac lover.[19] This is a perfect Ovidian deconstruction of the epic gaze: the ultimate inward-facing non-teleological prophetic situation, in which the act of attempting to gain a prophecy is the thing prophesied and the outcome, so the system of epic narrative collapses in on itself, and the masculine desire to perform heroic feats is subjugated to the desiring and grieving gaze of the woman left behind.[20]

In comparison, the two dreams of Pompey in Lucan are more conventional reversals. At the beginning of book 3 Pompey leaves Italy, his gaze lingering on the shore, just as Alcyone's gaze lingers on Ceyx' ship (*BC* 3.4–7).[21] The ghost of his dead wife, Caesar's daughter Julia, visits him in a terrifying dream, which finishes with an obscure prophecy of his death (*bellum te faciet ciuile meum*, 'Civil war will make you mine', 33–4), in a way which reads the war as serving the rivalry in love of Julia with Pompey's current wife Cornelia.[22] Although set up like a visitation dream, Pompey is not given guidance, but rather threats. Julia as a ghost intends to follow Pompey and join in the battle.[23] The power lies entirely with Julia, who takes on the prophetic role, viewing the underworld (*uidi ipse*, 14), as well as bending genres by recapitulating Propertius' Cynthia in 4.7, who returns to accuse her former lover of ignoring her, and to threaten him. At 9–11 the epiphany seems to be the action of Julia, who appears, rises and stands; at 28–30 she has avoided the effects of Lethe, and gained permission from the underworld powers to pursue him, in a sort of reverse katabasis. All Pompey can do in his panic (*trepidi . . . mariti*, 35; *terremur*, 38) is to try and claim to

---

[18] On connections with elegy, see Tränkle 1963, Fantham 1979: 336.
[19] The story of Protesilaus and Laodamia takes a similar slant-wise perspective on epic, and is mentioned in Prop. 1.1.
[20] On Alcyone's gaze from the shore, see below, p.225.
[21] Bruère 1951 sees resonances of Morpheus in the dream episode.
[22] She is also fury-like (*furialis*, 11), and resembles Allecto coming to Turnus.
[23] Rossi 2000: 574 links Julia to Creusa, in Pompey's reversal of the journey of Aeneas.

himself that it is only an empty dream (38).[24] Neither dream offers him any forward narrative momentum, and the ominous tone of the dream of Julia casts him rather as a tragic woman than an epic man.

To what extent are dreams part of the female gaze in epic? Scioli's recent exploration of the dream of Ismene in *Thebaid* 8 led her to conclude that the 'symbolic' dream opens a space for female viewing of epic material, and female discourse, connected by similarities to teichoscopy and weaving.[25] The female dream privileges the discursive over the narrative, watching over doing, emotion over decision. Do dreams offer an alternative space for a female gaze in epic? It is notable that prophets and dreamers, both male and female, are often passive in the face of a future inflicted upon them (or images and words inflicted upon them) and that there is a close connection between prophecy, dreams and sexual violence. In Ismene's dream complex sexual imagery is at work. Ismene, secluded in the house, dreams about her betrothed, Atys, whom she has unintentionally glimpsed only once before; in the dream the wedding ends in flames and Atys' mother chasing her. Meanwhile Atys has been violated and mortally wounded by Tydeus' careless spear, and when he is brought back to Thebes, Ismene's gaze is violated as she is brought to close his eyes in death. Scioli well demonstrates the problematic gendering of Atys' death; the shared name must surely evoke a connection with Catullus 63.[26] Another duo of lovers who may well offer something to the understanding of this passage are Cassandra and Coroebus in *Aeneid* 2. Ismene, unlike Cassandra, is given the opportunity to explain her presentiment to a sympathetic audience (her sister) but represses any understanding and refuses to allow Antigone to interpret it. The sense of violation in Ismene's gaze on her dying betrothed complicates the dream as a positive space for female discourse or viewing, but brings out the dream as a disturbance in the field of vision.[27] Dreams are not voluntary: the dreamer, unlike the weaver, or the viewer in a teichoscopy, does not choose to experience the dream. Dreams in ancient texts do seem to present subconscious processes

---

[24] At the beginning of book 7, Pompey dreams himself the object of the gaze of Rome in his theatre, being adored by the Roman people, a dream which is explicitly called a *vana imagine* at *BC* 7.8. Lucan describes the relationship between Pompey and Rome in terms of a love relationship (29–32), while also commenting on the possible prophetic function of the dream, as part of a number of alternative explanations (19–24).

[25] Scioli 2010: 235–6.

[26] For a tour of the intertexts lurking in this scene, see Micozzi 2001/2. There is generic complexity here too; for instance Micozzi 2001/2: 280–1 points out connections with the elegiac funeral scene.

[27] Augoustakis 2010: 74: 'Ismene is deflowered by Atys' gaze'; see also Hershkowitz 1998a: 290.

of desire, as well as grappling with the incomprehensibility of divine will and the movements of history.[28]

The dream of Atalanta (*Theb.* 9.570–636) shows a further level of powerlessness in the divine apparatus of the *Thebaid*. Her dream fits the 'tragic' or 'symbolic' pattern very closely: she purifies herself, and her prayer to Diana takes on the characteristics of the address to a confidante. The main dream is symbolic: an oak tree sacred to Diana has been defiled, wounded and bloodied (595–7). Atalanta herself takes on the role of interpreter: *simque augur cassa futuri* ('May I be an augur of the future in vain', 629). She has been disturbed by dreams for a while, and one of these is strikingly similar to the most disorienting part of Ilia's dream (577–8, wandering excluded from her normal places and connections; cf. *Ann*. 39–42 Sk.) Visual language is pervasive.[29] The build-up of dreams is typical of Statius' poetic tactics, surpassing and including previous dreams. Despite her power and agency, Atalanta continually focuses on sexual violation, looking back to Ovidian figures like Callisto who were blamed, punished and excluded for the crime of having been raped. Her anxiety dream about being excluded from the company of Diana's followers is the first hint of this (577–8); her speech demonstrates her faithfulness to Diana, touching in passing on her loathing of the conception of Parthenopaeus (*inuiso quamuis temerata cubili*, 613). She remains a virgin in spirit (*animumque innupta remansi*, 616), and has not hidden her *culpa* (blame, crime) but dedicated him too to Diana (617–21). Her power to see into the future and understand her own world is set against a complete impotence to do anything about it; even praying to Diana is signalled as vain (*nequiquam*, 607) before she even starts. The dream and Atalanta's emotional response represent the part of Statius' split voice that loathes the game of epic, that makes Parthenopaeus the emblem of the futility of war and epic heroism. This disturbance in the field of vision, underlined by sexual violence and social exclusion, is generically loaded.

More strikingly Diana is violated, too, by grief, and is reduced, like Diana in *Aeneid* 11, to the role of spectator. It is noticeable that just as Atalanta dreams that her hunting insignia liquefy (581), so Diana's statue dissolves in tears and grows wet after hearing her prayer (635–6). As Diana moves to Thebes, Statius emphasises her divine gaze:

---

[28] Although both Helen in *Iliad* 3, and Medea in Valerius Flaccus, are more or less compelled to go to the walls by divine forces. Subconscious processes of desire: Penelope in *Odyssey* 20; Medea in Apollonius 3; Ilia in Ennius; Pompey in Lucan 7.

[29] *uidebat*, 580; *uisa est*, 583; *cernit*, 595; *oculi*, 600; *lumina*, 601; *uidet*, 606; *signa*, 608; *occultare*, 617; *ostendi*, 618; *uisere . . . uisere*, 624–5; [*cernere*, 625a;] *aspicit*, 636.

> et in mediis frondentem Maenalon astris
> exuperat gressu saltumque ad moenia Cadmi
> destinat, interior caeli qua semita lucet
> dis tantum, et cunctas iuxta uidet ardua terras.
>
> (*Thebaid* 9.639–42)

> and she conquers with her step leafy Maenalus
> in the middle of the stars and takes the narrow path to
> the walls of Cadmus, where the inside way of heaven shines
> only for gods, and next to the heights she sees all the lands.

She meets Apollo, in mourning for Amphiaraus, who explains the powerlessness of his own gaze:

> en ipse mei (pudet!) inritus arma
> cultoris frondesque sacras ad inania uidi
> Tartara et in memet uersos descendere uultus;
>
> (*Thebaid* 9.653–5)

> Behold, I myself in vain watched the weapons and
> sacred wreaths of my own worshipper go down
> to empty Tartarus even though he had turned his face to me myself.

The extension of powerlessness from mortal to divine realm represents despair in the epic voice: it aligns the poet with the female gaze.

This section argued that dreams offer a female, centrifugal perspective on epic. Dreams are a marked space, interstitial, where aspects of other genres slip in, men can become women, and gods communicate partially with mortals. The Homeric Penelope shows a complex sense of unease; in post-Homeric epic the continuities between tragedy and epic are probably more important than the distance. Dreams often offer clear vision and emotional impact, but without logic or understanding. Dreamers, like prophets, are other-worldly.[30] The special connection with death and the divine makes dreamspace a source of power and a source of terror. Yet dreamers are essentially passive; if the dream leads to action, it is manly; yet more often, like ecphrasis, it leads to confusion and paralysis. If the dreamer's gaze is female, the association with deception, emotion and insubstantiality hampers any valorisation of the female gaze in epic. The dream-gaze is on the edges of epic.

---

[30] As Augoustakis 2010: 72 describes Statius' Ismene.

Teichoscopy

This section explores epic's female side further by looking at the institution of the 'teichoscopy' (viewing from the walls). Teichoscopy begins in *Iliad* 3, where Priam calls on Helen to point out the Greek heroes to him as they watch from the walls of Troy. A transgressive woman acts as narrator within this most masculine of genres. Teichoscopy is not a purely epic phenomenon, although it is marked as an epic intervention: Antigone watches from the walls at the beginning of Euripides *Phoenissae*;[31] Tarpeia in Propertius 4.4 falls in love with Tatius, and Scylla with Minos in Ovid *Metamorphoses* 8. In Flavian epic there are two episodes of teichoscopy: Statius *Thebaid* 7 and Valerius Flaccus *Argonautica* 6, and in Quintus Smyrnaeus *Posthomerica* 1 and Nonnus *Dionysiaca* 35 the women threaten to join in. I will examine these passages in more depth below, situating the observations of my earlier article in a broader context.[32]

Smaller moments describing women watching from the walls occur frequently and allude to this tradition. We have seen in Chapter 2 how the divine viewers act nearly all the time as a mediating audience. Non-combatants are another mediating audience, sometimes even when there are no walls for them to watch from.[33] The importance of the *Iliad* as code model means that siege warfare looms large in the imaginary of ancient epic. As well as the teichoscopy of Helen, Hecuba, Andromache and Priam (see below, p.226) are also often to be found on the walls of Troy. The implication seems to be that people would have been watching from the walls most of the time: certainly when Priam goes to Achilles to ask for the return of Hector's body, Cassandra sees him returning from her vantage point (24.699–702), and initiates the processes of mourning.

A good example from the *Aeneid* is the Latin women at 11.475–6: *tum muros uaria cinxere corona | matronae puerique* ('Then a varied group of mothers and boys garland the walls'), before they are called away to make prayers to Minerva, and then watch the eroticised figure of Turnus going out to fight (486–97). As the battle which leads to Camilla's death unfolds, internal audiences react, not just the other fighters (745–6), but also the women on the walls, who yearn to join in:

---

[31] Eur. *Phoen*. 88–201.
[32] For a more detailed examination of Valerius Flaccus and Statius, see Lovatt 2006.
[33] One example is the Colchian audience of Jason's feats at AR *Arg*. 3.1275–6, who sit on the Caucasian cliffs, although the gender of the viewers is not emphasised.

> ipsae de muris summo certamine matres
> (monstrat amor uerus patriae), ut uidere Camillam,
> tela manu trepidae iaciunt ac robore duro
> stipitibus ferrum sudibusque imitantur obustis
> praecipites, primaeque mori pro moenibus ardent. (*Aeneid* 11.891–5)
>
> The mothers themselves from the highest peak of the walls
> (true love of their fatherland shows them how, when they see Camilla)
> terrified they throw weapons by hand and they imitate steel
> with hard wooden fences and burnt stakes
> headlong, and they burn to die first on behalf of (or before) the walls.

The emotional impact of Camilla's death is emphasised by the decision of the mothers to join in battle and their desire to die.[34] References to the audience on the walls recur throughout book 12: at 131–3 the women and old men on the walls or by the gates are juxtaposed with Juno looking out from the Alban *mons* (134–7); at 595 Amata's view of the apparent death of Turnus and the imminent destruction of the city leads to her suicide; at 704–9 all gazes converge on the duelling pair, including those on the walls and the stupefied Latinus, while the Rutulians and the landscape combine to lament the death of Turnus at 928–9. Virgil's use of internal audiences seems to heighten engagement, sometimes by bringing all levels together (as in Feldherr's reading of *Aeneid* 5) but often offering multiple perspectives.[35]

The motif of women on the walls is even more pervasive in Statius' *Thebaid*, not just because of the siege context, but also because of the tragic and feminine slant of the narrative.[36] At 3.53–7 the mothers wait at the gates for the returning ambush; at 10.531–51 the Thebans defend themselves with missiles from the walls, echoing the Virgilian passage above (532–5). Book 11, like *Aeneid* 12, has many instances: at 49–56 Enyeus the trumpeter is defending the Argive fortifications when struck down, juxtaposed with the grieving gaze of Hercules (45–8); as the climactic duel approaches the audience layers are built up, including common people, old men and small children on the walls (416–19); the shout of the onlookers at 555–7 is echoed by the Theban landscape and deceives Polynices into thinking that Eteocles is dead, allowing the latter to make his deadly blow.

---

[34] Horsfall 2003 admits ambivalence in the phrase *pro moenibus*, and points to Quintus Smyrnaeus *PH* 1.436–9 as a possible imitation of the passage.
[35] Feldherr 1995.
[36] I am inclined now to agree with Dietrich 1999 on the importance of women in the *Thebaid*, although the female perspective does not offer an uncomplicated way out of the horrors of the poem.

Silius, too, reworks the passage from *Aeneid* 11: after the death of his female warrior, Asbyte (see below, pp.305–6), he stages an Iliadic race between her Saguntine killer, Theron, and Hannibal himself, watched throughout by the women on the walls: at *Pun.* 2.251–5 they watch as if at the games, long to open the gates, but are too terrified of Hannibal; at 256 Hannibal aims his victorious jaunt at the spectators on the walls, before driving off with Asbyte's horses. This whole passage is an epic intervention: neither Asbyte nor Theron exist in Livy.[37]

In historiographical siege narratives, non-combatants on the walls are mentioned, but there is rarely the same focus on viewing or on gender.[38] To take some examples from Livy, for instance: at 5.18.11 the Romans panic at rumours that the Veiientes may be on their way to attack Rome, and men rush to the walls, but the women, who are mentioned immediately afterwards go to pray in the temples; at 5.21.6–7 the Veiientes rush to the ramparts, but there is no mention of women, until, at 5.21.10–11 when the enemy are in the city, women and slaves throw tiles from the roofs;[39] at 6.28.3 the Praenestini are attacking Rome, and men hurry to the walls (but not women).[40] At 37.5.1 the townspeople of Lamia are defending themselves against the Romans, and women are involved in bringing weapons to the walls, but not viewing or fighting. Thucydidean historiography tends to avoid women, putting children first as the passive objects of the destruction of war.[41] Most similar to epic is Caesar *BG* 7.48, in which Gallic women first reach out to the Romans, and then inspire their menfolk to fight against them.[42] But these women are emphatically other (*more Gallico*, 'in the

---

[37] Whose entire Saguntum episode is over in only eight chapters (21.7 to 21.14). Many thanks to Luke Pitcher, Chris Pelling, Tapani Simojoki and Polly Low for advice on this material.

[38] On women and war, Loman 2004 gathers useful materials.

[39] On the topos of throwing tiles, see Barry 1996.

[40] Further: at 31.24.7 Philip attacks Athens, but the townspeople man the walls; Caesar *BC* 3.105.4 describes the citizens of Antioch going to the walls to defend it. An interesting variation at Caesar *BC* 3.9.6 in which the citizens of Salona use women and children on the walls to create the impression that they are still defended, while their true forces attack elsewhere; Sall. *Bell. Iugurth.* 67.1 describes the Numidian citizens of Vaga defeating the invading Roman forces with substantial involvement of women and children throwing missiles from the roofs. See also: Polyaenus 8.68–70 (Cyrenea); Plut. *Pyrrhus* 29.34; Plut. *Mor.* 245c, 248e; Diodorus 13.56.7, 15.83.3, 32.206. On Plutarch, epic and tragedy in the *Pyrrhus*, see Mossman 1992.

[41] Wiedemann 1983 argues that active engagement from women in Thucydides constitutes abnormality or marginality in historical discourse, particularly pointing to two episodes in which women on the walls join in the fighting; at Plataea, women and slaves hurl missiles from the rooftops (2.4.2); similar behaviour in Corcyra at 3.74 is termed contrary to nature (παρὰ φύσιν).

[42] *Quorum cum magna multitudo convenisset, matres familiae, quae paulo ante Romanis de muro manus tendebant, suos obtestari et more Gallico passum capillum ostentare liberosque in conspectum proferre coeperunt.* (Caes. *BG* 7.48)

Gallic custom') and Gallic mercenaries were particularly well known for taking their families with them.[43]

It is true that both men and women watch from the walls in epic too, but there seems to be a much stronger distinction between combatants and non-combatants in epic. In several of the historical examples, the city under siege has been taken by surprise, while in the *Iliad* it is assumed that all men of fighting age will be fighting. So although Priam watches from the walls, he and the other old men are denied the main index of epic virility: display of fighting prowess on the battlefield. The other main difference is between going to the walls to defend from above, and going to the walls to watch. By becoming passive spectators, the non-combatants lack agency and hence masculinity. However, epic puts a great deal of emphasis on actual women watching, and this is further emphasised by the female emotional perspectives adopted: lamentation and erotic viewing. If there is a core of epic spectacle in the theme of watching from the walls, however, the walls are inherently marginal spaces, and these episodes continually strain against the boundaries of genre: not just historiography, but also tragedy and elegy.

The original moment of epic teichoscopy is Helen on the walls of Troy in *Iliad* 3. The most striking aspect of this passage is that Helen takes the position of knowledge (and hence power?), becoming a surrogate of the narrator. Priam is represented as lacking knowledge: he needs Helen to tell him who is who and what is what. When Iris comes to bring Helen to the walls, she finds her weaving a cloak on which the *Iliad* itself is reproduced:

> τὴν δ' εὗρ' ἐν μεγάρῳ· ἡ δὲ μέγαν ἱστὸν ὕφαινε,
> δίπλακα πορφυρέην, πολέας δ' ἐνέπασσεν ἀέθλους
> Τρώων θ' ἱπποδάμων καὶ Ἀχαιῶν χαλκοχιτώνων,
> οὕς ἕθεν εἵνεκ' ἔπασχον ὑπ' Ἄρηος παλαμάων· (*Iliad* 3.125–8)

> And she found her in the hall. She was weaving a great web,
> double and purple, and she was weaving in many feats
> of both the horse-taming Trojans and the bronze-wearing Achaeans,
> which they were enduring for her sake at the hands of Ares.

Weaving, as many have pointed out, is a feminine equivalent of poetry;[44] and whereas Andromache at *Il.* 22.440–1 weaves a double purple cloth decorously adorned with varied flowers,[45] Helen takes over the

---

[43] Loman 2004: 50.
[44] See for instance Kennedy 1986, Bergren 1979. 'Helen is somehow like the bard … her action should be regarded as somehow reflective of the poetic process.' (Kennedy 1986: 5)
[45] Salzman-Mitchell 2005: 121–2 compares the two tapestries. See also Pantelia 1993.

quintessentially epic subject matter of battle, and turns it into a visual representation of her own significance.[46]

On the walls, Priam offers Helen a sort of acceptance and control by asking her to tell him who the Greek warriors are (*Il.* 3.162–70). At 229 she takes fuller control of the narrative and directs the gaze of both internal and external audience towards those she knows and wants to see: first, Idomeneus, guest friend of Menelaus, and then the absent figures of her brothers Castor and Pollux. She demonstrates a female gaze: while Priam wants to know about the men who look like important kings, Helen wants to see her own connections. She comes to the wall to view her former husband and her thoughts are of him at 139–40; at the end is her grief with the absence of her brothers at 236–42. However, as Scodel points out, Helen's initial desire is frustrated: we do not see her seeing her husband, and the main emotional pay-off of her viewing is an absence.[47] Even though Helen takes her own direction by looking at Idomeneus, she does not actually tell any stories; for Scodel 'the passage examines memory and its inadequacy' (80). It can be set in contrast to the objective, descriptive catalogue of book 2, in the voice of the primary narrator, and closely linking the narrator's vision with that of the gods.[48]

Yet Helen is also (obviously) a narrated object:[49] created and told by the poet, manipulated and ordered about by Aphrodite and Iris, she is a spectacle for those around her, and the prize over which both the duel and the entire war are fought. Helen's web shows a self-conscious awareness of her own significance for the battles, but equally she is an object of battle, as emphasised by Iris (*Il.* 3.136–8). When she arrives at the Scaean gates, she is a rival spectacle for the old men who are watching the battle (154–60). They look at her face and justify reactions to her beauty; they think of her as a cause, an abstract reason for what has happened and not as a person. They dwell on their own pain and suffering, in contrast to the narrator who focuses the reader on Helen's humanity, her inner thoughts and her own pain and suffering, both when Iris makes her long for Greece ("Ὡς εἰποῦσα θεὰ γλυκὺν ἵμερον ἔμβαλε θυμῷ / ἀνδρός τε προτέρου καὶ ἄστεος ἠδὲ

---

[46] Salzman-Mitchell 2005: 122 suggests that Helen's weaving fixes the mobile warriors with her female gaze, thereby disrupting the pattern of men causing women to become fixed. However, on another level Helen buys into epic ideology by putting heroic deeds on display.
[47] Scodel 1997: 79–80.
[48] See Chapter 2, pp.32, 42–3. On the whole passage, see Scodel 1997: 77–81.
[49] As Kennedy 1986 points out, particular oddities in the text of the episode (Iris' unmotivated action leading Helen to the wall; the chronological violations in the suggestion that Priam is viewing the Greeks for the first time) draw attention to the text's status as text: the presentation draws attention to itself and highlights the role of the poet. The chronological problems in particular set the *Iliad* up as a microcosm of the whole Trojan war in a self-conscious manner.

τοκήων· 'The goddess spoke thus and put into her heart a sweet longing for her former husband and city and her parents', 139–40) and in her speech to Priam (τὸ καὶ κλαίουσα τέτηκα. 'and I have melted with weeping', 176).

Priam's obvious sympathy for her, though mediated by his own preoccupation with himself and the gods, provides an authorising point of view within the text. The image of the elders as cicadas, chattering away with delicate lily voices, at 150–2, may be focalised through Helen, who, although she cannot hear their words, has clearly understood their meaning, as we can tell from her rather pointed speech to Priam. Priam begins by looking for the 'kingliest' man (170) – Agamemnon. Yet Helen uses her reply to explain her own feelings, only coming to Agamemnon at 178–80, where even so she relates him to herself: he used to be her brother-in-law.

With Odysseus, Helen takes on the objective tone of one passing on information, and Antenor takes over, ostensibly backing her up (204) but actually bringing his own knowledge and experience to the forefront. Most strikingly, the narrator underlines a gap between Helen's knowledge and his own, by finishing on the absence of her brothers, Castor and Pollux.[50] Helen attempts to explain to herself why she cannot see them (236–42), but the authorised explanation of the narrator is that they are dead: Ὣς φάτο, τοὺς δ' ἤδη κάτεχεν φυσίζοος αἶα / ἐν Λακεδαίμονι αὖθι, φίλῃ ἐν πατρίδι γαίῃ. ('Thus she spoke, but the life-giving earth already held them in Sparta there, in their dear fatherland.', 243–4). The text draws a strong contrast between what she says and what is really true, emphasising Helen's subordination to gods and narrator.[51] At the end of the passage, it is Priam who is called on to enter the action: to go down to the battlefield, and make the oath for the duel between Menelaus and Paris, while Helen is prize and object.[52]

Helen is both subject and object at once, both viewed and viewing. It is her status as woman and extraordinary marvel that both allows her to stand out, and makes her into an object.[53] She is allowed power, influence and freedom not accorded to ordinary women, but also made a victim of her

---

[50] Kennedy 1986: 12–13 reads the whole episode as a contest between visual and oral poetics: the 'bard' shows his superiority to Helen most clearly here – but surely there can't be any real competition between Helen and 'Homer'? She is a subsidiary part of the narrator, another aspect of the epic voice (and gaze).

[51] Scodel 1997: 81: 'The narrator stresses not her knowledge but her ignorance, and the painful gap between the present spectacle and the absent past.'

[52] Kennedy 1986: 9–10 suggests that the fact that Helen does not return to her tapestry after this episode could be read as an emblem of artistic or rhetorical failure.

[53] For an exploration of Helen in the literary tradition, see Maguire 2009: esp. 113–15 on Helen's agency and passivity in the *Iliad*.

own celebrity. The favour of Aphrodite both makes her like a hero in her closeness to the gods, and forces her against her will into Paris' bed.

This privileged subjectivity mirrors that of prophetesses, who take their place in public discourse, but at the price of bodily integrity and control. It is notable, then, that Helen in the *Odyssey* takes control of discourse in a number of marked public ways and displays a privileged and effective gaze:[54] she recognises Telemachus (4.138–46), when Menelaus himself has held back from naming him; she gives Telemachus a drug to ease his pain (219–32); she tells a story of her own recognition of Odysseus while in Troy (235–64), performing the reverse of her role in the teichoscopy, now reporting back on the Trojans to the Greeks; Menelaus doubles this story with his own narration about Helen herself and her insight into the Trojan horse, her failed attempt to make the men betray themselves. In book 15 when Telemachus is leaving, Helen doubles Menelaus' gift of a mixing bowl with her own gift of a robe she herself wove (15.123–30). Finally Helen takes Menelaus' place in interpreting the omen of an eagle and a goose: Peisistratus asks Menelaus to interpret it (166–8) but while Menelaus was pondering (169–70), Helen jumps in: 'Hear me! I shall be your prophet, the way the immortals put it into my heart, and I think it will be accomplished.' («κλῦτέ μευ· αὐτὰρ ἐγὼ μαντεύσομαι, ὡς ἐνὶ θυμῷ / ἀθάνατοι βάλλουσι καὶ ὡς τελέεσθαι ὀΐω.», 172–3). The Odyssean Helen is back in her element, and the *Odyssey* shows greater hospitality to female power and subjectivity.

We have seen the complexity of the teichoscopy from the outset. Helen is both viewer and viewed, narrated object and subjective narrator, poet figure, yet with limited knowledge. We look through her eyes and those of others simultaneously. Helen's beauty makes her stand out from other female characters, yet she still shares feminine concerns, and is more explicitly treated as an object because of her beauty. On the other hand, her insight and power are not wholly attributable to her beauty, especially in the *Odyssey*.

Teichoscopy is also used in tragedy: the fullest example is Antigone's view from the walls at Euripides *Phoenissae* 88–201.[55] This passage has been considered a possible interpolation (too epic?), although Mastronarde judges most of the arguments against it to be unconvincing.[56] There are a number of differences between Antigone's spectatorship and that of Helen:

---

[54] Like a man, she seems to have successfully repaired her marriage after an affair, suggesting that the power of her beauty and charisma have trumped Menelaus' masculinity.
[55] Scodel 1997 also discusses the *parodoi* of Euripides' *Hypsipyle* and *Iphigenia in Aulide*.
[56] Mastronarde 1994.

Antigone watches the battle on her own initiative, with the permission of her mother (88–91), not from the public space of the Trojan walls, but from the roof of the palace.[57] Even so, worry about her exposure frames the narrative (92–4, 99, 193–201). She is afraid and overwhelmed by the spectacle, and even though she seems to know more than Priam about the invading army, and asks to have specific warriors pointed out to her, she is subordinate in her ignorance to her informer, even though he emphasises his slavery. Her descriptions and responses, however, form an important mediation between narrator and audience: for instance at 128–30 she compares Hippomedon to a painting of a giant. Like Helen, she has her own narrative desire: to see her brother. And as in the *Iliad* that desire is largely frustrated, here by realistic inadequacy of vision: the slave points him out, but Antigone cannot see clearly and can only make out his shape (158–62). Scodel 1997: 93 analyses the effects of the tragic use of female viewers to mediate the overwhelming impact of the spectacle of an army on the point of battle in Brechtian terms: 'The audience, by seeing and hearing her, rather than the spectacle itself, can feel the impact of the sight without losing the ability to evaluate it. The limits of tragic spectacle thereby show themselves as advantages. The poet selects and re-presents, conveying an emotional impact that does not overwhelm.' In epic, too, of course, we cannot actually see the spectacle; narrative and description need the filter and refraction of internal audiences to bring them alive. Presenting a viewer's response can create both alienation and involvement, as do the similes which describe the gathering army. The use of internal viewers is one respect in which the *Iliad* foreshadows the tragic perspective, as Slatkin 2007 suggests of the encounter between Hector and Andromache in book 6; equally tragedy evokes and to a certain extent buys into the overwhelming spectacle of epic. Moreover, as Hesk points out, the lack of a ritual framework to defuse and contain can make epic even more overwhelming.[58]

In sum, it seems to me that there is more continuity between epic and tragedy than difference, and the presence of a female perspective, even if disempowered and on the margins, is an important part of the epic gaze. A simple opposition between the divine gaze (objective, knowledgeable, effective, leading to action) and the female gaze (subjective, fallible, ineffective, passive) is one of the structures at play in the visual dynamics of epic, but this opposition founders on the various scenes of gods disempowered, watching in painful frustration, while female viewers can validate the joy of epic.[59] Further, the subjective emotional and erotic viewing carried out by

---

[57] Scodel 1997: 85.   [58] Hesk forthcoming.   [59] See above, Chapter 2, on limits, pp.71–7.

women exposes them to danger, as well as complicating the epic focus on success in battle, personal glory and enduring memory.

Gazing at departing heroes

Women watch battles from the walls; they also watch as epic heroes leave in their quests for glory. We have seen above how the Ceyx and Alcyone episode of *Metamorphoses* 11 deconstructs the relationship of dreams and prophecy in epic. This episode also contains a climactic reworking of the female gaze at the departing hero, an important aspect of female viewing in epic, whether from the walls or from the shore (both marginal locations).

> sustulit illa
> umentes oculos stantemque in puppe recurua
> concussaque manu dantem sibi signa maritum
> prima uidet redditque notas; ubi terra recessit
> longius atque oculi nequeunt cognoscere uultus,
> dum licet insequitur fugientem lumine pinum;
> haec quoque ut haud poterat spatio summota uideri,
> uela tamen spectat summo fluitantia malo;
> ut nec uela uidet, uacuum petit anxia lectum
> seque toro ponit: renouat lectusque torusque
> Alcyones lacrimas et quae pars admonet absit.   (*Metamorphoses* 11.463–73)

> She lifted up
> her streaming eyes and first sees, standing on the curved stern
> giving a sign to her with his shaken hand, her husband
> and gives back well-known signs; where the land recedes
> further and her eyes cannot recognise the faces,
> while it is allowed she follows the fleeing ship with her gaze;
> when this also had been removed so that it could not be seen over the distance,
> then she watches the sail floating on the top of the mast;
> and when she does not see the sail, anxiously she seeks the empty bed
> and places herself on her couch; and the bed and the couch renew
> Alcyone's tears and remind her of the part that is not there.

This single sentence models the gradual process of separation, from exchanging signals, to the inability to recognise faces, to the ship and then sail disappearing, until finally the viewer herself is secluded in the most female space of the bedroom; it puts Alcyone's emotion in the forefront of the narrative. Her refusal to let go visually shows her desperation and disempowerment. Even though her vision shapes the narrative, the fact remains that she must stay, while her husband has the power to decide where and when to go. It is a close reworking of the elegiac separation of Protesilaus and Laodamia in *Heroides* 13.15–22, gesturing towards the Iliadic roots of the idea.[60]

The image of the abandoned woman straining her eyes after her beloved may well derive its importance in Latin poetry from Catullus 64: the ecphrastic description begins with Ariadne's gaze, at both Theseus and herself (52–7; see above, pp.162–5), and ends with it (249–50); at 126–7 Ariadne climbs a mountain to gaze after Theseus. This erotic trope, however, is also an epic scene. Lying behind many of these scenes is the farewell scene of Andromache and Hector in *Iliad* 6. Although not straightforwardly a teichoscopy, Andromache is on the walls when Hector finds her (*Il.* 6.372–3, 386–9); she had gone there like a madwoman when she heard that things were going badly for the Trojans (μαινομένη, 389), and the workings of vision in this passage give an important insight into the female gaze in epic. At 404, Hector looks at Astyanax (ἰδών), while Andromache's attention is focused on him: he avoids her direct emotional appeal, while setting dynastic continuity against duty/glory. Hector disregards Andromache's speech because of his awareness of his own exposure to the gazes of the Trojans and posterity (440–6: note the emphasis on shame and glory). While Astyanax is terrified by the visual power of his father in his armour (466–70), Hector's gaze at Andromache (482–5) is one of pity (ἐλέησε νοήσας, 484). He envisages her as the object of the conquering gazes of the Greeks (459), when he will have been reduced to a monument to his own heroism, unable to protect his family. His dismissal of her from the walls is an act of pity, so she will be protected from the horror and pain of watching battle, even if he phrases it in terms of decorum (war is men's work; women should stick to weaving: 490–3). Andromache's lingering gaze, looking back as she obediently leaves the walls (496), is the beginning of all the female gazes at departing heroes to come. Hector puts civic duty and epic glory above the welfare of his family (the 'choice of Hector'). The image at the beginning of book 7, at 4–7, which compares the relief felt by the Trojans at the arrival of Hector and Paris on the battlefield to the relief felt by sailors when they finally have a favouring wind, associates his return to battle with the act of setting out on a journey and makes Hector's departure seem more concrete.

After Ariadne, probably the most famous abandoned woman is Dido, and she too watches her beloved depart from high on the walls: first at

---

[60] This image is a frequent one in the *Heroides*, making the abandoned woman as the emblem of a new genre. Other examples: 2.91; 5.57–8; 6.65–74.

Aen. 4.401–12 she sees the Trojans making ready to go *arce ex summa* (410), from the height of her citadel which should be the site of her power; then at 586–7 she wakes to find them gone and watches the sails disappear *e speculis* ('from the watch-towers'). Her vertical perspective suggests an affinity with the divine gaze, but serves only to underline her powerlessness. The first of these moments is closely connected to Aeneas' initial vision of Carthage by an insect simile: the hard-working Carthaginians each carrying out different tasks are compared to bees doing the same at 1.430–7. Aeneas watches from a hill outside Carthage, but is not seen, too far away and enshrouded in mist by Venus; he feels a longing to match Carthaginian purpose and success. Similarly Dido watches the purposeful actions of the Trojans as they prepare to leave, and they are compared to ants:

> migrantis cernas totaque ex urbe ruentis:
> ac uelut ingentem formicae farris aceruum
> cum populant hiemis memores tectoque reponunt,
> it nigrum campis agmen praedamque per herbas
> conuectant calle angusto; pars grandia trudunt
> obnixae frumenta umeris, pars agmina cogunt
> castigantque moras; opere omnis semita feruet.
> quis tibi tum, Dido, cernenti talia sensus,
> quosue dabas gemitus, cum litora feruere late
> prospiceres arce ex summa, totumque uideres
> misceri ante oculos tantis clamoribus aequor!
> improbe Amor, quid non mortalia pectora cogis!
>
> (*Aeneid* 4.401–12)

> You would see them moving on and rushing from the whole city:
> and just as ants, mindful of winter, when they ravage
> a huge heap of barley relocate it from a building,
> a black column goes through the fields and they gather together
> booty through the grass on a narrow path; some struggle as they
> push weighty grains on their shoulders, others force the columns
> and rebuke delays, and the whole track seethes with work.
> What feelings for you, Dido, then, seeing such things,
> what groans were you giving, when you looked out from the high
> citadel on the shore widely seething, and you saw the whole
> sea churned up before your eyes with such great noise!
> Wicked Love, what do you not force on mortal hearts?

Smith's suggestion that the physical distance between Dido and Aeneas represents the spiritual distance between them is only part of the story;[61]

---

[61] Smith 2005: 111.

clearly Dido, unlike the distant viewer in Lucretius, does not feel distant. All of Virgil's poetic pyrotechnics are here working to embroil the reader with Dido and Dido with the Trojans. The reader is strikingly addressed at 401 (*cernas*, 'you would see'), and it seems that the narrator focalises the simile (or perhaps the divine audience); but instead at 408, with another address, this time to Dido, it becomes clear that Dido is the one thinking of the Trojans as ants, just as Aeneas had thought of the Carthaginians as bees. Now Dido resents the Trojans' purposeful hard work, carried out in order to abandon her, even as she (or the narrator) admires it.[62] Verbal repetitions link simile and context, viewer and viewed: the repetitions of *feruere* (407 and 409) and *cogere* (406 and 412) both inside and outside the simile undermine the distance.[63] Reed has effectively pointed out the way that allusion to Ennius and Accius, who describe elephants and Indians respectively using the phrase *it nigrum campis agmen*, according to Servius, links Carthage and Rome: 'Dido's gaze intertextually assimilates "plundering" Trojans – that is, proto-Romans – to Carthaginians attacking Roman territory, wreaking the queen's vengeance and fulfilling her curse.' (99)[64] While bees are domestic animals, ants are not: and even bees can be viewed threateningly, as they are in *Aen.* 12.584–92, about to be smoked out.[65]

Dido's viewing here is not powerless: she is being left behind, but she is about to initiate a series of events that will prove extraordinarily destructive to the Romans. However, the focus is on the effect of her vision on her: the power and energy of the Trojan departure is assimilated to the power and energy of her destructive love. Dido is enough of a Medea figure for us to understand that the destruction concerned is not just self-destruction: the disempowered female gaze is also a vengeful gaze. In the simile the Trojans are made 'other' by their lack of subjectivity; later when Aeneas meets Dido in the underworld, she turns the tables, becoming incomprehensibly other to him. He sees or thinks he sees her, like someone catching a glimpse of the

---

[62] Their organisation is described in military terms (*agmen, praedam, agmina cogunt*), and they are *hiemis memores*, 'mindful of winter' (403), setting them in opposition to the *immemor* Theseus. But does this make it worse? Aeneas has not forgotten about Dido; he has decided to leave anyway.

[63] *Feruet* and *feruere* both apply to the Trojans, as ants, and in the effect they have on the shore, but it is often an emotional word, and *sensus* puts the emphasis on Dido's emotions. Later, and crucially, Aeneas will be *feruidus* as he kills Turnus (12.951). Elsewhere in the poem the word is evenly distributed between Trojans and Italians. Of Turnus about to fire the ships at 9.72; Euryalus mid-slaughter at 9.350; 9.693 of the Trojans; 736 of Pandarus; 10.788 of Aeneas in his killing spree; 12.293 of the Italian Messapus; Turnus 12.325; Aeneas in pursuit 12.748; 12.894 Turnus' calls Aeneas' words *feruida*.

[64] Reed 2007: 98–100.

[65] At AR *Arg.* 4.1452–6 ants are paired with flies insatiably thronging around a drop of honey: here definitely a pest rather than a moral *exemplum*.

new moon (*qualem primo qui surgere mense | aut uidet aut uidisse putat per nubila lunam*, 6.453–4); in the same way, Lynceus catches a brief glimpse of Hercules at the end of Apollonius' *Argonautica*, just after the passage of another ant simile (4.1477–80). The uncertain nature of the vision emphasises the incomprehensibility of the other's desire. Hercules has passed beyond mortal vision, and Dido too achieves a sort of apotheosis, a separation in death from the mortal gaze, while Aeneas takes on the reader's unease in the grip of the complex and conflicting emotions the *Aeneid* creates.[66]

How epic is Dido's gaze? More perhaps than we might expect. In both Apollonius and Valerius Flaccus, women watch as the Argonauts leave: a crowd follow the heroes at AR *Arg*. 1.238–40 as they walk down to the ship, gleaming like stars; women in particular pray for their return at 247–9. This passage leads into the lament of Jason's mother, Alcimede (278–91), and as he leaves he is compared to Apollo (306–11), inspiring the onlookers to raise a shout. Jason is an erotic object because of his heroic ambitions. The fact that Valerius adds bereft and abandoned mothers pursuing the ships with their eyes shows how important this image was in Latin poetry:

> it pariter propulsa ratis; stant litore matres
> claraque uela oculis percussaque sole secuntur
> scuta uirum donec iam celsior arbore pontus
> immensusque ratem spectantibus abstulit aer.
>
> (VF *Argonautica* 1.494–7)

> The ship goes evenly propelled, mothers stand on the shore
> and follow the bright sails with their eyes and the shields of the heroes
> struck by the sun, until at last the sea is taller than the mast
> and the immeasurable air removed the ship from those watching.

The bright sail evokes Catullus 64, also the model for the anxious parent gazing out from the cliffs: Aegeus' speech to Theseus at 215–37 emphasises his desire and need to gaze on his son (220, 233, 236), and his vision of the wrong sails leads immediately to his suicide (243–4). The scene of the Argonauts' departure in Valerius Flaccus also draws in a reference to Hector and Andromache in *Iliad* 6, via the lines in which Peleus says goodbye to Achilles (VF *Arg*. 1.255–73, cf. *Il*. 6.474–81), as well as evoking Evander's farewell to Pallas at *Aen*. 8.558–84 in combination with the mothers on the walls of Pallanteum (*stant pauidae in muris matres oculisque sequuntur | pulueream nubem et fulgentis aere cateruas*, 'The mothers stand panicked on the walls and follow with their eyes the dusty cloud and the

---

[66] Similarly Aeneas at *Aen*. 8.18–30 is like Apollonius' Medea (AR 3.755–8).

230 The female gaze

squadrons gleaming with bronze', 592–3). The combination of distance (on land equating to the dusty cloud, on sea to the gradual disappearing of the sail) with the gleaming armour of heroes going to war links the glamour of war with the pain of separation.

The female gaze is tellingly juxtaposed with the divine gaze as Valerius' Argonauts depart; at VF *Arg.* 1.498–502, Jupiter, the gods and the fates also watch the departure (quoted above, Chapter 2, p.49). Zissos suggests that the divine gaze takes over as the mortal gaze fails.[67] The emphasis on the starriness of Jupiter's viewing point (498) foreshadows the Argo's eventual catasterism. The superlative *pulcherrima* transfers the physical beauty of the Argonauts, the source of wonder in Apollonius, onto the figurative beauty of their heroic achievements. Jupiter objectifies the Argonauts not through an erotic gaze, but by considering them the tools for his plan. The Argonauts are the object of the erotic gaze as they arrive at Lemnos (1.630–9). The Argonauts are the objects of the marvelling gaze, too, in Apollonius' Phaeacia at AR *Arg.* 4.1182–93, where women come in crowds to gaze at them (1182–3), wondering at their beauty and shapeliness (1192–3). These heroes are on display as erotic objects.

If the Argonauts are objects of desire and lament, so are Statius' Argives when they set out for war in *Thebaid* 4; the link is emphasised by a simile of sailors setting out on a journey (24–30). The book begins with the divine gaze: Phoebus (1–4); Bellona showing her torch and hurling a spear (5–7). The departure builds on that of Valerius Flaccus' Argonauts, with boys, brides and fathers crowding around, and families clinging to weapons. The simile evokes the abandoned woman:

> sic ubi forte uiris longum super aequor ituris,
> cum iam ad uela noti et scisso redit ancora fundo,
> haeret amica manus: certant innectere collo
> bracchia, manantesque oculos hinc oscula turbant,
> hinc magni caligo maris, tandemque relicti
> stant in rupe tamen; fugientia carbasa uisu
> dulce sequi, patriosque dolent crebrescere uentos.
>
> (*Thebaid* 4.24–30)

> Thus when by chance, a loving band cling to men about to go
> far over the sea, when already the winds are at the sails and the anchor
> returns from the severed sea-bed: they struggle to twine their arms
> around a neck, and kisses disturb their dripping eyes here,
> here the mist of the great sea, and at last they stand, abandoned,

---

[67] Zissos 2008: 302. See above, Chapter 2, pp.39–45 on the divine gaze and scene changes.

on the cliff nevertheless; it is sweet to follow the fleeing
sails with their gaze, and they grieve that their native winds grow stronger.

The vertical position of the women on a cliff is set against the imagery of liquefaction. So the agency of Bellona is set in contrast to the impotence of those left behind. In the catalogue that follows, Statius includes the figure of Argia on the tower:

> tamen et de turre suprema
> attonitam totoque extantem corpore longe
> respicit Argian; haec mentem oculosque reducit
> coniugis et dulces auertit pectore Thebas. (*Thebaid* 4.89–92)

> nevertheless from the final tower
> thunderstruck and standing far out with her whole body
> he looks back at Argia; she leads back his mind and eyes
> and the sight of his wife turns away sweet Thebes from his heart.

For Polynices the two competing forces are not glory and family, but one family in competition with another, Thebes versus Argos. The thought of Thebes is sweet, just as the sight of the receding sails is sweet in the simile (*dulce*, 30). Argia is thunderstruck (*attonitam*), and like Medea in Valerius Flaccus she is not afraid to be seen. These two details show her emotional state, but all this is focalised through Polynices. He is always on the point of turning back, and Argia is an important part of this sense of tragic causation. In book 11, which we will examine further below (p.244), a vision of Argia on the walls of the Argive encampment almost makes him decide not to fight Eteocles (11.140–50). While epic piles up causes which make the outcome inevitable, tragedy offers continual opportunities to avoid the one terrible event. Below we pursue the female gazes of Argia and Antigone at the end of the poem.

The *Achilleid* goes further, as one might expect, towards elegy, and offering a counterpoint to Homer. Deidamia watches the departure of Achilles for Troy:

Turre procul summa lacrimis comitata sororum
commissumque tenens et habentem nomina Pyrrhum
pendebat coniunx oculisque in carbasa fixis
ibat et ipsa freto, et puppem iam sola uidebat.
ille quoque obliquos dilecta ad moenia uultus
declinat uiduamque domum gemitusque relictae
cogitat: occultus sub corde renascitur ardor
datque locum uirtus. (*Achilleid* 2.23–30)

Far on a high tower, accompanied by a weeping crowd of sisters
and holding Pyrrhus, who had been entrusted to her and now had a name,
his wife was hanging and with her eyes fixed on the sails
she was now herself going down to the straits, and now she alone was seeing the ship.
He also turns his face aslant towards the beloved walls
and thinks of his widowed home and the groaning left behind:
the hidden fire is reborn in his heart
and *uirtus* gives way.

Deidamia's viewing is set up as part of the scenery by the imperfect tense: all this was going on while Achilles is looking. He is the real subject here, and perhaps it is only in his imagination that Deidamia figuratively throws herself after the ship. This passage dramatises strongly the competition between family connections (wife and son) and heroic glory (*uirtus*, emphasised by Odysseus' intervention which follows immediately afterwards at 30–48). Achilles' backward gaze is aslant, suggesting that he is not yet fully committed to his role as an epic hero, and still retains something of the femininity and passivity of the earlier parts of the poem. The *Achilleid* up to this point has famously been less than straightforwardly epic and martial. The rebirth of love might suggest that love would have remained an important force in the poem ahead too: or is *ardor* ripe for transformation into the burning gaze of the warrior? Would Statius have reconciled erotics and epic, or would this Achilles always have ended up on the margins?

The scenes of heroic departure might have been expected to show women as fixed, lacking power and left behind, while male heroes move off into their epic future without a backward glance. In fact, on the one hand, women often have power in these scenes; they make the men look back, and in the cases of Ariadne and Dido are actually threatening. But on the other hand women are marginalised by the emphasis on the male choice between glory and family, becoming an object in their turn of the male obsession with mortality, of the backward glance of epic.

Teichoscopy and the erotic: Propertius and Ovid

We have already seen the erotic charge in Iris' temptation of Helen out onto the walls (*Il.* 3.139–40, esp. γλυκὺν ἵμερον, 'sweet desire', 139). In Latin poetic responses to teichoscopy, eros takes centre stage. Epic has always had its erotic side, and can be read tendentiously as always already about love: Helen and Paris, Odysseus and Penelope, Jason and Medea, Aeneas, Dido and Lavinia, all these relationships underlie the reasons for battle.⁶⁸ Two Augustan episodes of erotic teichoscopy play with genre in similar ways: Propertius' Tarpeia poem (4.4) and Ovid's Minos and Scylla episode (*Met.* 8.1–151).

Propertius' fourth book is a tour de force of generic complication: he sets it up as something different from his previous Callimachean, deliberately anti-war and anti-epic stance, as something more Roman, more orthodox, more Augustan.⁶⁹ In 4.1a he claims to have given up erotic elegy, but in 4.1b he takes it up again.⁷⁰ Tarpeia is both a feature of the landscape and an elegiac heroine, an *aetion* and a traitor. The landscape, which begins with the aetiological marker (Tarpeia's tomb, 4.4.1–2) segues into an erotic *locus amoenus* (4.4.3–6).⁷¹ Tarpeia's initial *coup de foudre* is visual: she falls in love with Tatius as she catches sight of him (19–22). From her own hill she performs frequent teichoscopies: her speech begins and ends with the theme of viewing. At 31–4 she calls Tatius' armies and armour *formosa oculis meis* ('beautiful to my eyes') and wishes she could look on his face as a prisoner. At 65–6 she longs to see him in her dreams. But this female gaze leads to action: at 81–4 she meets the enemy (*conuenit*), makes a pact (*ligat*), climbs the hill and even kills the guard dogs with a sword (*occupat ense*). Her final reward is death and monumentalisation like an epic hero: *o uigil, iniustae praemia sortis habes* ('O watcher you have the reward of an unjust chance', 94). The ambiguity allows us either to sympathise with her death (it was unjust that Tatius had her killed, after the emotional pain of her all-night vigils) or to condemn it (it was unjust that a traitor, who should have been guarding the city, should have an important part of the Roman landscape named after her). Propertius plays on the theme of *militia amoris* throughout: love as wound (30); trumpets of war turned into trumpets of marriage (61–2). The irony is that just as the elegiac lover refuses a military career and perverts gender roles because of the force of love, so Tarpeia perverts gender roles by becoming an action heroine, and pursuing her beloved, going further than her mythological role models Scylla and Ariadne (39–42), who remain feminine. Warden suggests that Tarpeia bends genre as much as gender: starting from the lines which compare her to an Amazon with torn tunic (71–2), he finds layers of allusion to Virgil's Camilla, Amata and Dido.⁷² But her attempt to break the boundaries of gender and genre, successful inasmuch as she renders the boundary of

---

⁶⁸ See Keith 2000: 65–100. ⁶⁹ On Propertius 4 see: Janan 2001, Debrohun 2003, Welch 2005.
⁷⁰ On elegy and epic in Prop. 4.10 see Ingleheart 2007.
⁷¹ On landscape and metapoetry in this poem see King 1990. ⁷² Warden 1978.

Rome permeable, brings to her only death.[73] The juxtaposition with the *inclusus amatrix* Arethusa in 4.3, who is shut in away from her husband's wars on the edges of empire, is also productive.[74] Arethusa, too, desires to be an Amazon (4.3.43–4) and see the battle for herself; she has put a great deal of intellectual effort and imagination into following her husband metaphorically (35–40); her desire to know evokes a desire to see. If Tarpeia is a Helen figure, watching from the walls, and betraying her family for love, Arethusa is an Andromache figure, left behind in the domestic space, reduced to weaving (18, 33–4), and, apparently, writing; at least this letter, anyway. These female gazes evoke a space between epic and elegy, a mediation between opposites, which is typical of the interstitial nature of Propertius 4, and is taken up enthusiastically by Ovid in *Metamorphoses* 8.[75] These passages show that the female gaze is always on the edge of epic, but remains important for engaging with epic. Epic is elegy's 'other': the two worlds have opposing values and each offers incomprehensibility to the other.

When Ovid's Scylla watches Minos from the royal tower, she is closely modelled on her elegiac counterpart.[76] But where Tarpeia's initial vision of Tatius is quickly subsumed into speech and compressed, elliptical snapshots of narrative, Ovid lingers on the process of Scylla's viewing. She is on the walls anyway, playing with the 'musical' stones of the walls, when the war begins and she becomes knowledgeable by watching (*spectare*, *Met.* 8.20; *norat*, 21), until she knows Minos only too well (*noverat*, 23; *nosse*, 24). Ovid's description, and her viewing along with ours, begins with Minos in his helmet (25–6). Each element of his armour becomes attractive because he is wearing, and then using, it: the helmet, the shield (26–7), the spear (28–9), the bow (30–1). Her viewing takes the epic arming scene, already associated with erotics by Hera's erotic arming in the deception of Zeus (*Il.* 14.166–86), and gradually changes its character to make it more obviously erotic. But this body is attractive because it is active: his strength and skill in throwing the spear, the way he bends the bow: culminating in her comparison of Minos to Apollo.[77] And then he takes off his helmet, and the key word *nudauerat*, in combination with his eroticised control of his horse

---

[73] Debrohun 2003: 118–35 on liminality in Propertius 4; 146–9 on Tarpeia.
[74] Debrohun 2003: 196 makes this link: 'Tarpeia is almost a "would-be" Arethusa, deceived into believing that marriage can be a cure for war.'
[75] Both Janan 2001 and Debrohun 2003 read Propertius 4, and Tarpeia in particular, as the mediating element.
[76] See Tissol 1997: 143–53.
[77] Aeneas (*Aen.* 4.143–50) and Jason (AR *Arg.* 1.307–11) as Apollo in erotic contexts: Aeneas is viewed by Dido and the Carthaginians as they set out for the hunt; Jason is viewed by the crowd as the Argonauts go down to the boat.

(*premebat, regebat*, 34), brings her to a frenzy: *uix sua, uix sanae uirgo Niseia compos mentis erat* ('Scarcely did she belong to herself, scarcely was the Niseian virgin in her right mind', 35–6). Just as Ovid once longed to be the ring encircling Corinna's finger (*Am.* 2.15), so Scylla longs to be the spear in his grasp or the reins pressed by his hand. Associations with Ovidian elegy suggest that this is a less than entirely epic moment, but the erotic gaze has always been present in epic, too. It is the trappings associated with epic masculinity which are fetishised, yet their removal brings heightened arousal. Distance is what allows this gaze licence: if Minos could see her gazing, she would have to look away. But her desire focuses on collapsing the distance, first metaphorically, and then literally:

> impetus est illi, liceat modo, ferre per agmen
> uirgineos hostile gradus, est impetus illi
> turribus e summis in Cnosia mittere corpus
> castra uel aeratas hosti recludere portas,
> uel si quid Minos aliud uelit. (*Metamorphoses* 8.38–42)

> She has an impulse, if only it were allowed, to take her virgin
> steps through the enemy column, she has an impulse
> to send her body from the topmost towers into the Cretan
> camp or to open the bronze gates to the enemy,
> or anything else that Minos wants.

The repeated word *impetus* implies an attack, whether an attack on her, or her attack on the battlefield. She desires to join in the battle, or take revenge on the indifference of the object of her gaze by committing suicide. But this violent urge metamorphoses into the desire to let him in, to the town and her body.[78]

As for Tarpeia, Scylla's teichoscopy is a solitary event; the only confidant is not a nurse, but the night, called *nutrix* (81). She does not narrate, but rather makes soliloquies. In the second of these, when she responds to Minos' decision to abandon her, she calls herself *auctor* (*auctore relicta*, 108). He has left behind the one who was responsible for his victory. Only seven lines earlier Minos is *iustissimus auctor* ('most just ruler', 101) as he gives laws. By betraying her city, she has gained agency, but in doing so she has gone beyond the bounds of acceptable femininity (and humanity?) and Minos is validated in his rejection of her. Unlike Tarpeia, though, her agency is not literal; she does not become an epic hero. At the end of the

---

[78] Salzman-Mitchell 2005: 108–11 concentrates her reading of this episode on the breaking of boundaries, and how transgression through vision ends with woman as monster.

speech, she imagines herself in competition with other girls in love, going through flames and swords (76–8) but her brief flirtation with bravery and military heroism is over quickly: all she needs to do is dare to cut her father's hair. Vision continues to be important: Minos recoils from the sight of her crime (95–6), and Scylla is driven to violent anger when she sees that he is about to depart (105). Finally, in her metamorphic transformation, she does take her desire to dive, to fly into the action literally. Where heroines watch departing heroes and pursue them with their gazes (see above, pp.225–32), Scylla literally pursues the ship (*insequar*, 141; *consequitur*, 143), and when her transformed father attacks from above, she becomes a bird and flies. Salzman-Mitchell points out that she ends up permanently in a liminal space, neither heaven, earth or sea, neither dead or alive, and permanently objectified, a *monstrum* (in the eyes of Minos, 100) for all to see.[79] Unlike Tarpeia, she does not even keep her name. Yet the readers see epic from her point of view – on the margins. Love causes military success; female viewing is the point of the story. The result is a disturbing metamorphic phenomenon, a *monstrum*, in which unease attaches equally to lover and soldier.

Valerius Flaccus' Medea

Valerius Flaccus interweaves epic and *eros* even more closely in *Argonautica* 6.[80] While the Argonauts fight Aeetes' brother Perses, Medea watches. This episode is hardly mentioned in Apollonius Rhodius;[81] here it takes a whole book of narrative.[82] In my earlier article, I argued that Medea begins the teichoscopy episode as a model reader of epic (6.576), mixing wonder (484–5) at the spectacle with horror (503–6) and pity. Her desire to see her own connections (585) does give her a female gaze; Juno leads her to identify more and more with Jason, so that she proceeds from recognition (575–9), to following him everywhere with her gaze (579–86; 657–8), to almost becoming him (683–5), anticipating what will happen to him (686) and figuratively joining him on the battlefield (564–6). Imagery of burning (Jason: 601, 605; Medea: 658, 663, 669) and storm (Medea: 664–6; earlier in the book, war as storm: 353–7; 380–1; Jason: 685) links Jason and Medea, so she is like a reflection of her beloved, and intertextuality intensifies this

---

[79] Salzman-Mitchell 2005: 111.
[80] For a fuller discussion of this passage, and the passage of Statius below, see Lovatt 2006.
[81] AR *Arg*. 3.352–3 and 3.392–5 mention a possible war of conquest against the Sauromatae in exchange for the golden fleece. See Zissos 2002 on Valerius' complex appropriation of his various models.
[82] See Baier 1998.

effect: both are like both Dido and Aeneas.[83] By the end of the passage, however, Medea's viewing is quite unlike that of the normal reader of epic: her fear (659–60) contrasts with Jason's rejoicing at the sight of war (545–9), and she ignores both the pathos and the horror in her fixation on Jason alone (719–20). Her lack of self-control, combined with her potential power, makes her an incarnation of the monstrous female. I now develop this reading to focus in more depth on Medea's combination of power and passivity, particularly in relation to voice, speech, recognition and understanding; to explore how Valerius Flaccus mixes the epic gaze with elegy and tragedy in a provocative combination.

When Juno decides what to do, it is Medea's power that attracts her. At 439–54, Medea is described as a powerful witch: *nocturnis qua nulla potentior in aris* ('no one is more powerful than her at the dark altars', 440), and like Erichtho she has power over the cosmos (stars, sun, fields, rivers) as well as mortals (444–5). She inspires Phrixus and even her intertextual predecessor, Circe, to marvel (445–8), and Juno sees her as the hero who will defeat the bulls for Jason:

> non aliam tauris uidet et nascentibus armis
> quippe parem nec quae medio stet in agmine flammae.
> nullum mente nefas, nullos horrescere uisus:
>
> (VF *Argonautica* 6.451–3)

> She sees no other woman who is equal to the bulls, the weapons
> being born or to the flame which stands in the middle of the column,
> there is nothing unthinkable for her mind, and she shudders at no sight.

Despite this power, however, she is much more passive in the teichoscopy than many of her intertextual predecessors. Juno is utterly in charge: as she approaches, her divine radiance strikes Medea with panic (*pauor*, 480) and *horror* (481). She literally takes her hand and leads her to the walls, as Medea marvels (488–9). In comparison, Iris, disguised as Helen's sister-in-law, simply persuades her, and does not even accompany her when she goes (*Il.* 3.121–44).[84] Her passivity is echoed in her ignorance and innocence:

> ducitur infelix ad moenia summa futuri
> nescia uirgo mali et falsae commissa sorori;
> lilia per uernos lucent uelut alba colores
> praecipue, quis uita breuis totusque parumper
> floret honor, fuscis et iam notus imminet alis.   (VF *Argonautica* 6.490–4)

---

[83] Lovatt 2006: 71–2. In addition, the image of Jason as the Caucasus mountains (611–12) evokes Aeneas as Mount Athos (*Aen.* 12.701–3).

[84] Fucecchi 1997: 127, who also points out that she is like a victim led to sacrifice (Polyxena at Ovid *Met.* 13.450–2; Iphigenia at Lucretius 1.95–6).

> Unfortunate one, she is led to the heights of the walls, a virgin
> unaware of evil to come and entrusting herself to her false sister;
> just so, white lilies shine through the spring colours
> standing out, whose short life and undamaged honour only briefly
> flourishes and even now the South wind threatens with dark wings.

The lily image evokes her virginal purity and its imminent destruction. Lilies were the flowers gathered by Proserpina in Ovid, and recalls the imagery of epithalamia.[85] Lavinia's blush at *Aen.* 12.64–71 is important, although Valerius strikingly keeps only the white and removes the blush, emphasising that his Medea is not in love; instead her pallor suggests vulnerability and imminent suffering as well as innocence. However, given that we have already seen her as possible epic hero in the eyes of Juno, the connections via Ovid's Atalanta with Camilla and the paralysed gaze of Turnus, may also be relevant, so too the associations of this imagery with dying beautiful boys (see Chapter 7, pp.278–80). Ovid's Hyacinthus, broken off like a flower in death, is particularly closely associated with lilies. It is as if Juno is performing the role of rapacious male god (Pluto, Apollo, Mercury) by inseminating Medea with transgressive love which will overcome her *pudor* and defeminise her (just as the beautiful boys too cross the gender boundaries, and are feminised in death).[86] While Virgil and others have applied the imagery of defloration to death, here Valerius Flaccus applies the imagery of death to (potential and emotional) defloration. This image underlines Medea's powerlessness and her status as object of the gaze, particularly the divine gaze, but also the male gaze. However, Hecate too is watching, not malevolently, but as her divine sponsor, like Diana watching over Camilla at *Aen.* 11.841–9.[87] She promises Medea a monument (*monumenta*, 500) and stakes a rival claim to be recognised as Medea's teacher (*magistram*, 501), as Juno is later described (*Iunone magistra*, 578). She promises not to abandon Medea, as Ovid's Diana abandoned Callisto (*Met.* 2.441–65), but her promise of vengeance on Jason evokes Medea's tragic future, and the simile describing the paralysis of Medea and Juno as they are struck by the force of the battle (503–6), must also evoke the

---

[85] Medea has already been compared to Proserpina at VF *Arg.* 5.343–9; on this see Stover 2003: 127. Stover argues that hints of emasculation brought out by Jason's initial similarity to Salmacis are trumped by his heroic recuperation in book 6. Epithalamia: Stat. *Silu.* 2.1.46 *vernos . . . flores*; Catullus 61.185–8. On lily imagery, see Dyson 1999.
[86] Agri 2011 argues that Juno's destruction of Medea's *pudor* can be read as a sort of rape.
[87] Fucecchi 1997: 128–30 sees this link.

horrific effect of Medea's future tragic actions.[88] This simile also acts to connect viewers and fighters: an earlier bird simile at 260–4 compares Oncheus transfixed by a spear to a bird trapped in its trusted resting place by bird-lime and unable to move.

The relationship between Medea's gaze and the narrative is equally complex. Although initially she recapitulates Helen, she does not take on Helen's role as narrator. Instead Juno stages the whole spectacle for Medea as audience. After Juno's initial speech, Medea is not even given a chance to reply (*illa nihil contra*, 'She said nothing in reply', 488). When she does finally speak, at 588–90, her question attempts to hide her growing infatuation, but Juno's much longer speech in response is represented as driving her on like a pack animal: *contra aspera Iuno | reddit agens stimulis ac diris fraudibus urget.* ('In reply harsh Juno driving her applies the spurs and forces her with/into dreadful deceits', 590–1). The speech itself draws Medea in by her gaze (*aspicis*, 'you see', 595) and interprets her viewing to align it with Juno's agenda: Jason flashes out shining (*emicet effulgens*, 596), and by implying that this is an ephemeral spectacle, and that she should not miss a moment of it before Jason leaves Colchis (597–9), Juno evokes already the gaze of the abandoned woman at the departing hero. Finally at 675–9 Medea takes the initiative in her conversation with Juno (*ac prior his*, 'And thus first these things', 675); Juno takes this as the signal that her task is complete, and leaves in the middle of her speech (*medio in sermone*, 679), which emphasises the power of the goddess. Medea's verbal initiative is paralleled by her physical exposure:

> imminet e celsis audentius improba muris
> uirgo, nec ablatam sequitur quaeritue sororem.
>
> (VF *Argonautica* 6.681–2)
>
> She stands out from the high walls more daringly, the wicked
> girl, and does not follow or seek the sister who has been removed.

Here Medea is both threat and threatened, and continues the link with imagery from the earlier battle scene: at 383–5 Gesander, who has just been fighting Amazons, falls like a mountain or a city wall.[89] So Medea threatens her own city walls.[90] These lines also bring out the importance of

---

[88] On Medea's tragic connections in Valerius Flaccus, see Buckley forthcoming.
[89] *Imminet* may recall *supereminet*, which is a key word of Stover 2003's analysis of the initial meeting of Jason and Medea at 5.367 (130–1).
[90] Another moment of assimilation between Medea and Jason comes in the imagery of scattering: Medea at 584 scatters her gaze (*sparsit uaga lumina*) and Jason as a lion at 614 scatters his hunger (*spargitque famem*). Stover 2003: 143.

recognising (or not recognising) the goddess. Medea is so much in Juno's power at this stage that she no longer cares whether or not the figure who has been influencing her is her sister or a disguised immortal. Jason in contrast recognises the goddess's inspiration and strength (609–10), which leads into his conception of himself as ultimately epic: two similes, comparing him to a mountain (611–12), and a lion on the rampage (613–16), seem to be focalised through Jason himself.

Stover 2003: 143 points out the potential generic instability of this last lion simile: its Iliadic resonance (*Il.* 12.298–301) is compromised by its use in the *Odyssey* at 6.130–4 to describe Odysseus as he meets Nausicaa, complete with heroic fiery eyes. In the same way, Jason as Sirius evokes both Apollonius' Jason in the middle of his erotic encounters (3.956–9), and the centrally heroic figures of Diomedes (*Il.* 5.4–8), Achilles (*Il.* 22.25–32) and Aeneas (*Aen.* 10.270–5). Sirius is also important in erotic poetry (Tib. 1.1.25–8; Ovid *Fasti* 4.901–42; Hor. *Odes* 1.17), and Stover argues that this generic tension is at its strongest in Jason's meeting with Medea, when he is beautified by Juno and stuns Medea's gaze, while being fixated on her himself (VF *Arg.* 5.363–77). This tension is resolved, Stover argues, in book 6, in a '"reconciliation" between the poem's erotic and martial themes' (144). But as his final note points out, this reconciliation is not secure (146 n.57). In its rich and subtle use of the epic gaze, the poem plays similarly with generic tension and complication. The epic invocation at 6.515–16 is immediately followed by a brief *aristeia* of Absyrtus, as if Medea had actually taken charge of the narrative and was able to determine the poet's choice of hero on which to focus (despite Juno's pressure, she begins by looking for her brother).[91] The erotic potential of the star similes is brought out by the comparison of Aron to Lucifer (527–8), who has both military and erotic visual power, and wears a cloak (evoking the Jason of Apollonius' Hypsipyle episode) which burns at 526 (*chlamys ardet*). The following figure has an eerily Ovidian resonance: Armes wears horns, pretending to be the Lycaean god (530–3), and paralyses the enemy in astonishment at his appearance (534), only to be stripped of his costume by Aron, an Actaeon killed in battle, rather than torn to pieces by his own dogs. The battle scenes are lavishly supplied with both horror and pathos.[92]

---

[91] A link to the Iliadic Helen, and her inability to see her brothers?

[92] Body fragments and gore: scythed chariots at 345–70; in our passage, opening up the body at 551–2; entrails pouring out at 555–6; seeing his own lifeblood pour out at 572–4; decapitation and dismembering at 619–20. Pathos: Peucon as Crenaeus figure: 563–8; Colaxes son of Jupiter: 621–56; Caicus' wife and accidental death: 688–9; Myraces the Parthian and his eunuch: 690–724.

Juno's is not the only divine gaze to be in play: at 621–30 Jupiter laments that he must watch his son Colaxes die; Pallas stands ready to protect the Argonauts at 172–7, with Mars and Tisiphone, raising her head to the sky, on the other side (178–81); at 396–400 Pallas uses her aegis to panic the charioteers and throw them in confusion against their own side. Finally, the defeat of Perses' troops is described in terms of vision: they have seen enough (721) and the flight before their eyes of their leaders (723) causes them in turn to flee; Perses watches them and laments (*tuens*, 726), and evokes the tragic future once more by longing to see vengeance on Jason (*uideam*, 735). He then intends to perform an act of *deuotio* but Pallas sees and rescues him in a cloud (*uidisset*, 740; *nebulam*, 745).

However, the last lines of the book emphasise the erotic frame: this whole battle is a ploy devised by Juno to display Jason to Medea. Salzman-Mitchell, in her discussion of Scylla, claims that 'the main point of the warrior's existence is not to be looked at, as it is the case with women commonly, but to accomplish glorious deeds that place them beyond the personal in transcendent aspirations, to achieve *kleos* through action'. (109) But in the Ovidian narrative, and in Valerian teichoscopy, the battle exists only for the benefit of its female viewer, who is the point of the story. Jason will use Medea to achieve glory and pursue his transcendent aspirations, but his *kleos* will always be compromised by his association with Medea, and he will inevitably remain in her shadow. Valerius brings this out in the last few lines of the book, which come back to Medea and the tradition of erotic viewing:

> ut fera Nyctelii paulum per sacra resistunt,
> mox rapuere deum iamiam <in> quodcumque paratae
> Thyiades, haut alio remeat Medea tumultu
> atque inter Graiumque acies patriasque phalangas
> semper inexpletis adgnoscit Iasona curis
> armaque quique caua superest de casside uultus.   (VF *Argonautica* 755–60)

> As the Nyctelii for a little resist the god in their wild rites,
> but soon they seize the god and now, even now, the Thyiades
> are ready for whatever, not otherwise does Medea return to the battle,
> and among the columns of the Greeks and the phalanxes of her fatherland
> always she recognises Jason, her cares unsatisfied,
> and his weapons and his face which stands above the hollow helmet.

We have seen Tarpeia afflicted with Bacchic madness, at the same time as becoming an Amazon (Prop. 4.4.71–2);[93] the Bacchic connection is also erotic

---

[93] Fucecchi 1997: 264–9 points to the similarity with Tarpeia, but also Andromache compared to a Maenad at *Il.* 22.460.

(Dido, Prop. 1.3) and obviously tragic. For a moment it seems that Medea is doing what the women in Iphigenia at Aulis do (Eur. *IA* 164–302), and actually going down among the troops.[94] Instead, however, her gaze continues, ending with Jason's face awkwardly released from the helmet, the climactic moment of Scylla's viewing of Minos (*Met.* 8.32).[95] These lines make an emphatically un-epic ending to the book, and we have to ask why, if Valerius' main motivation was to rehabilitate epic in the panegyrical service of the new Flavian regime, did he choose such a complex, problematic and generically unstable story to tell?

Statius' Antigone

Statius' Antigone twice watches from the walls (in books 7 and 11) and we have already seen Argia.[96] By thinking about gender, genre, displacement and alienation in these episodes, I explore the importance of the tragic and female gaze in the *Thebaid*. Statius is an adroit reader of Homer, and his combination of catalogue and teichoscopy at 7.243–373 suggests that he, like Scodel, saw the two Homeric episodes as complementary.[97] McNelis has shown Statius' close engagement with the Homeric catalogue in this passage.[98] Passages of detailed reminiscence of *Iliad* 2 are interspersed with Callimachean and Ovidian digressions. The overall framework uses the characters of the Euripidean teichoscopy (Antigone and her *paidagogos*) but gives them a Homeric twist. As in Euripides, Antigone is not the narrator; nor are they viewing the enemy. But they are not viewing Thebans either: rather, as in the catalogue in *Aeneid* 7, they are viewing foreign allies. Similarly, Antigone does not do the narrating, but her interventions are assertive and powerful: at 7.247 she speaks first (like Priam, *Il.* 3.161–70); her instructions to Phorbas suggest an invocation (*dic, o precor*, 'tell me, I pray', 249), while the tropes of invocation are tangentially repeated by Phorbas at 282–9, but without actually creating any sense of epic authority for his narrative.[99] Furthermore, immediately after

---

[94] Scodel 1997: 88–91.
[95] Fucecchi 1997: 269 points to Tarpeia and Scylla, plus several Statian examples, and Sen. *Phoen.* 471–3.
[96] Since Lovatt 2006 two important interventions have occurred: McNelis 2007: 101–23 examines the poetics of the teichoscopy scene; he suggests that Statius moves between Iliadic catalogue and Callimachean/Ovidian digression until he settles on a Lucanian or Telchinic poetics of civil war for the second half of the poem. Bernstein 2004 dissects the dynamics of viewing in *Thebaid* 11, arguing that authorising viewpoints are removed (discussed above, Chapter 2, pp.71–7), leaving only unhealthy visual pleasure or impotent disavowal.
[97] Scodel 1997.   [98] McNelis 2007: 102, 111–12, 115–16, 118–19.
[99] McNelis 2007: 102–8 shows the anti-epic tendencies of this 'invocation'.

this 'proem in the middle', Antigone interrupts, to push the narrative towards tragedy, aetiology and Ovidian rape narrative. As in the *Iliad*, where Helen unsuccessfully looks for her brothers, and in the *Phoenissae*, where Antigone cannot really make out Polynices, here Antigone sees two men who are apparently brothers, but does not recognise their true relationship. A flurry of Ovidian myths follow: Narcissus cannot fight because he is now a flower; Niobe's children, too, represent an absent military force. The expression of poetic inability at 343–50 is made literal by Phorbas' recollection of the death of Laius, which causes him to stop talking. Statius has taken the absences at the heart of the Iliadic and Euripidean catalogues, and multiplied them many times. Not only does Antigone not look at her brother, she does not even gain the opportunity to try and look for him, and her poetic guide presents a tableau of poetic failure.

The passage is also riddled with tendentious and problematic allusions: the mention of Atalantean Schoenos at 267–8 highlights Statius' conflation of the two Atalantas (both Ovidian) throughout the poem; Shackleton Bailey points out that *tauro auito* at 279 is problematic, because it conflates the bull who seduced Europa with the bull which destroyed Dirce;[100] McNelis points out the non-military heritage of the Permessus, which makes it the wrong river for a military catalogue, and the mismatch of swans and the river Strymon, usually associated with cranes.[101] At 294–6, Phorbas' emphasis on the well-travelled nature of Antigone's confusion of Lapithaon and Alatreus might suggest that this is well known, but it is not elsewhere attested and appears to have been invented by Statius.[102] At 315–27 Phorbas seems to have picked a similarly tendentious version of the Boeotian river Asopus' rage against Jupiter for the rape of his daughter, also marked by numerous Alexandrian footnotes (*datur*, 315; *ferunt*, 319; *insignia*, 326).[103] All these things come together to make Phorbas an uncomfortable narrator, and the audience very much aware of the textuality of this passage, whether they are informed (and therefore confused by so much going on) or uninformed (and therefore just confused by the obscure and complex references).

Phorbas' final narrative breakdown, however, is dominated by reference to Theban tragedy: he cannot manage to tell what happened to Laius, just as

---

[100] Shackleton Bailey 2003: 419 n.40.
[101] We might also make the link with Propertius confusing Tarpeia as Amazon/Bacchant image at 4.4.71–2, which also mentions the Strymon, especially as Propertius at 2.10.25–6 uses the Permessus as a fount of anti-war poetic inspiration.
[102] McNelis 2007: 113.   [103] McNelis 2007: 112–15.

so many in Sophocles' *Oedipus rex* cannot tell, through ignorance, then fear and horror. His affection for Antigone equally foreshadows her own tragic future: she may be suitable for marriage (*thalamis habilem*, 366) and in one piece (*integram*, 366) but he will never see her married, while he is correct that he will see (*uisurus*) a repeat of the familial *nefas* between Laius and Oedipus, as the two team up to organise and motivate their descendants' mutual self-destruction. His failure of narrative is also a failure of the gaze: at 372 his gaze is blunted, and the orders of Eteocles silence Phorbas' narrative. Antigone has disappeared from our view, and even her response is an absence denied the audience for their narrative pleasure.

However, she does return. In book 11 she climbs the walls to make an appeal to Polynices not to fight his brother (11.354–87), parallel to Jocasta's appeal to Eteocles (315–53). The extreme circumstances lend Antigone determination and wings. In book 7 she is dignified but quiet:

> turre procul sola nondum concessa uideri
> Antigone populis teneras defenditur atra
> ueste genas; iuxtaque comes quo Laius ibat
> armigero; tunc uirgo senem regina ueretur. (*Thebaid* 7.243–6)

> Far on a lonely tower, not yet allowed to be seen
> by the people, Antigone defends her tender cheeks
> with a black cloak; next to her is her companion, who once
> was armour-bearer for Laius; then the royal girl revered the old man.

She is isolated, carefully kept from becoming the object of the gaze, far off and tender; she keeps by the side of her companion, and the emphasis is put on her respect and fear. In book 11 she goes further and faster:

> at parte ex alia tacitos obstante tumultu
> Antigone furata gradus (nec casta retardat
> uirginitas) uolat Ogygii fastigia muri
> exuperare furens; senior comes haeret eunti
> Actor, et hic summas non duraturus ad arces. (*Thebaid* 11.354–8)

> But in another part, maddened Antigone takes her silent steps
> through the intervening riot – and her chaste virginity does not
> slow her down – she flies raging to conquer the battlements
> of the Ogygian wall; her older companion Actor keeps with her
> as she goes, but he is not about to last out to the top of the citadel.

Like Argia in book 12 (at, for instance, 12.244–5), she will outpace her companion; she is both *furata* (maddened) and *furens* (raging), and her chaste virginity enhances a masculine hardiness to go with her feminine excessiveness. She looks from the wall for Polynices, at first with fallible gaze, as in the *Phoenissae*:

> utque procul uisis paulum dubitauit in armis,
> adgnouitque (nefas!) iaculis et uoce superba
> tecta incessentem, magno prius omnia planctu
> implet et ex muris ceu descensura profatur: (*Thebaid* 11.359–62)
>
> She hesitated a little as she looked at the weapons far away,
> and recognised (unspeakable!) Polynices with javelins and proud voice
> attacking the building, beforehand she fills everything
> with a great wail and addresses him from the walls as if about to come down:

Finally she eliminates the distance and makes contact with him: the power of her lament interrupts and anticipates him, filling the space as if through divine inspiration. Like Scylla, she seems about to cross the boundary of the wall, to move from being spectator to participant, and by speaking to Polynices she partially achieves that: she speaks but he is silent. She controls his gaze, by making him look back at her (*respice turrem*, 363) and demanding that he recognise her (*agnoscisne hostes?* 365), at the same time recognising the *nefas* of his attack. There is a hint of potential suicide in *descensura* (362) and *deuota* (371): Menoeceus looked out from the walls, as did Hero, who ended by killing herself, and Aegeus from the cliffs; Amata too kills herself after apparently seeing the death of Turnus, and Jocasta will follow this model (11.634–47). Antigone's speech mobilises the language of erotic teichoscopy:

> saltem ora trucesque
> solue genas; liceat uultus fortasse supremum
> noscere dilectos et ad haec lamenta uidere
> anne fleas.   (*Thebaid* 11.372–5)
>
> At least release your face
> and savage eyes; may it perhaps be allowed to know
> one last time your beloved face and to see whether you weep
> at these laments.

What she yearns for is reciprocity of emotional intensity, but the desire to see the face out of the helmet evokes Ovid's Scylla.

Extraordinarily, this teichoscopy is almost successful in eliminating the distance, and affecting the outcome. Polynices not only sees her, and recognises her, but even responds with reciprocal emotion, as Aeneas hesitates at the speech of Turnus:

> his paulum furor elanguescere dictis
> coeperat, obstreperet quamquam atque obstaret Erinys;
> iam summissa manus, lente iam flectit habenas,
> iam tacet; erumpunt gemitus, lacrimasque fatetur
> cassis; hebent irae, pariterque et abire nocentem
> et uenisse pudet. (*Thebaid* 11.382–7)
>
> At these words the madness had begun to grow limp,
> even though the Erinys interrupted with noise and stood in the way;
> now he turns his hands to hers sent down, slowly now he turns the reins,
> now he is silent; groans break out, and the helmet confesses
> tears; his anger grows blunt, and he is equally ashamed to go away guilty
> and to have come.

He does not take off the helmet, but tears are seen through it. His anger is blunted just as Phorbas' gaze was blunted. The shame that Medea lost through her teichoscopy is here restored through Antigone's. She has established an emotional connection by transgressing the boundaries of appropriate feminine behaviour, but doing so in the service of restoring morality and social or familial connections, rather than destroying them. But does this go too far? Is Antigone in danger of repeating the Theban incest narratives? Does she let herself go too far into the realm of the erotic? She is just as mad as he is, and her contest with Argia over his dead body, the way the two women act as doubles, continues this theme of Theban family relationships too close and too intense.

How does this episode of teichoscopy fit into the wider narrative of book 11? We have examined above the way the gods avert their gaze, and Bernstein's argument that this removes epic authority from the final duel. Antigone's first teichoscopy is juxtaposed with a scene of divine gazing: in book 7, the teichoscopy comes just after Bacchus' supplication of Jupiter, initiated by his viewing of the Argive expedition (*uiderat*, 'he had seen', 7.145). In book 11, Jupiter is watching the build-up to the battle at 11.119 (*illas ut summo uidit pater altus Olympo*, 'when the high father saw them from the top of Olympus') before he orders the Olympians to stop watching, leading into the series of attempts to prevent the duel (dream of Argia, Adrastus, Eteocles' sacrifice, Jocasta, Antigone). The unauthorised gaze which remains to see the final outcome of the duel is the marginal, disaffected gaze: women, furies, old men, ghosts and the common people. It is no coincidence that book 12 is dominated by women (even Theseus is surrounded by Amazons) and ends in the midst of lament.[104]

---

[104] For a largely positive reading of the feminine ending of the *Thebaid*, see Dietrich 1999.

Quintus and Nonnus: joining in battle

While Valerius gives us a Medea who figuratively joins in the fight, and Statius' Antigone threatens to leap from the walls, Quintus Smyrnaeus presents Trojan women who are spurred to heroic ambitions by the example of Penthesilea and decide to join in.[105] The Amazon queen, in the middle of her *aristeia*, while Achilles and Ajax are absent from the battlefield still lamenting Patroclus, is compared to a heifer destroying a garden (*PH* 1.396–402).[106] This takes the image of warrior as trampled flower and makes it comic by focusing on the hunger and delight of the heifer: to be properly heroic she would need to be a bull, and to fight other bulls rather than destroying vegetation. So Quintus takes the tradition of the warrior maiden and undercuts it by damning with faint praise. Similarly, the suggestion of a transgression more far-reaching than those of Valerius and Statius is only set up to be dismissed. The Trojan women are watching and wondering at Penthesilea, when a character called Hippodameia falls in love with the idea of war (404) and tries to persuade the other Trojan women to join in battle (409–35). She argues that eyes and light, along with food and air, are shared equally between men and women, so why should women not fight? She picks out Penthesilea as an example of a woman fighting even though it is not her city; the Trojan women have every reason to fight: to protect or avenge their families; to avoid enslavement (but there is no suggestion that epic glory inspires them: their connection to war is still female). The other Trojan women respond enthusiastically:

> Ὥς ἄρ' ἔφη, πάσῃσι δ' ἔρως στυγεροῖο μόθοιο
> ἔμπεσεν· ἐσσυμένως δὲ πρὸ τείχεος ὁρμαίνεσκον
> βήμεναι ἐν τεύχεσσιν, ἀρηγέμεναι μεμαυῖαι
> ἄστεϊ καὶ λαοῖσιν· ὀρίνετο δέ σφισι θυμός.
> Ὥς δ' ὅτ' ἔσω σίμβλοιο μέγ' ἰύζωσι μέλισσαι
> χείματος οὐκέτ' ἐόντος, ὅτ' ἐς νομὸν ἐντύνονται
> ἐλθέμεν, οὐδ' ἄρα τῇσι φίλον πέλει ἔνδοθι μίμνειν,
> ἄλλη δ' αὖθ' ἑτέρην προκαλίζεται ἐκτὸς ἄγεσθαι·
> ὡς ἄρα Τρωιάδες ποτὶ φύλοπιν ἐγκονέουσαι
> ἀλλήλας ὤτρυνον·   (*Posthomerica* 1.436–45)

These words filled them all with a passion for hateful fighting.
They were ready to rush out headlong from their walls

---

[105] On this passage, see Bär 2009.
[106] On Penthesilea and similes in Quintus, see Maciver 2012: 125–52.

> under arms, in their eagerness to defend
> their city and their people; so roused in them was their spirit.
> As bees inside a hive start humming loudly
> at winter's end, preparing to head for their pasture;
> they are no longer content to stay within;
> one challenges another to venture outside;
> so the women of Troy in haste to join the fray
> urged each other on.

The bee simile evokes complex imagery of peace and war, women and men, even if we assume that Quintus was not using Virgil.[107] At *Il.* 2.86–94 the gathering Greek armies are compared to bees gathering in swarms, and at *Il.* 12.167–72 Greeks defending their camp are like bees defending their hive. This simile is appropriate to the situation: the women are about to fight for the first time, gathering to march out, and they are determined to defend their city. These two examples seem to suggest that it really is a military image. However in Apollonius at AR *Arg.* 2.130–36 the Lemnian women saying goodbye to their men are compared to bees darting from flower to flower to gain the last honey. These potentially transgressive women are compared to the actually transgressive women of the Lemnian myth: but at a moment of normative erotic disturbance. If we can take Virgil into account, two moments seem important: first and most famously at *Aen.* 1.430–6, where Aeneas watches the Carthaginians building their city, like bees working hard for their queen; secondly at 12.584–92, where the besieged Latins are like bees being smoked out of their hive. Among the multiple resonances of these bee similes is the perspective: people look like insects when viewed from afar, and most of these similes are not focalised by an internal viewer (except for Aeneas looking at Carthage), but rather evoke the objectifying gaze of the epic narrator (or the gods). The main point of comparison is the noise of the bees, with the implication that this noise is an empty threat, like the chattering of the cicadas at *Il.* 3.150–2. This suggests a further objectification, a trivialisation of the bees. Further, Penthesilea and Helen in book 14 are closely linked, and both are described by similes which mix erotic desire with the desire for success in war *via* the idea of sailors on a journey: at 14.63–8 Helen returning to the Greeks is like their native land to returning sailors; at 1.633–9, Penthesilea's death is like a shipwreck for the Trojans as they return to the city, both drawing on the image of Odysseus' return to Penelope (*Od.* 23.233–40). Quintus radically links erotic desire and desire for success in battle, desire for salvation with

---

[107] Polleichtner 2005 explores bee similes from Homer to Virgil.

desire for a beautiful woman, bringing together the traditions of the female gaze in innovative ways.

After this simile, the priestess Theano persuades the Trojan women not to fight in the end, by arguing that they have not been trained for this kind of work. The emphasis on work (*PH* 1.451, 452, 453, 457, 459, 464, 466) evokes the bees as symbols of *labor*; the hard work of men and Amazons in training for war is what legitimates their right to fight, not their gender per se. This is a considerably more sophisticated approach than Hector's argument in *Iliad* 6 (above, p.226), in which he simply states that war is man's work. Her final argument recalls the historiographic tradition of women fighting as a last resort to try and save their city from destruction: we are not at that point yet, she argues (472–4), although the Virgilian resonances, with the link between Carthage and its inevitable destruction, and the city of Latinus, literally destroyed in the process of founding Rome, bring out the fact that the destruction of Troy (and the final enslavement of the Trojan women) is very much the *telos* of this epic.

In contrast, Nonnus' *Dionysiaca* plays complex games with gender, viewing and walls in book 35. In the absence of Dionysus, who has been driven temporarily mad, the Bacchic armies are faring badly. On the Indian side, king Deriades' right-hand man, and son-in-law, Morrheus, has fallen in love with an Amazonian warrior, Chalcomedea, whom he pursues. The desiring gaze of Morrheus is complicated by Deriades' order that no man should rape the Bacchants in case sexual desire turns them away from battle, and by the fact that he is married to Deriades' daughter. His illicit pursuit of love, then, frames an episode which plays with the theme of teichoscopy. At the beginning of book 35, Deriades has trapped the army of Bacchants within his city, and is attempting to slaughter them, while old men and the women of the city watch from the walls and roofs:

ἀκλινέες δὲ γέροντες ἀερσιλόφων ἐπὶ πύργων
φύλοπιν ἐσκοπίαζον· ὑπὲρ τεγέων δὲ καὶ αὐταί
θυρσοφόρον στίχα πᾶσαν ἐθηήσαντο γυναῖκες·
καί τις ὑπὲρ μεγάροιο περικλινθεῖσα τιθήνη
παρθένος ἑλκεσίπεπλος ἐδέρκετο θῆλυν ᾿ενυώ,
καὶ κταμένῃ βαρύδακρυς ἐπέστενεν ἥλικι κούρῃ. (*Dionysiaca* 35.11–16)

The old men were seated unmoving upon the high precipitous walls, watching the fray; the women also upon the rooftops gazed at the whole thyrsus-bearing throng, and many a longrobed maiden from her chamber above leaning upon her nurse marked this female warfare, and lamented with tears the slaughter of some girl of her own years. (trans. Rouse)

The battle is within the city rather than outside it, and the enemy are women rather than men. The watchers on the walls are now split by gender: the old men just watch, but the women empathise with the deaths of those they identify with, and see war itself as female. In an erotic digression, an unnamed Indian soldier wrestles with Deriades' order not to rape the Bacchants, falling in love with his dead enemy (17–78). At 79–97 there is a further twist: the watching Indian women decide to join in the fight. Protonoe avenges her husband Orontes, who was killed at 17.168–314; Cheirobie, the wife of Morrheus, and Orsiboe also attack the Bacchants. Each is compared to a Greek heroine: Atalanta, Meleager's sister, and Deianira, who Hercules armed when he was fighting Hylas' father, according to the scholia on Apollonius. Dionysus' destabilisation of gender is infecting his Indian enemies: but these women are still defined by their relationships to men, and are still represented as defending their city, rather than becoming epic fighters:

ἄλλη δ' εἰνοδίην ὑπεδύσατο δηϊοτῆτα,
παρθένος ἐγρεκύδοιμος, ὑπὲρ τεγέων δὲ καὶ ἄλλαι
λαϊνέοις βελέεσσιν ἐθωρήσσοντο γυναῖκες· (*Dionysiaca* 35.94–6)

Many a battlestirring maiden entered the fight in the street, other women on the roofs provided themselves with stony missiles. (trans. Rouse)

In the world of the *Dionysiaca*, in which the army is made up of Amazons, Bacchants, Pans and Sileni, the tropes of epic are turned upside down and inside out. By putting the battle within the city, women can join in the fight without crossing the boundary of the walls; by making those fighting in the city also women, the women who join in the battle seem much less transgressive. But the Indian women are wives and mothers, and despite their ethnic otherness, they must still be domesticated by comparing them to Greek examples of women legitimately fighting at the request of their menfolk or in a desperate situation. The generic resonances are with history rather than tragedy, and the erotic gaze is reserved for men looking at women. It is striking that both Quintus and Nonnus toy with the idea of turning teichoscopy into participation, and no surprise that Nonnus takes it further than Quintus.

Lament, aftermath and the female gaze

After Odysseus has slaughtered the suitors, the first person to see the dead bodies and the bloody hall is Eurykleia. Summoned by Telemachus she gives a female perspective on the epic violence of the *Odyssey*:

εὗρεν ἔπειτ' Ὀδυσῆα μετὰ κταμένοισι νέκυσσιν,
αἵματι καὶ λύθρῳ πεπαλαγμένον ὥς τε λέοντα,
ὅς ῥά τε βεβρωκὼς βοὸς ἔρχεται ἀγραύλοιο·
πᾶν δ' ἄρα οἱ στῆθός τε παρήϊά τ' ἀμφοτέρωθεν
αἱματόεντα πέλει, δεινὸς δ' εἰς ὦπα ἰδέσθαι·
ὣς Ὀδυσεὺς πεπάλακτο πόδας καὶ χεῖρας ὕπερθεν·
ἡ δ' ὡς οὖν νέκυάς τε καὶ ἄσπετον ἔσιδεν αἷμα,
ἴθυσέν ῥ' ὀλολύξαι, ἐπεὶ μέγα ἔσιδεν ἔργον·
ἀλλ' Ὀδυσεὺς κατέρυκε καὶ ἔσχεθεν ἱεμένην περ,
καί μιν φωνήσας ἔπεα πτερόεντα προσηύδα·
«ἐν θυμῷ, γρηῦ, χαῖρε καὶ ἴσχεο μηδ' ὀλόλυζε·
οὐχ ὁσίη κταμένοισιν ἐπ' ἀνδράσιν εὐχετάασθαι.» (*Odyssey* 22.401–12)

> There she found Odysseus among the slaughtered dead men,
> spattered over with gore and battle filth, like a lion
> who has been feeding on an ox of the fields, and goes off
> covered with blood, all his chest and his flanks on either
> side bloody, a terrible thing to look in the face; so
> now Odysseus' feet and the hands above them were spattered.
> She, when she saw the dead men and the endless blood, began then
> to raise the cry of triumph, having seen it was monstrous
> work, but Odysseus checked her and held her, for all her eagerness,
> and spoke to her and addressed her in winged words, saying:
> 'Keep your joy in your heart, old dame; stop, do not raise up
> the cry. It is not piety to glory so over slain men.'

The simile puts the emphasis on horror: Odysseus covered in gore, like a violent predator, is terrifying to look at (δεινὸς δ' εἰς ὦπα ἰδέσθαι). But Eurykleia's response is paradoxically happy: the emphasis on the corpses and endless blood lead to rejoicing and the appreciation that this is a great deed (the heroic core of the *Odyssey*). Yet Odysseus is the one to check her joy, with a sense of the propriety of lament and the respect needed for the dead. The last book of the poem will focus, like the end of the *Iliad*, on aftermath and reconciliation. Eurykleia's joy goes beyond the propriety of epic: she is more bloodthirsty than the hero himself. When at the beginning of book 23 Eurykleia wakes Penelope, she begins with the return of Odysseus, and recapitulates that first vision of the aftermath, including Odysseus as a lion (23.45–8). She insists that Penelope too would have rejoiced (ἰδοῦσά κε θυμὸν ἰάνθης, 'You would have been cheered to see him', 47), but Penelope resists taking any obvious pleasure; she still agrees to view the remains of the battle, but emphasises rather her need to see her son, above the dead bodies of the suitors and the man who killed them. The aftermath offers an opportunity for women to confront the male world of epic violence, and their responses to it are often complex. The importance of these scenes in the Homeric poems means that they are not the province of tragedy alone. Coming in after the action always limits the power of the gaze to stimulate agency, but many narratives are cyclical, and the response of women can be an important catalyst for further violence. Women may or may not buy into the ideology of personal glory gained in battle, but as audience to aftermath they mediate between narrator and readers in formulating different responses to epic narrative.

While the Odyssean scene is firmly within domestic space, even if women are excluded during the battle, and women are responsible for returning that space to domestic order, Iliadic lament is located on the walls. I will examine below the ways that Hector's heroism is closely tied to the beauty and integrity of his body (see below, Chapter 7, pp.262–5), but when he dies, the dirt and defilement of his body (22.401–4) is the visual moment which initialises the change of scene from Greek rejoicing to Trojan mourning, from Achilles creating a spectacle to Hecuba and Priam viewing it:

> Ὣς τοῦ μὲν κεκόνιτο κάρη ἅπαν· ἡ δέ νυ μήτηρ
> τίλλε κόμην, ἀπὸ δὲ λιπαρὴν ἔρριψε καλύπτρην
> τηλόσε, κώκυσεν δὲ μάλα μέγα παῖδ' ἐσιδοῦσα·   (*Iliad* 22.405–7)

> So all his head was dragged in the dust; and now his mother
> tore out her hair, and threw the shining veil far from her
> and raised a great wail as he looked upon her son

Mourning requires the removal of the covering veil, the exposure of female emotion. And although words and hearing are central to the process of lament, vision also has a part to play: Andromache hears the noise of mourning (447) and is again inspired to run to the walls like a maenad (460); the impact of the sight is the removal of her power to see: darkness of night mists over her eyes (462–7). Her lament is the climax, but Priam takes the initiative; as in teichoscopy, lament is for the non-combatants, but old men share this discourse with women.[108]

In the *Aeneid* too, the two great laments pair a mother and a father: both non-combatants, and one on the walls, Euryalus' mother (*Aen.* 9.481–97) and Pallas' father (11.152–81). Both are alerted by Fama and both laments are initiated by the sight of the dead body.[109] Euryalus' decapitated head in particular becomes an emblem of the horrors of war, and, as his death is a

---

[108] On spectatorship and mourning, Murnaghan 1999–2000.
[109] On the links between the two deaths and their involvement in a pattern of future generations cut off, see Reed 2007: 40.

death-in-love, so the viewing of his dead body is closely connected to the erotic teichoscopy. Virgil sends a particularly strong signal by repeating the two lines describing dawn which occur as Dido awakes to watch the Trojans depart:

> Et iam prima nouo spargebat lumine terras
> Tithoni croceum linquens Aurora cubile.
>
> *(Aeneid* 9.459–60; 4.584–5)
>
> And now Aurora first was scattering the lands
> with new light, leaving the yellow bed of Tithonus.

The calm and optimism of a new dawn is contrasted with the visceral horror and emotional shock of death and abandonment. Turnus focalises this dawn as his men see fully, and come to terms with, the slaughter wrought by Nisus and Euryalus before they died; it is in this context that they put the heads of the dead young men on display (*uisu miserabile*, 'a wretched sight', 465), mirrored by the extraordinarily effective half-line *Euryali et Nisi* (467) in which the pair of names equate simply to the pair of heads. The Trojans are on the walls:

ingentisque tenent fossas et turribus altis
stant maesti; simul ora uirum praefixa mouebant,
nota nimis miseris atroque fluentia tabo.   *(Aeneid* 9.470–2)

they hold the huge trenches and on the high towers
stand sorrowful; at the same time the faces of heroes fixed above were stirring them,
too well-known to the wretched men and flowing with black gore.

Those holding the walls are fighters, unusually, since Aeneas has ordered them not to leave their defences, and the way this compromises their masculinity is brought out by Numanus Remulus' insults (598–620). The Trojans trapped on their walls are feminised, reduced to spectators; Ascanius can only shoot an arrow in response, and if Apollo is watching (638–40), he is doing so in order to restrain. When Euryalus' mother, interrupted by rumour while weaving, in a close reworking of Andromache, runs to the walls, she abandons her femininity in grief, at the same time that it is emphasised by her extreme emotion:

> euolat infelix et femineo ululatu,
> scissa comam, muros amens atque agmina cursu
> prima petit, non illa uirum, non illa pericli
> telorumque memor   *(Aeneid* 9.477–80)

> she flies out, tragic, and with feminine wailing,
> torn hair, mad she first seeks the walls
> and the columns at a run, nor is she mindful of the men,
> nor the danger of weapons

Her first words emphasise vision: *hunc ego te, Euryale, aspicio*? ('Is this how I see you, Euryalus?', 481), and her speech comes to a climax with her demand to the Rutulians to shoot her down, or to Jupiter to strike her down with a thunderbolt, drawing attention to her exposed position on the walls. Her removal to the safety of domestic space (498–502), however, is designed to protect the emotionally vulnerable soldiers.[110]

For Fantham, Statius' *Thebaid* is the epic of lamentation.[111] How is Statius' emphasis on lament connected with his complex appropriation of the epic gaze? I have discussed elsewhere the terrifying lamentation of Ide in *Thebaid* 3, where she is compared to a witch (3.140–6).[112] This passage of the Thebans mourning for the soldiers killed in the ambush of Tydeus in book 2 reveals further material when put into the framework of this chapter. The lamenting people pour out from Thebes much like the Argives seeing off their army in the next book (3.114–18; 4.16–20; in particular the tricolon of *pueri nuptae patres* is repeated). They pour out from the walls (*moenibus*, 115), breaking the boundaries in order to view the battlefield (*uisere flagrant*, 'they burn to see', 118). The bloody sight inspires grief and madness (124–5). Their gaze is penetrative; they dig out and display the bodies (*scrutantur galeas frigentum inuentaque monstrant | corpora*, 'They scrabble in the helmets of the cold men and show off the bodies they have found', 127–8). Ide is powerful and terrifying in her grief, but also object and monster (136–7 in particular: *uerum | terror inest lacrimis*, 'but there is terror in her tears'). She recapitulates Euryalus' mother, in stereo, high definition, doubled:

> ut uidit lacrimisque oculi patuere profusis:
> 'hosne ego complexus genetrix, haec oscula, nati,
> uestra tuor?' *(Thebaid* 3.150–2)

---

[110] It is interesting that Smith 2005 does not discuss this passage, given his interest in the competing effects of vision and words. This passage seems to me to show the limitations of his thesis that vision is more constructive than words in the *Aeneid*. Here words and vision work together to create the same impact; Euryalus' mother articulates what the Aeneadae are already thinking, and intensifies the effect of the vision of the impaled heads. The lamenting voice of the *Aeneid* is also often taken to be anti-Augustan (or at least ambivalent): see for instance Perkell 1997.

[111] Fantham 1999: 225 'only in the late and somber *Thebaid* of Statius does lament become a counter-movement equal in force to the deaths that are its occasion, itself serving as occasion and stimulus to further conflict' ... 'lament in Statius' poem is thus seen as outweighing heroic action, as the epic suffocates in a world too conscious of the negative motivation of deeds of valor (*virtus*)'.

[112] Lovatt 1999.

When she saw, her eyes opened with streaming tears:
'Do I watch over these embraces, as a mother, these your kisses, sons?'

The death-in-love here becomes incestuous, the brothers both positive mirror-image of Polynices and Eteocles, and fatally embroiled in the familial tangling of the *Thebaid*. She calls them her power (*potentia matris*, 154), but the threat implied in the witch simile is never fulfilled: this mother just grieves and disappears.

We have examined above the teichoscopy scenes of Argia and Antigone: what happens when they intrude onto the physical space of the battlefield, in their joint search for Polynices' corpse? Augoustakis 2010 views the scene as a possibility for reconciliation, which founders as 'the madness of war has now penetrated into the hearts of women, who compete as their male counterparts have done in the previous books'.[113] Certainly their success in burying Polynices is qualified both by his continuing enmity to Eteocles after death, shown in the split flame, and in the apparent resumption of hostility between Argia and Antigone (or is it a desire for personal glory? or to protect the other woman?) at 457–62. However, if book 12 is the book of epic recapitulation, with the double of the Theban war carried out by Theseus, Argia seems to carry out an alternative epic recapitulation, and one in which her gaze is effective, with divine help, in clear contrast, for instance, to Turnus' failure of the gaze in *Aeneid* 12 (see below, p.319). When the Argive women come on the scene at 105–28 there is a mini-catalogue of the mourning wives, as if starting the poem again. Jupiter may have removed his gaze, and there is still no sign of him, but the female deities are there in force, watching this new epic departure (129–40). The encounter with Ornytus, who narrates the terrible situation from which he has narrowly escaped, acts as an analogy for the figure of Achaemenides in *Aeneid* 3, who joins Aeneas and enables them to escape the Cyclops, to avoid following too closely in the footsteps of Odysseus, an image of intertextual repetition.[114]

In a much-cited passage, at 177–82, Argia conceives an unfeminine love of *uirtus*, abandons her sex (*sexu relicto*) and undertakes an epic task (*immane opus*), going face to face with danger (*pericli | comminus*).[115] She is braver (and more transgressive?) than a Bacchant (181) or Colchian witch

---

[113] Augoustakis 2010: 80–5.
[114] Hinds 1998: 111–15 on Achaemenides and Ovid's re-recapitulation; Achaemenides is an emblem of epic re-duplication; see also Papaioannou 2005: 75–112.
[115] Agri 2011 discusses the connection between striding out and masculinity, and connects Argia's abandonment of *pudor* with the Medea of Valerius Flaccus, via their shared Proserpina similes.

(182). She is driven on by visions of Polynices (187–93), most importantly her memory of the departure in book 4 (him sad under his fierce helmet, like Hector, and the mutual gaze of their teichoscopic moment), and her own image of his ghost demanding burial, which marks her as an Achilles figure. Her speech to the other Argive women ends with a peculiar reminiscence of Ovid's Scylla: *ne tantum reuocate gradus. illo impetus ingens | auguriumque animi* ('Don't call back my steps, in the end; a huge impulse drives me to that place and the prophecy of my soul', 203–4; *impetus illi* is key phrase of *Met.* 8.38–9). She is both epic hero and mad prophetess, and it is no surprise that she becomes monstrous and an object of the horrified gaze of those who meet her (219–23). At 224–7 an image emblematic of otherness emphasises her gender- (and genre-)bending tendencies: she is like a eunuch servant of Cybele, the leader of a mad chorus (*dux uesana chori*), recalling Thiodamas' earlier comparison to a worshipper of Cybele (10.170–5). Both enter an uncanny space beyond gender; while Thiodamas is feminised by inspiration, Argia gains power and terror in the madness of grief. The emphasis on darkness and her conquest of it recalls the night-raids, not least those of Nisus and Euryalus (*Aeneid* 9) and Thiodamas, accompanied by Hopleus and Dymas (*Thebaid* 10, also on a quest to bury those they loved).[116] Yet the simile which compares her to Ovid's Ceres, searching for Proserpina, gaining light from the volcano (270–7) emphasises rather her femininity, maternal not erotic, moves away from heroic epic, and sets Polynices up as another young man violated by epic death (by analogy with Proserpina as rape victim). At 278–90 she is the object of the gaze in two ways, as Statius compares the Argive princess of former days, feared and watched because of her royal status, with the unaccompanied, terrified woman in the dark. He calls her *attonitam* at 278, recalling her previous appearance on the walls, at 4.90: now she is much more than a passive spectator. With a wise gaze (*uisu sagaci*), she rummages through the bodies, penetrating the battlefield and searching out her own connection, not with eyes but hands. Just after this, the scene switches to Juno on Olympus, looking back at Argia (*respexit*, 296), furtively stealing away from her husband at night, to help the Argive women; Juno has not abandoned the epic or the battlefield, and turns her face towards it (*aduertit uultum*, 298), joining in the grief (*indoluit uisu*, 297). The poem ends as if permanently marooned in the *Dios apate*, with Juno in charge as she was in book 10. Her appeal to the moon to see Argia results in such brilliance that she

---

[116] Darkness: *caligantibus* (231); *arcana* (233); *caecis* (234); *tenebrae* (242); *nigrantes tenebras* (254); *tenebris* (284); *gradu caeco* (286).

herself can hardly bear it, an odd reversal of Ovid's Semele episode (309–11). But this light results in the success of Argia's search: she finds Polynices, and recognises him (*noscit*, 313) by her own weaving. Like Andromache, her gaze now fails as she faints (317–18), and her lament at the sight recalls that of Euryalus' mother: *hunc ego te, coniunx, ... aspicio?* (322–4). At 325–8 she remembers the teichoscopy: now he cannot look at her, and he cannot take her within the walls of Thebes. This first half of *Thebaid* 12 does offer a powerful female gaze, goddesses and mortal women working together, replacing the masculine reconciliations of *Iliad* 23 and 24, even if it founders on the endlessness of lament, the figure of Theseus and yet another war.

Conclusions

This chapter has explored three different sites of female viewing: dreams, the walls, lament and aftermath. I finish by looking at an episode which combines the viewing of the departing hero with a dream, the separation of Hannibal and Imilce in Silius *Punica*, along with his gaze on the battlefield of Zama. What sort of viewer is Hannibal? Does his gaze become female?

Book 3, after the fall of Saguntum, represents the beginning of war proper, and a re-beginning of Silius' epic. At 3.406–9, Hannibal views his shining troops, leaves a shadow over the land, and is compared to Neptune, gliding over the sea, watched by the Nereids. He is transformed from the supremely controlling viewer (*lustransque sub armis, | qua uisu comprendere erat*, 'viewing their weapons, as far as it was possible to take in with sight', 407–8) into the object of the gaze, like the Argonauts at the beginning of Catullus 64. This Neptune simile also reverses the first simile of the *Aeneid* (1.148–53), in which Neptune calming the sea is compared to an orator calming a mob. Here the leader of the army is compared to Neptune, viewed in power and majesty, with a godlike gaze. Within this narrative movement, the departure scene recalls the departures of the Argonauts and Thebans in Valerius Flaccus and Statius, but complicated by the fact that Hannibal is sending away his wife Imilce to safety, as Lucan's Pompey sends away Cornelia (*BC* 5.722–815), rather than leaving himself.[117] In their exchange of speeches, Hannibal emphasises the dangers of crossing the Alps (90–2), and Imilce insists she could do it, taking up a well-worn trope of the erotic *propemptikon*.[118] She accuses Hannibal of only looking

---

[117] On Pompey and Hannibal: Tipping 2010: 84–9.
[118] Cf. for instance Prop. 4.3. Augoustakis 2010: 175 n.43 gives examples.

at her through her sex (*solo aspicimur sexu*, 114) but encourages him to go (*i ... i ...*, 116). She sees Hannibal's epic ambition as transgressive: *tibi gloria soli | fine caret* ('for you alone glory lacks a boundary/end', 122–3). Silius' Hannibal is a figure of excess, as Tipping has well demonstrated.[119] His excessive masculinity threatens to become feminine.[120] The departure scene does not clearly distinguish between husband and wife:[121]

> abripitur diuulsa marito.
> haerent intenti uultus et litora seruant,
> donec iter liquidum uolucri rapiente carina
> consumpsit uisus pontus tellusque recessit. (*Punica* 3.154–7)
>
> Torn away, she is snatched apart from her husband.
> The faces cling gazing and hold on to the shore,
> until, while the swift ship snatches the watery way,
> the sea consumes sight, and the land recedes.

abripitur diuulsa clearly describes Imilce, but the plural at 155 is more confused (at 17.214 *intentus uultus* is repeated as Hannibal looks back alone at Italy, there clearly singular), and the mixed lamentations of 152 (*dumque ea permixtis inter se fletibus orant*, 'While they persuaded each other in this way, mixed with tears') emphasise the mutuality of the emotional parting. Imilce's passivity is highlighted by the impersonal description of the gazing; when the sea steals sight, that might apply to either of them (the sea is in between them); similarly, the ship actively snatching suggests Hannibal's focalisation, as if the ship is taking his wife away.[122] Only when we reach the phrase *tellus recessit* does the focalisation settle on Imilce, watching the land disappear into the distance. Who is going, and who is left behind? Although Hannibal immediately gets on with the masculine business of warfare:

> At Poenus belli curis auertere amorem
> apparat et repetit properato moenia gressu.
> quae dum perlustrat crebroque obit omnia uisu,
> tandem sollicito cessit uis dura labori,
> belligerumque datur somno componere mentem. (*Punica* 3.158–62)

---

[119] Tipping 2010: 73.   [120] Loraux 1990.
[121] Augoustakis 2010: 151 n.136, and 152, suggests this ambiguity, and compares it to the departure scene in book 17: 'Hannibal's attachment [is] represented in a reversal of gender, which blurs the boundaries of male vs. female.'
[122] The combination of *carina* at the end of the line, and *consumpsit* surely evokes Catullus 64 (*carinam*, end line 249), plus imagery of satiation, see above, pp.202–3.

> But the Carthaginian made an effort to turn away love through the cares
> of war and seeks again the walls with hurried step.
> And while he thoroughly investigated them and went around all things
>   with frequent gaze,
> at last the tough force yielded to the worried work,
> and the war-like mind was handed over to sleep to settle.

The desperate gaze of an Alcyone is replaced by the workman-like, controlling gaze of the commander; rather than looking from the walls, he looks at the walls. Yet by using words interchangeably Silius assimilates the worries of war and the worries of love: *curis*, often used of love, here refers to war; *labori*, the quintessential opposite of the *otium* of the lover, is associated with the worries of love (*sollicito*). Like Alcyone, too, he ends up in his bed, having a significant dream.[123]

The dream, too, offers a number of markers of Hannibal's instability. It begins as a messenger dream, with Mercury sent by Jupiter (163–7). Mercury's initial rebuke (172–3) of Hannibal for being asleep recalls Agamemnon at *Il.* 2.23–5, as well as Aeneas in *Aeneid* 4, and the prophecy is deceptive. However, with the warning not to look back, the paradigm changes, and at 183–4 Hannibal is whisked off to Italy. The dream moves from an epic, masculine dream, to a tragic, feminine dream, and now he is most like Lucan's *matrona*. At 198–200 Silius even questions whether he is actually still dreaming, or is now having a waking vision. The snake which terrifies him and wreaks destruction (representing the war, or Hannibal himself) is clearly symbolic, and Hannibal himself is terrified of it.[124] As with Penelope, and Ilia, the disturbing dream is given a positive interpretation by a figure in the dream, in this case Mercury: yet Hannibal's terror at his own monstrosity aligns him with the unease of the female gaze. Is he raping or being raped?

In book 17, Hannibal's gaze is definitively feminised. His dream at 17.158–69 is a straightforwardly tragic anxiety dream, in which the ghosts of those Romans he conquered harry him from Italy. As he leaves Italy and looks back longingly at the shore and his epic ambitions receding into the distance (17.211–17), he is now assimilated to his departing wife from book 3; his comparison to an exile (216–17) recalls Ovid's reuse (or the mutual interconnectedness) of the Ceyx and Alcyone scene in *Tristia* 1.3, as well as Lucan's Pompey, leaving Italy in book 3, followed by his dream of Julia (see

---

[123] Also the Dido episode, in which Mercury rebukes Aeneas for paying attention to the wrong walls (*Aen.* 4.260–1, 265–7); the messenger element of Hannibal's dream is modelled on Aeneas' dream at *Aen.* 4.554–70.
[124] Tipping 2010: 72–9 on Hannibal's Herculean and snakish aspects.

above). The counter-intuitive image at 207–11, in which the relief of the Italians at Hannibal's departure is compared to the relief of sailors at the end of a storm, makes this a reverse *Odyssey*, as well as linking to the sailing images used of departing heroes elsewhere in the tradition. This image is one of the tactics of recommencing which saturate this book. The storm, too, started by Neptune, repeats and reverses the storm at the beginning of the *Aeneid*. The comparison of Hannibal to a lightning bolt at 474–8 evokes Lucan's description of Caesar at *BC* 1.151–7. Like Aeneas and Odysseus at their initial appearances in their epics (*Aen.* 1.94–101; *Od.* 5.299–312), Hannibal laments that he might die at sea rather than in battle (17.260–7). However, this new epic, like book 12 of the *Thebaid*, is going to reach an abrupt close: by 559–61 Hannibal is wishing that he had died in the storm after all. Hannibal's come-uppance at Zama is closely modelled on Turnus in the *Aeneid*. Juno deceives him by fashioning a phantom Scipio, and drawing him away from the battle. Like Juturna, she drives him all over the place, taking him away from epic, and at 567–80 becomes a pastoral shepherd (perhaps recalling the huntress Venus of *Aeneid*, 1) in order to permanently abandon him on the margins. Now he can only watch, powerless to intervene:

> At fessum tumulo tandem regina propinquo
> sistit Iuno ducem, facies unde omnis et atrae
> apparent admota oculis uestigia pugnae.   (*Punica* 17.597–9)

> But at last queen Juno stopped the tired leader
> on a neighbouring tomb, from which the whole sight appeared
> the traces of the black battle moved towards his eyes.

Not only is Juno active and Hannibal the object of the sentence, he does not even have control over his eyes: the *facies* appears and the signs go to his eyes. This impotence is specifically contrasted with his previous viewing of his victories (600–4). Now, as he watches from a tomb, all that remains to console him is the memory of his deeds (606–15). He finishes by going into the mountains not to find a vantage point, but to hide (616–17), and finally becoming a passive image in Scipio's triumphant parade (643–4).

This example shows that the female gaze is a useful category for thinking about epic. There are feminine ways of looking in epic, and they are important in defining the genre. Women on the walls, viewing the departing hero, the tragic, feminine side of dreaming, the lamenting gaze, all form part of a gendered reading of epic. The disempowered non-combatants who can look but not act are set in clear opposition to the divine gaze, looking askance from the margins, rather than looking down. When women take on the role of narrator, they can have a measure of influence, but often their effectiveness is circumscribed and limited. These tropes of feminine viewing are often situated at the edges of epic, with close links to other genres, particularly tragedy and elegy. From women as viewers I move to men as objects of the gaze, male bodies fragmented and fetishised, and epic heroes turned into art objects, stars and plants.

CHAPTER 7

Heroic bodies on display

As Achilles charges Hector, finally about to kill him, his spear is like the evening star:

> οἷος δ' ἀστὴρ εἶσι μετ' ἀστράσι νυκτὸς ἀμολγῷ
> ἕσπερος, ὃς κάλλιστος ἐν οὐρανῷ ἵσταται ἀστήρ   (*Iliad* 22.317–18)
>
> And as a star moves among stars in the night's darkening,
> Hesperus, who stands as the most beautiful star in the heavens

Achilles has already been compared to Sirius, at 22.26–32, as he runs across the plain towards Hector, watched from the walls by Priam, a star which has a baleful and threatening aspect.[1] Now it is not Achilles who is κάλλιστος in the heavens, but the brightness of his spear. As he approaches Hector he is gazing at his beautiful flesh (εἰσορόων χρόα καλόν, 321), with the intention of piercing it:[2]

> φαίνετο δ' ᾗ κληῖδες ἀπ' ὤμων αὐχέν' ἔχουσι,
> λαυκανίην, ἵνα τε ψυχῆς ὤκιστος ὄλεθρος·
> τῇ ῥ' ἐπὶ οἷ μεμαῶτ' ἔλασ' ἔγχεϊ δῖος Ἀχιλλεύς,
> ἀντικρὺ δ' ἁπαλοῖο δι' αὐχένος ἤλυθ' ἀκωκή·   (*Iliad* 22.324–7)
>
> yet showed where the collar-bones hold the neck from the shoulders,
> the throat, where death of the soul comes most swiftly;
> in this place noble Achilles drove the spear as he came on in a fury
> and clean through the soft part of the neck the spear point was driven.

Both heroes are characterised by their beauty, but Achilles is invulnerable, brilliant, heavenly, a reflection and extension of his deadly weapon, while

---

[1] The second half of line 28, μετ' ἀστράσι νυκτὸς ἀμολγῷ, is repeated here at line 317, making the connection between the two images even stronger.
[2] On Hector's neck, and other similar moments of femininity emerging through vulnerability, see Reed 2007: 23; Loraux 1989: 120–1, citing *Il.* 5.858, 11.352, 573, 13.830, 14.406, 15.316, 21.398, 22.321. Although the *Odyssey* is very different from the *Iliad* in its use of battle scenes, Odysseus' killing of Antinous specifically evokes Achilles' killing of Hector, by reusing *Il.* 22.327 at *Od.* 22.16.

Hector is vulnerable, fleshy, mortal. Further, when Hector lies dead on the battlefield and Achilles has addressed his corpse and stripped his armour, the other Greeks come to take part in his death:[3]

> ἄλλοι δὲ περίδραμον υἷες Ἀχαιῶν,
> οἳ καὶ θηήσαντο φυήν καὶ εἶδος ἀγητὸν
> Ἕκτορος· οὐδ' ἄρα οἵ τις ἀνουτητί γε παρέστη.
> ὧδε δέ τις εἴπεσκεν ἰδὼν ἐς πλησίον ἄλλον·
> «ὢ πόποι, ἦ μάλα δὴ μαλακώτερος ἀμφαφάασθαι
> Ἕκτωρ ἢ ὅτε νῆας ἐνέπρησεν πυρὶ κηλέῳ.»
> Ὣς ἄρα τις εἴπεσκε καὶ οὐτήσασκε παραστάς. (*Iliad* 22.369–75)

And the other sons of the Achaeans came running about him,
and gazed upon the stature and on the imposing beauty
of Hector; and none stood beside him who did not stab him;
and thus they would speak one to another, each looking at his neighbour:
'See now, Hector is much softer to handle than he was
when he set the ships ablaze with the burning firebrand.'
So as they stood beside him they would speak and stab him.

Hector is the object of the gaze of the Achaeans, passive because dead and no longer able to respond. The strong contrast between active action hero and passive object of the gaze is only undermined by his continuing beauty: this beauty is an important characteristic of the hero. When Priam pleads with Hector not to face Achilles earlier in the book, the climax of his speech is the contrast between the beautiful death of the young hero and the pitiful, disgusting spectacle of an old man torn to pieces:

> νέῳ δέ τε πάντ' ἐπέοικεν
> ἀρηϊκταμένῳ, δεδαϊγμένῳ ὀξέϊ χαλκῷ,
> κεῖσθαι· πάντα δὲ καλὰ θανόντι περ, ὅττι φανήῃ·
> ἀλλ' ὅτε δὴ πολιόν τε κάρη πολιόν τε γένειον
> αἰδῶ τ' αἰσχύνωσι κύνες κταμένοιο γέροντος,
> τοῦτο δὴ οἴκτιστον πέλεται δειλοῖσι βροτοῖσιν. (*Iliad* 22.71–6)

For a young man all is decorous
when he is cut down in battle, and torn with the sharp bronze,
and lies there dead, and though dead all that shows about him is beautiful;
but when an old man is dead and down and the dogs mutilate
the grey head and the grey beard and the parts that are secret,
this for all sad mortality is the sight most pitiful.

---

[3] On the passage see Richardson 1993: 144. Cf. Herodotus 9.25.1 on the beauty of the dead Masistios. Griffin 1980: 47 cites the view of a scholiast that this scene is designed to magnify the greatness of the dead man by 'the heroic contrast of the impassive corpse of Hector and the small malevolence of those who ran from him in life and can face him only when he is safely dead'.

The Homeric hero needs to be beautiful in order to be a hero, and beauty is confined to aristocratic heroes.[4] This chapter takes Vernant's concept of the 'beautiful death' literally.[5] Heroic death, and the epic hero himself, is not just noble or excellent, but aesthetically and erotically beautiful. How does later epic develop this idea from its Homeric instantiation?[6]

In this chapter, I explore the body of the hero as the erotic object of the epic gaze, the star of epic, the centre of attention. There are complications: the distinction between the mature hero and the boy on the brink of manhood; that between the powerful, active and controlling hero, and the passivity of the wounded and dying hero; the way these two distinctions combine in the beautiful young man, assimilated to the deflowered virgin in death;[7] the further complication of gender in the figures of transgressive female warriors: is it always different for girls?[8] The chapter begins with imagery: the star, the horse, the statue, and the olive tree.[9] Through this imagery we glimpse the complexity of epic attitudes to beauty. Heroes can become objets d'art, with divine sponsors acting as artists, both in battle and in erotic contexts; not only women become statues in the epic world. I situate these issues in the changing cultures of the ancient world: how do attitudes to beauty and displaying the body change? Is epic heroism radically reconfigured by viewing it in the context of gladiatorial spectacle? How do the aesthetics of violence change over time? Fragmented bodies and body parts take centre-stage in epic battle scenes from the *Iliad* onwards and replace the whole and active hero: can we see this as a sort of fetishisation? Does this tendency destroy 'the illusion of depth demanded by the narrative', as Mulvey suggests of fragmented images of female bodies in film?[10]

---

[4] Beauty seems also to be a heroic quality in the epic cycle: *Theb.* fr. 3 West describes Haemon as 'most beautiful and most desirable' (κάλλιστόν τε καὶ ἱμεροέστατον).
[5] 'Through a beautiful death, excellence no longer has to be continually measured against someone else or to be tested in combat. Rather, excellence is actualized all at once and forever after in the deed that puts an end to the hero's life.' (Vernant 1981: 51)
[6] Reed 2007: 32–3 argues for Bion's *Epitaph on Adonis* as the first real example of this topos. My conception of hero as erotic object is broader than Reed's, including the live, powerful, hero in motion, as well as the dead and objectified body, including both homoerotic and heterosexual desire. To a certain extent I agree that Homer is different, but not as different as Reed implies.
[7] Fowler 1987 was the starting point; Reed 2007: 16–26 explores the territory, and 26–31 points out the complexity of gaze and focalisation in an exemplary fashion. See also Jamset 2004 and Lovatt 2005: 67–75 on Statius. Reed argues that this complex of gendered and ethnic imagery is fundamentally concerned with the formation and negotiation of Roman identity (*passim*, but see especially 41–3). However, it (also) engages with a tension in masculinity (both Greek and Roman, if in slightly different ways) fundamental to the epic genre.
[8] For a provocative discussion of why defeated countries in statues are represented as women, see Vout 2007: 25–7.
[9] For a study of the epic simile, together with other figures, see Wofford 1992.
[10] Mulvey 1975 reprinted as Mulvey 1988: 63.

Are these body parts another disturbance in the field of vision for epic? Finally, the chapter finishes this exploration of masculinity, by considering femininity. What happens when the warrior concerned is actually female? Taking as case studies Camilla in the *Aeneid* and Penthesilea in the *Posthomerica*, the section asks whether there is any real difference between the feminine and the problematically masculine.

Images of beauty: epic heroes as objects of desire

Readers of epic are used to heroes compared to lions or rivers or storms: extended similes that convey violence, action and power. On occasion, however, the epic hero can become an aesthetic object. Scattered throughout the corpus of epic are images which evoke erotic discourse. Star images combine power and terror with outstanding beauty; other similes turn the male body of the hero into a consciously figured work of art or a cultivated plant or flower; horse images, beginning with Paris at *Il.* 6.506–11, place a particular focus on the physical beauty of the warrior in motion.

The 'star' is a dead metaphor in movie discourse: brilliant personalities, about whom films, careers and entire worlds can be built, were central to classic cinema, and are still significant in discussions of more recent film.[11] We have examined two images of Achilles as star, part of the fire and shining imagery that surrounds him in the *Iliad*.[12] But Achilles' beauty is not just deadly and semi-divine: it is also erotic. Many ancient readers of Homer read Achilles as the *eromenos* ('beloved') of Patroclus in a pederastic relationship.[13] The Hesperus image above in particular was used by later poets, both epic and non-epic, in erotic contexts.[14] Other star imagery in the *Iliad* refers to Sirius, and is much more clearly concerned with epic power and malevolence (Diomedes 5.4–7; Hector 11.61–6).[15] But Apollonius brings out the erotic element: Jason is twice compared to a star; once as he approaches

---

[11] See Vincendeau 2000, Austin and Barker 2003, Dyer 2004, Willis 2004.
[12] On this see Whitman 1958: 128–53, Moulton 1977: 108.
[13] For instance, Plato's Phaedrus at *Symposium* 179e–180b; others read him as the lover, others still deny that it is an erotic relationship. Mariscal and Morales 2003, Lovatt 2005: 59–67.
[14] Hesperus, or Lucifer, the evening star, was another name for the planet Venus, also the morning star. In love poetry, famously at Sappho fr. 104; Catullus 62.26; Apuleius *Apology* 10.8 cites an epigram purportedly by Plato; other epigrams: Meleager 100 (Gow 243, 4528–30); Rhianus 2 (Gow 174, 3204–7).
[15] Similarly, Silius describes Hannibal at *Pun.* 1.460–4 as both comet and star, before going on to compare him to a storm; here it is his opponent, Murrus, who is the beautiful boy (1.376–7) separating the two sides of the image. Quintus Smyrnaeus links Neoptolemus with his father's deadly brilliance: at *PH* 2.206–11 Achilles is the sun whose brilliance contrasts with the Trojans, compared to dark clouds of locusts. As Neoptolemus joins the expedition, he is compared to a star (7.347); later Thetis watches and rejoices, and he is compared to both the sun and Sirius (8.24–31).

Hypsipyle, wearing his brilliant cloak, he is like the star which love-sick girls watch as they dream (AR *Arg.* 1.774–80); the implicit baleful influence of the star is contrasted with Jason himself, modest object of the predatory gaze of the Lemnian women (782–6). Secondly, at 3.956–61, Jason approaches Medea as she waits in the temple, like Sirius, beautiful to see (καλός, 958, 960), but bringing suffering. The double-edged beauty of Achilles' violence and power has been assimilated into an erotic context. The same effect is achieved at 2.40–4, where Polydeuces is like the evening star in his erotic charm (here following the pederastic ideal), but despite the objectifying force of Amycus' hostile gaze (48–9), Polydeuces is marked as equally violent and threatening (his strength and rage are like that of a wild beast, 44–5). A particularly good example of a boy hero as object of the gaze is Pallas in the *Aeneid*. As the Trojan forces leave Pallanteum with their new allies, Pallas stands out:

> inde alii Troiae proceres, ipse agmine Pallas
> in medio, chlamyde et pictis conspectus in armis:
> qualis ubi Oceani perfusus Lucifer unda,
> quem Venus ante alios astrorum diligit ignis,
> extulit os sacrum caelo tenebrasque resoluit.
> stant pauidae in muris matres oculisque sequuntur
> pulueream nubem et fulgentis aere cateruas.   (*Aeneid* 8.587–93)

> Then the other Trojan leaders, and himself, in the middle, Pallas,
> of the column, marked out by his cloak and his painted weapons:
> just as when Lucifer drenched in the waves of Ocean,
> whom Venus cherishes above the fires of other stars,
> raises his sacred face in the heaven and dissolves the shadows.
> The mothers stand panic-stricken on the walls and follow with their eyes
> the dusty cloud and the squadrons gleaming with bronze.

His name stands out at the end of the line, set illustratively between *agmine* and *medio*; the cloak and the weapons mark him as a version of Jason, but also hint at his inevitable death.[16] The language of liquefaction in the star image suggests erotic exhaustion, and Lucifer here is the object of the desiring gaze of Venus;[17] yet the face, of and as the star, emanates light, and affects the world around it. The brightness of Lucifer is transformed

---

[16] Other examples of young men proud of their finery (and facing imminent death): Euryalus *Aen.* 9.488; Lausus 10.818, 832; Chloreus 11.768–77. Wiltshire 1989: 54, Reed 2007: 37.

[17] Putnam 1995c argues that this image contributes to the suggestion of sexual tensions in Pallas' relationship with Aeneas. I would argue that Pallas is rather the erotic object of a wider audience, both male and female, perhaps, but not markedly, including Aeneas, but also certainly including the readers of the poem.

Images of beauty: epic heroes as objects of desire 267

into the brilliance of weaponry, and the watching mothers do not desire, but fear on behalf of those going to war. Pallas should, like Jason, be approaching a beloved; instead he has premature heroic ambitions.[18]

The reception of this trope in Quintus and Nonnus offers a fresh perspective. Quintus makes the most of the erotic overtones, but applies them to a woman: Penthesilea, on her arrival in Troy, surpasses her entourage like the moon surpasses the stars (*PH* 1.35–41), and like Dawn surpasses the other seasons (48–51); her beauty is divine, dazzling, both active and passive:

> ἀμφὶ δὲ Τρῶες
> πάντοθεν ἐσσύμενοι μέγ' ἐθάμβεον, εὖτ' ἐσίδοντο
> Ἄρεος ἀκαμάτοιο βαθυκνήμιδα θύγατρα
> εἰδομένην μακάρεσσιν, ἐπεί ῥά οἱ ἀμφὶ προσώπῳ
> ἄμφω σμερδαλέον τε καὶ ἀγλαὸν εἶδος ὀρώρει,
> μείδιαεν ‹δ'› ἐρατεινόν, ὑπ' ὀφρύσι δ' ἱμερόεντες
> ὀφθαλμοὶ μάρμαιρον ἀλίγκιον ἀκτίνεσσιν   (*Posthomerica* 1.53–9)

> Round them the Trojans,
> running from everywhere, were astounded at the sight
> of the tireless war god's daughter in her long greaves,
> looking like one of the blessed immortals; in her face
> there was a beauty that frightened and dazzled at once.
> Her smile was ravishing, and from beneath her brows
> her love-enkindling eyes like sunbeams flashed.

The Trojans' reaction is compared to that of farmers in a drought who see approaching rain (63–9), and Priam is like a blind man who regains some of his sight (76–83).[19] She is a major hero arriving as a salvation to hard-pressed troops, but also distinctly eroticised. Her powerful gaze is one that kindles love, her eyes shoot rays and her beauty is itself a source of terror. Penthesilea's power is limited, and her heroically beautiful death will be subsumed in the story of Achilles' desire. Nonnus applies this image to the beauty of Dionysus at *Dion*. 17.8–14, with the twist that his divine beauty is precisely divine, and he outshines his entourage like the sun (not Hesperus, or even the moon) outshines stars, combining two different comparisons, to

---

[18] Other epic stars: VF *Arg.* 5.563–9; at the banquet with Aeetes, the Argonauts are described in erotic terms; the breeze is excited (*incita*) and the road blossoms (*floret*) and the group is like a chorus of stars rising from the sea; Aeetes mixes wonder with dismay (*maestissimus ira | miratur*). The many heroes are objects both of the predatory gaze of Aeetes and the desiring gaze of Medea. Lucretius characterises Epicurus as a star at 3.1042–4; his intellectual brilliance outshines that of others; this continues Lucretius' appropriation of epic tropes.

[19] See Bär 2009 *ad loc.*

create a much stronger effect, emphasising Dionysus' overwhelming brilliance (along with that of Nonnus, of course). The stars of epic, then, overpower with desire, along with heroic power and brilliance.

Star images are images of setting out, beginning, approaching. Horse images represent the hero in his full glory. Where the star image moves us very far from the physicality of the body, to focus on its visual impact on those watching, the horse simile gives us rather an impression of what it is like to be in the body of the hero, as well as representing him as erotic subject and object. The simile which describes Paris as he finally returns to battle at the end of *Iliad* 6 sets the pattern. Aphrodite has rescued him and forced Helen to sleep with him, and he has been rebuked by Hector:

ὡς δ' ὅτε τις στατὸς ἵππος, ἀκοστήσας ἐπὶ φάτνῃ,
δεσμὸν ἀπορρήξας θείῃ πεδίοιο κροαίνων,
εἰωθὼς λούεσθαι ἐϋρρεῖος ποταμοῖο,
κυδιόων· ὑψοῦ δὲ κάρη ἔχει, ἀμφὶ δὲ χαῖται
ὤμοις ἀΐσσονται· ὁ δ' ἀγλαΐηφι πεποιθώς,
ῥίμφα ἑ γοῦνα φέρει μετά τ' ἤθεα καὶ νομὸν ἵππων.   (*Iliad* 6.506–11)

As when some stalled horse who has been corn-fed at the manger
breaking free of his rope gallops over the plain in thunder
to his accustomed bathing place in a sweet-running river
and in the pride of his strength holds high his head, and the mane floats
over his shoulders; sure of his glorious strength, the quick knees
carry him to the loved places and the pasture of horses.

The focus of the simile is on the release and exuberance of the horse, especially in his exaltation in his own body as it moves: galloping, bathing, strength, the posture of the head, the movement of the mane over the shoulders, strength again and the movement of knees, all emphasise what it feels like to be a prime physical specimen with a fully functioning body, sensually connected to the world.[20] The frame of the simile makes it clear that this is precisely the connection with Paris who is 'confident in his quick feet' (ποσὶ κραιπνοῖσι πεποιθώς, 505) and runs, 'exalting, on his quick feet' (καγχαλόων, ταχέες δὲ πόδες φέρον, 514). Later versions of this simile, especially in Virgil, interpret the joy as almost sexual anticipation: the horses waiting in the pasture in the simile describing Turnus at *Aen.* 11.494 are specifically female (*equarum*).[21] The prominence of Aphrodite in book 6,

---

[20] Kirk 1990: 226 describes the simile as 'energetic and sumptuous' and says that it 'helps present Paris in a more glamorous light'. See also Graziosi and Haubold 2010: 225–9.

[21] Horsfall 2003: 292–4, with support from other readers, including Servius. He also comments: 'A simile that deserves a monograph'; see 292 for further bibliography.

and the fact that Hector's accusation of Paris is primarily that he was making love when he should have been making war, cast Paris in an unavoidably sexual light.[22] However, now he is returning to battle, his *jouissance* suggests that he can, on occasion, have the same delight in battle as he does in sex. The ambivalence of the Iliadic Paris stems largely from his erratic attachment to the 'heroic code' as exemplified by Hector.[23] Book 6 presents this in the strongest terms, by presenting Hector with three women offering three opportunities for escape and lingering, all of which he steadfastly refuses, while Paris is precisely lingering with the unwilling Helen. The second use of the same simile to describe Hector himself, at *Il.* 15.263–8, confuses these oppositions, and discourages us from seeing Paris as unique in his tendency to become a sexualised object of the gaze. The frame of the simile does not have the same strong emphasis on Hector's body, and the point of similarity with Paris may well be rather his revivification by Apollo after wounding, just as Aphrodite had recently rescued Paris, suggesting that he is more the object of the divine gaze than the erotic gaze. But, as we have seen above, Hector is beautiful, too, and the contrasts with Paris in book 6 serve also to remind us of the potential similarity between the two brothers.[24]

Paris is only one case of outstanding beauty in the *Iliad*; how is beauty used and represented in the *Iliad*? Achilles is also compared to a horse at 22.21–4, as he returns to battle, just before the star simile at 25–32. The horse simile is focalised through the Greeks, while there is an explicit change of focalisation to Priam at 25, which mediates the move to the much more threatening star simile.[25] Beauty is a characteristic of Achilles, used in his speech to Lycaon in book 21 as one aspect of his excellence, that nonetheless will not exempt him from death:

οὐχ ὁράᾳς οἷος καὶ ἐγὼ καλός τε μέγας τε;
πατρὸς δ' εἴμ' ἀγαθοῖο, θεὰ δέ με γείνατο μήτηρ·
ἀλλ' ἔπι τοι καὶ ἐμοὶ θάνατος καὶ μοῖρα κραταιή. (*Iliad* 21.108–10)

Do you not see what a man I am, how huge, how splendid
and born of a great father and the mother who bore me immortal?
Yet even I have also my death and my strong destiny;

---

[22] The prominence and positive portrayal of Paris in *Troy*, especially the casting of Orlando Bloom, suggests that twenty-first-century audiences find it difficult to separate erotic success from heroic and narrative success.
[23] On the ambivalence of Paris, see Collins 1987.
[24] Helen's attempt to detain Hector, in parallel with Andromache, suggests that she views him at this point as more attractive than Paris.
[25] The shining glory of Paris at *Il.* 6.513 reminds Graziosi and Haubold 2010: 229 of Achilles at the height of his powers.

Here beauty is one aspect of being *aristos*, along with size, noble descent and closeness to the gods.[26] Lack of beauty equates to moral turpitude and lack of nobility, as in the cases of Dolon (10.316) and, most famously, Thersites (2.216–19).[27] However, beauty is often separated from excellence, and its presence without the necessary fighting prowess is a frequent trope in rebukes.[28] This abuse focuses on the disjunction between appearance and reality; beauty, it seems, leads onlookers to expect heroic success, but beauty without fighting power becomes an active sign of disgrace. Epic warriors put themselves in the field of vision of others, and are always potentially exposed to the gaze of those watching; their masculinity can be compromised if they are not sufficiently active and successful to sustain it.

Male beauty was not just a fascination of the epic genre: Pindar equally associates it with excellence.[29] The existence of male beauty contests as part of the festival culture of ancient Greece show that men were 'to-be-looked-at' in a very different way from action heroes in films today.[30] It is particularly important that not all contests judged men for their strength and size in combination with beauty, but some focused on beauty alone; and also that there were contests for different age groups. Hawley argues, too, that male bodies become spectacles in Greek drama, when disempowered or in pain.[31] Changing attitudes to male beauty can be seen in visual representations of the naked male body.[32] By the Classical period, male

---

[26] Is beauty associated with aristocratic status, or a marker of it? Van Wees 1992: 78–9 remarks on the way that beauty is only allowed to princes in the *Iliad*. The difficulties of separating physicality from ethical and social characteristics in Greek thought make it complex to trace attitudes to physical beauty in particular. See also Donlan 1999: 106–7: 'Beauty was an important aspect of the Homeric ideal and a desirable aspect of the Homeric warrior (and of his women), and its possession contributed to a person's *arete*.' (106)

[27] On Thersites as an incarnation of blame poetry, see Nagy 1979: 259–64.

[28] Paris is the infamous recipient of this abuse, most dramatically at *Il*. 3.39–57, after he shrinks from the prospect of a duel with Menelaus, where Hector calls him: Δύσπαρι, εἶδος ἄριστε, γυναιμανές, ἠπεροπευτά ('Evil Paris, excellent in appearance, woman-mad, cajoling', 39); this line is repeated at 13.769. In book 3, Hector goes on to point out that his beauty (καλὸν εἶδος) is not supported by strength and might (44–5); and that the lyre-playing, the gifts of Aphrodite, his hair and beauty (εἶδος), will not stop him from rolling in the dust (54–5). However, Hector himself is the subject of a similar rebuke from Glaucus about abandoning the body of Sarpedon (17.142), and both Hera (5.787) and Agamemnon (8.228) rebuke the Greeks in similar terms.

[29] Donlan 1999: 107. *Olympian* 8.19–20, 9.94, 10.99–105, 14.5–7; *Isthmian* 2.3–5, 7.22; *Nemean* 3.19–20, 11.11–14. See also Donlan 1999: 200–1 on erotic references to beauty in the *Theognidea*.

[30] Crowther 1985 sets out the ancient evidence. See also Hawley 1998a: 38–9.

[31] Hawley 1998b, though his comparison with epic seems to me only skin deep. Perhaps there is less need to focus on the male body beautiful in the texts of Greek drama since physical bodies were present on stage. Whereas in epic, any sense of embodiment must be achieved by words.

[32] See Osborne 1997 for an exploration of the implications of nudity: 'the conventional asexuality of the unclothed beardless youth offered the male body for display only at the price of questioning his masculinity' (524). Osborne 2011: 27–54 on the 'athletic ideal' as stylised.

beauty was not straightforwardly heroic or divine (or even virtuous), if, indeed, it ever was. There is a clear distinction between mature, bearded men (clothed and decorous) and beardless youths (naked and the passive objects of desire), which suggests that ideals of pederastic desire informed the construction of masculinity. This offers another way to protect the masculinity of mature, elite males, but also shows that it was at risk from exposure. Without the hypermasculine glamour of heroism, men cannot securely allow themselves to become objects of the gaze.

There is definitely a step-change by the time we see the next complete epic, the *Argonautica* of Apollonius in the Hellenistic period. When Apollonius reworks the Homeric horse simile at 3.1259–61, he does not sequester it in safe reference to a hero of dubious standing, or even an enemy about to be defeated, but rather he uses it to describe his central heroic figure at the moment of his greatest success. After Jason uses Medea's *pharmaka*, his weapons become unbreakable and he gains invincible strength. His temporary heroisation is equivalent to Hector's revivification by Apollo, with the signficant difference that Apollo is returning Hector to his normal state after a knock, while Medea allows Jason a brief period in which he feels (and looks) truly Homeric. This makes him more like Paris, who acquires at the end of *Iliad* 6 an apparently temporary heroism, and some brief acknowledgement from his brother. The emphasis on Jason's body is strong: his hands at AR *Arg.* 1257–8 and his limbs at 1261 together frame the simile. In the simile itself Apollonius adds two parts of the horse's body not mentioned by Homer, the neck and the ears.[33] The association of Jason's leaping movements with dance might also compromise his masculinity, although the lightning simile at 1265–7 portrays uncompromising power. The emphasis on Aeetes, the Colchians and the Argonauts as audiences of Jason's feats, and the comparison of Aeetes to Poseidon going to the Isthmian games (1240–5), build Jason up as object of the gaze. Only with the help of the *pharmaka* can he make the transition from object to subject.[34] The brief comparison at 1282–3, where the narrator offers a rather uncertain perspective on Jason as like Ares, but also in some ways like Apollo, encapsulates his heroic ambivalence, especially with the emphasis on nakedness (1282, γυμνὸς δέμας).[35] He is both warlike and beautiful, inspiring terror and desire. Finally, as he charges on the earth-born men, who themselves shine like stars through a stormy sky

---

[33] See Hunter 1989: 237–9.
[34] Jason as subject of verbs of vision: AR *Arg.* 1284 (παπτήνας, ἴδε); 1289 (μαστεύων); 1293–5: other heroes terrified by the sight, but Jason stands steadfast; 1337–8 and 1346–7: keeping an eye out for the earth-born men.
[35] Hunter 1989: 241 makes reference to art, and also Pindar *Pyth.* 4.87–8.

(1359–63), he becomes an Iliadic, Achillean comet (1377–80).[36] With eerie appropriateness, the earth-born men are described as shoots broken off in an orchard, a simile clearly focalised through the disappointed gaze of Aeetes (1396–404). Jason's triumphant (temporary) masculinity feminises the earth-born men, and renders Aeetes a farmer rather than a fighter, reflecting back on its sender the unpromising heroic quality of the ploughing contest he has just undertaken. Hunter 1989 *ad loc.* points out that this section is 'unlike anything else in the poem' and that 'A. has compressed a whole *Iliad* into this final section.' This miniaturisation of Homeric epic is typically Hellenistic, and not unlike the narrative tactics of Callimachus, turning the heroic heart of epic into a game, a contest, to be watched, making Homeric epic subsidiary to Apollonius' erotic and aetiological concerns.

In the light of the literary one-upmanship on display, it makes perfect sense that Virgil, Valerius and Quintus should all later choose to capitalise upon it with their own play on epic masculinity. We can also, unusually, here see continuity in Ennius' *Annales*, where the Homeric simile recurs (*Ann.* 535–9).[37] Without a context, it is difficult to guess what function the image performs, but there is an emphasis on the strength, self-sufficiency and heat of the horse, without the explicit *equarum* of Virgil's reworking, which suggests a much more straightforward masculinity (though the hot breath hints at things to come). Virgil, however, is much closer to Apollonius, when he uses it of Turnus, released from the politicking of the council in *Aeneid* 11. The description of Turnus arming is juxtaposed with the female gaze: the women garlanding the walls (11.475–6); Amata with her retinue praying to Pallas Athene for help, accompanied by Lavinia with downcast eyes, marked as the passive object of the war (*causa mali tanti, oculos deiecta decoros*, 480). This offers us (at least) two potential focalisers of the arming scene, Amata and Lavinia.[38] The tone is initially violent and threatening (*furens*, 486; *aënis | horrebat squamis*, 487–8) but modulates into a more ambivalent key at 489:

> tempora nudus adhuc, laterique accinxerat ensem
> fulgebatque alta decurrens aureus arce
> exsultatque animis et spe iam praecipit hostem   (*Aeneid* 11.489–91)

---

[36] Though the earth-born men fall like pines or oaks (1375–6) at their own spears, not Jason's attack.

[37] *et tum, sicut equos qui de praesepibus fartus | vincla suis magnis animis abrumpit et inde | fert sese campi per caerula laetaque prata | celso pectore; saepe iubam quassat simul altam, | spiritus ex anima calida spumas agit albas.* 'And then, just as a horse, stuffed from the mangers, breaks off the bonds with his own great spirits and from there takes himself through the sky-blue of the plain and the joyful meadows with high heart; often he shakes his raised mane as his gasps drive white foam from his hot breath.'

[38] Even though they are not actually represented as watching, they are in the reader's mind as she reads the description.

Images of beauty: epic heroes as objects of desire 273

> his head is still naked, and he had girded his sword to his side
> and was shining golden as he ran down from the high citadel
> and he rejoices in his spirit and now with hope anticipates fighting the enemy

His naked head is part of the trope of the desirable warrior,[39] and his false hope, combined with the similarity to Laocoon,[40] mark him out as an object of pathos. This is another example of Turnus' ambivalent heroism, with Virgil evoking both Paris and Hector, along with Jason. He is an object of desire precisely because of his exuberant masculinity, but the excessiveness of his emotions renders him vulnerable, and tends to feminise him.[41] There is a pleasure for readers (and hearers) of epic both in identifying with the hero as subject of desire, and watching him (perhaps simultaneously) as object of desire. Desire is not restricted to erotic scenes, but is equally evoked in the glory and brilliance of battle. In the ancient world, it seems likely that this desiring audience would include both men and women, that men on display would not necessarily need to be marked or read as participants in pederastic relationships, in order to become objects of male desire, to be epic gays (as it were) to be under the epic gaze.

This section has explored the way that the body of the active hero can still be a site of desire despite its power and activity.[42] I turn now to images in which the warrior is more clearly passive: plant imagery and the idea of the hero created as an art object, often by a divine craftsman. We would expect this imagery of a beautiful woman, and these two tropes come together famously in the blush of Lavinia at *Aeneid* 12:[43]

> accepit uocem lacrimis Lauinia matris
> flagrantis perfusa genas, cui plurimus ignem
> subiecit rubor et calefacta per ora cucurrit.
> Indum sanguineo ueluti uiolauerit ostro
> si quis ebur aut mixta rubent ubi lilia multa
> alba rosa, talis uirgo dabat ore colores. (*Aeneid* 12.64–9)

---

[39] See above, Chapter 6, pp.234–5. [40] Horsfall 2003: 292.
[41] For Reed 2007, Turnus is the ultimate Adonis-figure, to whom all the other young deaths lead (44–55); on his feminisation see 60–72.
[42] Valerius Flaccus' reworking of the horse simile gives it a more bitter twist: it is inserted into the departure from Lemnos at VF *Arg.* 2.384–9, and here the emphasis is on the suppressed energy and potential violence of the horse, now a warhorse as in AR (*bellator equus*, 386). Jason becomes a Paris figure, while Hercules takes the role of Hector in his rebuke. The coldness and sluggishness of idleness are contrasted with the energy of war, expressed in its *clamor* and *fragor*. In Quintus Smyrnaeus, a horse image is used of Neoptolemus as he leaves Scyros (*PH* 7.315–27), framing Deidamia's grief at his departure with at the other end an image of the boy as star (7.347). Here the erotic charge of the hero is replaced by maternal grief. Quintus adapts the simile from a warhorse breaking free into a racehorse held in check by his mother's refusal to let him leave.
[43] On Lavinia's blush see Lyne 1983, Dyson 1999; Reed 2007: 20 reads it as the inverse of the death of Camilla.

> Lavinia heard the voice of her mother, with tears
> drenching her burning cheeks, a huge blush set her
> on fire and ran through her face, making it hot.
> Just as if some Indian dyed ivory with bloody red
> or when white lilies grow red with many roses
> among them, so the maiden gave colour to her face.

The erotic language is clear; the burning and the heat, not to mention that key word *uiolauerit*, which suggests sexual violation as well as coloration, stain as well as dye. Flowers are equally important in erotic discourse. Whether or not Lavinia is in love with Turnus, she is clearly an erotic object in this passage, though the active verb in line 69 (*dabat*) does suggest her agency; she is not straightforwardly passive. The exoticism and luxury of Indian ivory are also important. She is a rare object of immense value, the woman over whom the war is fought. Lavinia's blush takes its colour and the first half of the image from a simile in the *Iliad*, describing the wounded Menelaus:[44]

> Ὡς δ' ὅτε τίς τ' ἐλέφαντα γυνὴ φοίνικι μιήνῃ
> Μῃονὶς ἠὲ Κάειρα, παρήϊον ἔμμεναι ἵππων·
> κεῖται δ' ἐν θαλάμῳ, πολέες τέ μιν ἠρήσαντο
> ἱππῆες φορέειν· βασιλῆϊ δὲ κεῖται ἄγαλμα,
> ἀμφότερον κόσμος θ' ἵππῳ ἐλατῆρί τε κῦδος·
> τοῖοί τοι, Μενέλαε, μιάνθην αἵματι μηροὶ
> εὐφυέες κνῆμαί τε ἰδὲ σφυρὰ κάλ' ὑπένερθε.   (*Iliad* 4.141–7)

> As when some Maeonian woman or Carian with purple
> colours ivory, to make it a cheek-piece for horses;
> it lies away in an inner room, and many a rider
> longs to have it, but it is laid up to be a king's treasure,
> two things: to be the beauty of the horse, the pride of the horseman.
> so, Menelaus, your shapely thighs were stained with the colour
> of blood, and your legs also and the ankles beneath them.

The precise relationship between image and context is, as often, elusive; is the colour and the dyeing the only point of contact? Or is Menelaus a passive object, beautiful and to be treasured?[45] The emphasis on his thighs, legs and ankles brings the audience up close and personal. But this image is importantly focalised through Agamemnon, whose shuddering reaction fills the next two lines. Agamemnon sees Menelaus as someone who must be

---

[44] On the Menelaus similes, see Wofford 1992: 31–3. 'This simile ... makes the audience or readers briefly take the point of view from which the war seems painful but beautiful, a figurative move that deflects attention to the epic distance, displacing the violence and transmuting the war scene into a source of aesthetic contemplation.' (33)

[45] Moulton 1974b: 93 n.14 suggests that 'association with women and children ... begins to complicate our conception of Menelaus'; *contra* Kirk 1985: 346.

protected; he has just fought a duel with Paris and been exposed to Trojan treachery. If Athene had not diverted the arrow, Menelaus would be dead and the whole expedition would become an empty failure. Menelaus is further feminised by the image at 130–1 of Athene brushing away the arrow as a mother brushes away a fly from a sleeping child. This does not just emphasise the gulf between immortal insouciance and mortal danger but equally turns Menelaus into a dependent child. Menelaus, in a way, is equal and opposite to Helen as well as Paris, the beautiful treasure over whom the war is fought; Agamemnon is the king whose storerooms will keep him safe.⁴⁶ This simile is also focalised through Menelaus himself at 150–2: for him, perhaps, the blood itself represents the treasure of his own life. On another level the artist who dyes the ivory is a doublet of the poet, composing the simile, on whom, ultimately, both Menelaus and Agamemnon are equally dependent for their continuing existence in literary immortality. Menelaus here, then, is an object of the epic gaze: the story written on and through his body and blood is a work of art for our entertainment.⁴⁷

While the Maeonian or Carian woman (non-Greek, possibly meant to be a foreign slave) has no direct counterpart in the narrative surrounding the Iliadic simile, another cluster of images focuses on gods as craftsmen, forming heroes into works of art. Odysseus is made over in this way twice; the simile first occurs in *Odyssey* 6 with Nausicaa as privileged viewer and is repeated at 23.157–62 for Penelope:

τὸν μὲν Ἀθηναίη θῆκεν, Διὸς ἐκγεγαυῖα,
μείζονά τ' εἰσιδέειν καὶ πάσσονα, κὰδ' δὲ κάρητος
οὔλας ἧκε κόμας, ὑακινθίνῳ ἄνθει ὁμοίας.
ὡς δ' ὅτε τις χρυσὸν περιχεύεται ἀργύρῳ ἀνὴρ
ἴδρις, ὃν Ἥφαιστος δέδαεν καὶ Παλλὰς Ἀθήνη
τέχνην παντοίην, χαρίεντα δὲ ἔργα τελείει,
ὣς ἄρα τῷ κατέχευε χάριν κεφαλῇ τε καὶ ὤμοις.
ἕζετ' ἔπειτ' ἀπάνευθε κιὼν ἐπὶ θῖνα θαλάσσης,
κάλλεϊ καὶ χάρισι στίλβων· θηεῖτο δὲ κούρη. (*Odyssey* 6.229–37)

Then Athene, daughter of Zeus, made him seem taller
for the eye to behold, and thicker, and on his head she arranged
the curling locks that hung down like hyacinthine petals.
And as when a master craftsman overlays gold on silver,
and he is the one who was taught by Hephaistos and Pallas Athene

---

⁴⁶ Sammons 2009 argues that Agamemnon presents himself to a wider audience in his response to Menelaus' wound.
⁴⁷ Wofford 1992: 33: 'They are fighting a war that we, like the gods, are watching, and necessarily we sympathize at the same time that we stand aside and enjoy the story.'

> in art complete, and grace is on every work he finishes,
> so Athene gilded with grace his head and his shoulders,
> and he went a little aside and sat by himself on the seashore,
> radiant in grace and good looks; and the girl admired him.

Here Athene literally forms Odysseus, arranging his hair like that of a sculpture and gilding him with χάρις ('grace') as a jeweller overlays gold on silver.[48] It is only now that Nausicaa sees him erotically, not just looking at him, but gazing in wonder (θηεῖτο) and begins to think of him as a possible husband (244–6).[49] Odysseus has moved from being almost a beast (unwashed, hairy and naked) to being almost a god (243). He retains his virility, despite becoming the object of the female gaze, but he, too, like Menelaus, is in a situation of dependence: he is relying on Nausicaa not only to wash and clothe him but to ease his reception at the potentially hostile court of the Phaeacians. Equally for Penelope in book 23 he becomes an erotically charged vision of male beauty, where it is ultimately up to her to decide whether to accept him back. Athene's moulding of Odysseus reflects her moulding of the plot of the *Odyssey*, becoming a doublet for the poet in more than one way, as she intervenes to shape the reactions of Nausicaa/Penelope (and the audience). The hero is the object of her gaze, her plot and her intervention: of her creation.

In the *Aeneid*, too, when Aeneas reveals himself to Dido for the first time, he becomes a work of art:

> restitit Aeneas claraque in luce refulsit
> os umerosque deo similis; namque ipsa decoram
> caesariem nato genetrix lumenque iuuentae
> purpureum et laetos oculis adflarat honores:
> quale manus addunt ebori decus, aut ubi flauo
> argentum Pariusue lapis circumdatur auro.   (*Aeneid* 1.588–93)

> Aeneas stood still and shone out with a bright light,
> his face and shoulders were like a god's; for his mother herself
> had given grace to her son's hair and had breathed the dazzling glow
> of youth on him and joyful honours in his eyes:
> just as hands add grace to ivory, or when silver
> or Parian marble are surrounded by yellow gold.

The ivory of Menelaus is combined with the silver and gold of Odysseus, but the figure of the artist is eclipsed, falling back into the pluperfect tense

---

[48] χάρις recurs three times: 234, 235 and 237.
[49] Other characters beautified in the *Odyssey*: 2.12–13 (Athene makes over Telemachus about to face the council on Ithaca); 3.463–9 (Polykaste daughter of Nestor bathes him and dresses him so that he looks like an immortal); 18.187–99 (Athene beautifies Penelope before she faces the suitors). Beauty is a sort of armour against difficult situations.

and becoming disembodied hands. The contrast between white flesh and golden hair is brought out by the contrast between silver/marble and gold.⁵⁰ The impact on Dido is held back until after his speech (*obstipuit primo aspectu Sidonia Dido*, 'Sidonian Dido was struck dumb at first sight', 613). Aeneas, like Odysseus, is a combination of almost divine power with almost feminine vulnerability: he is a hero, like a god not just in the eyes of his female viewer, but in the words of the narrator; but he, too, is dependent on Dido's help. The representation of the hero as erotic object and work of art conveys passivity and vulnerability, yet also his power over his viewers.⁵¹

In contrast, women compared to statues are in much more desperate positions of passivity, and much more explicitly eroticised. A tragic example is Polyxena in Euripides' *Hecuba*, who is about to be sacrificed on the tomb of Achilles when she herself strips off her clothes, and the beauty of her breasts is compared to that of a statue: μαστούς τ'ἔδειξε στέρνα θ' ὡς ἀγάλματος / κάλλιστα ('She showed her breasts and a chest most beautiful like that of a statue', 560–1). Segal comments that readers are drawn into the dynamics of viewing, mixing the uncomfortable stirrings of desire with sympathy and admiration for her character, but that the image of the statue 'keeps the scene at a certain aesthetic distance' (117).⁵² He argues that the itemisation of body parts at 363–8 serves to rehumanise her (as her speech certainly does) in the actual moment of killing.⁵³ We have already seen above the example of Ariadne at Catullus 64.61, where the comparison with

---

⁵⁰ Aeneas is also characterised by his golden hair at *Aen.* 4.141–50, where he is compared to Apollo, the most beautiful among his companions (*ipse ante alios pulcherrimus omnis*, 'he most beautiful above all others', 4.141). This could also suggest comparison with a statue of Apollo: at *Dion.* 4.102–7 the disguised Aphrodite, in an attempt to persuade Harmonia to marry Cadmus, compares him both to Apollo himself (95–9) and to the Pythian type-statue of Apollo (102–7). Cadmus is not just like the statue, but exceeds it in beauty: Apollo has only a gold diadem whereas Cadmus is entirely golden. Jason is twice compared to Apollo in Apollonius' *Argonautica*, first as he sets out on his quest (1.307–11), and second as he sets out to fight the bulls in book 3 (1282–3).

⁵¹ Two Ovidian heroes, both of whom start as young men on the brink of passing into manhood, are compared to art objects, and both fail to hold onto their masculinity: Narcissus is compared to a statue at *Met.* 3.418–19, object of Echo's gaze, but fades away with desire for himself; Hermaphroditus is also a work of art at 4.353–5, object of the gaze of Salmacis, and about to lose his masculinity in her feminising waters. Hinds 2002: 138 notes that 'the invitation to view along with the characters is insistent, and once again the desiring gaze crystallizes at a crucial moment into an image of artistic connoisseurship'. This is not just characteristically Ovidian self-conscious reflection on art, but also a further play on ideas of epic heroism.

⁵² Segal 1990: 114 citing the reactions of Gellie 1980 and Rivier 1944: 173 on the 'warmth' generated by the death of a beautiful woman.

⁵³ Segal 1990: 118. Michelini 1987: 161–5 emphasises the sensational nature of Euripides' innovation in this passage; she regards the association between *eros* and *kalos* and the female body as too risky for tragedy, although (n.119) it is present in epic. 'Finally, the combination of apparent innocence and purity with sexual appeal permits us, as Talthybius does, to ogle Polyxene, even as we sympathise with her. The appeal to shameful pleasures is very satisfyingly blended with high moral tone.'

the statue of a Bacchant is the key moment of the reader's alienation from Ariadne's point of view, and leads into the removal of her clothes.[54] Ovid's Andromeda, too, at *Met.* 4.673–7, set out as a sacrifice to the sea monster, chained to a rock, is a paradigm of passivity and fixity, a damsel in distress waiting for Perseus to rescue her, and object of his desiring gaze. Generically, though, the aestheticised female body is not the proper province of epic: as we will see below, the Perseus episode is a key moment of Ovidian engagement with epic (Chapter 9, pp.347–53), but is not in any sense straightforwardly epic. In the battle of the Lapiths and the centaurs, too, Ovid parodies epic; here he presents the *liebestod* of two centaurs, Cyllarus and Hylonome (*Meto.* 12.393–428). Cyllarus is presented as an aestheticised epic hero: his beauty will not save him; his beard is just beginning to grow; he is compared to a statue (398). But this is immediately qualified by the fact that he is a centaur (*et quacumque uir est*, 'and in every respect in which he is a man', 399); the passage goes on to praise the half of his body which is a horse in terms used to praise epic horses. This is Ovid's slant-wise take on horse similes to convey the beauty and vigour of heroes elsewhere in epic, and it has the effect, as so often in the *Metamorphoses*, of creating alienation, underlining the artificiality of literary convention by pushing it to its extreme and beyond.

The mature hero, then, can be an erotic object as well as an aesthetic object:[55] this is even more clearly true of the adolescent hero, at that moment of almost becoming a man, characterised in the ancient world as the most desirable for an *eromenos*.[56] From Homer onwards a succession of heroes characterised by their youth and beauty come before the eyes of the readers only to be brutally cut down.[57] The imagery later used in erotic

---

[54] See above, Chapter 5, pp.162–5.

[55] The focaliser of this eroticisation of the mature hero is usually a woman: presumably many men in the ancient world would have found it uncomfortable to identify themselves with Nausicaa or Dido and look on Odysseus or Aeneas as erotic objects. They might, however, identify with Odysseus and Aeneas and gain pleasure from feeling the desiring gaze of the female audience upon them. Which suggests further that epic has a place for the female gaze, as an important part of constructing epic masculinity.

[56] On pederastic relationships in the ancient world, see the classic study of Dover 1978; Halperin 1990; more recently the controversial intervention by Davidson 2007; on visual material see Lear and Cantarella 2008; on attitudes to homosexuality in Rome, see Williams 1999.

[57] *Il.* 4.473–89 (Simoeisius as poplar); 8.300–8 (Gorgythion as poppy); 14.486–505 (Ilioneus as poppy); 17.50–60 (Euphorbus); *Aen.* 9.431–7 (Euryalus as poppy); 11.68–71 (Pallas as violet or hyacinth); 10.815–32 (Lausus; on his claim to be an Adonis-figure, see Reed 2007: 36–40); *Met.* 10.162–219 (Hyacinthus, beloved of Apollo; metamorphoses into flower); VF *Arg.* 6.690–720 (Myraces, oriental luxury; compared to olive tree); *Theb.* 8.554–654 (Atys), 9.877–83 (Parthenopaeus); *Pun.* 1.376–7, 4.515–17 (Murrus); *PH* 6.372–85 (Nireus as olive); *Dion.* 11.214–52 (Ampelos, who is turned into a vine). In the cyclic *Little Iliad*, Zeus gives a golden vine to Laomedon as compensation for the rape of Ganymede (fr. 6 West = scholion on Eur. *Troad. Women* 822).

epigram (often but not exclusively homoerotic) is applied to these heroes: they are young plants, flowers, or as we have seen above (pp.262–8), the morning or evening star, shining more brightly than its companions.[58] Two examples of the plant imagery from the *Iliad* show how much of this trope is there from an early stage, even before its enrichment with imagery from erotic poetry and the epithalamium. Gorgythion (*Il.* 8.300–8) is killed by accident by Teucer who was aiming at Hector; he is introduced with a description of the beauty of his mother (304–5) and compared to a drooping poppy:

> μήκων δ' ὡς ἑτέρωσε κάρη βάλεν, ἥ τ' ἐνὶ κήπῳ,
> καρπῷ βριθομένη νοτίῃσί τε εἰαρινῇσιν,
> ὣς ἑτέρωσ' ἤμυσε κάρη πήληκι βαρυνθέν. (*Iliad* 8.306–8)

> He bent, drooping his head to one side, as a garden poppy
> bends beneath the weight of its fruit and the rains of springtime;
> so his head bent slack to one side beneath the helm's weight.

This is a cultivated flower drooping from natural causes in the expected cycle of the seasons. In contrast, Euphorbus is compared to an olive tree which has been carefully cultivated by a gardener (17.53–4), with emphasis on beauty and blossom (55–6), which is torn prematurely from the ground by a storm (57–8). Euphorbus is much more explicitly eroticised, with the focus on the beauty of his hair along with the silver and gold of his armour:

> αἵματί οἱ δεύοντο κόμαι Χαρίτεσσιν ὁμοῖαι
> πλοχμοί θ', οἳ χρυσῷ τε καὶ ἀργύρῳ ἐσφήκωντο. (*Iliad* 17.51–2)

> his hair, lovely as the Graces, was splattered with blood, those
> braided locks caught waspwise in gold and silver.

His cultivated appearance is destroyed by the gore of battle. Care and beauty are overwhelmed by greater forces (storm and war).

Similarly, Simoeisius is introduced as ἠΐθεον θαλερὸν ('unmarried and in the bloom of youth', 4.474); at 473–6 there is a focus on his mother and how she conceived him by the Simoeis; however, he will not be able to look after her in her old age (477–8). The moment of death closes in on his body pierced, with the details of position emphasising the body (beside the right breast; going clean through the shoulder, 480–2). The simile which follows turns him into material for a craftsman:

---

[58] Some examples from book 12 of the *Greek Anthology*: 8 (boy blushes redder than rose); 40 (statue and rose); 56 and 57 (Praxiteles and the statue of love); 58 (rose outshines other flowers); 59 (sun that quenches the stars); 126 (Diophantus as sapling); 163 (boys as jewels and gold); 178 (Theudis like sun among stars); 196 (Lycinus' eyes shoot forth flame); 234 (rose as beauty); 256 (boys as flowers and olive).

> ὁ δ' ἐν κονίῃσι χαμαὶ πέσεν αἴγειρος ὥς,
> ἥ ῥά τ' ἐν εἰαμενῇ ἕλεος μεγάλοιο πεφύκει
> λείη, ἀτάρ τέ οἱ ὄζοι ἐπ' ἀκροτάτῃ πεφύασι·
> τὴν μέν θ' ἁρματοπηγὸς ἀνὴρ αἴθωνι σιδήρῳ
> ἐξέταμ', ὄφρα ἴτυν κάμψῃ περικαλλέϊ δίφρῳ·
> ἡ μέν τ' ἀζομένη κεῖται ποταμοῖο παρ' ὄχθας. (*Iliad* 4.482–7)

> He dropped then to the ground in the dust, like some black poplar
> which in the land low-lying about a great marsh grows
> smooth-trimmed, yet with branches growing at the uttermost tree-top:
> one whom a man, a maker of chariots, fells with the shining
> iron, to bend it into a wheel for a fine-wrought chariot,
> and the tree lies hardening by the banks of a river.

This simile combines the straightness and strength of a fine plant with a sense of the death as material for a craftsman. Does this simile offer a contrast between the pointless destruction of war and destruction with a constructive aim? Or does Simoeisius' death contribute to Ajax' reputation? Or is the narrator the analogue of the chariot-maker, turning Simoeisius into a finely wrought piece of poetry?[59] These plant images, then, turn heroes into objects, if living objects, beautiful to look at; they also show a certain self-consciousness, a distancing, even as they create pathos, and evoke generational continuity cut off, the mothers deprived of their sons, who will remain unmarried.

Beautiful boys are also compared to jewels. In the *Aeneid*, Ascanius, whose position as heir of Aeneas and ancestor of the Julian *gens* makes him inviolable, becomes a jewel or an ivory inlay, displayed on the walls of the Trojan camp in book 10:

> qualis gemma micat, fuluum quem diuidit aurum,
> aut collo decus aut capiti, uel quale per artem
> inclusum buxo aut Oricia terebintho
> lucet ebur; fusos ceruix cui lactea crinis
> accipit et molli subnectens circulus auro. (*Aeneid* 10.134–8)

> Just as a jewel flashes which divides the tawny gold,
> grace of neck or head, or as ivory shines
> inlaid by skill in box-wood or Orician
> terebinth; his milky neck receives his loose
> hair and a circlet wreathes it with soft gold.

---

[59] Ovid's Adonis episode presents the beautiful boy as object of desire and material for poetry; at the beginning of the episode he is like a cupid in a picture, with a self-referential allusion to his incorrect attributes (*Met.* 10.515–17); at the end he is transformed into an anemone.

Images of beauty: epic heroes as objects of desire 281

The beauty of Ascanius is not just that of a charismatic leader in the making, but also an object of desire, erotic and exotic in equal measure.[60] Like Menelaus, he represents the *raison d'être* of the expedition: Aeneas left Carthage for the sake of Ascanius' Roman destiny. In book 9 Ascanius longs to make the transition from boy to man, to join in battle, but he must remain a spectacle: Apollo stops him from taking action and becoming an epic subject rather than a passive object (9.653–6). Ascanius is in the process of being formed by his epic experiences, as Aeneas' didactic address in book 12 emphasises (12.435–40). Ascanius is the object of ecphrasis, but also one that looks back: he does succeed in shooting Numanus Remulus, even if he is not allowed to leave the walls. His beauty might normally indicate the imminence of death, but, like Menelaus and Helen, he has a special status and must be protected. Beauty here also indicates nobility and status.

Silius uses this image in his description of Piso, young, beautiful, with wisdom beyond his years, who is destined to die attacking Hannibal in the battle of Cannae (*Pun.* 10.250–9):[61]

> is primam ante aciem pictis radiabat in armis,
> Arsacidum ut fuluo micat ignea gemma monili.   (*Punica* 8.466–7)
>
> He was shining out, first before the column, in his painted weapons,
> as a fiery jewel flashes in a tawny necklace of a Parthian king.

Here Silius tars the Romans as they face defeat with the oriental otherness which the Trojans cannot entirely avoid in the *Aeneid*. This creates a degree of assimilation with the Carthaginians, especially the reference to the Parthians, still powerful enemies of Rome. That Piso dies, and becomes an emblem of Roman defeat, might suggest that only in Silius' epic do the Trojans finally become Roman: or on a more pessimistic reading, the future greatness of Rome is always compromised by future luxury and immorality. The jewel image has the added irony that works of art, like poetry, are not inevitably consigned to death in the cycle of the seasons, but should be able to escape the endless round of death and decay. Notable, then, that most of the heroes formed into divine works of art do survive their epics. Yet they are also more passive and more strikingly objectified than natural beauty, which moves, grows and dies of its own accord.

---

[60] Rogerson 2002: 67: 'so Ascanius' jewel-like presence on the walls of the Trojan camp is significant of the danger that he poses on the battlefield and the danger that he poses to Rome. It suggests the peril that he shares with the other, ill-fated young heroes of Virgil's epic by exposing himself in battle. And it draws the attention and incites the desire of his audience.'

[61] He is also one emblem of Roman loss at *Pun.* 10.403–4. Spaltenstein 1990 *ad loc.* on the link with Ascanius in the *Aeneid*.

Statius' Achilles in the *Achilleid* shows how important this imagery is for negotiating gender identity. At the key moment of book 1, when he sees Deidamia and agrees to be disguised as a woman, Statius piles on the imagery. At 277–82 after Thetis first proposes the disguise, he bridles, and his instinctive refusal is compared to the reaction of a wild horse in the process of being tamed, reversing the Virgilian (and Homeric) horse simile; this horse used to rejoice in his freedom, but now does not offer his body to submission. Achilles' proud masculinity is curbed when Thetis keeps him away from war, but the erotic implications remain. After he catches sight of Deidamia and immediately falls in love, Statius compares his blushing to an artefact dyed by a woman of the Massagetae (307–10), evoking both the wound of Menelaus and the blush of Lavinia, while Deidamia herself is a doublet of Nausicaa and Dido (293–6), and her appearance is also described in the language of heroic beauty (at 297–8 she blushes, and her jewels and gold have greater light – literalising the image, and making her the matching equivalent of Achilles). At 323–4 Achilles adopts the female gaze, looking askance at the girls (*obliquat*, 324), before Thetis forms him into a woman (325–31), and is compared to a craftsman moulding wax (332–4). This image particularly conveys the softening of Achilles, and the reversibility of the change, as well as Thetis' control of the plot and his life. Achilles is both object and subject of desire, feminised by emotion, yet destined to form and express his masculinity precisely in its containment.[62]

We have seen, then, boys as exotic art works, mature heroes as objects of the desiring gaze of women and the wound of Menelaus, which turns him into a reflection of Helen, the beauty over which the war is fought. In many ways the wound of Menelaus is the most striking of these objectifications of the heroic body, and I finish this section with Nonnus' reception of the Menelaus passage. In book 29, the middle of the *Indiad* section, in which Dionysus is battling with his arch-enemy Deriades, the beautiful boy Hymenaios appears, his name a self-conscious nod to the traditions of epithalamium imagery. He is like the morning star (*Dion.* 29.18–19) though rather than outshining other beauty, he is light in the midst of darkness represented by the black-skinned Indians. Dionysus falls in love with him in battle and plays with the idea that his arrows killing Indians are also the arrows of love shooting him (29.39–44). Zeus makes an arrow swerve aside from Dionysus and hit Hymenaios, and Aphrodite keeps the shot out of the flesh just like a mother driving off a fly from her child (29.84–6). This

---

[62] Heslin 2005: 129 argues that Thetis usurps the father's role by turning Achilles into a girl rather than initiating him into manhood.

image immediately activates the Menelaus episode in *Iliad* 4 (matching image at *Il.* 4.130–1), in case we had not already picked it up. Dionysus laments the wound, but like Agamemnon, takes courage from the sight of the barbs outside the flesh (*Dion.* 29.100–3, *Il.* 4.151–2). Ultimately he uses his divine powers to heal the thigh himself, now becoming the artisan who forms the flesh of his beloved boy, not an artist making luxury goods, but a goatherd making cheese (29.157–61). Nonnus has playfully reworked the Iliadic version and explicitly eroticised the whole episode by making the wound the equivalent of Dionysus' wound of love, focusing on the reddened thigh (*Dion.* 29.87 and 154) and the god's bodily contact with the boy. The erotically charged beautiful boy is here linked back to Menelaus wounded in battle, a literalisation of the implications in the Homeric passage; the generic play in the cheese image, however, shows a certain uneasiness in the reworking, a pastoralisation of a key epic moment.

Heroes and gladiators

The epic hero is often represented as beautiful and has a certain glamour derived from his closeness to death and his closeness to the gods. We have seen one tendency in epic imagery: to turn the hero into a literal aesthetic object, a tendency that runs through both Greek and Roman epic. What difference, however, does historical context make to the way the heroic body is viewed? One particular context which has been influential in the reading of Roman epic is that of gladiatorial spectacle.[63] Heuzé points out that the phrase *hoc habet!* ('he's had it!' *Aen.* 12.296), a gladiatorial phrase, is used by Virgil's Messapus when he wounds Aulestes.[64] Another marker is the tendency for all epic battles, no matter what their geographical location, to find their way on to the sand of the arena (*harena*).[65] Lucan makes much use of the idea of the gladiatorial pair (*par*), and this too is taken up by

---

[63] On Virgil, see Heuzé 1985: 174–93. Hardie 1986: 151–4 also suggests gladiatorial spectacle as one frame for the battle between Turnus and Aeneas. On Ovid, Hinds 2002: 139–40 brings out the amphitheatricality of, among others, the deaths of Pentheus and Orpheus. On Lucan, Leigh 1997: 234–91, building on Ahl 1976: 86–8 and Masters 1993. On Valerius Flaccus as a spectacle of disempowerment: Zissos 2003.

[64] *OLD s.v. habeo* 16 d (of a gladiator receiving a fatal or winning hit). Two possible echoes from Statius' *Thebaid*: at 11.557, when Polynices thinks he has killed Eteocles, his comment is *'Bene habet!'* This is a fairly common phrase ('all is well'), but punctuated differently as (*'Bene! habet.'* "Good. He's had it.'), it would follow on from other gladiatorial imagery. More convincing is the phrase at 12.705 (*prior hostis habet*, 'the first enemy got them'), when the Thebans are preparing for war against Theseus and all is in disarray after their 'victory' against the Argives. This metaphor implies that the Thebans are like a gladiator returning to the ring for a second battle when he was wounded in the first.

[65] *Harena* is used innovatively by Virgil four times in book 12 to refer to the dust of battle (276, 340, 382, 741). See Hardie 1986: 152 n.80. Leigh 1997: 244 points persuasively to Lucan *BC* 6.60–3, where the field of battle is both an *area* and a *harena* (both terms for the arena). In Flavian epic the use of *harena*

Flavian epic: most notably, Polynices and Eteocles in Statius' *Thebaid* are a *par infandum* ('unspeakable pair', *Theb.* 11.125).[66] Other arena spectacle equally forms and informs epic: the wild beast similes traditional in Homer, often evoking hunting, can also in later epic suggest the *venatio* in the arena, especially where the animals are exotic. Lucan's Scaeva is compared to a bear (*BC* 6.220–3), a leopard (6.180–4) and an elephant (6.208–13); read with all the other gladiatorial markers in this episode, he becomes a one-man wild beast spectacle.[67] Bears and other animals fighting each other (or compared to each other) equally form spectacular similes in Flavian epic.[68] Roman arena spectacle, then, influences the way that Roman writers rework epic; viewing gladiators shapes the development of the epic gaze.

Gladiators were not only significant in the Western empire, but became equally popular among Greeks under Rome.[69] This carries over into Greek imperial epic, where the traces of gladiatorial spectacle can also be found in Quintus Smyrnaeus. The Atreides surrounded by Trojans are compared to wild beasts in the arena:

τοὶ δ' ἐν μέσσοισιν ἐόντες
στρωφῶντ', εὖτε σύες μέσῳ ἕρκεϊ ἠὲ λέοντες
ἤματι τῷ ὅτ' ἄνακτες ἀολλίσσωσ' ἀνθρώπους,
ἀργαλέως δ' εἰλῶσι κακὸν τεύχοντες ὄλεθρον
θηρσὶν ὑπὸ κρατεροῖς, οἱ δ' ἕρκεος ἐντὸς ἐόντες
δμῶας δαρδάπτουσιν, ὅ τίς σφισιν ἐγγὺς ἵκηται

(*Posthomerica* 6.531–6)

Those two were caught in the middle turning
this way and that like boars or lions in an enclosure,
on a day when rulers gather people together
and cruelly shut them in to meet a dreadful death

as battle ground is pervasive: Valerius' boxing match at VF *Arg.* 4.30 and 264 takes place on the sand (both seashore and arena). At 6.711 Myraces is stretched out like an olive tree blown over on black sand. See also Silius Italicus *Pun.* 4.241; 14.160; Statius *Theb.* 3.334; 10.518. The link between gladiatorial spectacle and epic games is further highlighted by clusters of *harena* in Statius' and Silius' games (*Theb.* 6.525, 556, 848, 853, 874; *Pun.* 16.414, 485).

[66] On Lucan's *pares* see Leigh 1997: 244–5. In Statius' *Thebaid*, on Polynices and Eteocles, see Bernstein 2004, Lovatt 2005: 253–6, Coffee 2009. Antigone and Ismene are an odd pair at 8.608 (*par aliud*); Shackleton Bailey 2003 contrasts them to Polynices and Eteocles, but they might also be standing against Tydeus and Atys who have just been fighting. In Silius' *Punica*, Laevinus chooses his own gladiatorial match in Ithemon at 5.546.

[67] Leigh 1997: 243–4; he also reads Cato's snake episode in book 9 as a reverse *venatio* at 265–82.

[68] At VF *Arg.* 3.631–6, the Argonauts clamouring to set off without Hercules are compared to stag, boar, wolves and she-bear keen to fight as long as the tiger and lion are not there; Statius compares Tydeus and Agylleus wrestling in the games to bulls, boars and bears at *Theb.* 6.864–9; at 11.26–31 the Thebans taking advantage of Jupiter's thunderbolt are compared to bears, wolves and other animals taking advantage of the lion's successful hunting. At Silius' *Pun.* 4.563–6 Mago and Maharbal are bears attacking a bull; at 5.309–15 Appius is a lion to Mago's bull on the sand of the arena.

[69] The classic study is Robert 1940.

from the savage beasts that are penned in there with them
to tear apart any slave who happens to come too close.

This simile strikingly breaks the frame of the *Posthomerica* by making a truly post-Homeric reference: what starts out like a Homeric simile becomes that most Roman of institutions, execution by wild beasts, explicitly set up as a spectacle by a tyrannous ruler. To a Greek living in the Roman empire, then, epic spectacle cannot be hermetically sealed off from Roman spectacle. The brutality of epic battle is always potentially analogous to the glory of the arena.

What is the effect, then, of seeing the epic hero as a gladiator and epic battle as gladiatorial duelling? Leigh suggests that the effect in Lucan is simultaneously to distance and familiarise, break the frame and draw the viewer in, make them complicit and demand their outrage. He focuses on the effects of arena spectacle on political engagement, the 'bread and circuses' effect. But how does this imagery affect the way we think about the epic hero? The gladiator in Roman culture is a contradictory and emotive symbol. Barton has explored the way in which gladiators are simultaneously exalted and despised, hated and desired, *exempla* to be emulated and monsters to be destroyed.[70] Graffiti in Pompeii (and the imprint of the dead body of a rich woman discovered in the gladiators' barracks there) give potential substance to Juvenal's satiric portrait of women erotically obsessed by gladiators.[71] The gladiator can be read as a scapegoat and a fetish: anxiety about and threat of disempowerment and destruction is displaced onto the gladiator.[72] Aristocrats who no longer control their destinies in both Rome and the provinces find gladiatorial games compelling and repulsive. The gladiator offers an extreme example of the body on display for the use of others, penetrable and commodified, despite hypermasculine prowess and fighting performance.[73] By turning epic into a gladiatorial spectacle and the epic hero into a gladiator, Roman poets and readers complicate the role of epic in society. As a genre, it cannot straightforwardly produce propaganda for those in power: after Lucan, can the death of Turnus ever not be a gladiatorial

---

[70] Barton 1993.
[71] On desire and the gladiator, see Barton 1993: 47–83, especially 65, citing Petronius' *Satyricon* 126 and Juvenal 6.82–113. Beard 2008 debunks the idea that the body of a richly dressed woman found in the gladiators' barracks in Pompeii shows the truth behind this image: she is more likely to have been fleeing and taking refuge, than visiting her lover at the time of the eruption. But even if these accounts are exaggerated or fictional, they represent a Roman discourse about gladiators, a male fantasy, perhaps, about the fantasies of women.
[72] Wiedemann 1992: 34 discusses scapegoats; Barton 1993: 44–6.
[73] On the penetrability of the gladiator, Bartsch 2006: 152–6; in Juvenal 2, Gracchus putting himself on display as a gladiator is more scandalous (143–8) than offering himself as bride to his trumpet player (117–20).

spectacle? After Lucan and Virgil, can the death of Hector ever not be a gladiatorial spectacle? Although I will focus in this section on combats particularly marked as gladiatorial by language and imagery, the dynamics of gladiatorial viewing must affect all epic duels.

Watching gladiatorial spectacle could be a paradoxical experience: does it encourage dehumanisation of those fighting, or heightened emotion and identification? The emotional response of a massed crowd, fans and partisans, cheering and groaning, makes gladiators both more than and less than human beings. The other mode of viewing gladiatorial battle which is clearly on display in ancient descriptions and discussion of gladiators is a moral and judgemental mode.[74] For instance, Seneca uses the gladiator as an image for the committed Stoic:[75] *Illis licet arma summittere, misericordiam populi temptare: tu neque summittes nec vitam rogabis; recta tibi invictoque moriendum est.* ('To gladiators it is permitted to put down their weapons and try for the pity of the people; you will neither put them down nor plead for your life: you must die erect and unconquered.', Sen. *Epist.* 37.2). The mode of death contributes to the pleasure of the spectacle. Pliny insists in his *Panegyric* of Trajan that Trajan's gladiatorial spectacles were 'neither effeminate nor debauched, nor the sort that softens men's minds and breaks them, but the sort to set us afire for beautiful wounds and contempt of death, since even in the bodies of slaves and the guilty the love of praise and the desire for victory could be discerned'. (*Visum est spectaculum inde non enerve, nec fluxum, nec quod animos virorum molliret et frangeret, sed quod ad pulchra vulnera contemptumque mortis accenderet: quum in servorum etiam noxiorumque corporibus amor laudis et cupido victoriae cerneretur*, Pliny *Pan.* 33.1). Audiences are called to pass judgement on both good and bad deaths, good and bad spectacles, as well as their own good and bad responses to watching the spectacles. The pleasure of the arena exists in the tension between sadistic voyeurism and a stance of moral distance. To what extent is this also the pleasure of epic?

We can see the way that epic evokes the arena in an indirect fashion by looking at two moments in Ovid's *Metamorphoses*. Salzman-Mitchell 2005: 107 points out the way that Medea watches Jason perform his feats at *Met.* 7.134–8, and argues that there is a gendered contrast here between men who are watched in action, and women who are pictured statically. But

---

[74] Leigh 1997: 158–90 on exemplarity, read through Lucan's Scaeva episode.
[75] Bartsch 2006: 152–64 discusses the potential feminisation of orator and actor in Roman society, with reference to the gladiatorial paradigm of visual availability and penetrability; 165–82 examines philosophical responses to putting the body on display.

when Medea imagines watching Jason, in her speech before she meets him in the temple, she toys with the idea of a much more gladiatorial spectatorship: *cur non et specto pereuntem oculosque uidendo | conscelero?* ('Why should I not watch him as he dies and make my eyes accomplices by watching?', 7.33–4), complete with the idea of cheering on the bulls, the earth-born men and the dragon (34–5). In her decision about whether or not to help him, she is already like a gladiatorial audience deciding on the fate of the defeated fighter. Salzman-Mitchell argues that men are never completely objectified, since they are viewed in action, while women are fixed and passive. But this opposition is insecure. Jason is disempowered by his need for help, and his actions turn him into an avatar of Medea. Medea judges herself negatively for contemplating this gladiatorial viewing, although her erotic viewing is equally problematic. She recognises her own potential sadistic voyeurism, even as she exaggerates it for the purpose of persuading herself. The complex reception of the idea of women watching gladiators in paintings such as Simeon Solomon's *Habet!* (1865) is already present in embryo in Ovid's representation of Medea.[76]

An even more pointed reference to the arena comes at *Met.* 11.24–7, when the mob of Bacchants in the process of killing Orpheus are compared first to birds of daylight spotting a nocturnal bird, and then to dogs in the morning show in the amphitheatre making a stag their prey. Here there are two dehumanising gazes: that of the Bacchants at Orpheus, and that of the readers at the show. Orpheus is disempowered by his inability to protect himself with his song, and is targeted either as an object of female desire repudiated, or in vengeance for his hatred of women: he is the one who rejects women (*nostri contemptor*, 11.7). The desiring gaze here becomes the assaultive gaze, complicated by making a man its object. The women are both dehumanised and degraded by their comparison to dogs and birds, the traditional carrion creatures of epic; even if here they are killing, their defenceless prey renders them utterly unheroic, and this episode evokes unease rather than pleasure.

The moment of epic battle which most strongly evokes the arena is that crucial moment of life or death: Scaeva in Lucan, Eteocles in Statius' *Thebaid*, Turnus in Virgil's *Aeneid*, all beg for mercy in the moment before death and leave the decision between life and death up to the conqueror

---

[76] See Prettejohn 1999. The complexity of identification is shown by the way that historical male viewers discussed their own identification with the female desiring gaze (165–7): for instance, John Addington Symonds on Shakespeare's *Venus and Adonis*: '[Venus] only expressed my own relation to the desirable male. She brought into relief the overwhelming attraction of masculine adolescence and its proud inaccessibility' (cited by Prettejohn, 165).

(though for both Scaeva and Eteocles, it is a feint). I begin with Messapus and Aulestes in *Aeneid* 12. Messapus is one of the most important Rutulian leaders, a son of Neptune, and a key figure in the catalogue of the Italians.[77] The encounter occurs just after the truce set up for the duel of Turnus and Aeneas has been broken and Juturna has stimulated the Rutulian audience to intervene with a false portent. The first spear strikes down a young man outstanding in beauty and stretches him out on the tawny sand:

> hasta uolans, ut forte nouem pulcherrima fratrum
> corpora constiterant contra, quod fida crearat
> una tot Arcadio coniunx Tyrrhena Gylippo,
> horum unum ad medium, teritur qua sutilis aluo
> balteus et laterum iuncturas fibula mordet,
> egregium forma iuuenem et fulgentibus armis,
> transadigit costas fuluaque effundit harena.   (*Aeneid* 12.270–6)

> The flying spear, where by chance the nine most beautiful
> bodies of brothers had stood opposite, so many which one faithful
> Tuscan wife had given life for Arcadian Gylippus,
> to one of these in the middle, where the sewn belt rubs the belly
> and the clasp joining the sides bites,
> a young man outstanding in appearance and in shining armour,
> pierced through his ribs and poured him out on the tawny sand.

Virgil manipulates the visualisation of the readers in a strikingly cinematic manner: there is a pause between the spear and its impact, delaying and heightening the emotional response with a cut to its object and brief excursus to his brother and parents, then a close focus on the minutiae of his body, which surely encourages audience identification (we know what that rubbing *feels* like), yet also creates a certain numbness and dislocation (not the face or the body itself, but his clothes). Here the combination of beauty, death and the arena (implied by *harena*) combine to make this young man erotic object, source of pathos and gladiator. Messapus makes the next killing:

> Messapus regem regisque insigne gerentem
> Tyrrhenum Aulesten, auidus confundere foedus,
> aduerso proterret equo: ruit ille recedens
> et miser oppositis a tergo inuoluitur aris
> in caput inque umeros. at feruidus aduolat hasta
> Messapus teloque orantem multa trabali

---

[77] His appearance out of order in the otherwise alphabetical catalogue has stimulated Malamud 1998 to read him as a poet figure, representing an Ennian poetics of military epic. Sons of Neptune are often monstrous (Polyphemus, Amycus) but Messapus represents the decent face of Rutulian heroism, in contrast to Mezentius.

desuper altus equo grauiter ferit atque ita fatur:
'hoc habet, haec melior magnis data uictima diuis.'
concurrunt Itali spoliantque calentia membra.

(*Aeneid* 12.289–97)

> Messapus, greedy to overturn the treaty,
> terrifies the Tuscan king Aulestes who is wearing
> the regal sign, from his horse opposite; he rushes backwards
> and, wretch, is rolled over on the altar behind his back,
> head over heels. But Messapus, seething, hurls his spear
> at him, and as he begs greatly, with his huge beam of a weapon
> high on his horse strikes him heavily from above and speaks thus:
> 'He's had it; this is a better victim to give to the great gods.'
> The Italians run together and despoil his still warm limbs.

When Messapus says *hoc habet*, he is not just turning Aulestes into a gladiator, but himself also, as he delivers the final blow from on high, adopting the vertical, powerful, and arguably divine, gaze. The moral/judgemental mode of viewing is encouraged by implied authorial comment: Messapus is *auidus* ('greedy') to break the truce and Aulestes is a *rex* who attempts to retreat backwards and trips over an altar. Death on an altar evokes Priam (2.550–3), who exemplifies the opposite of the beautiful death, trembling and slipping as he struggles to the altar, further objectified as Neoptolemus grabs him by the hair.[78] The bathetic tone of Aulestes' death along with the greed and arrogance of Messapus, complicate any pleasure in this episode. Both men are compromised by the evocation of gladiators. Further, this episode has strong resonances with the final moments of the *Aeneid*: Turnus, like Aulestes, is cast by his despatcher as a sacrificial victim;[79] both Messapus and Aeneas are *feruidus* ('seething', 12.293 and 951) as they strike the blow. Both Aulestes and Turnus beg for mercy, but both are despatched nonetheless. This passage reverses and foreshadows the end of Turnus and brings out the gladiatorial frame of *Aeneid* 12.[80] The

---

[78] On the uneasy combination of old age and heroism in Priam's death, see Mills 1978.
[79] Williams 1973 *ad loc.* suggests that Aulestes is a better victim than the animals – but perhaps he is rather a substitute for Turnus who was also described like a sacrificial victim at 220–1. Or is he rather a reworking of Priam, killed on the altar by Neoptolemus?
[80] A recent exploration of *Aeneid* 12 as spectacle is that of Rossi 2004: 150–70. Rossi argues that the assimilation of Turnus and Aeneas is mirrored by the unification of the watching audience, thus setting up the end of the *Aeneid* as civil war, a version of the recent experience of Virgil's Roman readers, but with no sense of peace and reconciliation at its end. All these different aspects of the heroic body on display, erotic and gladiatorial, seem to converge on the end of the *Aeneid*; the passage is a profound reflection on the workings of epic as well as identity. Its prominence in Virgilian scholarship bespeaks its compelling force as ending and refusal of closure. Reed 2007 makes a strong case for Turnus as eroticised object of the gaze (44–72); Aeneas is more complex; he has associations with the heroine persona (186–93), and, like Menelaus, he is wounded (193–4). In the gladiatorial

Messapus and Aulestes episode separates the erotic and pathetic viewing (death of the son of Gylippus) from the moral, sadistic and bathetic viewing, elements which will be fused in the death of Turnus.

Aeneid 12 must be at the heart of Roman epic: the much-discussed *aristeia* of Lucan's Scaeva in contrast is the ultimate extreme. Scaeva is the posterboy of gladiatorial epic.[81] Leigh has established the gladiatorial framework of this episode: not only the exotic animal similes, but also the key phrase *parque nouum Fortuna uidet concurrere, bellum | atque uirum* ('and Fortune sees a new pair meet, a war and a man', *BC* 6.191–2), among other things, make it obvious that the viewing of both readers and internal audience, imagined and present (Caesar and the other Caesarians, Pompey), is intended to be gladiatorial.[82] Scaeva's performance engages with *aristeias* Iliadic and Virgilian.[83] *Fortuna* as viewer stands in for the divine gaze of epic, and the match between a war and a man evokes the *Aeneid* (*arma uirumque* stands as emblem of the whole poem), while undermining it: this really is one man taking on the whole war, while everyone else watches.[84] The episode inspires mixed responses: Hömke 2010 calls it 'one of the most repulsive passages in ancient literature'; the stylised violence alienates even as it shocks.[85] Lines 169–79 begin the show, which his fellow soliders are greedy to watch (*auidi spectare*, 167): a litany of varied weapons is rolled out (*euoluit*, 171 – possibly metapoetic?), beginning with dead bodies (*cadauera*, 170), ruined walls (*ruinae*, 172), beams, blocks of stone and himself (173), stakes and poles (174–5), sword (176), stone (176) and fire (178), to confront varied body parts: breasts (*pectora*, 174), hands (*manus*, 176), head and bones (*caput ossaque*, 176), brain (*cerebrum*, 177), hair and cheeks (*crinesque genasque*, 178), and finally eyes (*oculis*, 179). The landscape and the opponents are both disintegrating.

Hömke reads this passage cinematically, as if the 'narrating camera' was progressively zooming in, which, she suggests, is 'an aesthetisization (*sic*) of

---

framework he combines the figures of both master of ceremonies (analogous to emperor), hearing the plea for mercy and making the life or death decision, and gladiator (watched, judged, desired, despised). The final blow encapsulates the idea of the penetrative gaze as a moment of unease, a disturbance in the field of vision, in which power and identification are problematically embroiled, the fantasy of Augustan Rome as utopia is exploded.

[81] In particular he keeps coming back in Leigh 1997: 158–90 (as *exemplum*); 221–33 (on his relationship to the Roman culture of displaying wounds); 243–6 (as gladiator). Other important discussions: Conte 1974, Sklenář 2003: 45–58, D'Alessandro Behr 2007: 45–53, Hömke 2010.

[82] Leigh 1997: 243–6.

[83] D'Alessandro Behr 2007: 47 on links with Virgil's Mezentius; Sklenář 2003: 48–9 on Diomedes in the *Iliad*. Sklenář reads Scaeva as radically undermining epic.

[84] On Scaeva's bizarrely ineffective *paraceleusis*, which produces an audience rather than allies, see Leigh 1997: 181–4. On Scaeva and the epic *totus/unus* opposition, see Hardie 1993: 8, 35.

[85] For a comparison of Statian violence with the film of Tarantino, see Gervais forthcoming.

dying through an artificial and artistic expansion of the interval between life and death'.[86] The narrator's gaze seems to go progressively deeper inside the bodies, becoming haptic in its evocation of the sounds and textures of disintegrating bodies: the fragile skull (*fragili conpage*, 177); the shrieking of the eye as it burns (*strident*, 179). The eyes come as a climax, as they do in Scaeva's own disintegration in the next scene of the show. After the leopard simile, at 187–95 we again move from weapons to bodies, beginning with the blunting of his sword, going through the ringing of the shield, and the helmet collapsing and damaging the head it should be protecting, to his temples (*tempora*), innards (*nudis uitalibus*) and bones (*ossibus*). Some relief (alienation and textuality) comes from a series of comparisons, which turn Scaeva into a landscape of his own, a wall (201–2), the bearer of a forest (205–6), and again evoke the arena with the elephant simile (207–12). The return to the action is marked by *ecce* (214), as we follow the course of an arrow approaching from afar, evoking all those heroes wounded (and feminised) in this way (Menelaus, Camilla, Aeneas), to bring this sequence to a climax as it pierces his eyeball. The choice of the eye as the site of this show-stopping wound is important: will Scaeva's assaultive gaze now be compromised? Is this a literalisation of the evil eye? Or will he instead become monstrous, a revivified Polyphemus? Eye wounds are popular and frequent in epic, reflecting on the simultaneous power and vulnerability of the heroic gaze.[87] Scaeva, however, responds with hyperbolical disregard: he himself pulls out his own eyeball. The details of ligaments and muscles tearing (217) are trumped only by his gesture of scorn towards his own body, when he tramples the eye (219). This leads into the third arena simile (of a Pannonian she-bear fighting

---

[86] Hömke 2010: 103. This approach is similar to Most 1992a, who argues that dismemberment is characteristically Neronian. It is certainly taken to extremes here, but how different is it really from examples below in the *Iliad*, or less controversially, in the Hesiodic *Aspis*? See Martin 2005b.

[87] The blinding of Polyphemus (*Od.* 9.382–94) may well be the code model for this epic topos, which would explain Lucan's sound effects. Polyphemus' eye crackles and sizzles (σφαραγεῦντο, 390; σίζ', 394). The two images of Odysseus as craftsman (shipbuilder, 384–6; blacksmith, 390–3) take on a different resonance in view of his control of the gaze in this episode, connecting him even more closely to the poet as craftsman, and the gods. He forms Polyphemus by mutilating, creating his own story. However, there are a number of Iliadic examples: 13.617 (Peisander's eyes fall out and lie in the dust); 13.493–500 is fully worthy of Lucan (Peneleus spears Ilioneus in the eye, and goes through his head; he hacks off the head and with the spear stuck in the eye, displays the head to the Trojans like a drooping poppy); 16.741–2 (Cebriones' eyes fall into the dust). In Latin epic, there is *Aen.* 8.261 (Hercules squeezes out the eyes of Cacus – rather tangential, suggesting a certain squeamishness?); *Met.* 12.252–3, 268–70, 314–15 (all in the battle of the Lapiths and centaurs; that there should be so many examples so close together in Ovid's hyperbolic parody of epic battle must suggest that they represent an extreme of epic violence). After Lucan there are: VF *Arg.* 6.246 (Oebasus pierced in the eye); *Theb.* 7.647 (eyes look at body); *Pun.* 4.534–41 (Gracchus removes the sight of the one remaining eye of Cupencus); 5.447 (Giant Othrys gets an arrow in the eye); QS *PH* 3.155 (Achilles kills Hipponous); 8.318 (Deiophantes hit in the eye).

against a Libyan hunter), followed by the break in the fighting, in which he pretends to be fatally wounded, and appeals for gladiatorial mercy. We also step back to see the overall effect of his wounds (his face has been destroyed and he is now *informis*, formless) and the reaction of the watching Pompeians, whose united cheer strikes the heavens (*laetus fragor aethera pulsat*, 225), reminding us not only of the reactions of the Rutulians at *Aen*. 12.928–9, but also of the massed partisans of the gladiatorial arena. He uses his appeal for mercy to strike down one more gullible enemy with a sword like lightning (239), but is prevented from achieving the death he desires (*mortis amor*, 246), by the arrival of Caesar and reinforcements.

This is the ultimate epic *coitus interruptus*: neither the readers, nor the internal viewers, nor Scaeva himself receive the expected pay-off of the *aristeia*, the beautiful death. Nevertheless, his body is treated as a relic, in a scene which D'Alessandro Behr finds 'grotesque and slightly blasphemous'.[88] The Caesarian partisans compete to pull out the weapons from his body (*telaque confixis certant evellere membris*, 255), a reversal of the Greeks competing to stab Hector's corpse over and over at *Il*. 22.369–75.[89] In this episode, desire is transformed into disgust; Scaeva is not beautiful, though he is worshipped as if divine. He is not even a gladiator, but an animal (or a series of animals).[90] Object of all gazes, he nevertheless retains his own perverse subjectivity, transformed by his desire for death, going beyond any conceivable epic love of praise. The vivid, gut-wrenching violence is offset by the invasive textuality, the very showmanship itself. This episode is a brilliant example of McGowan's clash between fantasy and desire (see above, Introduction, p.9): fantasy comes with the hyperbolic over-the-top textuality of the reworking of epic; desire with the refusal of the ultimate epic pay-off, the beautiful death, the admirable or virtuous hero, the authorising audience (no gods, no Caesar). It is also a political statement, which fuses epic spectacle with political tyranny. If the *Aeneid* offers a subtle sense of unease that creeps unwanted into Roman triumphalism, Lucan shatters any attempt to integrate epic's validatory power.

The gladiatorial paradigm is a powerful one for exploring processes of identification and objectification. The heroes of the *Iliad* gain their power from the necessity of war; gladiators fight not to defend their city or their honour, but to entertain. Wild beast spectacles take this dehumanisation

---

[88] D'Alessandro Behr 2007: 52.
[89] For Leigh 1997: 221–33 this evokes and problematises the Roman tradition of worshipping the scarred body of the warrior who has fought for the state.
[90] On god–man–beast, see Hardie 1993: 69.

Fragmentation, fetishisation and the heroic body

further still. Readers must strive instead for exemplarity as a way of creating distance. The grotesqueness of Lucan's Scaeva episode (and its descendants in Flavian epic) presents a striking disturbance in the field of epic vision.

Fragmentation, fetishisation and the heroic body

Ultimately epic enshrines the body wounded, damaged and in pain. The gladiatorial context offers one way of reading these bodies. The subject matter of epic may be kings and great deeds, but an epic without battle scenes would be no real epic (both Ovid in the *Metamorphoses* and Nonnus in the *Dionysiaca* play with this generic expectation). Battle scenes focus on the bodies of men (and sometimes women) violently destroyed. This can make uncomfortable reading for twenty-first-century readers; it can also become a point of contact with film, especially mainstream horror and action movies.[91] Was it uncomfortable too for ancient readers? How does this representation of disintegrating bodies create different effects? How do battle scenes help to form the epic gaze?

I start with a series of deaths in the *Iliad*. Extreme violence in epic is often presented as decadent and non-Homeric, but the *Iliad* already shows many of the characteristics prevalent in later epic. Lucan may spend more lines per wound than Homer, but I am not convinced that violence in Roman epic is qualitatively different from that of earlier epic.[92] At *Il.* 13.540 we are in the middle of things: Zeus is putting into action his plan to honour Achilles by making sure the Greeks are defeated without him, and Poseidon is countering by attacking the Trojans. At 541–4, Aeneas spears Aphareus in the throat; he dies and segue to Antilochus slashing Thoon:

> Ἀντίλοχος δὲ Θόωνα μεταστρεφθέντα δοκεύσας
> οὔτασ᾽ ἐπαΐξας, ἀπὸ δὲ φλέβα πᾶσαν ἔκερσεν,
> ἥ τ᾽ ἀνὰ νῶτα θέουσα διαμπερὲς αὐχέν᾽ ἱκάνει·
> τὴν ἀπὸ πᾶσαν ἔκερσεν· ὁ δ᾽ ὕπτιος ἐν κονίῃσι
> κάππεσεν, ἄμφω χεῖρε φίλοις ἑτάροισι πετάσσας. (*Iliad* 13.545–9)

> Antilochus, watching Thoon as he turned about, dashed in on him
> and slashed at him, and shore away the entire vein
> which runs all the way up the back till it reaches the neck. This
> he shore away entire, so he sprawled in the dust backward,
> reaching out both hands to his beloved companions.

---

[91] See for instance Martin 2005b, Hömke 2010, Gervais forthcoming.
[92] Most 1992a collects statistics on numbers and types of wounds in epic in order to suggest that fascination with dismemberment is particularly Neronian and can be related to Neronian literary style, especially Seneca's abruptness.

The passage begins with a clear subject/object antithesis: we observe his victim along with Antilochus, and join in with the rush of his attack. This is a classic example of the assaultive gaze: a gaze that is part of the action, not just a precursor but part of his violent attack. The description of cutting away the artery has an alienating effect, especially with the repetition of πᾶσαν ἔκερσεν, a verb used of cutting hair (*Od.* 23.136). The detail of the location of the artery in 547 evokes medical discourse. Homeric scholarship has long been fascinated by Homer's apparently medical expertise.[93] The medical gaze creates distance and tends to objectify. It also foregrounds the narrator: the victim cannot see his own artery and the attacker would not think this specifically in the split second he brings down his sword. The victim and pathos are back in the foreground when Thoon stretches out his hands to his comrades.

Antilochus becomes the next object of the Trojan gaze as he tries to despoil his victim, but Poseidon protects him with a cloud. Adamas makes a failed attempt to kill him and attempts to retreat among his compatriots:

> Μηριόνης δ' ἀπιόντα μετασπόμενος βάλε δουρὶ
> αἰδοίων τε μεσηγὺ καὶ ὀμφαλοῦ, ἔνθα μάλιστα
> γίγνετ' Ἄρης ἀλεγεινὸς ὀϊζυροῖσι βροτοῖσιν.
> ἔνθα οἱ ἔγχος ἔπηξεν· ὁ δ' ἑσπόμενος περὶ δουρὶ
> ἤσπαιρ' ὡς ὅτε βοῦς, τόν τ' οὔρεσι βουκόλοι ἄνδρες
> ἰλλάσιν οὐκ ἐθέλοντα βίῃ δήσαντες ἄγουσιν·
> ὣς ὁ τυπεὶς ἤσπαιρε μίνυνθά περ, οὔ τι μάλα δήν,
> ὄφρα οἱ ἐκ χροὸς ἔγχος ἀνεσπάσατ' ἐγγύθεν ἐλθὼν
> ἥρως Μηριόνης· τὸν δὲ σκότος ὄσσε κάλυψε. (*Iliad* 13.567–75)

> but as he went back Meriones, dogging him, threw with the spear
> and struck between the navel and genitals where beyond all places
> death in battle comes painfully to pitiful mortals.
> There the spear stuck fast driven and he, writhing about it,
> gasped as an ox does when among the mountains the herdsmen
> have bound him strongly in twisted ropes and drag him unwilling.
> So he, stricken, gasped for a little while, but not long,
> until fighting Meriones came close and wrenched the spear out
> from his body, and a mist of darkness closed over both eyes.

We are following and watching with Adamas, until Meriones throws his spear, when we zoom in to the inner, most painful place of Adamas' body. Here we empathise with the victim, if not identify with him, writhing and gasping. His state is made even more vivid by the simile, which turns him into a beast (though it also offers an external perspective). The comment that he gasped for a little while, but not long, also suggests an external point

---

[93] Most 1992a: 397. See for instance Daremberg 1865, Friedrich 1956.

of view, perhaps that of Meriones, but the mist of darkness can only be seen from within. There is a double perspective throughout this scene, inside and outside, victor and victim: the reader of epic simultaneously takes both perspectives.

The end of Adamas is a break point and the narrative goes to and fro: from Helenus killing Deipyrus, to Menelaus keen for revenge, wounding Helenus, on whose behalf Peisander attempts to take revenge. Finally Menelaus and Peisander face each other with sword and axe:

> ἅμα δ' ἀλλήλων ἐφίκοντο.
> ἤτοι ὁ μὲν κόρυθος φάλον ἤλασεν ἱπποδασείης
> ἄκρον ὑπὸ λόφον αὐτόν, ὁ δὲ προσιόντα μέτωπον
> ῥινὸς ὕπερ πυμάτης· λάκε δ' ὀστέα, τὼ δέ οἱ ὄσσε
> πὰρ ποσὶν αἱματόεντα χαμαὶ πέσον ἐν κονίῃσιν,
> ἰδνώθη δὲ πεσών· ὁ δὲ λὰξ ἐν στήθεσι βαίνων
> τεύχεά τ' ἐξενάριξε καὶ εὐχόμενος ἔπος ηὔδα· (*Iliad* 13.613–19)

> They made their strokes at the same time
> and Peisandros chopped at the horn of the helmet crested with horse-hair
> at the very peak. Menelaus struck him as he came onward
> in the forehead over the base of the nose, and smashed the bones, so that
> both eyes dropped, bloody, and lay in the dust at his feet before him.
> He fell, curling, and Menelaus, setting his heel on
> his chest, stripped off his armour and spoke exulting over him:

The passage alternates between the perspectives of Menelaus and Peisander, characterised, as in lines 614, 615 and 618, by ὁ μὲν and ὁ δὲ, so that the sudden sickening disintegration of Peisander's face has an even greater impact. The smashing of the bones must be felt from Menelaus' point of view, and Peisander cannot see his own eyes falling in the dust. Menelaus is then attacked by Harpalion, who in turn becomes the object:

> Μηριόνης δ' ἀπιόντος ἵει χαλκήρε' ὀϊστόν,
> καί ῥ' ἔβαλε γλουτὸν κάτα δεξιόν· αὐτὰρ ὀϊστὸς
> ἀντικρὺ κατὰ κύστιν ὑπ' ὀστέον ἐξεπέρησεν.
> ἑζόμενος δὲ κατ' αὖθι φίλων ἐν χερσὶν ἑταίρων
> θυμὸν ἀποπνείων, ὥς τε σκώληξ ἐπὶ γαίῃ
> κεῖτο ταθείς· ἐκ δ' αἷμα μέλαν ῥέε, δεῦε δὲ γαῖαν. (*Iliad* 13.650–5)

> but as he went back Meriones let fly at him with a bronze-shod
> arrow, and hit him beside the right buttock, so that the arrow
> was driven on through under the bone to fix in the bladder.
> There, sitting among the arms of his beloved companions,
> he gasped out his life, then lay like a worm extended
> along the ground, and his dark blood drenched the ground in its running.

We start from the perspective of Harpalion, gesturing towards his soon to be bereaved father (643–5); he attacks Menelaus, fails and starts to retreat, looking about him. We do not see what he sees, however, and instead watch him with Meriones as he looks around. The focus on the fragment of his body and the arrow's progress inside it goes beyond the perspective of both victor and victim; here, too, the medical gaze of the narrator anaesthetises the reader, only to come back the more painfully to Harpalion's perspective, feeling the hands of his beloved companions and his gasping death. The simile, though, suggests the Greek perspective, as it denigrates and objectifies him.

These three deaths in just over a hundred lines of *Iliad* 13 show different epic tactics, sharpening and dulling the pain and pity of the reader/audience. Moments that evoke the humanity of the dead (or soon to be dead) balance those that strip it away. Each dying hero becomes the sum of his body parts: the artery in the back, the lower abdomen, the bones and the eyes, the buttock and the bladder. Mulvey argues that the fragmented body of the woman on display in film is a fetish that breaks the narrative frame: 'One part of the fragmented body destroys the renaissance space, the illusion of depth demanded by the narrative, it gives flatness, the quality of a cut-out or icon rather than verisimilitude to the screen.'[94] In Mulvey's argument, woman on display does not just give visual pleasure: she also threatens it; in Freudian terms, she reminds the boy of his first understanding that women do not have penises, and that he too might have his penis removed: woman therefore represents lack and the threat of castration. Mulvey posits two ways that classical cinema deals with this threat: sadistic voyeurism (voyeuristic looking, punishing and destroying the woman) and fetishistic scopophilia ('complete disavowal of castration by the substitution of a fetish object or turning the represented figure itself into a fetish').[95] Ellen Greene has used these ideas to read the display and fragmentation of the female body in love elegy.[96] Here in epic battle narratives we clearly see the fragmentation of bodies, changes of pace and perspective that might be read as analogous to the close-up in film, and the breaking or slowing down of narrative pace, especially by similes. But does this constitute the fetishisation of the heroic body? What difference does it make that the body concerned is male?

---

[94] Mulvey 1988: 62–3.   [95] Mulvey 1988: 64.
[96] Greene 1998: 82–4. 'The narrator's obsessively particularizing mode of describing Corinna's body in *Amores* 1.5 may thus constitute an analogue to the film close-up. . . . The *amator* thus dehumanizes his mistress not only through his dismemberment of her but also through a kind of decapitation that renders her lifeless. . . . As possessor of the gaze, the male speaker gathers up the scattered parts of Corinna's body; they are enfolded within his text and collected as *singula* for his remembering.'

One response might be to suggest that the failing, wounded or dying hero is feminised.[97] This is consistent with imagery of defloration discussed by Fowler.[98] It is also potentially banal: if 'feminine' is an epithet applied to the powerless and submissive half of a hierarchical relationship, of course the defeated warrior becomes feminine. It does not account for the mix of alienation and identification that we have seen in these scenes of violence, or elucidate the way that the epic gaze works here.

A useful strategy might be to move away from a Freudian analysis of fetishism. A theory of fetishism that goes beyond gender difference opens many possibilities: that of women fetishists, of male bodies as fetishes.[99] Fernbach discusses 'immortality fetishism', suggesting that the pre-Oedipal theory of fetishism as 'the disavowal of individuation' is linked to 'the disavowal of death and the fetishization of immortality', in which fetishists are 'disavowing the mortal flesh in order to construct a vision of transcendent technoimmortality and self-completion'.[100] When epic obsessively focuses on fragments of the heroic body, even though the body is in the process of dying, the poem subverts (for a moment) narrative time and places the fragmented body beyond death. This tactic allows the reader not to be paralysed by fear of death, to stand back from the imminence of their own death and watch that of others as aesthetic objects and with pleasure.

The play of alienation and identification in epic battle scenes, as in gladiatorial spectatorship, does seem to have a strong connection with ancient attitudes to mortality. We might then see ancient epic as working with a 'fetishism strategy'. Louise Kaplan in *Cultures of Fetishism* brings together many different aspects and interpretations of fetishism to perform a socio-cultural reading.[101] She posits five principles of fetishism, drawing on various thinkers from Freud and Marx to Derrida: first, that fetishism is a 'mental strategy or defense' which enables people to control the world by turning 'enigmatic energy and immaterial essence' into something tangible and real, and controllable (20). For our purposes, the heroic body can be read as the tangible and real representation of the energy and heroism of the warrior, the controllable, conceivable side of the pure energy represented by the fire imagery surrounding Achilles in the *Iliad*, for instance, and the

---

[97] See Lovatt 2005: 219–41 on gender, bodies and defeat in Statius. The bodies of dying heroes in Statius tend to be liquefied, to collapse and fragment, all signs of vanishing masculinity.
[98] See above. Fowler 1987.
[99] Fernbach 2002 argues (25) that 'fetishism can, in fact, have a subversive edge ... a culturally transgressive quality'. She focuses on 'decadent fetishism' which 'involves an identification with the Other and a fantasy of self-transformation that offers a critique, in a fashion, of hegemonic hierarchized binaries'. (27)
[100] Fernbach 2002: 31–2.   [101] Kaplan 2006.

unpredictable, dangerous power of the epic pantheon. Kaplan also argues that fetishism 'brings certain details into the foreground of experience in order to mask and disguise other features that are thus cast into the shadows and margins ... The powerful presence of the erotic surface disguises and covers over the absences that would otherwise remind us of something traumatic.' (21) The interplay between foreground and background in the treatment of epic battle scenes and the foregrounding of the injured and dying hero can be argued to occlude the sheer pointlessness of the destruction and the 'heroic code' itself. We become so caught up in our emotional and aesthetic responses to the bodies (and deaths) of heroes, that we can lose sight of the fundamental destructiveness of war, of the competition for status as a warrior and of the poetry which valorises and celebrates it. The eroticisation of the dying hero, then, is an important part of the process of maintaining the pleasure of the text.

Yet epic is characterised by its internal oppositions, its self-critical moves. Where a 'fetishism strategy', at least according to Kaplan, 'transforms ambiguity and uncertainty into something knowable and certain' (21), epic from the *Iliad* onwards embraces the complications in its own story world. The choice of Achilles, and the use of domestic imagery in similes, shows the way that opposition and uncertainty are set against the strong feeling of a community of values most clearly articulated by Hector. While the divine gaze can be argued to reinforce the values of epic, the marginal gaze of the women and non-combatants on the wall offer an oblique perspective. Finally, Kaplan's evocation of the Freudian death drive, as discussed by Derrida ('The death drive tints itself in erotic color. The impression of erogenous color draws a mask right on the skin', 23), makes me wonder to what extent the enjoyment of epic is tainted by the *amor mortis* of a character like Scaeva. Is enjoyment of epic much the same voyeuristic pleasure (and horror) as that which causes drivers to slow down as they pass the scene of a multiple pile-up, trying to catch a glimpse of death in action? Is it death itself which fascinates? Especially deaths eroticised and glamorised, hedged around with moral and political endorsements, millennia of canonisation? Or does the beautiful death allow us to disavow the disempowerment of the audience?

A further, complementary strategy is offered by masochism. Studlar re-evaluates gaze theory from the perspective of a nuanced reading of masochism: perhaps what we can see in epic battle narrative reflects a masochistic aesthetic? The way that epic cuts between victor and victim, offering the reader virtually simultaneous representations of inflicting and suffering violence, is similar to the play of masochistic fantasy, where 'there are dialectical shifts from inflicting to receiving pain'.[102] Separation and alienation, too, are a feature of masochistic desire.[103]

The masochistic aesthetic could well be at work in the epic gaze. It may not be the whole story, but pain and suffering are essential to epic. Clover has shown the way that horror films construct a victim–hero.[104] The androgynous female 'final girl' survives the slasher's murderous rampage and fights back to take control of the narrative. Simlarly, epic constructs a hero–victim. Every victor is always about to become a victim. The centrality of death to the construction of epic heroism is important here, but also the dynamics of narrative, where the hero is vulnerable after he has killed. In our hundred lines of *Iliad* 13, we see Antilochus threatened immediately after he kills Thoon, Helenus wounded after killing Deipyros, the structural equivalence of Peisandrus and Menelaus, who is attacked by Harpalion as he exults; Harpalion is killed in the act of attacking. Achilles figuratively dies in the shape of Patroclus; the poignancy of his killing of Hector rests on his own death made inevitable by his actions. He is, as Seaford has shown, a dead man walking: the ultimate hero is also ultimately a victim.[105] Aeneas is assimilated to Turnus, down to the echo in Turnus' moment of death (*soluuntur frigore membra*, *Aen.* 12.951) of Aeneas' first appearance in the poem, when he wishes that he had died in the *Iliad* (1.92).

These two approaches, fetishism and masochism, are not incompatible. Fetishism and sadomasochism have a close relationship.[106] Masochism emphasises the narrative movement between killer and victim, the shifting identification of readers and narrator, while fetishism focuses more on the close-up, the still, the image, the alienation and textuality.

In the light of the preceding discussion, I now examine some scenes from post-Homeric epic, starting with the *aristeia* of the Roman Scaevola at the battle of Cannae in Silius, *Punica* 9.370–400. Scaevola (and the other Romans) have accepted the inevitability of defeat and are focused on the beautiful death (367–9; *decori* ... *leti*, 377). Caralis is introduced as the grammatical object (*exultantem Caralim*, 380) even as he is focused on his own business, fixing spoils on a tree, and becomes the object of Scaevola's sword. The emphasis on the sword penetrating his body up to the hilt puts us in Scaevola's position. At 383–4 however we are thrust back into Caralis' consciousness as he bites the ground, thinking of it as enemy territory (or is

---

[102] Studlar 1988: 23.
[103] Studlar 1988: 27: 'Masochistic desire, by contrast, depends upon separation to guarantee a pain/pleasure structure.'
[104] Clover 1992: 21–64, and *passim*. [105] Seaford 1994: 144–90.
[106] Gebhard 1969, Freund, Seto and Kuban 1995, Hucker 2008: 255.

this the narrator's perspective intruding?), and is lost in the pains of death. Scaevola's next two kills, Gabar and Siccha, are presented bewildered in their subjectivity, but as moral exemplars: Gabar is surprised to see his hand cut off (the separation of *acer* from *dextram* suggests the time lag between happening and realisation), returning the focus from weapon to body part. Siccha's subjectivity comes to the fore as he rushes to help his friend (387–9) but in an unexpected twist is stopped in his tracks by treading on a sword with his naked foot. The emphasis on the vulnerable body part is made more telling by juxtaposing it with his continued subjectivity: he blames his own lack of boots (*damnauit*, 391). Now we cut from Scaevola's victims to his killer (Nealcas, 392–4) and follow the torn off rock hurled, as if by the torrent, into Scaevola's face. The rattle of teeth (with alliteration of *c* and *p*) is curiously intimate, but the face destroyed puts us further away with the narrator. His liquefaction is too haptic to see from a distance; the texture of blood and brains mixed with more solid matter bring us back in, and the scene reaches a climax with black gore flowing from crushed forehead and eyes. The beautiful death is thoroughly contaminated and pushed into the background, with the rush of internal fluids in the foreground, taking over the narrative. Then the narrative cuts away to a different pair, Marius and Caper, and a mini-biography, which takes off the immediate pressure of destruction. Here, as elsewhere, Flavian epic skirts the boundaries of the bearable, both by stylisation and hyperbole racking up the horror, and avoiding it.

This is not just Lucan and afterwards: as Virgil establishes Aeneas' credentials as an epic hero after he returns from his mission to Evander at *Aen.* 10.310–44 we can see a sequence of building violence. The first kill is Theron, slipped in as an ablative absolute (*occiso Therone*, 312), but developed with the sword penetrating armour and gold embroidered clothing, until finally it opens up his body (*huic gladio perque aerea suta, | per tunicam squalentem auro latus haurit apertum*, 'this man, with the sword, through the bronze joints, through the tunic bristling with gold, he drains the open side', 313–14). At 315–17 the focus moves from the dead warrior (Lichas) to the body of his dead mother; this move both displaces the violence, and links it with the violence of childbirth. The bodies of Cisseus and Gyas are brought into view with the adjectives *durum* (317) and *immanem* (318), before pulling back to talk about their connections with Hercules (319–22). At 322–3 sound and vision combine (*ecce* and *uoces*) and the line *intorquens iaculum clamanti sistit in ore* ('hurling a javelin he stopped it in his shouting mouth') vividly dramatises violence. Aeneas' action of hurling the javelin is set against the image of the static javelin, fixed and stopped even as the mouth continues shouting, the finite verb sitting in between the two parts of the participial clause. We then stand back a little from the destruction to focus on the eroticised body as Clytius is rescued by his brothers (324–32). The complexity of the mix between eros and battle is confusing here: Clytius is *infelix* and is pursuing his beloved, Cydon, whose body is described (*flauentem prima lanugine malas*, 'growing tawny on the cheeks with the first down', 324); the implication is that he in turn will be pursued, since he enters the narrative as grammatical object. We expect either or both to die the eroticised death of the beautiful boy; but in a sequence of deferral his seven brothers are interposed; they throw their weapons, but Venus turns them away. Finally Aeneas, with the help of Achates, sends his spear through shield, breastplate and chest of one brother (335–7, ending with the thumping *pectore rumpit*), and the same spear throw continues into the arm of another brother, and we focus on his now useless arm, hanging and dying at his side (*dexteraque ex umero neruis moribunda pependit*. 'the right arm about to die hung by its tendons from the shoulder', 341), in which the arm stands in for the whole person, and takes the foreground, while the dying man recedes into the background. Another spear is displaced from Aeneas onto Achates, also a graze (*perstrinxit*, 344; cf. *stringentia*, 331). A brief *aristeia* for Clausus, not involving Aeneas, is more bloody; he hits Dryops in the throat, who vomits out thick blood (*crassum uomit ore cruorem*, 349). But even here, Virgil pulls back from a continued build up of horror: at 350–2 he kills three men in three different ways, surely a perfect opportunity for a gladiatorial display. But we are not told what those three different ways were. The violence of the *Aeneid* is tempered by restraint and deferral; lists of names, mini-biographies and other tactics designed either to defer or to create pathos, intervene, so that Aeneas in particular is not associated with the most horrific bodily disintegration (for instance, Turnus' killing of Pandarus at 9.749–55). In contrast, the eroticisation of death is more prominent in Virgil, compared for instance with Lucan, suggesting that, while associations with defloration and rape can make it more horrific, it can offer a distractingly glamorous and attractive surface, employing a fetishism strategy to defer the direct confrontation of the reader with death and destruction.

We might look at any number of other passages: for instance, the sea battle at Massilia (*BC* 3.585–669), which has been well examined by others;[107] or the *aristeia* of Amphiaraus at *Theb.* 7.632–770, to see similar tactics at work and to gain a sense of the peculiarities of each epicist's reworking of the generic conventions of bodies on display. Ovid's battle of the Lapiths and centaurs at *Met.* 12.210–535 is particularly revealing for its

---

[107] Dinter 2006, Hömke 2010, cf. Bartsch 1997: 10–49 and Most 1992a.

combination of hyperbolic violence with black humour; we have touched on the parody of the eroticisation of death in the *liebestod* of the centaur lovers, Cyllarus and Hylonome; the complexities of gender are given a new slant in the transsexual Caeneus, with his impenetrable body.[108]

This section, then, has taken further the exploration of bodies on display in epic by looking at epic violence in conjunction with masochism and fetishism. Bodies are used both to make the narrative seem more real, to have an emotional impact on the reader, and also to dehumanise, to distance. By focusing on parts and details, the poet can skate on the surface of pain and displace the confrontation with death (or the confrontation with power) that underlies the epic genre. At other times, or in a different mode of reading, cuts between the perspective of victor and victim create a sadomasochistic narrative which takes pleasure precisely in pain and destruction.

Action heroines

The hero–victim is important for exploring the masochistic aesthetic of epic: but what difference does gender make in the end? In this section I want to see what changes when we approach the sexualised violence of epic from the perspective of female hero–victims, especially Camilla in the *Aeneid* and Penthesilea in the *Posthomerica*, and look at them as subjects and objects of the gaze. Heuzé discusses the deaths of Dido and Camilla in the *Aeneid* and suggests that the lingering descriptions of their agony are part of the fascination with the death of a beautiful woman, which as Poe famously said is 'the most poetical topic in the world'.[109] Clover quotes horror director Dario Argento: 'I like women, especially beautiful ones. If they have a good face and figure, I would much prefer to watch them being murdered than an ugly girl or man.'[110] Even when both men and women are being killed, the camera tends to linger on the gruesome murder of the beautiful, sexual woman.[111] This is not straightforwardly true of epic, *pace* Heuzé. We have seen above how the death of the beautiful young man is equally lingering, aesthetic and erotic. This reflects the differing sexualities of antiquity: the pederastic icon, a boy on the verge of manhood, first down powdering his cheeks, is just as much a sexual object as the beautiful woman. Epic does, however, complicate the rules of gender performance by including female heroes. Unlike Clover's 'final girl', the survivor who turns to slash the slasher, gender makes the epic heroine the exception rather

---

[108] Keith 1999 on gender; Lyne 1984 on wordplay. [109] Heuzé 1985, Poe 1970: 55.
[110] Clover 1992: 42 citing Schoell 1985: 54. [111] Clover 1992: 35.

than the rule in the genre; and almost inevitably, within the economy of epic, female heroes die.

Camilla has been read as both proto-feminist and the reinforcement of patriarchy, much like the action heroines analysed by Tasker.[112] Camilla strides onto the scene of the *Aeneid* in pole position at the end of the catalogue of Italians in book 7, where her extraordinary beauty and reputation for superhuman speed gather a fascinated audience:

> illam omnis tectis agrisque effusa iuuentus
> turbaque miratur matrum et prospectat euntem,
> attonitis inhians animis, ut regius ostro
> uelet honos leuis umeros, ut fibula crinem
> auro internectat, Lyciam ut gerat ipsa pharetram
> et pastoralem praefixa cuspide myrtum.   (*Aeneid* 7.812–17)
>
> At her all the young men, poured out from buildings and fields,
> and the crowd of mothers are gazing and looking eagerly as she goes,
> gasping with thunderstruck minds at the way royal honour
> veils her light shoulders with purple, the way the clasp interweaves
> her hair with gold, the way she herself bears a Lycian quiver
> and a shaft of pastoral myrtle with a spear point fixed at its head.

Their amazement surely registers not just awe at her beauty (or as one scholiast suggested, envy of her weapons) but surprise that she is there at all. Despite her treatment by Turnus as one of his most important allies, she never loses the shock value attached to simply being a woman warrior.[113] Her death in particular is sexualised and the gaze plays a crucial part. She is both Amazon (*Amazon*, 11.648; simile at 659–63) and huntress, devotee of Diana. The play of hunter and hunted is activated when she kills Ornytus the *uenator* ('hunter', 678). In her boast over his body, she not only accuses him of thinking he is still hunting, but reminds him that he has been killed by womanly arms (*muliebribus armis*, 687). With skilful riding, she turns the chase on Orsilochus *sequiturque sequentem* ('and pursues the pursuer', 695). At 721–3 she catches Ligus like a hawk catching a dove. Hunting is inevitably an erotic metaphor, and Camilla pursues it for all it is worth, distinctly a woman on top.

---

[112] Tasker 1993: 132–52. E.g. 'The phallic woman, that characters like Sarah Connor and Ripley represent, is seen as a male ruse, and a film like *Thelma and Louise* as "little more than a masculine revenge fantasy" whose "effect is perversely to reinforce the message that women cannot win".' Quoting Joan Smith in the *Guardian*, from a paper given by Jane Arthurs. On Camilla see Mitchell 1991, Boyd 1992, Keith 2000: 27–31, Reed 2007: 16–43.
[113] For instance, at *Aen.* 11.498–521.

However, she is also the object of the hostile gaze: first that of Jupiter at 725–6 who spurs on Tarchon to turn the tide of the battle, taking over in the process Camilla's role as bird of prey (751–6).[114] Then she is obsessively stalked by Arruns, who has been watching her for a while; his observation is described in detail at 759–67. He even tracks her footprints (*uestigia lustrat*, 763). Camilla opens herself to destruction by letting her instincts as a hunter (*uenatrix*, 780) and, Virgil suggests, as a woman (*femineo praedae et spoliorum ardebat amore*, 'she was burning with a feminine love of booty and spoils', 782) take over. She pursues the too luxuriously adorned Chloreus and, in her single-mindedness, does not see the *hasta* coming towards her:

> ergo ut missa manu sonitum dedit hasta per auras,
> conuertere animos acris oculosque tulere
> cuncti at reginam Volsci. nihil ipsa nec aurae
> nec sonitus memor aut uenientis ab aethere teli,
> hasta sub exsertam donec perlata papillam
> haesit uirgineumque alte bibit acta cruorem.   (*Aeneid* 11.799–804)

> So as the spear, sent by his hand, hissed through the breezes
> all the Volscians turned their keen minds and
> kept their eyes on the queen. She herself was not aware
> of breeze or sound or the weapon coming through the air,
> until the spear reached its mark under the uncovered breast
> and stuck, driven deeply in, and drank the virgin blood.

This moment has been read as both rape and defloration.[115] The sinister personification of the spear and the location of the wound in the breast combine to activate an image of perverse motherhood, feeding not a baby but a sexualised death.[116] Pathos and condemnation are mixed to mark her as a deeply ambivalent character: mothers bared their breasts to gain sympathy, Amazons bared their breasts as an index of otherness and transgression. In the same way we both look at her from outside (sympathetically, with the Volscians, 800–1) and share her lack of awareness, and, later, her pain (828–31). The further detailed description of the process of death (slipping, bright colour leaving her face, gasping, dropping the reins, liquefying, cold, drooping head and finally dropping her weapons) not only fits in with the patterns of feminisation in death shown in the *Thebaid*, but also echoes the eroticised deaths of young men such as Euryalus and Pallas.[117]

---

[114] She is also the object of the protective gazes of Diana and Opis (*Aen.* 11.532–96, 836–67).
[115] Heuzé 1985: 172, Fowler 1987: 195, Reed 2007: 19–20.
[116] Fowler 1987: 195, Heuzé 1985: 175–6. Reed 2007: 19: 'The spear is like a vampire baby.'
[117] Jamset 2004 in comparison with Parthenopaeus; Reed 2007 makes a strong case for reading these eroticised deaths together.

What difference, then, does gender make to the erotics of viewing epic? Less, perhaps, than we might expect: Camilla is marked as female, especially by the mention of her breast and the activation of images of motherhood. But this fits into the pattern of the eroticisation of death and the association between virginity and destruction.[118] Camilla is one more epic pin-up, marked out as a variation because she is a woman, but still essentially a hero–victim, killing and being killed like any other epic hero.[119] Reed analyses the gender ambiguities of Camilla's death in connection with those of Euryalus, and concludes that 'the phrase *femineo amore* implicitly feminizes – or at least extends her androgyny to – the men. . . . Her death, coming last in our series, does not so much reestablish her femaleness as confirm and retroactively exacerbate a tension of gender in all three scenes.' (24) In this way, perhaps, Virgil is a proto-feminist: the men are raped and violated in death just like the women.

Our sense of Virgil's complexity can be sharpened by comparison with Silius, whose Asbyte (*Pun.* 2.56–207) is a version of Camilla.[120] Asbyte is an African Amazon princess, who is descended from Iarbas, drives a chariot and shoots a bow. Despite the emphasis on her otherness, well traced by Augoustakis, including her virginity, she dies a relatively masculine death.[121] The episode abounds with doubles, fakes and false trails: like Camilla, Asbyte is both hunter and Amazon, and she is the object of the hostile gaze of Mopsus, also a hunter. We expect her to be shot down from afar, but instead the shot hits Harpe at her side, and she can reenact Camilla's death scene from the perspective of the observer, Acca, and avenge herself like Opis.[122] Even after the death of his two sons, Mopsus, rather than taking the expected vengeance, like Aegeus simply throws himself off the wall.[123] Theron is a failed imitator of Hercules, who takes on his beast-like tendencies, becoming a hunter who will ultimately be hunted.[124] Augoustakis points out that in the encounter between Theron and Asbyte, both 'absorb

---

[118] Mitchell 1991. Young men cut off before they can reproduce, like Camilla.
[119] The emphasis on her breast is a fragmentation of sorts, but she mostly seems to remain whole, and although she is objectified to a certain extent by the gazes of Jupiter and Arruns, she retains her subjectivity until the end, when her fleeing spirit groans like Turnus' spirit at the end of the poem.
[120] On Asbyte, see Uccellini 2006, Augoustakis 2010: 117–29, Keith 2010.
[121] She has chosen her horses herself, from amongst the *mapalia* (African huts); this affinity with animals and the Punic word links her to the African woman displayed on the shield, discussed in Chapter 5, at pp.191–7 above. On her virginity, see Augoustakis 2010: 118.
[122] The permeation of the boundary of the walls in this scene, and the gender reversal, which sees the woman fighting outside the walls, and the men shooting her from within, shows the radical reconfiguration of epic space in the Saguntum episode.
[123] A Daedalus who does not fly: the second son is named Icarus, and dies at 132–7.
[124] On Theron's name, Augoustakis 2010: 121–3; on his role as Hercules figure, see Tipping 2010: 19.

Camilla's traits and behaviour, in a game where the female has repudiated her femininity, while the male is lured by a woman's attire' (125). Both set their sights on each other: Theron at 164–8, at which point Asbyte eludes him in a provocatively oriental fashion, by swerving away. The horses sent suddenly off to the side evoke the oblique female gaze we have seen above (*obliquos detorquet equos*, 170). This allows her both to retreat and attack: when she returns *Therona uidet* ('she sees Theron', 189), turning him into the object of her gaze, and her battle-axe, as she in turn longs for his lion skin as a spoil. His mode of confronting her reasserts his masculinity: he terrifies the horses by rising up with his lion skin, so that he seems to become the lion of epic similes (but also evokes the monster which Apollo sends to derail Amphiaraus in *Thebaid* 6, and another round of fakery). Finally he breaks her skull and spatters the chariot with brains, then decapitates her to use the head as a trophy. The use of heads as trophies evokes the pairs of male heroes eulogised by Virgil and Statius (Nisus and Euryalus, *Aen.* 9.465–7; Hopleus and Dymas, *Theb.* 10.449–52). We thus see Silius move away from the eroticisation of death, and back to the fetishisation of the violent fragmentation of bodies. The substitution of the family romance of Mopsus and his sons for the literal romance of Achilles and Penthesilea shows Silius avoiding the erotic side of epic.

Quintus Smyrnaeus re-presents Camilla's archetypal model, Penthesilea: the Amazon queen, takes up the first book of the *Posthomerica*, a new version of the legend told in the cyclic *Aethiopica*. I have discussed her initial eroticisation above (p.267). She arrives in Troy, the mobile figure who will be fixed by Achilles' spear. Her arming scene marks her as a serious epic hero, not emphasising her femininity (the only body part described is her shins, *PH* 1.142), but her brilliance (144, 147–50 shield as moon); she shines like a thunderbolt (153–6). Her boast at 326–34 does not mention her own femininity, and much of the imagery that saturates her *aristeia* presents her as indistinguishable from a male hero (forest fire, 209–10; lioness pouncing on cattle, 315–18; wave, 320–3; storm, 355–6). The turning point comes at 376 when Ajax and Achilles enter the fray. Fate trumps the marvelling gaze of the Trojans at 353–4 with a malevolent and objectifying gaze (390–4). At that point Penthesilea is described as a heifer trampling plants, a clear link back to her own comrades, killed at 262–4 like heifers sacrificed by a strong man. She is not as different from the other Amazons as she first appeared. As a gale laying low the forest (488–93), her raw power is emphasised. But the comparison to a leopard (479–80) hints that she takes part in the amphitheatrical framework discussed above. Ajax and Achilles appropriate the masculine imagery of epic heroism: at 516–19 they are the

Aloides, threatening Olympus, explicitly a morale-boosting sight for the Greeks (515), lions (524–7) and a forest fire (536–7). She is still a leopard as she faces them (540–4).¹²⁵ Her moment of death comes quickly; a first spear-blow replicates Camilla's wound:

Αἶψα δ' ὑπὲρ μαζοῖο δαΐφρονα Πενθεσίλειαν
οὔτασε δεξιτεροῖο, μέλαν δέ οἱ ἔρρεεν αἷμα
ἐσσυμένως. Ἡ δ' εἴθαρ ὑπεκλάσθη μελέεσσιν,
ἐκ δ' ἔβαλεν χειρὸς πέλεκυν μέγαν· ἀμφὶ δέ οἱ νὺξ
ὀφθαλμοὺς ἤχλυσε καὶ ἐς φρένα δῦσαν ἀνῖαι.   (*Posthomerica* 1.594–8)

In a flash he pierced above the right breast the warrior
Penthesileia. Thereat a stream of dark red blood
gushed out, and the strength of her limbs was broken at once.
Her massive battle-ax dropped from her hand, and a mist of darkness
veiled her eyes, as agony penetrated her frame.

The subversive and sinister drinking spear is gone, however, and the blood is separated from her beauty. She is liquefied, but still treated as if a male warrior. She retains enough life to consider supplication, but Achilles finishes her off:

καί οἱ ἄφαρ συνέπειρεν ἀελλόποδος δέμας ἵππου.
Εὖτέ τις ἀμφ' ὀβελοῖσιν ὑπὲρ πυρὸς αἰθαλόεντος
σπλάγχνα διαμπείρῃσιν ἐπειγόμενος ποτὶ δόρπον,
ἢ ὥς τις στονόεντα βαλὼν ἐν ὄρεσσιν ἄκοντα
θηρητὴρ ἐλάφοιο μέσην διὰ νηδύα κέρσῃ
ἐσσυμένως, πταμένη δὲ διαμπερὲς ὄβριμος αἰχμὴ
πρέμνον ἐς ὑψικόμοιο πάγῃ δρυὸς ἠέ νυ πεύκης·   (*Posthomerica* 1.612–18)

In a flash he impaled her and her wind-swift horse together.
As a man might impale some innards on a spit
over a glowing fire, impatient for his meal;
or as a hunter might cast a deadly shaft in the mountains
with force enough for its weighty head to shear clean through
the belly of a stag and, flying on its course,
to be stuck in the trunk of a lofty oak or pine.

These images not only make her the prey pursued and slaughtered, like Camilla, huntress become hunted, but further objectify her, by turning her into meat to be cooked and eaten. The consumptive gaze, here conflated

---

¹²⁵ The leopard is an exotic animal, but not a traditional image of epic heroism. Penthesilea may also be figured as a female gladiator. The female gladiator is largely a figure of male fantasy, rather than historical reality. See Coleman 2000 on an inscription representing two female gladiators called Amazon and Achillia. For a more general survey, McCullough 2008.

with the assaultive gaze, prefigures Achilles' sexual desire to come. Hunting is a prelude to eating; chasing a prelude to rape. The long build-up of her *aristeia*, and the swiftness of Achilles' victory combine with this image of meat to reinforce the gender hierarchy. This could be read as polemically undoing Virgil's Camilla, or as exalting Achilles in the face of the triviality of Trojan hopes. Penthesilea retains her visual impact in death, like Patroclus. In fact she is explicitly compared to him at 708–21; when Achilles sees her and falls in love with her, his grief is as great as the grief he felt for his friend: the *Iliad* is subsumed already in the first book. At 621–3 she falls to the ground preserving her beauty, and she is compared to a tree, like the dead warriors above (625–9). As Achilles removes her helmet, her beauty makes the Argives marvel (657–62), assimilating her to other youthful heroes who remove their helmets and become erotic objects.[126] In a telling image, her dead body is compared to Artemis asleep (663–5). Achilles becomes a potential Actaeon, violating her with his gaze and presumably wishing for more, while Penthesilea is a version of Nausicaa (or Medea or Dido), both virginal and eroticised. She is not asleep, however, but dead. At 666–8, Aphrodite's personal handiwork reminds us of the male heroes beautified by goddesses above; but here the aim is not to protect Penthesilea, who is Hector as well as Patroclus, but to wound Achilles. She is a narrative appendage of Achilles, represented by Thersites as a second Briseis. This episode brings out a necrophilic impulse lurking in the epic beautiful death. Yet Thersites does not accuse Achilles of lusting after a dead body, but rather being woman-mad, like Paris, valuing love over war. Penthesilea does, however, gain a burial and monument (782–810), with the honour of being the first Hector figure in the long-drawn-out death-throes of Quintus' Troy.

We have seen, then, the complexity of Virgil's Camilla in contrast with Silius' avoidance of the erotic; Quintus takes both Penthesilea's masculinity and her objectification to the extreme. Each text offers a slightly different intersection between gender and the death of a beautiful hero.

Conclusions

The main aim of this chapter was to explore the representation of the hero in epic as object of the gaze, both erotic and otherwise. Using imagery associated with erotic poetry, and by transforming the hero into an art object, when he is in a situation of dependency, we can see mature epic heroes objectified, at least to a certain extent, even when active. Young men

---

[126] Parthenopaeus, Ascanius. See above, pp.3–5, 280–1 and Chapter 6, pp.234–6.

Conclusions

are much more vulnerable to the erotic gaze, to being fixed in their identity as boys, visually available (and, it is implied, sexually available).[127] The activation of a gladiatorial framework in the viewing of battle in Roman epic adds to the complexity of the epic gaze at male heroes. Gladiators are both *exempla*, to inspire identification, and abject, to be despised and destroyed. Further examination of the focus on bodies and body parts in violent battle scenes from different epics allowed us to see these complex spectatorial dynamics in action. Both fetishism and masochism offer productive ways of approaching epic violence. Epic can be viewed as using a fetishism strategy. The honour and glory, the nobility and admiration, enshrined in the heroic code, operate to distract readers (audiences) from the sheer, pointless destruction. The powerful erotic surface, the glamour, only serves as a defence mechanism in the face of the inevitability of death and the particular abjection of violent death. Ultimately, the beautiful death leaves the hero just that: dead.

Epic is aware of, glories in, the contradictions that this disavowal generates. Achilles in the *Odyssey* bemoaning his fate; Odysseus as he eludes and confuses with storytelling; the erotic escapades of Jason and his lack of self-sufficiency; the careful side-stepping of the *Aeneid* into eros and pathos; the parody and humour, the continual narrative divergence of Ovid; the absurdity, extremity and rhetoric of Lucan; the darkness of Statius; Silius' tangential manoeuvres; Quintus' reliance on and subversion of Homer and the playfulness of Nonnus: all in their different ways both perpetuate and undermine the disavowal at the heart of epic. Epic is not just a totalising genre; it is also a genre of fragmentation and disintegration.[128] The enormity of epic means that it is always potentially about to fall to pieces.

---

[127] Reed 2007: 23: 'In Euryalus and Pallas, the shadow of a feminine persona figuratively registers the loss of their adult male potential; the erotic light that falls on them in a sense confirms their now permanent status as boys, whose viewpoint was inconsequential and whose bodies were sexually possessable.'

[128] On totalising and epic, Hardie 1993: 1–3.

CHAPTER 8

The assaultive gaze

The book has moved from the active visual power of the gods through the compromised gaze of mortals and prophets to the object at the centre of the representation, the ecphrastic image. From this ultimate object we return via the compromised gaze of women and the heroic body as object, to the powerful, assaultive gaze of the epic hero. Heroes are not only the passive subject matter of the poem: they are agents in the story, and they have powerful gazes, on which they act. More than this, in fact: the literal power of the gaze is more extreme in ancient thought and literature than in modern film. This chapter will explore the eye as site of power in epic: the blazing eyes of the berserk warrior; other examples of the assaultive gaze, with or without fire; the evil eye exemplified by Medea: and battles of the gaze, in which conflict is carried out literally by looking.

This link between vision and violence has been explored by Carol Clover through analysis of the film *Peeping Tom*, in which a serial killer films and kills his victims simultaneously, stabbing them with a spike on his camera.[1] This thematises and literalises 'the assaultive gaze', viewing which leads directly to violence. In Mulvey's original formulation 'voyeurism ... has associations with sadism: ... Sadism demands a story, depends on making something happen, forcing a change in another person, a battle of will and strength, victory/defeat, all occurring in a linear time with a beginning and an end.'[2] The gaze which attacks, the battle of will and strength and the association with narrative drive are equally pertinent to ancient epic.

Ancient optical theory and folk ideas about vision combine to make ancient narrative even more receptive to these ideas.[3] Theories of sight, and ideas about it, tended to stress its haptic nature: whereas for us, light is insubstantial, in the ancient world seeing was akin to touching. Among the

---

[1] Clover 1992: 174–5. [2] Mulvey 1988: 64.
[3] See Introduction, pp.17–21 for more detail. For a summary of ancient theories of vision, see Bartsch 2006: 58–67; see also Simon 1988.

proliferation of different theories, intromission envisaged *simulacra* from objects entering the eyes and causing vision; extramission thought of the eye as emitting rays or a visual current. These two sides often worked together: the eye is both active and passive, emitter of fiery rays, and vulnerable window of the soul. While epic shows fewer traces of folk ideas about vision than other genres (for instance, the novel), the possibility of sight as literal weapon, affecting the world in a physical fashion, lurks beneath various tropes and recurring scenes. As we inhabit the space between figurative and literally assaultive gazes, poets play on the tension in different ways.

Blazing eyes

The essence of the assaultive gaze is looking at someone with the intention of committing violence against them; the step into folk models of vision occurs when we imagine that this look itself can carry out the violence. Epic heroes frequently have blazing (shining, glowing, fiery) eyes; this characteristic is often associated with an assaultive gaze.[4] This section examines the associations of blazing eyes in epic, and begins to explore the active visual power of the hero.

When Agamemnon hears Calchas' explanation of Apollo's anger at the beginning of the *Iliad*:

> μένεος δὲ μέγα φρένες ἀμφὶ μέλαιναι
> πίμπλαντ', ὄσσε δέ οἱ πυρὶ λαμπετόωντι ἐΐκτην·   (*Iliad* 1.103–4)

the heart within filled black to the brim with anger
from beneath, but his two eyes showed like fire in their blazing.

Later, when Pallas Athene restrains Achilles from killing Agamemnon, there are more blazing eyes:[5]

> θάμβησεν δ' Ἀχιλεύς, μετὰ δ' ἐτράπετ', αὐτίκα δ' ἔγνω
> Παλλάδ' Ἀθηναίην· δεινὼ δέ οἱ ὄσσε φάανθεν.   (*Iliad* 1.199–200)

---

[4] On 'glowing eyes' in archaic Greek *epos*, see Turkeltaub 2005. On the association between large eyes and divinity in Ptolemaic iconography, see Koenen 1993: 27 on Berenike II.

[5] Turkeltaub 2005 argues that two groups of phrases referring to glowing eyes can be distinguished by their syntax: the first group, as here, in which the eyes shine for a brief time, described by a verb; the second, in which an adjective describes the eyes as shining, in a way which implies it is a permanent characteristic. The first type of phrase is used only of mortals and animals, the second mainly of gods. On this basis, he suggests that it must be the eyes of Achilles which are glowing, and, as well as reflecting his anger and *menos*, that similarities of vocabulary and the close association with Athene bring out Achilles' semi-divine nature, at the moment when his movement towards death is assured. Other discussions of this line include: Nörenberg 1972 with further bibliography, Constantinidou 1994, Pulleyn 2000.

> Achilles in amazement turned about and straight away
> knew Pallas Athene; and the terrible eyes were shining.

Eyes in ancient epic do not just passively receive images: they can also emit light. This fire from the eyes is associated with power and violence. Blazing eyes are a sign of μένος, or life force, as well as intense emotion.[6] The might and anger of a hero (equally associated with gods and monsters) comes out through the eyes: not just the appearance of fire, but something more literal. In an instructive moment in Apollonius, Circe gives the reader an explanation for Medea's assaultive gaze:

> πᾶσα γὰρ Ἠελίου γενεὴ ἀρίδηλος ἰδέσθαι
> ἦεν, ἐπεὶ βλεφάρων ἀποτηλόθι μαρμαρυγῇσιν
> οἷόν τε χρυσέην ἀντώπιον ἵεσαν αἴγλην.
> (AR *Argonautica* 4.727–9)

> For the whole race of Helios were obvious to see
> since by the flashing of their eyes from afar
> they threw in front of them a golden radiance.

Medea is the granddaughter of the sun and she has in her gaze something of the sun's fire and power. We will come back to the figure of Medea in the final section of this chapter, in which we will examine battles of the gaze. Here Apollonius is playing with a pseudo-rational explanation of the magic powers of Medea and Circe, blurring the boundaries between divine and mortal, epic hero and female monster. Apollonius implies that it is acceptable for Medea to have an exceptional gaze, because of her descent from Helios. It is no coincidence that he makes this gesture of justification before pushing the idea of the assaultive gaze further than any other epic.

In this section I want to explore further the fiery eyes of heroes: what effects do these rays emitted from the eyes have on the world around them? Are they just a sign (of anger, mortality, or even divinity)? Or do they literally impact on the narrative? I focus first on the *Iliad*, the code model of epic, in which two figures stand out for their association with this phenomenon: at first, Hector is the hero whose eyes blaze most insistently; after the death of Patroclus, he seems to burn out, or at least to be eclipsed by the deadly brilliance of Achilles. Whitman has traced the progression of fire imagery in the *Iliad*, noting how images of

---

[6] Kirk 1985: 64, Turkeltaub 2005: 181: 'at their most basic level all glowing eyes index the vigor of the vital principle'.

sacrificial fire, blazing armour and forest fires permeate the poem.[7] He reads fire as 'a symbol of Greek heroism', with connections to both divinity and death.[8] In book 8 Hector is inspired by Zeus, and succeeds in making the Greeks retreat behind their fortification: the Greeks stand behind the ditch, praying in terror, while Hector prowls on the other side:

> Ἕκτωρ δ' ἀμφιπεριστρώφα καλλίτριχας ἵππους
> Γοργοῦς ὄμματ' ἔχων ἠδὲ βροτολοιγοῦ Ἄρηος.   (*Iliad* 8.348–9)
>
> while Hector wearing the stark eyes of a Gorgon or murderous
> Ares, wheeled about at the edge his bright-maned horses.

The μένος which Zeus has given him (335) is reflected in the power of his gaze, the equivalent of Athena's aegis, decorated with the Gorgon's paralysing stare, or a manifestation of Ares.[9] He is both godlike and monstrous. The Greeks are fixed, literally penned in and paralysed, while Hector moves and threatens with his gaze.[10] Hector momentarily transcends mortality, on the margins of heroism. We come back to Hector at the end of book 12, when he finally breaks through the Greek fortifications:

> ὁ δ' ἄρ' ἔσθορε φαίδιμος Ἕκτωρ
> νυκτὶ θοῇ ἀτάλαντος ὑπώπια· λάμπε δὲ χαλκῷ
> σμερδαλέῳ, τὸν ἕεστο περὶ χροΐ, δοιὰ δὲ χερσὶ
> δοῦρ' ἔχεν· οὔ κέν τίς μιν ἐρύκακεν ἀντιβολήσας
> νόσφι θεῶν, ὅτ' ἐσᾶλτο πύλας· πυρὶ δ' ὄσσε δεδήει.   (*Iliad* 12.462–6)
>
> Then glorious Hector burst in
> with dark face like sudden night, but he shone with the ghastly
> glitter of bronze that girded his skin, and carried two spears
> in his hands. No one could have stood up against him, and stopped him,
> except the gods, when he burst in the gates. And his eyes flashed fire.

Here the blazing eyes are the climax of this climactic moment. The description of Hector's face as dark like swift night evokes the anger of Apollo against Agamemnon (ὁ δ' ἤϊε νυκτὶ ἐοικώς, 'He came as night comes down', 1.47), and the blazing armour looks forward to his almost successful attempt to burn

---

[7] Whitman 1958: 128–53. '[L]urid flame seems to start from every portion of the poem.' (132) 'War itself is fire, yet here the real fire which threatens is the blaze of the tragic wrath.' (135) 'All the associations of the image – death, rage, heroic greatness, the fall of Troy, and divinity itself – now play against each other constantly.' (137–8) 'Throughout the arming scene, the single symbol of fire connotes directly all the anguish, semidivine glory, and utter isolation of Achilles. Less directly, it still flickers with intimations of rage, loss, and imminent death.' (139)

[8] Whitman 1958: 132.   [9] On the gorgon's stare, see below, pp.353–7.

[10] Though this image of Hector's power is straightaway undercut by making him the object of the malevolent gazes of Hera and Athene.

the ships. The fire in his eyes is an emblem of his destructive intent, and his triumphant life force.[11] The blazing eyes are juxtaposed with his penetration of the Greek camp; it is impossible to decide whether they respond to success or enact it. The last five lines of the book (467–71) show him communicating his urgency to the other Trojans and finish with the terrified response of the Greeks. After the Greek resurgence in books 13 and 14, Zeus makes Hector a terrifying figure again:

> μαίνετο δ' ὡς ὅτ' Ἄρης ἐγχέσπαλος ἢ ὀλοὸν πῦρ
> οὔρεσι μαίνηται, βαθέης ἐν τάρφεσιν ὕλης·
> ἀφλοισμὸς δὲ περὶ στόμα γίγνετο, τὼ δέ οἱ ὄσσε
> λαμπέσθην βλοσυρῇσιν ὑπ' ὀφρύσιν, ἀμφὶ δὲ πήληξ
> σμερδαλέον κροτάφοισι τινάσσετο μαρναμένοιο
> Ἕκτορος· *(Iliad* 15.605–10)

> He raged as when spear-shaking Ares or destructive fire
> rages among the mountains, in the dense places of the deep forest.
> A slaver came out around his mouth, under the lowering brows
> his eyes were blazing, the helm on his temples
> was shaken and thundered horribly to the fighting of Hector.

Here he is compared to the fire that he is bringing to the ships, and again to Ares, and his eyes blaze. Fire is an apt metaphor for the destructive gaze: combining light, life, destruction and terror (though he is also compared to water battering cliffs (618–21) as he attempts to penetrate the ranks of the Achaeans). With Zeus by his side, Hector is a predator bearing down on his prey, both god and beast, foaming at the mouth. The Achaeans 'flee in unearthly terror' (θεσπεσίως ἐφόβηθεν, 637). His assaultive gaze is also brought out in the simile (630–6) of a lion stalking cattle, springing and eating an ox. Hector kills Periphetes who has fallen over in the retreat:

> τῇ ὅ γ' ἐνὶ βλαφθεὶς πέσεν ὕπτιος, ἀμφὶ δὲ πήληξ
> σμερδαλέον κονάβησε περὶ κροτάφοισι πεσόντος.
> Ἕκτωρ δ' ὀξὺ νόησε, θέων δέ οἱ ἄγχι παρέστη,
> στήθεϊ δ' ἐν δόρυ πῆξε, φίλων δέ μιν ἐγγὺς ἑταίρων
> κτεῖν'· *(Iliad* 15.647–51)

> Stumbling on this, he went over on his back, and the helmet
> that circled his temples clashed horribly as he went down.
> Hector saw it sharply, and ran up and stood beside him,
> and stuck the spear into his chest, and killed him before the eyes
> of his dear friends.

---

[11] Though with connotations of divinity, the line seems to be designed to underline Hector's difference from the gods, the temporary quality of his assimilation to the divine (which will also be true of Achilles).

Hector's gaze is vertical, penetrative and powerful, leading directly to a killing, and making the watching Greeks powerless to help.[12] The blazing eyes of the hero, then, link him both to divinity and monstrosity, and his gaze seems to create paralysis in the audience, not just a sign of his threatening power, but aiding and transferred into physical action.[13] The boundary between watching and killing which is violated so vividly in *Peeping Tom* is equally violated by Zeus who is viewing at 599–600, driving Hector on at 603, and teamed (almost identified) with Hector as he kills at 637.

After the death of Patroclus, the fire imagery clusters around Achilles, and his eyes blaze, too. In particular, the arming scene in book 19 shows how essential the blazing eye is to the hero's ensemble. When he first sees his new shield (above, p.199), the Myrmidons are terrified, but Achilles not only gazes straight at it but takes on its fiery quality:

> αὐτὰρ Ἀχιλλεὺς
> ὡς εἶδ', ὥς μιν μᾶλλον ἔδυ χόλος, ἐν δέ οἱ ὄσσε
> δεινὸν ὑπὸ βλεφάρων ὡς εἰ σέλας ἐξεφάανθεν· (*Iliad* 19.15–17)

> Only Achilles looked, and as he looked the anger came harder upon him
> and the eyes glittered terribly under his lids, like a lightning flash.
> (after Lattimore)

The promise of power and divine favour given by the shield leads to an intensification of his anger and a reinforcement of his intention, to the extent that his blazing eyes have the destructive power of lightning. At the beginning of his arming, the whole Greek army shines, and Achilles in the middle is brightest of all:

> ἐν δὲ μέσοισι κορύσσετο δῖος Ἀχιλλεύς.
> τοῦ καὶ ὀδόντων μὲν καναχὴ πέλε, τὼ δέ οἱ ὄσσε
> λαμπέσθην ὡς εἴ τε πυρὸς σέλας, ἐν δέ οἱ ἦτορ
> δῦν' ἄχος ἄτλητον· (*Iliad* 19.364–7)

> And in the middle brilliant Achilles armed himself.
> And a clash went from the grinding of his teeth and his eyes
> glowed as if they were the stare of a fire, and the heart inside him
> was entered with sorrow beyond endurance. (after Lattimore)

Book 19 showcases the growing morale of the Greeks at the sight of Achilles, and the arming scene is full of light imagery. Fire and light work together in

---

[12] The phrase ὀξὺ νόησε is often used of gods: vision is implied by the modifier.
[13] Lonsdale 1989 argues that the verb παπταίνω conveys ideas of defensive looking about for means of escape and paralysing prey with a stare before killing them, when attacking. This second idea may also lie behind other words implying a terrifying gaze.

the Greek imagination. The brilliance of the sun and stars is light as well as fire, and so is the shining of Achilles' eyes (σέλας in the second example is explicitly the brilliance of fire, but can also apply to lightning). In particular, the shield is compared to the moon, leading into a simile of sailors gazing at a fire on the land (374–80); his helmet shines like a star (381); Automedon's whip shines (395) and Achilles in his armour shines like Hyperion (398). We have to wait until the next book and after the speech of Zeus to see the impact of the blazing Achilles on the Trojans, and by sight alone they are physically terrified:

> Τρῶας δὲ τρόμος αἰνὸς ὑπήλυθε γυῖα ἕκαστον,
> δειδιότας, ὅθ' ὁρῶντο ποδώκεα Πηλεΐωνα
> τεύχεσι λαμπόμενον, βροτολοιγῷ ἶσον Ἄρηϊ.   (*Iliad* 20.44–6)

> But the Trojans were taken every man in the knees with trembling
> and terror, as they looked on the swift-footed son of Peleus
> shining in all his armour, a man like the murderous war god.

Now Achilles is both godlike and monstrous, an Ares figure, an incarnation of the terror of war. The impact is a long-distance one, anticipating Hector's response to Achilles in book 22, when he cannot bear the sight and turns and flees:

> Ὣς ὅρμαινε μένων, ὁ δέ οἱ σχεδὸν ἦλθεν Ἀχιλλεὺς
> ἶσος Ἐνυαλίῳ, κορυθάϊκι πτολεμιστῇ,
> σείων Πηλιάδα μελίην κατὰ δεξιὸν ὦμον
> δεινήν· ἀμφὶ δὲ χαλκὸς ἐλάμπετο εἴκελος αὐγῇ
> ἢ πυρὸς αἰθομένου ἢ ἠελίου ἀνιόντος.
> Ἕκτορα δ', ὡς ἐνόησεν, ἕλε τρόμος· οὐδ' ἄρ' ἔτ' ἔτλη
> αὖθι μένειν, ὀπίσω δὲ πύλας λίπε, βῆ δὲ φοβηθείς.   (*Iliad* 22.131–7)

> So he pondered, waiting, but Achilles was closing upon him
> in the likeness of the lord of battles, the helm-shining warrior,
> and shaking from above his shoulder the dangerous Pelian
> ash spear, while the bronze that closed about him was shining
> like the flare of blazing fire or the sun in its rising.
> And the shivers took hold of Hector when he saw him, and he could no longer
> stand his ground there, but left the gates behind, and fled, frightened.

Achilles, armour shining like fire or the sun, is like a god of war again. Hector, too, is taken by trembling, and flees. Wars can be won on the field of vision. If your enemy turns and runs because of your visual impact, you have won. The hero's blazing persona has an important psychological impact on those watching. This is passive visual power, but blazing eyes represent a more active visual power, determination, anger, intention to do violence.¹⁴ The creation of terror in the enemy is a crucial part of the stare-down that is an epic confrontation. Achilles' blazing eyes, up close and intimate, embody his penetrative gaze. While epic avoids making this powerful and assaultive gaze too literal, there is significant emphasis on the visual impact of the hero, through imagery and by the focalisation of his approach through the watching enemy (or the viewers on the walls). The tendency to blur the boundary between active and passive vision, between being seen and using vision to affect those around, producing yourself as a spectacle designed to have an effect, makes the visual aspect of battle very important.

Turkeltaub suggests that glowing eyes are a permanent characteristic of gods in archaic *epos*, who in any case shine.¹⁵ In later epic, too, blazing eyes are an attribute of heroes, usually when they are at the height of heroic prowess, and almost transcending mortality in the glory of their *aristeia*.¹⁶ Gods themselves have eyes that shine, and eyes that blaze with anger.¹⁷ At the other end of the continuum are the monsters and animals: included by Turkeltaub with the mortal men, but some, like Hesiod's Typhon (*Theogony* 826–7) are closer to the gods than mortals.¹⁸ Perhaps the uncontrolled nature of the violence conveyed by blazing eyes makes it both more than, and less than, human. Similarly the intense and often destructive emotion of love can result in fiery eyes. Ariadne at Catullus 64.91–2 views Theseus with burning eyes; Odysseus is compared to a mountain lion with

---

¹⁴ In the cyclic *Iliou Persis*, a discussion of different types of doctors includes the blazing eyes of Ajax as a symptom of his madness and his violent intentions (fr. 2 West).

¹⁵ Turkeltaub 2005: 170; on shining gods Parisinou 2000: 6–7, Constantinidou 2010.

¹⁶ Some examples of heroes: *Il.* 13.435 (Alcathous); *Od.* 4.662 (Antinous); *Scutum* 72 (Cycnus); *Iliou Persis* fr. 4.8 (Ajax); AR *Arg.* 1.1296–7 (Telamon); *Aen.* 9.703 (Bitias), 9.731, 12.670 (Turnus); VF *Arg.* 4.235 (Amycus), 6.604–5 (Jason), 6.658 (Medea); *Pun.* 2.431 (Hamilcar), 5.275–6 (Appius), 8.560–1 (Scipio), 9.65 (Paulus), 11.219 (Hannibal), 327 (Perolla), 338–41 (Hannibal), 17.309 (Carthaginian), 398, 409 (Scipio); *PH* 1.59 (Penthesilea), 7.362, 464 (Neoptolemus). Other mortals: *Aen.* 2.405 (Cassandra dragged from the temple); *Met.* 8.466 (Althaea on the point of killing Meleager).

¹⁷ Turkeltaub 2005 distinguishes between the two by syntax, but the adjectival examples seem to be much more neutral in tone, with fewer intimations of anger and violence; I would not necessarily include all examples of 'shining' eyes as part of representation of the assaultive gaze. Some examples of gods (including personifications and furies): *Il.* 3.397 (Aphrodite); 13.3, 7, 14.236, 16.645 (Zeus); *Homeric Hymn to Hermes* 45 (Hermes compared to quick-thinking mortal); 278 (Hermes); *Scutum* 145 (Phobos); AR *Arg.* 4.54–65 (Diana); *Aen.* 2.111 (Palladion), 6.300 (Charon), 7.448–9 (Allecto); *Met.* 15.674 (Aesculapius); VF *Arg.* 2.184 (Venus); *Pun.* 9.444–5 (Pallas), 15.26–7 (Voluptas); *PH* 3.356 (Apollo); *Dion.* 18.261–2 (Kampe), 31.75 (Megaera).

¹⁸ Some animal references occur in similes describing heroes; others represent transformed men. Monster/animal: *Il.* 13.474 (Idomeneus as mountain boar); *Od.* 6.131–2 (Odysseus as mountain lion), 19.446 (boar about to scar Odysseus); *Scutum* 390 (Heracles as boar); AR *Arg.* 2.25–30 (Amycus as mountain lion), 2.405; *Aen.* 2.210 (snakes), 12.102 (Turnus as bull); *Met.* 1.239 (Lycaon as wolf, but emphasising continuity with his character before the change), 3.33 (dragon), 8.284, 356 (Calydonian boar), 11.368 (wolf); VF *Arg.* 4.235 (Amycus); *Theb.* 5.508 (dragon), 6.396 (chariot horses and riders), 11.532 (Polynices and Eteocles as boars); *PH* 7.488 (lions); *Dion* 4.379 (dragon).

blazing eyes when he meets Nausicaa (*Od.* 6.131–2);[19] Salmacis, the predatory nymph of Ovid *Metamorphoses* 4, watches Hermaphroditus with burning eyes (347); Medea's eyes blaze in both Apollonius and Valerius Flaccus. At AR *Arg.* 3.1008–25 there is great emphasis on the eyes of both Medea and Jason, but the flame of love from his eyes captures her flashing gaze:

> τοῖος ἀπὸ ξανθοῖο καρήατος Αἰσονίδαο
> στράπτεν ἔρως ἡδεῖαν †ἀπὸ φλόγα, τῆς δ' ἀμαρυγάς
> ὀφθαλμῶν ἥρπαζεν·   (AR *Argonautica* 3.1017–19)
>
> Such was the desire flashing its sweet flame
> from the blonde head of the son of Aeson, and it captured
> the bright sparkles of her eyes:

Despite the predatory sense of capturing, and the violence implied by the lightning strike of στράπτεν, the flame of love is present in the eyes of both. Later, at 4.16–17, when Medea is on the point of escaping from the palace, the fire in her eyes is much more akin to the heroic fire in the *Iliad*: ἐν δέ οἱ ὄσσε / πλῆτο πυρός ('her eyes filled with fire'), as she leaves the domestic realm, takes the initiative and grows towards the transgressive heroic stature which she will take later in the book. Valerius Flaccus plays different games: first, he makes Jason's blazing eyes a feature of his standard heroic *aristeia* at VF *Arg.* 6.604–5, along with a lion simile; then Medea too takes on this gaze as she watches, both transgressive heroine and lover:

> At regina uirum (neque enim deus amouet ignem)
> persequitur lustrans oculisque ardentibus haeret;
>   (VF *Argonautica* 6.657–8)
>
> But the queen (for the god does not banish the fire)
> pursues the hero with her gaze and clings with burning eyes;

Like an abandoned lover she follows and desires him; like a rival fighter she preys on him. Her evocation of Dido (*at regina*) emphasises destructiveness to come, as does the violent maddened gaze she directs at Venus in the following book (7.292–4). Finally at the moment of their meeting, they are compared to prey rather than predators, blind ghosts or funereal trees (7.400–5) and their mutual gaze at 7.511–12 is swallowed up by sick

---

[19] This is one of the most troubling instances: is his anger stimulated by the sight of someone who will help him achieve his aim (of vengeance against the suitors)? But it seems unlikely he should be thinking this, since he has not yet even seen the suitors. Does it imply that he might, like a violent and uncivilised beast, rape Nausicaa (or that he would like to)? Or that she thinks he might? De Jong 2001: 158 suggests that the image is focalised by the girls, in which case the blazing eyes indicate both his potential violence, his heroic status and his impressive life force.

shame. The tragic and destructive elements of the erotic gaze are much stronger in Valerius' version.

In this chapter, I have focused on the *Iliad* as master model, but it is clear that there are many differences between epics. The *Odyssey* has many fewer examples of this motif; Apollonius has only one straightforward hero with blazing eyes, but in a situation of conflict between comrades;[20] Ovid has mainly animals; Lucan none at all.[21] The *Aeneid* uses fire imagery and fiery eyes in the later books in a way that is closely related to the *Iliad*. At the height of his *aristeia*, when he is accidentally shut into the Trojan fortifications and compared to a tiger among the herd (730), Turnus gains a new influx of heroic energy:

> continuo noua lux oculis effulsit et arma
> horrendum sonuere; tremunt in uertice cristae
> sanguineae clipeoque micantia fulmina mittit: (*Aeneid* 9.731–3)

> Immediately a new light shone out from his eyes and his weapons
> clanged horrendously, his bloody crests tremble
> on his head and he sends out flashing thunderbolts from his shield.

The new light in his eyes, while not explicitly fiery, is matched by active rays of light sent out from the shield. When Aeneas arrives at *Aen.* 10.261–2, his shield famously burns as he stands on the prow of the ship (*stans celsa in puppi, clipeum cum deinde sinistra | extulit ardentem*). After the death of Pallas, Aeneas seeks Turnus with an obsessive burning gaze (*ardens*, 514), with the images of Pallas and Evander continually before his eyes (*Pallas, Euander, in ipsis | omnia sunt oculis*, 515–16); the flames foreshadow the pyre on which he will burn his captives (*flammas*, 520). In book 12, the fire imagery continues: Turnus, about to be compared to a bull, has eyes that flash flame:

> his agitur furiis, totoque ardentis ab ore
> scintillae absistunt, oculis micat acribus ignis: (*Aeneid* 12.101–2)

> Driven by these furies, burning sparks start
> from his whole face, he flashes with fire from his fierce eyes

at the start of the book; but just as Hector is eclipsed by Achilles, so Turnus' fire is put out by Aeneas. As Aeneas goes out to make the treaty, his shield is burning (*sidereo flagrans clipeo*, 167); but it is Turnus who blazes again when

---

[20] Telamon coming close to assaulting Tiphys over the abandoning of Heracles at 1.1296–7, drawing on Achilles' anger against Agamemnon.
[21] Although he does playfully distort the idea, showing typical self-conscious rejection of epic standards: at *BC* 1.154 Caesar is famously described as a lightning bolt, and is imagined attacking the eye with flame; at 6.179 Scaeva literalises the blazing eye by setting fire to his opponent's eyeballs. Perhaps Lucan's rejection of this idea should reinforce its connection with divinity.

the treaty is disrupted and he sees Aeneas retreating wounded (*subita spe feruidus ardet*, 325). Finally, when Aeneas cannot catch him, his gaze turns to the city (*aspicit*, 558) and he is lit up by an idea (*continuo pugnae accendit maioris imago*, 560); he is like a shepherd smoking out the bees (586–92). Turnus' metaphorical flames (669–71) become literal flames engulfing the city (672–3). The fire imagery around Aeneas at the end of the book is more subtle: he flashes his weapon at 887, and again at 919, like a thunderbolt (922), and he is lit up by the sight of the sword-belt (*accensus*, 946), until his heat (*feruidus*, 951) produces the coldness and darkness of death for Turnus (*frigore*, 951; *umbras*, 952 – last word of the poem). Virgil is careful to avoid attributing the full Homeric blazing eyes to Aeneas, skirting around them and gesturing towards them, but always pulling away short.

In comparison, Silius' *Punica* is striking because it focuses on heroic examples (though Hannibal and Hamilcar have a monstrous edge), and allows Scipio the same burning gaze as Hannibal. In the early books, Hannibal is associated with the assaultive gaze: his crest is compared to a destructive comet at *Pun.* 1.460–4; his spear and shield pour forth light and fire at 466–7, terrifying both armies.

A major cluster comes in book 11, in which the Capuans have decided to ally themselves with Hannibal, and take in the Carthaginians like Dido takes in the Trojans in *Aeneid* 1.[22] The one figure who resists is Decius, and when Hannibal hears of his resistance, his anger is extreme:[23]

> suffuderat ora
> sanguis, et a toruo surgebant lumine flammae.
> tum rictus spumans et anhelis faucibus acta
> uersabant penitus dirum suspiria murmur. (*Punica* 11.218–21)

> Blood flooded his face, and flames rose from his fierce eye;
> then he was foaming at the mouth and the sighs driven
> from his gasping throat expressed the dreadful murmur deep inside.

The intensity of his emotion and the power of his life force are clear; he also thinks of himself as approaching divinity (and Silius colludes in representing him in this way). In his speech the Alps are *uni calcata deo* ('trampled by one god', 218); later he sits on a high throne (*sublime sedentis*, 232) and thunders down at Decius (*tonat*, 233). When Decius has been taken away, all calms like Jupiter after a storm (*serenos | laetus circumfert oculos*, 'joyful he

---

[22] On this episode see Augoustakis 2010: 109–12.
[23] Similarly at Trasimene (*Pun.* 5.603–6) his anger boils over, but without the reference to flaming eyes, as he decides to kill Flaminius to avenge Sycchaeus.

looks around with peaceful eyes', 260–1). He is also an animal, however: at 243–6, Silius compares Hannibal to a lion springing down onto a herd of cattle recalling the description of Hector discussed above. This image vividly retains his vertical perspective. Decius then represents him as an almost cannibalistic figure: *sanguine laetum | humanum*, 'joyful in human blood', (250–1).[24] Later he is 'adorned like a god and received with divine honours' (*deum cultu et sacro dignatus honore*, 272) at the meal given by the Capuans, and one Capuan, elsewhere called Perolla, although unnamed in Silius, resolves to murder Hannibal. After his stirring speech to his father: *uibrabat ab ore | ignis atrox, animusque uiri iam bella gerebat* ('terrible fire was brandished by his face, and the spirit of the hero was already waging war', 327–8). Here the anger of Perolla reaches for heroic status, ironically threatening to make him a version of Hannibal, but his father steps in and tries to discourage him:

> tune illum, quem non acies, non moenia et urbes
> ferre ualent, cum frons propior lumenque corusco
> igne micat, tune illa uiri, quae uertice fundit,
> fulmina pertuleris? (*Punica* 11.337–40)

> Will you be able to bear him, whom neither columns, walls
> or cities are strong enough to stand up to, when his brow is closer and his eye
> flashes with glittering fire, will you bear those thunderbolts of that man,
> which he pours from his head?

Here is Hannibal made myth by his enemies, bristling with divine attributes – not just the blazing eye, but thunderbolts poured from his head.[25] Whether it is fear of Hannibal or his father's determination to kill himself in the process, Perolla decides not to go ahead with his assassination attempt. His brief brush with heroism is farcically unrealised: his gaze is unacted upon. Yet Hannibal, too, is ultimately toothless, despite his wrath on the divine scale: he never succeeds in punishing Decius, who is released by Ptolemy, and dies a peaceful death.

We have seen Hannibal's blazing anger; this heroic intensity is appropriated by the Romans in the final book of the poem.[26] Before the battle of Zama, Hannibal attempts to hold on to Carthaginian morale by evoking former victories, and attempts to make his soldiers visualise past successes: *cerno flagrantes oculos vultumque timendum* ('I see the blazing eyes and your face that must be feared,' 17.309). The blazing eyes for Hannibal are a mark of heroic success as much as heroic anger, and he is attempting to bring

---

[24] Tipping 2010: 64.   [25] Tipping 2010: 102–3 on the metapoetic apotheosis of Hannibal.
[26] Scipio's father kills a man with a Gorgon stare at the battle of Ticinus (*Pun.* 4.234).

success back for this battle too. However, Scipio is the figure who holds the fiery power when the two leaders confront each other at 17.391–8:

> ibat Agenoreus praefulgens ductor in ostro,
> excelsumque caput penna nutante leuabat
> crista rubens. saeuus magno de nomine terror
> praecedit, Latioque micat bene cognitus ensis.
> at contra ardenti radiabat Scipio cocco,
> terribilem ostentans clipeum, quo patris et una
> caelarat patrui spirantes proelia dira
> effigies; flammam ingentem frons alta uomebat.   (*Punica* 17.391–8)

> The Agenorean leader, shining out in purple, was coming
> and the red crest was lifting his high head
> with nodding plumes. Savage terror of his great name
> goes before him, and his sword, well known to Latium, flashes.
> But on the other side Scipio is radiant with burning scarlet,
> showing his terrifying shield, on which he had engraved
> dire images of father and uncle together breathing battle.
> His high forehead threw up huge flame.

The two are closely assimilated, but the fire predominates on Scipio's side; the evocation of thunderbolts is appropriate for Scipio as putative son of Jupiter.[27] Hannibal inspires terror because of his name. Though his sword flashes, he shines (*praefulgens*) rather than burning (*ardenti*). Scipio's flame recalls the arrival of Aeneas in *Aeneid* 10, and Virgil's description of Augustus at Actium on the shield of Aeneas (*Aen.* 8.680–1). Silius puts clear emphasis on their visual impact: at 399–400 he claims that the leaders hold all the hope of victory:

> sub tanta cunctis ui telorumque uirumque
> in ducibus stabat spes et uictoria solis.   (*Punica* 17.399–400)

> Even though there was such a great force of weapons and men
> all hope and victory was resting on the leaders alone.

Despite this emphasis on the leaders, here alone the blazing eyes are generalised to all the fighters:

> inde ensis propiorque acies et comminus ora
> admota ac dira flagrantia lumina flamma.   (*Punica* 17.408–9)

> Next the sword and closer battle-lines and faces moved
> to close quarters and eyes burning with terrible flames.

---

[27] Perhaps we are meant to remember the description of Scipio at *Pun.* 8.546–61, in which he has a burning but gentle gaze (*flagrabant lumina miti | aspectu, gratusque inerat uisentibus horror.* 'His eyes burn with a gentle appearance, and there was a welcome thrill for those looking at him.', 560–1)

When Hannibal is fighting, he is compared to lightning that seems to be everywhere (17.474–8):

> ut cum fulminibus permixta tonitrua mundum
> terrificant, summique labat domus alta parentis,
> omne hominum terris trepidat genus, ipsaque ob ora
> lux atrox micat, et praesens adstare uiritim
> creditur intento perculsis Iupiter igne. (*Punica* 17.474–8)

> As when thunder mixed thoroughly with lightning bolts
> terrifies the world, and the high home of the exalted parent slips,
> all races of men on earth are terrified, and the fierce light
> flashes in their faces themselves, and for each man
> present Jupiter seems to stand close, striking with aimed fire.

Hannibal's impact as a fighter is the same as the visual impact of lightning, and induces the same irrational terror and the same sense of standing out in the field of divine vision as being in the midst of a thunderstorm, where every lightning strike seems personal, and personally destructive. But Scipio remains on fire: *iamque ardore truci lustrans fortissima quaeque | nomina obit ferro* ('And now surveying with his fierce fire each of the bravest names he meets them with the sword', 491–2). His assaultive gaze functions clinically to wipe out the *nomina* of the Carthaginians, not just men on a battlefield, but epic warriors striving for *kleos*. The play on the one and the many is complicated by the fact that the two fiery warriors never meet. Instead, Roman fire is generalised to the whole army, as the destruction of the Carthaginians is compared to the destruction of a city by fire (17.504–8).[28] While Aeneas sets the city of Latinus on fire to smoke out Turnus, only the killing of Hannibal can satisfy the destructive desires of the Romans; even Carthage set on fire would not suffice (17.512–16). Scipio searches for Hannibal with a powerful and penetrative gaze:

> illum igitur lustrans circumfert lumina campo
> rimaturque ducem. iuuat in certamina summa
> ferre gradum, cuperetque uiro concurrere, tota
> spectante Ausonia. celsus clamore feroci
> prouocat increpitans hostem et noua proelia poscit. (*Punica* 17.517–21)

> Therefore scanning for him he sends his eyes around the plain
> and scrabbles to find the leader. It would please him to march towards
> a final showdown, and he desires to meet the hero in battle, with the whole

---

[28] The phrase *per culmina flammas* (506) echoes the figurative destruction of Carthage itself at *Aen.* 4.669–71.

of Ausonia watching. Rebuking with a fierce shout from on high
he calls the enemy forward and demands a new battle.

It could all start all over again: but this is the moment when Juno intervenes, to turn the poem back to *Aeneid* 10, to feminise and marginalise Hannibal and to deprive Scipio, the Italians, Silius and the readers, Roman and otherwise, of the climactic confrontation. Here Silius graphically dramatises the gap at the heart of epic, the Lacanian gaze which is the confrontation with the traumatic real, equally a generic confrontation between epic and history (historical knowledge forbids Silius from following his epic models, despite his reluctance). If the deaths of Hector and Turnus (and the flight of Pompey, the fratricide of Polynices and Eteocles) are ultimately unsatisfying, how much more satisfyingly unsatisfying is the refusal to stage the confrontation altogether?[29]

Blazing eyes are a sign of emotional power and intensity, the overflowing life force of the hero as he approaches divinity (and threatens monstrosity), which terrifies those watching. Fire from the eyes, with its potential to be read as a literal force, does more than symbolise the intent to cause violence, and the imminent breaking of boundaries. It leads to killing and destruction, is an image of violence, causes paralysis and terror among the objects of the fiery gaze, taking away their ability to act. Epic poets are careful not to take this too far; Virgil in particular associates the fiery gaze with Turnus, not Aeneas. There is a gap between what the fire from the eyes might achieve, and what it can actually be represented as doing. The fiery gaze is always ultimately a sign rather than a reality, a sign which, like all signs, is always unable fully to stand in for its referent. In the same way, the hero during his aristeia approaches but never achieves divinity.[30] Blazing eyes are not the only manifestation of the assaultive gaze in epic, though the image has proved a useful case study. In the following section I sketch other aspects of it, though time and space prevent me from exploring them fully.

Tropes of the assaultive gaze

The assaultive gaze is not a concept that can easily be pinned down to a single word, or even a single concept. Hence it is difficult to search comprehensively

---

[29] Achilles is not satisfied by killing Hector, but must extend his rage against the dead body; dissatisfaction with the end of the *Aeneid* is legendary; on closure and its limitations in Virgil and his successors see Hardie 1993: 1–18. 'The epic strives for totality and completion, yet is at the same time driven obsessively to repetition and reworking.' (1) See also Hardie 1997a. On Scipio and closure see Tipping 2010: 162–3; Scipio in general 138–92; see also Marks 2005.

[30] Most strikingly in the case of Statius' Tydeus, whose immortality Pallas Athene was bringing when she sees him cannibalistically savaging his enemy, in a battle of the gaze with the dead man's head.

for examples.³¹ Lonsdale examines the semantic range of the verb παπταίνω and suggests that it can suggest the use of the gaze to paralyse the prey before attacking. Examples in the Homeric epics suggest that this word is one possible marker of an assaultive gaze, though it is not always used in that way. Similarly, δέρκομαι, which means both 'to see clearly' (LSJ 1) and 'to shine' (2.11), according to LSJ 'seems properly to be used of sharp sight'.³² Δράκων is probably derived from it, and implies the powerful sight of dragons.³³ With various modifiers, such as δεινός, σμερδαλέος, ὀξύτατος, it is often found in contexts which suggest an assaultive gaze. In Latin, Esteves has argued that *torqueo*, which usually means 'twist' (*OLD* 1), but can also imply a more neutral 'turn (the eyes)' (6b), or a more dramatic 'torture' (3), or hurl (of weapons, 9) and cognates such as *detorqueo*, which has stronger implications of deception, can also be used of a hostile gaze, such as that of Jupiter at Carthage in *Aen.* 4.220.³⁴ Metaphors of throwing or casting the gaze (for instance, *Aen.* 12.483), images of shooting glances like arrows or spears,³⁵ glowering eyebrows: all these things can contribute to the representation of an assaultive gaze. While Jupiter's gaze is usually serene, the verb *torsit* at 4.220 suggests anger, the intention to destroy, and hostility, evoking Jupiter's thunderbolt, just questioned by Iarbas: Esteves points out that the other instances of *torqueo* used of gazing in Virgil are all associated with frenzy, and all but one also have burning eyes (the exception is Amata at 7.399. whose gaze is bloody).³⁶

Since the *Odyssey* often feels like an exception (or an alternative) to mainstream epic, I finish this section by examining the assaultive gaze of Odysseus. Odysseus is a master of words, but he is also a man of powerful vision, who uses disguise and concealment, and sees beneath the surface: he is famous for devising the wooden horse to bring about the fall of Troy by concealment; he defeats the Cyclops by depriving him of vision; his travels give him vision and knowledge of other worlds, including the underworld. The battle with the suitors in book 22 of the *Odyssey* is the climax of the

---

[31] Even for the more specific concept of glowing eyes, Turkeltaub 2005 makes use of the idea of traditional referentiality, to explain the lack of a single formula to convey it.

[32] This verb is often used of Apollonius' Argonauts as they pass various landmarks: for instance δερκόμενοι παράμειβον (at 2.660, 725); ἔδρακον (911). At 932–5 the Argo gliding over the sea is compared to a hawk high in a clear sky, with implications of predatory sight, as well as speed.

[33] On snakes and dragons see Ogden 2007: 65–104, especially fieriness at 81–2.   [34] Esteves 1982.

[35] Lonsdale 1989 points out that παπταίνω is only used of warriors attacking with arrows, javelins or spears, never swords (329), and is associated with many renowned archers in the Homeric poems: *Il.* 4.496–8 (Odysseus, even though here using a spear), 8.269 (Teucer), 13.649 (Meriones); *Od.* 11.607 (Heracles). He also argues that it represents a 'divinely radiant quality' and that 'sharp shining qualities associated with παπταίνω reinforce the quasi-divine vision intended by the verb'.

[36] Esteves 1982: 24: *Aen.* 7.448 (Allecto), 12.670 (Turnus); *Georgics* 3.433–4 (serpent), 4.451 (Proteus).

poem, and continually foregrounds Odysseus' assaultive gaze, Athene's divine gaze, the failure of the suitors' gaze, and the objectification of the suitors.[37]

Odysseus has already established his powerful vision, by shooting the arrow through the axes at the end of book 21. Book 22 begins with him taking a vertical perspective as he leaps up onto the threshold (2), and aims his bow at the suitors: the arrow which he shoots at Antinous (8) is given a sense of slow-motion as we move from Odysseus' perspective to that of Antinous, about to drink and not imagining that Odysseus could take on the challenge of facing so many men single-handedly (9–14). When it hits, however, we are vividly reminded of Achilles' predatory and almost erotic gaze at Hector:

τὸν δ' Ὀδυσεὺς κατὰ λαιμὸν ἐπισχόμενος βάλεν ἰῷ,
ἀντικρὺ δ' ἁπαλοῖο δι' αὐχένος ἤλυθ' ἀκωκή.   (*Odyssey* 22.15–16)

But Odysseus, aiming at this man, struck him in the throat with an arrow, and clean through the soft part of the neck the point was driven.

Line 16 is the same as *Il*. 22.327; the increased distance of the arrow perhaps adds to the impact of the gaze here, while a spear throw seems closer and more intimate. In both cases, the successful warrior needs to aim at the most vulnerable point of his enemy's body; the softness and tenderness of the penetrated body feminises it. The thick blood which spurts from Antinous' nostrils as he falls is a moment of abjection, and the focus on tables and feasting underlines the sudden violence. The suitors respond with panic, darting glances around like prey looking to escape (the other side of παπταίνω): πάντοσε παπταίνοντες (24), emphasising their failure of nerve and of the gaze.[38] Meanwhile Odysseus emphasises his intent to kill them all in vengeance, as he looks at them darkly: ὑπόδρα ἰδών (34, 60). Eurymachus, too, dies as Odysseus' arrow penetrates far inside his body (from breast, to liver: 81–3).

Odysseus' arrows always hit their mark (117–18), and his spear, along with those of his helpers, never fails (265–71, 280–5), while Athene turns aside the spear throws of the suitors (255–9, 272–80). Athene's appearance as Mentor (205–35) is typical of her Odyssean mode of action; but at 238–40 she makes herself look like a swallow and goes up into the rafters, to test Odysseus, turning him as well as the suitors into objects of her gaze. It is her aegis which inspires the final panic in the suitors (297–301), whose stampede is like that of cattle stung by an insect – not even dignified enough to be prey.

---

[37] De Jong 2001: 525 comments on the importance of 'embedded focalization' in the episode.
[38] Similarly at 43 they look around for a way to escape destruction: πάπτηνεν δὲ ἕκαστος ὅπῃ φύγοι αἰπὺν ὄλεθρον· And at 380, Medon and Phemios, who have been spared, are still acting like scared animals: πάντοσε παπταίνοντε, φόνον ποτιδεγμένω αἰεί. ('darting glances around everywhere, always expecting death'.)

In contrast Odysseus and his comrades are like vultures attacking smaller birds (302–6), with the emphasis on the birds descending from the mountains and plunging down on their prey. This pair of similes emphasises the suitors' failure of courage, understanding and vision, along with the contrasting sharp predatory sight of Odysseus. Finally, Odysseus' mastery, and the suitors' abjection, is complete: he looks around like a hunter assessing his haul, in the opposite sense of παπταίνω:

> Πάπτηνεν δ' Ὀδυσεὺς καθ' ἑὸν δόμον, εἴ τις ἔτ' ἀνδρῶν
> ζωὸς ὑποκλοπέοιτο, ἀλύσκων κῆρα μέλαιναν.   (*Odyssey* 22.381–2)
>
> Odysseus looked about his own house, to see if any man
> was still left alive, escaping the black destruction.

Medon had been hiding under a chair; only by escaping sight did he escape death, giving Telemachus time to vouch for him. The suitors are reduced to fish gasping to death on the shore (383–9), lying in piles so that not even the epic glory of a beautiful death remains.[39] Instead the imagery of food and banqueting is turned about on them, so that they become versions of the resources they have been squandering. The contrast between the two sides is much greater than in the *Iliad*; the power of the assaultive gaze is even more extreme; this is a massacre, even if they do gain a brief chance to arm themselves. The problematic interpenetration of domesticity and violence complicates the valorisation of epic violence: blood becomes dirt, and Eurykleia sees Odysseus as a lion covered in gore, a terrible thing to look at (δεινὸς δ' εἰς ὦπα ἰδέσθαι, 405). He has now become the monster which the girls imagine he might be in book 6 (130–4).[40]

This passage shows both sides of the verb παπταίνω, the association of the assaultive gaze with arrows and spears, and with the vertical gaze of the gods. It also brings together the attacking gaze of the hero with the objectification of his victims, whose unedifying deaths do not really glorify either themselves or him, and leave the house a site of pollution. On the other hand, this is the moment when Odysseus successfully claims the stature of an Iliadic hero, when the *Odyssey* becomes truly epic. The dehumanisation of his enemies brings out Odysseus' epic power, but also reveals the disturbance in the field of vision which characterises the epic gaze.

---

[39] De Jong 2001: 540 points out the unheroic comparison with fish, which expresses the suitors' helplessness and Odysseus' scorn for them.
[40] Possible hints also of the Cyclops at 9.294–5.

The evil eye

The hostile, attacking gaze of the hero, combined with terrifying visual power, is complicated by association with folk ideas about the evil eye. The evil eye looks askance, evoking feminine modes of viewing. The section explores the assaultive female gaze of Apollonius' Medea, and the way Ovid mixes the divine gaze with Invidia to look aslant once more at epic. The idea of the evil eye (a gaze that harms you simply by looking at you) is persistent and pervasive.[41] In both Greece and Rome it was a commonly held and frequently discussed belief.[42] Both Greek and Latin had words for the concept: βασκαίνω is to 'bewitch by the evil eye' (LSJ) and βασκανία represents both the malign influence of the evil eye, and the amulets used to ward it off. In Latin *fascinare* (from which the English 'fascinate' is derived) connotes not just 'To cast a spell on' (*OLD*) but specifically a visual spell; the *fascinum* (a phallus, often worn around the neck) is an apotropaic device for warding off the evil eye. Visual images showing the eye under attack from humans or from animals and weapons acted as 'graphic defences *against* the eye's potential to harm'.[43] The pervasiveness of the idea within Greek society can be seen in Pollux' discussion of metal-working vocabulary, which includes a discussion of objects hung in front of furnaces to avert envy, called βασκάνια.[44] The intellectual elite of the ancient world had an ambivalent attitude to the idea: for instance, in one of the most important ancient discussions, that of Plutarch at *Quaestiones convivales* 5.7 'On those who are said to cast an evil eye' (Περὶ τῶν καταβασκαίνειν λεγομένων), the passage begins by expressing scorn for the belief:

> οἱ μὲν ἄλλοι παντάπασιν ἐξεφλαύριζον τὸ πρᾶγμα καὶ κατεγέλων· ὁ δ' ἑστιῶν ἡμᾶς Μέστριος Φλῶρος ἔφη τὰ μὲν γιγνόμενα τῇ φήμῃ θαυμαστῶς βοηθεῖν
>
> While everyone else pronounced the matter completely silly and scoffed at it, Mestrius Florus, our host, declared that actual facts lend astonishing support to the common belief.

but goes on to propose various scientific explanations for it. Pliny (*HN* 7.16–18) brings the subject of the evil eye into an ethnographic description. Yet what he begins by attributing to African tribesmen, along with androgyny and miraculous immunity from snake-bites, he ends by bringing back to Cicero, his own society and generalising out into the whole of humanity:

---

[41] Spread throughout the modern world: Dundes 1981. For a general theory on the workings of the evil eye as a mechanism for healing disorder, see Siebers 1983.
[42] On the evil eye in Greek literature as a representation of the envy of the gods, see Rakoczy 1996. See also Dickie 1991, Bartsch 2006: 138–52.
[43] Bartsch 2006: 139. [44] Dickie 1993: 174.

> feminas quidem omnes ubique visuque nocere quae duplices pupillas habeant
> Cicero quoque apud nos auctor est. adeo naturae, cum ferarum morem vescendi
> humanis visceribus in homine genuisset, gignere etiam in toto corpore et in
> quorundam oculis quoque venena placuit, ne quid usquam mali esset quod in
> homine non esset.
>
> Also among ourselves Cicero states that the glance of all women who have
> double pupils is injurious everywhere. In fact when nature implanted in man the
> wild beasts' habit of devouring human flesh, she also thought fit to implant
> poisons in the whole of the body, and with some persons in the eyes as well, so
> that there should be no evil anywhere that was not present in man.

It is difficult to draw a clear dividing line between harmful magic in general and the specifically visual phenomenon of the evil eye, but the visual representations of the eye as threat and the commonness of apotropaic devices suggest that while it might not be intellectually respectable, many people in the ancient world were drawn in by the idea of a magically destructive gaze.

What is the significance of belief in the evil eye? Rakoczy in his important study of the topic, which ranges from Homer to early Christian writings, suggests that the evil eye is inextricably linked with the envy of the gods towards mortal success.[45] Yet, as we have seen, not only gods but humans also were believed to harm with their eyes. The idea of a malevolent divine gaze is significant in epic, as discussed above, but often the gods look down from above to help as much as to harm. Broader studies of the evil eye as cultural phenomenon, such as that by Tobin Siebers, situate it firmly in a social context: 'At the core of superstitious representations burns the violence of social relations.'[46] The evil eye superstition is interpreted by Siebers as a mechanism which works to contain the violence of social rivalry. Envy, accusation, demonisation: all are functions of relationships between humans. The idea of the evil eye represents an often-made but problematic connection between vision and causality: events that have no easily perceived cause activate the human need to create a narrative, to accuse and to blame. The line of sight is a connection which suggests causation.[47]

There is no doubt that in the ancient world the link between envy and vision is extremely important.[48] In Latin, Invidia is etymologically related to

---

[45] Rakoczy 1996.   [46] Siebers 1983: 144.
[47] Siebers 1983: 33–5 on 'accusatory logic': 'every cause has an effect and, more importantly, every effect has a cause'. This might be called 'over-coherent thinking'; Currie and Jureidini 2004 suggest that this is a function of the human brain's evolutionary requirement to make snap judgements about its surroundings.
[48] See Keith 1992: 127: 'the etymological play foregrounded by the collocation *Invidiam visaque oculos* vividly documents the action of "looking aslant," which is the primary meaning of *invidere*'.

videre. The figure of Invidia in Ovid's *Metamorphoses* is evil eye incarnate.[49] Invidia is a personification of envy, called upon by the goddess Minerva to punish Aglauros, the daughter of Cecrops. Aglauros had earlier usurped the powerful gaze by looking into the box which concealed Ericthonius. Now Mercury is in love with her sister and she is acting as *lena*. Minerva is jealous of her success:

> Vertit ad hanc torui dea bellica luminis orbem
> et tanto penitus traxit suspiria motu
> ut pariter pectus positamque in pectora forti
> aegida concuteret; subit hanc arcana profana
> detexisse manu, tum cum sine matre creatam
> Lemnicolae stirpem contra data foedera uidit,
> et gratamque deo fore iam gratamque sorori
> et ditem sumpto quod auara poposcerat auro.
>
> (*Metamorphoses* 2.752–9)

> The war-like goddess turned the sphere of her fierce eye to this girl
> and dragged sighs from deep within, with such great motion
> that she equally shook her breast and the aegis placed
> on her breast: it stole upon her that this was the girl who had uncovered
> mysteries with profane hand, then, when she saw the offspring
> of the Lemnian god, created without a mother, against the agreement made,
> and she would be thanked by the god now and by her sister
> and wealthy with the gold she had taken, which she had greedily demanded.

Salzman-Mitchell reads Aglauros as a woman who attempts to usurp the vertical gaze of male gods.[50] Yet it is not straightforwardly a narrative of punishment: Minerva is also infected by invidia, resentful of Aglauros' success.[51] Like the personification of Invidia, she both suffers from the symptoms and causes them in others. Her actively hostile gaze transforms into hostile action. Invidia is a process of contagion, a disease. When Minerva orders her to punish Aglauros, she uses this imagery: *infice tabe tua natarum Cecropis unam*, 'Infect with your gore one of the daughters of

---

[49] On this episode see Feeney 1991: 243–7, Keith 1992: 117–34, Hardie 2002b: 236–8, Salzman-Mitchell 2005: 38–42. A clear example of the evil eye belief in the *Metamorphoses* is the brief reference to the Telchines in Medea's journey in book 7: *Phoebeamque Rhodon et Ialysios Telchinas, | quorum oculos ipso uitiantes omnia uisu | Iuppiter exosus fraternis subdidit undis*. ('Phoebean Rhodes and the Ialysian Telchines, whose eyes destroyed everything with sight itself, Jupiter full of hate buried under his brother's waves.', *Met*. 7.365–7).
[50] Salzman-Mitchell 2005: 39: 'The vertical gaze is almost exclusive to male gods. While goddesses have the power to look down and control, mortal women are banned from this and their intrusive gazes are punished.'
[51] Feeney 1991: 247: 'When we look at Invidia, after all, we see her with Minerva's averted eyes.'

Cecrops' (2.784). Invidia's effect on the world around her is that of corruption and pollution:

> quacumque ingreditur florentia proterit arua
> exuritque herbas et summa cacumina carpit
> adflatuque suo populos urbesque domosque
> polluit　　　　　　　　　　　　　　　　(*Metamorphoses* 2.791–4)
>
> Wherever she goes, she lays low the flourishing fields
> burns off the grass and blasts the treetops
> and pollutes with her breath peoples cities and houses.

The moment of contact is not just inspiration but poisonous infection:

> inspiratque nocens uirus piceumque per ossa
> dissipat et medio spargit pulmone uenenum.
> 　　　　　　　　　　　　　　　　　　(*Metamorphoses* 2.800–1)
>
> She breathes harmful infection and spreads pitch
> through her bones and scatters poison in the middle of her lungs.

In ancient thought, vision is one way of passing on infection; visual contact can be as dangerous, infectious and polluting as touching or breathing. The abjection of Invidia, as personification and as process, is associated with averted (or at least indirect) vision. In the passage of Plutarch mentioned above, Mestrius Florus goes on to explain the evil eye by the contagiousness of vision: 'the glance, breath, or speech of people with the evil eye, upon contact with others, infects them as well'.[52] It is no coincidence that when Minerva first catches sight of Invidia, she averts her eyes (*uidet . . . Inuidiam uisaque oculos auertit*, 'When she had seen Invidia she turned her eyes away', 2.770). As Feeney says: 'The essence of Ovid's envy is that it comes from and feeds on "looking", but cannot bear to look, so that it must look askance, and therefore distorts everything in its field of vision.'[53] This is reflected in the anxiety and disgust which Invidia inspires: a Lacanian gaze in the Ovidian field of vision, which underlines the discomfort and bizarreness of representing gods, let alone personifications.

Mercury himself is not immune to this distortion: his gaze when he first sees Herse, flying over the fields after turning Battus into stone for betraying the hiding place of his rustled cattle, is the ultimate example of the rapacious

---

[52] καὶ γὰρ ἡ ὀσμὴ καὶ ἡ φωνὴ καὶ τὸ ῥεῦμα τῆς ἀναπνοῆς ἀποφοραί τινές εἰσι τῶν ζῴων καὶ μέρη κινοῦντα τὰς αἰσθήσεις, ὅταν ὑπ' αὐτῶν προσπεσόντων πάθωσι. (Plut. *Quaest. conv.* 680f); Bartsch 2006: 145. See also Calasiris in Heliodorus' *Aethiopica* 3.7. Bartsch 2006: 147: 'the evil eye involves the penetration of the body by a visually directed force from the exterior'.
[53] Feeney 1991: 247.

gaze of the male god.⁵⁴ However, the simile which immediately follows, describing Mercury as a kite hovering over a sacrifice, but frightened away by the priests, presents him in a rather less powerful and unsavoury light:⁵⁵

> inde reuertentes deus aspicit ales iterque
> non agit in rectum, sed in orbem curuat eundem.
> ut uolucris uisis rapidissima miluus extis,
> dum timet et densi circumstant sacra ministri,
> flectitur in gyrum nec longius audet abire
> spemque suam motis auidus circumuolat alis,
> sic super Actaeas agilis Cyllenius arces
> inclinat cursus et easdem circinat auras.   (*Metamorphoses* 2.714–21)

> The winged god caught sight of them returning and did not
> direct his way straight, but curved round, going in a circle.
> Just as a very swift and speedy kite who has seen entrails,
> while he fears and the packed crowd of priests stand around the rites,
> he is turned away in a circle but does not dare to go further away
> and hovers around his hope, greedy, with wings moving,
> so the active Cyllenian turns his flight above the Attic
> citadel and sketches a circle in the same breezes.

Mercury is clearly represented as predatory here, but the tentativeness of his circular movements is akin to the obliqueness of gaze which characterises Invidia later in the passage.⁵⁶ The extent to which his power is compromised by his need to seek mortal help (Battus' help in concealing his cattle rustling, Aglauros' help in accessing Herse) perhaps represents his status in the divine hierarchy.⁵⁷ There is a clear difference between the kite which preys on dead meat and is afraid to interrupt the sacrifice and, for instance, the eagle which snatches Ganymede from amongst his protectors (*Aen.* 5.250–7).⁵⁸ However, in both cases, his divine power is ultimately enforced by summary petrifaction: both Battus and Aglauros are turned to stone. Yet at the very end of the episode we return to the infection of the gaze: as Aglauros turns to stone, the hardness creeping through her veins is compared to an *immedicabile cancer* ('untreatable cancer', 825). Minerva's oblique exercise of her (female) divine power through the obliquely looking Invidia has caused Aglauros to provoke the divine punishment of Mercury,

---

⁵⁴ Salzman-Mitchell 2005: 39.
⁵⁵ The kite was regarded as a thief, appropriate for Mercury. See Hill 1985: 213. It is also part of a running theme of bird imagery in *Metamorphoses* 2: Keith 1992: 121–2.
⁵⁶ In particular *iterque non agit in rectum* of Mercury (714–15) is echoed by *nusquam recta acies* (776) of Invidia.
⁵⁷ See Keith 1992: 117–23 on the links with preceding episodes in book 2.
⁵⁸ On this ecphrasis see Putnam 1998b: 55–74, Hardie 2002a.

who has, as a result, lost the prize of his rapacious male gaze. The complexity of epic causation is on show in this episode, and it is causation that is at the heart of ideas about the evil eye.[59] Minerva surreptitiously watching Aglauros, Invidia infecting her, Aglauros watching Herse and Mercury, finally Mercury's abrupt glance as he touches her with his wand, all these lines of sight interact with each other and work together to cause her petrifaction, which is the *telos* of the story, but works to stop it in its tracks.

Ovid's Invidia episode also offers reflection on genre and the inevitable intertextual play, entwined with each other.[60] The passage is a miniature refraction of the *Aeneid* and a subversion of epic monumentality.[61] Herse becomes both Dido and Pallas when Mercury looks down on her:

> quanto splendidior quam cetera sidera fulget
> Lucifer et quanto quam Lucifer aurea Phoebe,
> tanto uirginibus praestantior omnibus Herse
> ibat eratque decus pompae comitumque suarum.
>
> *(Metamorphoses 2.722–5)*
>
> By as much as Lucifer shines more splendidly than the rest
> of the stars and by as much as golden Phoebe outshines Lucifer,
> by so much was Herse walking, more beautiful than all the
> maidens and she was the grace of the procession and of her own
> companions.

This image combines the description of Pallas as Lucifer at *Aen.* 8.589–91 with that of Dido as Diana at *Aen.* 1.498–502. Invidia takes on the dual Virgilian personas of Fama and Allecto.[62] When Aglauros is consumed by envy, her two potential plans of action might have turned her into a Dido or an Iarbas respectively:[63]

> saepe mori uoluit, ne quidquam tale uideret,
> saepe uelut crimen rigido narrare parenti; *(Metamorphoses 2.812–13)*

---

[59] Siebers 1983: 32: 'The line of sight serves as a thread connecting events that might otherwise remain disconnected. Events possessing a degree of coincidental causality become more firmly joined because of the patterns surrounding eyesight.'
[60] Keith 1992: 127–30 discusses the literary background of Invidia as a poetic threat.
[61] The Battus episode, too, draws on the *Aeneid*, specifically the Hercules and Cacus episode in *Aeneid* 8, in which Hercules too has stolen cattle; in this case, rather than informing on him, Cacus steals his stolen goods, and hides them with his own Hermetic craftiness (dragging them away backwards so their footprints point in the wrong direction). Hercules' monumental epic anger and immense violence contrast with Mercury's disguise and deceptiveness.
[62] On the connection with Fama, see Hardie 2002b: 236–8, Keith 1992: 130–1. Invidia as poet figure using *enargeia*: Tissol 1997: 67. On Allecto see Keith 1992: 130 n.34, Hill 1985: 214–15, Otis 1970: 120.
[63] Keith 1992: 131 suggests that these lines show Aglauros as another potential *index* (informer) in the sequence of punishments for tale-telling in book 2. Bömer 1969: 428 points out a verbal echo of *Aen.* 11.417: *ne quid tale uideret*.

> Often she wanted to die, so that she would not see anything else,
> often she wanted to tell the story as an accusation to her severe father.

The episode makes love the centre of epic; its presiding deity is the figure of Invidia herself, an inversion of epic's obsession with *kleos* or *gloria*. The inversion of love and war is emblematised by the simile comparing Mercury growing hot with love to a bullet growing hot in the air (2.726–9). Instead of love leading to war, or abandoned for glory, we have the perverse creation of a lasting monument to Aglauros' envy, not just the story in the *Metamorphoses* itself, but also the statue stained black by the venom in her heart. The struggle of the epic hero to obtain glory always leaves him open to the risk of inciting envy: the desire to be gazed at is a dangerous desire. This danger is one that carries over to the epic poet, who often identifies himself with his subject matter.

This episode both explores the workings of vision, power and monumentality in epic and encapsulates Ovid's own oblique vision of epic. The *Metamorphoses* is continually glancing sideways, and sometimes perhaps malevolently (and enviously?), at its epic predecessors. We will come back to Ovid's reflections on the epic gaze in the conclusion. In this episode we see contagion as an alternative mode of assault, deliberately anti-epic in its non-confrontational complexity. More direct, heroic and violent is the extraordinary gaze of Medea in subduing Talos in Apollonius *Argonautica* 4, to which we now turn.

Medea and Talos

In the Talos episode, the Argonauts are returning from Colchis and are desperate for food and water when they come to Crete, which is guarded by the bronze man Talos.[64] Talos looks down on the Argonauts from a cliff and pelts them with crags to stop them landing. Medea volunteers to take care of him. She prays to the *keres* and:

> θεμένη δὲ κακὸν νόον, ἐχθοδοποῖσιν
> ὄμμασι χαλκείοι Τάλω ἐμέγηρεν ὀπωπάς·
> λευγαλέον δ' ἐπὶ οἷ πρῖεν χόλον, ἐκ δ' ἀίδηλα
> δείκηλα προΐαλλεν, ἐπιζάφελον κοτέουσα.
>
> (AR *Argonautica*. 4.1669–72)

> Her mind set upon evil, she cast a spell upon bronze Talos' eyes with her malevolent glances; against him her teeth ground out bitter fury, and she sent out dark phantoms in the vehemence of her wrath.

---

[64] DeForest 1994: 136–8 reads Talos as the inspiration of the Colossus of Rhodes and a representation of Homeric epic, overcome by the Callimachean evil eye of Medea.

At this point the narrator exclaims his wonder (θάμβος) at the possibility of harming someone from afar, Talos knocks his vulnerable ankle vein on a sharp rock, his ichor flows out like melting lead, and he topples off the clifftop, like a pine tree blown over by the wind. This is Medea's epic *aristeia*, a battle of the gazes in which she takes on Talos' semi-divine vertical gaze (not just his height but his position on top of the cliff give him a powerful advantage over the Argonauts, vulnerable in their ship) and sends out δείκηλα from her eyes to attack him through his vulnerable eyes. Line 1670 represents this battle graphically with Medea's eyes at the beginning and those of Talos at the end. In fact, it is Talos' vertical gaze that proves his downfall: both his height (the distance between eyes and feet makes it easier for him to accidentally damage his ankle) and his position (once he has fallen he cannot possibly recover) contribute to his defeat. The position of power is also a position of vulnerability.

This episode is the only significant example in ancient epic of the evil eye as literal weapon. The language of the description is pseudo-scientific. δείκηλα is used of the phantoms/impressions which emanate from objects and enter the eyes in the intromissive model of vision.[65] The narrator's apostrophe of Zeus, however, uses the language of paradoxography to draw attention to the discourse of tall stories, superstition and disbelief.[66] The narrator's implied disbelief in his own story is continued in the simile, where the double causation of the pine tree's fall (both woodcutters and winds) reflects the problem of determining what caused Talos' fall: was it really Medea's enchantment or was it just a coincidence?

It is no coincidence that Medea is a woman and a barbarian: a figure of the other for the Greek readership of Apollonius (though also a character with whom we are encouraged to sympathise and identify). This intrusion of female, Colchian witchcraft goes beyond traditional θάμβος at the epic hero and the narrator is drawn into the act of denying his own epic authority. The opposite side of the coin is Medea's usurpation of epic heroism:

ὡς ὅγε χάλκειός περ ἐών ὑπόειξε δαμῆναι
Μηδείης βρίμῃ πολυφαρμάκου.   (AR *Argonautica* 4.1676–7)

So that man, bronze though he was, yielded to destruction through
the grim power of Medea, mistress of drugs.

---

[65] For instance Democritus B 123 DK. On Democritus' theory of vision see Dickie 1990: 272–5, 284–6, Taylor 1999: 37–117, esp. 39, 71–8, Powers 2002.
[66] Dickie 1990: 275–8, Powers 2002: 97.

Medea acquires a heroic-sounding epithet, while χάλκειός περ ἐών and δαμῆναι strongly evoke the language of the *Iliad*.[67] χόλον . . . ἐπιζάφελον κοτέουσα equally sets Medea in the Iliadic tradition of heroic anger.[68] The image of a warrior toppling like a tree is also a Homeric topos.[69] The confrontation between Medea and Talos is in effect the last battle of the poem, followed only by the Anaphe episode and Euphemus and the clod, before the Argonauts reach the end of their journey. If Apollonius is creatively misreading epic, is this episode the climax of his anti-Homeric polemic? One theme of book 4 is Medea's gathering power, while Jason gradually fades.[70] The Talos episode is an important part of the closural moves of the *Argonautica*.[71] The vertical gaze of the gods and the authority of the narrator are invested in creating an epic *telos* (goal/end). But what is the *telos* of the *Argonautica*? What sort of epic ending does Apollonius allow? True, they had a goal in the fleece, and another goal of returning home (in the Odyssean fashion). The final verse of the *Argonautica* (4.1781) looks back to *Od.* 23.238, a line from the simile describing Penelope's reaction to Odysseus' return as like that of shipwrecked men reaching land. This literalisation of the Homeric image removes the female response to male achievement, and compromises the sense of epic closure. The Argonauts' return to their beginnings lacks the emotional punch of Odysseus' *nostos*, and the lack of closural gestures makes us aware of all the story still to come. Medea's conquest of Talos underlines the complexities of the poem as a whole: the powerful gaze of the hero is distorted and deflected in favour of Medea's heroic yet disturbing powers which go beyond the propriety of the normal assaultive gaze of epic.[72]

---

[67] προΐαλλεν is also Homeric (*Il.* 8.365 of Zeus sending Athene down to help Heracles; at 11.3 of Zeus sending down Eris). Does this figure Medea's enchantments as a form of divine intervention?

[68] For instance, see *Il.* 9.525 (Phoenix' speech to Achilles) describing epic anger; κοτέουσα is also Homeric.

[69] See above, pp.278–80. Effe 2001: 157: 'Viewed against the background of a Homeric battle-scene, where a falling warrior is constantly compared with a falling tree . . . the specific quality of this "heroic deed" leaps to the eye: it is a woman's deed, accomplished with the aid of magical power. Thus the falling tree simile – the last in Apollonius' epic – marks as clearly the distance from the Homeric drawing of epic battle-scenes as the one which places the Argonauts' first warlike action in an unfamiliar light.' On tree similes in Homer, see Moulton 1977: 23, 56–7; *Il.* 4.482–7 (Simoeisius as poplar), 13.178–80 (Imbrius as ash), 13.389–91 (Asius as oak, poplar or pine), 17.53–8 (Euphorbus as olive tree).

[70] Dyck 1989.   [71] See Hunter 1993: 119–29.

[72] Medea is always the epic other (always threatening to be tragic), as well as ethnically other, female, divine and monstrous. ἐχθοδοποῖσιν is a tragic word (Soph. *Phil.* 1136; *Ajax* 932). For bibliography on the figure of Medea see Clauss and Johnston 1997 and Bartel and Simon 2010.

Battles of the gaze and the end of the *Aeneid*

Medea's use of the evil eye to win a battle, literalising the hero's fiery eyes, is unique: an aberration in epic. Other battles of the gaze, however, while less explicit in their use of active visual power, are much more clearly central to the epic world. We have already looked briefly at Achilles and Hector in the *Iliad*. The end of the *Aeneid* has recently been read as a visual encounter, with almost opposite conclusions.[73] For Smith the final encounter between Aeneas and Turnus stages a contest between vision and rhetoric which maps onto the transition from Republican rhetoric to the power of images in the age of Augustus. Thus Turnus' failure of vision is set against Aeneas' visual power, and the rhetoric of his final plea for mercy is an obfuscation that threatens to turn Aeneas away from his *telos*. But the visual impact of the sword-belt of Pallas (and Smith works hard here to draw a positive message from the destructive Danaids) trumps Turnus' attempt at verbal persuasion: vision causes action. Hardie reads the passage through the filter of Lucretius, unpacking dense layers of Lucretian allusion, re-entering the territory of Cosmos and Imperium but arriving at a very different place.[74] For Hardie, the revelation of the sword-belt contrasts with the philsophical revelation achieved by Lucretian intellect and underpinning Lucretian emotional detachment. Instead it inspires overwhelming passion and a re-identification with the divine gaze which Lucretius associates with malevolent *Religio*. Can our explorations of the hostile gaze in epic, and the epic gaze in general, generate a different perspective?[75]

The battle between Epicurus and Religio in Lucretius 1, examined above pp.99–101, is a battle of the gaze, nearly as extreme as that of Medea and Talos:

> humana ante oculos foede cum vita iaceret
> in terris oppressa gravi sub religione,
> quae caput a caeli regionibus ostendebat
> horribili super aspectu mortalibus instans,
> primum Graius homo mortalis tollere contra
> est oculos ausus primusque obsistere contra
>
> (*De rerum natura* 1.62–7)

> When human life was lying foully before our eyes
> trodden into the earth by oppressive superstition,

---

[73] Smith 2005: 167–75, Hardie 2009b.   [74] Hardie 2009b.
[75] This passage has generated a vast amount of scholarly literature, including: Johnson 1976: 114–34, Lyne 1987: 85–99, Galinsky 1988, Stahl 1990, Putnam 1995a, Harrison 1998, Thomas 1998. See now Tarrant 2012 for a judicious overview.

> who showed her head from the regions of the sky
> attacking mortals from above with her bristling gaze,
> a Greek man dared to be the first to raise
> mortal eyes against her and the first to stand against her

Lucretius equates the divine gaze of traditional religion, looking down from above and acting against mortals, with the gaze of the successful epic hero, looking down on the corpse of the enemy he has just killed.[76] In contrast, Epicurus displays the steadfast gaze equated with the act of standing fast in battle (*obsistere contra*). We, the readers of Lucretius, are invited to embody the epic hero by trampling on the corpse of Religio. This programmatic passage reads epic as a genre defined by battles of the gaze: not just the climactic duel of two heroes, but the competing gazes of mortals and immortals.

The link between this passage of Lucretius and the end of Virgil's *Aeneid* is that image of the successful epic hero standing over the soon-to-be-dead body of his arch-enemy, a hero who becomes a version of Jupiter when his spear becomes a thunderbolt (*Aen.* 12.922–3).[77] But is there a battle of the gazes in the duel sequence at the end of the *Aeneid*? Do Turnus and Aeneas face each other down like Hector and Achilles, Epicurus and *Religio*? I start with the moment at 12.665–71 when Turnus finally realises that he must face Aeneas:[78]

> obstipuit uaria confusus imagine rerum
> Turnus et obtutu tacito stetit: aestuat ingens
> uno in corde pudor mixtoque insania luctu
> et furiis agitatus amor et conscia uirtus.
> ut primum discussae umbrae et lux reddita menti,
> ardentis oculorum orbis ad moenia torsit
> turbidus eque rotis magnam respexit ad urbem.   (*Aeneid* 12.665–71)

> Turnus was struck dumb and thrown into confusion by the changed
> image of everything and he stood with silent gaze; huge shame seethes,
> mixed with mad grief in one heart,
> and love stirred up by rage and his self-conscious courage.
> As soon as the shadows had been shaken off and the light had
> returned to his mind,

---

[76] Brown 1984: 57: 'The military and the monster-slaying imagery implies a challenge to traditional epic values.'
[77] '[H]e, like the Dira, is Jupiter's agent'; Tarrant 2012: 329.
[78] Turnus' silent gaze and stupefaction here are another factor linking him to the Aeneas of book 1 who gazes at the images of the destruction of Troy with the same paralysis: *dum stupet obtutuque haeret defixus in uno* ('While he gazes and is held fixed in one gaze', 1.495). On the assimilation of Turnus and Aeneas see Thomas 1998.

he twisted the burning spheres of his eyes to the walls
deeply disturbed he looked back from his chariot at the great city.

Here the shadows of divine veiling are burnt off by the image of Aeneas destroying the Latin city.[79] He is fixated by the realisation of his own failure, and his blazing eyes represent not just his heroic *menos* in the tradition of Hector, but also his inner mania. They also reflect (quite literally) the burning of the city in the next few lines (672–5). The use of the verb *torsit* echoes the moment where Jupiter turns his gaze to Carthage in response to Iarbas' prayer at 4.220, emphasising Turnus' destructive passion and, perhaps, his self-torture.

He turns to face Aeneas and the duel finally begins, but Virgil keeps frustrating the reader's desire for their gazes to lock in the ultimate battle for epic mastery. First the focalisation shifts to the Trojan and Rutulian audience (704–7) and then Latinus himself (707–9). Even within the bull simile (715–22) the emphasis is on the watching herd. Then the text moves to sound (*fragor*, 724) and the perspective of Jupiter as incarnation of fate (725–7). Turnus' attempt at a deciding blow focuses in on the sword which shatters and from then on Turnus cannot hold onto the heroic gaze. After the reconciliation of Juno, the arrival of the *Dira* and the departure of Juturna, we finally return to the ultimate epic scenario: a warrior and his weapon (*telum coruscat*, 'the spear flashes', 887). Now Turnus seems incapable of looking Aeneas in the eye: he shakes his head (*caput quassans*, 894) and looks around for a tactic (*circumspicit*, 896). The famous dream simile, which likens the effect of the *Dira* on Turnus to the paralysis experienced by dreamers, also enshrines the failure of Turnus' gaze: *oculos ubi languida pressit | nocte quies* ('when torpid rest presses down the eyes at night'). Most striking is his reaction when he realises his rock has not hit the mark:

sic Turno, quacumque uiam uirtute petiuit,
successum dea dira negat. tum pectore sensus
uertuntur uarii: Rutulos aspectat et urbem
cunctaturque metu letumque instare tremescit,
nec quo se eripiat, nec qua ui tendat in hostem,
nec currus usquam uidet aurigamue sororem.   (*Aeneid* 12.913–18)

So for Turnus, wherever he sought a way with his courage,
the divine terror denied success. Then various feelings
are turned over in his heart; he catches sight of the Rutulians and the city

---

[79] See above, Chapter 3, pp.88–94.

and delays in fear and trembles at death pressing against him,
and he does not see any way to snatch himself away, nor any force
to attack his enemy, nor anywhere his chariot or his charioteer sister.

Here we have a vivid image of Turnus failing to look at Aeneas, desperately seeking with his eyes any way to escape from the situation, despite the *uirtus* which the text still emphasises. This whole failed attempt has had so little impact on Aeneas that Virgil returns to him with the same words as at 887; he is still standing flashing his spear, but now it is inevitable and fatal: *cunctanti telum Aeneas fatale coruscat* ('Aeneas flashes the fatal weapon at the delaying man', 919). Aeneas can and does own the heroic gaze: *sortitus fortunam oculis* ('obtaining his fortune with his eyes', 920).

Only after the conclusive thigh wound brings Turnus down and Aeneas stands over his vanquished enemy do their eyes finally meet: *ille humilis supplex oculos dextramque precantem | protendens* ('he, humble, suppliant, stretches out his eyes and his praying right hand', 930–1).[80] Virgil defers the key visual confrontation until after the battle: it is the moment of supplication which is the climactic moment of tension in the poem. Not will he win, but will he kill?[81] This ultimately complicates and goes beyond the economy of epic violence, asking the genre for something more, and inevitably not getting it. For Aeneas is now the one who cannot hold the gaze of his enemy: *uoluens oculos* ('his eyes rolling', 939), he takes on the hesitation which has characterised Turnus (*cunctanti* 919 is picked up by *cunctantem* 940).[82] It is his immersion in the emotionality of visual

---

[80] There are problems here with both text and interpretation. See Tarrant 2012: 330–1, who judges on word order and probability, especially in a situation of supplication that it is Turnus who is cast low (no longer *superbus*), not his eyes. There are parallels for the use of *protendere* with vision (Catullus 64.127, *Aen.* 2.405). Two readings of the line are possible, one in which Turnus is looking at the ground and one in which he is looking at Aeneas. If we take *humilis* as accusative plural agreeing with *oculos* we might translate as Putnam 1995a: 180 does: 'a suppliant, with eyes humbled and stretching forth his right hand in prayer', in which case the *humilis oculos* might suggest that he is looking at the ground, unable to meet Aeneas' gaze. Literature on supplication does not focus on the gaze of the supplicant: Naiden 2006: 44–62 describes the gestures associated with Greek and Roman supplication but does not comment on the gaze. But supplication is about making a persuasive connection with the person supplicated, so it seems most likely that supplicants would look at those they were supplicating. Two of Naiden's visual examples – fig. 2.3 (48) and fig. 2.9 (61) – do represent a meeting of the gaze. Looking up from below might also count as 'humble eyes'. The balance of probability seems to be on the side of Turnus looking at Aeneas in this line. If he is not, however, that would in many ways be equally interesting, showing the complete failure of Turnus' gaze.
[81] In many ways following on from the end of the *Iliad*: not will he win, but will he ultimately respect convention and return Hector's body? So arguably epic has always problematised its own central tropes. See Hardie 1993: 1–18 on closure and the lack of it.
[82] See Putnam 1995b. Tarrant 2012: 334 reads the rolling eyes as 'a sign of fierce concentration'.

response (*oculis postquam saeui monimenta doloris | exuuiasque hausit*, 'after he has drained with his eyes the reminder and spoils of a savage grief', 945–6) which confirms his epic limitations.[83] By deferring the battle of the gazes and making supplication the moment of truth, Virgil complicates epic values. When read in the highly political context of the *Aeneid*, this complication undermines the valorisation of epic as an authoritative political genre.[84]

Statius, Pietas and another final confrontation

I end this chapter by exploring Statius' multi-layered response to the end of the *Aeneid* and coming back to the problems associated with the divine gaze in epic.[85] In *Thebaid* 11 the central confrontation of the whole poem is played out: all the delaying strategies which have attempted to steer the narrative away from its fratricidal nadir have evaporated. The gods have officially declined even to view this unspeakable and unwatchable epic moment.[86] But the personification of Pietas is still watching:

> iamdudum terris coetuque offensa deorum
> auersa caeli Pietas in parte sedebat,
> non habitu quo nota prius, non ore sereno,
> sed uittis exuta comam, fraternaque bella,
> ceu soror infelix pugnantum aut anxia mater,
> deflebat, saeuumque Iouem Parcasque nocentes
> uociferans, seseque polis et luce relicta
> descensuram Erebo et Stygios iam malle penates.   (*Thebaid* 11.457–64)

Now for a long time Pietas had been sitting in an opposing part
of the heavens, offended by the earth and the gathering of the gods,
not in the dress by which she was formerly known, nor with an untroubled face,
as if she was the tragic sister of the fighters or the anxious mother
she was weeping and railing against savage Jupiter and the guilty
Fates, saying that she was about to abandon the poles and the light
and go down to Erebus and that now she would prefer a Stygian home.

---

[83] *Haurio* here suggests the immoderacy of his gaze: Dido in *Aeneid* 1, for instance, *longumque bibebat amore* ('drinks a long draught of love', 1.749) as she gazes at (and listens to) Aeneas; also 4.661–2, which uses *haurio*.

[84] Tarrant 2012: 334 points out that epic supplications are rarely if ever successful, but nevertheless finds the evocation of sacrifice problematic (339–40), and ends his commentary, like Virgil's text, with shadows: compared to other books that end with a death 'in sound and wording this last instance is also the darkest' (341).

[85] See Franchet d'Espèrey 1999: 261–77, Bernstein 2004: 81, Ganiban 2007: 170–5, McNelis 2007: 150–1, (on Pietas granting the episode exemplary status).

[86] See above, pp.71–7.

Here Pietas alienates herself deliberately from the gods,[87] whom Jupiter has ordered not to watch, and perversely claims that she is about to embrace the underworld instead, continuing Statius' overturning of Virgilian cosmic order.[88] Her mode of watching is not divine (in particular, unlike Jupiter, she does not have the characteristically serene and detached perspective of the gods) but female.[89] She is explicitly associated with women watching from the walls, and Antigone and Jocasta in particular, both of whom have attempted to stop the fight, and one of whom will be driven to suicide by the outcome.[90]

However, like Antigone and like other divine watchers, she is unable to resist the temptation to leave the walls and join the battle: *speculataque tempus | auxilio, 'temptemus,' ait, 'licet irrita coner,' | desiluitque polo* ('having spied a time for help, "let us try," she said, "though I try in vain," and jumped down from the pole', 11.470–2). Bernstein suggests that a series of male father figures, from Jupiter to Oedipus to Adrastus, take part in a 'pattern of disavowed authority' in *Thebaid* 11.[91] Pietas, despite looking down, has an oblique perspective, as a female god and a spy (*speculata*).[92] Her attempt at divine disguise (*arma etiam simulata gerens cultusque uiriles*, 'even bearing faked weapons and masculine dress', 477) is called 'deceit' (*fraudes*, 483) by Tisiphone. Pietas even suggests to the combatants that the gods are trying to stop the duel out of pity: *nonne palam est ultro miserescere diuos? | tela cadunt, cunctantur equi, Fors ipsa repugnat*. ('Surely it is obvious that the gods take pity of their own accord? Weapons fall, horses delay, Chance herself fights back', 480–1) when her earlier rant implies that she blames the gods as well as the humans for the atrocity (462, 465–6), acting more like a Juno and less like the embodiment of Roman decency.[93] Yet

---

[87] Ganiban 2007: 172–3 buys Tisiphone's criticisms and joins in: 'how can her self-righteous rebukes of the gods be taken at all seriously?'

[88] See Hardie 1993: 57–87 on the ordering of the epic universe and its disordering.

[89] McNelis 2007: 151 suggests that she 'marks the entire divine system as destructive'.

[90] Jocasta commits suicide by falling on the sword of Laius at *Theb.* 11.634–47. Ganiban 2007: 174: 'The implied resemblance to Jocasta and Antigone, also powerless characters, suggests that Pietas belongs with the defeated in Statius' world.'

[91] Bernstein 2004: 68.

[92] Juno is described similarly at VF *Arg.* 7.575 (*speculatrix*) and *Pun.* 17.341 (*speculantem*); Boreas at VF *Arg.* 1.575, who will fail to stop the Argonauts with a storm, like Virgil's Juno, is also described as *speculatus*.

[93] A comparison with the appearance of the personification of Virtus is revealing: where Pietas changes her feminine aspect for masculine dress, Virtus uses deceit (*fraude, Theb.* 10.640) to shed her masculine *horror* and *vigor* (641). The ambivalence of Statius' Virtus is signalled by the way both Pietas and Tisiphone share an intertextual resonance with her. The swiftness of Virtus' possession of Menoeceus is compared to a lightning bolt striking a cyprus (10.674–7) while Tisiphone notices Pietas *caelestique ocior igne* ('more swiftly than heavenly fire', 11.483). See Fantham 1997 on Virtus in

despite her partial assimilation to Tisiphone and her claim of imminent defection to the underworld, her battle of the gaze with Tisiphone establishes them as polar opposites:

> sic urguet, et ultro
> uitantem aspectus etiam pudibundaque longe
> ora reducentem premit stridentibus hydris
> intentatque faces; deiectam in lumina pallam
> diua trahit magnoque fugit questura Tonanti. (*Thebaid* 11.492–6)
>
> Thus she upbraids her, and attacks
> her with hissing snakes and straining firebrands as she voluntarily
> avoids her gaze itself and withdraws her shame-bound
> face far away; the goddess drags her downcast cloak
> over her eyes and flees to complain to the great Thunderer.

Pietas here loses both the battle of words and the battle of gazes without even attempting to stand her ground. She replays Juturna's flight from the *Dira* at *Aen.* 12.885–6, likewise covering her head but not even mustering the will for an oppositional voice, combined with an echo of the Homeric Aphrodite who is put to flight by Diomedes in *Iliad* 5, and rushes off to complain to Zeus.[94] The powerlessness of feminine attempts to hold the family together is compared with the masculine drive to obtain power and glory.[95] Yet the vengeful energy of the underworld is also gendered feminine. This battle of the gaze deflects our attention from the duelling heroes onto two semi-divine personifications, both female. In both cases the battles are not satisfyingly epic: Pietas gives in too easily, Polynices is caught by deception. The visual confrontation and the power of the gaze are both called into question, along with the authority of the divine gaze and the epic genre itself.

What happens when we apply our visual reading to the actual duel between Polynices and Eteocles?[96] How is Statius reworking Virgil and what does the whole episode tell us about the epic gaze and Statius' reading

---

Lucan and Statius, Ganiban 2007: 174 on the link between Virtus and Pietas: 'Pietas' resemblance to Virtus is thus strange, and made even more so by the deeply ambivalent presentation of Virtus, who herself resembles a Fury.'

[94] At *Il.* 5.347–51 Diomedes tells Aphrodite to keep away from battles which are the works of men, echoed by Tisiphone at 11.484–5; Aphrodite then complains to Dione and Ares; but Diomedes' comments are ultimately validated by Zeus at 5.426–30.

[95] Ganiban 2007: 173 suggests that the connection between Pietas and Juturna can 'only stain the moral purity of Statius' goddess', reading Juturna as a new Allecto and ignoring her liminal status as divine rape victim and goddess; he concludes effectively that '[p]erhaps nowhere in the poem do we see so clearly the subversion of the ideal of *pietas* from the Augustan *Aeneid* than here in book 11' (175).

[96] On the duel itself, see Bernstein 2004 and Ganiban 2007: 176–206; both readings focus on spectacle and internal audiences.

of it? The hallmark of this duel is failed vision on both sides. First Polynices wounds Eteocles' horse and both think the blood is Eteocles' own (*Theb.* 11.515–16); Polynices' ensuing charge is not only greedy but blind (*caecusque auidos illidit in aegrum | cornipedem cursus*, 'and blind he dashes his greedy charge against the sick horse', 517–18).[97] Their hand-to-hand fighting is characterised by entanglement and confusion:

> coeunt sine more, sine arte,
> tantum animis iraque, atque ignescentia cernunt
> per galeas odia et uultus rimantur acerbo
> lumine: (*Thebaid* 11.524–7)

> They join together against custom, without skill,
> only with anger in their minds, and they scrutinise fiery
> hatreds through the helmets and scour their faces with
> bitter eye.

The hostile gaze and the blazing eye are here presented in ultimate intimacy, scrabbling and probing at each other's faces, using vision as weapon simply because it is the only method of getting into the cracks of each other's armour.[98] Active and passive vision are combined and reflect off each other as they see hatred in fiery eyes and attempt to probe vulnerable eyes through helmets. Finally, Polynices' ultimate downfall is his failure to see that his brother is still dangerous and his desire to make his brother witness his own defeat (557–60), which brings him close enough to be killed before Eteocles dies.

If the *Aeneid* undermines epic success by staging supplication as a battle of the gaze, Statius goes much further: Juturna and Turnus at least represent a sort of heroic failure, while Statius' heroes are successful in embracing negativity, violence and destruction. Juturna, as a nymph raped, immortalised and exploited, is a deviant perspective on the divine gaze in the *Aeneid*, while Pietas sends the main voice of the *Aeneid* into the margins: and is herself compromised in her equivalence to Turnus. Even the alternative feminine perspective fails.

Not all battles of the gaze are military confrontations: a good example of a moral and philosophical test of steadfastness, focused on the gaze, is the story of Regulus in Silius' *Punica* 6.[99] When he is captured in ambush by

---

[97] For a reading of Polynices and Eteocles in economic terms, see Coffee 2009: 241–71.
[98] On *rimor* as key Statian word, see Henderson 1994.
[99] The battle with the snake has some elements of a battle of the gaze: Avens is blinded by fear (190); the snake's eyes flash fire (220); sight of snake is terrifying (245) but Regulus attacks single-handedly with his spear (247–8); arrows blind the snake (274).

Xanthippus, his excessive desire for glory is shown when he does not look back for help (*Pun.* 6.334–6). The humiliation of Rome is symbolised by the Carthaginians' power to look at Regulus (while the gods look at them): *te, Regule, uidit | Sidonius carcer! tuque huic sat magna triumpho | uisa es, Carthago, superis!* ('Did the Sidonian prison see you, Regulus? And did you seem great enough to the gods, Carthage, for this triumph!', 342–4). As the Carthaginian mission departs for Rome, Regulus' steadfastness in the face of humiliation undermines Carthaginian victory, turning the victorious viewers into lovers left behind, while he remains unmoved:

> omnis turba ruit, matresque puerique senesque.
> per medios coetus trahit atque inimica per ora
> spectandum Fortuna ducem. fert lumina contra
> pacatus frontem, qualis cum litora primum
> attigit appulsa rector Sidonia classe.   (*Punica* 6.366–70)

> The whole crowd rushed down, the mothers, boys and old men.
> Through the middle of the gathering and past the hostile faces
> Fortuna drags the leader, now a spectacle. He holds his gaze against them,
> with a peaceful brow, just as when he first touched
> the Sidonian shore, as ruler pushing on the fleet.

In defeat, he is still like a victor, calm, unbowed and in command of himself. Further still, Regulus has one face for all fortunes, good or bad (386–8). Marcia's appeal to his emotions is bound to fail: does this make him heroic or inhuman?[100] Regulus' calm gaze in the face of both the hostile Carthaginians and his emotional countrymen (especially his wife) is a disturbing distortion of the visual field: what seems initially admirable becomes so extreme as to be uncanny.

We have seen various battles of the gaze, from Achilles versus Hector, to Medea versus Talos, hero versus hero, to witch versus monster; Epicurus and *Religio* paves the way for a reinterpretation of Turnus and Aeneas, in which the moment of truth is not battle, but supplication. In Statius' *Thebaid*, Tisiphone, the personification of hellish energy, easily bests Pietas, the personification of Virgilian epic values: but their doublets, Polynices and Eteocles, implicate each other's gazes in a spiral of destruction. Regulus might perhaps offer an alternative to military success: but instead his invulnerable gaze is problematic in different ways.

---

[100] Augoustakis 2010: 156–95 examines both Regulus and Marcia in terms of otherness.

The hostile gaze in epic: some conclusions

Vision embodies epic power in various ways: the visual impact of the hero can itself win battles, but the blazing eyes of the hero, intimate and close at hand, are part of the exchange of force in the heroic duel. The figure of the successful epic warrior standing over his defeated enemy and looking down on his body while he penetrates it with the killing blow offers the epic hero a sort of apotheosis. But the gaze is vulnerable as often as it is powerful, and the only real example of death by vision, the evil eye of Medea, is activated by a female, barbarian and not entirely mortal. In taking the powerful gaze to excess, Apollonius feminises it; for Statius female characters are as much implicated as men, gods as mortals. The uncanny objectification of the dead by the successful warrior becomes instead an uncanny confusion of visual categories.

CHAPTER 9

Fixing it for good: Medusa and monumentality

This final chapter brings together the two sides of the gaze, powerful and disempowered, subject and object, same and other, male and female, to explore the end result of epic: the traces that are left behind. Just as Medea's powerful gaze is appropriated by the Argonauts in the service of their quest, yet Medea's tradition overshadows theirs, so Perseus and Medusa are locked into a complex interdependency. The chapter begins with Perseus as epic hero using Medusa to create monuments in Ovid and Nonnus, and moves on to Medusa's point of view: how does she kill and die in Ovid and Lucan? It then broadens out to investigate epic monumentality and to bring out the paradox at its heart: if an epic hero wants to gain monumental success, he must be transformed from doer to object, from viewer to viewed.

Perseus

Ovid's Perseid is the episode of the *Metamorphoses* in which the poem engages most vigorously with epic.[1] Perseus is also an embodiment of the male gaze: for Salzman-Mitchell, he is the mobile hero confronting the bound woman;[2] for Keith, 'the exemplary Herculean–Odyssean hero and an exponent of the epic virility to which Hermaphroditus aspires'.[3] The Perseid represents a key moment in the *Metamorphoses*, but nevertheless presents a problem of tone.[4] Ovid self-consciously sidesteps Perseus' most memorable feat to focus on the story of Perseus and Andromeda. This gives us a traditional epic hero, battling

---

[1] Otis 1970: 70 refers to 'the almost clamorously epic exploits of Perseus'.
[2] Salzman-Mitchell 2005: 77–84, though she emphasises the instability of Perseus' control of the gaze, and the possibility for 'the resisting reader' to 'disarticulate the viewer's fantasy and expose the strategies whereby Andromeda is constructed as a work of art and deprived of her own identity' (83).
[3] Keith 1999: 223. Keith also suggests that the episode is 'an exploration of the risks entailed by the male in his control of the gaze' (222). Wheeler 1999: 183–5 on Perseus as narrator: 'Perseus turns from the telling of miraculous stories to performing them, transforming his disbelieving audience into stupefied statuary – monuments of wonder, frozen forever as an object lesson in incredulity.' (185)
[4] Otis 1970: 159–65.

monsters with the aid of the gods, fighting a war over his bride, one man successfully defeating a multitude.[5] However moments of humour (his wings are waterlogged, he almost forgets to fly when mesmerised by Andromeda), his unsympathetic portrayal and his eventual reliance on the head of Medusa to extricate him from an impossible battle all serve to problematise his heroism.[6] But is the problem really with Perseus (or Ovid)? Or is Ovid playing around with deep tensions at the heart of epic?

Epic heroism centres on the desire to die gloriously and achieve *kleos*.[7] Epic itself is both monument to and tomb for its own protagonists. There is always an anxiety in epic that the hero might slip across the boundary from facing to courting death.[8] This is mirrored in the reader in the simultaneous anxiety about and desire for the act of looking death in the face. It is, as we have seen, not the killing but the dying that sets a seal on the hero's status.[9] The owner of the assaultive gaze must become an object to be looked at. What Ovid does in the Phineus episode is to literalise and thematise these anxieties by turning Perseus' victims into literal monuments. Backed into a corner by the ever-increasing hordes of foes, Perseus has no choice but to pull out the head of Medusa (*Met.* 5.177–80). Ovid has already presented the reader with a series of classic epic tableaux, ecphrastically fixing the heroes as they die: the beautiful Atthis and his lover Lycabas dying together (46–73); Emathion's tongue continuing to talk (99–106); Lampetides the bard killed as he plays the lyre (111–18); rich Dorylas deprived of his lands (128–36). The Gorgon's head then serves to take this process a step further, to turn poetic images into described statues: Thescelus aiming his spear (181–3); Ampyx lunging with his sword (184–6); Nileus boasting about his lineage (187–94); Eryx chastising his comrades and charging (195–9). Ovid dwells self-consciously on the paradoxes of vision and of battle: Aconteus is

---

[5] Perseid as reworking of *Aeneid*: Otis 1970: 159–65. The 'struggle between Perseus and Phineus is obviously meant to recall the Iliadic *Aeneid* and, more generally, the *aristeiai* of epic' (161).

[6] On the humour, see Solodow 1988: 102–3. The episode made Otis 1970 very uncomfortable indeed: 'Here Ovid's ingenuity is not so much amusing as gauche and repellent. ... Ovid had no taste for heroes and, certainly, no capacity for creating them. ... The *Phineus* is mitigated by neither humour nor brevity; it cannot be taken as anything but a hollow pretence of epic that, despite and indeed because of its ingenuities, degenerates into mere bathos. Here Ovid is at his worst and his worst is very bad indeed.' (163–4) Lowe 2007: 77–92 also focuses on the unsympathetic portrayal of Perseus.

[7] Not all epic heroes die: Aeneas survives his epic, only to die in battle later (according to tradition); quest epics like the *Argonautica* have the goal of survival and return (but also achieving posthumous fame). The elderly epic hero (like Nestor) is a bizarre, out-of-place confection.

[8] *Amor mortis* is important in Lucan, as in Rutz 1960, but draws on near-suicidal impulses from much earlier in the tradition, such as Achilles after the death of Patroclus (Antilochus is afraid that he will cut his throat: *Il.* 18.32–4). See *BC* 4.146–7 with Asso 2010: 143–4; also at 1.458–62, 4.280, 485, 544, 3.134, 240, 695, 6.246 with Hunink 1992 *ad loc*; 8.363–4 with Mayer 1981: 130.

[9] Vernant 1981. See above on the beautiful death, p.264.

killed by mistake even though he is on Perseus' side (200–2), and Astyages, unable to believe his enemy is a statue, is petrified with amazement on his face, immortalised as a permanent viewer of ecphrasis (203–6). Even more self-conscious is the comment of Perseus as he creates a permanent image of supplication out of Phineus:

> quin etiam mansura dabo monimenta per aeuum,
> inque domo soceri semper spectabere nostri,
> ut mea se sponsi soletur imagine coniunx.   (*Metamorphoses* 5.227–9)
>
> Instead I will give a monument that will remain through the ages,
> and you will be gazed upon for ever in the house of my father in law,
> so that my wife might console herself with the image of her betrothed.

Perseus creates a monumental Phineus who sets in stone the final scene of the *Aeneid*, a Turnus preserved forever in his moment of defeat to be the object of the gaze of his former beloved. His imagination of Andromeda's perspective suggests that she might be a Lavinia figure: in what way is she consoled by looking at the image of Phineus? Reassured that he will never have her? Or consoled for losing her lover? The imagined relationship of viewer to image underlines the fact that petrifaction both causes death and sidesteps death. Perseus' victims are simultaneously mortalised and immortalised.

Keith has analysed the gaze of Perseus as the ultimate male gaze.[10] But as Rimell points out he is assimilated to Medusa and ultimately adopts her gaze.[11] And his most severely objectified victims are men, not women. The hybrid Perseus/Medusa combination is a paradoxical poet-figure, exposing the epic hero to the gaze of both fellow heroes and women on the walls, as well as poets and readers. Epic heroes who achieve the beautiful death are inevitably immortalised in and as the moment of defeat. The whole episode enshrines the problem of the epic hero who wants to be doing, in control, owning the gaze, but the nature of epic poetry demands that he must also be the object of creativity, to-be-looked-at, often by a female audience. Even the hero who does not die, who successfully defeats his enemies, is often implicated in other ways in the centrality of death in epic.[12] Though Perseus holds Medusa's decapitated head his control of the gaze is insecure; he

---

[10] Keith 1999: 222: 'Ovid documents in the Perseus narrative the correlation between the male gaze and masculine subjectivity, which come together in the visual objectification of women ... and landscape ... to confirm the superiority of male over female.'

[11] Rimell 2006: 18 points out the way that Perseus and Medusa overlap, so much so that he '*becomes* her lethal gaze'.

[12] Epic ought to have a strong dichotomy between success and failure, staying alive and biting the dust, but in practice different factors combine to assimilate killer and killed. The death of Patroclus foreshadows and entails the death of Hector, which in turn foreshadows and entails the death of

becomes a Narcissus-style poetic hero, and dallies on the boundaries of genre,[13] abandoning his claim to traditional epic heroism by not dying, by taking the Medusan escape route. Perseus both is and is not an emblematic epic hero; in this, arguably the most epic episode in the *Metamorphoses*, Ovid prominently displays his exploration of the problematics of epic heroism. Ovid takes epic monumentality into the realm of the absurd, insists on his ability to take epic on, while going beyond it by freezing, distancing and deconstructing it.

Perseus is also a key figure in Nonnus' engagement with the epic genre. At *Dion.* 18.289–305 Dionysus' admiring host Staphylos sets Perseus and Dionysus up as parallel epic heroes: the head of Medusa is a fruit like the grape (both bring oblivion: 295–7); the Indian enemies of Dionysus are equated to both the Gorgon and the sea monster: ὅπως ἕνα κῶμον ἀνάψω Γοργοφόνωι Περσῆϊ καὶ Ἰνδοφόνωι Διονύσωι ('That I might hold one victory feast for Gorgonkiller Perseus and Indiankiller Dionysus', 304–5). In the central book of the epic, book 25, which starts the second half, the *Indiad*, Nonnus self-consciously reflects on his role as epic poet and second Homer. We have already looked at his version of the shield of Achilles in this book:[14] most of the first half is taken up with a tendentious and polarised comparison between Dionysus and the other sons of Zeus, Perseus and Hercules. Perseus represents the mundane face of epic masculinity (ἠνορέην, 25.29) that extraordinary, semi-divine, androgynous Dionysus is destined to surpass. Where Ovid creates a heroic but nonetheless unsympathetic Perseus, Nonnus strives in every way to do him down: from questioning his ability to fly (*Dion.* 25.33), ridiculing his mode of transport (34), presenting him as a killer of pregnant women (38–42) to emphasising his flight from the other Gorgons, Sthenno and Euryale (53–9); this Perseus is a robber (35) who has carried out only a womanly feat (θῆλυν ἄεθλον, 65). The climax of his tirade sets both heroes up as a spectacle for the heavens:

Ἀλλὰ φίλοι, κρίνωμεν· ἐν ἀντολίῃ μὲν ἀρούρῃ
Ἰνδοφόνους ἱδρῶτας ὀπιπεύων Διονύσου
Ἰέλιος θάμβησεν, ὑπὲρ δυτικοῖο δὲ κόλπου
Ἑσπερίη Περσῆα τανύπτερον εἶδε Σελήνη,

Achilles; Turnus is assimilated to Aeneas in the very moment of his death. The defeated body of the dead hero becomes an object to be exchanged and fought over, almost his own monument, while the victorious body of the hero is equally on display, to be looked at and desired by viewers and readers.

[13] Segal 1998: 20–1:'Through the combination of the elegiac/erotic and the epic contexts of the body/ statue confusion, Ovid enables his metamorphic theme both to embrace and contrast the discourses of love and war ... as the two scenes bring together the two genres, so they bring together male and female bodies, each in its characteristic role. The woman as statue is an object of stupefying beauty; the warrior as statue is arrested in the midst of violent martial acts.'

[14] See above, Chapter 5, pp.190, 195–7.

βαιὸν ἀεθλεύσαντα πόνον γαμψώνυχι χαλκῷ.
καὶ Φαέθων ὅσον εὖχος ὑπέρτερον ἔλλαχε Μήνης,
τόσσον ἐγὼ Περσῆος ἀρείονα Βάκχον ἐνίψω.
(*Dionysiaca* 25.98–104)

But friends, let us judge them: Helios marvelled
as he watched the sweats of Dionysus Indianslayer
on the Eastern soil, over the Western gulf
Evening Selene saw long-winged Perseus,
after achieving his labour with a curved piece of bronze;
and as much as Phaethon obtains a higher boast than the Moon,
by so much will I declare that Bacchus is stronger than Perseus.

The two heroes are evaluated by the stature of their divine audiences: the male gaze of the sun distinguishes Dionysus while Perseus is only impressive to the female gaze of the moon. This comparison twists together the epic trope of the divine audience with the erotic simile so well known from Homer and Virgil in which the hero or heroine is compared to Apollo or Diana standing out among their companions, making Perseus compete on Dionysus' androgynous territory. The victory of Dionysus over Perseus, however, is focused not on his own achievement of immortality but his ability to immortalise others: Semele and the crown of Ariadne are compared to the less fortunate Danae and Andromeda. Even though Andromeda has been set among the stars, she is still chased by the sea monster. Paradoxically Medusa's eye is mild as it sparkles among the stars. Now that the whole myth is transferred into the ultimate monument of the firmament, Medusa's eye has lost the power to paralyse and the monster, although fixed, still moves, while Andromeda is perpetually in motion as its prey. By choosing Perseus as the comparandum for Dionysus, Nonnus plays an Ovidian game with epic, setting himself as the climax of the tradition of going beyond the limits of epic.

The final battle between Dionysus and Perseus takes place in book 47 after Dionysus rescues and marries Ariadne. The city of Argos refuses to honour him because they are afraid of Hera, and an anonymous Argive praises Perseus in his place (47.498–532), overturning the narrator's comparison from book 25. Hera incites Perseus to fight Dionysus, and imagines him creating the ultimate spectacle for her eyes:

Βασσαρίδων δὲ
ὄμματι Γοργείῳ βροτέην μετάμειψον ὀπωπὴν
εἰς βρέτας αὐτοτέλεστον ὁμοίιον· ἀντιτύπῳ δὲ
κάλλεϊ πετρήεντι τεὰς κόσμησον ἀγυιάς,
Ἰναχίαις ἀγορῆσιν ἀγάλματα ποικίλα τεύχων.
(*Dionysiaca* 47.559–63)

> With the Gorgon's eye turn the mortal faces
> of the Bassarids into matching images self-made;
> With the beauty of the petrified copies decorate your streets,
> constructing varied wonders for the Inachian market places.

This picks up on the specifically Ovidian version of Perseus in which he makes artistic creations and becomes a version of the poet: ποικίλα ('varied') is a key word of Nonnian poetics.[15] Perseus' Nonnian epithet is κορυθαιόλος ('Flashing helmet', 47.537, 595) and Hera herself attacks Dionysus with light:

> καταιθύσσουσα δὲ Βάκχου
> ἀστεροπῆς μίμημα, θεόσσυτον ἁλλόμενον πῦρ,
> ῥῖψε κατὰ Βρομίοιο σελασφόρον αἴθοπα λόγχην.
>
> (*Dionysiaca* 47.609–11)
>
> She floated over Bacchus,
> an imitation of lightning, leaping fire sent by the gods,
> and hurled at Bromios her lightning-bearing flashing lance.

as if having a second attempt to strike Dionysus with lightning, after failing to incinerate him along with his mother.[16] As winged Perseus circles overhead, Dionysus levitates under his own power and grows to cosmic proportions, grasping the sun and the moon (655–63). Perseus is clearly outclassed in this final comparison, and flees to fight the women: ultimately, in this battle, the only person he petrifies with the head of Medusa is Ariadne, Bacchus' new bride (665–6), causing the extreme anger of Bacchus, who would have killed him, if Hermes had not ordered him to stop fighting Hera. Shorrock has pointed out the clear links between Dionysus' anger and both the end of the *Odyssey* and the beginning of the *Iliad*.[17] The description of his anger echoes Odysseus' anger at the suitors (*Od.* 24.526–30) and Hermes pulling him back echoes Athene restraining Achilles at *Il.* 1.197. Nonnus thus includes the whole Homeric corpus in a sort of miniature ring allusion. This Perseus flees, and instead of gazing in wonder at his own bride-to-be, who is *like* a statue, only succeeds in turning his enemy's bride into a statue. Nonnus literalises Ovid's image and takes the Ovidian commentary on epic heroism to the extreme. The only monument at the end of this battle (which contains and miniaturises the whole *Iliad* and *Odyssey*) is Ariadne's crown set in the stars, a monument to love, sex and divinity. Where Ovid's Perseus looks slant-wise at epic conventions, Nonnus redefines epic as building up to his Dionysus.

---

[15] On Perseus in Nonnus see Shorrock 2001: 101–4.
[16] The futility of this is immediately pointed out by Dionysus: if he survived the full thunderbolt of Zeus, how can some fiery spear damage him? (613–17)
[17] Shorrock 2001: 101–4.

Perseus exists to make Dionysus look good; Medusa has less supernatural power than Dionysus, this epic's protagonist. Rather than borrowing attributes of the gods, Dionysus is a god. Perseus' mortal monuments are outclassed by Dionysus' catasterisms, using the cosmos itself as a monument. Dionysus and the *Dionysiaca* literally outgrow the boundaries of epic poetry.

And Medusa

What then of the female gaze which gives Perseus his epic power? The myth of Medusa is familiar, iconic, pervasive: not just in ancient literature, but also modern culture.[18] But this familiarity masks a blind spot at the centre of the myth: how exactly did Medusa kill? And how did she die?[19] Medusa's eyes turn people to stone: but do they do it actively? Do they have a petrifying gaze? Or is it only passive? Is it the act of looking into Medusa's eyes that becomes the moment of death? This is an important question within our framework, because it reflects Medusa's ambivalent position as both powerful, monstrous female viewer and passive objectified artefact to-be-looked-at. Does she own a powerful gaze that trumps Perseus' heroism, or is she an object to be owned by the male hero?

The two main ancient accounts of the death of Medusa are in Ovid's *Metamorphoses* and Lucan's *Civil War*. These two texts have been persistently radical reinterpreters of the epic gaze. The fact that most of the surviving literary material on Medusa does not focus on this moment of truth may be a coincidence; or is it the blank point from which we must shy away?

Ovid seems to have used the myth in an original and innovative way.[20] Ovid's story focuses on Perseus' exploits after the death of Medusa (suggesting that a heroic account of the killing of Medusa existed, perhaps a *Perseid* of the sort that Callimachus despised) and invents a metamorphic origin for Medusa, turning her into a beautiful woman whose rape by Poseidon in Minerva's temple pollutes the gaze of Minerva, who punishes her by turning her beautiful hair into monstrous snakes. The *Metamorphoses* shies away from Medusa's death, and only offers a condensed and allusive account of Perseus'

---

[18] For a selection of reactions to Medusa, see Garber and Vickers 2003; for a recent classical reappraisal see Lowe 2007. Ancient versions of death of Medusa: Hesiod *Theogony* 270–83; Ps-Hesiod *Aspis* 220–7; Pindar *Pythian* 10.46–8, 12.11–19; Pherecydes fr. 11 Jacoby (cited by Schol. Apollonius 4.1515); Palaephatus *Peri Apiston* 31; Apollodorus 2.4.2; Heraclitus *Peri Apiston* 1 with Stern 2003. Modern culture: most notably as the symbol for Versace, see Garber and Vickers 2003: 276.

[19] Rimell 2006 uses Medusa as one of her touchstones for her study of the Ovidian poetics of desire. Rimell would like Medusa to have petrified herself: 'Like Narcissus, she enthralls, stupefies, and is finally killed (conceivably – we can never quite *see*) by her own glance' (16).

[20] Ovid as first to make Medusa's victims into statues: Solodow 1988: 211, Hardie 2002b: 178.

great feat. At the banquet celebrating his wedding to Andromeda he finally agrees to tell his story; readers perhaps might be expecting a two-book digression like Aeneas' tale in the *Aeneid* (or Odysseus' in the *Odyssey*); instead we receive an eighteen-line epitome in indirect speech, covering both heroic feat and heroic journey. He begins with his theft of the eye of the daughters of Phorcys and his approach through the grim landscape of the Gorgons:

> passimque per agros
> perque uias uidisse hominum simulacra ferarumque
> in silicem ex ipsis uisa conuersa Medusa;
> se tamen horrendae clipei, quem laeua gerebat,
> aere repercussae formam aspexisse Medusae,
> dumque grauis somnus colubrasque ipsamque tenebat,
> eripuisse caput collo;   (*Metamorphoses* 4.779–85)

> and everywhere through the fields and along the roads
> [he said] that he saw statues of men and beasts
> turned from themselves into stone by seeing Medusa;
> he however caught sight of the shape of the terrifying Medusa
> reflected in the bronze of his shield, which he bore on his left arm,
> and while heavy sleep held both her snakes and herself,
> he snatched away the head from its neck;

Medusa is caught in the mirror of the shield and already foreshadows her role on the aegis of Athena.

In this version it seems that looking at Medusa, or more specifically looking at her eyes, is the fatal error, although the ablative absolute (*uisa Medusa*) allows the precise relationship between Medusa and the petrified men and animals to remain vague. This still allows for the possibility of an actively malevolent and powerful gaze, because as we have seen above the evil eye was often understood as the passing of infection from one person to another through the connection of their eyes. This could explain the way that her gaze seems so much more active in Lucan's account.

Fantham has explored the varied dynamics of Medusa's gaze in Lucan and reads her as 'a new Stoic myth of heroism' and 'a double symbol of the unnatural evil of human overreach and the impiety of slaughter among kin' – thus more or less a symbol of Lucan's poem itself.[21] Lucan begins by describing her landscape:

> squalebant late Phorcynidos arua Medusae
> non nemorum protecta coma, non mollia sulco
> sed dominae uultu conspectis aspera saxis   (*Bellum civile* 9.626–8)

---

[21] Fantham 1992: 119.

> The wide fields of Medusa the daughter of Phorcys are rough
> not shaded by the leaves of trees, not soft from the plough
> but rough with rocks which had been seen by the face of its mistress

Here Medusa's active gaze seems to be transforming the landscape itself from agricultural land to stony desert.[22] At 638–9 Lucan marvels at the speed of death: *quem, qui recto se lumine uidit, | passa Medusa mori est?* ('What man, who saw her with straight eye, did Medusa allow to die?'). Lucan emphasises the way that petrifaction both is and is not death: it happens too fast for him actually to die. But there seems to be a difference between looking obliquely and looking her straight in the eye. It is the connection between the two pairs of eyes which is fatal. At 647–8 she threatens the sky and sea, and at 649–51 birds fall out of the sky and whole tribes are petrified. Lucan's emphasis on landscape and animals makes Medusa's gaze more active: the sky and sea cannot look back at her.[23] When Perseus comes into the story, he is little more than an embodiment of Pallas' ongoing destruction of Medusa; she not only tells him what to do (665–8) and gives him the shield (669–70) but physically directs his hand as he kills the sleeping Medusa (*ipsa regit trepidum Pallas dextraque trementem | Perseos auersi Cyllenida derigit harpen*, 'Pallas herself guides the panicking man and her right hand directs Mercury's trembling scimitar of Perseus who was turned away', 675–6). The metal that kills Medusa is thus radically overdetermined: held by Perseus, guided by Pallas and belonging to Mercury, it implements the ultimate conspiracy against Medusa. No coincidence that Lucan immediately gropes for Medusa's perspective: the one view no one could ever have is offered and simultaneously refused to the reader, the view of Medusa's dying face:

> quos habuit uoltus hamati uolnere ferri
> caesa caput Gorgon! quanto spirare ueneno
> ora rear, quantumque oculos effundere mortis!
> Nec Pallas spectare potest, uoltusque gelassent
> Perseos auersi, si non Tritonia densos
> sparsisset crines texissetque ora colubris.   (*Bellum civile* 9.678–83)

> What expression did the Gorgon have on her face as her head was cut off
> by the wound of curving iron! How much poison was breathed out
> from her mouth, I wonder, and how much death did her eyes pour out!

---

[22] Or are these rocks the remains of humans and animals who looked at her as in Ovid? We can never be completely sure. Fantham 1992: 99 says 'The reader's attention is firmly directed to Medusa, and her lethal gaze. Here, and repeatedly in the next thirty lines, to be exposed to the sight of Medusa, rather than to see her, is the hazard.'

[23] The birds could work either way: the image of the bird of prey looking down with its extraordinarily sharp sight and its predatory and active god's-eye view is a familiar one from Ovid's Perseus narrative.

> Pallas could not even look, and the face of Perseus turned away
> would have solidified, if Tritonia had not sprinkled
> the dense hair and covered the face with snakes.

In the moment of death her gaze seems to be at its most powerful, too much even for the divine gaze of Pallas, and, it is suggested, too powerful even to survive looking in a reflection. Her dying gaze pours out of her like blood or breath, assimilating her visual power to a physical effluence. Even at this, the most active moment of Medusa's vision, her gaze seems almost independent of her agency, as it will go on to be, continuing to petrify after her death, when she can certainly no longer be in charge.[24] Lucan's vision of Medusa's gaze as active is an aberration in the ancient material, a Lucanian inversion, a paradox, a personification.

It is, however, a foretaste of what was to come: Medusa's ambivalence is the secret of her attraction. She symbolises the monstrous–feminine, representing for psychoanalysts both the fear of castration and the possibility of phallic womanhood.[25] For feminists she is both 'a figure for the silencing of women' and 'an icon of resistance and rage at female subjugation'.[26] Sartre uses her as an emblem of the petrifying gaze of the other.[27] With her history of appropriation by psychoanalysis and her uneasy relationship with feminism, it is no surprise that Medusa makes herself felt in feminist film criticism.[28] De Lauretis turns Medusa into a pin-up for female objectification, demanding, as Ovid does, that we acknowledge Medusa as a woman. Yet she enters the world of epic as a device on a shield, the climactic apotropaic device in Athene's arming in *Iliad* 5: ἐν δέ τε Γοργείη κεφαλὴ

---

[24] Fantham 1992: 107 reads this as 'a stronger power of killing whatever her dead image confronts'; stronger though it may be, her death strips her of agency.

[25] Examples in Garber and Vickers 2003: Freud 1955 selection in Garber and Vickers 2003: 84–6; see also Irigaray 1985. Rimell 2006 suggests that '[s]he is not simply the horror of "nothing to see" ... but a complex, phallic-vulvic mystery that is never truly seen'. But I think Rimell overplays the empowering creative side of Medusa, who is after all dead when she creates her works of art.

[26] Rimell 2006: 17, along with examples in Garber and Vickers 2003: Sarton (1971) *The Muse as Medusa* (107–8) or Emily Erwin Culpepper (1986) *Experiencing my Gorgon Self* (238–46). Most significantly, perhaps, Cixous 1976. See also from a classical perspective: Joplin 1991.

[27] According to Sartre 1966: 555, the meaning of the myth of Medusa is 'the petrifaction of Being-for-itself in Being-in-itself by the Other's Look'. Barnes 1974 explains this thus: 'when another person looks at me, his look may make me feel that I am an object, a thing in the midst of a world of things. If I feel that my free subjectivity has been paralysed, this is as if I had been turned to stone.' Garber and Vickers 2003: 124–7. Medusa, like Medea, is also 'other' in the sense that she is African and situated in Libya.

[28] See for instance De Lauretis 1984 who moves from Freud to the politics of cinematic identification: 'My question then, how did Medusa feel looking at herself being slain and pinned up on screens, walls, billboards, and other shields of masculine identity, is really a political question that bears directly upon the issues of cinematic identification and spectatorship: the relation of female subjectivity to ideology in the representation of sexual difference and desire, the positions available to women in film, the condition of vision and meaning production, for women.' Garber and Vickers 2003: 199–200.

δεινοῖο πελώρου, / δεινή τε σμερδνή τε, Διὸς τέρας αἰγιόχοιο. ('and thereon is set the head of the grim, gigantic Gorgon, a thing of fear and horror, portent of Zeus of the aegis.', *Il.* 5.741–2), as we saw above.[29] The image, petrified and petrifying, of the mask-like female face surrounded by snaky hair is ubiquitous in ancient art and this *gorgoneion* was likely to have been the inspiration for the myth as told in Ovid.[30] Medusa then represents the feminisation of horror rather than the objectification of the female in the processes of mythology. Yet when we (as we inevitably do) read her through Ovid's humanisation, and its later receptions, we cannot help but see the female subjectivity trapped within the apotropaic icon. Medusa is a synecdoche for women in epic: monster, uncanny, associated with the divine, powerful, at the same time as she is raped, objectified, an object conquered and exchanged by men to give them power.

Monumentality

We have seen Medusa becoming a monument, pinned up on Athena's shield, creating monuments in Ovid's Perseus episode, and neutralised in the perversely fluid firmament of Nonnus' *Dionysiaca*. The same movement between active and passive, eerily powerful and uncannily powerless is encapsulated in epic monumentality. Epic heroes threaten to become monsters, but end up as monuments. Epic is deeply concerned with monument and memory. But how do monuments work? Why are monuments a particular concern of epic? How do epic heroes think about monuments? How do internal spectators view monuments? What do monuments represent for the reader and the poet of epic? Is the monument, like the epiphany, another encounter with the Lacanian gaze, a blank spot which fails to achieve the desires with which it is loaded?

A monument is a visible sign which stimulates an act of remembering: unlike a souvenir, it carries with it authority and creates cultural capital.[31] The physical monuments remaining from the ancient world represent it, as a repository of cultural authority, as a site of contested values.[32] That authority may be undermined (Fowler points especially to the way that Ovid turns Augustan monuments into sites for sexual assignations);[33] the monumental attempt to control interpretation is always open to

---

[29] See above, Chapter 5, p.199. [30] Lowe 2007; see also Lowe 2010.
[31] Tatum 2003: 1–32 on monuments, especially the Vietnam war memorial. See also Dyer 1995: 126–7 on the Lutyens Somme monument: 'Permanent, built to last, the monument has none of the vulnerability of the human body, none of its terrible propensity to harm.'
[32] Beard 2002 gives a stimulating case study of one monument: the Parthenon. [33] Fowler 2000c: 210.

358 Fixing it for good: Medusa and monumentality

contest.³⁴ In the same way, the monument's claim to permanence can always be challenged: in the words of Fowler '[t]he essence of the monument is paradoxically its lack of monumental stability, the way in which it is constantly reused and given new meaning' (211). However part of the impact of a monument, an essential part of monumentality, is that claim of permanence, that attempt to appropriate the controlling vertical gaze of the gods, to create and bestow authority.³⁵ Monuments are things we look up at: despite their lack of agency, they have the power to oppress as well as inspire. They also represent a sort of fixity, permanence but also rigidity.

Epic as a genre has a special relationship with monumentality. The analogy between *kleos* and tomb in Homer has long been established.³⁶ Tatum reads the shield of Achilles as both weapon and tomb.³⁷ One of the few fragments to remain from Ennius' monumental text is set in the context of his rebeginning, the beginning of the sixteenth book of the *Annales*, where he seems to be saying that the elite quest for immortality is less well served by physical monuments than by his own poetry:³⁸

> reges per regnum statuas sepulcraque quaerunt
> aedificant nomen, summa nituntur opum vi.
> postremo longinqua dies confecerit aetas.   (Ennius *Annales* 405–7 Sk.)
>
> Kings through their rule seek statues and graves,
> build a name, strive with highest force of resources.
> Finally the far-reaching age of the day will have finished them.

The quest for monumental immortality is set up in the same terms as epic battle.³⁹ In the *Aeneid*, the two major closural moments of the poem both focus on monuments: the last thing Aeneas sees before he plunges his sword into Turnus is the *saeui monimenta doloris* ('souvenir of savage grief', *Aen.* 12.945), the sword-belt of Pallas, adorned with images of the Danaids killing the fifty sons of Aegyptus;⁴⁰ the chronological end-point and the ultimate *telos* of the poem is Augustus viewing his own triple triumph from the temple of

---

³⁴ Fowler 2000c: 209 points out that critics who use monuments (such as Galinsky 1992) to give authority to univocal readings of texts fall foul of the same fallacy as historicists: monuments, like history, are texts, interpretations, that are always open to multiple readings.
³⁵ It is no coincidence that many monuments are set in high places, or built deliberately above the human scale. Tatum 2003 notes that the Vietnam war memorial is deliberately kept low.
³⁶ See also Sinos 1980: 47–51, Ford 1992: 131–71: '*Sema* as a figure for the monumental epic text, the tomb-like embodiment of its hero's fame.' (157)
³⁷ Tatum 2003: 139; 136–57 on the shield.   ³⁸ Fowler 2000c: 194, with Skutsch 1985: *ad loc.*
³⁹ Virgil later echoed Ennius' words at *Aen.* 12.552 (*pro se quisque uiri summa nituntur opum ui*, 'on his own behalf, each hero struggles with the highest force of his resources').
⁴⁰ *monimenta* is associated with 'monument' but has various meanings: for Turnus the sword-belt is a marker of his epic achievement, but for Aeneas, and the reader, it is a warning, a reminder, an intertextual marker of the tragic loss of young life.

Apollo (*Aen.* 8.720–8) on the shield of Aeneas – an emperor as monument embodied, viewing a memorialisation of his own achievements, set into armour that is equally a monument. Monuments are a central concern of epic and epic itself can be read as a monument.

In this concern, epic relates to wider literary concerns; the desire to be remembered surely lies behind every act of putting words into texts. Lyric poetry, history, even elegy and epigram: all aim to immortalise themselves and their subjects. Horace's *opus* is a monument as enduring as Virgil's:

> exegi monumentum aere perennius
> regalique situ pyramidum altius,
> quod non imber edax, non Aquilo impotens
> possit diruere aut innumerabilis
> annorum series et fuga temporum.   (*Odes* 3.30.1–5)
>
> I have constructed a monument more lasting than bronze
> and higher than the royal site/decay of the pyramids,
> which the voracious rainstorm, and the powerless North wind
> cannot tear down, nor the uncountable
> list of years nor the flight of time.

Is it simply that literature in general and poetry in particular are concerned with their ability to create a monumental record?[41] Or does Ovid recognise a particularly epic affiliation in this passage when he echoes it in his epilogue to the *Metamorphoses*?[42] Horace seems to be consciously setting himself up against the epic poet Ennius, whose name might be hinted at in the adjective *perennius*, when he reworks Lucretius' homage to Ennius at *DRN* 1.118 into his own claim of literary priority.[43] My attempt to define an 'epic gaze' is always calling attention to the problems of the very category 'epic'. Epic is a mode, a mindset, not simply a concatenation of metre and subject matter. Historiography, too, has a close relationship with monumentality, but Livy, for instance, avoids calling his history a monument, even though the process of viewing monuments is one important model for his readers.[44] Instead he

---

[41] On the ambiguity of *situs*, see Woodman 1974: 117–18, cf. Simonides (ed. Page) 531, lines 2–5.
[42] *Iamque opus exegi, quod nec Iouis ira nec ignis | nec poterit ferrum nec edax abolere uetustas* ('And now I have constructed a monument, which neither the anger of Jupiter, nor fire, nor the sword, nor voracious age can destroy', *Met.* 15.871–2).
[43] *detulit ex Helicone perenni fronde coronam* ('he brought down the crown from Helicon with its eternal leaf', Lucr. *DRN* 1.118) with the key word *perennius*, but also in 3.30.12–14: *ex humili potens | princeps Aeolium carmen ad Italos | deduxisse modos* ('powerful from humble beginnings, I was the first to bring down Aeolian song to Italian metres').
[44] Thuc. 1.22: κτῆμά τε ἐς αἰεὶ μᾶλλον ἢ ἀγώνισμα ἐς τὸ παραχρῆμα ἀκούειν ξύγκειται. ('In conclusion, I have written this as a thing for always, rather than a competitive piece for immediate listening.') See Jaeger 1997: 15–29: 'Unlike Horace's famous metaphor, which emphasizes the size, solidity and

contrasts poetic monuments with physical monuments available for the historian to scrutinise.⁴⁵ Any literature concerned with the past or looking to the future has a claim on monumentality: yet epic does seem to have a special relationship with monuments.⁴⁶

Epic monuments

Let us visit some epic monuments, beginning with the *Iliad*. Homeric *kleos* (the subject matter of Homeric epic is famously the *klea andron*, 'fames of men') is marked by and constitutes a tomb/monument.⁴⁷ Tombs dot the Homeric landscape and act as reminders of past heroes.⁴⁸ In *Iliad* 7, Hector challenges the Greeks to a duel and offers the loser the opportunity of epic fame along with death:

> εἰ δέ κ' ἐγὼ τὸν ἕλω, δώῃ δέ μοι εὖχος Ἀπόλλων,
> τεύχεα συλήσας οἴσω προτὶ Ἴλιον ἱρήν,
> καὶ κρεμόω προτὶ νηὸν Ἀπόλλωνος ἑκάτοιο,
> τὸν δὲ νέκυν ἐπὶ νῆας ἐϋσσέλμους ἀποδώσω,
> ὄφρα ἑ ταρχύσωσι κάρη κομόωντες Ἀχαιοί,
> σῆμά τέ οἱ χεύωσιν ἐπὶ πλατεῖ Ἑλλησπόντῳ.
> καί ποτέ τις εἴπῃσι καὶ ὀψιγόνων ἀνθρώπων,
> νηῒ πολυκληΐδι πλέων ἐπὶ οἴνοπα πόντον·
> «ἀνδρὸς μὲν τόδε σῆμα πάλαι κατατεθνηῶτος,
> ὅν ποτ' ἀριστεύοντα κατέκτανε φαίδιμος Ἕκτωρ.»
> ὣς ποτέ τις ἐρέει· τὸ δ' ἐμὸν κλέος οὔ ποτ' ὀλεῖται. (*Iliad* 7.81–91)

> But if I take his life and Apollo grants me the glory,
> I will strip his armour and carry it to sacred Ilium
> and hang it in front of the temple of far-striking Apollo,

---

durability of the poet's achievement and draws attention to his building activity (*exigere*), Livy's words stress the active role that his audience must play to comprehend the past' (23) and Feldherr 1998. Jaeger also points out the way that Livy manipulates Polybius' account of Paullus' tour of Greece to remove his famous comparison of Phidias' chryselephantine statue of Zeus to the Zeus of Homer and replace it with a reference to sacrifice on the Capitoline (1–3).

⁴⁵ Jaeger 1997: 168–72 on Livy's account of the statue of Ennius at the tomb of the Scipios in Rome. She concludes that 'poetry, represented by the statue of Ennius, serves as a marker for the absence of history' (170).

⁴⁶ Propertius' fascination with Roman monuments in book 4 is intimately bound up with his continuing generic negotiations: he is always self-consciously not writing epic, as if he has a sense that he is in epic territory. Janan 2001: 167 argues that the elusive *puella* undoes Propertius' attempt to build an 'androcentric, quasi-epic monument' in book 4. See also Welch 2005.

⁴⁷ Redfield 1994: 30–41 on *kleos*. 'In song events acquire a kind of permanence which confers on them something approaching immortality.' (35) 'There is thus a curious reciprocity between the bard and his heroes. The bard sings of events which have a *kleos*; without the heroes he would have nothing to sing about. At the same time, the bard confers on his heroes a *kleos*, without which they would have no existence in the later world.' (32) On the anti-funeral, 183–6. On tombs, Grethlein 2008: 28–32.

⁴⁸ Sinos 1980: 48. *Il.* 2.604 (Aipytios); 2.793 (Aisyetes); 10.415, 11.166–7, 11.371, 24.349 (Ilos).

> but his corpse I will give back among the well-benched vessels
> so that the flowing-haired Achaeans may give him due burial
> and heap up a mound upon him beside the broad Hellespont.
> And some day one of the late-born men will say
> 'This is the sign of a man who died long ago,
> who was one of the bravest, and glorious Hector killed him.'
> So will he speak one day and my glory will not be destroyed.

Both the armour and the tomb of the dead man become monuments, reminders, embodiments of story. The armour is equally a monument, set up as a threat as well as a votive offering, embodying the hostile gaze of Apollo, conveyed in the epithet ἑκάτοιο. Hector attempts to control the workings of monumentality, by imagining an authorised reading of the tomb, one that objectifies yet valorises the dead man, but is chiefly read as a signifier of his own glory. Our reading of the *Iliad* as monument both reinforces and undermines this optimism: the *Iliad* guarantees Hector's *kleos*, but we know he does not kill his opponent in the coming duel, and we also know that his death will stand as the ultimate guarantee of Achilles' glory. The monument is not securely a marker of glory: it can always potentially be reduced to a grave. By longing for indestructible *kleos*, the epic hero creates and pursues destruction, not only of others but also of himself; the marker that remains cannot be enjoyed by the hero; the reader and poet can rejoice in the bitter pleasure of controlling its interpretation.[49] Hector's tomb is also the closural image of the poem as we have it (*Il.* 24.788–804) so that the poem neatly enacts what it describes, burying Hector and perpetuating his *kleos*. But as it does so, it allows us to question this circularity, by revealing the emptiness at the heart of the tomb. Like Lacan's sardine can, the monument is a disturbance in the field of vision which reveal's the subject's inability to control meaning.

Roman epic is equally concerned with monumentality. When Virgil immortalises Nisus and Euryalus, the beautiful boys who die for each other, in *Aeneid* 9, he uses the same vocabulary of monumentality as Horace:[50]

> Fortunati ambo! si quid mea carmina possunt,
> nulla dies umquam memori uos eximet aeuo,
> dum domus Aeneae Capitoli immobile saxum
> accolet imperiumque pater Romanus habebit. (*Aeneid* 9.446–9)

---

[49] Reflection in the *Iliad* on the instability of monumentality: 2.811–14, 23.326–33, with Grethlein 2008: 30–1. See also Dickson 1995: 218, with further bibliography.

[50] In particular echoing *usque ego postera | crescam laude recens, dum Capitolium scandet cum tacita uirgine pontifex*. ('Until I will grow fresh with praise to come, as long as the priest with the silent virgin climbs the Capitol.', *Odes* 3.30.7–9). Hardie 1994: 153 points out close links with the passage of Ennius cited above. On the potential instability of the apostrophe, see Casali 2004.

> Blessed pair! If my songs can do anything,
> no day will ever erase you from the remembering age,
> while the house of Aeneas inhabits the unmoving rock
> of the Capitol and the Roman father holds his rule.

Virgil claims for poetry the same power to immortalise as physical monuments, suggesting that the names of his invented heroes will be inscribed in the annals of Roman myth.[51] The *Aeneid* stands in the Roman literary landscape like the Capitol dominates Rome, both to-be-looked at and looking down on you, a reassuring symbol of order, but always also potentially an image of oppressive power. So the father is both *paterfamilias* and emperor, situated in the Capitol, observing his subjects, whom he also protects.[52] In Roman epic, the fame and glory of the hero is closely tied to the imperial gaze: Rome's ability to inspect and control the other guarantees cultural power and the durability of Roman myth and literature. The emperor's gaze ensures the survival of poetry.

This passage has been reworked throughout Roman epic and gives a glimpse into the genre's changing relationship with Rome and political power. Statius' reworking names Nisus and Euryalus:[53]

> uos quoque sacrati, quamuis mea carmina surgant
> inferiore lyra, memores superabitis annos.
> forsitan et comites non aspernabitur umbras
> Euryalus Phrygiique admittet gloria Nisi.   (*Thebaid* 10.445–8)

> You also are sacred, although my songs rise
> from a lesser lyre, you will survive the mindful years.
> And perhaps Euryalus will not spurn your companion
> shades and the glory of Phrygian Nisus will grant you an audience.[54]

The connections to monumentality, the physical site of Rome and Roman political power are all gone. Now the *Aeneid* itself is the guarantee of immortality. Statius himself makes no claim on Rome or on political power, relying instead on the intertextual authority of Virgil. This passage is symptomatic of the *Thebaid*'s pessimistic approach towards power, poetry and monumentality: Statius monumentalises the infant Opheltes, but problematises the glory of his heroes at every turn. When Polynices and Eteocles kill each other, he offers them an anti-memorialisation (11.574–9)

---

[51] *Eximo* can mean 'remove from a list': *OLD* 3b.
[52] Hardie 1994: 154 on the ambiguity of *Pater Romanus*.
[53] On Statius' reworking of Virgil, see Ganiban 2007: 131, Markus 1997.
[54] Cf. *OLD s.v. admitto* 9: to admit to a status, include in a class or category, as well as 1, to admit or receive visitors.

hoping that only one day would witness such a crime, and Polynices' funeral, stealthy, at night, accidentally on his brother's pyre, proclaims the persistence of their enmity rather than the endurance of poetic glory.[55]

In contrast, Valerius Flaccus uses this *topos* to immortalise Hypsipyle, not just a woman, but always already a tragic heroine:[56]

> non ulla meo te carmine dictam
> abstulerint, durent Latiis modo saecula fastis
> Iliacique Lares tantique palatia regni.   (VF *Argonautica* 2.244–6)

> No age will remove you from your place in my song
> while the era endures in the Latin *fasti*
> and the Trojan household gods and the palaces of such a great reign.

Here Valerius Flaccus makes Roman control of time, religious continuity with the mythical (and epic) past, as well as monumental markers of wealth and power, the guarantors of poetic immortality, but confuses all this Virgilian material by applying it to a female, tragic subject.[57] He also draws on Lucan's personal relationship with his subject matter in his address to Caesar at the site of Troy:[58]

> O sacer et magnus uatum labor! omnia fato
> eripis et populis donas mortalibus aeuum.
> inuidia sacrae, Caesar, ne tangere famae;
> nam, siquid Latiis fas est promittere Musis,
> quantum Zmyrnaei durabunt uatis honores,
> uenturi me teque legent; Pharsalia nostra
> uiuet, et a nullo tenebris damnabimur aeuo.   (*Bellum civile* 9.980–6)

> O sacred and great toil of the poets! You snatch everything
> from fate and bestow the age on mortal peoples.
> May you not be touched with the envy of sacred fame, Caesar;
> for, if it is right to promise anything from Latin Muses,
> as long as the honours of Smyrna's poet endure,
> those to come will read us, me and you; our Pharsalia
> will live, and will be condemned to shadows by no age.

Lucan evokes Homer as the guarantee of poetry's power, just as Statius evokes Virgil; the physical remains of the Homeric monuments have not

---

[55] See Lovatt 1999 on links with Lucan and Pompey.
[56] See Clare 2004, Gibson 2004 on Hypsipyle.
[57] Silius Italicus also offers a Virgilian immortality to two sets of three brothers who kill each other at *Pun.* 4.396–400, but his poetic immortality is sufficient in itself and requires no Roman power, rather reversing the anxieties of Statius' anti-monumentalisation at *Theb.* 11.574–9 (*videre*, *Pun.* 4.399, *viderit*, *Theb.* 11.578).
[58] See Rossi 2001, Tesoriero 2005, Zwierlein 2010.

survived, but live on through the power of the *uates*.⁵⁹ Yet Lucan here equates himself with Caesar, violently ripping the dead from the natural processes of decay.⁶⁰ It is Caesar who threatens fame with envy (*inuidia*) not the other way around, in a reversal of the normal poetic pattern, usurping the gaze of posterity, and looking into the future with an evil eye. The simple equation of epic with monument, epic immortality with Roman political power, does not stay simple for long.

Pompey

Perseus and Medusa bring out the paradox in epic monumentality, that the active hero becomes a passive object, while reflecting on the hero's relationship to monstrosity and divinity. We have also seen the instability of monuments, which threaten to become markers of empty death, along with the anxiety of the relationships between epic poets, political power and the tradition. This chapter brings these themes to a climax with two epic deaths and their monuments: Pompey in Lucan, and Achilles in the *Odyssey* and *Posthomerica*.

The scene of Pompey's treacherous murder at the end of Lucan *Bellum civile* 8 is one of the climactic moments of the poem as it stands.⁶¹ Malamud reads Pompey's decapitated head as a version of the Gorgon's head, and an emblem of the poem.⁶² Her reading is already a visual one: Pompey is both actor and spectator at his own death, 'attempting to fix the image by which he will be memorialized in future texts'.⁶³ He aims at the transcendence of art, but in practice is exposed and mutilated, his dead eyes notably naked as they stare: *lumina nuda rigescunt* ('his naked eyes grow stiff', *BC* 8.683). Fixed and exposed, Malamud's Pompey is utterly disempowered. Finally, his embalmed head faces Caesar in a battle of the gaze, and Caesar becomes a demonic force who can face the gaze of the Gorgon unharmed (9.1032–9).⁶⁴ We can take this reading further by thinking about Pompey's grave. Lucan goes on from

---

⁵⁹ On this passage, see Spencer 2005 who suggests that Caesar freezes the circle of repetition and renewal and simultaneously makes ruins artificial and meaningless.

⁶⁰ As Erictho the witch resuscitates the dead in book 6: this idea of poetry as the violation of the grave recurs in the Pompey passage below.

⁶¹ On this passage see Mayer 1981: 167–90, Malamud 2003, Spencer 2005: 60–4, Erasmo 2005. 'When we consider Lucan's debt to earlier accounts of burial in epic, there is a risk that a modern interpreter will speak of an anti-heroic sensibility. In one way that is what we are dealing with, but not because Lucan faults such descriptions, rather he knows that they are irrelevant to his theme.' (Mayer 1981: 168–9)

⁶² Malamud 2003: 32: 'As a figure that presides over the boundaries between original and imitation, victor and victim, self and other, living and dead, and life and art, the Gorgon's head is an emblem not just of civil war, but of Lucan's own artistic production, *Civil War*.'

⁶³ Malamud 2003: 34.

⁶⁴ Following the argument of Malamud 2003, who points to Erichtho's invocation of a demiurge who can gaze directly on the Gorgon (*BC* 6.744–9) and the alignment of Pompeian forces with Pallas and

the section on Pompey's head to think about the fate of his headless corpse: in apposition to the fixed and mummified head, his body is battered by nature and identifiable only by its lack of identifying features (8.708–11).[65] Cordus decides to bury Pompey's headless body in an improvised grave, using borrowed fire: his monument is a stone in the sand with '*hic situs est Magnus*' ('Here lies the Great man', 8.793) inscribed by charred stick.[66] At 797 Lucan repeats *situs est* to suggest that his burial is provisional; he is fixed, but fixed on the edge of the flowing and changing ocean (*situs est, qua terra extrema refuso | pendet in Oceano*, 'he lies here/is sited here, where the end of the earth hangs on the Ocean poured back', 797–8). Throughout this passage Pompey like Medusa is both powerful and powerless, fixed and mobile, gazed upon and gazing. From the start of Lucan's portrayal Pompey has been a monument and a name, more to-be-looked-at than acting: *plausuque sui gaudere theatri, | nec reparare nouas uires, multumque priori | credere fortunae. stat magni nominis umbra;* ('he rejoiced in the applause of his own theatre, nor did he restore himself with new strength, and trusted greatly in his former fortune. He stands the shadow of a former name.', 1.133–5).[67] The metaphor in *reparare* (repair, renew, restore) suggests that Pompey is like his theatre. Interpretation of the famous tag *stat magni nominis umbra* has tended to focus on the pun on *magnus* and the idea of Pompey as an empty name: but read in context, and followed by the image of Pompey as a tree, loaded down with spoils *nec iam ualidis radicibus haerens | pondere fixa suo est* ('clinging by roots no longer strong and fixed by its own weight', 138–9), he becomes a neglected monument, worshipped but not repaired.

When we go back to Pompey's grave, the same play on monument and name continues: *Romanum nomen et omne | imperium Magno tumuli est modus* ('The Roman name and the whole empire is the limit of the grave for Magnus', 798–9) protests Lucan, resisting the fixing effect of his own poem. *omnia Lagi | arua tenere potest, si nullo caespite nomen | haeserit* ('He can possess all the fields of Lagus, if his name clung to no turf', 802–4).[68] The

---

the Gorgon as agents of cosmic stability (7.144–50, 567–73). 'Like Ovid's Perseus, who uses Medusa's head to turn his enemies into statues that monumentalize his own power, Caesar's acquisition of Pompey's head gives him a symbolic command over the process of signification.' (38)

[65] On Pompey's headlessness, and references to Virgil, Seneca and Ovid, see Malamud 2003: 35–6, Berno 2004.

[66] Spencer 2005: 61–2 notes the ambiguity of *situs*, here as in Horace, where it can refer to place or decay. It would be nice to see an echo of Horatian monumentality here, particularly with the Egyptian context, but the formulaic nature of *hic situs est* greatly undermines the possibility.

[67] On these lines see: Ahl 1976: 156–7, Rosner-Siegel 1983, Narducci 1985: 1533–4, Feeney 1986, Johnson 1987: 73–4, Rossi 2000: 573–4.

[68] Mayer 1981: 181 suggests that the comparison with Hercules and Bacchus here builds up towards an apotheosis of Pompey at the end of the book.

mixing of the positive present tense with the counterfactual conditional shows Lucan's continued paradoxical protests: he has arranged for Pompey's name to be inscribed on a makeshift tomb and he protests against it. Pompey can escape and yet his name is fixed.[69] At 806–15 the narrator lists all the achievements that would not have fitted on a gravestone, no matter how monumental, replicating Cordus' longing for the state funeral Pompey will never have (729–35), so that the poem does not just lament the lack of a monument and provide an incomplete monument, it also provides an imaginary virtual funeral and monument, of the sort Lucan felt Pompey should have had. The passage climaxes with the image of Pompey's name in monumental contexts:

> quis capit haec tumulus? surgit miserabile bustum
> non ullis plenum titulis, non ordine tanto
> fastorum; solitumque legi super alta deorum
> culmina et extructos spoliis hostilibus arcus
> haud procul est ima Pompei nomen harena
> depressum tumulo, quod non legat aduena rectus,
> quod nisi monstratum Romanus transeat hospes.   (*Bellum civile* 8.816–22)

> What grave captures these things? A pitiful tomb rises
> not full of any inscribed honours, nor such a great list
> of offices; and what we were used to read above the high roofs
> of the gods and upon arches built from enemy spoils,
> the name of Pompey, is not far from the sandy depths,
> put down on a burrow, which a traveller could not read standing upright,
> which a Roman visitor would pass by unless it was pointed out.

The name and its reputation are synonymous with the monuments on which they are inscribed:[70] Pompey's achievements set him up high with the gods and looking down on the enemy, while Lucan's version of his tomb is low and obscure, so that even the humble tourist must bend down to look down on it. Lucan's regret at Pompey's burial goes beyond his dislike of the tomb's inferiority: Lucan desires to remove Pompey from the processes of epic, while using epic to build him up. At 840–5 Lucan goes so far as to long to violate Pompey's tomb. The function of burial to pacify the enraged spirit of the dead is invoked only to be denied: at 772–3, Cordus suggests that someone may one day want to placate Pompey's spirit; at 781–2 Lucan calls Cordus' actions a crime, for which he will be granted undue fame; at

---

[69] Comparison with Plutarch's account suggests that Lucan did not invent the whole burial, though the character of Cordus is almost certainly Lucan's invention: see Mayer 1981: 171.

[70] Neither the placing of the name above the roofs of the temples nor the mention of arches was factual (Mayer 1981: 183–4): this seems to me to make Lucan's emphasis on monuments stand out more.

796–7, he asks *cur obicis Magno tumulum manesque uagantes includis?* ('Why do you fling a tomb at Magnus and shut in his wandering spirit?'). The narrator himself longs to violate Pompey's grave and undo his burial:

> quis busta timebit,
> quis sacris dignam mouisse uerebitur umbram?
> imperet hoc nobis utinam scelus et uelit uti
> nostro Roma sinu: satis o nimiumque beatus,
> si mihi contingat manes transferre reuolsos
> Ausoniam, si tale ducis uiolare sepulchrum.   (*Bellum civile* 8.840–5)

> Who will fear the burial place,
> who will fear to move the shade worthy of rites?
> Would that Rome might order this crime from me and be willing
> to make use of my embrace: enough, o too much, of a blessing,
> if it should happen to me to bring back to Ausonia the spirits
> torn away, to violate such a tomb of the leader.

Yet this is not the final note. Lucan's distrust of monumentality leads to a recuperation of Pompey's grave: because this grave is provisional and transitory, there will be no lasting proof of Pompey's death (865–9).[71] On the one hand, tourists will prefer placating Pompey's spirit to visiting the temple of Casian Jupiter (851–8); on the other hand, the modesty of his grave fits with a Roman rejection of gold and luxury. Finally the grave will become as mythical as Crete's claim on the tomb of Jupiter. This final section of book 8 skirts around an apotheosis of Pompey, competing with Jupiter, making Fortuna the ultimate deity (860–1), and equating his humble burial site with the worship of places where thunderbolts have struck.[72] Finally, at the beginning of book 9, his spirit is portrayed rising above the tomb and joining the *semidei manes* ('semi-divine shades', 9.7) in the firmament. Here Pompey regains his powerful gaze and instead of being fixed and set in the ground, attains a divine perspective:

> illic postquam se lumine uero
> inpleuit, stellasque uagas miratus et astra
> fixa polis, uidit quanta sub nocte iaceret
> nostra dies risitque sui ludibria trunci.   (*Bellum civile* 9.11–14)

---

[71] Mayer 1981: 180 notes the change in tone: 'a mean grave will serve Pompey well after all, for it must in time disappear and so contribute to his deification'.

[72] This looks back to the image of Caesar as thunderbolt, perhaps suggesting that Pompey has been struck by Caesar, or maybe rather inverting the imagery, to give Pompey that special relationship with Jupiter and making him the thunderbolt who has come to earth. Mayer (1981: 190) seems to lean towards the latter when he says 'Lucan sets Pompey alongside Jupiter.'

> There, after he had filled himself with true
> light, and wondered at the wandering stars and the constellations
> fixed on the poles, he saw how much our day
> lay under darkness, and laughed at the mockery made of his headless body.

Ultimately his spirit endorses Lucan's continuation of his epic, refusing to be contained by the monument but rather involving itself back in the action by entering the breasts of Cato and Brutus. Death does not fix Pompey; monumentality and near apotheosis are eschewed for action, just as Lucan's epic is more than simply a tomb for Pompey, instead a text that demands engagement. Lucan's epic works by undoing epic, achieves epic authority by denying it, and creates a monument through the deliberate destruction and erasure of epic tropes of monumentality.

The end of Achilles

I started with Achilles and now finish with him, as the emblem of ancient epic. The death of Achilles is the absent heart (and end) of the *Iliad*.[73] The funeral of Patroclus (*Il.* 23.161–257) foreshadows and replaces the funeral of Achilles; the connection is dramatised by Achilles' sacrifice to Patroclus of the locks of hair that he had vowed to the river Spercheios for his safe return (23.138–53). The actual narrative of Achilles' death and funeral must wait for later, supplementary texts. I want to examine here two gestures towards the completion of this Iliadic hiatus: the discussion between the ghosts of Agamemnon and Achilles in *Odyssey* 24, and the full epic account in Quintus Smyrnaeus' *Posthomerica* 3.

In *Odyssey* 24, Hermes is leading the ghosts of the suitors down to the underworld, when Agamemnon and Achilles discuss their own deaths: Achilles laments Agamemnon's unheroic death, and Agamemnon reassures him in contrast that his own death and funeral were truly worthy of him.[74] This account of Achilles' death is thus set in contrast with Agamemnon's death at the hands of Clytemnestra and the suitors' deaths at the hands of Odysseus. Does the *Odyssey* here question the heroic values of the *Iliad*?[75] Is

---

[73] On Achilles as virtually dead, see Seaford 1994: 166–72.
[74] On the debate about the authenticity of *Odyssey* 24 see Stanford 1965, Moulton 1974a, Wender 1978, Whitehead 1984: 119; see also commentaries by Heubeck, Russo and Fernandez-Galliano 1992, De Jong 2001: 565–73, who holds that 'the final scenes of the *Odyssey* are indispensable' (565).
[75] Whitehead 1984: 124 argues that it does: 'the shift from Achilles to Odysseus as paradigmatic figures underlines the transition from the heroic ethos of the *Iliad* to the more morally delineated universe of the *Odyssey*'.

The end of Achilles

it significant that these are insubstantial shades attempting to imagine and share scenes in the past that they can never truly experience (their own deaths and burials)? Agamemnon represents Achilles' body as monumental in its demise: its stature lies in contrast to the ephemerality of battle (σὺ δ' ἐν στροφάλιγγι κονίης / κεῖσο μέγας μεγαλωστί, 'you lay in the whirlwind of dust great in your greatness', *Od.* 24.39–40). Achilles' dead body is also marked, like Hector's, by its beauty (χρόα καλὸν, 'beautiful flesh', 44). The Danaans sensuously prepare the body for burial, and cut off their own hair, in a repetition of Achilles' gesture over the grave of Patroclus (43–6). Agamemnon's description continually involves Achilles as imagined (impossible) viewer: he refers to him as 'you' throughout, apostrophises him by name at 72, 76 and 94, and applies the terminology of ecphrasis: at 61–2, the power of the Muses' lament is emphasised: ἔνθα κεν οὔ τιν' ἀδάκρυτόν γ'ἐνόησας / Ἀργείων· ('There you could not have seen one of the Argives without tears'); at 87–90 he appeals to Achilles' previous experience of funeral games (no doubt most importantly those of Patroclus) to allow him to imagine by how much his own outmatched those of others (ἀλλά κε κεῖνα μάλιστα ἰδὼν θηήσαο θυμῷ, 'but seeing those [games] especially, you would have marvelled in your heart', 90). Achilles is included in his own funeral, but like the viewer of ecphrasis he is also excluded. The description of Achilles' tomb itself:

> ἀμφ' αὐτοῖσι δ' ἔπειτα μέγαν καὶ ἀμύμονα τύμβον
> χεύαμεν Ἀργείων ἱερὸς στρατὸς αἰχμητάων
> ἀκτῇ ἔπι προὐχούσῃ, ἐπὶ πλατεῖ Ἑλλησπόντῳ,
> ὥς κεν τηλεφανὴς ἐκ ποντόφιν ἀνδράσιν εἴη
> τοῖς οἳ νῦν γεγάασι καὶ οἳ μετόπισθεν ἔσονται. (*Odyssey* 24.80–4)
>
> And around them then we piled up a tomb great
> and excellent, the sacred army of the Argive spearmen,
> on a headland, by the broad Hellespont,
> so that it would be seen from afar on the sea by men,
> both those who now are and those who will be in later days.

depicts it as great, like Achilles, an object on view through space and time. Achilles, then, has the marker of fame that Hector desired (even echoing ἐπὶ πλατεῖ Ἑλλησπόντῳ, from his speech at *Il.* 7.86). Agamemnon finishes with an emphasis on Achilles' name and *kleos*:

> ὣς σὺ μὲν οὐδὲ θανὼν ὄνομ' ὤλεσας, ἀλλά τοι αἰεὶ
> πάντας ἐπ' ἀνθρώπους κλέος ἔσσεται ἐσθλόν, Ἀχιλλεῦ· (*Odyssey* 24. 93–4)
>
> Thus not even after you died is your name destroyed, but always for you will there be noble fame among all men, Achilles

finishing the line with his name, as if to underline the point. But the tomb, of course, is no guarantee of memory: even with an inscription, which can be erased or deleted. This speech, rather, performs the *kleos* that it describes. Whitehead 1984 argues that Agamemnon misunderstands and misrepresents Achilles with his emphasis on material goods and the 'heroic code': for him it is 'the transcendent knowledge which Achilles achieves [which] consists in the internalization of the meaning of death' that really matters. Certainly, when Achilles gives instructions for the burial of Patroclus, he asks for a modest tomb (τύμβον δ'οὐ μάλα πολλὸν, 'no huge mound', *Il.* 23.245). But he immediately qualifies that by asking them to build it broad and high (εὐρύν θ' ὑψηλόν, 247) after he is gone. Similarly, his famous statement at *Od.* 11.489–91, in which he appears to deny the importance of heroism and honour, to undo his earlier choice of glory over long life, by saying that he would rather be the servant of a humble man, and alive, than the king of the dead, is qualified by his joy at the heroic success of Neoptolemus, as reported by Odysseus (11.538–40). Does this passage, then, valorise the comparison between Odysseus' successful *nostos* and Agamemnon's failed one, over the comparison between Achilles' heroic death and Agamemnon's unheroic one? Rather, Achilles and Odysseus are different but evenly matched, each achieving exemplarity, but in different contexts and different ways. This dialogue of the dead provides a rather unsatisfying shadow of, repetition of, poetic fame, which, like the glory, and the funeral, does not really stand up to comparison with the intensity of the actual experience of war (or life). Glory (like true union with the beloved, or true return from exile) can only be desired, a desire which can never be fulfilled.

Quintus Smyrnaeus' account of Achilles' death and burial takes a whole book of the epic (and continues into the funeral games in book 4, and the contest over Achilles' weapons, including ecphrasis, in book 5). Quintus' Achilles is grander, more enormous, almost monstrous, and his funeral assumes similar proportions. The account of his death belittles Apollo and augments Achilles: Achilles is on the point of destroying the gates of Troy, when Apollo sees him, faces him, eyes blazing, and tries to stop him with a shout (*PH* 3.26–42). Achilles is not just unfazed: he shouts back, and orders him back to Olympus (3.43–52). He turns his back on the god in a clear gesture of contempt (53), treating him like Diomedes had treated Aphrodite, and Apollo hides in a cloud (60–2) to shoot him. In other versions of the myth, it is Paris, helped by Apollo, who shoots Achilles.[76]

---

[76] On stories surrounding the death of Achilles, see Burgess 1995, Barchiesi 1996; see also Heslin 2005, Burgess 2009.

The end of Achilles

When Achilles reacts to the wound, he laments that his opponent will not face him (69, 72, 77–8). He even pulls out the arrow and throws it back, symbolically returning Apollo's penetrative gaze, and the arrow miraculously goes back to its sender (83–9), whom the narrative follows to Olympus. There, we are aligned with the Danaan gods, particularly Hera, as Apollo becomes the object of their contemptuous gaze (96, 131–4), and cannot meet Hera's eyes.[77] Achilles is wounded (and it is implied that poison is the actual means of death at 33), but nonetheless continues fighting: his visual power is unimpaired.[78] Quintus attempts to recuperate and magnify Achilles' death and glory by all means possible, thereby underlining still further the instability of epic glory.

Achilles' body is itself like a monument, in its size, visual impact and memorable nature. When the arrow hits him in the ankle, he falls like a tower hit by a whirlwind in an earthquake (63–5); when he finally dies, he falls like a cliff (177); the lamenting Achaeans wail for him like the inhabitants of a sacked city lament for the walls which kept them safe (413–16). His death exposes them to danger, but is also closely linked (causally and in imagery) to the fall of Troy: when Calliope consoles Thetis (652–4), she points to the imminent destruction of Troy – and the returning Greeks – and Zeus, too, contemplates the necessity for the fall of Troy now that Achilles is dead (4.56–61). This inverts and repeats the relationship between Hector and his city, the defender of the city, assimilating Achilles to his arch-enemy in death.

The body is not just figuratively but also literally monumental in scale: when they carry him to the camp, they strain beneath the weight (385–6); Ajax notes his size (433–4); when she beautifies him, Tritogeneia makes him even bigger (540). In the burial of Patroclus, his bones stand out because of their position (*Il.* 23.238–42); those of Achilles, on the other hand, stand out because of their sheer size (*PH* 3.723–9); they are like the bones of a Giant (ἀλλ' οἷα Γίγαντος ἀτειρέος, 725). Achilles' direct opposition to Apollo also contributes to this image of him as a Gigantic figure; most strikingly, his dead body is compared to that of Tityos (389–401), who was also shot down by Apollo, as he tried to rape Leto. This simile is also used of the gigantic and Gigantic body of Capaneus (*Thebaid* 11.12–17), and contributes to the sense of Quintus' Achilles as not just godlike but also monstrous. So, when the Trojans gaze at his body on the battlefield, they gaze like sheep at a

---

[77] Hera speaks, and the coverage of the Greek gods goes from line 96 to line 134. The balancing Trojan gods, in contrast, are given only four lines, in which their subordination to Hera is emphasised.

[78] Immediately after the wound, he glares around (παπτήνας, 67); he is compared to a wounded lion whose eyes glare and roll (145–6); his spear is like lightning (150); he deals Hipponous an eye wound (155–6).

predator (179–85). When he is compared to a god, it is Ares struck down by Athene (419–21), a god noted for his monstrosity. Not all Trojans are sheep, though: Paris motivates them in their fight for his corpse, by imagining the grieving women of Troy rejoicing in the sight of his dead body, like lionesses or female panthers exulting in the death of a hunter (200–7), displacing the epic anger onto the watching women, who are simultaneously orientalised and made masculine. When Tritogeneia treats his corpse with ambrosia, she makes it untainted, but preserves his fierce gaze (537), so that the Argives are amazed that he is like a living man (541–3). Even his allies seem a touch afraid.

Achilles is not wholly monstrous: his gentleness and civility are also stressed by the women he captured (549–50). But he is not feminised in his death: instead the imagery of purple and white, beauty and vulnerability, is displaced onto the lamenting Briseis (551–8), who is also monumentalised as a version of Niobe (574–81), whose tears will never dry, like water running down a rock. Achilles' body is the object of all the epic gazes: the gods, not just Thetis and Calliope, but also the other Olympians (4.43–55), women on the walls and in the camp, his comrades and enemies.

The funeral itself, with all its surrounding laments, is an intensification and aggrandisement of those of Hector and Patroclus in the *Iliad*, and of Achilles himself in the *Odyssey*. Hector has three laments, from Helen, Hecuba and Andromache; Achilles has Ajax, Phoenix, Nestor, Briseis, Thetis (and arguably Calliope). Where Agamemnon mentions the songs of the muses, Quintus gives us direct speech from Calliope, as well as mentioning other songs. The pyre of Patroclus will not light and the winds must be called (*Il.* 23.192–216); here Zeus himself sends Hermes to bring the winds without the initial difficulties (699–710). The list of luxury goods is further increased (689–93). The description of the tomb reflects this trumping of earlier epic:

> Ἀργεῖοι καὶ σῆμα πελώριον ἀμφεβάλοντο
> ἀκτῇ ἐπ' ἀκροτάτῃ παρὰ βένθεσιν Ἑλλησπόντου
> Μυρμιδόνων βασιλῆα θρασὺν περικωκύοντες.   (*Posthomerica* 3.740–2)
>
> The Argives heaped an enormous barrow for his tomb,
> at the end of the headland close to the Hellespont's depths,
> while mourning for the Myrmidons' heroic king.

Its monstrous size reflects the body of Achilles, and its position on the headland is further along, with the Hellespont evoking the previous descriptions.

All this striving for size and effect, however, is its own undoing. By not describing Achilles' death and burial, the *Iliad* had already done it to death. The cyclic *Aithiopis* seems to have forestalled Achilles' burial when Thetis snatches the corpse from the pyre.⁷⁹ No grief can be great enough, no lament powerful enough, no tomb enormous enough. As if to prove this point, the tragedy of Ajax in book 5 repeats Achilles' death (a repetition self-consciously annotated at 5.601–3, 658) and burial in a different mode: again the Greeks lament the loss of their greatest protection (662–3); again a tomb on a headland (656–63), which ends the book, suggesting a suicidal, self-destructive edge to epic heroism. The epic itself will end with the destruction of Troy trumped only by the failed *nostoi* of the Greek heroes.⁸⁰ Quintus' sophisticated insertion of his own story into the gap between the *Iliad* and *Odyssey* allows a new reflection on the gap in the heart of epic.

Last words

This book began with the powerful gaze of Achilles in *Iliad* 18 and the uncovered head of Parthenopaeus, object of many gazes, in *Thebaid* 9. If Achilles is repetitively memorialised as a shadow of his former self, Parthenopaeus is the closing emblem of the *Thebaid*:⁸¹

> Arcada quo planctu genetrix Erymanthia clamet,
> Arcada, consumpto seruantem sanguine uultus,
> Arcada, quem geminae pariter fleuere cohortes.
> uix nouus ista furor ueniensque implesset Apollo,
> et mea iam longo meruit ratis aequore portum.   (*Thebaid*. 12.805–9)

> 'Arcadian boy', with what wailing shouts the Erymanthian mother,
> 'Arcadian boy', preserving his face with his blood consumed,
> 'Arcadian boy', whom twin cohorts lament equally,
> scarcely might a new madness fill me up for those things, and present Apollo,
> and my ship has now deserved the harbour after a long ocean.

Augoustakis reads this passage as 'the relegation of the female to the fringes of the epic landscape' causing 'the reinforcement of gender and generic boundaries'.⁸² In contrast, Markus suggests that 'Statius refashions the traditional ideology of epic ... and turns it into a locus not of memory, but of lament.'⁸³ This is a play on sound, not sight, the repeated *Arcada* merging the women's voices with that of the poet, those of his readers and reciters. The hint of a potential beginning might invite us to link Parthenopaeus with Achilles in the *Achilleid* to come, another boy,

---

⁷⁹ West 2003: 112–13.   ⁸⁰ On the end of Quintus, see Carvounis 2007.
⁸¹ Hardie 1993: 48: 'It is a good moment to stop, for Virgil had also ended with a dead Arcadian, Pallas.' Although the *Aeneid* really ends with Turnus, not Pallas.
⁸² Augoustakis 2010: 90–1. See also Henderson 1993: 188, Masterson 2005: 313.   ⁸³ Markus 2003: 467.

protected and pursued fruitlessly by his mother.[84] Statius has already used up the poet's traditional declaration of inability (797–9):[85] even if he had a hundred chests and a divine voice, he could not encompass the extent of the lament (and the monuments) required by the devastation of Thebes.[86] Yet still we focus in on the face of the desired boy (*uultus*, 806), consumed by epic narrative, an empty shadow of active beauty.[87] All the words of epic come down to one word, a name, repeatedly called, and bringing out only the emptiness of words.[88]

How does the epic gaze interact with epic acts of preserving and remembering? If we take the gaze as the disturbance in the field of vision which reveals the gap that troubles and draws us in, what is the gap in the epic monument? The gap must surely be indeterminacy, elusiveness, the way a monumental death and a monumental poem, no matter how big, can never really convey pain or replace destruction with glory. What in the end is the *jouissance*, the climactic moment of joy in epic? The joy that we must turn away from and never fully see? Surely it is death itself.[89] Ovid's Perseus sidesteps death for himself, and his victims, by taking them out of the world of doing and into the world of art, which is why Ovid's Perseid looks askance at the heart of epic. The appeal to apotheosis, so important in the closure of both Ovid's *Metamorphoses* and Lucan's Pompey episode, is always a step back from the moment of truth. This is why the end of the *Aeneid* remains so compelling. We watch in horror and delight as Turnus dies:

> ast illi soluuntur frigore membra
> uitaque cum gemitu fugit indignata sub umbras.   (*Aeneid* 12.951–2)

> But his limbs dissolve in the cold
> and his life flees with a groan, angered, into the shadows.

And we end in darkness, in which we can see no more.

---

[84] 'A programme to inspire another epic': Hardie 1993: 48.
[85] Hinds 1998: 91–8, Georgacopoulou 2005: 229–31.
[86] On epic and lament see Fantham 1999. Female voices: Dietrich 1999.
[87] Hardie 1993 emphasises the way that Parthenopaeus brings the two sides together: 'in the final count, the tripling of grief overbids the gemination of civil war' (48): but the potentially uncountable ongoing momentum of epic promises ever more war, ever more grief.
[88] McNelis 2007: 171 on the 'gap between the grand narratives of martial valour and heroism and more mundane stories about those who live non-heroic lives'. But the two reflect upon each other.
[89] On film and the death drive, see McGowan 2011.

Bibliography

Agri, D. (2011) 'Pietas, pudor and timor: heroic emotions and intertextuality in Flavian epic'. Diss., University of Nottingham.
Ahl, F. (1976) *Lucan: An Introduction*. Ithaca, NY.
Alden, M. (1997) 'The resonances of the song of Ares and Aphrodite', *Mnemosyne* 50: 513–29.
  (2000) *Homer beside Himself: Para-Narratives in the Iliad*. Oxford.
Allan, W. (2006) 'Divine justice and cosmic order in early Greek epic', *JHS* 126: 1–35.
Andersen, O. (1978) *Die Diomedesgestalt in der Ilias*. Oslo.
Armstrong, D. (ed.) (2004) *Vergil, Philodemus and the Augustans*. Austin, TX.
Armstrong, P. (2000) *Shakespeare's Visual Regime: Tragedy, Psychoanalysis and the Gaze*. Basingstoke, UK.
Armstrong, R. (2004) 'Retiring Apollo: Ovid on the politics and poetics of self-sufficiency', *CQ* 54: 528–50.
Ash, R. (2002) 'Epic encounters? Ancient historical battle narrative and the epic tradition', in *Clio and the Poets: Augustan Poetry and the Traditions of Ancient Historiography*, eds. D. S. Levene and D. P. Nelis. Leiden: 253–74.
Asso, P. (2010) *A Commentary on Lucan De bello civili IV: Introduction, Edition and Translation*. Berlin.
Augoustakis, A. (2010) *Motherhood and the Other: Fashioning Female Power in Flavian Epic*. Oxford.
Austin, R. G. (ed.) (1964) *P. Vergili Maronis Aeneidos Liber Secundus*. Oxford.
  (1977) *P. Vergili Maronis Aeneidos Liber Sextus*. Oxford.
Austin, T. and Barker, M. (eds.) (2003) *Contemporary Hollywood Stardom*. London.
Baier, T. (1998) 'Ursache und Funktion des Krieges gegen Perses in den Argonautica des Valerius Flaccus', in *Ratis omnia vincet*, eds. U. Eigler and E. Lefèvre. Munich: 319–36.
Bakker, E. J. (1993) 'Discourse and performance: involvement, visualization and "presence" in Homeric poetry', *ClAnt* 12: 1–29.
  (2005) *Pointing to the Past: From Formula to Performance in Homeric Poetics*. Cambridge, MA.
Baldo, G. (1995) *Dall' Eneide alle Metamorfosi: il codice epico di Ovidio*. Padua.

Bär, S. (ed.) (2009) *Quintus Smyrnaeus, Posthomerica 1: Die Wiedergeburt des Epos aus dem Geiste der Amazonomachie, Mit einem Kommentar zu den Versen 1–219*. Göttingen.
  (2010) 'Quintus Smyrnaeus and the second sophistic', *HSPh* 105: 287–316.
Bär, S., Baumbach, M. and Dümmler, N. (eds.) (2007) *Quintus Smyrnaeus: Transforming Homer in Second Sophistic Epic*. Berlin.
Barasch, M. (2001) *Blindness: The History of a Mental Image in Western Thought*. London.
Barchiesi, A. (1996) 'Simonides and Horace on the death of Achilles', *Arethusa* 29: 247–53.
  (1997) 'Virgilian narrative: ecphrasis', in *The Cambridge Companion to Virgil*, ed. C. Martindale. Cambridge: 271–81.
  (1998) 'The statue of Athena at Troy and Carthage', in *Style and Tradition: Studies in Honour of Wendell Clausen*, eds. P. E. Knox and C. Foss. Stuttgart: 130–40.
Barker, E. (2009) *Entering the Agon: Dissent and Authority in Homer, Historiography and Tragedy*. Oxford.
Barnes, H. (1974) *The Meddling Gods: Four Essays on Classical Themes*. Lincoln, NE.
Barry, W. D. (1996) 'Roof tiles and urban violence in the ancient world', *GRBS* 37: 55–74.
Bartel, H. and Simon, A. (eds.) (2010) *Unbinding Medea: Interdisciplinary Approaches to a Classical Myth from Antiquity to the 21st Century*. London.
Barton, C. (1993) *The Sorrows of the Ancient Romans: The Gladiator and the Monster*. Princeton, NJ.
  (2001) *Roman Honor: The Fire in the Bones*. Berkeley, CA.
Bartsch, S. (1994) *Actors in the Audience: Theatricality and Doublespeak from Nero to Hadrian*. Cambridge, MA.
  (1997) *Ideology in Cold Blood: A Reading of Lucan's Civil War*. Cambridge, MA.
  (1998) '*Ars* and the man: the politics of art in Virgil's *Aeneid*', *CPh* 93: 322–42.
  (2006) *The Mirror of the Self: Sexuality, Self-Knowledge and the Gaze in the Early Roman Empire*. Chicago, IL.
Beard, M. (2002) *The Parthenon*. London.
  (2008) *Pompeii: The Life of a Roman Town*. London.
Beck, D. (2007) 'Ecphrasis, interpretation and audience in *Aeneid* 1 and *Odyssey* 8', *AJPh* 128: 533–49.
Becker, A. S. (1995) *The Shield of Achilles and the Poetics of Ekphrasis*. London.
Beissinger, M., Tylus, J. and Wofford, S. (eds.) (1999) *Epic Traditions in the Contemporary World: The Poetics of Community*. Berkeley, CA.
Bergren, A. (1979) 'Helen's web: time and tableau in the *Iliad*', *Helios* 7: 19–34.
Bernadete, S. (1968) 'The aristeia of Diomedes and the plot of the *Iliad*', *Agon* 1: 10–38.
Bernidaki-Aldous, E. (1990) *Blindness in a Culture of Light: Especially the Case of Oedipus at Colonus of Sophocles*. New York.

Berno, F. R. (2004) 'Un *truncus*, molti re: Priamo, Agamemnone, Pompeo, Virgilio, Seneca, Lucano.' *Maia* 56: 79–84.
Bernstein, N. W. (2004) '*Auferte oculos*: modes of spectatorship in Statius' *Thebaid* 11', *Phoenix* 58: 62–85.
Berres, T. (1992) *Vergil und die Helenaszene mit einem Exkurs zu den Halbversen*. Heidelberg.
Bexley, E. M. (2009) 'Replacing Rome: geographic and political centrality in Lucan's *Pharsalia*', *CPh* 104: 459–75.
Billerbeck, M. (1985) 'Aspects of stoicism in Flavian epic', *PLLS* 5: 341–56.
Blundell, S. and Williamson, M. (eds.) (1998) *The Sacred and the Feminine in Ancient Greece*. London.
Blundell, S., Cairns, D. and Rabinowitz, N. (eds.) (forthcoming) *Greek Visions*. Special issue of *Helios*.
Bömer, F. (1969) *P. Ovidius Naso Metamorphosen*. Heidelberg.
Bordwell, D. and Carroll, N. (eds.) (1996) *Post-Theory: Reconstructing Film Studies*. Madison, WI.
Bouquet, J. (2001) *Le songe dans l'épopée Latine d'Ennius à Claudian*. Brussels.
Bowra, C. M. (1952) *Heroic Poetry*. London.
Boyd, B. W. (1992) 'Virgil's Camilla and the traditions of catalog and ecphrasis', *AJPh* 113: 213–34.
Boyle, A. J. (ed.) (1993) *Roman Epic*. London.
Braswell, B. K. (1982) 'The song of Ares and Aphrodite: theme and relevance to *Odyssey* 8', *Hermes* 110: 129–37.
Braund, S. (1997) 'Ending epic: Statius, Theseus and a merciful release', *PCPhS* 43: 1–23.
Braune, J. (1935) *Nonnos und Ovid*. Greifswald.
Brown, C. G. (1989) 'Ares and Aphrodite and the laughter of the gods', *Phoenix* 43: 283–93.
Brown, P. M. (1984) *Lucretius De Rerum Natura 1*. Bristol, UK.
Brown, R. (1987) 'The palace of the sun in Ovid's *Metamorphoses*', in *Homo Viator: Classical Essays for John Bramble*, eds. M. Whitby, P. Hardie and M. Whitby. Bristol, UK: 211–20.
Bruère, R. T. (1951) 'Lucan's Cornelia', *CPh* 46: 221–6.
Buchan, M. (2003) 'Politics in the *Iliad*', *CR* 53: 275–6.
Buckley, E. (forthcoming) 'Seeing the *Medea*: epiphany and *anagnorisis* in Valerius Flaccus' *Argonautica*', in *Epic Visions*, eds. H. V. Lovatt and C. Vout. Cambridge.
Bulloch, A. (2006) 'Jason's cloak', *Hermes* 134: 44–68.
Burgess, J. S. (1995) 'Achilles' Heel: the death of Achilles in ancient myth', *ClAnt* 14: 217–44.
 (2009) *The Death and Afterlife of Achilles*. Baltimore, MD.
Burkert, W. (1960) 'Das Lied von Ares und Aphrodite: Zum Verhältnis von Odyssee und Ilias', *RhM* 103: 130–44.
 (1981) 'Θεῶν ὄπιν οὐκ ἀλέγοντες: Götterfurcht und Leumannsches Missverständnis', *MH* 38: 195–204.

(1985) *Greek Religion: Archaic and Classical*. Oxford.
Butler, J. (1990) *Gender Trouble: Feminism and the Subversion of Identity*. New York.
Buxton, R. (1980) 'Blindness and limits: Sophokles and the logic of myth', *JHS* 100: 22–37.
Cairns, D. (2002) 'The meaning of the veil in ancient Greek culture', in *Women's Dress in the Ancient Greek World*, ed. L. Llewellyn-Jones. Swansea, UK: 73–94.
  (2005) 'Bullish looks and sidelong glances: social interaction and the eyes in ancient Greek culture', in *Body Language in the Greek and Roman Worlds*, ed. D. Cairns. Swansea, UK: 123–55.
Carvounis, K. (2007) 'Final scenes in Quintus Smyrnaeus, *Posthomerica* 14', in *Quintus Smyrnaeus: Transforming Homer in Second Sophistic Epic*, eds. S. Bär, M. Baumbach and N. Dümmler. Berlin: 241–58.
  (2008) 'Transforming the Homeric models: Quintus' battle among the gods in the *Posthomerica*', *Ramus* 37: 60–78.
Casali, S. (2004) 'Nisus and Euryalus: exploiting the contradictions in Virgil's *Doloneia*', *HSPh* 102: 319–54.
Chanan, M. (1996) *The Dream that Kicks: The Prehistory and the Early Years of Cinema in Britain*. London.
Chinn, C. (2010) '*Nec discolor amnis*: intertext and aesthetics in Statius' shield of Crenaeus (9.332–338)', *Phoenix* 64: 148–69.
Chodorow, N. (1994) *Femininities, Masculinities, Sexualities: Freud and Beyond*. London.
Christensen, J. P. (2007) ' The failure of speech: rhetoric and politics in the Iliad '. Diss., New York University.
Cixous, H. (1976) 'The Laugh of the Medusa', *Signs* 1.
Clare, R. (2002) *The Path of the Argo: Language, Imagery and Narrative in the Argonautica of Apollonius Rhodius*. Cambridge.
  (2004) 'Tradition and originality: allusion in Valerius Flaccus' Lemnian episode', in *Latin Epic and Didactic Poetry*, ed. M. Gale. Swansea, UK: 125–48.
Clarke, M. (2004) 'Manhood and heroism', in *The Cambridge Companion to Homer*, ed. R. Fowler. Cambridge: 74–90.
Clauss, J. J. and Johnston, S. I. (eds.) (1997) *Medea: Essays on Medea in Myth, Literature, Philosophy and Art*. Princeton, NJ.
Clavel-Lévêque, M. (1984) *L'Empire en jeux: espace symbolique et pratique sociale dans le monde romain*. Paris.
Clay, J. S. (1997) *The Wrath of Athena: Gods and Men in the Odyssey*. Lanham, MD.
  (2011) *Homer's Trojan Theater: Space, Vision and Memory in the Iliad*. Cambridge.
Clover, C. J. (1992) *Men, Women and Chainsaws: Gender in the Modern Horror Film*. London.
Coffee, N. (2009) *The Commerce of War: Exchange and Social Order in Latin Epic*. Chicago, IL.
Colakis, M. (1985) 'The laughter of the suitors in *Odyssey* 20', *CW* 79: 137–41.

Coleman, K. (2000) 'Missio at Halicarnassus', *HSPh* 100: 487–500.
Collins, D. (2004) *Master of the Game: Competition and Performance in Greek Poetry*. Cambridge, MA.
Collins, L. (1987) 'The wrath of Paris: ethical vocabulary and ethical type in the *Iliad*', *AJPh* 108: 220–32.
Connell, R. (1995) *Masculinities*. Cambridge.
Constantinidou, S. (1994) 'The vision of Homer: the eyes of heroes and gods', *Antichthon* 28: 1–15.
  (2010) 'The light imagery of divine manifestation in Homer', in *Light and Darkness in Ancient Greek Myth and Religion*, eds. M. Christopoulos, E. D. Karakantza and O. Levaniouk. Lanham, MD: 91–109.
Conte, G. B. (1974) *Saggio di commento a Lucano: Pharsalia VI 118–260, l'Aristia di Sceva*. Pisa.
  (1986) *The Rhetoric of Imitation: Genre and Poetic Memory in Virgil and other Latin Poets*. Ithaca, NY.
Copjec, J. (1994) *Read my Desire: Lacan against the Historicists*. Cambridge, MA.
Cowan, R. (2007) *The Headless City: The Decline and Fall of Capua in Silius Italicus' Punica*. Available: http://ora.ouls.ox.ac.uk/objects/uuid:dceb6b5a-980c-46ca-ac9e-088615e7fbea.
Cribiore, R. (2001) *Gymnastics of the Mind: Greek Education in Hellenistic and Roman Egypt*. Princeton, NJ.
Crowther, N. B. (1985) 'Male beauty contests in Greece: the *euandria* and the *euexia*', *AC* 54: 285–91.
Currie, G. (1995) *Image and Mind: Film, Philosophy and Cognitive Science*. Cambridge.
  (2010) *Narratives and Narrators: A Philosophy of Stories*. Oxford.
Currie, G. and Jureidini, J. (2004) 'Narrative and coherence', *Mind and Language* 19: 409–27.
Cuypers, M. P. (1997) 'Apollonius Rhodius Argonautica 2.1–310'. Diss., Leiden.
Cyrino, M. S. (2010) *Aphrodite*. New York.
D'Alessandro Behr, F. (2007) *Feeling History: Lucan, Stoicism, and the Poetics of Passion*. Columbus, OH.
Daremberg, C. (1865) *La médicine dans Homère*. Paris.
Davidson, J. (2007) *The Greeks and Greek Love: A Radical Reappraisal of Homosexuality in Ancient Greece*. London.
Davis, P. J. (2009) 'Remembering Ovid: the Io episode in Valerius Flaccus' *Argonautica*', *Antichthon* 43: 1–11.
De Jong, I. J. F. (1987) *Narrators and Focalizers: The Presentation of the Story in the Iliad*. Amsterdam.
  (1996) 'Sunsets and sunrises in Homer and Apollonius of Rhodes: book-divisions and beyond', *Dialogos* 3: 20–35.
  (2001) *A Narratological Commentary on the Odyssey*. Cambridge.
De Lacy, P. (1964) 'Distant views: the imagery of Lucretius 2', *CJ* 60: 49–55.
De Lauretis, T. (1984) *Alice Doesn't: Feminism, Semiotics, Cinema*. Bloomington, IN.
Deacy, S. and Villing, A. (eds.) (2001) *Athena in the Classical World*. Leiden.

Debrohun, J. B. (2003) *Roman Propertius and the Reinvention of Elegy.* Ann Arbor, MI.
DeForest, M. M. (1994) *Apollonius' Argonautica: A Callimachean Epic.* Leiden.
Delvigo, M. L. (2005) 'La rivelazione di Venere (*Aen.* 2, 589–623)', *MD* 55: 61–75.
Depew, M. and Obbink, D. (eds.) (2000) *Matrices of Genre: Authors, Canons and Society.* Cambridge, MA.
Desmet, P. M. A. (2002) *Designing Emotions.* Delft.
Detel, W. (1998) *Foucault and Classical Antiquity: Power, Ethics and Knowledge.* Cambridge.
Devallet, G. (1992) 'La description du bouclier d'Hannibal chez Silius Italicus', in *L'Univers Epique,* ed. M. Woronoff. Paris: 189–99.
Dewar, M. (1994) 'Laying it on with a trowel: the proem to Lucan and related texts', *CQ* 44: 199–211.
Dickie, M. (1990) 'Talos bewitched: magic, atomic theory and paradoxography in Apollonius *Argonautica* 4.1638–88', *Proceedings of the Leeds International Latin Seminar* 6: 267–96.
  (1991) 'Heliodorus and Plutarch on the evil eye', *CPh* 86: 17–29.
  (1993) '*Baskania, probaskania* and *prosbaskania*', *Glotta* 71: 174–7.
Dickson, K. (1995) *Nestor: Poetic Memory in Greek Epic.* New York.
Dietrich, J. (1999) 'Thebaid's feminine ending', *Ramus* 28: 40–53.
Dinter, M. T. (2006) 'Lucan's epic body: corporeality in the Bellum civile'. Diss., Cambridge.
Dixon, S. (2001) *Reading Roman Women.* London.
Doane, M. A. (1982) 'Film and masquerade: theorising the female spectator', *Screen* 23: 74–87.
  (1988) 'Masquerade reconsidered: further thoughts on the female spectator', *Discourse* 11: 42–54.
  (1991) *Femmes Fatales: Feminism, Film Theory, Psychoanalysis.* New York.
Dominik, W. J. (1994) *The Mythic Voice of Statius.* Leiden.
Dominik, W. J., Garthwaite, J. and Roche, P. A. (eds.) (2009) *Writing Politics in Imperial Rome.* Leiden.
Donlan, W. (1999) *The Aristocratic Ideal and Selected Papers.* Wauconda, IL.
Dover, K. J. (1978) *Greek Homosexuality.* London.
Due, O. S. (1974) *Changing Forms: Studies in Ovid's Metamorphoses.* Copenhagen.
Dundes, A. (ed.) (1981) *The Evil Eye: A Folklore Casebook.* New York.
Dyck, A. R. (1989) 'On the way from Colchis to Corinth: Medea in book 4 of the *Argonautica*', *Hermes* 117: 455–70.
Dyer, G. (1995) *Missing of the Somme.* London.
Dyer, R. (2004) *Heavenly Bodies: Film Stars and Society,* 2nd edn. London.
Dyson, J. (1996) 'Dido the Epicurean', *ClAnt* 15: 203–21.
  (1999) 'Lilies and violence: Lavinia's blush in the song of Orpheus', *CPh* 94: 281–8.
Edwards, C. and Woolf, G. (2003) *Rome the Cosmopolis.* Cambridge.
Edwards, M. W. (1991) *The Iliad: A Commentary,* vol. 5: *Books 17–20.* Cambridge.
  (2002) *Sound, Sense, and Rhythm: Listening to Greek and Latin Poetry.* Princeton, NJ.

Effe, B. (2001) 'The similes of Apollonius Rhodius: intertextuality and epic convention', in *A Companion to Apollonius Rhodius*, eds. T. D. Papanghelis and A. Rengakos. Leiden: 147–69.
Egan, R. B. (1996) 'A reading of the Helen–Venus episode in *Aeneid* 2', *ECM* 15: 379–95.
Elley, D. (1984) *The Epic Film: Myth and History*. London.
Ellsworth, J. D. (1988) 'The episode of the Sibyl in Ovid's *Metamorphoses* (14.103–56)', in *East Meets West: Homage to Edgar C. Knowlton*, eds. R. L. Hadich and J. D. Ellsworth. Honolulu, HI: 47–55.
Elm von der Osten, D. (2007) *Die Konzeption der Göttin Venus in den Argonautica des Valerius Flaccus*. Stuttgart.
Elsner, J. (ed.) (1996) *Art and Text in Roman Culture*. Cambridge.
  (1998) *Imperial Rome and Christian Triumph: The Art of the Roman Empire AD 100–450*. Oxford.
  (2002) 'The genres of ekphrasis', *Ramus* 31: 1–18.
  (2007) 'Viewing Ariadne: from ekphrasis to wall-painting in the Roman world', *CPh* 102: 20–44.
Elsner, J. and Masters, J. (eds.) (1994) *Reflections of Nero*. London.
Erasmo, M. (2005) 'Mourning Pompey: Lucan and the poetics of death ritual', *Studies in Latin Literature and Roman History* 12: 344–60.
Esrock, E. J. (1994) *The Reader's Eye: Visual Imaging as Reader Response*. Baltimore, MD.
Esteves, V. A. (1982) '*Oculos ad moenia torsit*: on *Aeneid* 4.220', *CPh* 77: 22–34.
Faber, R. (2006) 'The description of Crenaeus' shield in *Thebaid* IX, 332–38 and the theme of divine deception', *Latomus* 65: 108–14.
Fabre-Serris, J. (2008) *Rome, l'Arcadie et la mer des Argonautes: essai sur la naissance d'une mythologie des origines en Occident – mythes, imaginaires, religions*. Villeneuve d'Ascq.
Fantham, E. (1979) 'Ovid's Ceyx and Alcyone: the metamorphosis of a myth', *Phoenix* 33: 330–45.
  (1992) 'Lucan's Medusa-Excursus: its design and purpose', *MD* 29: 95–119.
  (1997) 'The ambiguity of Virtus in Lucan's *Civil War* and Statius' *Thebaid*', *Arachnion* 3: www.cisi.unito.it/arachne/num3/fantham.html.
  (1999) 'The role of lament in the growth and death of Roman epic', in *Epic Traditions in the Contemporary World: The Poetics of Community*, eds. M. Beissinger, J. Tylus and S. Wofford. Berkeley, CA: 221–36.
  (2003) 'The angry poet and the angry gods: problems of theodicy in Lucan's epic of defeat', in *Ancient Anger: Perspectives from Homer to Galen*, eds. S. Braund and G. Most. Cambridge: 229–49.
  (2006) 'The perils of prophecy: Statius' Amphiaraus and his literary antecedents', in *Flavian Poetry*, eds. R. R. Nauta, H.-J. van Dam and J. J. L. Smolenaars. Leiden: 147–62.
Faraone, C. A. (1999) *Ancient Greek Love Magic*. Cambridge, MA.
Feeney, D. C. (1986) '*Stat magni nominis umbra*: Lucan on the greatness of Pompeius Magnus', *CQ* 36: 239–43.

(1990) 'The taciturnity of Aeneas', in *Oxford Readings in Vergil's Aeneid*, ed. S. J. Harrison. Oxford: 167–90.
(1991) *The Gods in Epic*. Oxford.
Feldherr, A. (1995) 'Ships of state: *Aeneid* 5 and Augustan circus spectacle', *ClAnt* 14: 245–65.
(1998) *Spectacle and Society in Livy's History*. Berkeley, CA.
(2009) 'Delusions of grandeur: Lucretian 'passages' in Livy', in *Paradox and the Marvellous in Augustan Literature and Culture*, ed. P. Hardie. Oxford: 310–29.
(2010) *Playing Gods: Ovid's Metamorphoses and the Politics of Fiction*. Princeton, NJ.
Fenik, B. (1974) *Studies in the Odyssey*. Wiesbaden.
Fernbach, A. (2002) *Fantasies of Fetishism: From Decadence to the Post-Human*. Edinburgh, UK.
Finiello, C. (2005) 'Der Bürgerkrieg: Reine Männersache? Keine Männersache! Erichtho und die Frauengestalten im *Bellum Ciuile* Lucans', in *Lucan im 21. Jahrhundert*, ed. C. Walde. Munich: 155–85.
Fish, J. (2004) 'Anger, Philodemus' good king, and the Helen episode of *Aeneid* 2.567–89: a new proof of authenticity from Herculaneum', in *Vergil, Philodemus, and the Augustans*, eds. D. Armstrong, J. Fish, P. A. Johnston and M. Skinner. Austin, TX: 111–38.
Fitzgerald, W. (1995) *Catullan Provocations: Lyric Poetry and the Drama of Position*. Berkeley, CA.
Foley, J. M. (2005) *A Companion to Ancient Epic*. Oxford.
Ford, A. (1992) *Homer: The Poetry of the Past*. Ithaca, NY.
(1999) 'Reading Homer from the rostrum: poems and laws in Aeschines' *Against Timarchus*', in *Performance Culture and Athenian Democracy*, eds. S. Goldhill and R. Osborne. Cambridge: 231–56.
Foucault, M. (1979) *Discipline and Punish: The Birth of the Prison*. Harmondsworth, UK.
(1980) 'The eye of power', in *Power/Knowledge*, ed. C. Gordon. Brighton, UK: 146–65.
Fowler, A. (1982) *Kinds of Literature: An Introduction to the Theory of Genres and Modes*. Oxford.
Fowler, D. (1987) 'Vergil on killing virgins', in *Homo Viator: Classical Essays for John Bramble*, eds. M. Whitby, P. Hardie and M. Whitby. Bristol, UK: 185–98.
(1991) 'Narrate and describe: the problem of ekphrasis', *JRS* 81: 25–35.
(1997) 'Virgilian narrative: (a) Storytelling', in *The Cambridge Companion to Virgil*, ed. C. Martindale. Cambridge: 259–70.
(2000a) 'Epic in the middle of the wood: *mise en abyme* in the Nisus and Euryalus episode', in *Intratextuality*, eds. A. Sharrock and H. Morales. Oxford: 89–113.
(2000b) 'Even better than the real thing: a tale of two cities', in *Roman Constructions*, ed. D. Fowler. Oxford: 86–108.
(2000c) 'The ruin of time: monuments and survival at Rome', in *Roman Constructions*, ed. D. Fowler. Oxford: 193–217.

(2002) 'Masculinity under threat? The poetics and politics of inspiration in Latin poetry', in *Cultivating the Muse*, eds. E. Spentzou and D. Fowler. Oxford: 140–59.
Franchet d'Espèrey, S. (1999) *Conflit, violence et non-violence dans la 'Thebaide' de Stace*. Paris.
Franklin, J. L. (1997) 'Vergil at Pompeii: a teacher's aid', *CJ* 92: 175–84.
Fredrick, D. (ed.) (2002) *The Roman Gaze: Vision, Power and the Body*. Baltimore, MD.
Freedman, B. (1991) *Staging the Gaze: Postmodernism, Psychoanalysis, and Shakespearean Comedy*. Ithaca, NY.
Freud, S. (1955) 'Medusa's head', in *The Standard Edition of the Complete Psychological Works of Sigmund Freud*, ed. J. Strachey. London: 273–4.
Freund, K., Seto, M. C. and Kuban, M. (1995) 'Masochism: a multiple case study', *Sexuologie* 4: 313–24.
Friedländer, U. (1895) *De Zoilo Aliisque Homeri Obtrectatoribus*. Königsberg.
Friedrich, W.-H. (1956) *Verwundung und Tod in der Ilias*. Göttingen.
Fucecchi, M. (1990) 'Empietà e titanismo nella rapprezentazione siliana di Annibale', *Orpheus* 11: 21–42.
    (1997) *La teichoscopia e l'innamoramento di Medea: saggio di commento a Valerio Flacco Argonautiche 6,427–760*. Pisa.
Furby, J. and Randell, K. (eds.) (2005) *Screen Methods: Comparative Readings in Film Studies*. London.
Gale, M. (1997) 'The shield of Turnus', *G&R* 44: 176–96.
    (2006) 'Review of Syed, *Vergil's Aeneid and the Roman Self*', *CR* 56: 106–8.
Galinsky, G. K. (1975) *Ovid's Metamorphoses: An Introduction to the Basic Aspects*. Berkeley, CA.
    (1988) 'The anger of Aeneas', *AJPh* 109: 321–48.
    (1992) 'Venus, polysemy, and the Ara Pacis Augustae', *AJA* 96 457–75.
    (1994) 'How to be philosophical about the end of the Aeneid', *ICS* 19: 191–201.
    (1998) 'The speech of Pythagoras in Ovid's *Metamorphoses* 15.75–478', *PLLS* 10: 313–36.
Gamman, L. (1988) 'Watching the detectives: the enigma of the female gaze', in *The Female Gaze*, eds. L. Gamman and M. Marshment. London: 8–26.
Gamman, L. and Marshment, M. (eds.) (1988) *The Female Gaze: Women as Viewers of Popular Culture*. London.
Ganiban, R. (2007) *Statius and Virgil: The Thebaid and the Reinterpretation of the Aeneid*. Cambridge.
Gantz, T. (1993) *Early Greek Myth: A Guide to Literary and Artistic Sources*. Baltimore, MD.
Garber, M. and Vickers, N. J. (2003) *The Medusa Reader*. New York.
Garstang, J. B. (1963) 'Aeneas and the Sibyls', *CJ* 59: 97–101.
Gärtner, U. (2005) *Quintus Smyrnaeus und die Aeneis*. Munich.
    (2009) 'Laokoon bei Quintus Smyrnaeus', in *Laokoon in Literatur und Kunst*, eds. D. Gall and A. Wolkenhauer. Berlin: 128–45.
Gebhard, P. H. (1969) 'Fetishism and sadomasochism', *Science and Psychoanalysis* 15: 71–80.

Gell, A. (1998) *Art and Agency: An Anthropological Theory*. Oxford.
Gellie, G. H. (1980) 'Hecuba and tragedy', *Antichthon* 14: 30–44.
Georgacopoulou, S. (2005) *Aux frontières du récit épique: l'emploi de l'apostrophe du narrateur dans la 'Thébaïde' de Stace*. Brussels.
Gervais, K. (forthcoming) 'Viewing violence in Statius' *Thebaid* and the films of Quentin Tarantino', in *Epic Visions*, eds. H. V. Lovatt and C. Vout.
Gibson, B. (2004) 'The repetitions of Hypsipyle', in *Latin Epic and Didactic Poetry*, ed. M. Gale. Swansea, UK: 149–80.
Gigante, M. (1979) *Civiltà delle forme letterarie nell'antica Pompei*. Naples.
Gildenhard, I. (2004) 'Confronting the beast: from Virgil's Cacus to the dragons of Cornelis von Haarlem', *PVS* 25: 27–48.
Gillespie, S. and Hardie, P. (eds.) (2007) *The Cambridge Companion to Lucretius*. Cambridge.
Glinister, F. (2009) 'Veiled and unveiled: uncovering Roman influence in Hellenistic Italy', in *Votives, Places and Rituals in Etruscan Religion*, eds. M. Gleba and H. Becker. Leiden: 193–215.
Goldhill, S. (1994) 'Representing democracy: women at the Great Dionysia', in *Ritual, Finance, Politics: Athenian Democratic Accounts Presented to D. M. Lewis*, eds. R. Osborne and S. Hornblower. Oxford: 347–96.
  (1995) *Foucault's Virginity: Ancient Erotic Fiction and the History of Sexuality*. Cambridge.
  (2001) *Being Greek under Rome: Cultural Identity, the Second Sophistic and the Development of Empire*. Cambridge.
  (2007) 'What is ekphrasis for?' *CPh* 102: 1–19.
  (2009) 'Review of Webb, *Ekphrasis, Imagination and Persuasion in Ancient Rhetorical Theory and Practice*', *BMCR* 2009.10.03.
Goldhill, S. and Osborne, R. (1994) *Art and Text in Ancient Greek Culture*. Cambridge.
Goold, G. P. (1970) 'Servius and the Helen episode', *HSPh* 74: 101–68.
Gowers, E. (2005) 'Virgil's Sibyl and the "many mouths" cliché (*Aeneid* 6.625–7)', *CQ* 55: 170–82.
Gransden, K. W. (ed.) (1976) *Virgil Aeneid VIII*. Cambridge.
Graziosi, B. (2002) *Inventing Homer: The Early Reception of Epic*. Cambridge.
  (2008) 'The ancient reception of Homer', in *A Companion to Classical Receptions*, eds. L. Hardwick and C. Stray. Malden, MA: 26–37.
Graziosi, B. and Haubold, J. (2010) *Iliad: Book 6*. Cambridge.
Greene, E. (1998) *The Erotics of Domination: Male Desire and the Mistress in Latin Love Poetry*. Baltimore, MD.
Grethlein, J. (2008) 'Memory and material objects in the *Iliad* and the *Odyssey*', *JHS* 128: 27–51.
Griffin, J. (1978) 'The divine audience and the religion of the *Iliad*', *CQ* 28: 1–22.
  (1980) *Homer on Life and Death*. Oxford.
  (1985) *Latin Poets and Roman Life*. London.
Grillone, A. (1967) *Il sogno nell'epica latina: tecnica e poesia*. Palermo.

Guillory, J. (1993) *Cultural Capital: The Problem of Literary Canon Formation*. Chicago, IL.
Habinek, T. (1998) *The Politics of Latin Literature: Writing, Identity and Empire in Ancient Rome*. Princeton, NJ.
  (2002) 'Ovid and empire', in *The Cambridge Companion to Ovid*, ed. P. Hardie. Cambridge: 46–61.
Habinek, T. and Schiesaro, A. (eds.) (1997) *The Roman Cultural Revolution*. Cambridge.
Hadjittofi, F. (2007) 'Res Romanae: cultural politics in Quintus Smyrnaeus' *Posthomerica* and Nonnus' *Dionysiaca*', in *Quintus Smyrnaeus: Transforming Homer in Second Sophistic Epic*, eds. S. Bär, M. Baumbach and N. Dümmler. Berlin: 357–78.
Halliwell, S. (2011) *Between Ecstasy and Truth: Interpretations of Greek Poetics from Homer to Longinus*. Oxford.
Halperin, D. M. (1990) *One Hundred Years of Homosexuality and Other Essays on Greek Love*. New York.
  (1995) *Saint Foucault: Towards a Gay Hagiography*. Oxford.
Hammer, D. C. (2002) *The Iliad as Politics: The Performance of Political Thought*. Norman, OK.
Hardie, P. (1986) *Virgil's Aeneid: Cosmos and Imperium*. Oxford.
  (1990) 'Ovid's Theban history: the first 'Anti-*Aeneid*?' *CQ* 40: 224–35.
  (1993) *The Epic Successors of Virgil*. Cambridge.
  (1994) *Virgil: Aeneid IX*. Cambridge.
  (1995) 'The speech of Pythagoras in Ovid *Metamorphoses* 15: Empedoclean epos', *CQ* 45: 204–14.
  (1997a) 'Closure in Latin epic', in *Classical Closure: Reading the End in Greek and Latin Literature*, eds. D. H. Roberts, F. M. Dunn and D. Fowler. Princeton, NJ: 139–62.
  (1997b) 'Questions of authority: the invention of tradition in *Metamorphoses* 15', in *The Roman Cultural Revolution*, eds. T. Habinek and A. Schiesaro. Cambridge: 182–98.
  (1999) 'Metamorphosis, metaphor, and allegory in Latin epic', in *Epic Traditions in the Contemporary World: The Poetics of Community*, eds. M. Beissinger, J. Tylus and S. Wofford. Berkeley, CA: 89–107.
  (2002a) 'Another look at Virgil's Ganymede', in *Classics in Progress*, ed. T. P. Wiseman. Oxford: 333–61.
  (2002b) *Ovid's Poetics of Illusion*. Cambridge.
  (2005) 'Nonnus' Typhon: the musical giant', in *Roman and Greek Imperial Epic*, ed. M. Paschalis. Herakleion: 117–30.
  (2006) 'Virgil's Ptolemaic relations', *JRS* 96: 25–41.
  (2009a) *Lucretian Receptions: History, the Sublime, Knowledge*. Cambridge.
  (2009b) 'Lucretian visions in Virgil', in *Lucretian Receptions*. Cambridge: 153–79.
Harries, B. (1990) 'The spinner and the poet: Arachne in Ovid *Metamorphoses*', *PCPhS*: 64–82.
Harris, W. V. (1989) *Ancient Literacy*. Cambridge, MA.

(2009) *Dreams and Experience in Classical Antiquity*. Cambridge, MA.
Harrison, E. L. (1990) 'Divine action in *Aeneid* book 2', in *Oxford Readings in Vergil's Aeneid*, ed. S. Harrison. Oxford: 46–59.
Harrison, S. (ed.) (1991) *Vergil: Aeneid 10*. Oxford.
  (1992) 'The arms of Capaneus: Statius *Thebaid* 4.165–77', *CQ* 42: 247–52.
  (1998) 'The sword-belt of Pallas: moral symbolism and political ideology (*Aen.* 8.630–728)', in *Vergil's Aeneid: Augustan Epic and Political Context*, ed. H.-P. Stahl. Swansea, UK: 223–42.
  (2001) 'Picturing the future: the proleptic ekphrasis from Homer to Vergil', in *Texts, Ideas and the Classics*, ed. S. Harrison. Oxford: 70–92.
  (2007) 'The primal voyage and the ocean of epos: two aspects of metapoetic imagery in Catullus, Virgil and Horace', *Dictynna* 4: 2–17.
  (2010) 'Picturing the future again: proleptic ekphrasis in Silius' *Punica*', in *Brill's Companion to Silius Italicus*, ed. A. Augoustakis. Leiden: 279–92.
Harrisson, J. G. (2010) 'Cultural memory and imagination: dreams and dreaming in the Roman Empire 31 BC to AD 200'. Diss., Birmingham, UK.
Harsh, P. W. (1950) 'Penelope and Odysseus in *Odyssey XIX*', *AJPh* 71: 1–21.
Hawley, R. (1998a) 'The dynamics of beauty in classical Greece', in *Changing Bodies, Changing Meanings*, ed. D. Montserrat. London: 37–54.
  (1998b) 'The male body as spectacle in Attic drama', in *Thinking Men: Masculinity and its Self-Representation in the Classical Tradition*, eds. L. Foxhall and J. Salmon. New York: 83–99.
Heath, J. (1994) 'Prophetic horses, bridled nymphs: Ovid's metamorphosis of Ocyroe', *Latomus* 53: 340–53.
Heerink, M. (2007) 'Going a step further: Valerius Flaccus' metapoetical reading of Propertius' Hylas', *CQ* 57: 606–20.
Heiden, B. (1998) 'The placement of "book divisions" in the *Iliad*', *JHS* 118: 68–81.
  (2000) 'The placement of "book divisions" in the *Odyssey*', *CPh* 95: 247–59.
  (2008) *Homer's Cosmic Fabrication: Choice and Design in the Iliad*. Oxford.
Heinrich, A. (1999) '*Longa retro series*: sacrifice and repetition in Statius' Menoeceus episode', *Arethusa* 32: 165–95.
Heinze, R. (1993) *Virgil's Epic Technique*. Bristol, UK.
Hejduk, J. (2009) 'Jupiter's *Aeneid*: *fama* and *imperium*', *ClAnt* 28: 279–327.
Henderson, J. (1987) 'Lucan/the word at war', *Ramus* 16: 122–64.
  (1991a) 'Statius' Thebaid/form premade', *PCPhS* 37: 30–80.
  (1991b) 'Women and the Athenian dramatic festivals', *TAPhA* 121: 133–47.
  (1993) 'Form remade/Statius' *Thebaid*', in *Roman Epic*, ed. A. J. Boyle. London: 162–91.
  (1994) 'To recognise Bosnia/Statius, *Thebaid* 11.407–8', *LCM* 19: 25–7.
  (2002) 'A doo-dah-doo-dah-dey at the races: Ovid *Amores* 3.2 and the personal politics of the Circus Maximus', *ClAnt* 21: 41–65.
Hershkowitz, D. (1998a) *The Madness of Epic: Reading Insanity from Homer to Statius*. Oxford.
  (1998b) *Valerius Flaccus' Argonautica: Abbreviated Voyages in Silver Latin Epic*. Oxford.

Hesk, J. (forthcoming) 'Heroic manoeuvres in the dark: visuality and perception in *Iliad* 10', in *Epic Visions*, eds. H. V. Lovatt and C. Vout. Cambridge.
Heslin, P. J. (2005) *The Transvestite Achilles: Gender and Genre in Statius' Achilleid*. Cambridge.
Heubeck, A., Russo, J. and Fernandez-Galliano, M. (eds.) (1992) *A Commentary on Homer's Odyssey*, vol. 3, Books XVIII–XXIV. Oxford.
Heuzé, P. (1985) *L'image du corps dans l'oeuvre de Virgile*. Paris.
Hexter, R. (2010) 'On first looking into Vergil's Homer', in *A Companion to Vergil's Aeneid and its Tradition*, eds. J. Farrell and M. C. J. Putnam. Malden, MA: 26–36.
Hill, D. E. (ed.) (1985) *Ovid Metamorphoses I–IV*. Warminster, UK.
Hinds, S. (1987) *The Metamorphosis of Persephone*. Cambridge.
  (1998) *Allusion and Intertext*. Cambridge.
  (2000) 'Essential epic: genre and gender from Macer to Statius', in *Matrices of Genre*, eds. M. Depew and D. Obbink. Cambridge, MA: 221–46.
  (2002) 'Landscape with figures: aesthetics of place in the *Metamorphoses* and its tradition', in *The Cambridge Companion to Ovid*, ed. P. Hardie. Cambridge: 122–49.
Hömke, N. (2010) 'Bit by bit towards death: Lucan's Scaeva and the aesthetisization of dying', in *Lucan's 'Bellum Civile': Between Epic Tradition and Aesthetic Innovation*, eds. N. Hömke and C. Reitz. Berlin: 91–104.
hooks, b. (1996) *Reel to real: race, sex and class at the movies*. New York.
Hopkinson, N. (1994) 'Nonnus and Homer', in *Studies in the Dionysiaca of Nonnus*, ed. N. Hopkinson. Cambridge: 9–42.
Horsfall, N. (ed.) (1995) *A Companion to the Study of Virgil*. Leiden.
  (2003) *Virgil, Aeneid 11: A Commentary*. Leiden.
  (2008) *Virgil Aeneid 2: A Commentary*. Leiden.
Hübner, W. (1970) *Dirae in römischen Epos: Über das Verhältnis von Vogeldämonen und Prodigien*. Hildesheim.
Hucker, S. J. (2008) 'Sexual masochism: psychopathology and theory', in *Sexual Deviance: Theory, Assessment and Treatment*, eds. D. R. Laws and W. T. O'Donohue. New York: 250–63.
Humm, M. (1997) *Feminism and Film*. Edinburgh, UK.
Hunink, V. (1992) *Bellum Civile Book III: A Commentary*. Amsterdam.
Hunter, R. (2009) *Critical Moments in Classical Literature: Studies in the Ancient View of Literature and its Uses*. Cambridge.
Hunter, R. L. (ed.) (1989) *Argonautica Book 3*. Cambridge.
  (1993) *The Argonautica of Apollonius*. Cambridge.
  (2006) *The Shadow of Callimachus: Studies in the Reception of Hellenistic Poetry at Rome*. Cambridge.
Ingleheart, J. (2007) 'Propertius 4.10 and the end of the *Aeneid*: Augustus, the *spolia opima* and the right to remain silent', *G&R* 54: 61–81.
Irigaray, L. (1985) *Speculum of the Other Woman*. Ithaca, NY.
Jaeger, M. (1997) *Livy's Written Rome*. Ann Arbor, MI.
  (2008) *Archimedes in the Roman Literary Imagination*. Ann Arbor, MI.

James, A. (2004) *The Trojan Epic: Posthomerica*. Baltimore, MD.
  (2007) 'Quintus Smyrnaeus and Virgil', in *Quintus Smyrnaeus: Transforming Homer in Second Sophistic Epic*, eds. S. Bär, M. Baumbach and N. Dümmler. Berlin: 145–58.
James, S. (2003) *Learned Girls and Male Persuasion: Gender and Reading in Roman Love Elegy*. Berkeley, CA.
Jamset, C. (2004) 'Death-loration: the eroticization of death in the *Thebaid*', *G&R* 51: 95–104.
Janan, M. (1994) *When the Lamp Is Shattered: Desire and Narrative in Catullus*. Carbondale, IL.
  (2001) *The Politics of Desire: Propertius IV*. Berkeley, CA.
  (2009) *Reflections in a Serpent's Eye: Thebes in Ovid's Metamorphoses*. Oxford.
Jensen, M. S. (1999) 'Dividing Homer: when, where and how were the *Iliad* and *Odyssey* divided into songs?' *SO* 74: 5–35.
Johnson, P. J. (1996) 'Constructions of Venus in Ovid's *Metamorphoses* v', *Arethusa* 29: 125–49.
Johnson, W. R. (1976) *Darkness Visible: A Study of Vergil's Aeneid*. Berkeley, CA.
  (1987) *Momentary Monsters: Lucan and his Heroes*. Ithaca, NY.
Jolivet, J.-C. (2005) 'Les amours d'Arès et d'Aphrodite, la critique homérique et la pantomime dans l'*Ars amatoria*', *Dictynna* 2.
Joplin, P. K. (1991) 'The voice of the shuttle is ours', in *Rape and Representation*, eds. L. A. Higgins and B. R. Silver. New York: 35–66.
Jung, C. G. (2002) *Dreams*. London.
Kaplan, E. A. (1997) *Looking for the Other: Feminism, Film and the Imperial Gaze*. New York.
Kaplan, L. J. (2006) *Cultures of Fetishism*. Gordonsville, VA.
Keith, A. M. (1992) *The Play of Fictions: Studies in Ovid's Metamorphoses Book 2*. Ann Arbor, MI.
  (1999) 'Versions of epic masculinity in Ovid's *Metamorphoses*', in *Ovidian Transformations*, eds. P. R. Hardie, A. Barchiesi and S. Hinds. Cambridge: 214–39.
  (2000) *Engendering Rome: Women in Latin Epic*. Cambridge.
  (2007) 'Imperial building projects and architectural ecphrases in Ovid's *Metamorphoses* and Statius' *Thebaid*', *Mouseion* 7: 1–26.
  (2010) 'Engendering orientalism in Silius' *Punica*', in *Brill's Companion to Silius Italicus*, ed. A. Augoustakis. Leiden: 355–73.
Kennedy, G. A. (1986) 'Helen's web unraveled', *Arethusa* 19: 5–14.
Kessels, A. H. M. (1978) *Studies on the Dream in Greek Literature*. Utrecht.
King, K. C. (2009) *Ancient Epic*. Chichester, UK.
King, R. (1990) 'Creative landscaping: inspiration and artifice in Propertius 4.4', *CJ* 85: 225–46.
Kirk, G. S. (1985) *The Iliad: A Commentary*, vol. 1, *Books 1–4*. Cambridge.
  (1990) *The Iliad: A Commentary*, vol. 2, *Books 5–8*. Cambridge.
Kirk, G.S., Raven, J. and Schofield, M. (1983) *The Presocratic Philosophers*. Cambridge.

Knight, V. H. (1995) *The Renewal of Epic: Responses to Homer in the Argonautica of Apollonius*. Leiden.
Knox, P. E. (1988) 'Phaethon in Ovid and Nonnus', *CQ* 38: 536–51.
Koenen, L. (1993) 'The Ptolemaic king as a religious figure', in *Images and Ideologies: Self-Definition in the Hellenistic World*, eds. A. Bulloch, E. S. Gruen, A. A. Long and A. Stewart. Berkeley, CA: 25–115.
Konstan, D. and Raaflaub, K. A. (eds.) (2010) *Epic and History*. Chichester, UK.
Krevans, N. (1993) 'Ilia's dream: Ennius, Virgil and the mythology of seduction', *HSPh* 95: 257–71.
Kristeva, J. (1982) *Powers of Horror*. New York.
Kronenberg, L. (2005) 'Mezentius the Epicurean', *TAPhA* 135: 403–31.
Küppers, J. (1986) *Tantarum Causas Irarum: Untersuchungen zur einleitenden Bücherdyade der Punica des Silius Italicus*. Berlin.
Lacan, J. and Miller, J.-A. (1978) *The Four Fundamental Concepts of Psychoanalysis*. New York.
Lada-Richards, I. (2004) '"Cum femina primum ...": Venus, Vulcan, and the politics of male *mollitia* in *Aeneid* 8', *Helios* 33: 27–72.
Laird, A. (1993) 'Sounding out ecphrasis: art and text in Catullus 64', *JRS* 83: 18–30.
Lambert, M. (2001) 'Gender and religion in Theocritus *Idyll* 15: prattling tourists at the Adonia', *AClass* 44: 87–103.
Lamberton, R. and Keaney, J. J. (eds.) (1992) *Homer's Ancient Readers: The Hermeneutics of Greek Epic's Earliest Exegetes*. Princeton, NJ.
Lane Fox, R. (1988) *Pagans and Christians*. Harmondsworth, UK.
Larmour, D. H. J., Miller, P. A. and Platter, C. (eds.) (1998) *Rethinking Sexuality: Foucault and Classical Antiquity*. Princeton, NJ.
Latacz, J. (1977) *Kampfparänese, Kampfdarstellung und Kampfwirklichkeit in der Ilias, bei Kallinos und Tyrtaios*. Munich.
Lateiner, D. (1995) *Sardonic Smile: Nonverbal Behavior in Homeric Epic*. Ann Arbor, MI.
Lattimore, R. (1951) *The Iliad of Homer*. Chicago, IL.
  (1967) *The Odyssey of Homer*. New York.
Laudizi, G. (1989) *Silio Italico e il passato tra mito e restaurazione etica*. Galatina.
Leach, E. W. (1974) 'Ekphrasis and the theme of artistic failure in Ovid's *Metamorphoses*', *Ramus* 3: 102–42.
Lear, A. and Cantarella, E. (2008) *Images of Ancient Greek Pederasty: Boys Were their Gods*. London.
Leigh, M. (1997) *Lucan: Spectacle and Engagement*. Oxford.
  (2006) 'Statius and the sublimity of Capaneus', in *Epic Interactions*, eds. M. Clarke, B. Currie and R. O. A. M. Lyne. Oxford: 217–42.
Létoublon, F. (2010) 'To see or not to see: blind people and blindness in ancient Greek myths', in *Light and Darkness in Ancient Greek Myth and Religion*, eds. M. Christopoulos, E. D. Karakantza and O. Levaniouk. Lanham, MD: 167–80.
Linares, L. A. and Saconi, P. M. (1996) 'Iliada E: Diomedes y el limite del poder', *AFC* 14: 149–55.

Lindberg, D. C. (1976) *The Fire within the Eye: A Historical Essay on the Nature and Meaning of Light.* Princeton, NJ.
Llewellyn-Jones, L. (2003) *Aphrodite's Tortoise: The Veiled Women of Ancient Greece.* Swansea, UK.
Loman, P. (2004) 'No woman no war: women's participation in ancient Greek warfare', *G&R* 51: 34–54.
Lonsdale, S. H. (1989) 'If looks could kill: παπταίνω and the interpenetration of imagery and narrative in Homer', *CJ* 84: 325–33.
Loraux, N. (1989) *Les expériences de Tirésias.* Paris.
  (1990) 'Herakles: the super-male and the feminine', in *Before Sexuality: The Construction of Erotic Experience in the Ancient Greek World*, eds. D. M. Halperin, J. J. Winkler and F. I. Zeitlin. Princeton, NJ: 21–52.
Lorenz, K. (forthcoming) 'Split screen visions: Heracles on top of Troy in the Casa di Octavius Quartio in Pompeii', in *Epic Visions*, eds. H. V. Lovatt and C. Vout.
Lovatt, H. V. (1999) 'Competing endings: re-reading the end of Statius' *Thebaid* through Lucan', *Ramus* 28: 126–51.
  (2002) 'Statius' ekphrastic games', *Ramus* 31: 73–90.
  (2005) *Statius and Epic Games: Sport, Politics and Poetics in the Thebaid.* Cambridge.
  (2006) 'The female gaze in Flavian epic: looking out from the walls in Valerius Flaccus and Statius', in *Flavian Poetry*, eds. R. R. Nauta, H.-J. van Dam and J. J. L. Smolenaars. Leiden: 59–78.
  (2007) 'Statius, Orpheus and the post-Augustan *vates*', *Arethusa* 40: 145–63.
  (2010) 'Interplay: Statius and Silius in the games of *Punica* 16', in *Brill's Companion to Silius Italicus*, ed. A. Augoustakis. Leiden: 155–78.
  (forthcoming-a) 'Competing visions: prophecy, spectacle and epic in Valerius Flaccus *Argonautica* 1 and Silius Italicus *Punica* 4 and 5', in *Religion and Ritual in Flavian Epic*, ed. A. Augoustakis. Oxford.
  (forthcoming-b) 'Following after Valerius: Argonautic imagery in the *Thebaid*', in *Brill's Companion to Statius*, eds. W. J. Dominik and C. Newlands. Leiden.
  (forthcoming-c) 'Hesiod and the divine gaze', *Helios*.
Lowe, D. (2007) 'Monsters in Augustan poetry: compromised identities'. Diss., Cambridge.
  (2010) 'Snakes on the beach: Ovid's Orpheus and Medusa', *MD* 65: 75–8.
Lowrie, M. (2009) *Writing, Performance and Authority in Augustan Rome.* Oxford.
Lyne, R. O. A. M. (1978) 'The neoteric poets', *CQ* 28: 167–87.
  (1983) 'Lavinia's blush: Vergil, *Aeneid*, 12. 64–70', *G&R* 30: 55–64.
  (1984) 'Ovid's *Metamorphoses*, Callimachus and *l'art pour l'art*', *MD* 12: 9–34.
  (1987) *Further Voices in Vergil's Aeneid.* Oxford.
Lyons, D. (1997) *Gender and Immortality: Heroines in Ancient Greek Myth.* Princeton, NJ.
Maciver, C. (2012) *Quintus Smyrnaeus' Posthomerica: Engaging Homer in Late Antiquity.* Leiden.
Macleod, C. (1983) 'Thucydides and tragedy', in *Collected Essays.* Oxford: 140–58.

Maguire, L. (2009) *Helen of Troy: From Homer to Hollywood*. Oxford.
Malamud, M. A. (1998) 'Gnawing at the end of the rope: poets on the field in two Vergilian catalogues', *Ramus* 27: 95–126.
    (2003) 'Pompey's head and Cato's snakes (Lucan's use of the Medusa myth from Ovid's *Metamorphoses* Book 4, in the *Bellum Civile*)', *CPh* 98: 31–44.
Mariscal, G. L. and Morales, M. S. (2003) 'The relationship between Achilles and Patroclus according to Chariton of Aphrodisias', *CQ* 53: 292–5.
Marks, R. (2005) *From Republic to Empire: Scipio Africanus in the Punica of Silius Italicus*. Frankfurt.
    (2008) 'Getting ahead: decapitation as political metaphor in Silius Italicus' *Punica*', *Mnemosyne* 61: 66–88.
Markus, D. (1997) 'Transfiguring heroism: Nisus and Euryalus in Statius' *Thebaid*', *Vergilius* 43: 56–62.
    (2000) 'Performing the book: the recital of epic in first century CE Rome', *ClAnt* 19: 138–79.
    (2003) 'The politics of epic performance in Statius', in *Flavian Rome: Culture, Image, Text*, eds. A. J. Boyle and W. J. Dominik. Leiden: 431–67.
Marti, B. (1945) 'The meaning of the Pharsalia', *AJPh* 66: 352–76.
Martin, R. (1997) 'Similes and performance', in *Written Voices, Spoken Signs*, eds. E. Bakker and A. Kahane. Cambridge, MA: 138–66.
    (2005a) 'Epic as genre', in *A Companion to Ancient Epic*, ed. J. M. Foley. Oxford: 9–19.
    (2005b) 'Pulp epic: the *Catalogue* and the *Shield*', in *The Hesiodic Catalogue of Women: Constructions and Reconstructions*, ed. R. Hunter. Cambridge: 153–75.
Masters, J. M. (1993) *Poetry and Civil War in Lucan's Bellum Civile*. Cambridge.
Masterson, M. A. (2005) 'Statius' *Thebaid* and the realisation of Roman manhood', *Phoenix* 59: 288–315.
Mastronarde, D. J. (ed.) (1994) *Euripides Phoenissae*. Cambridge.
Mayer, R. (ed.) (1981) *Lucan Civil War VIII*. Warminster, UK.
Mayne, J. (1998) *Cinema and Spectatorship*. London.
McCullough, A. (2008) 'Female gladiators in Imperial Rome: literary context and historical fact', *CW* 101: 197–209.
McGowan, T. (2003) 'Looking for the gaze: Lacanian film theory and its vicissitudes', *Cinema Journal* 42: 27–47.
    (2007) *The Real Gaze: Film Theory after Lacan*. New York.
    (2011) *Out of Time: Desire in Atemporal Cinema*. Minneapolis, MN.
McNelis, C. (2007) *Statius' Thebaid and the Poetics of Civil War*. Cambridge.
Mench, F. (1969) 'Film sense in the *Aeneid*', *Arion* 8: 380–97.
Menninghaus, W. (2003) *Disgust: The Theory and History of a Strong Sensation*. Albany, NY.
Merkelbach, R. (1961) 'Aeneas in Cumae', *MH* 19: 83–99.
Merleau-Ponty, M. (1968) *The Visible and the Invisible*. Evanston, IL.
Metz, C. (1982) *The Imaginary Signifier: Psychoanalysis and Cinema*. Bloomington, IN.

Michelini, A. N. (1987) *Euripides and the Tragic Tradition*. Madison, WI.
Micozzi, L. (2001/2) 'Eros e pudor nella *Tebaide* di Stazio: lettura dell'episodio di Atys e Ismene (*Theb.* VIII.554–565)', *Incontri Triestini di Filologia Classica* 1: 259–82.
Miller, J. F. (1994) 'The memories of Ovid's Pythagoras', *Mnemosyne* 47: 473–87.
Miller, J. F. and Woodman, A. J. (eds.) (2010) *Latin Historiography and Poetry in the Early Empire*. Leiden.
Miller, P. A. (2004) *Subjecting Verses: Latin Love Elegy and the Emergence of the Real*. Princeton, NJ.
Mills, D. H. (1978) 'Vergil's tragic vision: the death of Priam', *CW* 72: 159–66.
Minchin, E. (2001) *Homer and the Resources of Memory: Some Applications of Cognitive Theory to the Iliad and the Odyssey*. Oxford.
Mitchell, R. N. (1991) 'The violence of virginity', *Arethusa* 24: 219–38.
Mitchell, W. J. T. (1992) 'Ekphrasis and the Other', *South Atlantic Quarterly* 91: 695–719.
Modleski, T. (1988) *The Women who Knew too Much: Hitchcock and Feminist Theory*. London.
Moi, T. (ed.) (1986) *The Kristeva Reader*. Oxford.
Moore, S. (1988) 'Here's looking at you, kid!', in *The Female Gaze*, eds. L. Gamman and M. Marshment. London: 44–59.
Morales, H. (1996) 'The torturer's apprentice: Parrhasius and the limits of art', in *Art and Text in Roman Culture*, ed. J. Elsner. Cambridge: 182–209.
  (2004) *Vision and Narrative in Achilles Tatius' Leucippe and Clitophon*. Cambridge.
Mori, A. (2008) *The Politics of Apollonius Rhodius' Argonautica*. Cambridge.
Morrison, J. V. (1997) 'Kerostasia, the dictates of fate and the will of Zeus in the *Iliad*', *Arethusa* 30: 276–96.
Mossman, J. M. (1992) 'Plutarch, Pyrrhus, and Alexander', in *Plutarch and the Historical Tradition*, ed. P. A. Stadter. London: 90–108.
Most, G. (1992a) '*Disiecti membra poetae*: the rhetoric of dismemberment in Neronian poetry', in *Innovations of Antiquity*, eds. R. Hexter and D. Selden. New York: 391–419.
  (1992b) 'Il poeta nell'Ade: catabasi epica e teoria dell'epos tra Omero e Virgilio', *SIFC* 10: 1014–26.
Moulton, C. (1974a) 'The end of the *Odyssey*', *GRBS* 15: 153–69.
  (1974b) 'Similes in the *Iliad*', *Hermes* 102: 380–97.
  (1977) *Similes in the Homeric Poems*. Göttingen.
Mulvey, L. (1975) 'Visual pleasure and narrative cinema', *Screen* 16.3: 6–18.
  (1988) 'Visual pleasure and narrative cinema', in *Feminism and Film Theory*, ed. C. Penley. New York: 57–68.
Murgatroyd, T. W. H. (2007) 'Geo-politics in Lucan's Bellum civile'. Diss., Cambridge.
Murgia, C. E. (2003) 'The date of the Helen episode', *HSPh* 101: 405–26.

Murnaghan, S. (1999–2000) 'The survivor's song: the drama of mourning in Euripides' *Alcestis*', *ICS* 24–5: 107–16.
Myers, K. S. (ed.) (2009) *Ovid Metamorphoses Book XIV*. Cambridge.
Myers, T. A. (forthcoming) *Homer's Divine Audience: The Iliad's Reception on Mount Olympus*.
Nagy, G. (1979) *The Best of the Achaeans: Concepts of the Hero in Archaic Greek Poetry*. Baltimore, MD.
Naiden, F. S. (2006) *Ancient Supplication*. Oxford.
Narducci, E. (1985) 'Ideologia e tecnica allusiva nella Pharsalia', *ANRW* II.32.3: 1538–64.
Neill, A. (1996) 'Empathy and (film) fiction', in *Post-Theory: Reconstructing Film Studies*, eds. D. Bordwell and N. Carroll. Madison, WI: 175–94.
Neri, V. (1986) 'Dei, Fato e divinazione nella letteratura latina del I sec. d.C.' *ANRW* II.16.3: 1974–2051.
Newman, J. K. (1967) *The Concept of Vates in Augustan Poetry*. Brussels.
Nicolet, C. (1991) *Space, Geography and Politics in The Early Roman Empire*. Ann Arbor, MI.
Nightingale, A. (2004) *Spectacles of Truth in Classical Greek Philosophy: Theoria in its Cultural Context*. Cambridge.
Nix, S. (2008) 'Caesar as Jupiter in Lucan's *Bellum Civile*', *CJ* 103: 281–94.
Norden, E. (ed.) (1916) *P. Vergilius Maro Aeneis Buch VI*. Leipzig.
Nörenberg, H.-W. (1972) 'Zu Homer, Ilias A', *Hermes* 100: 251–4.
O'Gorman, E. (1995) 'Shifting ground: Lucan, Tacitus and the landscape of civil war', *Hermathena* 159: 117–31.
O'Hara, J. J. (1990) *Death and the Optimistic Prophecy*. Princeton, NJ.
  (2007) *Inconsistency in Roman Epic*. Cambridge.
O'Higgins, D. (1988) 'Lucan as *vates*', *ClAnt* 7: 208–26.
Oberhelman, S. M., Kelly, V. and Golsan, R. J. (eds.) (1994) *Epic and Epoch: Essays on the Interpretation and History of a Genre*. Lubbock, TX.
Oberrauch, L. (2005) 'Metempsychose, Universalgeschichte und Autopsie: Die Rede des Pythagoras in Ovid, *Met*. XV als Kernstück epischer Legitimation.' *Gymnasium* 112: 107–21.
Ogden, D. (2001) *Greek and Roman Necromancy*. Princeton, NJ.
  (2007) *In Search of the Sorcerer's Apprentice: The Traditional Tales of Lucian's Lover of Lies*. Swansea, UK.
Oliensis, E. (2009) *Freud's Rome: Psychoanalysis and Latin Poetry*. Cambridge.
Olson, S. D. (1989) 'Odyssey 8: guile, force and the subversive poetics of desire', *Arethusa* 22: 135–45.
  (1995) *Blood and Iron: Stories and Storytelling in the Odyssey*. Leiden.
Osborne, R. (1997) 'Men without clothes: heroic nakedness and Greek art', *Gender and History* 9: 504–28.
  (2007) *Debating the Athenian Cultural Revolution: Art, Literature, Philosophy and Politics, 430–380 BC*. Cambridge.
  (2011) *The History Written on the Classical Greek Body*. Cambridge.
Osborne, R. and Tanner, J. (eds.) (2007) *Art's Agency and Art History*. Oxford.

Otis, B. (1970) *Ovid as an Epic Poet*. Cambridge.
Padel, R. (1995) *Whom Gods Destroy: Elements of Greek and Tragic Madness*. Princeton, NJ.
Pagel, J. F., Kwiatkowski, C. and Broyles, K. E. (1999) 'Dream use in film making', *Dreaming* 9: 247–56.
Papaioannou, S. (2005) *Epic Succession and Dissension: Ovid, 'Metamorphoses' 13.623–14.582, and the reinvention of the 'Aeneid'*. Berlin.
Papanghelis, T. (1989) 'About the hour of noon: Ovid *Amores* 1.5', *Mnemosyne* 42: 54–61.
Parisinou, E. (2000) *The Light of the Gods: The Role of Light in Archaic and Classical Greek Cult*. London.
Park, D. (1997) *The Fire within the Eye: A Historical Essay on the Nature and Meaning of Light*. Princeton, NJ.
Parke, H. W. (1988) *Sibyls and Sibylline Prophecy in Classical Antiquity*. London.
Paul, J. (2013) *Film and the Classical Epic Tradition*. Oxford.
Pavlock, B. (1990) *Eros, Imitation and Epic Tradition*. Ithaca, NY.
  (2009) *The Image of the Poet in Ovid's Metamorphoses*. Madison, WI.
Pelling, C. (1996) 'The urine and the vine: Astyages' dreams at Herodotus 1.107–8', *CQ* 46: 68–77.
Penley, C. (ed.) (1988) *Feminism and Film Theory*. New York.
  (1994) 'Feminism, psychoanalysis and the study of popular culture', in *Visual Culture: Images and Interpretations*, eds. N. Bryson, M. A. Holly and K. Moxey. Hanover, NH: 302–24.
Perkell, C. (1997) 'The lament of Juturna: pathos and interpretation in the Aeneid', *TAPhA* 127: 257–86.
Perutelli, A. (1994) 'Il sogno di Medea da Apollonio Rodio a Valerio Flacco', *MD* 33: 33–50.
Pitcher, L. V. (2008) 'A perfect storm? Caesar and his audiences at Lucan 5.504–702', *CQ* 58: 243–9.
Platt, V. J. (2002) 'Evasive epiphanies in ekphrastic epigram', *Ramus* 31: 33–50.
  (2011) *Facing the Gods: Epiphany and Representation in Graeco-Roman Art, Literature and Religion*. Cambridge.
Poe, E. A. (1970) 'The philosophy of composition', in *Great Short Works of Edgar Allan Poe*, ed. G. R. Thompson. New York: 528–42.
Polk, M. L. C. (1997) 'Reversing the gaze: when women look back in Susan Glaspell's *Trifles* and Jonathan Demme's *The Silence of the Lambs*', in *Film and Literature: Points of Intersection*, ed. P. Davison. Lewiston, NY: 123–52.
Polleichtner, W. (2005) 'The bee simile: how Vergil emulated Apollonius in his use of Homeric poetry', *Göttinger Forum für Altertumswissenschaft* 8: 115–60.
Pomeroy, A. (2000) 'Silius' Rome: the rewriting of Vergil's vision', *Ramus* 29: 149–68.
Porter, J. I. (2006) 'Foucault's antiquity', in *Classics and the Uses of Reception*, eds. C. Martindale and R. F. Thomas. Malden, MA: 168–79.
Powers, N. (2002) 'Magic, wonder and scientific explanation in Apollonius' *Argonautica* 4.1638–93', *PCPhS* 48: 87–101.

Prettejohn, E. (1999) '"The monstrous diversion of a show of gladiators": Simeon Solomon's *Habet!*' in *Roman Presences: Receptions of Rome in European Culture, 1789–1945*, ed. C. Edwards. Cambridge: 157–72.
Pribram, E. D. (ed.) (1988) *Female Spectators: Looking at Film and Television*. London.
Prier, R. A. (1989) *Thauma idesthai: The Phenomenology of Sight and Appearance in Archaic Greek*. Tallahassee, FL.
Pucci, P. (1987) *Odysseus Polutropos: Intertextual Readings in the Odyssey and the Iliad*. Ithaca, NY.
  (1994) 'Gods' intervention and epiphany in Sophocles', *AJP* 115: 15–46.
  (1997) *The Song of the Sirens: Essays on Homer*. Lanham, MD.
  (2002) 'Theology and poetics in the *Iliad*', *Arethusa* 35: 17–34.
Pulleyn, S. (ed.) (2000) *Homer: Iliad Book One*. Oxford.
Purves, A. C. (2010) *Space and Time in Ancient Greek Narrative*. Cambridge.
Putnam, M. C. J. (1995a) 'Anger, blindness and insight in Virgil's *Aeneid*', in *Virgil's Aeneid: Interpretation and Influence*. Chapel Hill, NC: 172–200.
  (1995b) 'The hesitation of Aeneas', in *Virgil's Aeneid: Interpretation and Influence*. Chapel Hill, NC: 152–71.
  (1995c) 'Possessiveness, sexuality and heroism', in *Virgil's Aeneid: Interpretation and Influence*. Chapel Hill, NC: 27–49.
  (1998a) 'Dido's murals and Virgilian ekphrasis', *HSPh* 98: 243–75.
  (1998b) *Virgil's Epic Designs: Ekphrasis in the Aeneid*. New Haven, CT.
Quint, D. (1993) *Epic and Empire*. Princeton, NJ.
Quiter, R. J. (1984) *Aeneas und die Sibylle: Die rituellen Motive in sechsten Buch der Aeneis*. Königstein.
Raaflaub, K. A. (1998) 'Homer, the Trojan war, and history', *CW* 91: 386–403.
Rakoczy, T. (1996) *Böser Blick, Macht des Auges und Neid der Götter: Eine Untersuchung zur Kraft des Blickes in der griechischen Literatur*. Tübingen.
Ready, J. L. (2008) 'The comparative spectrum in Homer', *AJPh* 129: 453–96.
Reckford, K. J. (1995–6) 'Recognising Venus (1): Aeneas meets his mother', *Arion* 3: 1–42.
Redfield, J. (1994 (1st edn 1975)) *Nature and Culture in the Iliad: The Tragedy of Hector*. Durham, NC.
Reed, J. D. (2007) *Virgil's Gaze: Nation and Poetry in the Aeneid*. Princeton, NJ.
Richardson, N. (1993) *The Iliad: A Commentary*, vol. 6, *Books 21–24*. Cambridge.
Richardson, S. (1990) *The Homeric Narrator*. Nashville, TN.
Richlin, A. (1992) 'Reading Ovid's rapes', in *Pornography and Representation in Greece and Rome*, ed. A. Richlin. New York: 158–79.
Ricottilli, L. (2000) *Gesto e parola nell'Eneide*. Bologna.
Rimell, V. (2006) *Ovid's Lovers: Desire, Difference and the Poetic Imagination*. Cambridge.
Rinon, Y. (2006) 'Mise en abyme and tragic signification in the *Odyssey*: the three songs of Demodocus', *Mnemosyne* 59: 208–25.
Rivier, A. (1944) *Essai sur le tragique d'Euripide*. Lausanne.
Robert, L. (1940) *Les gladiateurs dans l'Orient Grec*. Paris.

Rogerson, A. (2002) 'Dazzling likeness: seeing ekphrasis in *Aeneid* 10', *Ramus* 31: 51–72.
  (2007) 'Review of Smith, *The Primacy of Vision in Virgil's Aeneid*', *CR* 57: 389–91.
Rosati, G. (1999) 'Form in motion: weaving the text in the *Metamorphoses*', in *Ovidian Transformations*, eds. P. R. Hardie, A. Barchiesi and S. Hinds. Cambridge: 240–53.
Rosner-Siegel, J. A. (1983) 'The oak and the lightning: Lucan BC 1.135–57', *Athenaeum* 61: 165–77.
Rossi, A. (2000) 'The 'Aeneid' revisited: the journey of Pompey in Lucan's *Pharsalia*', *AJPh* 121: 571–91.
  (2001) 'Remapping the past: Caesar's tale of Troy (Lucan *Bellum Civile* 9.964–999)', *Phoenix* 55: 313–26.
  (2004) *Contexts of War: Manipulation of Genre in Virgilian Battle Narrative*. Ann Arbor, MI.
Rouse, W. H. D. (1940) *Nonnos Dionysiaca*. Cambridge, MA.
Rozokoki, A. (2001) 'Penelope's dream in book 19 of the *Odyssey*', *CQ* 51: 1–6.
Rubin, D. (1995) *Memory in Oral Traditions: The Cognitive Psychology of Epic, Ballads, and Counting-Out Rhymes*. New York.
Rutherford, R. B. (ed.) (1992) *Homer: Odyssey Books XIX and XX*. Cambridge.
Rutz, W. (1960) 'Amor mortis bei Lucan', *Hermes* 88: 462–75.
Salzman-Mitchell, P. B. (2005) *A Web of Fantasies: Gaze, Image and Gender in Ovid's Metamorphoses*. Columbus, OH.
Sammons, B. (2009) 'Agamemnon and his audiences', *GRBS* 49: 159–85.
Sartre, J. (1966) *Being and Nothingness*. New York.
Schiesaro, A. (2003) *The Passions at Play: Thyestes and the Dynamics of Senecan Drama*. Cambridge.
Schmit-Neuerburg, T. (1999) *Vergils Aeneis und die antike Homerexegese: Untersuchungen zum Einfluss ethischer und kritischer Homerrezeption auf imitatio und aemulatio*. Berlin.
Schoell, W. (1985) *Stay out the Shower: Twenty-Five Years of Shocker Films Beginning with Psycho*. New York.
Scioli, E. (2010) '*Incohat Ismene*: the dream narrative as a mode of female discourse in epic poetry', *TAPhA* 140: 195–238.
Scodel, R. (1997) 'Teichoscopia, catalogue and the female spectator in Euripides', *ColbyQ* 33: 76–93.
Seaford, R. (1994) *Reciprocity and Ritual: Homer and Tragedy in the Developing City–State*. Oxford.
Segal, C. (1969) *Landscape in Ovid's Metamorphoses*. Wiesbaden.
  (1990) 'Violence and the Other: Greek, female and barbarian in Euripides' *Hecuba*', *TAPhA* 120: 109–31.
  (1998) 'Ovid's metamorphic bodies: art, gender and violence in the *Metamorphoses*', *Arion* 5: 9–41.

(2001) 'Intertextuality and immortality: Ovid, Pythagoras and Lucretius in *Metamorphoses* 15', *MD* 46: 63–101.
Shackleton Bailey, D. R. (2003) *Statius Thebaid*. Cambridge, MA.
Shapiro, H. A. (1980) 'Jason's cloak', *TAPhA* 110: 263–86.
Sharrock, A. (2002) 'An a-musing tale: gender, genre, and Ovid's battles with inspiration in the *Metamorphoses*', in *Cultivating the Muse*, eds. E. Spentzou and D. Fowler. Oxford: 207–28.
Shelton, J. E. (1974) 'The storm scene in Valerius Flaccus', *CJ* 70: 14–22.
Shorrock, R. (2001) *The Challenge of Epic: Allusive Engagement in the Dionysiaca of Nonnus*. Leiden.
(2011) *The Myth of Paganism: Nonnus, Dionysus and the World of Late Antiquity*. London.
Siebers, T. (1983) *The Mirror of Medusa*. Berkeley, CA.
Silverman, K. (1988a) *The Acoustic Mirror: The Female Voice in Psychoanalysis and Cinema*. Bloomington, IN.
(1988b) 'Masochism and male subjectivity', *Camera obscura* 17: 30–67.
(1992) *Male Subjectivity at the Margins*. New York.
(1994) 'Fassbinder and Lacan: a reconsideration of gaze, look and image', in *Visual Culture: Images and Interpretations*, eds. N. Bryson, M. A. Holly and K. Moxey. Hanover, NH: 272–301.
Simon, G. (1988) *Le regard, l'être at l'apparence dans l'Optique de l'Antiquité*. Paris.
(2003) *Archéologie de la vision: l'optique, le corps, la peinture*. Paris.
Sinos, D. (1980) *Achilles, Patroklos and the Meaning of Philos*. Innsbruck.
Sklenář, R. (2003) *The Taste for Nothingness: A Study of Virtus and Related Themes in Lucan's Bellum Civile*. Ann Arbor, MI.
Skutsch, O. (ed.) (1985) *The Annals of Quintus Ennius*. Oxford.
Slatkin, L. (2007) 'Notes on tragic visualizing in the *Iliad*', in *Visualizing the Tragic: Drama, Myth and Ritual in Greek Art and Literature*, eds. C. Kraus, S. Goldhill, H. Foley and J. Elsner. Oxford: 19–34.
Small, J. P. (1997) *Wax Tablets of the Mind: Cognitive Studies of Memory and Literacy in Classical Antiquity*. London.
Smith, A. C. and Pickup, S. (eds.) (2010) *Brill's Companion to Aphrodite*. Leiden.
Smith, A. M. (1999) 'Ptolemy and the foundations of ancient mathematical optics: a source-based guided study', *TAPhA* 89: 1–172.
Smith, M. (1996) 'The logic and legacy of Brechtianism', in *Post-Theory: Reconstructing Film Studies*, eds. D. Bordwell and N. Carroll. Madison, WI: 130–48.
Smith, M. S. (ed.) (1975) *Petronii Arbitri Cena Trimalchionis*. Oxford.
Smith, R. A. (2005) *The Primacy of Vision in Virgil's Aeneid*. Austin, TX.
Smith, W. (1988) 'The disguises of the gods in the *Iliad*', *Numen* 35: 161–78.
Smolenaars, J. J. L. (1994) *Statius Thebaid VII: A Commentary*. Leiden.
Solodow, J. B. (1988) *The World of Ovid's Metamorphoses*. Chapel Hill, NC.
Solomon, J. (2001) *The Ancient World in the Cinema*. New Haven, CT.
Spaltenstein, F. (1990) *Commentaire des Punica de Silius Italicus*. Geneva.

Spencer, D. (2005) 'Lucan's follies: memory and ruin in a civil-war landscape', *G&R* 52: 46–68.

Spentzou, E. and Fowler, D. (eds.) (2002) *Cultivating the Muse: Struggles for Power and Inspiration in Classical Literature*. Oxford.

Squire, M. (2009) *Image and Text in Graeco-Roman Antiquity*. Cambridge.

(2011) *The Iliad in a Nutshell: Visualising Epic on the Tabulae Iliacae*. Oxford.

Stacey, J. (1994) *Star Gazing: Hollywood Cinema and Female Spectatorship*. London.

Stahl, H.-P. (1990) 'The death of Turnus: Augustan Vergil and the Political rival', in *Between Republic and Empire*, eds. K. A. Raaflaub and M. Toher. Berkeley, CA: 174–211.

(1998) *Vergil's Aeneid: Augustan Epic and Political Context*. London.

Stanford, W. B. (1965) 'The ending of the *Odyssey*: an ethical approach', *Hermathena* 100: 5–20.

Stanley, K. (1993) *The Shield of Homer*. Princeton, NJ.

Steiner, D. (1995) 'Stoning and sight: a structural equivalence in Greek mythology', *ClAnt* 14: 193–221.

(2001) *Images in Mind: Statues in Archaic and Classical Greek Literature and Thought*. Princeton, NJ.

Stephens, S. (2003) *Seeing Double: Intercultural Poetics in Ptolemaic Alexandria*. Berkeley, CA.

Stern, J. (2003) 'Heraclitus the paradoxographer: Περὶ Ἀπίστων, *On Unbelievable Tales*', *TAPhA* 133: 51–97.

Stewart, A. (1993) *Faces of Power: Alexander's Image and Hellenistic Politics*. Berkeley, CA.

Stok, F. (2010) 'The life of Virgil before Donatus', in *A Companion to Vergil's Aeneid and its Tradition*, eds. J. Farrell and M. C. J. Putnam. Oxford: 107–20.

Stover, T. (2003) 'Confronting Medea: genre, gender, and allusion in the *Argonautica* of Valerius Flaccus', *CPh* 98: 123–47.

(2008) 'The date of Valerius Flaccus' *Argonautica*', *PLLS* 13: 211–29.

(2009) 'Apollonius, Valerius Flaccus and Statius: Argonautic elements in *Thebaid* 3.499–647', *AJPh* 130: 79–83.

(forthcoming) *Rebuilding Epic and Empire: Valerius Flaccus and Lucan*. Oxford.

Studlar, G. (1988) *In the Realm of Pleasure: Von Sternberg, Dietrich, and the Masochistic Aesthetic*. New York.

Syed, Y. (2005) *Vergil's Aeneid and the Roman Self: Subject and Nation in Literary Discourse*. Ann Arbor, MI.

Syme, R. (1939) *The Roman Revolution*. Oxford.

Taplin, O. (1992) *Homeric Soundings: The Shaping of the Iliad*. Oxford.

Tarrant, R. J. (ed.) (2012) *Virgil Aeneid Book XII*. Cambridge.

Tasker, Y. (1993) *Spectacular Bodies: Gender, Genre and the Action Cinema*. London.

Tatti-Gartziou, A. (2010) 'Blindness as punishment', in *Light and Darkness in Ancient Greek Myth and Religion*, eds. M. Christopoulos, E. D. Karakantza and O. Levaniouk. Lanham, MD: 181–90.

Tatum, J. (2003) *The Mourner's Song: War and Remembrance from the Iliad to Vietnam*. Chicago, IL.
Taylor, C. C. W. (1999) *The Atomists Leucippus and Democritus: Fragments – A Text and Translation with a Commentary*. Toronto.
Tesoriero, C. (2005) 'Trampling over Troy: Caesar, Virgil and Lucan', in *Lucan im 21. Jahrhundert*, ed. C. Walde. Munich: 202–15.
Thalmann, W. G. (1998) 'Thersites: comedy, scapegoats and heroic ideology in the *Iliad*', *TAPhA* 118: 1–28.
Thomas, R. F. (1998) 'The isolation of Turnus: *Aeneid* book 12', in *Vergil's Aeneid: Augustan Epic and Political Context*, ed. H.-P. Stahl. Swansea, UK: 271–302.
Thornham, S. (ed.) (1999) *Feminist Film Theory*. Edinburgh, UK.
Tipping, B. (2010) *Exemplary Epic: Silius Italicus' Punica*. Oxford.
Tissol, G. (1997) *The Face of Nature: Wit, Narrative and Cosmic Origins in Ovid's Metamorphoses*. Princeton, NJ.
Too, Y. L. (ed.) (2001) *Education in Greek and Roman Antiquity*. Leiden.
Tränkle, H. (1963) 'Elegisches in Ovids Metamorphosen', *Hermes* 91: 459–76.
Turkeltaub, D. (2005) 'The syntax and semantics of Homeric glowing eyes: *Iliad* 1.200', *AJPh* 126: 157–86.
  (2007) 'Perceiving Iliadic gods', *HSPh* 103: 51–81.
Uccellini, R. (2006) 'Soggetti eccentrici: Asbyte in Silio Italico (e altre donne periculose del mite)', *GIF* 58: 229–53.
Vaage, M. B. (2009) 'The role of empathy in Gregory Currie's philosophy of film', *British Journal of Aesthetics* 49: 109–28.
Van Erp Taalman Kip, A. M. (2000) 'The gods of the *Iliad* and the fate of Troy', *Mnemosyne* 53: 385–402.
van Hoorn, W. (1972) *As Images Unwind: Ancient and Modern Theories of Visual Perception*. Leiden.
Van Wees, H. (1992) *Status Warriors: War, Violence and Society in Homer and History*. Amsterdam.
  (1997) 'Homeric warfare', in *A New Companion to Homer*, eds. I. Morris and B. Powell. Leiden: 668–93.
Venini, P. (1991) 'Lo scudo di Annibale in Silio Italico (Pun. 2.406–52)', in *Studi di filologia classica in onore di Giusto Monaco III*. Palermo: 1191–200.
Vernant, J.-P. (1981) 'A "beautiful death" and the disfigured corpse in homeric epic', in *Mortals and Immortals: Collected Essays*, ed. F. I. Zeitlin. Princeton, NJ: 50–74.
Vessey, D. W. T. C. (1973) *Statius and the Thebaid*. Cambridge.
  (1975) 'Silius Italicus: the shield of Hannibal', *AJPh* 96: 391–405.
Vian, F. (2008) 'Echoes and imitations of Apollonius Rhodius in late Greek epic', in *Brill's Companion to Apollonius Rhodius*, eds. T. Papanghelis and A. Rengakos. Leiden: 387–412.
Vincendeau, G. (2000) *Stars and Stardom in French Cinema*. London.
Vout, C. (2007) *Power and Eroticism in Imperial Rome*. Cambridge.
Walde, C. (2001) *Die Traumdarstellungen in der griechisch–römischen Dichtung*. Munich.

(2006) 'Caesar, Lucan's *Bellum Civile* and their reception', in *Julius Caesar in Western Culture*, ed. M. Wyke. Oxford: 45–61.
Warden, J. (1978) 'Another would-be Amazon: Propertius 4.4.71–2', *Hermes* 106: 177–87.
Watson, P. and Watson, L. (1996) 'Two problems in Martial', *CQ* 46: 586–91.
Webb, R. (2009) *Ekphrasis, Imagination and Persuasion in Ancient Rhetorical Theory and Practice*. Farnham, UK.
Welch, T. S. (2005) *The Elegiac Cityscape: Propertius and the Meaning of Roman Monuments*. Columbus, OH.
Wender, D. (1978) *The Last Scenes of the Odyssey*. Leiden.
West, M. L. (ed.) (2003) *Greek Epic Fragments*. Cambridge, MA.
Wheeler, S. M. (1999) *A Discourse of Wonders*. Philadelphia, PA.
  (2000) *Narrative Dynamics in Ovid's Metamorphoses*. Tübingen, PA.
Whitehead, O. (1984) 'The funeral of Achilles: an epilogue to the *Iliad* in book 24 of the *Odyssey*', *G&R* 31: 119–25.
Whitman, C. H. (1958) *Homer and the Heroic Tradition*. Cambridge, MA.
Wiedemann, T. (1983) 'ἐλάχιστον ... ἐν τοῖς ἄρσεσι κλέος: Thucydides, women and the limits of rational analysis', *G&R* 30: 163–70.
  (1992) *Emperors and Gladiators*. London.
Wijsman, H. J. W. (1996) *Valerius Flaccus Argonautica, Book v*. Leiden.
Williams, C. (1999) *Roman Homosexuality: Ideologies of Masculinity in Classical Antiquity*. New York.
Williams, R. D. (ed.) (1973 (repr. 1987)) *The Aeneid of Virgil: Books 7–12*. London.
Willis, A. (ed.) (2004) *Film Stars: Hollywood and Beyond*. Manchester, UK.
Wilson, C. H. (1979) 'Jupiter and the Fates in the *Aeneid*', *CQ* 29: 361–71.
Wilson, D. F. (2002) *Ransom, Revenge and Heroic Identity in the Iliad*. Cambridge.
Wiltshire, S. F. (1989) *Public and Private in Vergil's Aeneid*. Amherst, MA.
Winkler, J. J. (1990) *The Constraints of Desire*. New York.
Winkler, M. M. (ed.) (1991) *Classics and Cinema*. London.
  (2004) *Gladiator: Film and History*. Malden, MA.
  (2007) *Troy: From Homer's Iliad to Hollywood Epic*. Oxford.
  (2009) *Cinema and Classical Texts: Apollo's New Light*. Cambridge.
Wofford, S. (1992) *The Choice of Achilles: The Ideology of Figure in the Epic*. Stanford, CA.
Woodman, A. J. (1974) '*Exegi monumentum*: Horace, *Odes* 3.30', in *Quality and Pleasure in Latin Poetry*, eds. D. West and A. J. Woodman. Cambridge: 115–28.
Wyke, M. (1997) *Projecting the Past: Ancient Rome, Cinema and History*. New York.
Zanker, G. (2004) *Modes of Viewing in Hellenistic Poetry and Art*. Madison, WI.
Zanker, P. (1988) *The Power of Images in the Age of Augustus*. Ann Arbor, MI.
Zetzel, J. E. G. (1989) 'Romane memento: justice and judgement in *Aeneid 6*', *TAPhA* 119: 363–84.

Zissos, A. (2002) 'Reading models and the Homeric program in Valerius Flaccus' *Argonautica*', *Helios* 29: 69–96.
  (2003) 'Spectacle and elite in the *Argonautica* of Valerius Flaccus', in *Flavian Rome: Culture, Image, Text*, eds. A. J. Boyle and W. J. Dominik. Leiden: 659–84.
  (2004) 'Terminal middle: the *Argonautica* of Valerius Flaccus', in *Middles in Latin Poetry*, eds. S. Kyriakidis and F. De Martino. Bari: 311–44.
  (2008) *Argonautica Book 1: Valerius Flaccus*. Oxford.
Zwierlein, O. (2010) 'Lucan's Caesar at Troy', in *Oxford Readings in Lucan*, eds. C. Tesoriero, F. Muecke and T. Neal. Oxford: 411–32.

Index locorum

Apollonius
  Argonautica
    1.547–9, 48
    1.742–6, 187
    1.782–5, 181
    2.197–207, 150
    2.317–407, 140
    3.6–10, 44, 57
    3.1008–25, 318
    3.1259–61, 271
    3.222–34, 169
    4.257–93, 194
    4.421–34, 183
    4.428–9, 201
    4.727–9, 312
    4.956–60, 51
    4.1182–93, 230
    4.1477–80, 229
    4.1669–72, 334
    4.1676–7, 335
    4.1731–45, 208

Catullus
    64.50–67, 162

Ennius
  Annales
    34–50 Sk., 209
    72–91 Sk., 142

Euripides
  Phoenissae
    88–201, 223

Homer
  Iliad
    1.53–6, 55
    1.103–4, 311
    1.197–200, 82
    1.199–200, 311
    1.597–600, 46
    2.5–34, 206
    3.125–8, 220
    3.243–4, 222
    4.141–7, 274
    4.482–7, 280
    5.3–415, 88
    5.127–32, 85
    5.596–600, 86
    5.741–2, 199
    5.855–9, 87
    6.372–476, 226
    6.506–11, 268
    7.81–91, 360
    8.300–8, 279
    8.348–9, 313
    11.2–603, 33–4
    11.36–7, 199
    12.200–50, 141
    12.462–6, 313
    13.545–9, 293
    13.567–75, 294
    13.613–19, 295
    13.650–5, 295
    14.153–60, 56
    14.224–30, 64
    15.13–30, 56
    15.605–10, 314
    15.647–51, 314
    16.462–507, 73
    17.51–4, 279
    18.202–48, 1–3
    18.491–6, 186
    18.516–19, 175
    19.14–15, 199
    19.19, 201
    19.15–17, 315
    19.364–7, 315
    20.22–3, 34
    20.44–6, 316

21.108–10, 269
21.388–90, 34
22.131–7, 316
22.21–4, 269
22.71–6, 263
22.131–7, 200
22.158–66, 45
22.317–18, 262
22.324–7, 262
22.369–75, 263
22.405–7, 252
Odyssey
4.138–264, 223
4.795–841, 207
5.73–4, 201
5.282–90, 126
6.131–2, 318
6.229–37, 275
7.91–4, 169
7.133–4, 201
8.266–369, 46
10.487–574, 140
11.100–49, 140
11.489–91, 370
11.608, 181
15.172–3, 223
19.535–62, 207
20.87–90, 209
20.345–57, 134
22.15–16, 326
22.381–2, 327
22.401–12, 251
23.157–62, 275
24.80–4, 369
24.93–4, 369
Homeric Hymn to Demeter
275–83, 79
Homeric Hymns
5.168–90, 79

Lucan
Bellum civile
1.53–9, 115
1.624–8, 142
1.638–40, 143
3.4–38, 213
3.88–168, 119
5.97–222, 146–7
5.165–9, 146
5.211–13, 147
6.1–3, 113
6.742–4, 155
7.192–206, 113
7.445–55, 112

7.447–8, 37
7.475–84, 114
7.557–81, 118
7.649–51, 116
7.680–4, 117
7.698–702, 117
7.796–9, 119
8.798–815, 365
8.816–22, 366
8.840–5, 367
9.11–14, 367
9.626–8, 354
9.678–83, 355
9.980–6, 363

Lucretius
De rerum natura
1.62–7, 337
1.62–71, 99
1.102–6, 123
1.1115–7, 100
2.1–19, 101
2.308–32, 101
3.14–19, 93
3.28–30, 100

Nonnus
Dionysiaca
17.8–14, 267
18.289–305, 350
25.98–104, 351
25.326–9, 196
25.352–60, 196
25.429–50, 190
25.560–2, 197
29.157–61, 283
31.3–12, 63
31.124–8, 64
32.9–37, 64
32.110–13, 64
35.11–16, 249
35.94–6, 250
47.559–63, 351
47.609–11, 352

Ovid
Metamorphoses
1.163–245, 50
1.605, 66
2.1–30, 169
2.178–81, 103
2.401–10, 69
2.633–75, 147
2.714–19, 66

404 Index locorum

Ovid (cont.)
  2.714–21, 332
  2.722–5, 333
  2.752–9, 330
  2.791–4, 331
  2.800–1, 331
  2.812–13, 333
  3.253–315, 80
  3.316–38, 156
  4.420–7, 66
  4.464–7, 67
  4.673–7, 278
  4.779–84, 354
  4.798–801, 75
  5.227–9, 349
  5.356–61, 68
  5.362–72, 70
  5.420–4, 70
  7.33–4, 287
  8.38–42, 235
  8.338–42, 180
  9.241–58, 50
  11.24–7, 287
  11.410–748, 211
  11.463–73, 225
  12.393–428, 278
  14.101–57, 129
  15.62–8, 101
  15.143–52, 102
  15.840–2, 104
  15.877–9, 123

Propertius
  4.4, 233–4

Quintus Smyrnaeus
  Posthomerica
  1.53–9, 267
  1.396–402, 247
  1.436–45, 247
  1.594–8, 307
  1.612–18, 307
  2.490–513, 53
  3.740–2, 372
  6.531–6, 284
  12.389–499, 152
  12.437–43, 54
  12.525–39, 131
  12.540–51, 132
  13.415–30, 75

Silius Italicus
  Punica
  1.17–19, 62

  1.29–33, 62
  2.56–207, 305–6
  2.251–5, 219
  2.429–31, 198
  2.437–45, 192
  2.449–52, 181
  3.154–7, 258
  3.158–62, 258
  3.163–200, 259
  3.406–9, 257
  3.492–569, 52
  4.324–30, 198
  5.420–2, 123
  6.366–70, 345
  8.466–7, 281
  9.370–400, 299
  11.218–21, 320
  11.337–40, 321
  12.628–9, 96
  12.668–730, 94–8
  12.682–5, 97
  12.719–25, 96
  14.341–52, 106
  14.665–71, 107
  14.676–8, 107
  15.421–34, 185
  17.158–69, 259
  17.211–17, 259
  17.341–3, 62
  17.391–8, 322
  17.399–400, 322
  17.408–9, 322
  17.474–8, 323
  17.517–21, 323
  17.597–9, 62, 260

Statius
  Achilleid
  1.277–82, 282
  1.325–31, 282
  2.23–30, 231
  Thebaid
  1.197–302, 51
  2.269–305, 171
  3.150–2, 254
  3.462–5, 143
  3.499–500, 144
  3.549–51, 144
  4.24–30, 230
  4.405–645, 156
  4.468–72, 156
  4.520–2, 157
  4.540–3, 158
  4.579–87, 158

4.89–92, 231
7.34–63, 171
7.243–6, 244
7.243–373, 242–4
7.564–78, 180
8.254–8, 151
8.760–6, 76
9.333–5, 188
9.519–20, 61
9.570–636, 215–16
9.639–55, 216
9.698–713, 3–5
9.731–5, 5
10.56–64, 184
10.70–83, 61
10.160–75, 138
10.445–8, 362
10.589–605, 159
10.640–77, 84
10.840–2, 109
10.860–3, 109
10.883–11.8, 51
11.119–35, 76–7
11.130–3, 74
11.354–8, 244
11.359–62, 245
11.372–5, 245
11.382–7, 246
11.416–19, 218
11.457–64, 341
11.492–6, 343
11.524–7, 344
11.587–93, 151
12.177–82, 255
12.203–4, 256
12.481–511, 204
12.665–71, 204
12.805–9, 373

Valerius Flaccus
Argonautica
1.111–20, 60
1.149–50, 170
1.207–33, 135
1.494–7, 229
1.498–502, 49, 230
2.216–19, 123
2.244–6, 363
2.408–17, 183
3.487–91, 60
4.68–71, 105
4.547–52, 136
4.631–5, 137
4.667–85, 51

5.407–56, 170
5.418–24, 194
6.451–3, 237
6.490–4, 237
6.657–8, 318
6.681–2, 239
6.755–60, 241
7.189–92, 59

Virgil
Aeneid
1.223–6, 35
1.254–6, 58
1.257–96, 125
1.402–9, 83
1.464–5, 202
1.494–5, 202
1.588–93, 276
2.268–97, 210
2.589–92, 90
2.604–7, 88
2.622–5, 89, 93
3.84–120, 141
4.208–10, 97
4.220–1, 36
4.401–12, 227
4.584–5, 253
5.252–7, 189
6.46–51, 128
6.453–4, 229
6.563–5, 129
6.580–5, 129
7.286–91, 67
7.789–92, 188
7.812–17, 303
8.587–93, 266
8.592–3, 230
8.626–8, 168
8.657–62, 194
8.698–706, 176
8.720–8, 176
9.126–58, 142
9.446–9, 361
9.459–60, 253
9.470–2, 253
9.477–80, 253
9.731–3, 319
10.3–4, 36
10.11–113, 125
10.96–9, 50
10.134–8, 280
10.261–2, 319
10.270–5, 200
10.310–44, 300

Virgil (cont.)
   10.466–73, 73
   11.475–6, 217
   11.486–97, 217
   11.489–91, 272
   11.799–804, 304
   11.891–5, 218
   12.64–9, 273
   12.101–2, 319
   12.244–56, 142
   12.270–6, 288
   12.289–97, 289
   12.665–71, 338
   12.913–8, 339
   12.945–7, 203
Georgics
   3.339–48, 192

General index

abject
  and Invidia, 331
  in Kristeva, 9
Achilles
  and beauty, 269
  and Deidamia, 232
  and fire imagery, 297
  and Hector, 262–4
  and monumentality, 368
  and Penthesilea, 308
  and star imagery, 262
  and the oblique gaze, 232
  blazing eyes, 315–17
  death in Quintus Smyrnaeus, 370
  in Statius as object of desire, 282
  on the walls, 1–3
Aeneas
  and blazing eyes, 319
  and the divine gaze, 88–94
  and the female gaze, 211
  as art object, 276
  as dissatisfied viewer, 203
  as interpreter, 142
  as narrator, 92
  as passive viewer, 203
  vertical perspective, 93
  viewing Carthage, 227
Agamemnon, 274, 311
Aglauros, 329–34
alienation, 34, 53, 178, 188, 224, 242, 278, 291, 297, 299
Amphiaraus, 143–5
Andromache, and Hector, 226
Andromeda, 278
anger
  of Juno, 61
Antigone
  and Argia, 255
  in Statius, 242–6
Antinous, as object of the gaze, 326
anxiety, 61, 104

and apotheosis, 104
and disgust, 331
dream, 259
poetic, 122
Aphrodite. *See also* Venus
  and Diomedes, 86
  controlling Helen, 221
Apollo, 45
  and Cassandra, 148
  and Diomedes, 86
  and Manto, 160
  and Ovid's Sibyl, 148
  and Phemonoe, 146
  and Virgil's Sibyl, 147
  epiphany of, 80
  on the shield of Aeneas, 176
  taming the Sibyl, 128
Apollonius and epic, 208
apotheosis, 229, 368
  of Caesar, 104
  of Ovid, 104
Arachne, 79, 183
Archimedes, 106–8
Ares
  and Aphrodite, 46–8, 78
  wounded by Diomedes, 87
Argia
  and Antigone, 255
  as object of the gaze, 256
  in *Thebaid* 12, 255–7
Argonauts, as objects of the gaze, 229–30
Ariadne
  and ecphrasis, 163–5
  in Nonnus, 352
Asbyte, 305–6
Ascanius, 253, 280
assaultive gaze, 310–46
  of Hannibal, 320
Atalanta, 3, 75
  dream of, 215–16

407

Athena
    and Achilles, 3, 82
    and Aglauros, 330
    and Diomedes, 85–8
    and Medusa, 353
    as artist, 276
    protectress of Telemachus, 5
Athene. *See also* Athena
    and Odysseus, 325–7
audience
    admiring, 3
    and identification in tragedy, 121
    authorising, 292
    desiring, 273
    in ecphrasis, 186
    interpreters of the future as internal, 124
    mediating, 217
    multi-layered, 5
    of Furies, 195
    of gods, 32
    of poetry, 14
    paralysed, 315
    participation, 44
    Zeus as mediating, 34
Augoustakis, 9
Augustus, 14
aural, the, and the visual, 23
averted gaze, 71, 77

Bacchus, as partisan, 52
battle scenes, 293–302
battles of the gaze
    Achilles versus Hector, 52, 317
    Aeneas versus Turnus, 337–41
    Capaneus versus Jupiter, 108–11
    Epicurus versus *Religio*, 99, 337
    Hannibal versus Jupiter, 53, 97
    Medea versus Talos, 334–6
    Odysseus versus the suitors, 325–7
    Pietas versus Tisiphone, 341–4
beautiful boy, 3, 5, 23, 142, 188, 189, 265, 280, 282, 301
beautiful death, 264, 349
bird's-eye view, 42, 71
blazing eyes, 98, 198, 311–24
    in *Aeneid* 12, 319–20
    in Silius' *Punica*, 320–4
blindness, and prophecy, 149–54
body, in pieces, 293–302

Caesar
    and the divine gaze, 118–20
    as Capaneus, 119
    as divine viewer in Ovid, 104
    divine perspective, 119

Calchas, 122, 140
Callisto, 68
Camilla, 218, 303–5
    as object of the gaze, 304
Capaneus
    and Amphiaraus, 145
    and the divine audience, 51
    and the mortal gaze, 108–11
Cassandra, 130–2, 148
Catullus, and ecphrasis, 163–5
Ceyx and Alcyone, 211–13, 225
change of scene, 2
    and the divine gaze, 39–45
Circe, 140, 312
cloak
    and cosmos, 183
    as feminine, 4, 182–5
consumptive gaze, 20, 67, 202, 307
contagion, and vision, 330
controlling gaze, 33, 39, 46, 58, 77, 259

deferral, and the *Aeneid*, 301
defloration, and death, 238
Demodocus, 153
departing heroes, in Statius, 230–1
desire
    and disgust, 292
    and fantasy, 139
    and frustrated viewing, 221
    and glory, 370
    and rape, 146–9
    and terror, 271
    and the insatiable gaze, 201
    body of hero as site of, 273
    for knowledge, 154, 234
    in dreams, 215
    masochistic, 299
    of the gods, 209
    of the other, 9, 229
destructive gaze, 86, 314, 329
Diana
    and Atalanta, 215
    and Parthenopaeus, 4
Dido
    and the prophetic gaze, 165
    as ecphrastic object, 202
    hostile gaze, 228
    watching the departure, 226
Diomedes, and the divine gaze, 85–8
Dionysus, outgrowing epic, 353
Dios apate (Deception of Zeus), 56
    in Nonnus, 63
Dis, as object of the gaze, 70
disavowal, 29, 77, 99, 242, 296, 297, 309
divine audience, 45–54, 65

and Capaneus, 110
and mediation, 32
as audience at games, 45
as fractious, 51
as Lucretian, 100
cannot bear to watch, 73
gladiatorial, 113
in later epic tradition, 48
in Lucan's apostrophes, 112
in Quintus Smyrnaeus, 54
in Silius Italicus, 52
laughter of, 46
divine council
  in Statius, 51
  in the *Metamorphoses*, 50
divine gaze, 341–4
  and vulnerability, 76
divine rape, 68, 79, 183
dream
  of Atalanta, 215–6
  of Ilia, 359
  of Ismene, 214–5
dreams
  and the female gaze, 206
  tragic and epic, 207

ecphrasis, 10
  and its undoing in *Thebaid* 12, 204
  and narrative, 165
  and paralysis, 201
  and the divine gaze, 168
  and the imperial gaze, 191–7
  and the tragic gaze in Lucan and Virgil, 174
  breaking the frame, 180
  definition of, 10
  ecphrastic failure, 190
  ecphrastic hope, 190, 202
  makers, 172
  of cloaks, 167, 182–5
  of places, 167
  of shields, 166
  rhetorical theories of, 20
ekplexis. *See* wonder
elegy, and Lacan, 9
enargeia, 159
  rhetorical theories of, 20
Ennius, 272, 359
  on monumentality, 358
epic
  and Catullus 64, 163–5
  and elegy, 233–4
  and epinician, 270
  and history, 62
  and monumentality, 358
  and politics, 126, 292

and the sublime, 48, 90
and tragedy, 224
as confrontation with death and/or power, 302
as cultural capital, 16
as mode, 359
causation, 87, 333
definitions of, 5
Iliadic and Odyssean, 6, 35, 166
modern usage of term, 25
totalising and fragmented, 309
epic authority
  and Lucan, 368
  and Ovid, 65–71
  and prophecy, 122, 161
  and the divine gaze, 111
Epicurus, 18, 26, 52, 53, 93, 99, 106, 108, 133, 337
  and Amphiaraus, 145
epiphany, 79–85
  and authority, 89
  in Apollonius, 79
  in the *Iliad*, 79
Erichtho, 154–5
erotic viewing, 5, 220, 234, 241, 287
eroticisation of death, 305, 388
Eteocles, 156
ethnicity, 194
evil eye, 328–36
  ancient theories of, 328–9
eye wounds, 291

Fama, 60, 84, 252, 333
  and Juno, 60
fantasy, 9, 31, 164
  and prophecy, 122
Feeney, Denis, 13, 111
female audience, 55, 349
  passivity, 186
female gaze, 353
  at the departing hero, 225–32
  existence of, 205
female prophets, and madness, 130–3
female readers of epic, 14
fetish, 285, 296
fetishism, 297, 301, 309
  in Mulvey, 7
fire imagery, in the *Iliad*, 312
Fitzgerald, William, 163–5
focalisation, 57, 98, 222, 228, 274
Foucault, Michel, 10
Freud, Sigmund, 8

Ganymede, 189–91
gaze
  definitions of, 7–11
  not always visual, 23

gender
  and action heroines, 302–8
  and power, 55
  and Statius' Achilles, 282
  and the gods, 55
  cloaks and shields, 184
  destabilisation in Nonnus, 250
  objects of ecphrasis, 185
genre, 5
  and boundaries, 220
  and gender, 207, 233, 256
  and madness, 139
  definitions of, 5–6
  edges of, 149
  erotics and epic, 233
  pastoral on the margins, 260
gigantomachy, as marker of the sublime, 52
gladiators, 5, 193, 283–93
  and desire, 285
  as abject, 309
gods
  and agency, 73
  and blazing eyes, 317
  and prophecy, 125–6
  as defining feature of epic, 29
  as source of epic authority, 31
  in ecphrasis, 175–7
Gorgon, 155, 364
grief, 61, 68, 203, 273
  and madness, 254, 256
  and the female gaze, 206
  of Euryalus' mother, 253
  of Helen, 221
  violating divinity, 215

Hannibal
  and blazing eyes, 320
  and Imilce, 258
  and the divine gaze, 94–8, 320
  and the female gaze, 257
  as *contemptor deorum*, 96
  as resisting viewer, 98
  breaking the frame, 182
  crossing the Alps, 52
Hasdrubal, 185
Hector
  and Achilles, 262–4
  and Andromache, 299
  and monuments, 361
  and Paris, 269
  and the beautiful body, 262–4
  as model, 5
  as object of the gaze, 263
  blazing eyes of, 312–15
  ghost of, 211

Helen
  as narrator, 220
  in the *Odyssey*, 223
  on the walls, 220–3
  veiled, 15
Helen episode, 89
Hephaestus. *See also* Vulcan
  as object of the gaze, 46
Hera. *See* Juno
Hera and Athene, 44
  as joint audience, 44, 55
  with Hephaestus, 51
Hercules, 60–1, 63
heroes
  as art objects, 273–8
  as erotic objects, 265–83
  as gladiators, 283–93
  as jewels, 280–1
  as plants, 278–80
heroic beauty, 262
history, and epic, 6
horror, 77, 149, 152, 179, 201, 226, 240, 251, 253, 293, 299, 357, 374

identification, 7, 16, 21, 121, 188, 224, 292, 297, 299, 337
  and epiphany, 81
  and gladiators, 286
  and internal audiences, 218
Ilia, dream of, 209
imperial gaze, 25, 68, 69, 70, 115, 118, 119, 121, 166, 194, 362
  and divine rape, 68
  and the shield of Aeneas, 177
  ecphrasis, 191–7
imperial Greek epic, and knowledge of Latin literature, 12–13
incomprehensibility, 26, 31, 84, 115, 124, 139, 146, 207, 215, 229, 234
insatiable gaze, 202
inspiration, as emasculation, 146
investigatory gaze, 64
Invidia, 329–34
Io
  and Juno's gaze, 65
  on the shield of Turnus, 188

Jason
  as horse in Apollonius, 271
  as star, 265
Juno
  and Allecto, 67
  and Dionysus in Nonnus, 62
  and Hannibal, 59, 260
  and Hercules, 59

and Jupiter in Ovid, 65–71
and Medea, 236–42
and Semele, 80
as alternative centre of power, 65
as emotional viewer, 57
as protectress of the Argonauts, 59
gaze of, 65
   downcast, 61
   as male, 67
   jealous, 65
   ox-eyed, 3
   structural, 56, 62
   vertical perspective of, 56
grief, 68
in Apollonius, 56
in Flavian epic, 59–62
in Nonnus, 65
in Silius Italicus, 62
in the *Aeneid*, 59
in the *Iliad*, 55–6
in the *Thebaid*, 61–2
in Valerius Flaccus, 59–61
Jupiter
ambivalence and power, 77
and Capaneus, 110
and fate, 72
and Juno, 65
and narrative, 72
and other gods, 54
and Phaethon, 103
and Prometheus, 105
and Semele, 80
and the *Dira*, 36
and Venus, 71
as autocratic, 51
as poet figure, 74
as rapist, 55
clemency, 106
gaze of, 39
   controlling, 33
   averted, 72
   panoptic, 126
   pitying, 45
in Silius Italicus, 37
in the *Metamorphoses*, 36, 50, 65–71
in the *Thebaid* 7, 37–9
in Valerius Flaccus, 37, 49
prophecy, 125
under attack from Hannibal, 53
Jupiter and Juno, 55
in *Aeneid* 12, 58–9
tensions between, 55

kleos, 55, 88, 241, 323, 334, 348, 358, 360, 361, 369, 370
Kristeva, Julia, 9, 149

Lacan, Jacques, 8, 149, 361
Lacanian gaze, 9, 26, 124, 139, 161, 324, 327, 331, 357
lament
   and Statius, 254–7
   and the female gaze, 220, 250–7
Laocoon, in Quintus Smyrnaeus, 33, 152
Lavinia, 273
Leigh, Matthew, 22, 113, 285
lines of sight, 6, 22, 329
Livy, 107, 219
   in contrast to Silius, 95
Lucan
   absence of divine audience, 111
   augury and divination, 142–3
Lucretius
   and later Latin epic, 99–111
   and the divine gaze in *Aeneid*. 2, 93–4
   and the sublime in Silius, 52
   and viewing from a distance, 100, 265

male gaze, 77, 205, 238, 333, 347
Manto, 156–61
Mars, as partisan, 52
masochism, 299, 309
McGowan, Todd, 9, 30–1, 139
Medea, 195
   and dreams, 208
   and ecphrasis, 171
   and genre, 240
   and Talos, 334–6
   and teichoscopy in Valerius Flaccus, 236–42
   as audience, 239
   as descendant of the Sun, 312
   as heroic, 336
   as object of the gaze, 238
   as other, 335
   as powerful, 237
   as prophet in Pindar, 208
   blazing eyes, 318
medical gaze, 153, 294, 296
Medusa, 353
   as feminist icon, 356
   as object, 353
   powerful gaze, 353
Menelaus, as art object, 274
Menoeceus, 84
   and Capaneus, 109
Mercury, 66
   as predator, 331
Messapus, 283, 288–90
Minerva. *See* Athena
monsters, and blazing eyes, 317
monumentality, 333
   empty tomb for Laocoon, 153

monumentality (cont.)
  in Roman epic, 362
  in the *Iliad*, 360
Mopsus and Idmon, 135
mortal vision, conditions of, 53, 90
mortality, 5, 32, 77, 102, 263, 297, 317
  and Oedipus, 152
  and Phineus, 151
  and power, 55
Mulvey, Laura, 7–8, 31, 205, 264, 296, 310

narrative
  and ecphrasis, 163–5
  objectivity, 32, 154
  omniscient, 48, 71, 112
    Caesar appropriating, 119
narrative transition. *See also* change of scene
  and ecphrasis, 164
    in Ovid, 177
  and the divine gaze, 37
narrator
  aligned with Juno, 67
  and Muses, 71, 78
  and similes, 3
  and Zeus, 33
  in the *Metamorphoses*, 178
  protesting ignorance in Lucan, 115
  revelation and authority, 90
  split voice of Statius, 77
Nausicaa, 275
navigation, 139–41
Neptune, peaceful gaze of, 57
Nero, 115
Nonnus, going beyond epic, 351
non-verbal behaviour, 71

objectification, 26, 56, 117, 146, 163, 185, 202, 203, 292, 326, 327, 356
objet petit a, as distortion in the field of vision, 9
oblique gaze, 110, 182, 328, 332
  and the female gaze, 260
  of goddesses, 25
  of Juno, 66
  of Ovid at epic, 148, 334, 374
Ocyrhoe, 147–8
Odysseus
  and the assaultive gaze, 325–7
  as art object, 275
  as monster, 327
  in bloody aftermath, 250
  veiled, 15
Oedipus, and the abject, 151–2
Orpheus, 287
otherness, 281
  and ecphrasis, 165, 191–7

in Kristeva, 9
  of the divine, 147
Ovid, deconstructing epic, 213, 350

Palinurus, 141
paradox, 77, 115, 156, 356, 364
  and disturbance in the visual field, 147
  and emotional viewing, 46
paralysed viewer, 68, 84, 116, 238
paralysis
  and grief, 203
  of prey, 315, 325
Paris, 268
Parthenopaeus, as object of desire, 3–5
passive visual power, 1, 85, 316
Patroclus, as model, 5
Penelope, 207, 251, 275
penetrative gaze, 88, 254
  and the gods, 61, 84, 86, 100, 371
  and violence, 142
  hostile, 198, 317, 323
  of narrator, 291
  of prophets, 26
Penthesilea, 247, 267, 306–8
performance, 24
Perseus, 144
  and monumentality, 348
  as poet-figure, 349
  in Nonnus, 350
Phaethon, 69, 103, 169
Phemonoe, as rape victim, 146
phenomenology, 8
philosophy
  and epic, 17
  and the divine gaze, 99–111
Phineus
  in Apollonius, 140, 150–1
  in Statius, 151
  in Valerius Flaccus, 136
Pietas
  and the female gaze, 342
  and Tisiphone in Statius, 341–4
pity, 1, 5, 35
  and horror, 236
  and pain, 296
pitying gaze, 226
poetic anxiety, 124
poetic authority, prophecy and the *si non vana* motif, 122–4
poetic failure, 243
poetic immortality, 104
political context, and divine councils, 51
pollution
  and objectification, 47
  and the divine gaze, 74–7

General index 413

Polynices, and Eteocles, 343–4
Pompey
  and his grave, 364
  and the divine gaze, 115–17, 367
  as godlike, 116
  as monument, 365
  as object of the gaze, 117, 364
  dreams of, 213
Poseidon. *See* Neptune
power, competitively acquired by gods, 55
Priam, and teichoscopy, 222
Prometheus, in Valerius Flaccus, 105–6
prophecy
  and madness, 130–9
  and the abject, 149–54
  and the divine gaze, 125–6
  omens and auguries, 141–5
prophetic gaze
  in Catullus 64, 165
prophetic madness
  and inspiration, 138
  in Flavian epic, 135
prophets
  as objects of the gaze, 145
Proserpina, 69
Pythagoras, 101–3
  as prophet and poet figure, 102

Quintus Smyrnaeus, and the divine audience, 53

Regulus, 344–5
returning the gaze, 164, 197–203

Salmoneus, 119
Salzman-Mitchell, Patricia, 7, 66, 178
Sarpedon, 73
Sartre, Jean-Paul, 8
Scaeva, as gladiator, 290–2
Scipio, and blazing eyes, 322
scopophilia, 296
Scylla, and Minos, 234–6
sea imagery, in Silius, 53
shield
  and cosmos, 173
  as apotropaic, 201
  of Aeneas, 187, 193
  of Agamemnon, 199
  of Ares in Apollonius, 187
  of Crenaeus, 188
  of Hannibal, 172–5, 191
  of Theseus, 204
  of Turnus, 188
Sibyl, 125
  and sexualisation, 147
  as witness, 129

gaze of
  penetrative, 128
  powerful, 127
  in Ovid, 129, 148
Silverman, Kaja, 8
similes
  and heroic beauty, 265–83
  and objectification, 296
  art objects, 273–8
  as distancing devices, 91
  as signs, 3
  bees, 248
  gladiatorial animals, 291
  horses, 268–73
  jewels, 280–1
  plants, 278–80
  stars, 265–8
Smith, R. A., 10
spectacle, 10, 161, 286, 317
Statius
  and tragedy, 243
  divination, 143–5
subjectivity, 4, 30, 88, 188, 191, 223, 228, 292, 300, 357
sublimity
  and divine audience in Silius, 52
  and prophecy, 129
  and Valerius Flaccus, 51
  as authorisation, 92
  deconstructed by Lucan, 113
  of Phaethon, 103
supplication, 340, 349
  Prometheus, 105
suture, 7, 21
  and epiphany, 81

Talos, 334–6
Tarpeia, and the female gaze, 233
teichoscopy, 27
  and participation, 250
  and the female gaze, 217–25
  in tragedy, 223
  of Antigone in Euripides, 223–4
  of Antigone in Statius, 242–6
  of Helen in the *Iliad*, 220–3
  of Medea in Valerius Flaccus, 236–42
Telemachus, 5, 44
textuality, 243
Theoclymenus, 134
Thiodamas, 138
Tiresias, 140, 156–61
  and structure in Ovid, 156
  in Statius, 156–61
Tisiphone, and Juno, 67

tragedy
    and blindness, 154
    and epic, 6
    and prophetic madness, 130
Turnus, 142
    and blazing eyes, 319
    as gladiator, 289
    as horse, 272–3
    as object of the gaze, 217

veiling, 15
Venus
    and rhetoric, 91
    and the imperial gaze, 70
    as erotic object, 187
    as object of the gaze, 47
    as partisan, 52
    epiphany, 83, 90
vertical gaze, 25, 35, 57
    of Archimedes, 106
    of Juno, 61, 66
    of Jupiter, 35
    of Talos, 335
    of the gods, 327, 330, 336, 358
virginity, 5, 244, 305
Virtus, epiphany, 84–5

vision
    ancient theories of, 18–19, 310–11
    and causation, 329
    and envy, 329–34
    and violence, 310
    metaphors of, 19
voyeurism, 186, 286, 287, 296, 310
    in Mulvey, 7
Vulcan, as maker of ecphrastic objects, 168

women
    as objects of ecphrasis, 164
        on the shield of Achilles, 186
    as statues, 277
    as unseen, 15
    on the walls, 219
        in historiography, 219
        in Nonnus, 249–50
        in Quintus Smyrnaeus, 247–9
wonder, 335
    and epiphany, 80
    and pity, 1
    and terror, 199
    and the gods, 29

Zeus. *See* Jupiter